# AN
# ECONOMIC HISTORY
# OF MODERN BRITAIN

## FREE TRADE AND STEEL
### 1850–1886

# AN
# ECONOMIC HISTORY
# OF MODERN BRITAIN

## FREE TRADE AND STEEL
## 1850–1886

By

SIR JOHN CLAPHAM

CAMBRIDGE
AT THE UNIVERSITY PRESS
1967

CAMBRIDGE UNIVERSITY PRESS
Cambridge, New York, Melbourne, Madrid, Cape Town, Singapore, São Paulo, Delhi

Cambridge University Press
The Edinburgh Building, Cambridge CB2 8RU, UK

Published in the United States of America by Cambridge University Press, New York

www.cambridge.org
Information on this title: www.cambridge.org/9780521046664

First published 1932
Reprinted 1952, 1963, 1967
This digitally printed version 2008

*A catalogue record for this publication is available from the British Library*

ISBN 978-0-521-04665-7 hardback (volume 1)
ISBN 978-0-521-10107-3 paperback (volume 1)
ISBN 978-0-521-04666-4 hardback (volume 2)
ISBN 978-0-521-10100-4 paperback (volume 2)
ISBN 978-0-521-04667-1 hardback (volume 3)
ISBN 978-0-521-10108-0 paperback (volume 3)
ISBN 978-0-521-75798-0 paperback (3 volume set)

# PREFACE

THIS volume has not followed quite so quickly on the heels of the first as I had hoped, mainly, I think, because the material is not very well suited for quick handling. It is at once heavy and incomplete; and much of it has been imperfectly sifted. Then, the further one advances towards the present age of full social and economic statistics, the more difficult does the writing of certain sections of the narrative become. As Britain gets more deeply involved in a 'world economy' the treatment must be something more than insular. After 1870, Alfred Marshall used to say, you cannot write *English* economic history: he might have given an earlier date. How far the adjustment of statistics to narrative, and of England to the world, has been successful is for readers to decide. The attempt to make it has certainly taken time.

Material is incomplete partly because the Mid-Victorians, living in a world which was demonstrably getting more comfortable and was running without too much friction, did not appoint so many Commissions and Committees of Inquiry as the Early Victorians. It has been said that reliance on these accumulated inquiries, concerned as they were primarily with economic and social pathology, has warped our view of the early nineteenth century. I rather think it has, sometimes. But the reports, carefully read, tell almost as much about normal as about diseased social tissue. For instance; one of the comparatively few reports of the earlier type from the Mid-Victorian era, that on child labour in the 'sixties of which Karl Marx made so much use, is full of incidental information about the organisation of industry. So is the trade union inquiry of the same decade. Fortunately the Late-Victorians of the 'eighties and 'nineties became socially and economically anxious, and resumed inquiry into all sorts of things on a scale so huge as to be almost daunting. There is ample retrospective information in the four or five folios on the *Depression of Trade and Industry*

of the 'eighties; more still in the sixty-seven folio parts of the
*Report of the Royal Commission on Labour* of the 'nineties—
beautifully indexed, to the student's great advantage—or in the
nine volumes of Charles Booth's *Life and Labour of the People
in London*.

Where official and other strictly original sources fail, the lack
of enough first-rate local and trade monographs is acutely felt.
I have in mind books of the class of G. I. H. Lloyd's *The
Cutlery Trades* (1913), C. Wright and C. E. Fayle's *History of
Lloyd's* (1928) or G. C. Allen's *Industrial Development of
Birmingham and the Black Country* (1929). The appearance of
the last two, and of many other books and articles used, including 'the Webbs' on the Poor Law, since my first volume was
published, shows how much the second might have gained by—
shall we say?—another ten years at a finishing school. But I
cannot afford ten years; and I believe that the material which
I have used is trustworthy, if still incomplete.

For this volume I owe a special debt to Alfred Marshall.
Some years before he died he entrusted to me the bound files
of the *Economist*, from the 'forties to the 'seventies, to be kept
until I had written beyond them and then transferred to the
Marshall Library. It is an uncommon privilege to stroll about
the business world of the 'sixties and 'seventies with Walter
Bagehot, the editor of those years, literally at one's elbow. He
is more vivacious than most economists, trade historians, or
secretaries of Commissions; and wiser too.


For procuring information in Glasgow, Liverpool, and
Grimsby I am indebted to Mr A. M. Stephen, Mr J. H. Hubback and Mr Joseph Bennett. I owe to Mr A. H. Moberly
information about the suburban architecture of the 'eighties
used and quoted on p. 498. Of my colleagues at King's, I must
thank Professor Pigou, for loans of books and for—what he has
quite forgotten—encouragement when the economist in me got
impatient with the task of his much bulkier room-mate the
historian; Mr John Saltmarsh, for information extracted for
my use from our muniments; Mr W. H. Macaulay, who allowed

me to draw on his hunting memories and on his complete knowledge of the works of Surtees; and Mr Hamilton McCombie, who checked my references to the chemical industries. I owe special thanks to the last-named because I hold, with conviction, that a writer whose habit is tiresomely detailed has no right to plague his friends with his proof-sheets, but should take his own risks of blundering. For all other passages, and for these, I hereby take mine.

I have decided not to be deterred from thanking my wife for some very heavy work on the Index by the appearance of a monograph entitled *1066 and All That*. English contemporaries will understand the reference; and should my book keep afloat for half a generation, foreigners and learned posterity may profitably inquire into it.

J. H. CLAPHAM

*Cambridge*
  *1 May, 1932*

# CONTENTS

# BOOK III

## FREE TRADE AND STEEL

PLATES AND DIAGRAMS

The following maps are available for download from www.cambridge.org/9780521101004

# BOOK III

∽

## FREE TRADE AND STEEL

This is no longer the age of mystery. No longer the age of artificial protection to national industry.

PROF. LEONE LEVI, 1863

The ferruginous temper...which...has changed our Merry England into the Man in the Iron Mask.

JOHN RUSKIN, 1880

August 18, 1865. The Atlantic cable has snapped. The Great Eastern is fishing about for the ends.

March 18, 1878. Off to see the telephone and phonograph. The former is nothing to compare with the latter for wonderfulness. *Diary of Mary Gladstone*

*Progress and Poverty*, by Henry George (New York, 1879: London, 1881).

# CHAPTER I

## BRITAIN AND THE NATIONS, 1848–53

"OUR Parliament is to be prorogued on Tuesday and dissolved the same day," Victoria wrote to her Belgian uncle on June 29, 1852. "Lord Derby himself told us, that he considered Protection as quite gone. It is a pity they did not find this out a little sooner; it would have saved so much annoyance, so much difficulty."[1] Fourteen months earlier she and her Consort and England had held their triumph of industry and peace under the "blazing arch of lucid glass" at the Great Exhibition. All three felt confident and generous towards the world, as they walked among the exhibits.

> Look yonder where the engines toil:
> These England's arms of conquest are,
> The trophies of her bloodless war:
>> Brave weapons these.
> Victorious over wave and soil,
> With these she sails, she weaves, she tills,
> Pierces the everlasting hills,
>> And spans the seas.[2]

Let the engines and the engine-minders be fed, and let the art and wealth of the nations come into England—freely. "Albert's name is immortalised, and the wicked and absurd reports of danger of every kind, which a set of people, viz. the *soi-disant* fashionables and the most violent Protectionists, spread, are silenced."[3]

What had "quite gone" in 1852 was the prospect of a reversal of Peel's economic policy as carried forward by the Whigs since 1846, the policy which, in spite of the survival of long lists of dutiable articles in the tariff, had disposed of effective protection to the staples of agriculture, the extractive industries and nearly all manufactures. Ships imported to be broken up paid 25 per cent. *ad valorem* and artificial flowers also 25 per cent.; but the most favoured British manufacture of importance, silk,

---

[1] Martin, Theodore, *The Life of His Royal Highness The Prince Consort*, II. 451.

[2] Thackeray, W. M., *May-Day Ode*.

[3] Martin, *op. cit.* II. 368.

had now no more than a 15 per cent. duty to shelter it, as against absolute prohibition thirty years earlier. No other manufacture had more than 10 per cent.; and many industries, or parts of industries, had none at all. Iron, wool and hides could come in free; so could coal had anyone wished to send it; also litharge and "live creatures illustrative of natural history," with "magna grœcia ware," manna and manures. Colonial timber could come at 1s. a load, or about 2 per cent. *ad valorem* for the commoner sorts; wheat at 1s. a quarter, or slightly more than 2 per cent. at the prices current in 1850–52[1]. In effect Britain was an open market for nearly everything which she produced except alcohol; and home-made alcohol had to carry the excise. The last of those export duties on which the kings of medieval England had lived vanished, as a corollary to the repeal of the Navigation Laws, in 1850. It was the duty on coal exported in a foreign ship.

The opened market had done its work well throughout the Irish famine; although during the years 1850–52 farmers were dissatisfied with the prices of grain[2]. Imports of grain and flour of all sorts into the United Kingdom had been at their maximum in 1849, when the Irish potato area had not recovered from the blight and something like 1,400,000 people in Ireland, nearly a quarter of the surviving population, were still in receipt of poor relief[3]. The course of the import trade as conditions became more normal was as follows. The figures are those of the Board of Trade for 'Grain, Flour and Meal as Grain,' entered for home consumption, in millions of quarters[4]:

| 1849 | 11·9 | 1852 | 7·8 |
| 1850 | 9·1 | 1853 | 10·1 |
| 1851 | 9·7 | 1854 | 7·8 |

Except in 1849, when shipments of the maize with which the famine had been stanched were still abnormally large, rather more than half the imports were of wheat or wheaten flour. The

[1] For the customs of this period see *Customs Tariffs of the United Kingdom from 1800 to 1897* (c. 8706 of 1897), p. 717 *sqq.* There were a number of specific duties on silk goods: 15 per cent. was the general maximum rate when levied *ad valorem.* Prices are in Tooke and Newmarch, *History of Prices*, vol. v and in the weekly price-current of the *Economist*.

[2] See vol. i. p. 455.

[3] Pauperism figures are in the *Statistical Abstracts for the United Kingdom*.

[4] All figures are from the Board of Trade's monthly and annual statements. It has not seemed necessary to give references for each from the *Accounts and Papers* of the various years. The statements are also available in full in the files of the *Economist*.

rest was principally oats and maize, neither of which was much eaten by the people of Britain. What the import of a yearly average of about 4,900,000 quarters of wheat, for the triennium 1850–52[1], meant in terms of dependence on the foreigner statisticians were not certain: they did not know how much wheat was grown at home or how much oat and barley meal was eaten. But their calculations went to suggest that perhaps so many as from 5,000,000 to 6,000,000, out of the 21,185,000 people alive in Britain in the year of the census and the Great Exhibition, already 'lived on foreign bread,'[2] or that about a quarter of every one's bread was foreign. The heavy imports and high prices of 1853 showed how desperate the position might have been had the foreign share been excluded.

Whenever wheat had been imported at all, at any time during the previous fifty years and more, some had come as flour. Barrelled flour from America was a standard commodity, especially in the Liverpool trade. A very sharp—though, as it proved, short-lived—rise in the imports of this half-manufactured food-stuff occurred in 1851, provoking some anxious discussion among protectionists and millers[3]. In 1849 the wheat flour imported into the United Kingdom for home consumption had not risen above the figure, already considerable, of 197,000 tons. In 1850 it was rather less. In 1851 the figure jerked up to 270,000 tons. Quite early in the year there was noted "a suspension to some extent of the mill power in this country, but especially in Ireland."[4] Irish mills often bought English and other wheat, and sent the flour to England. Now they were being cut out of this trade by very efficient millers in Rouen and Paris. The comment of the free traders was apposite and prophetic. They admitted "some difficulty which flour mills will have to encounter, placed far from any port, without a local supply of wheat," like those of Ireland; they said it was "generally admitted that the French millers" were "superior to the English...in their mode of management"; but they argued that our "large steam flour mills," with their cheap coal and good machinery, would learn their lesson—were in fact already learn-

---

[1] It was a triennium of rather poor harvests. Tooke and Newmarch, *History of Prices*, v. 223–5. In 1853 wheat prices rose steadily from 45s. to 80s.

[2] See the estimates, in Porter, G. R., *Progress of the Nation* (edition of 1851), p. 143. Lawes, J. B. and Gilbert, J. H., in the *J.R.A.S.* 1880, estimated that for the years 1852–9 imported wheat formed 26·5 per cent. of the consumption.

[3] See the article in the *Economist*, quoted below.

[4] The *Economist*, March 29, 1851.

ing it—and would beat the French[1]. Free trade was producing
its normal results—tiresome but wholesome stimulus for all;
for the weak and ill-placed, the gulf that lies beyond 'the
margin' of the economists; for the powerful and adaptable, more
power. A fall in the imports of wheat flour, to an annual average
of 180,000 tons for the five years 1852–6, came in support of
the free traders' argument[2].

Compared with the imports of wheat, those of other essential
and competitive foodstuffs were still relatively insignificant.
True, the live cattle of all kinds imported rose from 66,000 in
1850 to 127,000 in 1853, and the sheep from 135,000 to 249,000;
but Britain had several millions of cattle and many millions of
sheep, and she drew from 150,000 to 200,000 of each yearly out
of Ireland, with plenty of butter[3]. With the recovery of Ireland
after the famine, imports of taxed foreign butter, which had
reached 15,000 tons in 1847, remained stationary until 1853,
when they rose to 20,000 tons. The imports of cheese were
growing even more slowly; those of salted and preserved meat
were trifling; and the five taxed foreign eggs per head of the
population per annum, which was about the consumption of the
early 'fifties, cannot have affected much the market for British
and Irish eggs. Nearly all the foreign livestock, with the farmyard and dairy produce, came by steamer across the Channel
and the North Sea; and most of it went into the Thames to feed
London. Lancashire and the Clyde had Ireland close at hand.
In 1852 the total imports of foreign livestock—cattle, sheep and
swine—were returned at 334,000. The weekly reports of arrivals
on the London market give a total of no less than 268,000 of
these delivered there[4]. Holland was perhaps the most important single source of cattle and dairy produce: her Friesland
butter was the standard London quotation. Few animals came
from north of the Skaw or south of Finisterre: the arrival of
some "very superior oxen" from Oporto was a matter for
comment in a market report, usually jejune, of February, 1854[5].

The opening of the British grain market had made the grain

---

[1] The *Economist*, as above.
[2] There had been no important change in the sources for the supply of wheat
and wheat flour given in vol. i. p. 500 for the year 1847.
[3] The imports from Ireland are in a return of 1854, *Accounts and Papers* LXV.
367. The cattle in Great Britain may have been 6,000,000 or rather less, the sheep
28,000,000 or rather more. Regular agricultural returns had not begun.
[4] Reckoned from the weekly Smithfield Market reports in the *Economist*.
[5] *Economist*, February 11, 1854.

imports almost rival in bulk what had been the only regular bulk import trade thirty years earlier, that in timber. So far had British forestry declined very long ago; so insistent had been the demands of the Royal Navy, whose official spokesmen were saying in 1851 that "iron does not appear to be applicable for ships of war,"[1] that there had not been any real question of protecting home-grown timber for years. The issue had been between the foreign and the imperial. Peel had left a duty of 15s. a load, which would often work out at over 20 per cent. *ad valorem*, on foreign hewn timber: in 1851 this duty was halved, but it remained an obstacle to trade. Nevertheless the natural convenience of supply from Scandinavia and the Baltic was re-asserting itself[2]. By 1853, out of the total import of 2,404,000 loads of timber into the United Kingdom, very little more than half came from British possessions.

What weight of timber was felled at home is not known: all told it must have been great. Many estates, perhaps most, were nearly self-sufficing for ordinary estate purposes. British ash had no rival for hafts and handles. British oak and beech had many recognised uses. Oak, ash, beech, and the hard-working elm, against which house carpenters had long been turning in favour of soft-working fir timber, each held unchallenged that place in the country wheelwrights' and waggon-builders' scheme which it was not even to begin to lose for another thirty years[3]. There was an immense consumption of wood, much of it no doubt home grown, for railway carriages and waggons. The planta-tions of young larch and spruce which had angered Cobbett might, when conveniently placed, be felled for pit props, though the larger pitwood often came from overseas. The naval authori-ties still kept some sort of watch, at least in the remainder royal forests, on the great timber of oaks planted during the American War of Independence and now ripening for use. Yet in spite of its stubborn prejudice in favour of English oak, the Admiralty, which had almost cleared the country of 'navy oak' during the French wars, was now filling up its yards more and more with substitute woods—teak, Baltic oak, Italian oak, pitch pine and fir. Deptford yard in 1855 had in store 4596 loads of these

---

[1] Captain Washington in the 1851 *Exhibition Lectures*, I. 563.

[2] For the diversion of the trade to British North America since 1800 see vol. I. p. 237–8.

[3] See Sturt, George, *The Wheelwright's Shop* (1923), for the position in the 'eighties.

substitutes against only 1868 of English oak[1]. The railways were mostly laid on sleepers of imported fir. Little else was used in town building. The commercial shipbuilder, though he still used plenty of British timber, had taught the Admiralty the value of the substitutes. For none of the major uses was the British timber essential; which was as well, for there was not enough of it well placed for bulk felling to meet any of them, and apparently nobody thought it likely that there ever would be.

In wool the open market continued to work smoothly for producer, consumer and dealer, and to illustrate beautifully the territorial division of labour and the principles of a free international trade as lately restated by John Mill. Certain classes of wool were regularly sold by the United Kingdom to its continental neighbours, particularly the French. The weight in 1850 was 12,000,000 lbs., and the declared value £624,000—the highest figures ever recorded[2]. This came from an annual clip (including the skin wool from slaughtered sheep) which was estimated by one authority at 157,500,000, and by another at 228,000,000 lbs.—estimates which reveal the real ignorance[3]. Foreign and colonial wool imported had risen in 1850 to 73,000,000 lbs. of which over 14,000,000 lbs. was re-exported, again mainly to France. Every continent and almost every country sent some wool to England, but by 1850 more than half came from Australia, which had taken the place of Germany as the main source of fine wool since 1835. The best 'Electoral' (Saxon) wool still fetched the highest prices, and Spanish wool was quoted first in the antiquated ritual of market reports; but the import from Spain was nearly dead, and the import from all Germany in 1850 was not half what it had been in 1840, and only a third of what it had been in 1830. In 1835 more than half the imported wool had been German: by 1855 the proportion was barely one-sixteenth, as the figures, taken at five-year intervals, show[4].

The growth of the re-export trade between 1845 and 1855 marks the final establishment of London as the distributing centre for Australian wool[5]. Competition of French buyers in

---

[1] Albion, R. G., *Forests and Sea Power* (1926), p. 403.

[2] A very small amount of the wool was Irish: no figures are available.

[3] The first is that of Prof. Low quoted in James, J., *History of the Worsted Manufacture* (1857), p. 542; the second that of Southey, a London wool-broker, in Forbes, H., *The Worsted Manufacture*; 1851 *Exhibition Lectures*, II. 321.

[4] See Table, p. 7.

[5] See Shann, E., *An Economic History of Australia* (1930), book I, especially ch. VI, "John Bull's Greater Woolsack."

London kept up the prices, both of imported and of British wools. Lincoln long wool rose by more than 22 per cent. between January, 1851 and January, 1853, and good Southdown wool, the nearest in character to the Australian, by 25 per cent. Here was nothing to tempt anyone to reverse a patently successful policy.

|  | Exports of British wool in millions of lbs. | Total imports in millions of lbs. | Imports from Germany. | Imports from Spain. | Imports from Australia. | Re-exports of wool. |
|---|---|---|---|---|---|---|
| 1835 | 4·6 | 42·2 | 23·8 | 1·6 | 4·2 | 4·1 |
| 1840 | 4·8 | 46·9 | 21·8 | 1·3 | 9·7 | 1·0 |
| 1845 | 9·1 | 75·5 | 18·5 | 1·1 | 24·2 | 2·6 |
| 1850 | 12·0 | 75·3 | 9·2 | ·4 | 39·0 | 14·4 |
| 1855 | 16·2 | 99·3 | 6·1 | ·07 | 49·1 | 29·4 |

Nor was there anything in the state of the extractive industries to suggest that the free traders were wrong. Indeed no protectionist said they were; and some extractive industries, copper and tin mining for instance, were still lightly protected[1]. The Cornish mines were splendidly active. Though some 5000 tons of copper, unwrought and part-wrought, and over 40,000 tons of copper ore, were imported annually in 1850 and 1851, more than 6500 tons were exported raw 'in bricks and pigs'; nearly 12,000 tons in sheets, nails and other simple forms; and beyond that all the copper and brass manufactures. Lead was like copper; the exports still greatly exceeded the imports. Tin was not in quite so strong a position, viewed crudely. A few hundred more tons were imported in the ingot, and retained for home consumption, than were exported unwrought; but the tinplate trade raised its exports to £1,000,000 worth in 1851. Tin also entered into many manufactured exports. The prices of English tin were good and they were rising, and employment in Cornwall and Devon grew. In coal and iron Britain was supreme. The position won in the first quarter of the century was retained and improved. Coal exports were growing slowly —they fluctuated between 3,250,000 and 4,000,000 tons in the early 'fifties—but of coal import there was never any question. Exports would have grown rather quicker, but for the protective policies of some other nations. France not only laid a heavy

[1] Copper duties were now negligible: copper ore paid 1s. a ton, and raw copper 2s. 6d. The price rose to above £100 a ton in 1853. Down to 1848 the duty had been protective, working out at about 10 per cent. *ad valorem*. The duty on foreign tin was still about 6 per cent. *ad valorem* (£6 a ton) in the early 'fifties.

duty on all coal, but gave a tariff preference to the land-borne coals of Belgium[1]. The considerable import of iron—30,000 to 40,000 tons—was rather a measure of the prosperity of Sheffield than of effective foreign competition with the British iron-masters: it was the charcoal bar from Sweden or Russia, specially suitable for cutlery; and its value in 1850–53 was much less than that of the steel, largely made out of it, which Britain was exporting unwrought, over and above the edge tools and cutlery.

The produce of British blast and puddling furnaces and roll-ing mills was pouring abroad in what seemed impossible quan-tities, as country after country entered the railway age. A ship-ment of 554,000 tons of the cruder forms of iron—pig, cast and wrought—had been remarkable enough in 1849; for in 1839 the figure had been only 191,000 tons[2]. By 1853 shipments had reached 1,260,000 tons, and of this two-thirds was not pig or cast iron but the more valuable puddled iron—bar, bolt, rod and wrought of all kinds. America remained the great buyer: Yankee clippers left the Mersey heavy with Staffordshire bar[3]. Exports of finished iron and steel goods grew less rankly, yet healthily. There were no imports of manufactured iron, none at least which were inserted in the regular trade returns of the early 'fifties. The customs officials now added from time to time items to the list of commodities described as 'principal articles of foreign and colonial merchandise.' They inserted a number of headings between 1848 and 1853, as the character of the im-ports changed with the changes in the productive capacities of the nations, and in the British tariffs. But they did not think it necessary to add to the two traditional iron categories—'iron in bar, unwrought' and 'steel unwrought.' The former con-tained the record of the charcoal bar for Sheffield; the latter, once very important[4], was now almost empty.

That geological variety and geographical lay-out which have made the small area of Britain an almost complete show-case of the geological formations, ringed about by the near sea, are

---

[1] The French coal tariff was very complex: there were different rates for land and sea-borne coal, and short-haul sea-borne coal paid more than long-haul. See Dunham, A. L., *The Anglo-French Treaty of Commerce of 1860 and the Progress of the Industrial Revolution in France* (1930), p. 9, 19.

[2] See the diagram in vol. I. p. 483.

[3] From the memories of an iron-merchant who arranged some of the ship-ments.

[4] See vol. I. p. 150.

particularly favourable to her extractive industries. Much of her iron lies close to her coal, or close to the sea, or both. Copper lies deep by the sea which washes the edge of the Welsh coalfield. The salt of the Keuper beds in the trias of Cheshire, Stafford and Worcester—about Northwich, Shirleywich and Droitwich—is all near to coal measures[1]. Easily worked at every successive level of civilisation, it had been worked and moved with special ease in the new age of canals, steam and railways. A little salt still came in from 'the Bay,' but the export grew steadily. It was nearly twice as great in 1852–3 as it had been in 1842–3, though worth only some £250,000 a year. On the shoulders of the salt trade stood, very literally, the trade in soda, with its headquarters in South Lancashire and on the Clyde. The exports, from very small beginnings about twenty-five years earlier, had grown to nearly £500,000 a year by 1853. They were associated with other, though less valuable, exports of the heavy chemicals and industrial acids, whose raw materials were home-extracted pyrites and salt, with some imported pyrites and sulphur.

Provided she could count on her regular food supplies from Ireland, Britain was still reasonably self-sufficient in the narrow commissariat sense, when corn crops were pretty good, in spite of the millions who in average years now ate foreign bread. She could have kept alive for the best part of a year, with an effort perhaps from harvest to harvest, even if she had lost control of the outer seas. But as the world then was, and indeed essentially, this is a most unimportant conclusion. Her control of the outer seas was almost as complete as her control of the Solent. A coalition which might have threatened it was unthinkable in 1851. What naval dangers there were—some there were bound to be, with a Napoleon rising again—were almost all localised in the Channel. Had some unthinkable coalition completely mastered the seas, south, east and west, she would have been forced to peace for lack of cotton, hemp, timber, sugar, tobacco, saltpetre, markets and empire some time before she might have been forced to it by a shortage of meat or bread. It is easy to overrate the value of the corn laws as insurance policies. Insurance against a mere interruption in British control of the sea was hardly necessary: at nearly every season of the year there were bread and meat in Britain for months.

[1] Woodward, H. B., *The Geology of England and Wales*, p. 240.

Insurance against the ultimate, and very remote, dangers of a desperate war was to be found only in an overwhelming fleet, a shrewd balance-holding diplomacy, or a consistently pacific policy. The free traders believed that what had lately been done under their inspiration was a contribution to such a policy.

Some of the leaders were no doubt too sanguine in their estimate of the strength of a good international precedent. Even the cautious Peel, who had "no guarantee to give that other nations will immediately follow our example," was convinced that it would "ultimately prevail." He saw "symptoms of it already" in 1846[1]. But the free-trade leaders did not suppose that Britain, with her new cheap food, her coal and iron and machines and capital, had entered on an eternity of industrial and commercial leadership. An age of leadership, yes, but how long? They knew about America, as their master Adam Smith had known, when he faced the possibility of a transfer of the capital of the Empire across the Atlantic "in the course of little more than a century."[2] "Here," Cobden, not yet a politician, had thought in 1835 as he looked from Laurel Hill over the valley of the Monongahela where it flows north towards Pittsburg, "here will one day centre the civilisation, the wealth, the power of the entire world."[3]

"The people there," his newspaper ally, the *Economist*, wrote in 1851, "have our knowledge, our skill, and more than our activity...they have an immense continent at their command, and they continually receive accessions of capital and population from England and from every country in Europe. From the relative progress of the two countries within the last sixty years, it may be inferred that the superiority of the United States to England is ultimately as certain as the next eclipse."[4]

"Ultimately": did the economist, in his mind, give the ultimatum seventy years to run or only fifty? Or did he, as is much more likely, think no more about it because it would not run out in his day, and because there was no question about British superiority in 1851? In an earlier article that same year he, or a colleague, had been discussing the balance of trade[5].

[1] Jan. 27, 1846. Hansard, Third Series, LXXXIII. 277–8. The Corn Law repeal speech.
[2] *Wealth of Nations* (ed. Cannan), II. 124.
[3] Morley, J., *The Life of Richard Cobden*, I. 31.
[4] *Economist*, March 8, 1851.
[5] *Ibid*. January 11, 1851. The article is a very early, perhaps the earliest, complete though necessarily unstatistical analysis of the items in the modern balance of trade.

He deplored the lack of relevant statistics. We knew, he wrote, the declared values of our exports. For the imports we had correct quantities, but only the old official values which were "notoriously no indication whatever of the present value." So alarmists could always argue that the balance was against us. He was sceptical of the possibility of ever securing all the necessary information; but his notes on the information lacking are eloquent of British strength. To the declared value of the exports he added a hypothetical eighth for freights, "the great proportion of which are paid...to British shipowners": in spite of the Yankee clippers, Britain did most of her own carrying. Next he referred to a great unknown sum for "the profit, whatever it may be, obtained abroad on those goods, shipped on account of British houses" (Britons handled much of this trade at both ends. There were British firms in all important Baltic towns, and British banks in every Mediterranean port[1].) Then he spoke of the unknown earnings of "the enormous amount of British capital employed in different parts of the world," and of the remittances of unknown amount from profits and from incomes of public servants overseas. "Most of the banks in Australia, the West Indies and Canada, are conducted with British capital"; so is "a considerable part of the cultivation of our colonies." He went on to enumerate loans to America, investments in European railways, and the rest. These were familiar facts, he said, or should have been. But perhaps the most important fact of all bearing on the balance of trade was "too often entirely overlooked." "As a rule England gives credit to all the world and takes none." "In India, China, North America and all our foreign markets, though in a much less degree in our continental trade"—an important qualification—credits "extending over many months" were given when we exported; when we imported, the goods were drawn against at once by the seller abroad, and the drafts were "usually paid about the time or shortly after the arrival of the cargoes. Practically speaking, then, England gives long credits on her exports, while the imports are paid for in ready money."[2] And the commercial life of the planet, he might have added, was therefore dominated by the bill on London, an international

[1] See Jenks, L. H., *The Migration of British Capital to 1875* (1927), p. 188-9.
[2] For more critical and balanced statements see the evidence of D. B. Chapman, of Overend and Gurney, before the *S.C. on the Bank Acts*, 1857, x. Q. 4840 *sqq.*, especially Q. 5130-46.

currency, and was largely financed through London. "English credit supplied the capital of almost the whole world."[1] He did not quote the blessing in Deuteronomy xxviii. 12–13, but it would spring to the mind of many Victorian merchants who knew their Old Testament: "and thou shalt lend unto many nations, and thou shalt not borrow. And the Lord shall make thee the head, and not the tail."

Undisputed superiority in commerce and in money-lending went with a superiority in manufacturing which was the more marked because it was shown most in the making of those things which the world chiefly needed. That it would be shown at every point was not to be expected. Already the well-informed knew that an American was more likely than an Englishman to get tiresome and expensive handicraft operations done for him by machinery. This, to take an outstanding instance, had been shown long before, though most British manufacturers had not yet noticed it, in connection with a critical stage in the business of wool spinning. The 'condensing' process, in which the gauzy film of carded wool is stripped mechanically from the carding rollers and delivered in loose ropes ready for the mule, had been fully worked out by John Goulding of Massachusetts before 1832[2]. It got rid of the belated handicraft operation of slubbing, *i.e.* preparing the loose ropes on a hand-worked 'billy,' which came in between machine carding and mule spinning and spoilt the team-work of the machinery. It also got rid of the billy roller with which the brutal slubber so often beats the piecers in the early stories of factory cruelty. By 1850 Goulding's condenser, which has been called "almost as great an advance in wool manufacture as the spinning jenny itself,"[3] was widely, if not universally, used in New England; for several years it had been coming into use in Galashiels and Hawick, where its merits had been advertised in the 'thirties by a local

---

[1] *S.C. on the Bank Acts and the recent Commercial Distress*, 1857–8, v. Evidence of John Ball, Q. 1702.

[2] See Cole, A. H., *The American Wool Manufacture* (1926), 1. 102–3. Goulding, like Arkwright, seems to have been more an organiser of inventions than an inventor. He bought important notions from others. Patents for mechanical condensing had been taken out in England in 1834 (see vol. 1. p. 144) but had not come into general use.

[3] By Hayes, G. L., *Bulletin of American Wool Manufacturers*, 1894, p. 329, quoted in Cole, *op. cit.* 1. 103.

man who had been to America[1]; but it was hardly known elsewhere.

The lag behind America was not only in wool spinning. New types of cotton spindle, the 'cap' and the 'ring' spindles, were of American origin; and the critics of the Ten Hours Act of 1847 were threatening England with the competition of unregulated cotton factories, which "rivalled if they did not exceed" her own[2]. Americans had shown more interest than Englishmen in the devising of machinery for making such things as pins and screws. It was an American reaping machine, McCormick's, which attracted most attention at the Great Exhibition and afterwards, when tried before twelve hundred farmers at Cirencester in September, 1851[3]. A second good American type was shown; of English types, only one and some models. So great a stir was made about the American invention, which was far from new in 1851, that Scotsmen were forced to point out how Bell's machine had really reaped corn in the Carse of Gowrie for fourteen years. Patriotic propaganda gave an impetus to the use and improvement of the Bell type[4]; but there can be little doubt that the American types were better and more readily improved. The world's principal reapers of to-day have evolved from them.

A very different labour-saving machine was also shown in the American section in 1851, but it aroused rather less interest. There is no mention of it in the series of lectures by which eminent men tried to spread the chief results of the Exhibition. But some of the papers noted it. "There is a sewing machine which works with astonishing velocity," said the *Economist*[5] in a long philosophical article on national industrial characteristics as revealed at the Exhibition. This machine was selected, together with a grease-removing soap which could be used either in salt water or fresh, and the "unbounded...uses to

[1] Bremner, D., *The Industries of Scotland* (1869), p. 160–2. And see below, p. 83.

[2] Hume in Hansard, LXXXIX. 1077 (Feb. 10, 1847). For the spindles see Chapman, S. J., *The Lancashire Cotton Industry*, p. 71 n., Priestman, H., *Principles of Worsted Spinning*, p. 23.

[3] *Economist*, September 13, 1851. It is claimed that McCormick used the notions of John Common, of Denwick, Northumberland (Wood, Sir H. T., *A History of the Royal Society of Arts*, p. 129) just as Arkwright used his predecessors' notions.

[4] See 1851 *Exhibition Lectures*, II. 15; Prof. Wrightson in *British Manufacturing Industries* (1876), VIII. 153.

[5] Of June 28, 1851.

which caoutchouc is put," as a representative revelation of the American spirit. "Their agricultural implements, their Daguerrotypes, and other applications of modern discoveries, not behind their Eastern competitors, we pass over." American inventors, impelled by the need for economy of effort in the American home, had been hammering at the sewing machine for years, in succession to and side by side with English, German and French pioneers. America had the responsive demand. In 1850 Isaac M. Singer made in twelve days what "is said to have been the first machine satisfactory to manufacturers."[1]

Inventive as Americans were, their most typical inventions were hardly competitive with British manufacturing industry. They supplemented it; went beyond it; or met needs which it had not yet been called upon to meet. Hitherto the imports of all of them, or of things made by them, had been trifling and had left no mark on the trade returns. This was not true of some European manufactures. A few, a very few, had been able to compete on the British market when tariffs were still high, and without the smugglers' help. "I am of opinion that if the duty on toys were 100 per cent. it would not be a protection; and I find that almost all the toys used in this country...come from Switzerland and Bavaria and the central states of Germany." So John McGregor told the Committee on Import Duties in 1840[2]. He was thinking of the wooden dolls and Noah's Arks and other products of a hard-living peasantry's winter evenings. Many French fancy goods and articles of fashion were in the same category for a different reason. "In all matters of taste the French appear to excel us," said another witness, himself a silk manufacturer[3]. Sometimes taste, fashion and craftsmanship had combined to bring the French article in over a stiff tariff. "I never wear an English boot"—it is McGregor again speaking—"I do not find any that I like; I pay the 30 per cent. duty

---

[1] Bolles, A. S., *Industrial History of the United States* (1881), p. 245. For the early history see *ibid.* p. 243–5; Levasseur, E., *Hist. des classes ouvrières et de l'industrie en France de 1789 à 1870*, II. 550; Leno, J. B., *The Art of Boot and Shoe Making* (1885), p. 160 *sqq.*; Sewell, *The Birth of the Sewing Machine* (1892). It was only by accident that an excellent French machine, Thémonnier's, was not in the 1851 Exhibition: Leno, p. 160. On the whole subject of American machinery see Burn, D. L., "The Genesis of American Engineering Competition," *E.J.* (*Econ. Hist.*), Jan. 1931.

[2] In answer to Q. 186.

[3] T. F. Gibson, Q. 2274.

and import my own boots from Paris, not so much on account of the price, but of the quality of the leather."[1]

When duties on fine goods dropped to a standard 10 per cent., while those on some rougher manufactures disappeared, it became possible, after a time, to gauge their capacity for penetrating the British market. For the first few years there was not much evidence to go on; but, as Europe settled down to work after 1848, a commercial equilibrium appropriate to the new tariff conditions was gradually established. Most of her debts to England the continent, like the rest of the world, paid in food, raw materials and non-competing commodities such as French or Spanish wines and Italian oils. But its fine manufactures came in increasing quantities, mainly from France and Switzerland. With few exceptions, they were not products of some variant of the new machine industry but of cheap, skilled and tasteful handicraft directed and organised by commercial middlemen. There was little or no machinery used in French tanneries or in French shoe-making and glove-making, but, as John McGregor would have anticipated, there was a growing import of French boots, shoes and gloves. By 1853 the imports of "women's boots and calashes; women's shoes with cork or double soles; and women's shoes of silk, satin, stuff, or leather"[2] had risen to 184,000 pairs, nearly all "entered for home consumption." Of men's boots and shoes 84,000 pairs were imported, but these were mostly re-exported. The gloves for home use had reached the figure, astonishing when the probable number of glove-users in a population of some 22,000,000 is considered, of 3,000,000 pairs. An import of 600,000 pairs of what the customs called 'boot fronts' is not self-explanatory. This is the explanation. "It is found by experience," Charles Babbage wrote in 1851[3], "that the upper leather of Boots made in France is better...than the upper leather manufactured in England." Of sole leather the reverse was true, so you imported the uppers, the 'fronts.' Experience had justified McGregor and furnished the economists with another neat illustration of the territorial division of labour under free trade, which memory says they never used.

Cheap French and Swiss clocks and watches, made by an elaborately divided and subdivided handicraft system, formed another important group of imports. Until 1853 the returns are

[1] Q. 152.        [2] The customs classifications in the Board of Trade returns.
[3] *The Exposition of* 1851 (2nd ed.), p. 8.

worthless, being the official values; but after Gladstone modified the duties in that year the numbers began to be recorded. In the first seven months (June–December, 1853) 135,000 clocks and 43,000 watches came in. In 1854 the clocks numbered 228,000 and the watches 79,500. As these are the figures for home consumption, it would seem that English mantelpieces were filling up rather rapidly with French clocks and English pockets with Swiss watches.

There was a growing import of foreign glass of many kinds and from many countries—window, plate, flint, but above all cut, coloured and fancy, from France, Italy, Bohemia and Saxony. The customs returns of the early 'fifties do not permit any exact study of the trade: the values remain worthless and the weights, square feet of plate glass and so on, cannot be compared with any figures of domestic output or consumption. But there can be no doubt that this was, at least in some branches, an important competitive, not merely a supplementary, import. In 1840, when the glass duties were so high as to mean prohibition of the ordinary sorts, and the British manufacturer was protected against smugglers because his goods were "of great bulk and precarious carriage," the glass manufacturers were "among the very few" who were really interested in protective duties[1]. At that time their industry was still subject to the excise; and there is no doubt that the working of the excise had stunted it, ossified it, and made it unadaptable. Optical glass, for example, was nearly all imported because the excise rules did not permit the only methods by which it could properly be made[2]. Cooksons of South Shields made some lenses and prisms for lighthouses between 1831 and 1845, but they were not first-rate and the work did not pay. Most manufacturers in 1840 knew little about the foreign industry except its reputation, and feared the unknown. McGregor, no doubt a witness with a free trade bias, thought that they asked "for protection from ignorance of the matter."[3] In 1845 Peel abandoned the excise and lost nearly £600,000 of revenue in so doing. British glass-making sprang forward at once. Chance Bros. of Stourbridge began to produce lighthouse equipment in 1845, and continued previous experiments with optical glass.

[1] *Report on Import Duties*, Q. 80, 82.

[2] Porter, *op. cit.* p. 256; Powell, H. J:, *Glassmaking in England* (1923), p. 108, 110.

[3] Q. 83. According to Gladstone, McGregor was "loose minded." See vol. 1. p. 491, n. 2.

But it is said that "little progress was made"[1] in either, until Bontemps and Tabouret, French experts, came to England as refugees in 1848 and worked as heads of departments at Stourbridge. So the Chances made, not only the sheets for the "blazing arch" of 1851, but a complete lighthouse equipment and telescope discs for show under it. With the possible exception of the Pilkingtons of St Helens, who made other things, they were the strongest glass firm in the country. Weaker firms contracted output or closed down as foreign competition became keener.

It was in textiles inevitably that competitive imports were most heard of. French silks waited at the door for each fall in the tariff. That was why silk kept its extra 5 per cent. And French skill and taste were not confined to silks. In cottons neither France nor any other country, except perhaps India, could face Lancashire and Clydesdale. East India piece goods to the declared value of £190,000 were still imported in 1853. There were some European cotton gloves and stockings and yarns, most of which were re-exported; also a block of 'other articles' unspecified, worth £75,000 to £100,000 a year. But this was little to set against an export of cotton goods and yarns worth over £30,000,000, distributed over the whole face of the earth; and these insignificant imports were rather complementary than competitive. Manchester and Glasgow did not worry about any of them. The imports of wool manufactures were also in part complementary; but they were complementary in a sense of which England had no reason to be proud— there was a valuable field of manufacturing where she could not stand up to France, and she admitted it. Sometimes her experts gave technical, sometimes fiscal, sometimes commercial and sometimes artistic reasons. Finally a section of them fell back on a mystical or fatalistic one. The goods in question were called *merinos*, because made of French or French and Australian merino wool, and also *mousselines de laine*, colloquially delaines. The wool was combed, power-spun, and hand-woven. The delaines came mainly from Roubaix, Rheims and the St Quentin country, where the firm of Rodier, which rules the trade to-day, started at Bohain precisely in 1853[2], a year in

---

[1] Powell, *op. cit.* p. 110, on which this account is based. Georges Bontemps of Choisy-le-Roi, author of *Le guide du verrier*, had previously co-operated with the Chances: his stay in England was only short.

[2] Brunhes, J., *Géographie humaine de la France* (1920), II. 545.

which the value of wool manufactures imported into the United Kingdom rose suddenly by nearly 60 per cent.

The technical reasons given for French success were that the wool was worked 'dry,' *i.e.* without oil, and so took the colour better; that after being combed it was 'prepared' for spinning in a specially effective way; that it was spun on the mule and not on the more strenuous throstle and so made softer and more delicate yarn. The fiscal reason was an important one: French policy encouraged the export of these goods. The commercial reason was also important and relevant: "it has always been the rule acted upon by the British manufacturer, rather to produce a large quantity of goods at a small percentage of profit, than a small quantity at a greater percentage"[1]: these fabrics *de luxe* were made in small quantities with necessarily wide margins of profit: they were not his sort, were in fact hardly competitive so long as he had plenty of work for his throstles and power looms, as in the early 'fifties he generally had. The steady increase in the number of worsted mills showed it. The fatalistic reason was given in a report of a Deputation from the Bradford Chamber of Commerce in 1855, as paraphrased by the great Bradford manufacturer Titus Salt.

The French produce...goods which by their intrinsic beauty of texture and dye leave every competitor hopelessly in the rear. The prices...are such that we have long since abandoned their manufacture; and the Deputation, unable to find out the cause of this undeniable superiority, were obliged to ascribe it to the well-known truth that a trade once established in a certain locality cannot be carried on with the same success at another place, though the latter may, to all appearances, possess even superior advantages[2].

France had applied to these newly devised and expensive combed-wool fabrics the taste, craftsmanship and commercial enterprise which had made her silk industry so formidable. For wool-working she had called in the new machinery. She had, indeed, in Josué Heilmann of Mulhouse[3], the inventor of the combing machine without which the delaines could not have come so "good cheap" to market; but not much fresh machinery had appeared in the Lyons trade since Jacquard's loom, a hand-loom, established itself there between 1810 and 1825. A little

---

[1] Forbes, H., 1851 *Exhibition Lectures*, II. 325.

[2] James, *op. cit.* p. 526 n. Comments on the report are in the *Economist*, December 8, 1855.

[3] He died in 1848. See Burnley, J., *Wool and Woolcombing* (1899), ch. IX, for his life.

steam-power was used to supplement water-power in the throwing mills. Experiments were made with the power-loom for
plain silks in 1843–4; but even thirty years later there were only
about 6000 power-looms to 110,000 hand-looms in Lyons and
its neighbourhood[1]. This slow adoption of power was England's
opportunity. She had in fact been holding off French competition by power ever since Huskisson opened her market—by
power, and East India raw silk, and the study of French fabrics,
and the 30 per cent. or 15 per cent. duty. English power-driven
throwing machinery was believed to be "superior to that of any
other country" in 1840[2]. Since the 'thirties, Manchester had
woven some cheap silk and mixed fabrics by power[3]. In the
'forties, Macclesfield and other places were turning Bengal silk,
of which Britain had "the exclusive possession," into bandanna
handkerchiefs, and actually exporting them, with some other
silk goods, to France, a fact which seemed to G. R. Porter "not
the least surprising of the effects which have followed the total
alteration of our system in regard to this manufacture."[4] These
shipments to France were only a small, though a very important,
part of a general body of exports of silk and part-silk yarns and
fabrics, the maintenance and apparent growth of which were
most satisfactory to free traders, who had been forced to reply
to prophesyings of total ruin for the British industry whenever
the old barriers about it had been touched. The export of British
manufactured silk and part-silk goods had been worth £736,000
in 1845 and £838,000 in 1846. With raw material at about the
same price as in 1845–6[5], the figure for 1852 was £1,156,000 and
for 1853 it was £1,595,000. The imports of European manufactured silk for the years 1852–3 may have been worth nearly
twice as much; but no figures of values are available, so that the
result has to be reached roughly by multiplying the recorded
weights in pounds by at least £3, which was Porter's minimum
figure for the average value of silk goods per pound, and by making
some allowance for smuggling[6]. Evidently French, and some

---

[1] From estimates for 1873 in the *Enquête sur l'état de l'industrie textile* of 1904,
III. 46.          [2] *Report on Import Duties*, Q. 2236.
[3] See vol. I. p. 196, 554.          [4] *Progress of the Nation*, p. 219.
[5] The standard silk quotations were if anything a shade lower in 1852–3 than
in 1845–6. The *Economist's* weekly price current, *passim*.
[6] Porter, *op. cit.* p. 573. At £3, the recorded imports for 1852–3 would be
worth £3,981,000 against £2,751,000 of exports. As the imports were largely
fine French silks £3 is probably too low. There was no doubt some smuggling.
Eastern silks, entered not by the pound but by the piece, are excluded from this
calculation.

other, continental manufacturers were making full use of their new opportunities and were doing a good business in England. It is equally clear that the British industry was active, more adaptable than it had been under the pre-Huskisson hot-house regime, and in a position to adapt itself further—though probably with trouble and loss—should it be required to sacrifice the special protection which had been assigned to it. From the standpoint of the whole national economy, it was a secondary industry at best; but then so were all those industries with which foreign competition was real; for it was only one section of one division of the wool manufacture which was dominated by France.

Over her chosen ground, the ground where her engines toiled, England's control was in fact almost complete. Engines toiled in America too; but not much on goods for export[1] and hardly at all on goods for export to England. Belgian machinery was abundant and good; but Belgium was very small. French machinery was relatively scantier and worse, all things considered. Holland was hardly thought of as a manufacturing country: she had turned late to the new industrial technique and had no 'heavy' industries[2]. German machinery, and indeed German manufacture generally, was, as a whole, inferior and imitative—such at least was the impression produced on some visitors to the Exhibition who had no anti-German bias. "In machinery—except perhaps field-pieces...the Germans appear very deficient" the *Economist* wrote[3]. It went on to quote a correspondent of the *Allgemeine Zeitung*: "I cannot deny that German industry has no peculiar character. In the Exhibition (from which alone we judge) it appears as if every national characteristic were carefully avoided. Everywhere German industry appears to lean on some foreign industry and to imitate it....Here one beholds the supporting hand of France, there that of England." This is not a complete or final verdict on the German industry of 1850–51[4]. But it was the verdict which Englishmen naturally gave or repeated, and there was truth in it.

[1] American cotton manufactures were exported in fair quantities to considerable distances. It was this that alarmed Lancashire in 1847. There was also a miscellaneous export of manufactures to Canada, Mexico, the West Indies, etc.; but America bought vastly more than she sold.

[2] Baasch, E., *Holländische Wirtschaftsgeschichte* (1927), p. 415 *sqq*. For Belgium and France, Clapham, J. H., *The Economic Development of France and Germany*, p. 59, 63, 70 and *passim*.

[3] June 28, 1851.                    [4] See below, p. 111.

The course of America's economic evolution was predicted by men of long sight. That of France was clearly determined by her past, and was predictable. That of Germany was obscure. Of other countries Britain might utilise the products, value the markets, or respect the arts; she did not affect to place them in an economic category with herself.

# CHAPTER II

## THE INDUSTRIAL FIELD IN 1851

BRITAIN had turned her face towards the new industry—
the wheels of iron and the shriek of the escaping steam.
In them lay for the future not only her power and wealth
but her very existence. She must take the risks of the 'industry
state,' which lives by the export of its manufactures, because she
could do no other[1]. Many Englishmen bore those risks proudly,
like the industrial free traders of the North. Most bore them
ignorantly, seeing to-day's cheaper loaf or to-morrow's good
balance-sheet. Educated men of the older country stocks were
apt to shoulder them with reluctance, regretting that not ill-
adjusted life of town and country which was passing away.
Those who had followed Peel with open eyes, like Sir James
Graham, had done so because population was growing "at the
rate of 300,000 per annum."[2] It had been a question of time, a
race between life and food. To such men free trade was a need
to be faced, not a treasure to be won.

The course was set towards the 'industry state,' but the
voyage was not half over. England lived by her ships, but not even
yet quite as the Dutchmen of the seventeenth century had lived
by their ships—"the which except they stir, the people starve."[3]
Agriculture was still by very far the greatest of her industries.
Including landowners, agents, farmers and labourers of all sorts,
26 per cent. of the men of twenty years old and upwards were
engaged in it directly. The male agricultural labourers of all
ages and all kinds numbered 1,284,000 out of a male population
above ten years of age of 7,616,000. To these would have to be
added most of the 279,000 farmers and graziers and an unknown number of their sons to get an exact estimate of the male
working force of agriculture.[4] Out of 10,736,000 women

---

[1] For the economic conception of the 'industry state' see the German controversies of two generations later when Germany in turn reached the parting of
the ways, especially Wagner, A., *Agrar- und Industriestaat* (1901 and 1902).

[2] Graham to Peel, Dec. 30, 1842. Parker, C. S., *Life and Letters of Sir James
Graham*, I. 332.

[3] Mun, T., *England's Treasure by Forraign Trade* (ed. Ashley), p. 107.

[4] *Census of 1851. Ages and Occupations* (1852-3, LXXXVIII. Parts I and II) for
all figures in this section.

71,000 were outdoor agricultural labourers, 128,000 were in-door farm servants, and 28,000 were farmers. Judged merely by numbers, the industry which came next to agriculture was domestic service[1]. The total of domestic servants of all ages was: male, 134,000; female, 905,000, or almost exactly 1 in 9 of all girls and women from ten years old and upwards. These two great groups may be compared with the main groups of the extractive and manufacturing industries and some important groups of handicraft trades, dealers and middlemen, to give a rough picture of the industrial balance of the country on its human side as Britain moved towards the 'industry state.' The groups vary greatly in composition[2]. Coal-mining and cotton are filled mainly with wage-earners; shoe-making and tailoring largely with small masters and shopkeepers; the blacksmiths are nearly all handicraftsmen with their mates and apprentices. The building crafts also contain many small masters, working either as jobbers or as sub-contractors under builders; and so on. The figures for building and railway work, and some other figures to a less degree, are affected by the fact that 367,000 men and 9000 women were returned simply as labourers, many of whom no doubt worked in different industries at different times of the year. Such facts provide the uncertainties always connected with an occupational census. Further, as the census of 1851 was much the most elaborate yet taken, and as Britain still contained a high proportion of illiterates, there is a wider margin of error than is to be expected in a census to-day. There is also a small arbitrary element in the selection of trades for insertion in the groups given on p. 24[3]. But the outline picture is probably a more accurate one of its kind than can be drawn of any country at any earlier date.

The occupations not specially characteristic of the machine age come high on the list, partly because machinery was setting people free to follow them. Coal-miners had increased greatly since 1831—they had not yet passed the shoe-makers, however[4]

[1] Including coachmen, gardeners, inn-servants; excluding charwomen, professional or institutional nurses, male and female, and farm servants.

[2] The census groups contain all persons 'working or dealing in' coal, iron, leather, etc.

[3] Certain groups in the census have been thrown together to get better industrial comparisons. The census figure for seamen, being necessarily defective, is replaced by the figure from the *Statistical Abstract* for 1851 which refers to the United Kingdom. This involves a slight overstatement, but is preferable to the much understated census figure of seamen within reach of the enumerators.

[4] See vol. I. p. 73.

## Principal occupation groups in Britain in 1851
### in order of size

| | Male | Female |
|---|---|---|
| Total population . . . . . . . | 10,224,000 | 10,736,000 |
| Population of ten years old and upwards . . . | 7,616,000 | 8,155,000 |
| Agriculture: farmer, grazier, labourer, servant . . | 1,563,000 | 227,000 |
| Domestic service (excluding farm service) . . | 134,000 | 905,000 |
| Cotton worker, every kind, with printer, dyer . . | 255,000 | 272,000 |
| Building craftsman: carpenter, bricklayer, mason, plasterer, plumber, etc. . . . . . . . | 442,000 | 1,000 |
| Labourer (unspecified) . . . . . . | 367,000 | 9,000 |
| Milliner, dress-maker, seamstress (seamster) . . | 494 | 340,000 |
| Wool worker, every kind, with carpet-weaver . . | 171,000 | 113,000 |
| Shoe-maker . . . . . . | 243,000 | 31,000 |
| Coal-miner . . . . . . . | 216,000 | 3,000 |
| Tailor . . . . . . . . | 135,000 | 18,000 |
| Washerwoman . . . . . . . | | 145,000 |
| Seaman (Merchant), pilot . . . . | 144,000 | |
| Silk worker . . . . . . . | 53,000 | 80,000 |
| Blacksmith . . . . . . . | 112,000 | 592 |
| Linen, flax worker . . . . . . | 47,000 | 56,000 |
| Carter, carman, coachman, postboy, cabman, busman, etc. . . . . . . . . . | 83,000 | 1,000 |
| Iron worker, founder, moulder (excluding iron-mining, nails, hardware, cutlery, files, tools, machines) | 79,000 | 590 |
| Railway driver, etc., porter, etc., labourer, plate-layer | 65,000 | 54 |
| Hosiery worker . . . . . . . | 35,000 | 30,000 |
| Lace worker . . . . . . . | 10,000 | 54,000 |
| Machine, boiler maker . . . . . | 63,000 | 647 |
| Baker . . . . . . . . | 56,000 | 7,000 |
| Copper, tin, lead-miner . . . . . | 53,000 | 7,000 |
| Charwoman . . . . . . . | | 55,000 |
| Commercial clerk . . . . . . | 44,000 | 19 |
| Fisherman . . . . . . . | 37,000 | 1,000 |
| Miller . . . . . . . . | 37,000 | 562 |
| Earthenware worker . . . . . | 25,000 | 11,000 |
| Sawyer . . . . . . . . | 35,000 | 23 |
| Shipwright, boat-builder, block and mast maker . | 32,000 | 28 |
| Straw-plait worker . . . . . . | 4,000 | 28,000 |
| Wheelwright . . . . . . . | 30,000 | 106 |
| Glover . . . . . . . . | 4,500 | 25,000 |
| Nailer . . . . . . . . | 19,000 | 10,000 |
| Iron-miner . . . . . . . | 27,000 | 910 |
| Tanner, currier, fellmonger . . . . | 25,000 | 276 |
| Printer . . . . . . . . | 22,000 | 222 |

—for though a miner fed machinery and was lifted from his work by it, he used none when at the coal face. Cotton workers had not increased very fast in the twenty years in spite of the huge growth of the trade: spinning machinery was far more efficient and the normal weaver now tended two power-looms. If some allowance be made for builders' labourers, the non-mechanical building trade, as might be expected, must have been more important numerically in relation to cotton than in 1831[1]. None of the 340,000 milliners, dress-makers and seam-stresses used sewing machines, it may be assumed; nor did the tailors, nor the shoe-makers. Handicraft blacksmiths were more numerous than the men of the great iron works, even though some men returned as blacksmiths were actually smiths in textile mills or strikers in engineering shops. On the figures— which at this point, however, are specially uncertain, though the fact is probable enough—more men were employed about horses on the roads than in all the work of the young railway system. Machine making is vaguely and generally entered in the returns; yet a few of the specialised textile machinery trades separate themselves out—reed-makers; card-makers; shuttle-makers; gill-makers—and the total also contains over 4000 tool-makers[2]. It is rather remarkable how comparatively few tanners and shipwrights served the needs of nearly 21,000,000 people. A good deal of leather was no doubt im-ported, but not many ships. The nineteen female commercial clerks will not be overlooked, nor the fifty-four female railway servants, nor the twenty-three women sawyers. The latter, to-gether with other small groups of women found in unlikely occupations—of which the units are given in the table—are probably widows carrying on businesses without necessarily labouring in them.

Any geographical picture of the distribution of occupations such as was attempted, on the whole with great success, for the census commissioners in 1851, necessarily suffers from the diffi-culty of handling those occupations which are distributed in almost exact proportion to population and so have no distinctive homes. These included at that time a majority of the main women's callings together with building, shoe-making, tailor-ing, blacksmithing, the work of the sawyer, the wheelwright

[1] See vol. I. p. 71–2.
[2] Not makers of machine-tools but of files and so on.

and the printer, and all mercantile, retail and internal transport business. The ingenious map designed by Augustus Petermann to illustrate the report of the census, which omits all these, is therefore less a map of occupations—though that is what it is called—than a map of industries working for other than the local market[1]. Shoe-making, for example, is indicated by Wellington boots in Northamptonshire, which contained 13,000 shoe-makers and worked for 'export,' but not in counties where the trade might be bigger but supplied mainly local needs. Stafford-shire, also something of an 'export' county, is not dotted with boots on the map, presumably because its population of shoe-makers was not much above the normal for the country—1 in 63 of the population against 1 in 76: Northampton had 1 in 16. One graphic method adopted for England and Wales—the in-sertion of a symbol in every Poor Law Union where an industry existed "to any extent"—tended to exaggerate the importance of outliers from a localised industry[2]. The map gives the im-pression that the wool manufacture was of some importance in Cornwall and South Wales, the six counties from Cardigan and Radnor to the Bristol Channel. In fact only about 450 people in Cornwall and about 2500 in the six counties were in any way connected with it; whereas Devon, which does not look much more important than Cornwall on the map, had 4300 wool workers. Fortunately linen is the only industry besides wool for which this method of mapping is likely to mislead. Taken as a whole, Petermann's map is as illuminating as it is ingenious. Supported by the census figures already given, indicating the occupations which were in the first rank numerically, it tells the whole story which it set out to tell—that of the localisation of manufacture about the end of the early railway age.

Nothing is more remarkable than the complete localisation of some textile industries and the attainment by others of a locali-sation which, although not complete, was not to be altered appreciably during the next half-century. Under pressure of bad times in the 'forties, cotton had fallen back on South Lancashire and the adjacent parts of Cheshire and the West Riding, leaving a strong detached force in Clydesdale and various

[1] Census of Great Britain, 1851, *Population Tables II. Ages, Civil Conditions, Occupations and Birth-place of the People, Volumes 1 and 2*, BPP 1852-53, LXXXVIII (1854). Map is available for download from www.cambridge.org/9780521101004
[2] For Scotland these symbols are inserted for counties and important towns.

weak ones in other districts. From nearly a dozen English and Scottish counties came complaints of local falls in population resulting from the closing down of cotton mills[1]. The area with the better competitive facilities had come best through a spell of bad trade. Of approximately 527,000 cotton workers in the country, some 312,000 were in Lancashire, 55,000 in Cheshire and the West Riding, and 58,000 in Lanarkshire[2].

The most complete concentration was that of the worsted industry into the West Riding. Its oldest home, Norwich, had been losing ground ever since the eighteenth century, but was still a fairly active manufacturing centre in 1831, though it had adopted little modern machinery, if any. By 1841 the trade was nearly dead: during that decade the population of Norwich had stood still. About 1840 a belated attempt to recover the old industry was made by the establishment of spinning mills[3]. Norwich had been buying yarn from Yorkshire and she wished to end this dependence. It was much too late; for in the next few years Yorkshire perfected combing machinery and went ahead again. In 1850 the factory inspectors reported nearly 865,000 worsted spindles and 32,617 power-looms for worsted in England: there were hardly any in Scotland or Wales. Of the spindles 746,000, and of the looms 30,850, were in Yorkshire. Norfolk had 19,216 spindles and 428 looms[4]. The thing was done, a clean decisive defeat. Worsted had become the Yorkshire industry which it would remain.

The woollen manufacture had almost reached the pitch of concentration which it showed in the twentieth century. It was, and is, less concentrated than cotton and much less concentrated than worsted. Of 138,000 people who described themselves as engaged in it in 1851 only 56,000 were in the West Riding; 15,000 in Scotland; 11,000 in Lancashire; 9000 in Gloucestershire; 7000 in Wiltshire—and the rest scattered over the remaining counties of England and Wales as the industries map suggests, Devon being the county next to Wiltshire in order of importance. Fifty years later the West Riding had still only half the woollen spindles in the kingdom, which implies only a

---

[1] Redford, A., *Labour Migration in England*, 1800–50 (1926), p. 9, 111.

[2] "Cotton worker" is here used in the comprehensive sense adopted in the table on p. 24 above.

[3] Blyth, *The Norwich Guide and Directory*, 1842, p. 62. Clapham, J. H., "The Transference of the Worsted Industry from East Anglia to the West Riding," *E. J.* 1910, p. 195 *sqq.*

[4] *F. J. Reports*, 1851, *A. and P.* XXIII. 117.

slight increase of concentration during that long and economically decisive age[1].

Just as cotton had drawn into Lancashire and wool into the West Riding, so flax was drawing northward into Scotland—and out of Great Britain altogether into Ulster. It had already ceased to be a really important English industry; for of some 103,000 people engaged in it in Britain no less than 77,000 were Scots, largely hand-loom weavers.

Silk still held out against the mechanical and geographical forces which were making for concentration. There were indeed more silk workers in mechanical Lancashire than in any other county[2], whereas Lancashire had hardly been reckoned a silk county at all thirty years earlier. In Cheshire the old nucleus of workers had grown with the aid of machinery to 22,000. But there were many about Coventry, where power was little used: there were still 16,000 in London and from 2000 to 6000 in each of six other counties. In nearly every place where there was any textile manufacturing, some silk was worked and the industry persisted in a few places where there was no other.

It is not easy to exaggerate the importance of the textile manufactures in the industrial life of the country. Although not even that of cotton was completely mechanised—there may have been still 40,000 to 50,000 cotton hand-looms at work[3]—they stood as the representative industries of the age of machinery and power, even though coal-mining and metallurgy had more final significance. Because they were so much mechanised their output was prodigious. Because they were not completely mechanised they carried with them in their march, and often left to fall by the wayside, a host of those who had now become handworking camp-followers. Not counting hosiery and lace, they found employment for—or should we say gave a trade name to?—nearly eleven hundred thousand people.

Their social importance can perhaps be best brought out by a comparison of 1851 with 1901. The comparison is not statistically exact at all points, but is quite exact enough for purposes of illustration[4]:

[1] Clapham, J. H., *The Woollen and Worsted Industries* (1907), p. 20.

[2] But many of them were hand-loom weavers, whose occupation survived to be hurt by French imports under the 'Cobden' Treaty of 1860.

[3] See vol. I. p. 554.

[4] The 1901 figures are from the *Survey of Industrial Relations* (1926) reproduced in the *Eighteenth Abstract of Labour Statistics*, 1926, p. 20. The heading

|  | 1851 | 1901 |
|---|---|---|
| Population of Great Britain . . . . . | 20,960,000 | 37,000,000 |
| Cotton workers (in 1851 with printers, dyers, etc.) . | 527,000 | 544,000 |
| Wool workers . . . . . . . . | 284,000 | 235,000 |
| Silk workers . . . . . . . | 133,000 | 37,000 |
| Linen and hemp workers (in 1901 with jute) . . | 134,000 | 99,000 |
| Textile printers, dyers, etc. . . . . . |  | 79,000 |
|  | 1,078,000 | 994,000 |

That is to say, the trades, or their nearest equivalents, which at the opening of the twentieth century employed 1 in 37 of the population had employed 1 in 19 in the year of the Great Exhibition. The hand-working camp-followers outside the mills, and the relative imperfection of machinery inside, account for the astonishing figures of 1851. It is to be remembered that, although there were nearly 250,000 power-looms in the cotton industry in 1850, there were less than 33,000 in worsted, less than 10,000 in woollen, barely 6000 in flax and not 1200 in silk[1].

Even in spinning, mechanisation was not complete, though true hand-spinning was dead in the factory districts, and nearly all the decisive inventions had been made. About 1830, American inventors had introduced the cap and the ring spindles[2], which were to become important in the worsted and cotton industries. But neither was economically decisive, for neither affected industrial organisation or greatly extended the empire of the machine; they were just improvements on the flyer spindle which Arkwright had borrowed from the spinning wheel. Nor had either gained a secure footing in Britain by 1850, and thereafter their progress was slow. That of the British-invented self-acting mule had not been quick, nor was it to become so; a fact of special interest because only with the arrival of the self-actor did mule-spinning become completely automatic. In the old 'hand mule,' although power supplied the main motive force, the 'carriage' on which the spindles are ranked was pulled out and pushed back by the spinner, the yarn being drawn out fine and twisted on the outward run and wound on to the bobbin on the return. It was the toil of this pushing and pulling that a deputation of cotton-spinners once

'Linen and Hemp Workers' includes those classes from the 1851 Occupations census (used on p. 24, above) most closely comparable with those under the heading 'Flax, Hemp, Jute, Rope, Canvas and Canvas Goods' in the 1926 *Survey*. Jute was not a distinct industry in 1851. See below, p. 84.

[1] Vol. I. p. 544.          [2] Above, p. 13.

illustrated to Lord Palmerston with a heavy arm-chair in his
own drawing-room[1]. The effective self-actor had been invented
by Roberts of Manchester in 1825. By 1834 his firm had made
520 self-actors with over 200,000 spindles, and they were hoping
to double the number in 1834–5[2]. But like so many new
machines, the self-actor was for a long time too rough for the
finest work—it did not wind the yarn well on the bobbin, for one
thing—and too dear for the smaller spinners. When the great
New Lanark mills were sold, for the second or third time, in
1851, they contained 28,900 self-actor spindles, but also 13,600
'hand-mule spindles.'[3] "On account of the excessive cost very
few firms were able to purchase the self-actor," a secretary of
the Oldham Master Spinners wrote long after, "and therefore
hand-mules were the rule and self-actor mules the exception."[4]
In the early 'fifties few self-actors were used in fine-spinning
districts such as that of Bolton, and they were far from universal
in the districts which span the medium and coarse counts[5].

In woollen spinning, as has already been noted, the operation of slubbing, which Andrew Ure had called a handicraft in
1834, had been little changed. The original 'slubbing billy' was
a hand-worked machine like the original jenny. Child piecers
rubbed together gauzy strips of wool from the carding engine, to
be roughly spun on the billy before going to their final spinning on the jenny or mule. By 1850 the billy might be power
driven, but the arduous piecing work for it remained. Even
eight years later Edward Baines of Leeds, when describing the
local industry before the British Association, treated the billy as
normal, though he spoke of a "new machine called the condenser" which would cut out billy and piecers and link the
carding machine direct to the mule[6].

Precisely in the year 1851 a textile invention perhaps more
decisive than that of the self-acting mule was completed for
England: Donisthorpe and Lister perfected a wool-combing
machine which became at once commercially successful. There

[1] Hodder, *Life of Lord Shaftesbury*, II. 19–21, quoting Grant, P., *The Ten Hours Bill* (1866).

[2] Baines, E., *History of the Cotton Manufacture* (1835), p. 207–8.

[3] Advertisement in the *Economist*, December 27, 1851.

[4] From a paper read before the British Association in 1887, quoted in Chapman, S. J., *The Lancashire Cotton Industry*, p. 69.

[5] Chapman, *op. cit.* p. 70.

[6] From a paper read in 1858 printed in his *Yorkshire Past and Present*, II. 632. Cf. p. 12, above and p. 83, below.

had been combing machines since Cartwright's day, but his Big Ben, though it had alarmed the hand-combers, neither ruined them nor made a fortune for Cartwright. They could still do better work than any machine. Down to about 1840 their position was reasonably safe—safe from machinery if not from themselves; for their trade was easily learned and the immigrant Irish took to it, with other unskilled and half-skilled men[1]. Then came the effective machines. All through the 'forties in England and France the inventors ultimately successful were at work—Donisthorpe, Heilmann, Lister, Holden, Noble. Heilmann succeeded first, and his patents were sold most profitably to English firms for use not only in the worsted but also in the cotton and flax industries. Lister and Donisthorpe adopted one of his central principles; and though Lister claimed that they had mastered all the difficulties connected with the invention "before M. Heilmann's patent was heard of," Heilmann's representatives secured a verdict for infringement against them in 1852. Next year the comb named after Noble—though it seems to have been mainly the work of Donisthorpe—came on the market; and a few years later Holden, a second collaborator with Lister, perfected another type of comb upon which he had first worked in 1847–8 or earlier[2].

These two men were not simple inventors: they were industrial organisers and combatants of the first rank, and Lister, a gentleman born, started with some capital. They had a European view. In conjunction they had started a combing mill at St Denis in 1849. Within a few years Lister dominated the industry. He sold machines to spinners for a royalty of £1000 each. By 1855 he had five English, three French and one German mill combing on commission for spinners. Never before had a factory industry been more quickly born, once the long gestation was over; nor did one ever grow more quickly. By 1857 James, the contemporary historian of the worsted industry, could write that "by far the larger proportion of the wool worked up in the worsted branch is combed by machinery," and could add that "far the greater proportion of all the wool …now combed is combed by Lister's machine."[3] A single

---

[1] James, *op. cit.* p. 501.

[2] The technical story of the patents is most fully told in Burnley's *Wool and Woolcombing*. Lister's claim to have anticipated Heilmann is from a public speech quoted by Burnley on p. 221.

[3] *Op. cit.* p. 564, 573: for the Lister and Holden mills, Burnley, *op. cit.* p. 275, 300.

Lister comb would do the work of a hundred skilled men easily, and do it very much better. Thus wool-combing was mechanised.

In the hosiery and lace industries, which rested on the primary textiles, very advanced hand-driven mechanisms had existed for generations. To these power had been applied, but only sporadically and much more often for lace than for hosiery. Lace-making by machine had developed, between 1760 and 1770, out of the making of fancy stockings on the knitting frame[1]. A little later came the 'warp' machine which combined, as its name implies, the longitudinal threads of a loom with the looped stitches of knitting. Many elaborate types of lace and net machine followed. It was fifty-five of these—John Heathcot's 'traverse bobbin net machines'—which Luddites smashed in Heathcot's factory at Loughborough in 1816. James Towle, their leader, was hanged at Leicester for attempted murder, "in presence of an immense multitude...singing a hymn with seeming fervour."[2] Heathcot bought an old mill at Tiverton, where the Devon cloth industry was decaying[3], and drove his new machines by power. His firm employed 1200 workpeople by 1836, and in the 'fifties between that and 2000. Meanwhile a number of other 'bobbin net' manufacturers had imitated his factory methods, especially about Nottingham. By 1831 there were 22 power factories in the country supposed to contain about 1000 machines employing directly about 3000 people. There were also hand-machine factories with some 5000 machines and there was a complicated system of out-work for finishing and embroidering the net[4]. Perhaps the area of power in the early 'fifties was four times what it had been in 1831; but in dealing with so intricate an industry, much subject to fashion, precision is difficult. A factory might use power and be half full of hand-workers. Its goods might be given out by 'finishing houses' to 'mistresses,' who overworked groups of young girls in 'drawing, scalloping, carding'; and as the whole

[1] The general narrative is in Felkin, W., *History of the Machine Wrought Hosiery and Lace Manufactures* (1867). For the early nineteenth century see also Ure, *The Cotton Manufacture*, II. 342 sqq., 420.

[2] Felkin, *op. cit.* p. 238.    [3] See vol. I. p. 45, n. 3.

[4] Felkin, *op. cit.* p. 340. These are the personal estimates of Felkin, who was in the trade. By 1840, in one factory inspector's district the hand machines were to the power machines as 2½ : 1. *S.C. on Mills and Factories*, Q. 3085. In 1843 "above half" of the lace machines were hand-worked. *R. on the...Lace Manufacture [and]..the Factory Act* (1861, XXII. 461), p. 6.

industry was relatively small the absolute amount of power factory work was inconsiderable.

In hosiery it was still almost negligible. There had long been 'shops of frames'—small factories without power—and a few power-knitting factories existed before 1840[1], but when William Felkin of his own initiative took a frame census in 1844 he found that throughout the whole industry—silk, cotton and wool— "the number of frames under one roof averaged...rather more than three."[2] There were about 15,000 masters to 33,000 journeymen. The masters as a class were not economically independent. Most of them worked for hosiers or hosiers' middlemen, but they were not factory hands. It would have been far better for them had they been. Power was, however, being applied here and there in the late 'forties and early 'fifties, to the 'rotary' frames for knitting wide goods and to the circular knitter which makes a seamless knitted tube, a machine invented by Isambard Brunel the elder in 1816, neglected for thirty years from conservatism and fear of trouble with the knitters, and only introduced effectively after 1847[3].

The very imperfect mechanisation of most of the remaining British industries is shown whenever the capital equipment or the numbers employed can in any way be tested. There were gigantic iron works in which Nasmyth's steam-hammer had now been added to the equipment, and there were integrated firms covering the whole field from the coal and iron mine to the finished article; but the iron business with one or two rather small blast furnaces was more typical[4]. Right through the light metal and cutlery trades in their infinite variety the small non-mechanised, or power hiring, business predominated. A trade here and there was transformed. Twelve steel-pen making firms in 1849 employed an average of 154 workpeople each[5]; but what Léon Faucher wrote of Birmingham industry in 1845 remained generally true of all the industries which lay in and about Birmingham—"like French agriculture" they had "got into a state of parcellation."[6] There and elsewhere mechanical

---

[1] S.C. on Mills and Factories, 1840, x, Q. 3108: "Stocking frames have recently been worked by power."    [2] Felkin, op. cit. p. 464.    [3] Op. cit. p. 496-9.
[4] See vol. I. p. 428-30. But in 1848, 22 per cent. of the 'ironworks' made 57 per cent. of the pig-iron. Fong, H. D., Triumph of Factory System in England (Tientsin, 1930), p. 140.
[5] Birmingham and the Midland Hardware District (1866), p. 49.
[6] Quoted in vol. I. p. 175.

engineering proper was moving swiftly and its greatest firms were growing fast. Yet out of the 677 English and Welsh engine and machine makers who made returns of the number of men they employed at the census of 1851, although 14 each employed more than 350, 537 employed less than 20, and another 72 less than 50[1].

At the ports and in the greatest towns were found the large steam flour mills which the *Economist* relied on to beat French competition[2]. It did not notice that they had neither adopted the French system of 'high grinding' nor tried the grinding rollers which had for some years been successful in Pesth[3]. Nor did it mention the thousand or two local water mills whose sizes and sites had not changed much since Domesday, in which the representative milling firm, the miller, employed one or two men. The demand for railway timber had encouraged the erection or extension of steam-driven sawmills at the ports: a group of timber-merchants and sawyers considerable in proportion to the size of the trade described themselves as employing more than 20 men; but only 4 out of 416 making returns claimed more than 50; and certainly the great sawmill was not a common thing.

The employment returns here quoted must be used with care. "Many employers of labour—in some trades nearly the whole number—omitted to attend to"[4] the instruction to make them; but they cover nearly three-quarters of a million workpeople; they are the only general figures from which exact information about the size of business units other than textile mills in the middle of the century can be derived; and for some important industries the returns are numerous enough to provide a very fair statistical sample. Only those are quoted in the condensed table given on p. 35[5] which do provide such a sample, which relate to trades of first-rate importance, and which agree with the facts of industrial organisation as otherwise roughly known. The figures in the third column are ambiguous. They include both those masters who said they had no workpeople and those who did not trouble to state the number of their

---

[1] *Census of 1851. Ages and Occupations*, I. cclxxvi. The Scottish returns under this head were so defective that they were not tabulated. See vol. I. p. 448.

[2] Above, p. 3.

[3] Bennett, R. and Elton, J., *A History of Corn-Milling* (1898–1904), III. 296 *sqq.* for the early history of roller-milling. There were English patents for it in the eighteenth century. [4] *Census of 1851*, as above.

[5] The original contains more numerical subdivisions and many more trades.

workpeople. Judging by the trades where the figures of this group are highest and lowest (*e.g.* the shoe-makers and the builders) it seems to be composed mainly of solitary working masters, though the figures under cotton manufacture do not allow of this interpretation. How many of these masters were really outworkers for a giving-out employer the figures do not show. Nor did the employer state whether or not his men worked on his premises. The figures are sign-posts in the field of industrial organisation, not a map of it; but they are useful sign-posts.

*Employers making returns and employed in certain trades in England and Wales, 1851*

| I<br>Trade | II<br>Masters making returns | III<br>No men or number not stated | IV<br>1 or 2 men | V<br>3–9 men | VI<br>10–19 men | VII<br>20–49 men | VIII<br>50–99 men | IX<br>100 and upwards |
|---|---|---|---|---|---|---|---|---|
| Tailor | 10991 | 4239 | 3852 | 2456 | 343 | 80 | 10 | 1 |
| Shoe-maker | 17665 | 7311 | 6016 | 3644 | 444 | 181 | 38 | 31 |
| Engine and machine maker | 837 | 160 | 152 | 295 | 90 | 72 | 49 | 34 |
| Builder | 3614 | 292 | 417 | 1541 | 701 | 498 | 113 | 52 |
| Wheelwright | 2057 | 670 | 982 | 373 | 20 | 11 | 1 | — |
| Tanner | 349 | 31 | 41 | 147 | 68 | 39 | 8 | 5 |
| Woollen cloth manufacture | 1107 | 131 | 199 | 329 | 156 | 179 | 41 | 82 |
| Worsted manufacture | 154 | 27 | 14 | 24 | 20 | 26 | 12 | 31 |
| Silk manufacture | 272 | 36 | 30 | 72 | 22 | 37 | 29 | 46 |
| Miller | 2394 | 403 | 1147 | 722 | 84 | 23 | 13 | 2 |
| Brewer | 776 | 120 | 228 | 319 | 67 | 34 | 3 | 5 |
| Lace manufacture | 317 | 58 | 54 | 123 | 28 | 26 | 9 | 19 |
| Cotton manufacture | 1670 | 482 | 81 | 174 | 124 | 216 | 172 | 411 |
| Earthenware manufacture | 378 | 68 | 68 | 112 | 31 | 56 | 7 | 36 |
| Blacksmith | 7331 | 2282 | 4035 | 967 | 31 | 15 | 1 | — |

Evidently for some old-fashioned crafts in which the terms master, journeyman, apprentice were still quite clear, the figures though not exhaustive are almost perfectly representative. The black smiths' and wheelwrights' figures illustrate this. The tailor ' and shoe-makers' are more difficult, for into them the outworking and shopkeeping elements enter; but they show clearly enough the rarity of large tailors' businesses and the co-existence in boot and shoe-making of a fair number of big—in fact outworking—businesses and innumerable cobblers and small handworking retailers. The engineering figures have been discussed already. Those for building are an invaluable contribution to the history of a trade whose movements are particularly hard to follow with any steady vision[1]. They show quite clearly the master bricklayer or master carpenter starting as a builder with his handful of men; often failing or getting no further; sometimes becoming a substantial employer; occasionally rising into the group of great building contractors. Five firms returned themselves as employers of more than 350 men.

The tanners were beginning to move. Thirty years earlier they had been without exception, so far as is known, in a very small way of business[2]. They had not yet come under the influence either of machinery or of change. As Lyon Playfair said facetiously, if Simon the Tanner whose home was by the seashore at Joppa had lived to compete at the Great Exhibition "no doubt he would have carried off a medal."[3] But the demand for leather never slackened, especially in the industrial North, where it was so much used for machine belting and a thousand other purposes. Therefore, although the typical tanner was still an employer of from three to nine men, a few had pushed into the highest groups.

Among the textile figures those for worsted are obviously defective, though probably representative, those for woollen very illuminating when compared with those for cotton. The full woollen columns IV and V contain surviving domestic clothiers, VI and VII the small factories, which are also well represented in cotton. The contrast between woollen VIII and IX and cotton VIII and IX is overwhelming. Cotton IX contains 113 firms with employment figures of 350 and upwards, woollen IX, 21. Hosiery manufacture figures are not given here because the commissioners mixed up manufacturing and retailing hosiers.

Earthenware shows a well-developed factory system, though it was a system which made little use of power owing to the nature of the processes. The figures suggest a slightly greater amount of industrial concentration than in woollen, not so much as in worsted, and not nearly so much as in cotton. In milling the contrast is marked between a very small group of what are

---

[1] There are some tolerable figures for the London building trades of 1860 in the *Social Science Association's Report on Trade Societies* of that year, p. 53.
[2] See vol. I. p 170.    [3] *1851 Exhibition Lectures*, I. 175.

clearly large steam mills; a group of about a hundred fair-sized mills, probably all steam driven; a larger, more indeterminate group (V), in which the water drive was probably general; and the mass of the old mills run by the miller, his mate and his lad. In the brewing figures there are evidently important omissions at the top of the scale; but thirty or forty men can work a very considerable brewery of the old type, so that most of the concerns in columns VII to IX might be classed as large units. The high figures in column IV, and perhaps some of those in column V, register the widespread survival of what has been called the handicraft brewer, the victualler who brewed his own beer and had provided most of the beer sold in many parts of the country twenty years earlier[1]. There were, in fact, in 1853 in all England and Wales 2470 brewers, who consumed 21 million bushels of malt, and 31,000 brewing victuallers and beersellers, who consumed 11 million bushels. London had 79 brewers, 1 brewing victualler and 61 brewing beersellers[2]. In this case the sample of the trade given in the 1851 figures is inadequate and tends to underrate the importance of the small concern, probably because many of the victuallers and beersellers did not naturally describe themselves as brewers.

There had been a time, not so many years back, when engineering would have left little trace on an occupational census and might not have been marked on an industrial map such as Petermann's. Similarly, in 1851, a few young industries of special significance for the future had no official memorial, partly because they were numerically weak, but mainly because their importance had not yet impressed the official mind. Chief among them were those which handled waste products hitherto neglected or raw materials hitherto intractable or unknown. There had been waste-product industries since animal refuse was first made into glue or linen rags into paper; and one of them, paper-making, had acquired a certain well-bred eminence in spite of its connection with the dust-bin and the 'rag and bone' man; but it was only in the nineteenth century, and generally speaking only late in it, that waste-product industries came into their own. As the world saw it, two very different figures were working to promote them—the man with the muck rake turning over heaps of garbage in search of cheap substitutes and of

---

[1] Vol. I. p. 170–1.
[2] Excise returns for 1853, *A. and P.* 1854, LXV. 325.

gain; the man of science seeking the truth and utility of things and believing that none of them is common or unclean. Perhaps the two should seem to the historian only aspects of a single figure, since gain and utility are cousins and the cheapening of things has been the handmaid of cleanliness.

Cheap substitutes, especially in cloth-making, were a reputed abuse against which gilds and government had made laws for centuries. They had been used most in poor outlying districts where gilds were few and laws ran with difficulty. Yorkshire clothiers in Elizabeth's day made their cloth mostly of coarse wool "and ffloxe and thrummes."[1] Before the last of the laws which had tried to make them do something else was repealed, in 1821[2], they had begun to use the modern 'adulterant'—torn-up rags, shoddy. Yorkshire tradition gave the year 1813 as that of the discovery of shoddy, a very appropriate date for the introduction of a cheap substitute—the peak price year of the century[3]. Machines for grinding up rags to make flocks for saddlery had been used before this in London. It is the very plausible conjecture of the first and only historian of shoddy that they were modifications of the rag-grinding machine which had come from the continent into the English paper trade about 1770[4]; or perhaps they were connected with a Scotsman's patent of 1801 "for preparing wove silk...from articles that have been wore," by grinding them up[5]. The first Yorkshire users of the machines, in Batley, Dewsbury and Brighouse, were characteristically secretive.

By 1828 the new 'adulterant' had come within the view of parliament. A London woolstapler told the Lords' Committee on the Wool Trade of that year that there was already a considerable import of foreign rags for use in Dewsbury. The shoddy went, he said, into "low carpets and low druggets," "goods made for sale not for wear." A second witness said that it never went into goods "for outer wear." A third, who used it, admitted that clothes "for workhouse purposes" were

[1] Heaton, H., *The Yorkshire Woollen Industry* (1920), p. 145: see also p. 97, 131.
[2] Vol. I. p. 339.
[3] Jubb, Saml., *The History of the Shoddy Trade* (1860), p. 17: "ten or fifteen years" before 1828, evidence of John Nussey of Birstall before the *Lords' S.C. on the Wool Trade*, 1828, p. 248.
[4] Jubb, *op. cit.* p. 19. For the paper machine, Spicer, A. D., *The Paper Trade* (1907), p. 55-7.
[5] Warner, Sir F., *The Silk Industry of the United Kingdom* (n.d. actually 1921), p. 426.

made of it, and that a proportion of it, with thrums, was blended with the new wool to make cheap " duffil" cloth "for the lower order of people who cannot get better goods." The machine that made it, one of these witnesses explained, was called "the manufacturers' devil."[1]

This name, with its derivative "devils' dust," was a godsend for men of letters out of love with their own day and for Chartist orators. Printers and barristers had devils, and rag-grinding machines made dust. The shoddy, used in reason, was no worse than the other forms of wool-waste which had always gone into cheap cloth, nor than the rag-waste which went into paper. "Duffil" kept "the lower order of people" warmer than its alternatives, cotton fustians, second-hand clothes, or the coarse linens of Thomas Carlyle's "Past." The shoddy was not always used in reason: rag-grinding is an unpleasant and used not to be a healthy job; the word shoddy probably deserved the connotation which it acquired. There was fraud and that 'illicit' profit which presumably there had been when rag-paper displaced vellum. But the thing rag-wool had nothing hellish about it. Had it not been discovered, the later nineteenth century would have been chillier or dirtier, or both.

Between 1828 and 1850 its use, which remained an English monopoly, was spreading obscurely and a little shamefacedly in the 'heavy woollen district' between the valleys of the Calder and the Aire. At first only soft rags such as stockings and flannels had been torn into shoddy. From about the mid 'thirties the devil was put at hard rags of fulled and felted cloth, old uniform coats, broadcloths and tailors' clippings. It tore them more slowly into 'mungo.' The seams and untearable bits, rotted, went with the true devils' dust, the unspinnable residuum, to manure hopyards. By the 'fifties the dust was beginning to be preserved in its separate colours, for use in making 'flock' wall papers. And so, the unique historian wrote, a few years later, "not a single thing belonging to the rag and shoddy system is valueless or useless."[2]

The close and rather secret association of the rag-wool with the pure wool manufacture made factory inspectors and census officials omit it from their statistics. But there was already

[1] *Lords' S.C.* p. 86, 54, 141.
[2] Jubb, *op. cit.* p. 24. Jubb's traditional date for 'mungo' is 1834. The traditional derivation is that, when the workmen said the hard rags would not go, the Yorkshire employer said "they mun go."

a distinct commercial and industrial organisation. By the side of the new railway through Batley, regular rag sales were organised in the early 'fifties, "on a precisely similar plan to the London colonial wool sales."[1] Rags were imported in quantity and were even 'ground' abroad by migrants from Batley and Dewsbury. Special groups of rag-sorting and shoddy-dealing firms had grown up. The latter either owned 'devils' or got rags ground for them on commission. Originally the cloth manufacturer had ground his own, and often he continued to do so; but now much rag-wool was sold and used outside the district where the business had originated; for in the 'fifties 'mungo' was "insinuating itself into the very seats of the fine cloth manufacture."[2] Hence the specialists to purvey it. The bulk of the rag-wool, however, either went without much admixture of new wool into the paddings, druggets, "workhouse cloths," "convict cloths," "slave cloths" and cheap blankets for which it had first been used, or—and perhaps predominantly—with a fair stiffening of new wool into the very serviceable "pilot cloths" which had become the staple manufacture of the district.

As a young waste-product industry the shoddy trade was lonely in its success. The paper-makers had long since adopted cotton rags as a standard high-grade raw material, using linen alone only for such things as bank notes. For their brown and wrapping papers almost any vegetable waste fibre would serve; but there had been no important recent innovation, except perhaps the 'overloading' of some papers with china clay, not a waste product[3]. Since most continental countries now tried to keep their good paper rags at home, the country was very thoroughly searched for suitable materials. No new waste ones had been found, though there had been experimental makings of straw-board. Glue-makers, size-makers, horn and bone workers, lampblack-makers, catgut twisters, plasterers with their cow hair, and the like, had learnt nothing fresh about the standard uses of animal refuse, though bone-manure making as an industry was only of recent growth[4]. For the most part Britain let her waste products run to waste. All the reserved utilities in her tar had not yet been revealed by the chemists.

[1] Jubb, op. cit. p. 36.         [2] Such as Huddersfield: ibid. p. 30.
[3] See Spicer, op. cit. p. 13, 26; also vol. I. p. 325–6.
[4] Vol. I. p. 456.

She sent her coal half-consumed in thousands of tons into the air, to blacken the skies and destroy the health and buildings of her cities, as she sent the rich fats from her wool-washing troughs and much of the fertilising domestic refuse of her towns to defile her streams and canals. Some intelligent farmers, however, had irrigated fields near Holyrood, long before 1850, from the Foul Burn which carried "the contents of a large proportion of the sinks, drains and privies" of Edinburgh[1]. Her coke was often made by burning piled coal in the open and never with any regard to economy of heat or by-products[2]. Her blast-furnaces flamed superbly and wastefully into the night. At "scarcely half-a-dozen" of them was any use made of "the waste gases" in 1851[3]. Here at least was a beginning, if a small one; but not of a new industry.

Of the industries dependent on new raw materials, or on materials newly made available, and still young and small enough to slip through the ordinary statistical meshes, that of caout-chouc—as the educated and even the industrialists still wished to call it[4]—was certainly first in importance. Caoutchouc is "now almost a necessity of life" one of the 1851 Exhibition lecturers said[5]. Yet it left no trace on the very elaborate census figures of that year[6], and the foreign trade returns showed an import of this necessary which had only grown from 150 tons in 1846, when the published records first took account of it, through 290 tons in 1848, to 380 in 1850. The industry was then rather more than five and twenty years old. Men of vision had seen the possibilities of the odd substance almost as soon as it be-came really known to science during the second quarter of the eighteenth century. South American Indians had shown the way. "On en fait des bottines impénétrables à l'eau, des balles qui rebondissent avec beaucoup de force," Turgot wrote in

---

[1] Chadwick's *Report on the Sanitary Condition of the Labouring Population*, 1842, p. 48.

[2] See Lowthian Bell's protests against this form of waste so late as 1881 in *Trans. Inst. Mech. Eng.* 1881, p. 432; and again in 1884 in his *Principles of the Manufacture of Iron and Steel*, p. 50.

[3] Playfair, Lyon, 1851 *Exhibition Lectures*, I. 169.

[4] See for its early history, Hancock, T., *Personal narrative of the origin and progress of the Caoutchouc or India Rubber manufacture in England*, 1857; also Collins, J., in *British Manufacturing Industries*, 1876, VII. 97.

[5] Solly, E., *India rubber or Caoutchouc*, I. 255.

[6] The numbers employed have always been relatively small: they only rose above 25,000 in the decade 1911–21. 18*th Abstract of Labour Statistics*, p. 27.

1769[1]; elastic bottles, too, which "peuvent servir de seringues." You might make flexible pipes, surgical bandages, valves for "la machine pneumatique," waterproof clothes and tents and a multitude of useful things. Unhappily, he said, "la gomme élastique" was still very rare: he might have added, had he known, that it was mechanically intractable and chemically perverse.

For fifty years a few chemists experimented with it, a few inventors took out vain patents for utilising it, and other people rubbed out pencil marks with it. In 1820 one of the inventors, Thomas Hancock of London, filed a patent for an elastic wrist band. Three years later Charles Macintosh of Glasgow patented his waterproof varnish, based on the fact already known to chemists that caoutchouc would dissolve in naphtha. Hancock really founded the industry by making the caoutchouc mechanically tractable. He could not get the bits of the stuff to unite readily, and so could not get the sizes he wanted, until he had torn them and pressed them in his 'masticator'—a toothed solid cylinder working in a toothed hollow one, not altogether unlike the shoddy-maker's devil. For something like twelve years he kept the creature working for him in secrecy, while he patented things that Turgot had foreseen—surgical bandages, hose pipes, water-beds. Barclays the brewers first took up his pipes after "a vast amount of opposition from the leather hose-makers."[2] One after another the now familiar uses were marked down. By 1835 the rather simple secret of the masticator was out, but the Hancocks still led the little industry.

All this time rubber goods suffered from the chemical defects of a material which became rigid at a rather early point of cold, decomposed at a rather early point of heat, and was dissolved at varying speeds in different kinds of grease including—though here dissolution was slow—human sweat. These facts may help to explain medical opposition to the early macintoshes and rubber shoes. Thomas Hancock was always at work trying every kind of chemical combination with his rubber. From about 1840 he carried on secret experiments with sulphur, and by 1843 he was patenting his process of 'vulcanisation' which yielded—among other things—the rubber statues of the Great Exhibition[3]. He always asserted that it was a mistake to suppose

---

[1] *Œuvres* (ed. Schelle), III. 103.

[2] The *Personal narrative*, p. 61. Hancock and Macintosh are in the *D.N.B.*

[3] It is said that he examined in 1842 some rubber "cured" by a secret process by his American contemporary, Charles Goodyear, for whom it is customary in

that rubber was not largely used before this last invention. As early as 1837–8, he said, his firm "often" used three to four tons a week[1]. But he did not say how often, and the import figures show when the real rise in consumption began. His 'elastic vulcanised rubber' resisted temperatures, both up and down, which would have ruined plain rubber. Hence its position as a necessary in a mechanical age. Its use for valves, to take a single instance famous at the time, greatly helped the adoption of high-speed screw marine engines[2]. The rigid vulcanised rubbers also, in their various grades, were finding innumerable uses; so that rubber imports, which had stood at 150 tons in 1846, for the years 1850–59 were to be:

| | Tons | | Tons | | Tons |
|---|---|---|---|---|---|
| 1850 | 380 | 1854 | 1380 | 1857 | 1100 |
| 1851 | 760 | 1855 | 2230 | 1858 | 1250 |
| 1852 | 980 | 1856 | 1440 | 1859 | 1060 |
| 1853 | 870 | | | | |

From 1846 the Hancocks had rubber works at Stratford-le-Bow. There they also handled an even newer raw material, gutta-percha[3]. It had only been brought to public notice in England in 1842 by Dr Montgomerie of Singapore, but by 1845 there was demand keen enough to produce reckless tree-felling in Malaya. That was the year of the first regular sales in London. The Hancocks took up the new material, tested it, treated it and began to sample its surgical and other uses. This was the time of experimental under-water telegraphy, and gutta-percha at once commended itself to Werner Siemens as a coating for cables. He used it on a trial cable across the Rhine in 1847 and at Kiel harbour in 1848. It was employed for the Hudson cable of 1849 and the Dover-Calais cables of 1850–51. William Siemens had recommended it to the British Electric Telegraph Company in March, 1850, and had made arrangements for

America to claim the invention (e.g. Bolles, A. S., *Industrial History of the United States*, p. 483). There is also a German claimant, Hindersdorf: *British Manufacturing Industries*, VII. 136. It is perhaps safest, with Levasseur, E., *Hist. des classes ouvrières et de l'industrie...de* 1789 à 1870, IV. 556 n., to divide the credit between Goodyear and Hancock: though Goodyear certainly used sulphur before Hancock patented its use. It is significant that both machinery and capital for the North British Rubber Co. of 1855 came from America. Bremner, D., *The Industries of Scotland* (1869), p. 363.

[1] *Personal narrative*, p. 140.
[2] 1851 *Exhibition Lectures*, I. 409.
[3] There is a first-hand account of the early use by Collins in *Brit. Man. Industries*, VII. 72 *sqq.* For the Hancock works, *V. C. H. Essex*, II. 495.

its manufacture[1]. Conditions were ripening for the growth
of big industrial units. In 1852 S. W. Silver and Co. moved
their waterproofing works across the Thames from Greenwich,
joined the Hancocks, and began to work rubber and gutta-
percha on a great scale. At first their advertisements of 'vulcanised and unvulcanised india-rubber in every form' were
issued from 'North Woolwich'; by 1858 the heading was
'Silvertown.'[2]

The rising, indeed the risen, cement industry of the mid
nineteenth century can hardly be classed with industries based
on raw materials hitherto waste or new or intractable, though
there had been an element of intractability. But like shoddy and
rubber it was overlooked by the enumerators of 1851, who
tabulated what were presumably the smaller industries of die-
sinking and dealing in feathers and quills. Like rubber, it
borrows from its future an importance out of line with whatever
may have been the size of its occupation group, or of its business units, in 1851. Its past and present were those of a rule of
thumb, trial and error, rather small, very slightly mechanised
industry. It had grown with the new harbour, canal and railway
works of the previous sixty years[3]. The eighteenth century
knew no 'hydraulic' (water-resisting) cements, though by burning clayey limestones there had been produced what are now
called hydraulic limes, some of which came very near to modern
Portland cement in composition. On the London clay of the
Thames estuary the limey nodules common in that formation
must often have gone to the limekilns. Probably some accident
showed that, after calcination, they yielded a cement. The clay
which had worked into their cracks furnished, with the limestone, that combination of lime, silica and alumina which, when
heated to the point of chemical combination and then ground,
is the raw stuff of all hydraulic cements. In 1796 James Parker
of Northfleet in Kent patented this very simple handling of
what came to be called 'cement stones.'[4] With a fine instinct
for publicity he had called his product Roman Cement.

[1] Pole, W., *The Life of Sir William Siemens* (1888), p. 86, 113; Jeans, W. T.,
*Creators of the Age of Steel* (2nd ed. 1885), p. 194; Bolles, *op. cit.* p. 436; Clapham, J. H., *Economic Development of France and Germany*, p. 157.

[2] Advertisement in the *Economist, e.g.* March 27, 1858.

[3] Art. "Cement," *Encyc. Britt.* 11th ed.; Butler, D. B., *Portland Cement*
(1899). For harbour works, below, p. 520 *sqq.*

[4] *V. C. H. Essex*, II. 405.

The average 'cement stone' of the London clay does in fact contain, along with a good many other things, the essentials of a very quick setting but not very strong cement[1]. So the hunt for cement stones began. They could be dug or, more cheaply, dredged for. The easiest digging was in the clay cliffs of Essex. These suffered much in consequence. Dredging became an important industry on the Thames, the Blackwater and the Stour in the early nineteenth century: about 1850 some hundreds of smacks still lived by it, though by that time the trade was falling off[2].

The demand for 'Roman Cement' declined before the almost equally well named 'Portland Cement,' a name apparently adopted by Joseph Aspdin, a Leeds stonemason who took out his patent in 1824, because Portland stone was a fine thing and so was his cement and looked rather like it[3]. It was originally just an artificial mixture of the materials—lime and clay, calcined and ground—which nature had mixed in the cement stone. Aspdin made a true Yorkshire secret of it; and legend shows his son working at Wakefield behind twenty-foot walls. Meanwhile others had been attacking the rather obvious problem on the Thames. As they solved it while Aspdin was hiding his dusty knowledge in what is not naturally a good cement-making region, the priority of his patent is not historically very important. By about 1830 Major-General Sir C. W. Pasley at Chatham and the firm of Frost at Northfleet had made good cements from the abundant local materials—chalk and Medway mud[4]. Chemical knowledge of the ingredients was incomplete; their calcination and their chemical combination were defective; grinding was very defective; but the process with the controlled materials prevailed in time over that which accepted any cement stone as good enough. By trial and error, the mixture which produced the maximum strength was found out; the cement was made reasonably uniform; and, about 1850, the 'Portland' industry, which was growing in its first natural home on the Medway, began to work for export.

At first the customs authorities made no returns; but it is known that there was an export of 21,000 tons, worth £64,000, in 1853, which had risen to 79,000 tons, worth £215,000, by 1860[5].

[1] Butler, *op. cit.* p. 3.    [2] *V. C. H. Essex*, II. 405.
[3] See the centenary notices in the press of 1924, *e.g. Observer*, Nov. 7, 1924.
[4] Butler, *op. cit.* p. 2–3.
[5] *Annual Statement of Trade*, 1854–5, LI; 1861, LX. The export in the 'fifties was largely to France.

From the side of organisation the cement industry of the mid century falls into line with such plain unskilled-labour industries as chalk-quarrying and lime-burning. Most of the men in it probably returned themselves as simple labourers in 1851. The calcined material, which had been man-handled before calcination, was broken up with hammers by hand; barrowed to the grinding millstones; and barrowed again to the dumps. No important labour-saving device was introduced for another twenty years; the great business unit was far in the future; and the imperfectly calcined and ill-ground product was of a quantity which "the veriest speculative builder"[1] would have rejected forty years later. But such as it was, like much other British produce of the 'fifties, it had no foreign competition to face at home and something like a monopoly of the export market.

[1] Butler, *op. cit.* p. 4. The first important labour-saving device did not come till 1872.

# CHAPTER III

## THE COURSE OF INDUSTRIAL CHANGE, 1850–86

LOOKING back on English life from the year 1880 over the thirty-one years since he first published *The Seven Lamps of Architecture*, John Ruskin wrote of "the ferruginous temper" which he then "saw rapidly developing itself, and which, since that day, has changed our Merry England into the Man in the Iron Mask."[1] (While he wrote the mask was turning visibly into steel.) The "ferruginous temper" went back far beyond 1849, as he implied and we know. In the 'twenties foreigners had seen it manifested in the "enormous iron cylinders" which rolled English garden walks[2]. In 1848–9, when the temper was only developing, Great Britain made perhaps half the pig iron of the world, and in 1853 doubts were expressed of her power to maintain so huge an output[3]. Yet she almost trebled it during the next thirty years, continuing to make more than the whole of a far more industrial world for eighteen of them. Further, she had passed from an age of empiricism and from a technique which—at least in the primary processes of iron and steel making—had made no important progress since 1828[4] into an age in which irons, slags, cokes, gases, steels and temperatures could be studied by exact methods, and in which the whole range of scientific problems connected with the inventions of Bessemer, Siemens and Thomas was faced, if not many of its peaks had been mastered. Led by Joseph Whitworth, the metal workers were learning precision. Metallurgy and the metal workers have an absolute primacy in the history of modern manufacturing industry. In no generation is that primacy more obvious.

During the twenty years between 1830 and 1850, the West of Scotland, once an insignificant producing area, had become the producer of more than a quarter of Britain's pig iron. In Staffordshire, furnaces had gone out of blast; South Wales had lost its dominating position[5]. But Scotland's best ironstone,

---

[1] *The Seven Lamps of Architecture* (ed. of 1880), p. 70 n.
[2] Dupin, *The Commercial Power of Great Britain* (Eng. ed. 1825), I. 165.
[3] See vol. I. p. 425.
[4] When Neilson introduced the hot-blast. Vol. I. p. 51, 426.
[5] Vol. I. p. 425–6, 428–30.

the 'blackband,' was known to be limited. It was this knowledge, combined with the instinctive conviction that the head-
long pace of the early railway age must be a transitory thing,
which made the iron-historian of that age suppose, in 1853,
that "we must retrograde"...."unless mineral fields at present
unknown come into operation."[1] Yet Scotland managed to
increase her 'make' of iron for another seventeen years, though
she never again had so large a share of the whole British 'make'
as she had when he was writing[2]; and the new mineral fields
were already in use. For many years South Wales, where native
coal-measure ironstones were limited and not very rich, had
drawn upon the 'pockets' of hematite ore in Cumberland and
Furness[3]. When official mineral statistics were first collected,
for 1854, it appeared that over 500,000 tons of this ore, with an
average content of something like 55 per cent. of iron, had been
raised in the year, and nearly all shipped away, some to Staffordshire and Scotland, most to Wales[4]. Since 1836 the much poorer
lias ironstone of Cleveland—it averages only 30 per cent. of
iron—had been regularly worked in the valley of the Esk, above
Whitby, and shipped first to the Tyne and then to the Tees, for
smelting mixed with the local coal-measure ironstones[5]. By
1850 the iron output of the North-Eastern area had risen to
something like 150,000 tons. In that year John Vaughan ascertained that the main seam of the lias ironstone came through
the Cleveland hills till it got into touch with tide-water and
South Durham coke at Middlesbrough. His firm had built
furnaces at Witton Park, near the coke and the clay-band iron
ore, four years earlier. To these furnaces Cleveland ironstone
began to move in 1851. Soon the furnaces came to Middlesbrough[6]. Thereafter the rise or fall of the main iron areas, as

[1] Scrivenor, *History of the Iron Trade* (ed. of 1854), p. vi.

[2] Lowthian Bell calculated that the Scottish 'make,' which had been 5·52 per
cent. of the whole in 1830, was 28·69 per cent. in 1852, 25·74 per cent. in 1855,
20·5 per cent. in 1870, and 13·53 per cent. in 1880. See Table I of his Memorandum to the *Second Report of the R. C. on Depression of Trade and Industry*
(1886), part 1. p. 320. The Memo. was reprinted as *The Iron Trade of the U.K.
compared with that of the other chief iron-producing nations*, 1886, and is quoted
below as Bell, *The Iron Trade*, with the paging of the book.

[3] Vol. 1. p. 50, 189.

[4] The first mineral returns in *A. and P.* 1856, LV. 469 *sqq.*

[5] Bell, Lowthian, in *The Reign of Queen Victoria*, II. 203–4 and in *The Industrial Resources of the Tyne, Wear and Tees* (1864), p. 79.

[6] Tomlinson, W. W.,*Hist. of the North-Eastern Railway*, p. 405, 507; Head, J.,
"Recent Developments in the Cleveland Iron and Steel Industry," *Trans. Inst.
Mech. Eng.* 1893, p. 225.

ore-producers and iron-producers, was in rough outline as follows[1]:

| | Tons of | 1855 | 1865 | 1875 | 1885 |
|---|---|---|---|---|---|
| Staffordshire | Ore raised | 2,500,000 | 1,485,000 | 1,654,000 | 1,830,000 |
| | Pig iron made | 855,000 | 899,000 | 712,000 | 545,000 |
| Wales and | Ore raised | 1,665,000 | 485,000 | 538,000 | 68,000 |
| Monmouth | Pig iron made | 871,000 | 917,000 | 597,000 | 833,000 |
| Scotland | Ore raised | 2,400,000 | 1,470,000* | 2,452,000 | 1,838,000 |
| | Pig iron made | 827,000 | 1,163,000 | 1,050,000 | 1,004,000 |
| Yorkshire: | Ore raised | 255,000 | 575,000 | 354,000 | 127,000 |
| West Riding | Pig iron made | 91,000 | 123,000 | 267,000 | 166,000 |
| North Eastern | Ore raised | 1,155,000 | 2,882,000 | 6,182,000 | 5,972,000 |
| District | Pig iron made | 298,000 | 1,012,000 | 2,049,000 | 2,478,000 |
| Shropshire | Ore raised | 365,000 | 274,000 | 240,000 | 178,000 |
| | Pig iron made | 122,000 | 117,000 | 121,000 | 45,000 |
| Cumberland and | Ore raised | 538,000 | 1,504,000 | 1,983,000 | 2,438,000 |
| Lancashire | Pig iron made | 17,000 | 312,000 | 1,045,000 | 1,384,000 |
| Derbyshire | Ore raised | 409,000 | 350,000 | 218,000 | 18,000 |
| | Pig iron made | 117,000 | 189,000 | 272,000 | 361,000 |
| Lincolnshire and | Ore raised | 74,000 | 489,000 | 1,660,000 | 2,349,000 |
| Northampton | Pig iron made | — | 26,000 | 192,000 | 426,000 |
| Foreign iron ore used | — | — | — | 738,000 | 3,313,000 |

* A possible serious error in this figure.

As the average iron-content of British ores worked in this period varied from about 30 per cent. to about 34 per cent., except the hematite of Cumberland and Furness which averaged 55 per cent., a district which, like Staffordshire or Scotland in 1855, has an ore figure about three times the size of its iron figure is smelting its own ore and not much else. When the iron figure rises well above a third of the ore figure, as in Wales and Monmouth throughout, ore imports from another district are indicated, in this case from Cumberland—or, latterly, from abroad. As the North-Eastern district never exported ore, the fact that its iron was well below 30 per cent. of its ore in 1855 suggests either bad smelting, or ore accumulating to await fresh furnaces, or error in a new and difficult piece of statistical collection. Cumberland and Lancashire had about got to the point of consuming all their own ore (at 55 per cent.) by 1875. Barrow had come into existence[2]. The Lincolnshire and Northamptonshire mines, at Frodingham, about Kettering, and elsewhere, lie on the curve of the lias beds sweeping from Cleveland down to Oxfordshire, Gloucestershire and the South-West.

[1] Bell, *The Iron Trade*, p. 11, and the *Mineral Returns* for 1886.
[2] Stileman, F. C., "On the Docks and Railway Approaches at Barrow-in-Furness," *Trans. Inst. Mech. Eng.* 1880.

Their development followed the rise of the lias ironstone industry at Middlesbrough; but owing to their distance from coke they remained primarily ore-export districts throughout the period, supplying Derbyshire, the West Riding and the Black Country[1]. Foreign ore, which began to arrive in appreciable quantities before 1870, went first to South Wales, for obvious reasons; later to Scotland and the North-East coast, for reasons connected with the history of steel[2].

The rise of the Middlesbrough industry had given opportunity for the application of the best known methods of smelting. A few furnaces in South Wales had already adopted, and improved, the French device of using the waste gases of combustion, not to illuminate the countryside but to raise steam and heat the blast[3]. This practice was introduced at Middlesbrough from the start, with an economy estimated ultimately at nearly a million and a half tons of coal a year. The furnaces first built were not bigger than the best then at work, the height being from 45 to 50 feet and the capacity some 5000 cubic feet[4]; but by utilising waste gases and increasing temperatures they were soon made to yield 220 tons a week, against a maximum of something like 120 tons from a hot-blast furnace elsewhere in the late 'forties. In 1864 John Vaughan tried a 75-foot furnace, with a view to increasing the weekly 'make.' He found that it not only made more iron but had a better iron-fuel ratio than the smaller structures. Soon 80 feet for height, and 20,000 cubic feet for capacity, became standard sizes. "Before long all the small furnaces on the banks of the Tees were demolished."[5] By 1870 the 80-foot monsters had been made yet hotter and their output driven up to between 450 and 550 tons a day, at an expenditure of two tons of coal per ton of iron made. After that, for over twenty years, there was "no great change in the size, form, or performance of the then best designed furnaces."[6]

What might be called Middlesbrough practice was naturally adopted in other new iron smelting areas, such as the Barrow

[1] Dove, G., "The Iron Industry of Frodingham," *Trans. Inst. Mech. Eng.* 1885. See also *J. of Iron and Steel Inst.* 1876.
[2] Bell, *The Iron Trade*, p. 16. The first Spanish ore came to the N.E. coast in 1861. Tomlinson, *op. cit.* p. 576.
[3] Bell, Lowthian, *Principles of the Manufacture of Iron and Steel* (1884), p. 23, quoted below as Bell, *Manufacture of Iron*; also *Reign of Queen Victoria*, II. 215.
[4] Vol. I. p. 428.
[5] Bell, *Manufacture of Iron*, p. 24. Eighty feet remained the standard size in 1907. Bell, Lady, *At the Works, a Study of a Manufacturing Town*, p. 23.
[6] Head, J., in *Trans. Inst. Mech. Eng.* 1893, p. 231.

district and North Lincolnshire. Older areas were more conservative. The gases flared to waste at nearly 90 per cent. of the Black Country furnaces in 1866[1]. In 1869 "the good folks of Coatbridge [still] had their streets lighted without tax or trouble" by "the flames of no fewer than fifty blast furnaces," which could be seen from the steeple of the parish church. "The flames have a positively fascinating effect. No production of the pyrotechnist can match their wild gyrations."[2] In 1876 the writer of a popular handbook on the iron industry spoke of only "the most modern furnaces" utilising their waste gases: his picture of a typical furnace—conceivably borrowed from some earlier work—showed one that did not[3]. In West Yorkshire it was an article of popular faith among ironmasters in the 'eighties that the very best malleable iron could only be made in the old way by the cold blast; though Lowthian Bell was reminding them that no "complete and systematically conducted course of experiments" had ever proved it, and was attributing the undisputed excellence of "best Yorkshire" iron, not to the temperature of the blast but to "the extraordinary care used in the forge and mill."[4]

As for coke-making, Bell wrote in 1884 that "until very recently, no kind of progress had been made in the process for the last fifty years."[5] In Durham, the chief coking county, not only was the yield of coke from the coal nearly 15 per cent. below what it should have been, owing to bad manipulation, but there was a shocking waste of heat accompanying "the immense volumes of smoke and flame which issue from a Durham cokework, blackening and desolating the country around it."[6] Yet ever since the year 1860, or even earlier, discreditable waste of this kind had been avoided in the scientific and economical coking practice of a few firms in France and Belgium. In 1884, only Bell himself and certain collieries at Wigan were attempting to economise the heat and save the precious by-products of coke-making. The county of Durham was sending 45,000 tons of sulphur into the atmosphere yearly from its coke ovens alone[7].

---

[1] *Birmingham and the Midland Hardware District*, p. 59–68. Of 170 furnaces, of which 119 were in blast, "about 20" utilised the waste gases.

[2] Bremner, *The Industries of Scotland*, p. 36.

[3] Williams, W. M., in *British Manufacturing Industries*, I. 15.

[4] Bell, *Manufacture of Iron*, p. 148, 154.         [5] *Ibid.* p. 47.

[6] *Ibid.* p. 50; and similar complaints in the *Trans. Inst. Mech. Eng.* 1881, p. 432.                        [7] Bell, *Manufacture of Iron*, p. 49–53.

When the first mineral returns were issued the new page in the history of steel had not been turned. Steel was made slowly and expensively, and was used only for tools, weapons, springs and various special purposes. Railways really were *chemins de fer*; engines built of iron plates ran on iron rails; and steamers' shafts were welded and wrought. The puddler, sweating at his furnace with his "underhand" to make the malleable iron, was the key-man of the metallurgical arch[1]. His displacement during the next thirty years was very slow, even when the new steel page had been turned. For nearly twenty of them he was not displaced at all; steel met part of a growing demand, and the rest was met by more puddling. The output of puddled iron in the early 'eighties was larger, probably much larger, than it had been in the 'fifties and 'sixties[2]. It is not even certain that it had fallen in the decade 1873–83. In 1855 the total British 'make' of pig was 3,218,000 tons and in 1865 it was 4,819,000 tons. When steel making in bulk was well established, as much as 50–55 per cent. of the pig was turned either into puddled iron or into steel; but there is no reason to think that the proportion was so high while the steel output was insignificant or small. A maximum for puddled iron would be perhaps 1,250,000 tons in 1855 and 1,750,000 tons in 1865. In the early 'seventies it was no doubt much higher, for a fairly trustworthy figure puts the 'make' in 1874, a year of depression, at 1,800,000 tons[3]. Lowthian Bell, however, doubted whether more than 3,000,000 tons had ever been produced in a year, even at the height of trade activity in 1872–3. Quite trustworthy figures for the early 'eighties run as follows:

|  | 1881 | 1882 | 1883 | 1884 |
|---|---|---|---|---|
| 'Make' of puddled iron in millions of tons | 2·7 | 2·8 | 2·7 | 2·2 |

The drop in 1883–4 was to mark the beginning of a steady decline. There were 4577 puddling furnaces in operation in Great Britain in 1884, when their gross output was still comparable with that in the best days of the trade: in 1885 there were only 3876[4].

By that time the puddlers were concentrating in districts

---

[1] Vol. I. p. 149, 189, 426–7.

[2] There are not trustworthy figures of output for the 'fifties and 'sixties; but from 1860 the number of puddling furnaces increased steadily up to 1873–5. It had not fallen to the figure of 1860 in 1884. Bell, *The Iron Trade*, p. 20 n.

[3] *Ibid.* p. 61.        [4] Mineral Returns, *A. and P.* 1886, LXXI. 225.

remote from the sea. True, there were 438 furnaces in Durham; but more than 1500 out of the 3876 were in Staffordshire, another 382 in the West Riding, and 133 in Shropshire. In Wales, where puddling had once been called the Welsh method of making iron, it was nearly extinct—only 192 furnaces in Glamorganshire and 56 in Monmouth being left. Fifteen years earlier these counties had been the chief seats of the iron rail trade. Their abandonment of the puddling furnace registered the victory of the steel rail. The North-Eastern Railway—to take one example—ceased buying iron rails in 1877; though even in 1884 Lowthian Bell was asserting, rather as part of an argument than as a self-evident proposition, that "steel, to the entire exclusion of iron, must be henceforward looked upon as the proper material for railroads."[1]

While the puddler dominated iron-making, the problem of how to dispense with this most laborious and costly manual process naturally occupied economical and inventive minds. Almost as soon as it was founded, in 1869, the Iron and Steel Institute set up a Committee on Mechanical Puddling to report on such experiments as the revolving furnace at Dowlais, which was to do for the iron by its motion what the puddler does by stirring it[2]. In 1871 the Institute sent a special commission, led by G. J. Snelus the Dowlais works chemist, to Cincinnati, where a mechanical puddler invented by Samuel Danks was said to be achieving remarkable results[3]. Rather later, a Middlesbrough firm took from the North-Eastern Railway a heavy order for rails made of iron refined in a rotating furnace. But in the late 'seventies, the possibility began to present itself that puddling, if it survived at all, might survive mainly as a method of making high-grade bars for which quality not cheapness was essential. "The altered state of public opinion respecting the future of puddled iron," Bell wrote in 1884, "has greatly diminished the interest felt in questions connected with its production,"[4] although even two years later he was informing a Royal Commission that "fully one half the iron [or steel] required in the malleable form continues to be made in the puddling furnace."[5]

It was then thirty years since Henry Bessemer, an inventor by profession, had read his paper on "The Manufacture of Iron

---

[1] Bell, *Manufacture of Iron*, p. 378: for the rails, below, p. 57.
[2] *Transactions*, Vol. I. of 1871, p. 392.
[3] Vol. II. of 1871, p. 258; Vol. I. of 1872, p. 1.
[4] *Manufacture of Iron*, p. 370.          [5] *The Iron Trade*, p. 16.

without Fuel" before the British Association at Cheltenham:
Aug. 11, 1856[1]. In the interval both Siemens' open-hearth
steel-making process and the Thomas-Gilchrist modification
of the Bessemer process had been made almost perfect.

The fuel to which Bessemer referred in his challenging title
was not that needed for smelting but that used in puddling,
cementation, or the making of crucible cast steel; for his original
plan was to run fluid iron straight from the blast furnace into
a 'converter'; to burn away all the chemical impurities—mainly
silicon and carbon—by a powerful air blast driven through the
molten mass from below, if he wanted malleable iron; and to
burn out all but an appropriate proportion of carbon, if he
wanted steel. "At a certain period of the process any quality of
metal can be obtained," he told his Cheltenham audience. That
iron could be refined with the aid of an air blast was part of the
oldest empirical knowledge of the metal worker. The novelty
was the pouring of air from below in great quantity and at great
speed into the iron when molten. In old-fashioned refining for
steel, as in puddling, the iron was at most viscous. In Bessemer's process, the rapid combustion of the silicon and the
carbon was to raise the temperature and keep the mass perfectly fluid.

At first, as early critics pointed out, Bessemer forgot the
phosphorus, which is very commonly present in British iron.
By chance his experiments had been made with an iron remarkably free of it. When repeated with phosphoric irons, his
process failed to eliminate the phosphorus, more than a very
minute proportion of which makes the metal non-malleable.
Failure from such a cause came to him, he said, "as a bolt from
the blue."[2] He began to look for non-phosphoric iron, and found
what he wanted in the Cumberland hematite, henceforward a
'Bessemer' ore. This problem, with other difficulties, provided
him with some three years' work before he was ready to attack
the market himself, after nearly all those who had taken out
licences to use his first patent had thrown in their hands discouraged. There were two other main difficulties. He found no
effective way of ascertaining the moment of 'the blow' at which
his metal had in it just enough carbon to be steel. So he purified
it completely, and then added iron which contained known

[1] Bessemer, Sir Henry, *Autobiography* (1905), p. 156 *sqq.*: *The Times*, Aug.
14, 1856.
[2] *Autobiography*, p. 170.

quantities of carbon and manganese, or the mixture known as ferro-manganese. The value of manganese in steel-making had long been recognised, if not understood, especially on the continent. "It was a matter of universal knowledge," he wrote later[1]. Another difficulty was mechanical. His first converters were fixed. But to secure exact results he must be able to stop or restart the full blast at will, and during a stoppage under a fixed converter the air-pipes might get clogged. The converter was therefore swung on an axis so that it could be tilted until the pipes led in above the surface of the molten metal.

During the early years (1856–9) Bessemer's mind ran on steel more than on wrought iron, perhaps because steel left the maximum margin of profit to the inventor. His decision to start making it in Sheffield had important technical and economic consequences. Years afterwards he explained why he took that decision[2]. No Sheffield man would try his method or pay the licence fees for his patent; therefore he must go there and "force the trade to adopt it by underselling." He took a partner and went in 1858. They produced some tool steel; but the things which they made most successfully were such as had hitherto been made, not of tool steel and not at Sheffield, but of the finest Yorkshire or Black Country wrought iron—cranks for locomotives, axles, propeller shafts, railway tyres. For these they employed pure Swedish iron. Later they used English 'Bessemer' iron. As neither was smelted in Sheffield, the plan of running the molten iron from blast furnace to converter had to be dropped. They must melt the pigs. So steel was not made "without fuel," though it was made very cheaply. Again, although Bessemer believed from the start that his steel would be fit for plates, rails, joists and all kinds of economical uses— he read a paper on "Cast Steel and its Application to Constructive Purposes" in 1861[3]—his own firm was so "crammed with orders"[4] for things in which there was more profit that they left the plain work for licencees to take up at their own pace. Some continental licencees, such as Krupp, were quicker that the English. Meanwhile Bessemer's own firm, during the fourteen years of the partnership (1858–72), made profits at a rate which, as he conjectured, had never been equalled "in the history of commerce." Including the selling price of the business at the end, but excluding the immensely profitable sales of licences,

---

[1] *Autobiography*, p. 264.          [2] *Ibid.* p. 175.
[3] *Trans. Inst. Mech. Eng.* July, 1861.          [4] *Autobiography*, p. 225.

the profit on the original capital throughout the fourteen years averaged "nearly cent. per cent. every two months."[1]

The new material had been tried for almost every use in the early days. John Brown and J. D. Ellis, of the Atlas works, the first men in Sheffield to trust it, rolled steel rails in 1860. They were not cutlers but steel-makers with a young and adaptable business[2]. Experimental Bessemer rails, made under licence by the Weardale Company at Tudhoe, were laid on the Newcastle High Level Bridge in April, 1862. In the following May, the London and North-Western tried some Bessemer rails at Camden Town[3]. At the Exhibition of 1862 Bessemer's firm showed, besides every kind of tool and weapon, shafts, tyres, bars, rods, rails and steel wire for ropes. In 1863 the screw steamer *Pelican* of 329 tons was built of steel plates: by the end of 1865 seventeen other steel ships of various sorts had been launched, among them the sailer *Clytemnestra* of 1251 tons. For years Bessemer spent his strength against the iron-bound obstinacy of the War Office and the Admiralty, whilst Napoleon III observed his guns with keen attention, and the French Ministry of Marine investigated the use of his steel for ships of war[4]. But there were obvious limitations to a very rapid extension of the mass uses. First, his high charge for patentee's licences, which settled down at £1 a ton on steel rails and at £2 a ton on steel for all other purposes[5]. Second, the relatively expensive 'Bessemer' raw material, which, with the licence, made the early steel plate or rail much dearer than its iron competitor. Third, the year-long tests of endurance on the permanent way, in the boiler or the ship, necessary to prove that the dearer material was really the more economical[6]. Finally, the gigantic lock-up of capital and human capital skill in puddling, and the as yet undisputed dominance of the British iron industry in the world's markets, were all against rapid change. The loss of this semi-monopolistic position and the accompanying economies in pro-

[1] *Autobiography*, p. 179.

[2] John Brown had originally been a cutlery factor. He became a steel-maker in 1844. From that time forward his firm was always pioneering. In 1860 it made experimental armour plate. Jeans, W. T., *The Creators of the Age of Steel* (1885), p. 275–86.

[3] *Engineering*, Jan. 5, 1866; Bessemer, *Autobiography*, p. 335; Tomlinson, *The North-Eastern Railway*, p. 648.

[4] All from the *Autobiography*.        [5] Jeans, *op. cit.* p. 282.

[6] See evidence of Seymour Clarke, General Manager of the Great Northern, before the *R.C. on Railways*, 1867 (XXXVIII. pts. I. and II.), Q. 12933: "it is a question of cost."

duction—partly enforced—during the decade 1870–80 were the deciding factors in the ultimate transition.

High among the economies came the development of steel-making in association with smelting, as Bessemer had originally proposed, mainly on the Welsh, North-West, and North-East coasts. Intimately connected with this partial shift from Sheffield to tide-water was the growth of the import of ore. The relatively high price of the limited stock of English hematite might have kept down steel production, had not the spread of the Bessemer and allied methods coincided with growing ore imports—mainly of the Spanish 'rubio' ore. When hematite prices rose "speculators of all kinds rushed off to Spain"[1] to get concessions. In 1870 the total import of ore was only 400,000 tons and the make of steel ingots was 240,000 tons; in 1880 the import of ore was 3,060,000 tons and the make of steel 1,250,000 tons. The economies in production, and the now proved merits of steel for heavy work, had led to the mass conversion of the railway companies during the decade. In 1872 the North-Eastern, in spite of its experiments ten years earlier, only used steel rails at points and crossings. By 1877 it had ceased to give orders for iron rails[2]. The final turn over from iron to steel—for new rails—was "virtually complete in three or four years from its commencement."[3] By 1875 all the locomotive boilers on the North-Western were made of steel plates and the Company had its own Bessemer plant at Crewe[4]. Here quality may have been the determining factor; with the rails that factor was price. The North-Eastern reduced its working expenses in the bad trade year 1879 by buying its steel rails dirt cheap; and when, in 1884, Lowthian Bell declared that steel "must be henceforward looked upon as the proper material for railroads," he led up to his declaration by pointing out that new rails could now be made of steel "even from a comparatively expensive hematite ore...more economically than a good quality of rail" could "be produced in iron from the cheaper ironstone of Cleveland."[5]

When the British 'make' of steel stood at about 240,000 tons, in 1870, 225,000 tons are said to have been made in the Bessemer converter and 15,000 by some form of the 'open-hearth'

---

[1] Lowthian Bell, quoted in Jeans, *op. cit.* p. 300.
[2] Tomlinson, *op. cit.* p. 648; Bell, *Manufacture of Iron*, p. 379.
[3] Head, J., Presidential Address, *Trans. Inst. Mech. Eng.* 1885, p. 309.
[4] Bessemer, *Autobiography*, p. 250.   [5] *Manufacture of Iron*, p. 378.

process connected with the name of Sir William Siemens. Late in the 'seventies came Thomas's basic process. The course of production thenceforward was as follows:

|             | 1878    | 1880      | 1883      | 1884      | 1885      |
|-------------|---------|-----------|-----------|-----------|-----------|
| Bessemer    | 800,000 | 1,000,000 | 1,550,000 | 1,300,000 | 1,250,000 |
| Open-Hearth | 174,000 | 251,000   | 455,000   | 475,000   | 610,000   |
| Basic       | —       | ?         | 121,000   | 179,000   | 140,000   |

The steady upward course of the open-hearth steel in so fluctuating an industry is sufficient witness to the efficiency of the process[1].

In his old age Bessemer recalled that he himself had made open-hearth experiments in the 'fifties and had even taken out a patent in October, 1855, for the "fusion of steel in a bath of cast iron," an essential feature of what came to be known as the Siemens-Martin process, patented in England by M. Martin of Sireuil just ten years later. Bessemer said that he doubted his own wisdom in dropping these experiments[2]. Apparently he half foresaw the abandonment of his ingenious but elaborate converter during the thirty years that followed his death[3]. But he was careful not to rob Siemens and Thomas of their honour. For Siemens—a master of applied science, and a general inventor like himself—he had a special regard. Siemens' main contribution to metal working was a by-product of a lifelong preoccupation with the economy of energy[4]. From economy in engines he passed—at the suggestion, it is said, of his brother Frederick—to economy in furnaces. The result of many years work was the regenerative gas furnace first used industrially in 1861 at Lloyd and Summerfield's flint-glass works in Birmingham, and then at Chance's Stourbridge works, where Michael Faraday saw it. In it, a current of burning gas, which may be of many kinds and is always cheap, heats the fire-brick labyrinth of the regenerative chambers: through them the next incoming currents of gas and air go, sucking in heat, to burn at a far higher temperature than the first current: and so on. Currents and

[1] The figures for the earlier years are rather uncertain. Those given in Bell, *Manufacture of Iron*, p. 432, based on reports of the Iron Trade Association, do not always agree with the official Mineral Statistics. I have followed the Mineral Statistics.

[2] Bessemer, *Autobiography*, p. 141.

[3] He died in 1898. Since 1893 more steel had been made on the open-hearth than in the converter. By 1925 only 6 per cent. was made in the converter, which by 1930 had disappeared.

[4] Pole, W., *The Life of Sir William Siemens* (1888); Obach, E., *Sir Wm. Siemens als Erfinder und Forscher* (1884); *D.N.B.*

temperatures can be exactly controlled and as much heat generated as the fabric of the furnace will stand. The principle can be applied to furnaces for every purpose, and was so applied within seven or eight years all over the world. From the first Siemens had suggested that it might be used not only for the melting of steel, for which it was obviously suited, but for its making[1].

Early experiments by licencees failed; but in 1865 the Martins of Sireuil made cast steel successfully by melting scrap steel in a bath of molten pig iron on an open Siemens hearth, and took out their patent. In that year Siemens started his Sample Steel Works in Birmingham to make his process known. Three years later he and a group of supporters founded the Siemens Steel Company at Landore, Swansea, where his own method— more fundamental than the Martins—was adopted. Into the molten pig, at full heat, was fed a pure ore in relatively small quantities. During the resultant combustion, carbon escaped as carbonic oxide and silicon as silica passed into the slag. The perfect control of the gaseous fuel and of the temperature in a Siemens furnace enabled the steel-makers to work very exactly. Ore was fed in so as to keep ebullition constant. The content of the furnace was sampled at intervals. At the right moment, it was 'physicked,' as the old Sheffield steel-makers used to say, with manganese[2].

The Landore works began to make steel about the middle of 1869, and turned out 75 tons a week. Three other important works were using the process that year[3]. By 1873 Landore had its own blast furnaces and collieries and could make 1000 tons a week, using sometimes the pure Siemens, sometimes the Siemens-Martin process. During the remaining ten years of his life Siemens worked hopefully at a still more fundamental process which had long fascinated him—steel-making direct from the ore without any use of previously smelted pig iron. On the face of it, this was a simpler thing than many which he and his generation had mastered. His metallurgical friends treated it most seriously; but Lowthian Bell wrote in 1878—" I have a kind of instinctive opinion that the Blast Furnace will be difficult to exterminate."[4] It still stands. Meanwhile the slow

---

[1] Pole, *op. cit.* p. 143.
[2] There is a description in Bell, *Manufacture of Iron*, p. 431.
[3] Pole, *op. cit.* p. 154; Jeans, *op. cit.* p. 159.
[4] Quoted in Pole, *op. cit.* p. 199.

extermination of the Bessemer converter had begun, as the steel-making figures show.

Yet it was in a model converter that Gilchrist Thomas, the young clerk in the Thames Police Court with a classical education and a passion for metallurgy, and his cousin Percy Gilchrist, an iron-works chemist in South Wales, tried their experiments with the basic process[1]. The aim was to render phosphoric ores available for the new steel-making. All the metallurgical world knew that there was a fortune in it: there had been innumerable experiments and some patents. The best opinion of the early 'seventies, that of Lowthian Bell, held that the high temperature and short duration of 'the blow' in the Bessemer converter were responsible for the retention of phosphorus in the iron. Thomas tracked the trouble to the silicon in the converter's lining of fire-brick, which would not unite chemically with the phosphorus. He determined to substitute something which would, something calcareous—bricks of powdered limestone or the like. There were great difficulties of manipulation. These were not overcome in the half-size experiments made at Blaenavon, where Gilchrist was working, and at Dowlais in 1877–8. Then E. W. Richards, manager of the Bolckow-Vaughan works at Middlesbrough, put his resources and experience at the inventors' disposal and the thing succeeded—in 1879. For economy's sake, to save wastage of the lining of magnesian limestone in the converters, more basic material, in the form of lime, was mixed with the charge to take up the phosphorus[2].

The world is so full of phosphoric ores, and the problem had been so much before the minds of metallurgists everywhere, that the announcement of its solution was an international incident. "Middlesbrough was soon besieged by the combined forces of Belgium, France, Prussia, Austria and America."[3] Would-be licencees from abroad called on Thomas before breakfast[4]. Operations were started at once, faster abroad than in Britain; for Britain had a fair supply of Bessemer ores of her own, and a fully developed commercial organisation for bringing foreign ore from mines close to the sea in Spain to furnaces close to the sea at Middlesbrough, or at Swansea, or on the Clyde. By 1882 there were twelve converters in Britain adapted to the new process—six of them at the Bolckow-Vaughan works—and ten

---

[1] Burnie, R. W., *Memoir and Letters of Sidney Gilchrist Thomas* (1891).
[2] See Richards' address to the Cleveland Institution of Engineers, Nov. 15, 1880, quoted at length in Jeans, *op. cit.* p. 307–13.
[3] Bell, *Manufacture of Iron*, p. 407.     [4] Burnie, *op. cit.* p. 128–9.

others were being prepared[1]. Thomas's principles could be applied without great difficulty to the open-hearth method of steel-making, but for some years, in England, basic converters predominated[2]. In the half-year Sept. 30, 1882—March 31, 1883, 281,000 tons of steel were produced by one or other application of the new process[3]. But of this tonnage only 58,000 was British; no less than 152,000 was German. Bad trade kept both Bessemer and basic converters relatively idle in Great Britain during 1884–5. But as he travelled over the world in those years, famous but dying of consumption, Thomas saw what he had accomplished, what he must have known that he would accomplish, for he was no mere trial and error inventor but a fully educated man who apprehended his problem and its implications. To Britain he had given the free use of her almost unlimited phosphoric ores: concurrently he had lowered the value which her insular position gave her in the Bessemer years. To America he had given little: she had such vast non-phosphoric reserves. To France and Central Europe, above all to the debatable land of Lorraine, he had given everything—for there nearly all the most abundant and accessible ores were phosphoric, and the sea was remote.

The remarkable maintenance of the output of puddled iron during the decade 1873–83[4], in face of competition from the converters and the open-hearths, and in spite of the abandonment of iron railway metal by all the great companies before 1879, was due principally to a great expansion of the demand for iron plates and angles in shipbuilding. The change over is well illustrated by output figures collected in 1883 for what was by that time the principal iron-producing and iron-shipbuilding district in Britain, the North-East coast[5]. They are not quite exhaustive but they tell the story:

|            | 1873        | 1882        |
|------------|-------------|-------------|
| Rails      | 374,000 tons | 7,000 tons  |
| Plates     | 191,000 „    | 498,000 „   |
| Angle bars | 51,000 „     | 150,000 „   |

[1] Mineral Returns, A. and P. 1884, LXXXV. 535 sqq.

[2] The first important application only came in 1888, when Maximilian Mannaberg installed a basic open-hearth plant at Frodingham in Lincolnshire: see the obituary notice of Mannaberg, The Times, Dec. 21, 1929. At the time of his death 70 per cent. of the British steel was made in such plants.

[3] Gilchrist's figures supplied to Bell, op. cit. p. 407.

[4] Above, p. 52.

[5] Bell, Manufacture of Iron, p. 459. In 1872 "no steel of any kind" was made on the N.E. coast: Head, "Recent Developments in the Cleveland Iron and Steel Industry," Trans. Inst. Mech. Eng. 1893, p. 226.

Through all the vicissitudes of the years following the boom-year 1873—in 1877 the total output of the three classes of manufactured iron in Cleveland was more than 35 per cent. lower than it had been in 1873—the proportion of plates to the total output rose quite steadily. The situation in the ship-building industry is shown by the numbers of sea-going ships of all kinds, sail and steam, on hand at June 30th, 1882. They were: wooden 55, steel 100, iron 625. Steel was coming rapidly into use in the 'eighties. On September 30, 1875, there had been no steel ships building at all. The tide turned in 1876–7. In 1880 Lloyd's surveyors inspected a steel tonnage of 35,000; in 1885 a steel tonnage of 166,000—but also 934,000 tons of iron ship-ping[1]. This late arrival of steel is at first sight surprising, for, as has been seen, a number of vessels of various sorts had been built of Bessemer steel in the years 1863–5. The largest of them, the clipper *Clytemnestra*, had come through the Calcutta cyclone of October, 1864, with credit. But the firm which had done the building got into difficulties and, in spite of financial assist-ance from Bessemer himself, went into liquidation. Steel was dear as compared with iron. If it was to be adopted it must be proved markedly superior. Proof was not forthcoming; and "for the next ten years steel shipbuilding was almost unheard of."[2] No doubt, as Bessemer always and inevitably believed, sheer conservatism in the shipyards explained much. The con-servatism of the Admiralty was there to back it. At Chatham, in 1864, elaborate tests of Bessemer steel plates had shown them to be stronger than iron as a rule but more erratic in fracturing. In 1868 Lloyd's surveyors, instructed to classify ships made out of steel "of approved quality," had tested some Bessemer plates—not of Bessemer's make—and had rejected them[3]. Seven years later, at the Institute of Naval Architects, the chief Admiralty constructor made much of the "uncertain-ties and treacheries" of steel. If makers would give him plates "as regular and precise" as plates of copper, he was ready to build "the entire vessel, bottom plates and all, of steel." Besse-mer traversed the whole chain of argument, adducing the *Clytemnestra* and the steel locomotive boilers. Siemens set him-

[1] See Head in *Trans. Inst. Mech. Eng.* 1885, p. 314; *Annals of Lloyd's Register* (1884), p. 123; Holmes, Sir G. C. V., *Ships Ancient and Modern*, ii. 40: Cornewall-Jones, R. J., *The British Merchant Service* (1898), p. 120.

[2] Jeans, *op. cit.* p. 100.

[3] Pole, *Siemens*, p. 192; *Annals of Lloyd's Register*, p. 118.

self to meet the Admiralty challenge, and satisfied their most exacting requirements with a uniform mild steel which was adopted for the despatch vessels *Iris* and *Mercury* in 1876: hence what was called in the shipping world the "resurrection" of steel about the year 1877[1].

By the 'eighties steel uniform enough and cheap enough for some mercantile requirements was being made by both processes. By 1885 marine boilers were "scarcely ever built of iron."[2] The general adoption of steel for the hull had become simply a matter of cost. "No one questions the superiority of steel over iron for naval architecture. The only barrier to its exclusive use is one of price, which is due to considerations of a mechanical order in the rolling mill itself." This was Lowthian Bell's opinion in 1884[3]. Next year, his successor in the Presidency of the Institution of Mechanical Engineers was pointing out that "steel bars, angles or plates...of the quality required by Lloyd's ...cost about 46 per cent. more than if of ordinary wrought iron."[4]

The reluctance of shipbuilders to experiment much with steel plates before the mid 'seventies is easily understood. Iron had not been generally adopted for steamers before the decade 1855–65; only for some of the best sailing ships during the decade 1860–70. Quick change to yet another more expensive, more experimental, material was hardly to be expected in so ancient a craft, in view of the policy and rulings of Lloyd's and the Admiralty. There were even a few little wooden steamships on the stocks on September 30, 1875[5].

The iron sailing ship was known twenty-five years earlier. The Liverpool-built *Ironside* of 1830 is generally reckoned the first, because she was the first rated at Lloyd's[6]; but very possibly iron barges had gone under sail before that. The iron steamer was well known. So early as 1844 B. G. Willcox, managing director of the Peninsular and Oriental, had prophesied its victory, and in 1848 Money Wigram of the Blackwall

---

[1] The phrase is used in the *Annals of Lloyd's Register*, p. 119; for the Admiralty episode see Price, J., "On Iron and Steel as constructive Material for Ships," *Trans. Inst. Mech. Eng.* 1881, p. 553, and the discussion of the paper.

[2] Head in *Trans. Inst. Mech. Eng.* p. 319.    [3] *Manufacture of Iron*, p. 460.

[4] Head, as above, p. 311.

[5] In fact six, of an aggregate tonnage of 1065. Cornewall-Jones, *op. cit.* p. 120.

[6] See *e.g.* Lubbock, Basil, *The Colonial Clippers* (1921), p. 200; *Annals of Lloyd's Register*, p. 75.

yard had allowed its great utility for "propeller ships," then recently introduced[1]. But of the 3,400,000 tons of sailing ships and the 170,000 tons of steamers registered under the red ensign in 1850, only a very tiny proportion was iron-built. The best-known steamers were not, except one or two belonging to the Peninsular and Oriental. The British and North American Royal Mail Steam Packets, as they were still officially described, although named popularly after their promoter and director Samuel Cunard, were all built of wood. The government which subsidised them required that they should be: it did not relax its requirement until 1856, when the iron *Persia*—paddle-wheel, 3766 tons—was built and engined by Robert Napier on the Clyde[2]. But, without any such constraint, their chief American rivals from 1850 to 1858, the Collins line of steamships, were also wood-built—of American live-oak and pitch pine[3].

At that time the wooden American clipper packets, the liners under their famous house flags, were still running in competition with steam. In the early years of the Cunard (1840–5) they had held their own without much difficulty, sometimes making their crossings in twelve to fourteen days—their captains, so it was believed in Liverpool, risking *delirium tremens* by keeping awake on black coffee[4]. As steamship competition began to tell, in the later 'forties, some of them were taken off the Liverpool beat and put into the new and immensely profitable trade round the Horn to California and the gold. But one of the most famous in chronicles of the sea, the *Dreadnought* of the Red Cross Line, was only launched in 1853 and only beaten out of the Atlantic trade by steam ten years later[5].

Wooden shipbuilding in Britain, throughout the age in which she won control of the world's seas by war and commerce, has an odd and, until its very last chapter, not a very glorious technical history. It is agreed that French warship design in the eighteenth century was better than English. Even in 1845 a British *Sanspareil* was planned on the lines of the *Sanspareil*

---

[1] Vol. I. p. 441.

[2] Napier had engined the Cunarders from the first and had helped to raise the original capital of the company in order that they might be as strong as he advised. Of the £270,000 initial capital Cunard had contributed £55,000. Napier, J., *Life of Robert Napier* (1904), p. 124 *sqq.* For the *Persia*, *ibid.* p. 192 *sqq.*

[3] Cornewall-Jones, *op. cit.* p. 134–5; Holmes, *op. cit.* II. 22, 29.

[4] Personal reminiscences of a Liverpool merchant: Lubbock, Basil, *The Western Ocean Packets* (1925).

[5] Lubbock, *The Colonial Clippers*, p. 12; *The Western Ocean Packets*, p. 59 *sqq*

captured in 1794 from the French[1]. It has been suggested that American clipper design goes back to French models. Whether it does or not, there is no doubt about the superiority of American builders, at least down to the decade 1840–50. During more than twenty years after Waterloo the British mercantile marine grew little, if at all[2]. Building was for replacement; there was a good deal of replacement by 'colonial builts'; and design made no progress. The East Indiamen were fine bits of shipwrights' work, built expensively of the best materials, but built on old-fashioned lines. The Company's *Waterloo* looks as if she might have driven with Hawke into Quiberon Bay[3]. As the Company gradually ceased to do business in India, there was some falling off in the size and quality of the ships which carried the eastern trade[4]. Meanwhile the large purchases of 'colonial builts' were giving business and experience in design to the yards of Quebec, Nova Scotia and New Brunswick[5]. A few British owners were already building in the United States. James Aiken of Liverpool did so some time before 1833, because prices in Massachusetts were 30s. a ton lower than in Liverpool, where, it may be recalled, the shipwrights' union was difficult to deal with[6]. In 1844 another Liverpool owner had said that it was only possible to compete in the North Atlantic trade by "having North American ships.... We could not sail British ships in that trade."[7]

There remained, however, the eastward trades—the Mediterranean, the Cape, India, and especially after the gold discoveries the rush trade to Australia. Here was room enough. Some of the finest ships in the Australian trade of the 'fifties were American built for British owners. American-built and American-owned clippers joined in the tea races from China until 1859; but ever since the early 'forties there had been effective British-built competitors. The years between 1837 and 1848 had seen a revival in British design[8],

---

[1] She was never launched. Clowes, *History of the British Navy*, VI. 191. And see Holmes, *op. cit.* I. 125, 486–7.   [2] Vol. I. p. 1–2.

[3] See her picture in Morse, H. B., *The Chronicles of the East India Co. trading to China* (1926), Vol. IV. frontispiece.

[4] Lubbock, Basil, *The Blackwall Frigates* (1922), p. 44.

[5] For Canadian ship-building see *Cambridge Hist. of the British Empire*, VI. (1930), 569 *sqq.*; Wallace, F. W., *Wooden Ships and Iron Men* (1924); *In the Wake of the Wind Ships* (1927); *Record of Canadian Shipping* (1929).

[6] *S.C. on Commerce and Industry*, 1833 (VI. 1), Q. 7172 *sqq.* For the Union, Vol. I. p. 212–13.

[7] *S.C. on British Shipping*, 1844 (VIII. 1), Q. 770.

[8] See Cornewall-Jones, *op. cit.* p. 233; Lubbock, *The China Clippers*, p. 144 *sqq.*

which had been preceded by the cheapening and improvement of all the innumerable adjuncts of a wooden ship which are not made of wood. A ship is not made all of wood, "like a box," as Cobden used to say to those who argued that the dearness of timber in Britain justified both dear building and protection[1].

Historians of ships date the beginning of the revival from the launch of the *Seringapatam* from Green's Blackwall yard in 1837[2]. She headed the long and glorious line of the Blackwall frigates, built for first-class passenger and cargo traffic and for speed. They were not technically clippers; rather vastly improved East Indiamen. 'Dicky' Green died in 1863. "Whilst he lived iron ships were not even hinted at in the Blackwall yard."[3] Within a few years of the launch of the *Seringapatam*, ships of the same type were being built by Laing and by Marshall, both of Sunderland. The 'Blackwallers' at first were small as compared with the old East Indiamen; well under 1000 tons against the East Indiaman's normal 1300. By the end of the 'fifties a representative group of them averaged 1050 tons. Laing built up to 1500 tons, and the last Blackwaller built on the Thames was of 1857 tons. She was launched in 1875—and she was of iron[4].

As their name implies, Green's ships had points in common with the newer type of Royal Navy frigate, designed for speed since the close of the French wars. The British ships which first challenged the American clippers in style, though not in size, were those built by Hall of Aberdeen in the early 'forties[5]. When the Australian passenger trade suddenly rose into importance in 1851–2 Liverpool owners, with their long experience of American building, placed their principal orders in Massachusetts, Nova Scotia and New Brunswick—above all, Massachusetts[6]. It was Donald McKay, a Nova Scotian domiciled in Boston, who built for James Baines' Black Ball line perhaps the most famous all-wood sailing ships of the 'fifties, among them the *Donald McKay* herself, launched in 1855 while Bessemer was working at his steel problem, a ship which on six consecutive voyages

---

[1] Speech of June 9, 1848. Hansard, xcix. 605.
[2] Lubbock, *The Blackwall Frigates*, p. 150; Chatterton, E. K., *The Ship under Sail* (1926), p. 134.
[3] Lubbock, *The Blackwall Frigates*, p. 103.
[4] Lubbock, *ibid.* p. 274, 290; Chatterton, p. 134.
[5] Lubbock, *The China Clippers*, p. 108.
[6] Lubbock, *The Colonial Clippers*, p. 22 *sqq.*

from Liverpool to Melbourne averaged eighty-three days[1]. But some of the Aberdeen clippers of the later 'fifties, of the Aberdeen White Star Line, though smaller, were at least as good. Among them the *Maid of Judah* passed the heads at Sydney seventy-eight days out from London in 1860. From Hall's yard in Aberdeen had come also the first British tea clippers for the China trade, the *Stornoway* and *Chrysolite* of 1851[2].

These are only a few names from the last and the great age of the British sailing ship. How active construction and purchase were are shown by the figures of the shipping register. In the quarter of a century preceding 1850 British sailing tonnage had grown from some 2,400,000 to 3,400,000: during the next fifteen years, in spite of a rapid increase of steamer tonnage, it reached its absolute maximum of 4,936,776 tons, manned by 158,000 seamen (1865). There were important purchases of American clippers from bankrupt American firms after the commercial collapse in the United States in 1857[3], and purchases in British America were continuous; but there was also very great building activity on the Thames, the Mersey, the Wear, the Clyde and the Dee, and on many a lesser estuary and harbour. Shoreham in 1850 could build up to 500 tons, ships "remarkable for swift sailing."[4] There were seventy-one builders of wooden ships at Sunderland in 1857[5]. Rye was still able to launch a 200 tonner in the early 'seventies[6]. In years of active building such as 1863–5, 1868–9, or 1875–6 the United Kingdom could turn out a sailing tonnage of 230,000 and more. The absolute maximum was 275,000 tons in 1864[7].

Since the 'forties there had always been a few iron sailing ships on the register. By 1865, although people did not build with iron at Shoreham or Rye, its use was familiar in the greater places. Iron steamers had shown the way. The difficulty of procuring 'great timbers' for vessels of any size had long harassed the Admiralty[8]. To the mercantile builder of big clipper ships iron came as a cheap and most efficient substitute. Experience showed that an iron-framed ship could be driven

---

[1] Lubbock, *The Colonial Clippers*, p. 83–4; Cornewall-Jones, *op. cit.* p. 230; McKay, R. C., *Some Famous Sailing Ships and their builder Donald McKay* (1928).

[2] Lubbock, *The China Clippers*, p. 110; *The Log of the Cutty Sark*, p. 46; Cornewall-Jones, *op. cit.* p. 230.

[3] Lubbock, *The Colonial Clippers*, p. 113.    [4] *V.C.H. Sussex*, II. 234–5.

[5] *V.C.H. Durham*, II. 304.    [6] *V.C.H. Sussex*, as above.

[7] *Tables Showing the Progress of Merchant Shipping*, 1902 (Cd. 329), p. 56.

[8] Albion, *Forests and Sea Power, passim.*

harder into a head sea, but that copper-sheathed wood fouled less, and so sailed quicker, than the iron-plates of those days. As racing clippers must be driven hard and brought home quick, the composite structure—planks on an iron frame—had much in its favour. The method came in with the new half-century, the first composite on Lloyd's list being the *Tubal Cain* of 1851[1]. Among the earlier composites to acquire notoriety was the *Red Riding Hood* of 1857 built by a Rotherhithe firm[2]. From 1863, a series of composite clippers was ordered by the Aberdeen Orient Line from this same firm and from Hall of Aberdeen. In 1867 came the *Thyatira* of 962 tons, the first composite clipper of the Aberdeen White Star Line. And so to the composite *Cutty Sark*, laid down by a Dumbarton firm that failed, and finished there by Denny in 1869, the surviving memorial of this great shipbuilding era[3].

Composite building was a by-product of the transition from wood to iron, and it became specialised to the racing clippers. Among other groups of high-class sailing vessels the transition went straight forward. By 1855 Lloyd's Register had issued complete and satisfactory rules for the survey and classification of iron ships. The rules were intended for steamers, but they facilitated the building of iron sailing ships. It is significant that the draft on which they were based was sent in by Lloyd's surveyors on the Clyde, now the headquarters of an industry which in earlier years had been more prominent on the Mersey and the Thames[4]. Apart from its cheapness and strength, the iron sailing ship was in far less danger from fire than the old wooden ship; and what that meant in reduction of human misery, and of insurance, a very little acquaintance with the stories of fire on the high seas will show. Plates of a maximum thickness of $1\frac{1}{16}$ ins. and light girder framework gave the iron ship great carrying capacity. In no country could it be built so cheaply and so well as in the United Kingdom.

Although many iron sailing ships were launched in the

---

[1] *Annals of Lloyd's Register*, p. 84. But the partial use of iron framing went back to 1810–15. Wood, Sir H. T., *A Hist. of the Royal Society of Arts*, p. 255.

[2] Lubbock, *The Colonial Clippers*, p. 147.

[3] Lubbock, *The Log of the Cutty Sark*, p. 31–2.

[4] *Annals of Lloyd's Register*, p. 76; vol. I. p. 439–40. Robert Napier, who at first built only engines, began iron shipbuilding in 1841. *Life*, p. 149. William Denny was his draftsman, John Elder his engine-shop manager; "most of the leading firms on the river were founded by men who had worked with him and his cousin David." *Ibid.* p. 243. Cp. Glover, J., "On the decline of shipbuilding on the Thames," *S. J.* 1869; where the causes are discussed.

'fifties, their great age was the twenty years from 1860 to 1880, and their principal beat the Australian trade. Throughout this period, and much later, they ran the southern wool. But they sailed on all seas. In 1866 Blackwall yard built the *Superb* of iron, 'Dicky' Green being dead[1]. When T. H. Ismay bought the flag of the Liverpool White Star clippers in 1867, he and his partners ran iron sailing ships for a time[2]. The Aberdeen White Star built its first iron clipper in 1869. The Orient Line followed in 1873. In 1875—the year in which the last Sunderland-built wooden ship was launched[3]—there was built on the Clyde what was believed to be the finest sailing ship afloat, the iron *Loch Garry* of 1500 tons, the first of a line of *Lochs* very prominent in the long-haul trades of the late nineteenth century. For about another ten years such vessels were built of iron. Then began the hybrid age of steel and sails; for to the very end of the nineteenth century there were "many branches of commerce in which sailing ships" might "be more profitably employed than steamers."[4] There may still be a few.

Profitable employment for iron ocean steamers was a little uncertain when, in the early spring of 1850, Tod and MacGregor had launched the screw steamer *City of Glasgow* of 1600 tons. Four years later she put to sea with nearly five hundred souls and was heard of no more; but in her short life she had acted as pioneer to the first line of Atlantic iron steamers—the Liverpool, New York and Philadelphia Steamship Company, the creation of William Inman. Built as a speculation, she was bought by the Company late in 1850. Next year, Tod and MacGregor supplied the bigger *City of Manchester*, which was followed by a succession of *Cities*—among them a solitary *Kangaroo*—with clipper bows and bowsprit and square-rigging on the fore and main masts. When the wooden Collins line broke down, under stress of an abnormal series of losses at sea and the American financial crisis of 1857, Inman adopted their sailing days, started a weekly service from New York, and secured the contract for the United States mail. By that time the Cunard was building of iron, but its first iron screw steamer for the Atlantic trade, the *China*, was not ordered until 1862[5].

[1] Lubbock, *The Blackwall Frigates*, p. 282.
[2] Kennedy, J., *The History of Steam Navigation* (1903), p. 301.
[3] *V.C.H. Durham*, ii. 304.     [4] Cornewall-Jones, *op. cit.* (1898), p. 237.
[5] Kennedy, *op. cit.* p. 106, 107, 227. Kennedy wrote from Liverpool with local knowledge. Holmes, *op. cit.* ii. 30.

It is not easy to determine exactly what effect the extraordinary episode of the *Great Eastern*, at once an example and a warning, had on the transition to the iron screw passenger steamer. The designing in 1852–3 of an iron steamer with both paddles and screw, 675 feet long and 83 feet wide as against the *City of Manchester's* 274 by 38 feet, showed what could be dared and accomplished. She was launched in January, 1858, or rather floated off sideways by a spring tide, at the fourth attempt; for her builders had decided to put that huge length into the Thames broadside on[1]. She had a thirty years' life. But she ruined her builder, Scott Russell of Millwall, and a multitude of shareholders who could not pay their calls; and she was sold unfinished, in the year of her launching, for little more than the launching had cost. She was completed with the aid of capital subscribed by "persons in the humblest ranks of life, domestic servants, costermongers, greengrocers and labourers."[2] Her completion had become a point of national honour, a sporting event which must be brought off; but she never paid the costermongers. After eight years of unprofitable uses, ten of considerable utility as a cable layer (1866–75) led to an inglorious old age on the Mersey as a floating signboard for a great retail "department" shop. She was broken up in 1888. "Her owners at this time were probably the only persons who ever realised a handsome profit out of her."[3] During her lifetime, first-rate Atlantic steamers had grown from the 274 × 38 feet of the *City of Manchester* to the 515 × 52 feet of the steel-built Cunarder *Servia*, with compound engines and incandescent electric lamps, the wonder-ship of the early 'eighties[4]. The *Great Eastern* was well before her time; but the mere building of her had been among the chief mechanical feats of the century.

The wooden paddle steamer before 1850 had carried passengers, mails and valuable cargoes, both on the narrow seas and the oceans, but had not touched bulk cargoes. By 1850–51 the new railways were damaging the coal trade between the North-East coast and the Thames. To meet this competition C. M.

---

[1] This was not a novelty. James Napier, Robert's brother, had prophesied failure on the basis of his own experience with broadside launches. *Life of Robert Napier*, p. 42.

[2] *The Illustrated London News*, Aug. 13, 1859. The *I.L.N.* is one of the best sources for the story of the *Great Eastern*. And see Kennedy, *op. cit.* p. 119 *sqq.*

[3] Kennedy, *op. cit.* p. 127. The shameful end of the *Great Eastern* came almost as a personal disgrace to schoolboys of the 'eighties who had learnt all about her from such books as Kingston, W. H. G., *The Boys' Own Book of Boats*.

[4] Kennedy, *op. cit.* p. 230.

Palmer of Newcastle had an iron screw collier built and named *John Bowes*. In five days' steaming she did work which two sailing colliers could not have done in a month. Neither prejudice nor the vested interests of the very ancient coastwise sailing trade could resist such obvious efficiency. Besides, the screw colliers solved the commissariat problem in the Crimean War. By 1864 they carried over 900,000 tons of coal to London alone, one of them, the *James Dixon*, with a crew of twenty-one, doing in a year work which would have occupied sixteen sailing colliers and 144 men. Iron steamers, Palmer wrote in that year, did "most of the carrying trade of the Baltic and Mediterranean"[1]—a great exaggeration, but true of that coal export business on which the British bulk-cargo steamer trade of the late nineteenth century was founded.

The iron screw liners of the 'fifties and 'sixties, like their wooden paddle predecessors, were primarily passenger and mail boats. But in 1863 the National Steam Navigation Company was started at Liverpool with a special view to cargo— the carrying trade of the seceded Southern States of the American Union. The trade was not as anticipated; but the Company did well; ran the biggest steamers of the 'sixties; and put into one of them, the *Italy* of 1868, the first compound engines ever used on an Atlantic liner[2].

'Compounding,' the use of the expansive power of steam at different pressures in two or more cylinders, had been patented by Jonathan Hornblower in 1781. Boulton and Watt broke him, on a different count, for infringement of patent. In 1810 Arthur Woolf, who had been a millwright under the great Bramah, patented another two-cylinder engine. But compound expansion, "the only great improvement which the steam engine had undergone since the time of Watt,"[3] did not come into general use during the early railway age, on land or sea— partly because of the dangers of high-pressure steam in the weak boilers of those days. For beam engines of the ordinary Watt type it was revived by M'Naught in 1845. Factory and other engines were 'M'Naughted,' made more powerful and more economical, by the addition of a small high-pressure cylinder. Then, in 1854–6, John Elder applied the principle to the marine engine on the Clyde. But this was only a beginning:

---

[1] *Industrial Resources of the Tyne, Wear and Tees* (1864), p. 247. Palmer's article on iron shipbuilding.

[2] Kennedy, *op. cit.* p. 109, 301.

[3] Ewing, J. A., *The steam-engine and other heat engines* (1894 ed.), p. 24.

great advances in engine and boiler making were necessary before the compound could drive out its predecessors. Boiler-pressures, for example, in the early 'fifties were seldom above 20 or 25 lbs. to the square inch. Twenty years later, when compound engines were really coming in, they ranged from 45 to 65 lbs.; in 1881, with the advent of triple-expansion, a list of typical new engines gives a mean of 77 lbs.[1]

The Peninsular and Oriental Company put compound engines into the *Mooltan* in 1860–1. There was considerable fuel economy and the experiment was repeated. But the engines proved untrustworthy and were all pulled out. Only in 1869 did the Company secure a set of "high and low pressure machinery which could be regarded as thoroughly satisfactory."[2] Between 1863 and 1872, the fuel consumption of good new marine engines was reduced by one half[3]: that left room for cargo. Meanwhile the Suez Canal had offered all the seas of the East to the iron or steel ship and the compound engine.

Movement became swift, and steam took over the heavy carrying on route after route. It is possible that even the 901,000 steamship tons on the British register in 1865 did more transport work than the 4,937,000 sailing tons of the same year; certain that the 1,900,000 steamer tons of 1875 did more than the 4,200,000 sailing tons of 1875. In 1882 the mounting curve of the steamer tonnage crossed the descending curve of the sailing ships. By 1885, the nearly 4,000,000 steamer tons with their 108,000 men may have done from six to seven times the work of the 3,400,000 tons of sailers and their 91,000 men.

While the mercantile marine was being thus transformed, the fishing fleet had changed more in the size, disposition and functions of its units than in their material or motive power. In the 'thirties and early 'forties the British fisheries had, as a whole, been in a poor way. Boats were small; deep-sea work was neglected; fishermen and their advocates were wailing about foreign competition—Frenchmen well within the three mile limit; even dragging our bays for bait at seasons which were closed in their own. In 1833 it was the considered opinion

---

[1] Marshall, F. C., "On the Progress and Development of the Marine Engine," *Trans. Inst. Mech. Eng.* 1881, p. 449 *sqq.* See also Wyllie, R., *ibid.* 1886, p. 473 for triple-expansion in the early 'eighties. For Elder, the *D.N.B.* He introduced the triple-expansion engine in 1881. For the compound locomotive, below, p. 180.

[2] Kennedy, *op. cit.* p. 54, quoting Sir Thos. Sutherland of the P. and O.

[3] Jeans, *Creators of the Age of Steel*, p. 147.

of a Select Committee that from Yarmouth to the Land's End the fisheries had been gradually declining since the peace[1]. Trawling, well known in the West Country, especially to the men of Brixham, was hardly practised in the North Sea at all, and it was declining in the Channel. At Hull the first trawler was seen in the year of the Reform Bill[2]. The trade had come up from the West by way of Ramsgate. Trawlers were pushing out beyond the Inner Silver Pit and the Sole Pit in the late 'thirties. In the hard winter of 1843 they first worked the Great Silver Pit under the Dogger Bank with amazing results. But they were still few and small. Hull's twenty-one fishing smacks ran only from 23 to 32 tons in 1844–5; by 1883 she had four hundred first-class trawlers, of from 65 to 90 tons, and some hundreds of lesser craft[3]. Grimsby had more, first-class trawlers and line cod-fishing smacks. Trawling only began there in 1858, "when four or five smacks migrated thither from Hull,"[4] the year before the railway to Grimsby was completed; but the deep-sea line fishing was older. From Yarmouth and Lowestoft and many other ports on the East coast, especially Peterhead and Aberdeen, the herring drifters went out in their season as they had long gone. Their numbers and size also increased and their design improved from about 1850, though they never ran so big as the trawlers. Some West coast fisheries also developed, but the great activity and improvement was on the East. By 1878, out of 176,000 tons of fish carried inland by rail in England and Wales, 124,000 came from Grimsby, Hull, Yarmouth and Lowestoft, and 59,000 from Grimsby alone[5].

Apart from the railway, nothing had done more to develop deep-sea trawling than the use of ice, introduced by Samuel Hewett for his trawler fleet based on Yarmouth about 1855[6]. The ice was imported from Norway or stored in ice-houses from English winter supplies. Last came steam; but its work was subsidiary down to the 'eighties. Between 1865 and 1875 the cutter rigged carriers which raced the fish home to market began to be replaced by steamers, and tugs helped drifters and

---

[1] Vol. I. p. 322: *S.C. on British Channel Fisheries*, 1833 (XIV. 69), an excellent report.

[2] *R.C. on Trawling*, 1885 (XVI. 471). Evidence of A. Rollit for the Hull smack-owners, Q. 8648. See in general Holdsworth, E. W. H., *Deep Sea Fishing and Fishing Boats*, 1874, based on the *Commission on Sea Fisheries* of 1866, of which Holdsworth was secretary.

[3] *R.C. on Trawling*, Q. 8631, 8627.     [4] Holdsworth, *op. cit.* p. 251.

[5] *R.C. on Trawling*, *App.* C IV.     [6] Holdsworth, *op. cit.* p. 244–5.

trawlers out and back. Late in the 'seventies—when trawling had got to the Great Fisher Bank off Jutland, and the trawlers at times could "almost sight the Naze of Norway"[1]—the steam trawler appeared, first in numbers on the Forth, where trawling of any sort was a recent development. Between 1879 and 1883 twelve steam trawlers were registered at Leith; between 1881 and 1883 nine at Granton, where there was a trawler-owning company. By the end of 1883 there were said to be about thirty in all Scotland[2]. Hull, with its four hundred first-class boats, had "none that go by steam except the carriers and cutters," and Grimsby had a single one[3]. Nor was there much progress in the years 1883–6. Prices were falling and boat-building of all sorts was slack. Only four steam trawlers were built in Scotland in 1886; and when an Inspector of the Fisheries for England and Wales issued a first jejune report in the following year, all that he found to say about trawlers and steam was that most of the trawlers were "fitted with steam capstans" for hauling in the nets[4].

The metal-built ship of the 'eighties, with its improved engines, would hardly have been possible, would certainly not have been possible at the price, but for the exact methods and the new ways of handling steel introduced into British engineering by Whitworth, and the extended use of hydraulic machinery which is connected particularly with the name of Armstrong. Whitworth had employed his true planes in his own Manchester workshop in the 'thirties; had made his methods public in 1840; and had communicated to the Institute of Civil Engineers his scheme for standardising screws, screw threads, and other mechanical essentials in 1841; but, ten years later, when his whole series of patented machine tools, his gauges adjusted to the ten-thousandth part of an inch, and his system of standardised screws and machine parts were praised in chorus by the jury of the Great Exhibition, although the jurymen spoke of the "great extension" which his system of standards had "already obtained," what evidently most impressed them was

---

[1] R.C. on Trawling, Q. 8655.    [2] Ibid. Q. 5410 and passim.
[3] Ibid. Hull, Q. 8640; Grimsby, Q. 9182. I am informed however that the Grimsby and North Sea Trawling Coy. formed in 1881 had two, the Aries and the Zodiac, before 1883.
[4] There had been regular Scottish reports for several years and Irish for many. The English and Scottish for 1887 here quoted are in A. and P. 1887, XXI. 147 and 245.

the vast field still to be occupied, and the "confusion and delay" of an unstandardised mechanical world. This too was what most impressed Dr Whewell when he was summoned to lecture on the Exhibition to the people[1].

From the height of, an established renown Whitworth was preaching to his fellow engineers in the 'fifties. "I cannot impress too strongly on...this institution," he told the Mechanical Engineers in 1856, "and upon all in any way connected with mechanism, the vast importance of possessing a true plane, as a standard for reference. All excellence in workmanship depends upon it....Next in importance to a true plane is the power of measurement,"[2] which his measuring machine and his gauges provided. This is hardly the tone which a preacher uses to the converted. In the matter of the bolts and screws he had eventually a very complete success. "Now," an admirer wrote in 1885, two years before Whitworth's death, "every marine engine and every locomotive in this country has the same screw for every given diameter. His system...has been adopted throughout the world, wherever engines and machinery are manufactured, the dies for producing the whole series having been originally furnished from his works at Manchester."[3] Working to gauge also spread rapidly in the 'fifties and 'sixties, so that in the more advanced sections of the engineering industry, such as textile engineering, machine parts became perfectly interchangeable. It was no longer necessary, as it once had been, to fit each several spindle in a cotton mill into its bolster by hand. Yet so late as 1886, the President of the Institution of Mechanical Engineers, when recapitulating to his colleagues those things which had "impressed themselves strongly upon" them in their recent visits to engineering shops of the first rank, laid special stress on the practice of "working to gauges throughout."[4] Evidently that practice was not yet among the things which no one need mention.

The individualistic and wilful young engineering industry and the users of engines, during the third quarter of the nineteenth century, were willing to accept the standardisation of a few essentials such as screws, but no more. Perhaps this was a

[1] The report is quoted in most accounts of Whitworth, *e.g.* Jeans, *Creators of the Age of Steel*, p. 228. And see vol. I. p. 446. Much of Whitworth's work was based on that of Maudslay, *e.g.* the 'Whitworth' true plane. *James Nasmyth, an Autobiography* (2nd ed. 1885), p. 144.

[2] *Trans. Inst. Mech. Eng.* 1856, p. 127.

[3] Jeans, *op. cit.* p. 224.    [4] *Trans. Inst. Mech. Eng.* 1886, p. 225.

good thing, if premature rigidity of machine types was to be avoided. Yet the multiplicity of types and specialities, natural as it was in an age of development, had great drawbacks. An extreme instance is that of the locomotive. Before 1850, in the hands of Robert Stephenson and others, it had attained a relatively high level of perfection, as the long lives of some early locomotives and the slight differences between an average locomotive of 1845–50 and one of 1880–85 show. Stephenson's *North Star*, sold to the Great Western in 1837, ran, with a new boiler, until 1870. A long-boiler engine built by him for the Great Eastern in 1847, and rebuilt in 1867, worked on into the 'eighties. An engine of Bury's, built in 1838, served the Furness Railway for sixty years. Yet this almost stabilised machine continued to be turned out to innumerable patterns[1]. "Probably five distinct classes of locomotives would afford a variety sufficiently accommodating to suit the varied traffic of railways," an expert wrote in 1855, "whereas I suppose the varieties of locomotive in actual operation in this country and elsewhere are very nearly five hundred." He suggested standardisation of classes but doubted "if such an arrangement could be worked out unless there were entire amalgamation of railway interests."[2] Seventy years later some such arrangement was being discussed in Britain and attained in Germany after the compulsory transfer of old-fashioned locomotives to the victorious allies.

William Armstrong, a lawyer by profession, had already patented an hydraulic crane and made other inventions when he took over the management of the Elswick works in 1847. There he proceeded to develop hydraulic machinery of every kind— cranes, lifts, capstans, swing and draw-bridges, lock-gates and sluices, grain elevators, pumps, pit winding engines, and mechanism for the movement of land and sea turrets[3]. The work was spread over a generation during which, after the first ten years, more of Armstrong's energies were directed towards munitions and ordnance than towards the things of peace. This side of his work culminated in the opening of the Elswick yard for the building of warships in 1882. Whitworth had been brought into official contact with munitions problems by the

---

[1] Warren, J. G. H., *A Century of Locomotive Building by Robert Stephenson and Coy.* (1923), p. 339, 355, 329.

[2] Clark, D. K., *Railway Machinery*, 1855, p. vii, quoted in Warren, p. 414.

[3] Important papers by or about Armstrong and his works are in the *Trans. Inst. Mech. Eng.* for 1858, 1868, 1869, 1874, 1881. And see the *D.N.B.*

invitation given him in 1854, at the time of the establishment of the government factory at Enfield, to construct rifle-making machinery for the state. He had decided that it was first necessary to find out experimentally what sort of a rifle ought to be made, and had evolved the type that bore his name, which the state did not adopt. From rifles he proceeded to Whitworth guns, which had their earliest, and very successful, field trials on the Confederate side in the American Civil War. By 1868 he had built a gun of position which could throw a shot weighing 250 lbs. to a distance of six miles and a half.

Meanwhile the small-arms demand had quickened mass-production and team work by machines. America began it. The government armouries of the United States had experimented with machine-made interchangeable parts in the 'twenties. About 1840, Blanshard's lathe for cutting irregular forms had been applied to gun-stocks at the Springfield arsenal. Samuel Colt's revolver, invented in the 'thirties, got its first mass demand from the Californian "forty-niners," and fascinated the old Duke of Wellington at the Great Exhibition. Colt used machinery and made his parts interchangeable. After the Exhibition he brought the machinery to England for use in a factory at Pimlico[1]. Before the government small-arms factory was founded at Enfield, a commission of inquiry was sent to the United States. In 1858 the factory was equipped with American machinery[2]. At Leeds a team of twenty-one machines had been installed earlier to meet the Crimean demand for cartridges[3]. Subsequently, at Birmingham, the Small Arms Trade Association of masters in the wonderfully subdivided Birmingham handicraft gun trade set up the first B.S.A. factory, with stock-making machines from America and rifling and boring machines from Leeds[4].

The story of munitions and ships of war is a thing apart; but its significance for industrial history, great at all times and

---

[1] Nasmyth's *Autobiography* (ed. 1885), p. 348.

[2] Bolles, *Ind. Hist. of the U.S.A.*, p. 254–6. *Birmingham and the Midland Hardware District* (1886), p. 396 *sqq.* Allen, G. C., *The Industrial Development of Birmingham and the Black Country* (1929), p. 188 *sqq.* Burn, D. L., "The Genesis of American Engineering Competition, 1850–70," *E. J. (Ec. Hist.)*, 1931.

[3] Meysey-Thompson, A. H., "On the History of Engineering in Leeds," *Trans. Inst. Mech. Eng.* 1882, p. 270.

[4] *Birmingham and the Midland Hardware District*, p. 403 *sqq.*; Goodman, J. D., "On the Progress of the Small Arms Manufacture," *S. J.* 1865, p. 494.

in all stages of industrial development[1], was never greater than during the early years of the age of exact workmanship, hydraulic machinery, and steel. The war departments of states were the metal-working inventor's ideal clients, clients whose demand for absolute strength of material and absolute perfection of workmanship was, or at least should have been, completely inelastic at all times, and in war time might become unlimited. As President of the Institute of Mechanical Engineers in September, 1856, Whitworth had welcomed the prospect which Bessemer's recent announcement held out of securing "iron and steel of a better quality."[2] His later experiments with ordnance convinced him that neither any kind of iron, hitherto exclusively used for gun-making, nor the new hard Bessemer steel in its ordinary state was what he required. Throughout the 'sixties he worked at the problem of compressing steel by hydraulic machinery while it was still fluid. His patent was taken out in 1865, but he was not ready to begin work on a commercial scale for another four years. By that time the uniform metal produced by the Siemens-Martin process was just coming on to the market[3]. It was the best material yet offered to be squeezed by Whitworth's hydraulic plungers into a compressed steel with a maximum both of strength and of ductility[4].

Devised primarily for guns, compressed steel soon found other uses. As ships of all kinds grew bigger, better material than wrought iron was needed for engine and propeller shafts. Compressed steel was used for the propeller shafts of the *Inflexible*, then the heaviest ship in the British navy, in 1876. Within a few years, Whitworth's shafting, made hollow like a gun so as to combine lightness with strength, was being employed in the mercantile marine. It was not merely light and strong. "The surface presented by a steel shaft to the bearings," F. C. Marshall of Newcastle wrote in 1881, "is also—it is not too much to say—almost infinitely more perfect than by the forged iron shaft, with its reeds, open texture, and iron cinder, from which engineers suffer so much. The friction must there-

---

[1] See the argument in Sombart, W., *Krieg und Kapitalismus*, 1913, and the modified argument in his *Moderne Kapitalismus*, 3rd ed. 1919, *passim*, and especially vol. I. p. 750 *sqq*.

[2] *Trans. Inst. Mech. Eng.* 1856, p. 126.          [3] Above, p. 63.

[4] See *inter alia* Carbutt, E. H., "Fifty years progress in Gun Making," *Trans. Inst. Mech. Eng.* 1887, p. 167.

fore be greatly reduced."[1] He spoke from experience, having just finished six pairs of engines with steel shafts. He was still using wrought iron piston and connecting rods, but was of opinion that, for large steamers, "steel-built crank shafts must come more and more into use. The constant failure of iron cranks...is too serious a question for the shipowner to let alone long." The *City of Rome*, the second largest steamship afloat, just launched for the Inman Line, had a hollow built-up crankshaft of Whitworth compressed steel[2]. So the transition of the 'eighties to the steel ship proceeded alongside of the transition to the all-steel engine within it.

Whitworth died—in 1887—before compressed steel had occupied more than a small part of the available field. He was anxious to see it employed in the construction of railway rolling-stock, because its use would lead to a great reduction in the dead weight hauled. But it was not at this time, nor in Britain, that the compressed steel underbody was generally adopted for railway vehicles[3]. Whitworth did however see in his last years great extensions in that making of machines by machines which his work had done so much to facilitate, even though "working to gauges throughout" was not yet universal. Wood-working machinery of all kinds, stimulated to rivalry by a rush of American machines in the late 'seventies, was making especially rapid progress in the early 'eighties[4]. In some ways it called for more ingenuity in the making, and more skill in the handling, than metal-working machinery; because the cutting tools of the latter move at fairly constant paces, at angles which vary little, through a material tolerably uniform; whereas no two woods are alike in density or grain; they must be cut at different angles; and tool speeds may vary, or rather did vary at that time, from 500 to 8000 feet a minute[4]. In average metal-working shops, although the "leading tools," the lathe and the plane, had

[1] "On the Progress and Development of the Marine Engine," *Trans. Inst. Mech. Eng.* 1881, p. 475.

[2] *Trans. Inst. Mech. Eng.* 1880, p. 341: an account of the ship while building at Barrow.

[3] There were very few in 1885. Head, J., Presidential Address: *Trans. Inst. Mech. Eng.* 1885, p. 321.

[4] Richards, G., "Recent Improvements in Woodcutting Machinery," *ibid.* p. 77 *sqq.* See also the *Trans.* for 1886, p. 275, the Presidential Address. The extensive use of wood-working machinery in America had been reported on by Wallis and Whitworth, commissioners to the New York Exhibition of 1853-4, in 1854; and America continued to lead during the next twenty years. Burn, D. L., in *E. J. (Ec. Hist.)*, Jan. 1931, p. 294, 299.

been altered very little "from their original forms,"[1] hydraulic machinery was coming in both for flanging and riveting; multiple punching and multiple drilling were becoming common and were displacing labour; and the rapid growth of the cycle industry at Coventry was providing fresh work for that stamping machinery which, in its simpler forms, had long been regularly used by the light metal trades of the Birmingham area[2].

The revolution in steel-making and the more exact engineering of the generation which followed the Great Exhibition reacted continuously on the older mechanised industries. Wood was not used in any new textile mill except for a few special purposes. Driving engines became steadily more powerful and more efficient. By continuous minor improvements, the driven machinery was made more completely automatic. The beautiful accuracy of its steel parts turned out to gauge made quicker running easy, and replacement swift. All through the labour story of these years runs the problem of 'speeding up.' But, in the cotton industry at least, there was no outstanding mechanical innovation, unless the introduction of Heilmann's comb in the early 'fifties, in place of the final carding process for cotton destined for the finest yarns, or that of ring-spinning on the frame, from America in the 'seventies, be so regarded. The comb, once introduced, changed little in thirty years; but it was used for coarser and coarser counts—down to 40's and 30's instead of 200's or 300's as at first—and, like all other machines, it was much speeded up[3]. Ring-spinning of warp yarns, well established in the United States before 1860, was still experimental in Britain in the late 'seventies. We cannot yet say "what is [its] proper position...in the economy of the cotton trade," an expert wrote in 1880[4]. Its really rapid introduction began only with the 'nineties.

Meanwhile the self-acting mule made steady, if slow, progress. "Before the cotton famine (1861–4) some hesitancy existed in people's minds as to whether [it] was a complete

[1] Meysey-Thompson, A. H., in *Trans.* 1882, p. 269.

[2] Head's Presidential Address, 1886; *Trans.* p. 275 *sqq.*

[3] See Platt, J., "On Machinery for the Preparing and Spinning of Cotton," and Spencer, Eli, "Recent Improvements in the Machinery for Preparing and Spinning Cotton"; *Trans. Inst. Mech. Eng.* 1866 and 1880.

[4] Spencer, Eli, as above, p. 527; and see Chapman, S. J., *The Lancashire Cotton Industry*, p. 71 n.

success, and it was only the more venturous spinners who would order a complete concern of self-actors."[1] Thereafter its final conquest of coarse spinning was rapid; of fine spinning long drawn out. "For spinning the finest counts...the hand-mule has been brought to great perfection," Eli Spencer of Oldham wrote so late as 1880[2]. He added that it was becoming more automatic; that the spinner had only "to supply the little power required to control some of the motions"; and that, even so, "men of first class ability as spinners became scarcer year by year." Two years later the operatives' secretary for the Bolton area, a home of the very finest spinning, reported that in the five years since 1877 the number of pairs of hand-mules in his district had fallen from 1300 to 516, and that their ultimate extinction was certain[3]. Extinction is said to have come in Glasgow about 1887. In English Pennine valleys a very few hand-mules could still be found at the opening of the twentieth century[4].

Meanwhile, taking the spinning industry as a whole—mules and frames and all preparing machinery—the changing relation of labour to machines, and the changes in the machines themselves, had produced these results[5]:

|  | Number of operatives in spinning mills | Yarn produced per operative in lbs. |
|---|---|---|
| 1844–6 | 190,000 | 2,800 |
| 1859–61 | 248,000 | 3,700 |
| 1880–82 | 240,000 | 5,500 |

As an effective element of the industry, the hand-loom had long been extinct. True, even in 1891–2, a German inquirer found a few grey-headed men and women, in well-lighted cellars at Bolton, weaving by hand "counter-panes of peculiar patterns ...with words woven in, mostly Bible verses." They had an "almost fanatically out-spoken determination to be the last of their trade, and to teach their handicraft to no younger person." The grandchildren worked in the factories, where they earned "three times as much" as their grandparents[6]. But so early as 1856 the cotton hand-looms which had survived the turn of the

[1] Andrew, S., *Fifty Years of the Cotton Trade* (1887), quoted in Chapman, *op. cit.* p. 70.    [2] As above, p. 516.
[3] Chapman, *op. cit.* p. 71.    [4] From personal information.
[5] Schulze-Gävernitz, G. von, *The Cotton Trade in England and on the Continent* (Eng. trans. 1895), p. 99, based on Ellison, T., *The Cotton Trade of Great Britain* (1886), p. 66, 68.
[6] Schulze-Gävernitz, *op. cit.* p. 105.

century had fallen to a few thousands; by 1885 it was a matter of hundreds. Between those years, the power looms had increased from 299,000 to 561,000, and they were running far quicker, probably more than 50 per cent. quicker. Whereas in 1850 there had been one weaving operative for 1·6 looms, in 1878 there was one for 2·1; in 1882 one for 2·2. The result, in the form just given for spinning, was:[1]

| | Number of operatives in weaving mills | Cloth produced per operative in lbs. |
| --- | --- | --- |
| 1844–6 | 210,000 | 1,700 |
| 1859–61 | 203,000 | 3,200 |
| 1880–82 | 246,000 | 4,000 |

The worsted industry had followed hard after cotton, of which it had almost become a part, because, between about 1840 and 1870, most of its women's dress fabrics had come to be made with cotton warps[2]. Indeed, as soon as it had assimilated the revolution in combing, that is to say from about 1855[3], it was perhaps more completely mechanised even than cotton. It did not use the mule at all, and so had no hand-mule spinners[4]. When John James wrote his *History* of the industry, in 1857, hand-loom worsted weavers were hardly to be found except in places like Wuthering Heights. Some of them hung on into the 'seventies, perhaps later. But even before James's time it had become impossible to quote general figures of their earnings, for they were no longer an industrial class. In the mills, iron looms clanged faster, steel spindles and gill-boxes and combs worked more smoothly, and labour was saved just as in cotton. Minor improvements were continuous—but it would hardly be too much to say that from the 'sixties to the 'eighties leaders of the industry, having got a complete mechanism, were content with it[5].

In the woollen industry, more varied and more scattered, things were different. Down to 1850, the mule itself had been little used in the Cotswold valleys: spinning was done on the

---

[1] Schulze-Gävernitz, *op. cit.* p. 108, 112, based on Ellison, *op. cit.* p. 66, 69. The 'weaving operatives' figure includes all those who worked in and about the weaving sheds.

[2] See, for example, the evidence of W. H. Mitchell before the *R.C. on the Depression of Trade and Industry*, 1886, Q. 3860.        [3] Above, p. 31.

[4] To be exact, it had not used it at all. 'French spinning' with modern mules was coming in a little in the 'eighties. *R.C. on the Depression of Trade, etc.*, 1886, Q. 6731 (Sir Jacob Behrens).

[5] The 'cap' spindle was one of the improvements, or variations; above, p. 13.

hand-jenny[1]. The decisive improvement of mechanical 'condensing' came in very slowly everywhere. The leading districts had adopted it generally by 1870[2]; but, according to the factory inspectors, there were only five 'condensers' in England and Wales, outside Yorkshire, in 1871. Returns of 'billy spindles' were still being made in 1875[3]. At that time in the still numerous company mills of the small Yorkshire clothiers there was much antiquated machinery; more in remote Welsh or Scottish carding and spinning mills. Within a few miles of Leeds, about Calverley and Farsley, a strong body of hand-loom weavers worked right through the 'seventies. "I went out of business in 1876," a retired Calverley manufacturer said in 1902, "and our firm had never had a single piece woven by power."[4] It was the same in the important fancy woollen trade of the Huddersfield district—the district which produced, among other things, the dashing Victorian waistcoats of John Leech's pictures, and which, with the Tweed towns, was the pioneer of all modern fancy fabrics for men's wear, as opposed to the old broadcloths, friezes and pilot-cloths. In 1866 the hand weavers managed about a quarter of the looms in the trade: they still had some importance twenty years later[5]. In the carpet trade of Kidderminster, power came in with disastrous rapidity in 1855–6; and so in 1866 a Power Loom Weavers' Association was founded among the men for defence. But in 1868 the much older English [Handloom] Carpet Weavers' Association had over 3000 members, in Yorkshire and elsewhere, including some in the Kidderminster area; and it was only after 1876 that this union, which in the interval had spread to Scotland, began to decline, with its trade, before the competition of floor-cloth and linoleum and the power-woven carpet[6]. That the hand-loom was at work in Wales, the Highlands, and the Hebrides many years later needs no demonstration here.

In the British flax industry, still more in the jute industry

---

[1] *V.C.H. Gloucester*, II. 194. Mules had not been adopted even by Gott of Leeds till 1829. Crump, W. B., *The Leeds Woollen Industry*, 1780–1820 (1931), p. 264.

[2] Baines, E., *Yorkshire Past and Present*, II. 665.

[3] For 'condensing' and the hand-worked 'billy' see above, p. 12, 30. The Inspectors' statistics quoted are in *A. and P.* 1871, LXII. 105; 1875, LXXI. 57. In the next series, *A. and P.* 1878–9, LXV. 201, there are no 'condenser' or 'billy' figures.

[4] Personal information.

[5] Clapham, J. H., "The Decline of the Handloom in England and Germany," *Bradford Textile Journal*, June, 1905, p. 45.

[6] Trade Union facts from *Webb MSS*. London School of Economics. Industrial facts, *V.C.H. Worcester*, II. 298 *sqq.*

which was splitting from it after 1850, the power-loom had gained much ground, and machinery for heckling, drawing and spinning had been improved in detail and pace. There had been only 6092 linen power-looms in 1850 against 32,617 for worsted and 249,627 for cotton[1]. The 6092 includes jute looms. Jute had been known since the Great Wars, when the East India Company had imported it experimentally as a substitute for hemp. Tried first in England, it got to Dundee in the 'twenties, but the machinery then running was not well suited to it. Importing merchants pressed it on manufacturers in vain for some years; but between 1833 and 1848 it came gradually into use for weft yarn, with a hemp or linen warp, in the manufacture of sacking and other rough goods. Not until 1848 were the technical difficulties of using it for the warp finally overcome, and the ground cleared for a pure jute industry. By about that time also, the spread of heckling machinery from Leeds into Scotland got rid of the bottle-neck of a handicraft operation in a preliminary process[2]. The jute industry was not yet, however, really distinct from that of flax. The machinery was almost identical; mills built for the older material went over to the new without difficulty; and so late as 1864, their historian was writing, in words which could hardly have been used twenty years later, that "the Linens manufactured in Dundee comprise flax, hemp and jute goods."[3]

After that date the separation became more marked every year[4]. By 1867 the import of jute into Dundee, for the use of the town and of adjacent towns in Forfar, Fife and Perth, was 64,000 tons—against 1100 in 1838—at a time when the whole national import of 'China Grass, Jute, and other Vegetable Substances of the nature of Hemp,' which was the most accurate figure that the national statistics provided, was only 80,000 tons. In that year there were in Scotland alone 20,000 power-looms for flax, jute and hemp, of which 8000 were in Dundee—considerably more than there had been in all Britain seventeen years before. The hand-loom, though by no means yet extinct in Dundee, was "fast disappearing"[5] even from the

---

[1] Vol. i. p. 554.          [2] See vol. i. p. 146.

[3] Warden, A. J., *The Linen Trade Ancient and Modern* (1864), p. 630. For jute origins see *ibid.* p. 50 *sqq.* and Bremner, *The Industries of Scotland* (1869), p. 251 *sqq.*

[4] For the later history the best source is the evidence of three Dundee witnesses before the *R.C. on Depression of Trade*, 1886, Q. 6175 *sqq.*

[5] Warden, *op. cit.* p. 557.

finer industry of Dunfermline, where much table-linen was made. Its disappearance had been heralded there by a short-lived factory hand-loom system. In England there were never many power-looms in this group of trades, because flax weaving was stationary or declining, and a large scale jute industry did not grow up. Even mill spinning of flax was stationary in the 'sixties at Leeds, where it had started[1]. In England as a whole the flax spindles had begun to fall by, or before, 1860. Ulster gained more than all that Britain lost, and Eastern Scotland gained in jute far more than she lost to Ulster in flax. England alone lost absolutely. Her flax power-looms crawled up to a maximum of 5600 in 1875, but had fallen to 4000 ten years later, hand-looms declining all the while. Her factory spindles fell from 442,000 in 1857 to 118,000 in 1885.

In 1885 the balance of power-driven flax machinery in the three sections of the then United Kingdom was as follows:

|  | England and Wales | Scotland | Ireland |
| --- | --- | --- | --- |
| Spindles | 118,000 | 221,000 | 817,000 |
| Looms | 4,000 | 21,600 | 22,000 |

Scotland's flax mills employed 39,000 people to England's 11,000; her jute mills another 36,000 to England's 4400. In addition each had a few thousand factory hemp-workers[2].

While factory conditions were intensifying, and factory location changing, in hemp, flax and jute, hosiery was just becoming a factory industry, and that slowly. In 1850 it had been an out-work industry with central warehouses, a number of non-power 'frame shops,' and a handful of experiments with power[3]. Ten years later, the Nottingham Chamber of Commerce reported that there were only 3000 to 4000 factory workers at all the rotary, circular, or 'warp' machines, against over 50,000 domestic framework knitters of the old sort[4]. In 1862, when the Commissioners on Children's Employment estimated that 120,000 people were connected with the hosiery industry, only 4487 were within the Factory Law. The latter figure was

---

[1] But Leeds still had 29 factories with 8000 workpeople in 1871. Baines, *Yorkshire Past and Present*, III. 193.

[2] Factory Returns, *A. and P.* 1875, LXXI. 57; 1884–5, LXXI. 1087.

[3] Above, p. 33.

[4] Felkin, W., *History of the Machine wrought Lace and Hosiery Industries*, p. 514.

no doubt exact[1]. In 1866 Felkin, the historian of knitting machinery, said that "even now the absorption of narrow hand-machines into large masses can scarcely be said to have more than commenced." He was speculating on the consequences of an age of power, how it might depopulate villages and "change local residence," much as some public-spirited cotton lord might have speculated seventy years earlier[2]. With the 'seventies, a parliamentary factory group, headed by Joshua Fielden, began to promote bills for checking evils in the hosiery industry incidental to an outwork system, especially the old standing abuses of frame-renting by middlemen hosiers. They were well advised, because the Inspectors had reported only 129 hosiery factories with 9700 workpeople in 1871. Of these factories, 74 were in Leicester, 45 in Nottingham, 3 large ones in Roxburgh. Many of them still contained great numbers of hand-frames, and so far were only glorified frame shops[3]. The success of Fielden and his group in getting on to the Statute Book the Act 37 and 38 Vict. c. 48 of 1874 helped the factories by interfering with the sweating of outworking knitters by the middleman. This is the course of factory development as reported by the Inspectors[4]:

|  | Hosiery factories in Great Britain | Persons employed in them |
|---|---|---|
| 1871 | 129 | 9,700 |
| 1878 | 185 | 14,900 |
| 1885 | 227 | 19,500 |

The accompanying decline in hand-frames outside the inspected factories has no such exact record; but it is known that, from the reputed 50,000 of 1850, they had fallen to a reputed 5000 in the Midlands by 1892. By that time more of them were in shops than in homes. It appears that, apart from the few making knitted gloves or doing very high grade work, they were kept going mainly because the War Office had an antiquated specification for military pants. The middlemen were still there and the Trade Unions were trying to drive the trade into the factories[5].

[1] It is from the Factory Inspectors' Report, A. and P. 1862, LV. 629. The estimate is in Second Report of the Children's Employment Commission, 1864, XXII. p. xxxii.

[2] Op. cit. p. 464.

[3] Factories and Workshops Return, A. and P. 1871, LXII. 105.

[4] A. and P. 1871, LXII. 105; 1878–9, LXV. 201; 1884–5, LXXI. 1087.

[5] R.C. on Labour, 1892, XXXVI. part 2, Q. 12,668 sqq. (machine workers), Q. 13,324 sqq. (hand workers). The pants are in Q. 13,358.

In the complex machine lace industry there was no decisive technical revolution. It was necessarily a sort of factory industry, because its machines were big and expensive. But its factories might well be, and often were, less mechanical and more workshop-like than the hosiery mills[1]. They grew in numbers between 1871 and 1885 about as fast as the hosiery mills; but they were on the average a great deal smaller at both dates. They were mostly in and about Nottingham. The figures are

|      | Lace factories in Great Britain | Persons employed in them |
|------|------|------|
| 1871 | 223  | 8,300  |
| 1885 | 431  | 15,000 |

Very prosperous during the decade 1873–83, mainly because of Victorian lace curtains, the English mills did not take up the most remarkable invention of that time, the lace embroidery machine. The period closes with their representatives explaining to a Royal Commission that this machine was at work in St Gall and Plauen, while Nottingham was making the plain net for it to embroider[2].

Silk, the oldest of power-factory textile industries and the last to make effective and extensive use of the hand-loom; whose yarns were combined with Lancashire cotton and Yorkshire worsted; woven on Coventry ribbon looms and knitted on the frames of Leicester and Derby; employed by craftsmen for the richest brocades and hurried by power into cheap handkerchiefs; the industry which believed itself ruined by the 'Cobden' Treaty of 1860, yet survived, if shorn and crippled, doing some of its old work in its old way, even in Spitalfields—silk was both unchanged and changed fundamentally between 1850 and 1885. Coventry millinery ribbons, made much as they always had been, enjoyed a "last really good spell of business" in the late 'eighties[3]; and when the leading firm of Macclesfield first got the order for silk handkerchiefs for the Navy, in 1883, it made them all on hand-looms[4]. But meanwhile the spun-silk industry, a waste-product machine industry, had been created.

[1] Above, p. 32.
[2] *R.C. on Depression of Trade*, 1886, Q. 6595 *sqq.*
[3] Warner, Sir F., *The Silk Industry of the United Kingdom*, p. 125. For the organisation at Coventry see vol. I. p. 197–8, 553–4 and *E.J.* XVII. 352–3.
[4] Warner, *op. cit.* p. 136.

Silk waste had always been too valuable to be thrown away; so the broken ends of thrown silk, and the short fibres from damaged cocoons, had been carded and spun into 'floretta' silk time out of mind in Italy, and to some extent, it would appear, in England before the invention of spinning machinery. In the early machine age the process had been adapted to the new conditions. In the 'forties a number of mills about Manchester span waste silk for cheap shawls on cotton-spinning lines. In 1836 two Glasgow silk throwsters had taken out a patent for handling waste silk—because of the length of its fibres—on flax or worsted, as opposed to cotton, lines[1]. A variant of this process, coupled with many inventions and ingenious modifications in spinning and weaving and the resolute use of the very cheapest waste cocoons, made one of the several fortunes of the effective creator of the English spun-silk industry, Samuel Cunliffe Lister the woolcomber.

In 1855 a silk broker sent Lister some unsaleable waste to see if he could comb it. With the aid of a co-inventor, Warburton, he did so and span it—in two years at a cost of £360,000. The material was so bad that, as Lister wrote later—"a...silk-spinner would at once have said: 'there is plenty of good waste; why bother with this rubbish?'"[2] Its very badness was his strength, for it left a margin for costly experiment and in the end made popular goods. In time, when the original silk comb had been superseded and all processes revised, Manningham Mills became one of the giant factories of Europe—sending silk sewing thread all over the world, making velvets and softly draping silks fitted to the taste of the 'eighties, with imitation sealskins and furs, very popular indeed. The mills were transferred to a Limited Company in 1889 for near £2,000,000[3].

Round about 1850 the world's oldest mechanical industry, corn-milling, comprised in Britain a few big steam units and innumerable little water mills on their ancient sites. But though in the great towns the motive power had changed, the art and craft of milling had not. The stones might be bigger, but the essentials were what Chaucer's miller would have understood. Not that the metal-age notion of grinding with fluted iron rollers had escaped English inventors. Isaac Wilkinson, iron-

---

[1] Warner, *op. cit.* p. 403, 417.
[2] As quoted in Warner, *op. cit.* p. 227.
[3] Warner, *op. cit.* p. 228.

master of Cartmel, had patented it in 1753; but nothing had come of the patent[1]. After 1820 the system had been tried experimentally on the continent, while the Corn Law protected the British miller. Shortly after 1846, he felt for a time the competitive effects of the system of 'high grinding' first practised—though not with rollers—in Austria-Hungary, and taken up in France. By that time rollers were being used successfully for the primary grinding, but stones for the finishing, in Pesth. However, when British millers began to inquire into the matter, in the late 'fifties and the 'sixties, the system was rather under a cloud. It had been recklessly applied to unsuitable wheats, and was not then making much headway even at Pesth. Also there were still many improvements needed before its general adoption was likely[2].

From 1862 onwards, experiments were being made with imported roller machinery. By 1870 one firm of Liverpool millers had got rid of stones entirely[3]. But the modern mill, fully equipped with steel rollers, 'centrifugal dressers' and other automatic machinery, only came some ten years later. The firm mainly responsible for its introduction dated it from 1881[4]. Automatic machinery was coming in about the same time in the United States, and no doubt there was interchange of notions. From 1881, aided by the growing concentration of corn-milling at the ports and the competition of American flour, the transformation of the industry and the growth of its representative unit, the great waterside automatic mill, went on very swiftly. By 1886 the steel rollers had "superseded almost entirely the use of mill-stones"[5]—in great mills only, it should be added. "The completeness of the revolution," the responsible engineer wrote in 1889, "is exemplified by the fact that practically in less than ten years the machinery and methods of corn-milling have been...entirely altered. The best kind of roller-mills...resemble ...in the accuracy of their construction the highest class of machine-tools."[6] He came from Manchester, where the high-class machine-tool had been developed by Whitworth.

[1] Bennett and Elton, *A History of Corn Milling*, III. 296.
[2] Bennett and Elton, III. 299 *sqq.*
[3] Bennett and Elton, III. 304.
[4] Simon, H. (the head of the firm), "On the latest Developments of Roller Flour Milling," *Trans. Inst. Mech. Eng.* 1889. See also Simon's paper in *Proc. Inst. Civ. Eng.* 1882, and the criticism in Bennett and Elton, III. 307.
[5] Head's Presidential Address, *Trans. Inst. Mech. Eng.* 1886, p. 286.
[6] Simon, *op. cit.* p. 148.

Almost contemporary with the revolution in milling came the industrial and commercial uses of artificial refrigeration. The physics of refrigeration had long been known. Sir John Leslie had actually made a little laboratory ice at Edinburgh about 1810[1]. English patents for ice-making by compression went back to the 'thirties; but artificial ice was not available in 1855. The transformation in the fish trade which set in in that year was based on the use of natural ice, such as any gentleman might have stored in an ice-house in his grounds to cool his summer drink. Only in 1861 came what has been claimed as "probably the earliest application of a refrigerating machine to manufacturing,"[2] and what was almost certainly the earliest in Britain, when a Harrison ether machine, patented in 1857, was used in the extraction of solid paraffin from shale oil. Next year a similar machine was tried for ground freezing, but not in Britain. It was in Germany that Poetsch finally developed the use of ground freezing for sinking coal pits through water-bearing strata, about the year 1880[3].

Refrigeration in its bearing on food problems was much discussed in the 'sixties, and invention went forward[4]. In 1867 came Reece's freezing machine, one of the early ammonia machines, which, as perfected twelve or fifteen years later, could make fifteen tons of clear block ice a day with a ton and a half of coal. Experiments in the freezing of meat were being made early in the decade by T. S. Mort and E. D. Nicolle in New South Wales. Mort certainly started the first freezing works in the world at that time; but it was not until February 2, 1880, that the *Strathleven* brought a cargo of frozen Australian meat into London docks[5]. Just five years earlier the first trial shipment of 'chilled' meat had come from New York. It had been kept cool by natural ice and a hand-worked fan; but that method had soon been improved upon[6]. By 1880, many types of refrigerating machinery were on the market. Windhausen of

[1] See Ewing, J. A., *The Mechanical Production of Cold* (2nd ed. 1921); Lightfoot, T. B., "Refrigerating Machinery," *Trans. Inst. Mech. Eng.* 1881 and 1886; the *D.N.B.* for Leslie; Critchell, J. T. and Raymond, J., *A History of the Frozen Meat Trade* (1912).

[2] Lightfoot, *op. cit.* p. 231. But Critchell and Raymond point out that a Harrison machine was used in a Bendigo brewery in 1851 and was patented in Australia in 1854–5. *Op. cit.* p. 22–3.

[3] *The Engineer*, Nov. 30, 1883, p. 417.

[4] Wood, Sir H. T., *A History of the Royal Society of Arts* (1913), p. 460–3.

[5] Wood, *op. cit.* p. 462; Critchell and Raymond, *op. cit.* p. 19.

[6] Bolles, *Industrial History of the United States*, p. 123.

Berlin had patented a complete vacuum pump type of ice-maker in 1878: it was tried at the Aylesbury Dairy, Bayswater, in 1881, but was not much imitated[1]. Far more important in the general history of refrigeration were a variety of compression machines patented here between 1873 and 1878—Giffard's, the Bell-Coleman, Lightfoot's—for these were the most easily applicable to cold storage on land or sea. The *Strathleven* had a Bell-Coleman installation. The London and St Katherine Dock Company used a Giffard machine for its first little cold store— to hold 500 frozen sheep—in 1882. Four years later, this and other stores had grown enormously, and even "retail butchers" were "now adopting...stores of their own."[2]

In 1866 the Royal Society of Arts had set up a committee to report on the food of the people, with special reference to "the production, importation, and preservation of substances suitable for food."[3] It took evidence not only about refrigeration but about the still rather experimental business of 'canning' or 'tinning' foods. There were no important novelties in the basic tin-plate industry itself between 1850 and 1886, except the introduction in the 'sixties of an efficient and economical device for spreading the tin, and the replacement of charcoal iron for the plates by Siemens steel between 1880 and 1886[4]; but all the time and in all countries the canning industry grew. There was Australian tinned mutton at the Great Exhibition. Foods preserved in tins had been used long before that, but only by soldiers and sailors and explorers. The committee of 1866 tried a navy tin forty-one years old. After turning aside for a few years from mutton and tin to gold, Australia turned back to them; and in the late 'sixties Australian meat extract and tinned meat began to come into general consumption. In the late 'seventies came the 'compressed cooked meats,' as Americans called them, from Chicago—tongues and corned beef and the rest. American fruits had already begun to arrive, and there was now a large consumption of miscellaneous British and European tinned foods. And every single tin plate which Australia or California or Chicago used was British made[5].

[1] Hopkinson, J., *Journ. R.S. of Arts*, 1882, p. 20.

[2] Lightfoot, *Trans. Inst. Mech. Eng.* 1886, p. 234. For the compression machines generally, Critchell and Raymond, *op. cit.* p. 336 *sqq.*

[3] Wood, *op. cit.* p. 461.

[4] Jones, J. H., *The Tinplate Industry* (1914), p. 10, 17; Cowper, E. A., *Trans. Inst. Mech. Eng.* 1881, p. 420.

[5] For Australian tinning, Critchell and Raymond, *op. cit.* p. 9–11; for American, Bolles, *op. cit.* p. 125; for the British tin-plate monopoly, Jones, *op. cit.* p. 20.

When the *Economist*, in June 1851, called public attention to the "astonishing velocity" of an American sewing machine[1], it noted in the journalists' style of the day that this invention threatened "to extinguish the occupation which dwarfs a race into the ninth part of its normal type." The proverbial philosophy here invoked would also have supplied a saying about "threatened men living long." Tailors are not extinct; but mechanical revolution was rightly foreseen in two of the greatest industrial groups in the country, nearly half a million seamstresses and tailors, and more than a quarter of a million of shoemakers. Neither had been even touched by machinery since the dawn of civilisation. There is also the revolution in domestic sewing to be borne in mind; but this the historian cannot easily follow out.

In Leeds, the town which was to become perhaps the most important home of the clothing factory, it is said that machinery was first introduced "to any extent" in 1857[2]. There, as elsewhere, the thing started simply, obviously, but obscurely when some enterprising man bought a batch of hand sewing machines and set girls to work them. By 1863 one of the pioneers at Leeds had 50 girl machinists on his premises and 200–300 female outworkers[3]. From some such simple beginning, at first without any use of power, and in close touch with contemporary developments in America, the complete factory evolved in the course of the next twenty-five years—borrowing devices from other industries and perfecting the uses of its own characteristic implement, the sewing machine. The evolution was slow and halting. In 1871 the Inspectors were aware of only fifty-eight tailoring and clothing factories in Britain. These were fair-sized concerns for they averaged 136 workpeople each; but they were said to have only 65 h.p. of steam between them. Presumably their 2600 sewing machines—not quite forty-five per factory—were hand-driven, a little power being harnessed

[1] Above, p. 13; *Economist*, June 26, 1851.
[2] Meysey-Thompson, "On the Hist. of Engineering in Leeds," *Trans. Inst. Mech. Eng.* 1882, p. 272. See also *V.C.H. Yorkshire*, II. 426; *V.C.H. Essex*, II. 25, for the Colchester industry.
[3] John Barran, *Children's Employment Commission*, 1864 (xxII), p. 2: "I began in a very small way," he said; adding, "in my retail business I only employ men." Not all the early machines were American. "Shortly after 1850" F. W. Harmer, a Norwich merchant, began to use machines "invented by a tailor named Thomas...like large fret-saws worked by treadles." *F W. Harmer and Coy.*, 1825–1925, p. 7.

for heavier jobs such as cutting or pressing[1]. The making of clothes did not become, and has not yet become, a pure factory industry: sub-contractors and individual outworkers always took jobs for which machinery had not yet been devised, or for which a particular firm might not be large enough to carry the appropriate machines; but the leading firms had a very complete mechanical installation by the early 'eighties. The clothes were cut out from innumerable piled up layers of material, on the top layer of which the pattern was chalked, by a power-driven band-knife working vertically. Sewing machines in ranks ran up to a maximum pace of two thousand stitches a minute. An iron set on the end of a jointed mechanical arm needed human guidance but not human driving; the button-holes were button-holed and all the buttons sewed on by machinery[2].

This was for low grade mass-production. As the quality improved, the amount of hand-work put into it, inside or outside the factory, increased. Such was the industry which was replacing what they called the making of slop clothing when Tom Hood wrote his *Song of the Shirt* for *Punch* in 1843. Women still plied needle and thread on market work: the factory had by no means absorbed all the clothes, and by no means all the work of the factory was machine-work; but there was less stitching "in unwomanly rags" than there had been forty years back. Night work had long disappeared from the Leeds trade. "The machines have saved all that," an employer said, even in 1863[3]. It was in the smart 'rush' trade of the West End season that there was most need for reform in the 'seventies and 'eighties.

The wholesale boot trade of 1850 had its factories, but they had neither machinery nor power. A device for riveting the soles to the uppers had been invented during the French wars by D. M. Randolph. Brunel the elder took it up and added other machines in an army boot factory. Once again the standardised demand for the forces had given the stimulus to mass-

---

[1] *Return of Factories and Workshops*, 1871 (LXII. 105). Harmer's of Norwich were called "The Steam Clothing Factory" apparently in the 'fifties: *op. cit.* p. 7. For American developments see Cole, A. H., *The American Wool Manufacture*, I. 293, and sources there quoted.

[2] Meysey-Thompson, *op. cit.* p. 272–3. Thomas's machine of the 'fifties ran at twenty stitches a minute; *F. W. Harmer and Coy.* as above.

[3] *Children's Employment Commission*, 1864, p. 7.

production. But like his team of block-making machines, Brunel's mass-production methods in boot-making went out of use, and almost out of memory, with the peace[1]. In the factories of the early 'fifties, under the master's eye, uppers might be cut carefully and soles roughly. Goods would be inspected there at the various stages of manufacture, and warehoused there; but nearly all, if not all, the actual making was done by 'binders,' who sewed together the parts of the upper at home, and by out-working master shoe-makers, who took apprentices just like the men in the bespoke trade, and did the heavy work with sole and heel leather by which the boot was 'made.'[2] By 1855–6 the Singer Company of New York was pushing a sewing machine for leather on the British market. It was a clumsy treadle machine and it made slow progress. At Stafford there was a shoe-makers' strike against machine-closed uppers; but with the aid of girl labour, machines got forward everywhere in time, first for light work sewn with a dry thread, then, with the necessary but not easy modifications, for sewing heavy wet-resisting uppers with a waxed thread[3]. About the year 1858, other treadle machines for cutting the butts (sole leather) and for stamping soles out of them were brought from America. Crick of Leicester reintroduced the system of riveting the sole to the upper by machine, a much simpler mechanical proposition than sewing it, and a very important step towards factory production. At Street in Somerset, William Clark devised and worked for a long time "in great privacy" the first simple machinery for building up and attaching the heels[4].

America and the needs of fighting men always set the pace. It has been said that the War of Secession, with its stupendous demand for army boots, "gave an opportunity to the boot-stitching machine which precipitated its introduction by many years."[5] Blake's decisive machine for sewing on the soles, invented in America and known in Britain before the war, only

[1] For the invention see Doolittle, W. H., *Invention in the [Nineteenth] Century* (1903), p. 367. For Brunel block-making machines, vol. I. p. 153.
[2] An excellent short account in *One Hundred Years' History of Shoes...at Street, Somerset* (Messrs C. and J. Clark), 1925, p. 6.
[3] Clark, *op. cit.* p. 8. For strikes at Stafford and elsewhere see *Trades Societies and Strikes* (*Nat. Ass. for Social Sci.*), 1860, p. 1. For damage done by these strikes to the Northampton trade, *R.C. on Labour*, 1892, XXXVI. part 2, Q. 12,076.
[4] *Op. cit.* p. 7.
[5] Swaysland, E. J. C., *Boot and Shoe Design and Manufacture* (Northampton, 1905), p. 8.

became thoroughly successful as a result of improvements made public during the war, in 1864[1]. It gave its manufacturers "a virtual monopoly of sole-sewing machinery for some years."[2] This, and Crick's riveting machine, were the first machines of importance special to boot-making, the closing of uppers being a fairly straightforward problem in sewing. With the Blake machine as basis, "the full team system of shoe-making was worked out in America" during the next ten years[3]. Leading firms in Britain kept in touch with American practice and imported the machinery. British machine-makers, mainly at Leicester, sometimes improved on it.

Down to the 'eighties—and for that matter much later— factory boot-making was far from being a complete power industry. In 1871 there were only 400 h.p. of steam in 145 boot and shoe factories; more than in clothing, but still not much[4]. Though the gas engine was coming into use during the next decade, steam remained the obvious power; few machines could be made really automatic; and new light ones for all kinds of sub-processes were constantly being tried. So only the heaviest and most certainly permanent machines, such as those for cutting butts or doing very stiff sewing, were as yet regularly power driven. The rest, as shown in contemporary designs, all have handles or treadles[5]. There was a fresh influx of American machines for the various finishing processes from about 1880. Hitherto machinery had helped only 'making,' in the narrowest sense of the word. Now edge-parers, levellers, ironing machines again roused trade union fears, and had to be introduced with discretion. With them came Goodyear's 'sew-round machine,' which produced the first exact replica of a hand-sewn welted boot. Each stage in boot-making had its team of machines, often simple ones easily replaced by hand processes in small factories; each team, of machines or processes, had its specialists with their new names—heel-builder, heel-breaster, heel-attacher, and the like[6].

There was still a vast deal of hand-work and home-work in

[1] Clark, op. cit. p. 9. Leno, J. B., The Art of Boot and Shoe Making (1885), p. 183. The actual manufacturer was Colonel McKay.

[2] Clark, as above.

[3] Clark, p. 9; Leno, op. cit. p. 186.

[4] Return of Factories and Workshops, as above.

[5] As, for example, in Leno's book of 1885.

[6] Leno, op. cit. p. 186. See Dictionary of Occupational Terms, compiled in connection with the census of 1921 (1927).

boot-factory centres, and more in London. So much boot-making was done at home, and by the piece, in 1886, that trust-worthy statistics of boot-makers' earnings could not be com-piled, even in the great centres[1]. The Kettering Co-operative Boot and Shoe Factory, founded in that year, installed "the ordinary run of machinery—not what is known as the American system though."[2] Even six years later, in the "heavy medium strong" boot trade of Leeds, "nearly half the work" was "done at the people's homes in the finishing department." There had been recent strikes against American machinery. And the whole London trade was "cut up between little employers," with a maximum of hand-work and home-work[3].

There is an odd, half-accidental, connection between the sewing-machine industries and a new industry of mid-Victorian times which had a future—the manufacture of cycles. Engineers of those times "universally accredited" the invention of the cycle to Gavin Dalziel of Lesmahagow, who put cranks in a hobby-horse in 1836. They were not at all clear about the credit for a much more decisive invention, which really started the industry, the suspension wheel; but they found it specified, together with wire-spokes, rubber tyres, and roller bearings, in a patent by E. A. Cowper of 1868[4]. It happened that at this time distress in the silk trade was driving people out of Coventry: population fell by 7 per cent. between 1861 and 1871. Possibly the presence of a large body of trained watch-makers in the town suggested to someone the idea of starting a new light metal industry, the manufacture of sewing machines. This was round about the year 1870. The factories must have had a hard struggle against their large-scale American competitors; but competition did not go on for long. Cycling became a gentle-manly pastime, and soon undergraduates were to return to the Universities pushing their "high bright bicycles" through the crowds at the railway station[5]. The occasion was seized at Coventry: "not only the human but even the mechanical por-tion of the equipment of the sewing-machine factories was

[1] *Stat. Tables and Report on Trade Unions*, 1886 (1887, LXXXIX. 715), p. 40.
[2] *R.C. on Labour* (1892, XXXVI. part 2), Q. 14,505.
[3] *Ibid.* Q. 11,984–5 and 15,010.
[4] Phillips, R. E., "On the Construction of Modern Cycles," *Trans. Inst. Mech. Eng.* 1885, p. 467.
[5] Anstey, F., *Vice Versa* (1882).

adapted, so far as possible, to the processes of the dawning industry."[1]

According to the census returns of 1881 only 1072 people in the whole country were employed in cycle-making; but this was probably an underestimate and would not include all the makers of accessories and cycle parts. Four years later it was claimed that there were more than 170 firms making cycles only; that there were 500 different types of cycles; that 3000 men in Coventry itself, and at least 5000 in the United Kingdom, got their living by the trade; that 40,000 cycles were turned out yearly; and that the average price of a machine was £20. Division of the output by the number of types, or of the employment figure by the number of firms, yields significant quotients. The expert who made these estimates in 1885[2] also classified the types. In Class 2c he placed "safety [*i.e.* low built, and geared] bicycles with steering wheel in front." He noted that "the steering was rather sensitive and consequently erratic." Type 2c was the machine which, when other types were forgotten and when its average cost had come something below £20, was to spin men down the grooves of change in England and in Uganda and Gwalior. Neither agricultural labourers nor Asiatics, it is believed, ever made a practice of riding high bright bicycles.

Cycle-making was an offshoot from those light metal trades of the Birmingham area which, like Sheffield cutlery-making, had been hardly mechanised at all before 1850, and were only sporadically mechanised during the succeeding generation. It is true that half-way through that generation (in 1865–6) the young, and already prosperous, Joseph Chamberlain wrote of the "revolution" which since 1850 had been "assimilating the town [of Birmingham] to the great seats of manufacture in the North and depriving it of its special characteristic, viz. the number of its small manufacturers."[3] He had particularly in mind his own industry, that of wood-screw-making, in which the introduction of self-acting machinery from America in 1854 had paved the

[1] Leppington, C. H. d'E., "The Evolution of an Industrial Town," *E.J.* 1907, p. 352. For Coventry watchmaking see vol. i. p. 48, 177.

[2] Phillips, *op. cit.*

[3] *Birmingham and the Midland Hardware District* (1866), p. 604. Though the screw-cutting lathe went back to Maudslay (Nasmyth, *Autobiography*, p. 128 and vol. i. p. 153) and had been used in the Midlands (Editor's note to Chamberlain's article, p. 605) wood-screws in 1850 normally had the thread "filed out by hand" (Chamberlain).

way for the final absorption, in 1866, of almost all the business into the factories and firm of Nettlefold and Chamberlain; but he could have given illustrations of big or fair-sized factories from many other trades of the city and district—locks in Wolverhampton, tinned and enamelled hollow ware at Wolverhampton and elsewhere, brass-tube-making and electro-plating in Birmingham itself, the new type of small-arms manufacture, steel-pen-making and the rising metal bedstead and cheap jewellery trades. There were also great concerns in the heavy industries of the Black Country, and in some branches of engineering proper; and there were large makers of railway rolling-stock. But the size of the large concerns was not always intimately connected with decisive mechanical innovations; and these big businesses rose from the Birmingham democratic industrial plain of small businesses with simple mechanism, and small working masters with little or none[1]. Their roots and suckers spread far beneath it. Chamberlain's process of 'assimilation' went on, but not rapidly, during the 'seventies and early 'eighties. In 1885 the speakers of the Birmingham Chamber of Commerce, whilst recording the rise of the great concerns and their recent transformation into private limited companies, were also calling the attention of Royal Commissioners to the still huge numbers of "small workers." "They take a house and commence to work in the upper part and so on," they explained[2].

The machine, aided by foreign competition, had crippled if not killed one bad old Black Country country trade, that of the outworking nailers. There were supposed to have been 50,000 people in it in 1830, a round figure probably too high. The census of 1851 gives 29,000. A Birmingham expert in 1865 thought 20,000. Wire nails, machine-cut nails, and Belgian competition in overseas markets, were the assigned causes of the decline. The decline continued; but the trade, a home of the worst forms of truck and of the blackguardly exploiting 'nail foggers,' was liable to be flooded in times of depression by unemployed colliers and iron-workers who had learnt it when

[1] *Birmingham and the Midland Hardware District, passim.* It is the report on the district prepared for a meeting of the British Association. Compare *Third Report on Children's Employment* (1864, XXII. 319), p. xi, most children hired by adult piece-workers; p. 7, not more than six or seven factories in lock and key trade; in saddlers' ironmongery "a vast number of small shops," etc.

[2] *R.C. on Depression of Trade and Industry*, Q. 1591.

young. So it was in 1878–9. This flooding, with the continued use of hand-made nails for boot soles and other special purposes, kept some 1500 workers in the trade in the Bromsgrove district at the end of the 'eighties[1].

About Sheffield, though great steel works were rising and factory organisation was making headway in the cutlery trade, there was certainly no cutlery revolution. In 1864 most even of the "large cutlery men" had "part of their work done out" and many cutlers who worked in factories—hiring the power—worked "on their own account or for other masters." When the Factory Acts were extended to cutlery in 1867, the inspectors had grave difficulty in finding 'factory owners' among the small master grinders and cutlers who hired power in little doses and employed a journeyman and a lad or two. With the workshop cutler they were not directly concerned. Even in 1901 there was only an average of six adults to each cutlery 'factory' on the inspectors' lists in the United Kingdom, in spite of the introduction of saw-grinding machinery from America in 1858, of file-cutting machinery about 1875, and of various types of mechanical hammer for blade forging before 1885. File-cutting machinery had been in use at Manchester, at Birmingham and abroad long before 1875. It is significant that men from Sheffield were indicting it before the Commissioners in 1886, and that a prominent manufacturer explained that he supplied both the machine-cut and the hand-cut file. No doubt his industry was a mixed factory-outwork, capitalist-small-master trade, like so many in Hallamshire and the Birmingham area[2].

Behind and beneath the technical development of all the industries lay the coal and the technique of collier and mining engineer. To those who, in 1865, spoke of an age of Iron or an age of Steam, Stanley Jevons replied that "coal alone can command in sufficient abundance either the iron or the steam; and coal, therefore, commands this age."[3] In his classical "inquiry concerning the progress of the nation and the probable exhaustion

---

[1] Ball in *Birmingham and the Midland Hardware District*, p. 110 *sqq*. *Fact. Ins. Rep.* 1868, p. 295–7 (1868–9, XIV. 75); 1879, p. 18 (1880, XIV. 93). *R.C. on Labour* (1892, XXXVI. part 2), Q. 18,378 *sqq*.

[2] *Fourth Report on Children's Employment*, p. 47, 201 for 1864; *Fact. Ins. Rep.* 1868, p. 12–13, for 1867; Lloyd, G. J. H., *The Cutlery Trades* (1913), p. 182, for 1901; *Ibid.* 186–7, 198, for the inventions; *R.C. on Depression of Trade*, Q. 1150 *sqq.*, Q. 3333, for 1886.

[3] *The Coal Question*, p. viii.

of our coal supplies,"[1] he argued that the annual consumption of coal, which he believed to have been 57,000,000 tons for 1851 and knew to have been 83,600,000 in 1861, would probably rise to 166,300,000 in 1881 and to 234,700,000 in 1891. In fact, owing to progressive fuel economy in steam raising, smelting and the like, and in spite of a fast growing export, the former figure was not reached until 1888 and the latter not until 1905. This slackening growth was not accompanied by anything very revolutionary in technique down to the 'eighties. Though there were a few important innovations, and everything got bigger or deeper, or stronger, the work of mining engineers was concentrated mainly on the problem of raising coal from the increasing depths, without increasing either the cost or the risk, and on spreading the best practice of the later 'forties[2].

In the years just before 1850 greater depths had been sounded everywhere, and explosions of fire-damp invariably followed. Before 1845, serious explosions had been rare, except in the deep pits of the North, but now (1845–50), in South Wales, Warwickshire, Lancashire, South Yorkshire, a series of terrible disasters—Risca, Rounds Green, Coppal, and the Oaks and Darley Main collieries at Barnsley—kept parliament busy with inquiries and led to the Act of 1850 (13 and 14 Vict. c. 100), the first of a long series which provided for or extended the 'Inspection of Coal Mines in Great Britain.'[3] The Acts had technical as well as preventive effects. The making and maintenance of correct plans of all collieries became a statutory obligation: the inspectorate provided a body of men with wide specialised knowledge and an uncommercial interest in efficient and safe mining practice. J. J. Atkinson, one of the earliest inspectors, to take a single example, in papers read before the North of England Mining Institute between 1854 and 1863, "laid for the English speaking races the scientific basis of modern mine ventilation."[4]

[1] The sub-title of *The Coal Question*.

[2] See vol. I. p. 432 *sqq*. For the slow spread of the best practice in some districts, Lones, *A Hist. of Mining in the Black Country* (1898), quoted in Allen, G. C., *The Industrial Development of Birmingham and the Black Country* (1929), ch. 6.

[3] For the accidents, Galloway, R. L., *History of Coal Mining* (1882; Galloway's later and fuller book, *Annals of Coal Mining*, was not carried beyond 1850), p. 234 *sqq*. Inspection had been provided for in the Act of 1843 (5 and 6 Vict. c. 99; see vol. I. p. 575–6) and Tremenheere had been appointed inspector; but this was inspection of labour, to see that women remained above ground, etc., not of the mine itself.

[4] Bulman, H. F. and Redmayne, R. A. S., *Colliery Working and Management* (2nd ed. 1906), p. 8.

All the deepest sinkings of the period were on the Lancashire and Cheshire coalfield. In 1858 the Astley deep pit at Dukinfield touched 2100 feet—exactly the reputed depth of the deepest pit of the early railway age, the Apedale in North Staffordshire. Near Wigan, 2448 feet was reached in 1869. Twelve years later, the Ashton Moss Colliery near Manchester sank a new pit to the 'great mine' coal at 2688 feet, the deepest sinking of the early 'eighties. Though Lancashire sank deepest, other districts were always deepening[1].

Deep pits needed great winding engines such as the new steel engineering could easily supply. In the 'forties an engine of 175 h.p. had been counted great: by the early 'eighties 1500 h.p. was sometimes required. The wicker corves for hoisting the coal and the miners were everywhere driven out by metal cages made at first of iron; but, "on account of its superior strength and lightness," steel had "come to be employed to a considerable extent...in the construction of winding ropes and cages, as well as for numerous other purposes" by 1882[2].

Urged on by the inspectors and the law, mining engineers took pains with ventilation. In 1850 there had been numberless pits, in those fields where shallow workings were normal, with no ventilating arrangements at all. On the Northern field, furnace ventilation, accompanied by the device of 'splitting the air,' i.e. the use of two air-currents, had been carried to a high level of perfection, and had proved superior in practice to Goldsworthy Gurney's device for producing air-currents by the discharge of jets of high-pressure steam. It was arguable in 1859 that no known mechanical device was better than a well-laid-out system of furnace ventilation[3]. Ten years earlier Struve's air-pump and Brunton's fan—devices based on French and Belgian practice—had succeeded simultaneously in South Wales. By 1852 fans had reached South Yorkshire, where they were tried by Biram, the 'viewer' of Earl Fitzwilliam's collieries near Rotherham. In 1858, J. J. Atkinson was defending not only the utility but the economy of the fan system before the mining engineers of the Northern field; and about two years later the first fan was erected there, at Twisdale Colliery, Durham[4].

[1] Galloway, *op. cit.* p. 265; *V.C.H. Lancashire*, II. 354; vol. I. p. 436.

[2] Galloway, *op. cit.* p. 259 and, for the winding engines, p. 266. The corves were not abandoned in one Cumberland pit till 1875. *V.C.H. Cumberland*, II. 353.

[3] See vol. I. p. 438 n. Also Galloway, *op. cit.* p. 150, 152, 251.

[4] Galloway, *Annals*, II. 296; *History*, p. 253.

The inspiration had come from abroad. So did the actual machines which decided the victory of mechanical ventilation all along the line. In 1862, Guibal of Mons patented the fan which finally converted the engineers of the North. Another foreign type, the Schiele, followed immediately. These two, together with one bearing a British name—the Waddle—were the dominant types of the period 1864–85. The first Guibal was tried at Elswick about two years after it had been patented. "Within ten or twelve years no fewer than two hundred were at work...in different parts of the kingdom."[1] In Eastern Scotland there was only one fan of any sort in 1873: there were over ninety in 1879[2]. About the same time Guibals were being installed in place of furnaces in the Earl of Lonsdale's Whitehaven collieries. The 'viewer' responsible for this was also getting rid of corves, and introducing another valuable innovation, already tried on the more fully mechanised fields, compressed air haulage underground[3]. By the 'eighties, although few even of the most primitive mining practices were literally extinct in Britain, most of the coal was raised from pits with a complete mechanical equipment for winding, ventilation and, at least on the main 'roads,' underground haulage. Thus a diminishing return to labour, at increasing depths, at greater distances from the shaft, and under worse atmospheric conditions was counteracted. Even an appreciable increase in return was secured. Yet there was nothing to be compared with the labour economy of a cotton mill. Very much labour was saved on the movement of men and coal from the face to the pit-bank, but hewing remained a handicraft.

Though not for lack of attempts to alter it. Even in the eighteenth century, invention had grappled with the process of 'holing' or 'kirving,' that is undercutting the coal seam so that it shall collapse by its own weight, the job for which the pitman crouches or, in a thin seam, lies on his side. But no coal-cutting machine had even approached success until the compressed-air drive had become practicable—with the aid of rubber. In the early 'sixties, a percussion type of machine, in which a piston instead of a human arm drives a pick, succeeded at the West Ardsley Colliery, Leeds. The patent was of 1861 and stood in the names of Donisthorpe, Firth and Ridley. Some

---

[1] Galloway, *History*, p. 255.     [2] *Ibid.* p. 256.

[3] The 'viewer' was Mr R. F. Martin. *V.C.H. Cumberland*, II. 365. There had long been steam haulage underground: compressed air was dearer but safer.

ten years after the first success, one of the patentees claimed that forty-eight men with the machine could do the work of sixty without it—a useful saving but no revolution[1]. Experiments were conducted systematically with this and other types of machine during the 'sixties and 'seventies. There were successes besides that at Ardsley. Some of the rotary cutters, in which the work is done by a toothed wheel placed parallel and close to the floor, were said to be "well spoken of" in 1876[2]. But there were all kinds of manipulative difficulties, besides those connected with the transmission of the power. Machines are never easily worked on a much tilted, a much faulted, or an uneven lying seam, or in one with a weak roof. A great deal "depends on the care and skill and energy of the men employed with them,"[3] qualities which, for obvious reasons, could not always be counted on. There was no risk of coal imports, and very little competition with British coal in overseas markets as yet. The upshot was that only some very tiny fraction of that coal was cut by machinery in the 'eighties. No important part was so cut even forty years later[4].

Figures of the mining population and of the output of coal at successive dates measure very roughly the extent to which machinery, organisation, and large-scale workings increased the efficiency of the miners' craft from the 'fifties to the 'eighties:

|      | British Coal Output, tons |  | Coal-Miners (Census figures) | Tons per Miner |
| --- | --- | --- | --- | --- |
| 1851 | 57,000,000 (Jevons' estimate) |  | 216,000 | 264 |
| 1861 | 84,000,000 (Mineral returns) |  | 280,000 | 300 |
| 1871 | 117,000,000 | ,, ,, | 314,000 | 373 |
| 1881 | 154,000,000 | ,, ,, | 382,000 | 403 |
| 1891 | 185,000,000 | ,, ,, | 517,000 | 358 |

The figures neglect changes in the working day and in the intensity of work, and many other matters which would require attention in an exact statistical treatment; but they tell the broad story. A great accession of mechanical and organising efficiency, and a growth of the normal mining business, increase the product of labour by 41 per cent., in spite of nature's

[1] Bulman and Redmayne, *op. cit.* p. 119; Galloway, *History*, p. 262.
[2] Williams, W. M., in *Brit. Man. Industries*, I. 113.
[3] Bulman and Redmayne, p. 114 (written in 1896).
[4] The use of pneumatic picks and drills was reported from only 557 mines even in 1927: most of these were used for driving headings and boring, not for coal-getting. *Seventh R. of the Sec. for Mines* quoted in *Labour Gazette*, Aug. 1928, p. 281. For the 'eighties, Galloway, *History*, p. 263.

reluctance, between 1851 and 1871. There is increase, but slower, for another decade: then retrogression sets in[1].

External conditions were hostile to mechanical progress in the metalliferous mines, except in the iron mines, and of these few were deep or highly organised. Lead-mining was shrinking into the lonelier hills and attracting little capital[2]. Copper, the glory of Cornwall, was still magnificently prosperous in the 'fifties—but not much later. Its mines had been equipped for pumping by Boulton and Watt themselves. Then steam had been applied to winding and stamping the ore, but not to hoisting the men. In the 'forties came Michael Loam's curious 'man engine,' meant to save the men such ladder climbs as the 228 fathoms of Dolcoath. But there were only eight man engines installed by 1862; and in 1881, though the Dolcoath engine went down 240 fathoms, the bottom was now at 362. A mine captain of seventy explained with pride in 1864 that 200 fathoms of ladders gave him no trouble[3].

By that time the shadow was falling on the mines of the Duchy. The best copper ore was giving out: Rio Tinto copper was being worked with British capital: the abundant copper ores of Lake Superior were to come soon. Though there were plenty of tin mines and stream works, Cornwall at that time lived primarily by its copper[4]. The decade 1871–81, in which at least a quarter of the miners emigrated, and the Cornish population fell by nearly 9 per cent., was no time for re-equipment. There were only ladders still for the 266 fathoms of West Wheal Seton in 1887[5]. Engines of Watt's pattern and boilers of Trevithick's remained in position. Some observers, their backward-looking fancies tickled by the simple uncontentious labour conditions

[1] From the census figures women are omitted; also the group 'miner undefined' in the censuses of 1861 and 1871. It was not large in either. The figures for 1881 and 1891 are those used in the *Survey of Industrial Relations* and reproduced in the *Eighteenth Abstract of Lab. Stat.* 1926, p. 22.

[2] For the one really great iron mine, Hodbarrow near Millom, see *V.C.H. Cumberland*, II. 396. By 1881 there were only 871 lead-miners in Derbyshire, and by 1901 only 285. *V.C.H. Derby*, II. 348. In Durham the lead output of 1905 was about one-tenth of what it had been in the 'fifties. *V.C.H. Durham*, II. 352.

[3] Jenkins, A. K. H., *The Cornish Mines* (1927), p. 222, 333. See also Price, L. L. F. R., "West Barbary or Notes on...the Cornish Mines," in *S.J.* 1888.

[4] Jenkins, p. 304. For the high number of tin-mines (82 out of less than 200 mines of all sorts in Cornwall and the South-West generally) *Fact. Ins. Rep.* 1879 (1880, XIV. 93), p. 84.

[5] Jenkins, p. 182.

of the Duchy, were saying that it seemed "to have escaped the disturbing influence of the Industrial Revolution,"[1] whilst, partly because of this happy escape, other revolutions had sent Cornishmen to the ends of the earth, and would send more.

Two allied elemental industries grew without conspicuous change while coal-mining was being re-equipped and copper-mining stunted. Both witnessed to Jevons' saying of 1865 that "coal commands this age." One, the gas industry, had revealed —most imperfectly—what was in coal; the other, the heavy chemical industry, had used coal to extract from salt its component parts and combine them with other elements, principally the carbon of the coal itself. Neither had been important before 1830. Neither was conspicuous as an employing industry in 1851, nor very conspicuous even in 1881; though the coal used in gasworks had grown from perhaps 600,000 tons in 1850 to 8,400,000 in 1885[2]. But their economic and social weights, like those of the rubber and some other industries, had no relation to numbers. Both, when Jevons wrote, had points of contact, but too few, with the fine chemistry of drugs and essences and the growing chemical science of the laboratories. A fresh contact with chemical science had been set up in 1863 when, under the first Alkali Act (26 and 27 Vict. c. 124), the state appointed an inspecting chemist to make soda manufacturers condense the hydrochloric "acid mist" with which some of their works had polluted the country[3]. The state also controlled gas works, their prices and dividends, and the illuminating power of their product—but not their chemistry. The alkali inspector, becoming "rather weary of the monotony as well as of the narrowness"[4] of his sole task, that of testing chimney gases for hydrochloric acid, began to study the general problems of air defilement, national health, and by-product economy. He secured an extended Alkali Act after eleven years (1874; 37 and 38 Vict. c. 43); but it was another seven before his dream of inspection for all 'emitting' industries—chlorine, cement, manure works and so on—was attained[5]. Some of his leisure had been spent in advocating, with little effect, the use of by-product ovens in coke-making, so as to gain such fertilisers as

[1] Price, op. cit. p. 498.
[2] For 1850, the estimate in Porter, *Progress of the Nation*, p. 582; for 1885, Thorpe, Sir E., in *Dic. of Applied Chemistry* (ed. 1922), s.v. Coal Gas.
[3] First *Rep. of the Alkali Inspector*, 1864 (1865, xx), p. 15.
[4] *Report of* 1872 (1873, xix).          [5] *Report of* 1882 (1883, xviii).

sulphate of ammonia[1]. The chemical affinities of the coal industries were at least being made public.

For many years, while gas works had multiplied, gas-work chemistry remained primitive. Far too much sulphur went into the gas. The coke was sold cheap, rich with unextracted hydro-carbons[2]. Coal-tar was a superabundant by-product for which it was hard to find an effective demand. So, for a time, was the hydrochloric acid which the soda makers no longer sent into the air. They found an outlet for some of their acid early by turning it into the bleaching powder (chloride of lime) for which the expanding cotton and paper industries had a sustained demand. Coal-tar meanwhile went unanalysed into the obvious baser uses; and much sulphur and lime waste went to generate sulphuretted hydrogen in the made ground on which part of Widnes was being built[3]. Then, between 1856 and 1870, came the discoveries of William Perkin and others, which were to transform dyeing; reveal the almost infinite chemical contents of coal; and stimulate the coke makers to save and handle their by-products, which contained many things besides chemical ferti-lisers. Perkin's 'Tyrian purple', vulgarly mauve, of 1856; the fuchsine of 1859, called also 'magenta' as a selling device; and the first alizarin—'turkey red'—which German chemists iso-lated in 1868, and Perkin more satisfactorily in 1869; these were the initial discoveries on which an industry was gradually based during the 'seventies and early 'eighties, but based more firmly in Germany than in Britain.

The manufacture of heavy chemicals was an industry of large localised units, easy mass output, and rather conservative routine. Owing to the magnificent location of the principal works, near salt, coal and tide-water—when inspection began, of 84 soda-makers, 38 were in South Lancashire and North Cheshire and 19 on Tyneside[4]—they had early secured control of the world's markets. Owing to concentration—nearly half the rock salt 'roasted' at that time was handled by 10 out of the 84[5] —and the huge Lancashire demand, they were able to work cheaply and, if necessary, dump surpluses abroad. From the start they had used the Leblanc process, or chain of processes, to make the sodium carbonate (washing soda), bicarbonate

[1] *Report of* 1878 (1878–9, xvi).
[2] Bone, W. A., *Coal and its Scientific Uses* (1918), p. 272.
[3] *Alkali Report of* 1874 (1875, xvi).
[4] *Alkali Report of* 1864.          [5] *Ibid.*

(cooking soda) and hydroxide (caustic soda), from the chloride which is common salt. Down to the 'sixties, when the world-power of the British makers was at its height, this was the only commercial 'process known. But in 1863 the Belgian chemical manufacturer Solvay borrowed from English laboratory chemists the so-called ammonia process, which turned out purer soda more cheaply. The strength of the main English firms, and their hold of the markets, prevented this competition from telling on them seriously, or forcing them to consider a change of process, for a decade or more. In 1875–6 more salt was 'roasted' for alkali-making in Widnes, a town most of which was only twelve years old, than in all Prussia[1]. But the trade disturbances and the competition of the later 'seventies so shook the British alkali trade that, in 1881–2, many firms were contemplating its abandonment. The next years saw the struggle of the processes begin in Britain itself. The Leblanc still held its own, especially in Lancashire, in 1886, in which year it consumed over four times as much salt as its rival[2].

The gas industry at that moment was approaching its first difficult corner. Consumption and expansion had gone on quite steadily, with continuous improvement in technique but no fundamental change, since William Murdoch lit up Boulton and Watt's Soho works in the year 1800. Throughout, high illuminating power in gas to be consumed on an open burner had been the sole desideratum. Now came the first flickerings of competition from electricity; Welsbach's invention of the incandescent burner in 1885; a rapidly extending use of gas for cooking and heating, and demands for a cheaper gas for use in internal combustion engines. The companies or municipal works with their comfortable monopoly areas, and no Belgians or Germans to fear, began to feel a little wind of change blowing among their retorts and coke heaps.

To the close of the third quarter of the century, electricity, although it had exerted power in the world by way of the telegraph since the middle of the second quarter, was not 'power.' As light it was still only the intense and rather unlovely glare which Faraday and Holmes had thrown out from the South Foreland on the evening of December 8, 1858. Even in 1881, all that the President of the Institute of Mechanical Engineers found to say about a main aspect of the electricity problem was:

---

[1] *Report for* 1875–6 (1878–9, XVI), p. 14.
[2] *Reports for* 1882 (1883, XVIII) and 1886 (1887, XVII).

"it is possible, and even probable, that one of the great uses to which Electric Force will be applied eventually, will be the simple conveyance of power by means of large wires."[1] Siemens and Halske had already mounted an experimental electric tramway in Berlin (1879). The full-grown 'dynamo machine,' as it was still called, whose principle had been given to the world almost simultaneously by William Siemens, Wheatstone and Varley, in 1867, had for some time been available, and had just (1880) received an important improvement from Siemens[2]. The President of the Engineers, before he began to speak of the transmission of power, had congratulated his colleagues on the recent arrival of "the elegant and steady domestic light of Mr Swan." A little later (1882) Siemens was telling the Society of Arts that electricity "must win the day as the light of luxury."[3] Graham Bell had demonstrated his telephone to Queen Victoria at Osborne, and the first telephone exchange had been opened in America, in January, 1878. Next year there were exchanges in London and about eight other British towns. In several of the towns 'electric light and telephone' companies were being formed in the early 'eighties. The combination is interesting[4]. William Siemens in his last years—he died in November, 1883—was immersed in the experimental application of electricity to metallurgy[5]. Its use in the chemical industries, but for which the world would have had no commercial aluminium, was to come soon. In America, Edison, very far from death, was pushing into field after field of electrical application and invention. In Germany, Emil Rathenau, a retired iron-founder bitten by electricity, had floated in April, 1883, the Deutsche Edisongesellschaft to exploit the carbon filament lamp[6].

Everything, in short, was ready for electrical industries and an electric age, but, apart from the telegraph industries, neither had arrived. Britain, her critics were telling her, was behind America and Germany. The Birmingham telephone exchange had only 312 subscribers in 1886. Telephone apparatus was

---

[1] *Trans. Inst. Mech. Eng.* 1881, p. 419 (E. A. Cowper).

[2] See *D.N.B.*, Siemens, and Jeans, W. T., *Creator of the Age of Steel*, p. 175–7, 182, 211.

[3] Quoted in Jeans, *op. cit.* p. 178.

[4] Baldwin, F. G. C., *The Hist. of the Telephone in the United Kingdom* (1925), p. 15, 23, 119. The first central electricity station was in Holborn in 1882.

[5] See *inter alia* Geipel, W., "On the Position and Prospects of Electricity as applied to Engineering," *Trans. Inst. Mech. Eng.* 1888, p. 103.

[6] Kessler, W. R., *Walther Rathenau* [Eng. trans. 1929], p. 12.

THE COURSE OF INDUSTRIAL CHANGE, 1850–86   109

nearly all turned out by hand, and usually designed and made by each separate company. Although the uses of electricity in collieries seemed obvious; although a Scottish colliery is believed to have been the first in the world to be lighted by electricity and fitted with a telephone, in 1881[1]; and although a pit in the Forest of Dean was even pumped by electricity in 1882[2]; five years later such enterprise remained unusual. At that time two out of the four United Kingdom experiments in electric traction were Irish: on the continent and in the United States there were many more. In contrast with the few and small British electric light works, nearly all in large towns, there was "hardly a city or town of 20,000 inhabitants in the United States which had not a central station for arc or incandescent lamps"; and "on the continent large central stations" were "already in operation in competition with gas."[3]

All the most interesting early experiments in the transmission of power over relatively long distances had been made abroad. Siemens had directed the attention of the Institute of Civil Engineers in 1883 to the way in which M. Marcel Deprez had managed to transmit as much as 3 h.p. to a distance of 25 miles through ordinary telegraph wires[4]. Electric power had been used by foreigners, though without long transmission and through small motors, in a number of industrial processes—for printing, tailoring, and the like at Boston; for the light metal industries at Geneva; and so on[5]. Such things were not unknown in Britain: electromagnetic riveters were installed at Dumbarton shipyards in 1886–7; but it was agreed that Britain was not the pioneer[6]. Electricity and dynamos and motors were expensive. British towns had not the "arrowy Rhone" flowing through them like Geneva. British factories had their steam engines, belts and shafting in good running order. Trade conditions in the early 'eighties were seldom such as to encourage capital expenditure on novelties. Coal was cheap. It had served my father very well. Why should I think of change just yet? The argument for delay was probably sound in more than nine cases out of ten—if a short view was taken.

[1] Baldwin, *op. cit.* p. 9: the Earnock Colliery, Hamilton.
[2] Trafalgar Pit, the first in England. *V.C.H. Gloucester*, II. 235.
[3] Geipel, *op. cit.* p. 103.      [4] Jeans, *op. cit.* p. 212.
[5] Geipel, *op. cit.* p. 78.
[6] Very important work on electric transmission, in connection with light companies, was however being done in London by Ferranti in 1886. See his obituary notice in *The Times*, Jan. 1, 1930.

It was enforced by the ease with which the lighter British industries could install, and in fact already had installed, the new low power internal combustion engines. You could get gas anywhere in a British industrial area, and these were gas engines. Scientific experiments with internal combustion were nothing new; but the first gas engine to go into industry was Lenoir's of 1860, a very wasteful type judged by later standards[1]. It was followed quickly by Hugon's of 1865 and by Otto's first, so-called 'atmospheric,' engine of 1866. Ten years later this rather "noisy and spasmodic" affair was superseded by the 'silent' Otto, an efficient machine with a four-stroke cycle. None of these names is British; nor were the engines which preceded the silent Otto of 1876 much used in this country. But when an English firm took over the manufacture of the improved Otto, it came into use rather fast, fastest where it was most needed, in the light metal industries. By 1882 its introduction had already had "a marked effect in increasing the number of factories" in the Birmingham area[2]. About that time Clerk's two-stroke cycle engine came as a not very formidable competitor with the now established Otto. Experiments were being made with other fuels than coal gas. Compared with coal it was expensive, but the engine was generally small like the steam engines of sixty years earlier[3]. The convenience and economy in supervision of the little apparatus which could be hitched on to the ubiquitous gas-pipes fully justified its use for all sorts of odd and end industrial purposes in every kind of 'factory.'

A whole generation had run since Thackeray sang in his May Day Ode of the toiling engines, "England's arms of conquest." There was discomfort in the body economic, a tang of doubt in the air. Enemies of "the snorting steam and piston stroke" there had always been. The author of that contemptuous phrase[4] was just turning from a Democratic Federation to a Socialist League, which should rid the world of piston-dom and piston-lords, if not of pistons. But that is not for discussion in this place. Nor are those forces, political, geographic, commercial, monetary, demographic, which had changed the position of Britain among the nations. The question which is

[1] Ewing, Sir J. A., *The Steam Engine and other Heat Engines* (4th ed.), p. 585 *sqq.* Clerk, Sir D., *The Gas, Petrol and Oil Engines* (1909).
[2] Survey of Birmingham industry, 1871–82, by a retiring factory inspector: *Inspector's Report* for 1883 (1884, XVIII. 181), p. 52. Also quoted in Allen, *op. cit.* p. 229.     [3] Vol. I. p. 443.
[4] From the prologue to William Morris' *Earthly Paradise*.

relevant here is that of the engines themselves and of all the economic power for which they stood in the minds of those who used or valued them. Was there the old justification for pride in England's arms of conquest? Was any other nation so well equipped; or perhaps better; at any points; or at all? Not at all: that was certain. But even in 1851 the United States had been better equipped for some purposes—such as stitching, reaping, revolver-making, wool-spinning; and ever since, the adoption, though very likely with improvement, of American machinery for one thing or another had been curiously frequent; so frequent that the historian is tempted to adopt from it some general formula of technical progress in late revolutionised industries, which shall simplify his narrative and his causal explanations. This is not permissible. But it would be even less permissible, in any general summary, to minimise the contribution of the nimble American 'engine' to the industrial life of that generation[1].

Continental nations had enjoyed industrial superiorities over Britain in 1851, but they were not 'engine' superiorities. Even in 1840, it had been reported to Lord Palmerston that the states of the German Commercial Union were "in some respects" ahead of Britain in their "means of manufacture." The "means" suggested were "the arts of design"; metal working; and, as might have been expected among a definitely better educated people, "chemical knowledge in its various branches."[2] In what senses, if any, Germany had really been superior to Britain in metallurgy at that time need not be determined. She was at least ready to take her full share in the metallurgical and mechanical progress of the next forty years, as she had opportunity. Krupp's name was known in Britain before 1851. It was very well known indeed, and not only in connection with guns, by 1886. Her superiority in "chemical knowledge" Germany retained into the era in which the alliance between exact science and 'the engines' became of greater moment every year. Some of it she exported to Britain in human form— Siemens was born in Hanover; some in actual engines, as Otto's; some in processes, as Poetsch's system of sinking mines in ground artificially frozen[3].

---

[1] Above, pp. 12–14, 77, 89, 94–5, 97, 99. Another instance is the Hoe printing-press, first made by Whitworth from American designs, and from 1869 at the firm's London factory. Burn, D. L., in *E.J.* (*Ec. Hist.*), Jan. 1931, p. 302.

[2] Bowring, J., *Report on the Prussian Commercial Union*, p. 55.

[3] Above, p. 90.

Belgium, earliest industrialised of all continental nations, was making returns to Britain for what she had borrowed when the Englishman Cockerill introduced the new metal-working methods and powers at Seraing in 1798–1813, and when British capital and engineers helped to build her railways and her gas industry, from the 'thirties onwards. Solvay paid Britain the compliment of borrowing to undersell; the ventilation of her mines owed more to Guibal of Mons than to any other single inventor; those methods of utilising the by-products of her coke ovens which she was so very slow to adopt had been worked out for her mainly by two Belgian mining engineers, Coppée and Carvès[1].

To France the direct mechanical or industrial debt, in this generation, was perhaps somewhat less—though admirers of the Heilmann comb might dispute this. Certainly it was less than it might have been had France not been so busy with revolution and *coup d'état*, with war for prestige and war for life, between 1848 and 1873. The approximate completion of her railway network came late, later than in Germany, and this held industrialism back[2]. She continued to excel most in the least mechanical crafts, and she was not as yet able to compete with England in any one of the industries specially characteristic of the age, except in certain branches of wool-preparing and spinning. In spite of all this, French names and French processes recur in even a summary account of inventions affecting British industry[3]. In a story of thought and its final significance for economic life there would be more.

Indisputably, Britain still led the world's industrial motion. Still the only true 'industry state,' she had her immense accumulations of mechanical productive power; her cotton industry; her coal industry; with a dozen others supreme in mechanism; and she had large exports of every sort of machine—though there was some dispute whether this last was an asset or a risky liability, and whether some of her mechanical accumulations might not with advantage be scrapped because obsolescent. The basic engineering inventions had been nearly all British, the great steel inventions all. Single-handed, Britain had created modern shipbuilding. As it happens, shipbuilding is greatly

[1] Bone, W. A., *op. cit.*, p. 307. Above, p. 51.
[2] Clapham, J. H., *The Economic Development of France and Germany*, 1815–1914, pp. 146–7, 150.
[3] Above, p. 14 n. 1, 59, 109.

depressed in 1885, but the secretary of the trade union of the
men who made the iron and steel ships says "so far as competition with England is concerned there is practically none."
Asked, "Have we got it all our own way?" he answers, "Quite
so."[1] But it will not be "quite so" very many years longer. The
mechanical and industrial movement has become once for all
international, and there is very little echelon in the advance.
British mechanical deputations to the United States; continen-
tals besieging Gilchrist Thomas before breakfast for licences to
work his invention; Rathenau founding his *Edisongesellschaft*;
or the careers of the brothers Siemens, planted in two countries
yet working together, are symbolic of the new age. Engines are
toiling indifferently for all. Mechanical or scientific industrial
monopolies are short lived. Some people, and they not poets,
are thinking that the world has too many engines, too many
in certain uses at least, and that in spite of John Stuart Mill
general over-production, or something which might with reasonable accuracy be so described, may after all exist if only in what
economists call 'the short period.'

[1] *R.C. on Depression of Trade*, Q. 14,760–1, Robert Knight.

CHAPTER IV

# THE DEVELOPMENT OF INDUSTRIAL ORGANISATION

THE era of metal and machinery had brought with it bigger industrial units all along the line. In the early 'twenties the largest and most famous of the old Thames shipyards, that of Wigram and Green, had employed perhaps 600 men "when...in full run."[1] In 1870 the average iron shipbuilding yard on the North-East coast employed rather more, and the average Scottish yard employed 800[2]. This is an industry in which the revolution had been carried through from start to finish during that half century, and in which the actual thing turned out, the ship, had grown hugely. Exactly how much the industrial unit in general grew, over any given period preceding the 'eighties, it is only possible to say for those textile industries about which returns of employment and machinery were made at fairly frequent, if irregular, intervals. It is known, for instance, that the average cotton factory in which spinning was done increased the number of its spindles by 30 per cent., and that the average worsted factory had a corresponding increase of 81 per cent., between 1850 and 1875[3]. What the representative, as opposed to the average, unit was at different dates there is no means of ascertaining with certainty. To the historian's great loss, the attempt made at the census of 1851 to collect and tabulate employment statistics for all industries was not repeated in succeeding censal years. A single return, of 1870–1, does however throw light on the average size of industrial establishments in all, or nearly all, the manufacturing industries, revealing those in which the factory had become normal and those in which the units were a mixture of factories and workshops. There are also some relevant special statistics, besides those for textiles. The return of 1871 was issued by the Home Office after two years' grappling with the Factory Acts

[1] Vol. I. p. 69.
[2] *Return of Factories and Workshops*, 1871 (LXII. 105). Figures collected in Nov.-Dec. 1870.
[3] *Fact. Ins. Rep.* 1875 (XVI. 251), p. 9. The figures may refer to whole factories (spinning mills) or to the spinning departments of what in Germany are called conveniently 'spin-weaveries.'

Extension Act and the Workshops Act of 1867 (30 and 31 Vict. c. 103 and c. 146). These were the Acts which brought nearly all the power-using metal industries, and also paper, glass, tobacco, printing and some others, under the Factory Inspectors, together with all places in which fifty or more persons were employed in manufacturing. They also put workshops under the inspection of the local authority, provided they contained women, children or young persons[1].

Though this return does not apply precisely to the conditions of the early 'eighties, it must do so very nearly. There is no reason to think that there was any important change in the scale of industrial operations in the interval. In 1870-1 the average British cotton factory employed 180 workpeople; in 1885, 191. Even in the hosiery industry, which the factory was just conquering and in which it was therefore likely to be specially expansive, the corresponding increase is only from 71 to 86[2]. The external conditions of most manufacturing industries, especially of the 'heavy' industries in which the units were the largest, were not encouraging between the crisis of 1873 and the early 'eighties[3]. This was not the sort of era in which businesses grow fast. Moreover, social averages of any sort seldom change much in ten years. It may be taken, therefore, that the 1871 returns give reasonably exact measurements of the statistical skeleton of British industrial organisation as it remained in the 'eighties; with the provisos, first, that the size of the localised industrial unit in the average industry may have grown by from 5 to 10 per cent. in the interval; and, second, that in some few industries, such as hosiery and bootmaking, the rapid progress of factory conditions may have increased that percentage to 20 or rather more.

The returns have a special interest of their own. They fall very near three culminating points in modern economic history —those of the age of steam; of the age of non-joint-stock industrial organisation; and of the age of undisputed British international supremacy in the old commerce and the new industry. Water power, so important in the earliest factory days and still of some significance in the 'forties, was now really of none; it furnished only 4·5 per cent. of all the h.p. (991,000)

---

[1] For the Acts see below, p. 416. The *Return* is that quoted above, 1871, LXII. 105.

[2] The 1885 figures from the *Return* in 1884-5, LXXXI. 1087.

[3] Below, p. 385.

which came under the view of the inspectors. Gas engine power had not begun to tell and electrical power was unknown. Joint-stock manufacturing companies existed in 1871, but they were rare and unimportant, except the public utility companies with which these returns do not deal. They grew rapidly in numbers during the next fourteen or fifteen years, but not in ways which markedly affected the scale of industrial operations[1]. That British economic superiority was near its nineteenth-century culminating point in or about the decade 1870–80 has been suggested in the narrative of industrial change and will be illustrated in other narratives. Here it is assumed.

The inspectors reported in 1871 on 2,417,000 employed persons of ten years old and upwards, and on 127,000 separate working places, 'works' they called them, in Great Britain. They claimed, and it would seem with reason, that for every place which came under the Factory Acts these returns might "be considered as nearly as possible accurate." Comparison with the census figures of the same year confirms this claim for the completely 'factorised' industries. For a few trades, the returns of workshops, which the inspectors procured from local authorities "in many cases disinclined to move,"[2] are remarkably full and seem certainly representative. But from some counties, and unfortunately from London, the workshop returns are lacking or quite inadequate. Even so, the sample of industrial organisation provided is of high value. It ignores all mining; all agriculture; a great part of the food and drink, clothing and building trades; and such scattered country trades as those of the miller, blacksmith and wheelwright. The inspectors had no oversight of outworkers, a fact which explains the inadequacy of their returns for the clothing trades, in which outwork is general.

The largest average unit recorded is in iron ship-building: 78 firms employed an average of 570·5 workpeople each: among these the 30 Scottish firms averaged 800. Primary iron-making 'works'—blast-furnaces, puddling-furnaces and rolling mills, separate or in combination—averaged 209 workpeople; but in Glamorgan and Monmouth 26 'works' of this class averaged 650. The general figure was brought down by Staffordshire, where the single blast-furnace firm and the small iron-mill were common. Contrasts within the metallurgical industries are illustrated in the table below. Industries printed in italics are

[1] Below, p. 138 sqq.  [2] Return, p. 105. For the local authorities, below, p. 416.

those returned by the inspectors as being carried on partly in factories, as defined by the Acts, partly in workshops. The term 'works' covers both.

### Metal-working industries of Great Britain, 1870-1

| | No. of 'works' | No. of workpeople | Average |
|---|---|---|---|
| All metal manufactures . . | 18,000 | 622,000 | 34·5 |
| Iron making . . . | 761 | 166,700 | 219 |
| Iron ship-building . . | 78 | 44,500 | 570·5 |
| Manufacture of machinery . | 1,933 | 163,600 | 85 |
| Nails and rivets . . . | 1,604 | 13,200 | 8 |
| Cutlery, files, saws, tools . | 1,143 | 24,600 | 21·5 |
| Miscellaneous articles of metal | 7,900 | 75,400 | 9·5 |

The last three groups illustrate the Sheffield, Birmingham, and Black Country trades, with a rare factory to swell the average and a host of workshops, or factories by definition only—i.e. small power-using, probably power-hiring, businesses—to keep it down. The figures must exaggerate the size of the average unit somewhat, because inspectors who seldom missed a factory no doubt failed to learn about many workshops. A relatively low figure for engineering proper, the ruling industry of the age, suggests, at first sight, that the little country machine shops are cancelling out the great firms of the industrial areas. This is no doubt a partial explanation. But as the Lancashire average (80) is below the national average, the main cause is evidently the existence of many small specialised shops in the industrial areas themselves.

The textile figures had not changed much since 1851, and not very much since the early days of factory inspection[1], though in all the industries the unit was growing.

### Chief Textile Industries of Great Britain, 1870-1

| | No. of factories | No. of workpeople | Average |
|---|---|---|---|
| Cotton | 2,469 | 436,000 | 177 |
| Woollen | 1,768 | 124,000 | 70 |
| Worsted | 627 | 109,500 | 175 |
| Flax | 346 | 70,000 | 202 |
| Jute | 58 | 16,900 | 291 |
| [Silk | 692 | 47,000 | 68] |
| [Lace | 223 | 8,300 | 37] |
| [Hosiery | 126 | 9,000 | 71] |

[1] In 1838 the average (mean) number of persons employed per factory was: cotton, 137; woollen, 46; worsted, 76. For elaborate statistical analyses of the inspectors' figures of this period, including calculations of the median as well as the mean, see Fong, *Triumph of Factory System in England*, p. 18 and *passim*. The medians in 1838 were: cotton, 92; woollen, 19; worsted, 57.

Three of the industries are bracketed because they are not in the same category as the rest. The silk 'factories' include 334 weaving businesses in Warwickshire averaging only ten workpeople each. But for these little Coventry ribbon shops—nearly half the 'factories' of the trade, with but one-fifteenth of its workpeople—the picture would be quite different. Lace and hosiery were still largely outwork, or factory-cum-outwork, industries, and the figures in this table refer to factories only. There was an outwork element of hand-loom weavers in every textile industry, but hardly great enough now, even in woollen, flax or silk, to affect the general factory character of the occupations. The low factory figures for woollen—much lower than for silk, if the Coventry figures are omitted—are such as had marked the industry throughout the century. It was not merely that tiny carding and spinning mills survived in Wales and Scotland. Yorkshire's average business was very little above the British average, because Yorkshire still contained a few of the old company mills and a great many small concerns near the borderline of the woollen and shoddy industries[1].

One textile entry in the inspectors' returns rouses a curiosity which it does not fully satisfy. They tabulated 12,800 'works,' and 44,000 workers, under hand-loom weaving unspecified. Of these 43, with 4700 workers, were called factories because of their size; the rest, workshops. The hand-loom factories were mainly in East Anglia—10 in Suffolk alone—and ranged, as is known from other evidence, from delicate silk to various other very rough fabrics. As the definition of a person 'employed' in a workshop under the Act was 'occupied with or without wages,' the remaining 'works,' in which the average employment figure is barely 3, are probably for the most part homeworking families of weavers in all the industries, with a sprinkling of small employers' loom shops. Nearly 13,000 in 3800 'works' were in Yorkshire; 4300 in 2300 'works' in Lancashire; 3300 in 800 'works' in Ayr; 4700 in 1100 'works' in Lanark; and more than 1000 in each of Stirling, Renfrew, Forfar, Cheshire, Warwick and Suffolk. It is unfortunate that the workshop figures from Middlesex (Spitalfields silk) and some other counties are defective. The sustained importance of the

---

[1] For the company mills see vol. I. p. 194–6; for the shoddy mills, which the inspectors did not distinguish, above, p. 39. The Yorkshire average in 1870–1 was 74. It was only 80 in 1899: Clapham, J. H., *The Woollen and Worsted Industries*, p. 131.

hand-loom in Scotland, which contained 20,000 out of the reported total of 44,000 hand-loom workers, is notable. There it turned out mainly linens, with some woollens. In England there was not much linen, a good deal of woollen, and a great deal of silk.

Some selected miscellaneous industries give the following results. Italics as before denote an industry in which factories and workshops existed side by side.

### *Miscellaneous Industries of Great Britain, 1871*

| | No. of 'works' | No. of workpeople | Average |
|---|---|---|---|
| Boot and shoe . . . . . | 9,500 | 62,000 | 6·5 |
| (Factories in ditto . . . . | 145 | 18,200 | 125·5) |
| *Tailoring and clothing* . . . | 8,000 | 43,000 | 5·4 |
| (Factories in ditto . . . . | 58 | 77,000 | 132·8) |
| *Millinery, etc.* . . . . . | 11,300 | 52,400 | 4·6 |
| Pottery . . . . . . | 537 | 45,000 | 83·8 |
| Bricks . . . . . . | 1,770 | 22,500 | 12·7 |
| Letterpress printing . . . | 3,550 | 48,300 | 13·6 |
| *Tanning and currying* . . . | 670 | 12,200 | 18·2 |
| *Baking* . . . . . . | 6,316 | 20,800 | 3·3 |
| Rubber and gutta percha . . | 39 | 5,700 | 146·1 |
| *Manufactures connected with building* (*builder, carpenter, cabinet-maker, etc.*) . . . . . . | *19,800* | *152,800* | 7·7 |

For factory industries, such as pottery and rubber, these figures are no doubt almost complete. Judging by the census returns of the same year, they furnish a good sample for tanning and currying and for printing, and a fair sample for baking. They are sure to include all large urban tanyards and the larger bakehouses, so that the employment figures yield maximum averages[1]. Of the clothing trades outside the factories they do not tell much, partly because the samples are small, partly because there are such complications of outwork in all these trades. The figures of 'manufactures connected with building' tell still less; for they mix up builders with cabinet makers and apparently exclude all craftsmen who work for a builder outside his yard.

[1] Some returns of the Typographical Association in 1860 (*Trades Societies and Strikes: R. of the Assoc. for Social Science*, p. 91–2) give an average employment figure of only 7: they do not include London but do include Manchester, Liverpool and Leeds. About 1890 it was estimated that the average staff of a London bakery was 5 (*R.C. on Labour*, 1893–4, XXXIV. Group C, Q. 29,572). In 1891 the figure for baking and confectionery was 6. Booth, C., *Life and Labour of the People in London*, IX. 55.

Unfortunately no other figures or records help much to determine the sizes of the various types of representative firms in the building trades, either in 1871 or later. The trade-group grew fast, easily holding its old position as the group which contained more men than any other except agriculture. The builders and their associated craftsmen—bricklayer, mason, plasterer, carpenter, plumber and so on—increased in numbers from 634,000 in 1871 to 761,000 in 1881. To these must be added probably not less than 250,000 labourers. (Compare the 531,000 males in all textile industries whatsoever; the 735,000 in conveyance of every kind; or the round 520,000 working in and about the coal-mines, in 1881.) The scale of operations in building varied extraordinarily and no statistical picture of an average building business could be true. But the fact that, when the census began to differentiate between employers and employed, in 1891, there were in London itself only thirty-six members of all the building crafts to each person who described himself as an employing builder is at least a reminder of the recurrent emergence, and the continued if precarious vitality, of the small building 'undertaker.' This great group of trades still offered a career to talent. "Are not most of the master-builders men who have been workmen originally?" a competent witness was asked about this time. "Nearly all of them," he replied[1].

In the basic industry of coal-mining, the growth of the physical unit of operations, the colliery or pit, had been accompanied by an expansion of the average colliery firm or company. What might be called the feudal colliery enterprises—the Earl of Durham's or Lord Londonderry's; the Earl of Dudley's; Earl Granville's in North Staffordshire, or those of the Duke of Bridgewater's trustees in South Lancashire—had expanded by deepenings and fresh sinkings and were now among the greatest business concerns of the country[2]. In 1886 the Bridgewater trustees controlled 15 collieries; the Earl of Durham, 13; Earl

---

[1] *R.C. on Labour*, Group C, Q. 32,095. Cp. Booth, C., *Life and Labour*, v. 30 *sqq.* The census officials of 1891, it should be noted, regarded their new returns of employer and employed as "excessively untrustworthy" (*Census*, 1893-4, CVI. 36). They express surprise that under the heading 'Builder' there appeared more masters than men. If this was a reason for distrusting these particular results, it is a poor one; 'men' in the building trades do not call themselves builders as a rule.

[2] *Mineral and Mining Statistics for* 1886 (1887, LXXIX).

Granville, 8; Lord Londonderry, 5 very large ones. Comparable with these, or sometimes on a still larger scale, were such firms as James Joicey and Co. with 11 important collieries, and Bowes and Partners with 14, on Tyneside; Pease and Partners with 14 in South Durham; Andrew Knowles and Son with 11 on the edge of Manchester; the Wigan Coal and Iron Co. with no less than 29—many small; or the great new steam coal companies of South Wales, such as the Powell Duffryn with its 13 separate collieries. At the other end of the scale, curious but quite unrepresentative, were such enterprises as that of a certain John Lewis, "the owner of a small colliery at Thurgoland, and on the 5th of March [1885] he lost his life in it. He and two others were the only persons in the pit."[1]

Between these extremes came the normal coal mine of the 'eighties, of considerable size but owned by a firm which owned no other. In North and East Lancashire, a highly developed area which contained, besides the 26 Bridgewater and Knowles mines, 12 belonging to Colonel Hargreaves' executors, there was an average of only 2 "mines or collieries" to each of the 151 owners or companies, including the Hargreaves, Knowles and Bridgewater group. In North Staffordshire there were only 1·6 "mines or collieries" to each owner or company. In the West Midland coal areas, in Yorkshire and in Scotland the ratio was still lower; and even in Durham, North and South combined, it was only 2·2 separate collieries or mines per firm.

The representative mine varied with the character of the mining, being smallest where the seams were shallowest. Fairly representative of average conditions, in a well-developed district of moderately deep workings, would be those of West Lancashire, the country of the Wigan Coal and Iron Co. There, in 1885, the average number of persons employed "in and about" each of 151 separate mines was 213. Not many miles away, on the North Welsh fields of Flint and Denbigh, the figure was not much more than half this[2].

The growth of the average colliery enterprise, in a district which had been technically rather backward down to the 'seventies, is shown by some Scottish returns for the decade 1875 to 1885. They cover the Eastern inspecting district of Scotland, which stretched from Lanark through the Lothians to Fife, Clackmannan and Kinross. In 1875 the inspector had

[1] *Report of Inspectors of Mines for* 1885 (1886, XVI. 1), p. 165.
[2] *Ibid.* p. 255.

to deal with 218 firms, 144 of which each raised less than 40,000 tons a year, and 23 of which each raised more than 150,000 tons. Ten years later the number of firms had fallen to 171 and the number raising less than 40,000 tons a year to 80. Meanwhile the number raising more than 150,000 tons a year had risen to 31, the four largest of them raising more coal than all the 80 at the bottom put together. Besides illustrating the growing concentration of the industry, the figures bring out the wide diversity of its business units[1]. Some of the 80 small pits may have resembled John Lewis's "colliery" at Thurgoland.

The metalliferous mines, among which those of Cornwall had been outstanding examples of large-scale production fifty, and even thirty, years earlier, were no longer representative of the extractive industries. Dolcoath was still raising over 2000 tons of "black tin" in 1886[2]. Just over the Cornish border, the Devon Great Consols Mine, Tavistock, yielded 6000 tons of dressed copper ore. Foxdale lead mine in Man had an output of 4000 tons; and a few of the iron mines, such as Hodbarrow by Millom, were really big. But the total output of 53,000 tons of lead ore came from well over 200 separate mines; while to furnish 14,000 tons of "black tin," 78 mines, 4 open works, and a number of foreshore and river washeries were pottering away in Cornwall. All the metalliferous mines put together only employed 41,000 workers against 520,000 "in and about" the coal mines. No concentration of ownership or growth of the productive unit is perceptible.

In brewing, concentration can be traced very clearly over a period of years by the average brewer's growing consumption of malt, the accompanying slight decline in the number of brewers, and the marked decline in those brewing victuallers and beersellers who have been called the handicraft brewers[3]. The figures for England and Wales are as follows:

|  | 1853 | 1864 | 1886 |
|---|---|---|---|
| Brewers . . . . . | 2,470 | 2,295 | 2,242 |
| Bushels of malt used . . . | 21 millions | 28 millions | 39 millions |
| Brewing victuallers and beersellers | 31,000 | 34,000 | 12,000 |
| Bushels of malt used . . . | 11 millions | 11 millions | 5 millions |

The concluding twenty years are the critical age: the handicraft brewer declines everywhere except in remote areas such as

[1] R. of Inspectors for 1885, p. 102.
[2] Mineral Returns, as above: "black tin" is dressed tin ore.
[3] Vol. I. p. 170–1; and above, p. 37.

Carmarthenshire. Down to 1853, and even to 1864, he had dominated many parts of the country, though he had long been squeezed out of London and Norwich. The Birmingham district, for example, true to its character as the home of small industries, got nearly all its locally brewed beer from 1700 brewing victuallers and beersellers in 1864. They used fifteen times as much malt as the brewers. By 1886 this was all changed. There were still nearly a thousand of the small men; but six-sevenths of the malt now went into the vats of twenty-six Birmingham district brewers[1].

Fifty years earlier brewing had been in places what baking still was over wide areas, a household industry in which producer and consumer are one. Curious search might well find some domestic brewing, if only by Colleges of ancient Universities, in the Britain of the 'eighties; but if found it would be a survival without much meaning. Domestic baking as a habit of the people was far from meaningless in the North: it was perhaps declining, but not yet rapidly. In 1831 there had been, according to the census, only one adult baker to every 2200 of the population in Cumberland, against one to every 295 in Berkshire[2]. In 1881 there was a baker of some sort to every 600 in Cumberland; to every 83 in Berkshire; to every 263 in London, where the average bakehouse, it is to be presumed, was bigger than either in Berkshire or in the North[3].

Though an age of easy communications works inevitably against the endurance of 'household' industry, the system in which the household makes for its own use, it is not certain that a machine age always does. The sewing-machine probably gave the system fresh life between 1855 and 1885. But though the search for vigorous remnants, or revivals, of household industry about the latter year might not prove merely an insignificant bit of antiquarianism, like the search for beer-consumers' brewhouses, it is one upon which the historian need not enter—partly because the facts are very elusive, partly because, although they are elusive, it is certain that over the whole field of domestic consumption, and especially among the urban wage-earners, the use of factory-made and shop-handled goods was increasing.

[1] *Excise Returns A. and P.* 1854, I.XV. 325; 1865, L. 701; 1887, LXXV. 79.
[2] Vol. I. p. 158.
[3] *Census of* 1881 (1883, LXXX), occupation summaries by county.

It is possible, but much less certain, that the working up of the consumers' raw material or half-finished goods by the craftsman, either on the consumers' premises or on his own, had declined in the sixty years since 'customer-weavers' of homespun linen and wool had been still fairly common in many parts of Britain[1]. There is an element of 'customer-work' in the endless jobbing repairs which the craftsman or craftswoman may carry out in other people's houses. Almost beyond question, the amount of such work had grown, not only absolutely but relatively, with the growing complexity of the Victorian home. There were hardly any plumbers in Sir Walter's Scotland: there was a plumber to every 508 of the population in the London of 1881[2]. Many of these were employed by builders, but many were small masters working on the customer's premises. A new and considerable industry in which, even in the 'eighties, "most of the masters had been workmen themselves,"[3] had been created by the consumer's necessity, in the full day of industrial concentration and Victorian capitalism.

The plumber type of jobbing workman was not exactly the 'customer-worker' of definition[4], because he supplied some at least of the material— if a plumber, lead piping and washers. Much closer to the definition were the scores of thousands of dressmakers and sewing women, whose work on the customer's premises, and often on the customer's materials and with her implement, the sewing-machine had certainly facilitated. What their exact number was in 1881 there is no means of determining; but even forty years later there were still 73,000 dress and blouse makers and milliners "working on their own account," that is, working either at home or on the customer's premises, and with no employer over them[5]. It is considerations such as these which would permit an argument, though not a proof, that customer-work as a whole had actually gained ground since 1850.

At all stages of economic evolution customer-work shades away into true handicraft—the system in which the working

---

[1] Vol. I. p. 159–62.

[2] *Ibid.* p. 164: *Census of 1881*, as above.

[3] Anderton, T., Sec. of the Operative Plumbers, before *R.C. on Labour* (1892, XXXVI. part 3, p. 43).

[4] The definition is German (*Kundenarbeiter*) and the system is commonest in fairly simple economic societies in which the craftsman owns little besides his skill and his tools.

[5] From the 1921 census: see *Eighteenth Abstract of Labour Statistics*, p. 11.

master owns tools and raw material, and sells finished goods or expert service or both, like the country blacksmith or the saddler. Horses still ruled the fields and the roads in the 'eighties, and London bus-horses had to be shod. The blacksmiths—men and sturdy lads—had not changed their functions much since 1851, or for that matter since 1551, although the census group included an uncertain number of men, perhaps a third of the whole, who were not shoeing and jobbing blacksmiths but just smiths associated with a variety of trades[1]. The total was no less than 132,000 in 1881. Even in London "little masters" still retained the bulk of the trade[2]. Down to 1871 the blacksmiths had grown almost as fast as the population. Between 1871 and 1881 they hardly grew at all. The ebb was soon to come.

The ancient handicrafts of the coach-builder, wheelwright and saddler were still almost intact. Twelve men to one employer in coach-building, and seven to one in saddlery, were the London figures in 1891[3]. The national averages in the 'eighties would be very much less. But these were threatened handicrafts, and already they had been linked up with industries of another sort. Saddlers had long drawn on the localised saddlery industry of Walsall, and country wheelwrights were forgetting how to make a new wooden axle for an old dung-cart. They had already forgotten how to make a wooden harrow, at least in Surrey[4]. The iron had entered deep into their trade.

Wheelwright, saddler, blacksmith, plumber; small carpenter, dressmaker or baker—the list might be lengthened— are typical survivals, or re-creations, of the producer who deals direct with the consumer either as customer-worker, repairing workman, or selling handicraftsman. Behind them was now usually some factory or other large-scale industry to supply their half-finished goods—iron axles; saddlers' ironmongery; iron bar; lead piping; sawn plank; sewing thread; flour—but they had the satisfactions, such as they are, and the risks, of economic independence and access to the ultimate consumer. Their journeymen and their lads had some fair prospect of succeeding

[1] "We do not cultivate having shoeing-smiths," the Sec. of the Assoc. Blacksmiths of Glasgow said to the R.C. on Labour (1893, XXXII. Group A, Q. 23,534).

[2] Booth, Life and Labour, v. 328.

[3] Booth, op. cit. IX. 55. Booth and his collaborators trusted the master and men statistics of 1891 about which the census officials were sceptical (above, p. 120, n. 1). That is why they are used here.

[4] Sturt, The Wheelwright's Shop, p. 20. Sturt went into business in 1884.

to these inheritances. Together they formed an important, though not an exactly measurable, part of the industrial population.

But most of the small masters who had survived, or come into existence, had some middleman or middlemen between them and the consumer; inevitably when the consumer was overseas and usually when he was not. In Birmingham the remains of the divided and sub-divided trade of gun-making, now that military demand had gone to the factories, worked for gun shops and those export merchants who kept half-savage tribes supplied. (They were suffering much from the suppression of slave-raiding and the checking of tribal war in Africa[1].) The declining watch-makers of Clerkenwell and their fellows in Coventry and other places, specialists who made not a watch but a main-spring, a hair-spring or a fusee chain, were hardly more than outworkers for the 'watchmaker' whose name stood on the dial[2]. Small masters in all the Birmingham, Black Country and Sheffield trades—they were still many—normally had their factor or merchant; or they might do jobs for a factory the doors of which had already closed on some of their fellows[3]. Above all in the cheap tailoring, furniture-making, and other London East-End industries, which were reproduced on a smaller scale in other great towns, there was every grade of small master and independent worker, in all sorts of different relationships with factories or with middlemen. In the East-End furniture trade the "typical producer" was a "man of small means, working with from three to six under him, and with little capital and no machinery."[4] This sort of man was on the increase in the late 'seventies and the 'eighties. Sometimes he would get material from "some superior employing firm or some intermediary."[5] There were also non-employing home workers, who supplied their own material and so might by courtesy be classed as independent handicraftsmen; though they were dangerously near common piece-paid outworkers. Below these were home workers using an employer's material, outworkers pure and simple.

In that unstable economic world men were always moving

---

[1] Allen, *The Industrial Development of Birmingham and the Black Country*, p. 265.

[2] Cp. vol. I. p. 177 n. 3. Booth, *op. cit.* VI. 26.

[3] *Birmingham and the Midland Hardware District* (1866), p. 454 n. Allen, *op. cit.* p. 327.

[4] Booth, *op. cit.* IV 164.     [5] *Ibid.* IX. 204: for the increase 1875–90, IV. 163.

from class to class. They start as wage-earners. They try as independent workers. Perhaps when out of work they make the thing they know how to make, and sell it cheap to the dealer, so beating down the market. They may or may not succeed in getting enough business to become masters of men. If things go wrong, they try again as wage-earners. The simpler and cheaper the trade, the easier it is to experiment in independence. "The cabinet-maker...can start operations, albeit inadequately, and insecurely, with only £2 or £3 in hand, and with fish curers, makers of cheap magic lanterns and toys, of sweet-stuffs, gingerbeer and many other things, an even smaller capital is required."[1] It is to be remembered that in those clubs of queer trades which were East London, East Leeds, and North Manchester, new members from the Polish ghettos had brought with them a knowledge of simple economic conditions and a terrible passionless grasp of how such conditions can be handled for gain.

While Jewish immigrants were giving an unwholesome stimulus to all varieties of domestic industry in the slums, the last of the half-rural domestic clothiers of the North had gone. There were still a fair number of them in the 'fifties, especially in the smaller places. "Pudsey had never so many small manufacturers of woollens" as about 1860[2]; but even then, machinery had taken over at least half the business of cloth-making, machinery in the company-mills which the clothiers had clubbed together to build, or in the cloth-finishing mills run by, or for, the merchants to whom they sold. For a long time only jenny-spinning and weaving had been done at home. As the jenny finally gave way before the mule, prosperous domestic men got control of, or shared, little mills and had the weaving done 'out.' Prospering more, they built a weaving-shed and installed power-looms. Others went where the unprosperous go. For some years the domestic survivors, with those who had become small manufacturers, sold their pieces in the cloth-halls at Leeds in the old way. When in 1868 the North Eastern Railway wished to invade the site of the White Cloth Hall, it was forced to compensate the owners and frequenters by building another. But business in the new one was always

---

[1] Booth, *op. cit.* IX. 207.
[2] Lawson, J., *Progress in Pudsey* (1887), p. 86. The statement, introduced by a "perhaps," refers to "twenty to thirty years" before 1887. For 1858 see vol. I. p. 193.

slack. During the 'eighties it ceased. It was in the 'eighties also that an Act was passed authorising the trustees of the Coloured, or Mixed, Cloth Hall to sell their building to the Corporation. It was no longer wanted for trade and was an obstacle to traffic. The Corporation pulled it down: widened streets and a Post Office occupy its site. Thus the commercial shell of domestic clothing was broken. It had for some time been empty[1].

If domestic clothiers passed into the mills, as overlookers or ordinary wage-earners, the fact is not on record, though presumably a few did[2]. As the factory system gained ground in the Birmingham area, however, a parallel transition was quite common. "I was a little master locksmith for 22 years....We nearly all work in large shops now," a man working for Chubbs said in 1863[3]. The small masters, Joseph Chamberlain wrote in 1866, were becoming "overlookers or foremen in large establishments."[4] The Birmingham, Black Country, and Sheffield trades showed more traces in their organisation of the absorption of 'masters,' or of methods natural in a field where small enterprise had been the rule and many masters had been absorbed, than any other trades in the country, except the building trades. Such methods were not at all new. The coalmine 'butties,' pilloried by Disraeli in *Sybil*, were a class of sub-contracting small master-miners hardly known outside the Midlands[5]. Sub-contract was very general in the old-established Midland ironworks. "The puddlers employed their own underhands; the shinglers, the rollers, the mill-rollers, the saw-men, all employed their own assistants, varying in number from one to four. The sheet-mill was under a sub-contractor employing half a dozen subordinates; the hammerman had three; the iron-moulders, thirteen in number, were under a

---

[1] Heaton, H., *The Leeds White Cloth Hall* (*Thoresby Soc.* vol. XXII. 1913); *The Yorkshire Woollen and Worsted Industries* (1920), p. 391–2.

[2] Early in the century Benjamin Gott had five "manufacturers" in his great mill at Bean Ing, Leeds, with weavers under them. They made cloth to his order and paid him a commission to cover their overhead charges. *The Leeds Woollen Industry*, 1750–1820 (*Thoresby Soc.* ed. W. B. Crump, 1931), p. 34, 307. Whether anything like this happened later is not yet known. The clothiers vanished so slowly that there was no crisis: their places were simply not filled up.

[3] *Third Report on Children's Employment* (1864, XXII), p. 25.

[4] *Birmingham and the Hardware District*, p. 605. Cp. Allen, *op. cit.* p. 159 *sqq.*, where the system is fully illustrated.

[5] The system extended into Derbyshire. See *R.C. on Labour* (1892, XXXIV), Group A, Q. 7190 *sqq.*, 7463 *sqq.*

sub-contractor. The coal was brought in and the ashes removed by sub-contractors."[1]

In the Birmingham light metal trades, factory charges for "standings and light," though perhaps sometimes introduced as a way to make profit, suggest the master who came into a factory for convenience and had perhaps previously been in the habit of hiring power[2]. "Brass overhands" and "head brass-casters" were in much the same position as shinglers and rollers in the iron-mills, either sub-contractors out and out, or what have been called piece-wage foremen, who are their first cousins. The same conditions were found at Sheffield, where middlemen employing "cheap labour" often took on jobs "in the employer's factory."[3]

In iron ship-building, sub-contract, the master under the master, was no doubt a development from the old master-shipwrights' practice of taking on jobs in small groups, at a bargain price, and hiring what extra help they might need at a wage[4]. It was strongly approved of by pioneers of the new ship-building, like William Denny of Dumbarton, who described in 1876 the "bands of workmen in a ship-yard, engaged in the larger operations of plating or framing an entire ship and paid by one or more superior trades men."[5] As practised in Welsh slate-quarries, where the sub-contractors supplied tools and gunpowder but not expensive plant, it had stirred the enthusiasm of the economist Cairnes, and was to lead a much later apologist to compare the contracting quarryman to a "tenant-farmer under a kind of metayer system."[6] It was endemic—here the metaphor from disease is certainly warranted—in the cheap clothing trades. In railway building and other works of construction it had always been very widely used. But its spread was widest and its national importance greatest in the building trade.

The separate building crafts had never blended into one body of wage-earning artisans under an employing builder, though

[1] Schloss, D. F., *Methods of Industrial Remuneration* (1892), p. 118.

[2] Allen, G. C., "Methods of Industrial Organisation in the West Midlands," *E.J. (Ec. Hist.)*, 1929, p. 543.

[3] *R.C. on Labour* (1892, XXXVI. part 2), Group A, Q. 19,020. And see above, p. 117. In the decade 1920–30 the tenacious Sheffield "little mesters working in tenement factories" were actually gaining ground. *Factory Report for 1927* (Cmd. 3144, 1928), p. 45.     [4] Vol. I. p. 177.

[5] Denny, W., *The Worth of Wages*, p. 18, quoted in Schloss, *op. cit.*

[6] Cairnes, J. E., "Cooperation in the Slate Quarries of North Wales," *Macmillan's Magazine*, 1865; *R.C. on Labour* (1892, XXXVI. part 1), Group A, Q. 9040.

the tendency was in that direction. A large number of important building firms were "competent to do everything necessary in connection with their work from beginning to end,"[1] directing the various groups of wage-earning craftsmen through wage-earning foremen, generally recruited from among the joiners. This arrangement was commonest in London. But even in London sub-contracts, particularly with master-plumbers, master-painters, and master-plasterers—themselves employers —were common enough. In the North they were very much commoner. The ordinary Lancashire practice was for a building to be 'taken' by a master-joiner. He let out mason's, bricklayer's, plumber's, painter's work to other masters, who were in fact sub-contractors. The same arrangement is reported from the Yorkshire and South Welsh industrial areas. No doubt it was common elsewhere. But it was an unstable arrangement, for the more successful of these contracting master-carpenters were always turning into 'builders,' direct employers of all, or nearly all, the crafts[2].

In the late 'eighties and early 'nineties there was much discussion of sub-contract in its relation to the rather elusive industrial vice of 'sweating.' From the men's side, in the building trades, objection was very seldom, if ever, raised to genuine subcontract under a small capitalist master. They regarded the finding of material, i.e. a measure of capitalism, as the test of the genuine master, whose acceptance of sub-contracts was 'legitimate.' What they all disliked was "sub-letting to the men," to mere "piece-masters," in which the sub-contractor's gain came from speeding up the work or breaking down the standard wage[3]. Obviously a 'legitimate' sub-contractor might also do these things: the things might or might not be abuses from the standpoint of national economy: the fact of interest here is the instinctive loyalty of the men to that small master system which was traditional, and still strong, in the building crafts. In spite of the great contractors, for the whole

[1] See evidence of Dew, G., Sec. of London Building Trades Committee, before *R.C. on Labour* (1892, xxxvi. part 2), Group C, Q. 17,380 *sqq.*

[2] The question of sub-contract was specially investigated by the *R.C. on Labour*, Group C. See especially 1892, xxxvi. part 2, Q. 18,463; 1893–4, xxxiv. Q. 32,061 and the Précis of evidence on the building trades in 1892, xxxvi. part 3, p. 34–48. See also Booth, *op. cit.* v. 40 *sqq.*, 151 *sqq.*

[3] *R.C. on Labour*, evidence of Dew, G., as above; of Otley, A., of the Operative Plasterers, especially Q. 17,295—objection to piece-masters "who do not find their material, but simply take work for labour only"; and the Précis, as above.

of those crafts, the crude ratio of masters of all kinds to men in London was only 1:13, at the census of 1891. For England and Wales, including London, it was 1:12 and for Scotland 1:10[1].

Some industries in which the small master flourished were also full of piece-paid outworkers. They were trades of the East London type, light and lightly skilled, in which as has been seen the two classes ran together. But the two most expansive trade groups in the country, during the generation which ended in 1885-6, building and coal-mining, had no place for the outworker; and in others there had been a continuous encroachment of factory work on outwork. Hand-loom weaving, woolcombing, frame-work knitting, lace-making, wholesale clothing, and boot and shoe making are the obvious instances. Little need be added to what has been said of these industries in the narrative of industrial change. The true outworker was still common in the bespoke boot-making and tailoring trades. There was a great deal of outwork on the fringes of factory tailoring, dress-making, boot-making, hosiery, and lace-making. A 'little mester' in Sheffield, and the man who corresponded to him in Birmingham, like the watch-maker of Clerkenwell or the homeworking cabinet-maker in a street off the Curtain Road, was often no better than an outworker for some factory, or for some Birmingham factor turning manufacturer. These, however, were not growing cells in the body economic. More people were wearing factory boots, factory watches, factory clothes, every year. "There are now [1887] even in the good class bespoke trade [of London], but few masters who get their tops cut out and closed in the primitive manner by men working in their homes. More and more it is becoming the custom to make use of uppers made up in a factory."[2] Soon Goodyear's 'sewround' machine, already known, would imitate the hand-sewn welted boot and annex another process from the pure handworker, so again diminishing the possible field of outwork. In factory centres, boot-making and hosiery trade unions were beginning to insist on factory work, because of the difficulty of enrolling and supervising the outworker[3]. Outwork tailoring for the bespoke trade had a longer expectation of life than outwork boot-making; outwork sewing and milliners' work an

---

[1] *Census of* 1891 (1893-4, CVI), p. xvi; Booth, *op. cit.* v. 153. The figures exclude builders' labourers.

[2] Schloss, D. F., in Booth, *op. cit.* IV. 71.

[3] *R.C. on Labour*, Group C; Leeds bootmakers, Q. 11,984-5; Midland Hosiery Federation, Q. 12,774 *sqq.* in 1892, XXXVI. part 2.

expectation longer still. But none of these groups except the last was numerically strong. And for the last long life was not greatly to be desired.

In some of the rural outwork industries there was still considerable vitality. Buckinghamshire chair-making, with its centre at High Wycombe, was in the main a mixed industry of small factories and workshops. It had grown remarkably since the 'thirties. As an export industry it was at its height about 1870. There were some fifty chair-making employers at Wycombe in 1885; but for miles around, in the cottages, tiny capitalists who had lathes, just as stockingers had once had frames, were supplying the simple beechen 'turned stuff' for front-legs and cross-bars. Backs, hind-legs, and seats were now always made in the factory[1]. North-East of the chair-country, along the Chilterns, lay the straw-hat country. The shadow of imported plait—first Italian and then Chinese—had already fallen across it. Cottage plaiting had declined conspicuously before 1880, in outlying districts where once it had flourished, such as the South-West corner of Suffolk and Western Essex. Even about Luton, which had won the headship of the industry from Dunstable by its earlier possession of a railway, there was less teaching by old women in plaiting schools and less frequenting of the Luton Plait Halls, in the early 'eighties, than there had been in the early 'seventies; yet outwork plaiting was still an important affair. As it contracted, other outworking jobs connected with the hat trade took its place, so that the villages of the Bedford-Buckingham-Hertford angle continued to be full of work[2]. There was also an important domestic or outwork pillow-lace industry in Bedfordshire, which still gave employment to nearly 5000 people at the census of 1881, after which date decline set in[3].

No important change had occurred in the industrial organisation of glove-making in the West, which still relied on outworking villages grouped round cutting-out shops and warehouses in Worcester, Woodstock, Yeovil, and Sherborne. The Sherborne industry had always been small. That of Yeovil had

---

[1] *Fact. Ins. Rep.* 1885 (1886, XIV. 797), p. 19 *sq.*; *V.C.H. Bucks*, II. 110–11. Cp. vol. I. p. 47, n. 2.

[2] County occupation figures in the *Census of* 1881 (1883, LXXX); *V.C.H. Suffolk*, II. 260; *V.C.H. Bedford*, II. 119 *sqq.*; statement of the Luton Chamber of Commerce in *R.C. on Depression of Trade* (1886), I. 96; for the earlier period vol. I. p. 47.

[3] *V.C.H. Bedford*, II. 123.

employed many thousands of women outworkers in the late 'fifties. There had been vicissitudes since, but no transformation. The Worcester trade, which had been in rather low water in the early 'fifties, had made a good recovery and sent out its parcels of gloves to be stitched in the cottages over a wide area. What proportion of the 13,000 women who returned themselves as connected with glove-making in 1881 were outworkers it is impossible to say; but probably the proportion was high. To them must be added some unknown figure for women who did a little 'gloving' but did not call themselves glovers, and for girls who helped their mothers yet might be returned as simply children without special occupation. Glovers' outworkers were not the most capable fillers up of a census schedule[1].

Southward over the downs from Yeovil, the rope, twine and net trade of Bridport—based originally on the fine Dorset hemp which was no longer grown—had been invaded by the machine and the competition of other districts, but not conquered. Sail-cloth had gone and rope was going; but netting flourished as an outwork cottage industry, because no machine could yet make square mesh or nets of irregular shape. Villages were specialised, not to the service of some master, but in the making of some particular size of mesh. It was all women's work. The men of the net-making families were mostly agricultural labourers, with a sprinkling of fishermen and miscellaneous coast workers[2].

These rural outworking industries are interesting but their aggregate demand for labour was small[3]. It is possible, but not very likely, that there were so many as 20,000 outworkers in straw-plait and hat-making, the greatest of them; certain that there were not 2000 in net-making, the least. One second-rate Lancashire cotton town could out-employ them all.

For over a century, the family business firm or small common-law partnership, with unlimited liability for all partners and un-limited freedom for dominating personalities, had cleared the way for industrial change. Some forms of enterprise required companies, but manufacturing had generally done without them. There were whole tracts of industry of which this was still true

[1] V.C.H. Oxford, II. 225; V.C.H. Worcester, II. 304; V.C.H. Somerset, II. 427–8; V.C.H. Dorset, II. 329; Census of 1881, as above.

[2] V.C.H. Dorset, II. 351 sqq.

[3] There were many others as interesting but smaller; cp. FitzRandolph and Hay, Rural Industries in England and Wales (1927).

in the 'eighties. "We have none in our district. I cannot remember one," a Bradford witness said of limited liability companies in 1885[1]. He was thinking, not of railways, gasworks or
banks, but of ordinary manufactures. Until very recently there
had been a curious, and no doubt largely irrational, reluctance
in the manufacturing world to adopt modifications in the
traditional type of business organisation, a reluctance which the
tardiness of the state to permit any general system of limited
liability had encouraged[2]. There had been experiments in
manufacturing on a joint stock ever since one of the very earliest
English joint-stock companies, the Elizabethan Mineral and
Battery Works, first made wire at Tintern and 'battery' ware,
that is to say hammered hollow ware of copper or brass, in
London[3]. Jacobean patentees and many later patentees, especially since the repeal of the Bubble Act in 1825, had sought
charters of incorporation to exploit their inventions with a joint
stock. Companies of various kinds had always been common
in the extractive industries, though most of them in the eyes of
the law were only extended partnerships. Informal and legally
irregular companies had been formed by the domestic clothiers
of Yorkshire, to help them in their struggle against the dominating personalities furnished with capital[4]. But when nineteenth-
century legal reformers first began to facilitate and regulate the
creation of companies, and to make guarded general provision
for limited liability, the response from British industry was uncommonly slow, though there were many industrial bubble
promotions, as might have been foreseen.

Take for example the working of the Act of 1837 (1 Vict.
c. 73), usually called the Letters Patent Act because it empowered the crown to give to companies by Letters Patent
certain of the privileges which hitherto had only been attainable
by Charter of Incorporation or Act of Parliament. Under it, in
the next sixteen years, applications were made by such varied
organisations as the Royal Mail and the Peninsular and Oriental
Steamship Companies; St Augustine's Missionary College, Canterbury; the Chemical Society and the College of Preceptors;

[1] *R.C. on Depression of Trade*, Q. 6791 (Sir Jacob Behrens).
[2] For this tardiness see Shannon, H. A., "The Coming of General Limited
Liability," *E.J.* (*Ec. Hist.*), 1931.
[3] Scott, W. R., *Early History of Joint Stock Companies*, II. 413 *sqq.*; Hamilton,
H., *The English Brass and Copper Industries to* 1800, ch. 1-3.
[4] For coal-pit ownership in eighths, and down to sixty-fourths, see vol. I.
p. 434; for the company mills, vol. I. p. 194-6.

the Canterbury Association which colonised New Zealand, Lord Ashley's Model Dwellings Society, several of the early Submarine Telegraph Companies, the East India Iron Company, and the Chartered Bank of India. The solitary home manufacturing Company whose application succeeded was the British Plate Glass of 1841, though applications were received from Shott's Iron Company, the Norwich Yarn Company—a scheme of 1838 to save the East Anglian worsted industry—and the Royal Conical Flour Mill, unsuccessfully promoted by the Earl of Essex and other gentlemen of rank in 1853[1]. In this latter year, which may serve to illustrate the position in the early 'fifties, out of 339 applications for provisional registration on behalf of projected companies of every kind except banking, 80 were railway projects; 54 gas projects; 35 were for insurance; 33 for all other public works; 32 for mining; and only 30 were proposals for "conducting manufactures, working patents, etc." Of these last, much the greater part never ripened[2]. In that year Henry Scrivenor was revising his *History of the Iron Trade*. He allowed to stand in it a passage from the first edition of 1840 in which he had asked the question, "Are Joint Stock Companies incompatible with success in iron making?" The lamentable results of those which had been projected or tried had seemed to suggest an answer in the affirmative. They ought not to be incompatible, Scrivenor went on to argue, given enough concentration of effort and enough working capital. These, he noted, were just the things which had generally been lacking[3]. To the serious industrialist, even when discussing iron-making, closely linked as it was with the extractive industries in which association of capital had long played a part, the words joint stock company still connoted irresponsible management, defective finance—actual fraud. He thought perhaps of that Northampton mining company of the late 'thirties which sank a pit three hundred yards deep and brought out coal which it had first put in, or of that Northern Coal Mining Company whose shareholders lost the whole capital of £500,000, and as much more, because of unlimited liability[4].

[1] "Return of all Applications for Charters with Limited Liability under 1 Vict. c. 73," *A. and P.* 1854, LXV. 611.

[2] "Registrations for 1853," *ibid.* p. 597. Registration had been provided for under 7 and 8 Vict. c. 110 of 1844. Legislation at that date had mainly railways in view. The printed lists are however incomplete. See Shannon, H. A., "The First Five Thousand Limited Companies and their Duration," *E.J.* (*Ec. Hist.*), 1932.  [3] Scrivenor, *op. cit.* p. 282.  [4] Vol. I. p. 434.

The government tradition of the early nineteenth century had been that, in order to establish a claim to a charter with limited liability, an enterprise must have one or more of certain 'notes' not found in the average manufacturing concern of the day—special risks, like that of a mining venture overseas; great size, like a canal or railway; need for a widely extended responsibility, as in insurance; or inability to exist at all without a large membership, like the College of Preceptors or the Chemical Society[1].

With a view to combining the maximum freedom of investment with reasonable security for careful management, in businesses which lacked these 'notes,' Benthamite legal reformers had tried to acclimatise the continental partnership *en commandite*, with unlimited liability for managing partners and limited liability for dormant partners. John Austin was praising it in 1825 and John Mill always praised it. But average British opinion was against them. In the year of Victoria's accession another legal reformer, Bellenden Ker, in a report to the Board of Trade which became classical, had summed up on the side of average opinion. His summing up was given wider publicity, at least in parliamentary and legal circles, when it was reprinted by a Select Committee on Joint Stock Companies in 1844[2].

Meanwhile companies were promoted recklessly or fraudulently whatever the law might say; for since the repeal of the Bubble Act mere promotion was not illegal[3]. Fortunes could be made and families ruined without any official having been asked to decide whether a project deserved Letters Patent or Parliament asked to adjudicate on a private Bill. So some cried for regulation. Others, whose voices were dominant after 1850, spoke of the desirability of relaxing "any restraints...on the free action of individuals or application of capital."[4] "All parties have advocated unrestricted competition. Why limit it in

---

[1] See Levi, L., *History of British Commerce* (1872), p. 289.

[2] *S.C. on Joint Stock Companies*, 1844 (VII. 1), App. I. For Austin's advocacy, *ibid.* p. 261. For Mill's, *Principles*, Bk v. ch. 9, § 7. Ker's report of 1837 was the basis for 1 Vict. c. 73. Cp. Holdsworth, W. S., *History of English Law*, VII. 195–7 on *commenda* and *commandite*. The system only came definitely into English law in 1907 by 7 Ed. VII, c. 24. The 1844 report led to the requirement for provisional and final registration of all joint-stock companies under 7 and 8 Vict. c. 110. The Act had in view unlimited companies.

[3] Decisions quoted in Holdsworth, *op. cit.* VIII. 221. Cp. a solicitor's evidence before the *S.C. on Companies Acts*, 1877 (VIII. 419), Q. 794 *sqq.*

[4] *S.C. on Law of Partnership*, 1851 (XVIII. 1), p. ix.

partnership?"[1] Why should not any company "as a matter of right, that is without a charter, engage in business without risking the fortune of each of its members?"[2] In the long debates, and the longer series of Acts, by which company creation was steadily made easier during the 'fifties, regulation and *commandite* were alike forgotten. Individualists wrote about "the unwarranted supposition that Parliament must make regulations for trade"[3]—any regulations at all, even that registration of companies which had been provided for in 1844. The upshot was the decisive Companies Act of 1862 (25 and 26 Vict. c. 89) under which any seven or more associates, provided their object was lawful, might constitute themselves a company, either with limited or unlimited liability, by simply subscribing a memorandum of association. Registration went on, but the Registrar had smaller powers than under the Act of 1844, and his register was soon cumbered with dead, still-born, or abortive companies[4]. In 1867 (30 and 31 Vict. c. 131) the legislators authorised a type of company in which directors might have unlimited, the rank and file of shareholders limited, liability. But such companies were never founded. The perfect liberty of the Act of 1862 was more attractive than this essay in *commandite*. As the wisest of Victorian fools sang:

> Some seven men form an Association
> (If possible, all Peers and Baronets)
> They start off with a public declaration
> To what extent they mean to pay their debts.
> That's called their Capital[5].

Perhaps it is not surprising that the average sober manufacturer remained suspicious or indifferent far into the 'seventies and 'eighties. If he was sober he could always get aid from a bank. The British banks "collected every particle of capital"[6] and meant to use it. By permitting overdrafts to men whom

---

[1] *Economist*, July 1, 1854.

[2] *S.C. on Companies Acts*, 1877, p. i.

[3] *Economist*, August 25, 1855. For the acts and debates of 1850–61 see Levi, *op. cit.* p. 337, and Shannon in *E.J.* (*Ec. Hist.*) 1931, as above; also articles "Commandite," "Joint Stock Company," "Partnership" in *Dic. Pol. Econ.*

[4] *S.C. on the Limited Liability Acts*, 1867 (x. 303), Q. 373. Under the 1844 Act the Registrar could not give final registration until he was satisfied with the deed of settlement for the government of the company. The 1862 procedure was more summary. In 1867 the Registrar (Hon. E. C. Curzon) wished to return to the 1844 practice. His successor was complaining in 1877 (*S.C. on Companies Acts*, Q. 5) that companies were often dead for years before he knew about it.

[5] Gilbert, W. S., *Limited Liability*.     [6] *Economist*, July 1, 1854.

they trusted, they were very like shareholders in many business concerns in the industrial areas. That was why the country did not need *commandite*, and why limited liability, as shrewd critics had foreseen[1], made no quick revolution and did most of its good work at first in fields for which companies had always been either essential, customary, or defensible. Its bad work was done where bad company work invariably had been done, among the blind and greedy.

Some great industrial firms operating in the appropriate fields made early use of the new Acts. Some new firms of the same class were created as limited companies. The Thames Ironworks was founded in 1857 under the older laws[2]. Before 1867, Ebbw Vale was a limited coal and iron company with a capital of £4,000,000; Palmer's Shipbuilding Company had a capital of £2,000,000 "held all over the country"; Bolckow Vaughan had £2,500,000 "held to a large extent in Manchester."[3] John Brown and Co. and Cammell and Co. of Sheffield, the Staffordshire Wheel and Axle Company, the Staveley Coal and Iron Company, and the Fairbairn Engineering Company of Leeds, are other illustrations of the spread of company organisation during the first five years after the Act of 1862 in those heavy trades among which Scrivenor had supposed, twenty years earlier, that companies ought to flourish, but did not[4]. He was thinking of businesses created as companies; and though, with the new facilities, there were successful creations in the years 1857–67, such as the Thames Ironworks, most of these big companies were private firms converted.

Gradually the many conveniences of the joint-stock with limited liability attracted the Victorian industrial leaders, especially when they wished to expand their businesses with lessened risk, and when they grew old. Men with large interests in some business, a prominent investing agent explained in 1877, "express a desire to limit that interest, and the only mode to do it is by forming a joint-stock company."[5] Perhaps they wanted to

---

[1] *E.g.* the *Economist*, as above.

[2] "Return of all J.S. Companies formed...since 18 and 19 Vict. c. 133," *A. and P.* 1864, LVIII. 289.

[3] *S.C. on the Limited Liability Acts*, 1867, Q. 857, 2342.

[4] For these companies and their dates see the "Return" of 1864, the *S.C. of 1867*, and the App. to the *S.C. of 1877*.

[5] Evidence of David Chadwick before the *S.C. on the Companies Acts*, 1877, Q. 2074 and *sqq.*; Chadwick gave similar evidence before the *S.C. on the Limited Liability Acts*, 1867, Q. 835 *sqq.* See the discussion of the work of the investing agents, below, p. 360.

divide the business among their family, or to "make it go on for ever." They would consult an investing agent, and with him they would find the seven men for the association. They themselves would be among the seven, with some friends of the agent's who would engage to put up capital. Sometimes all the capital would be found in the family and the company would be a private one. In this way Lowthian Bell's firm was 'limited' in 1873[1]. Next year Joseph Whitworth's great pioneering business followed[2]. The movement gathered way, especially in metallurgy and engineering. Even Birmingham witnesses, in 1885, while testifying to the persistent vitality of the small and the private firm, were able to give "a long...list of trades that have developed under the Limited Liabilities Act on a very large scale"; but they added that "almost without exception" these were private firms converted—Nettlefold, Tangye, Muntz, Perry—not new creations[3]. A process which was becoming familiar may be illustrated from a famous case outside industry. The Cunard Line became a limited company in 1878: shares were first offered to the public in 1880: three-fifths of the nominal capital remained in the hands of three families[4]. In the five years preceding October 1885, about 560 private firms were converted into companies, of which about 400 were still carrying on business at the latter date. A great many, probably a considerable majority, of these were not industrial. There had, for example, been numerous transformations among the textile warehouses in the neighbourhood of St Paul's Churchyard. But the proportion of 'industrials' must have been appreciable[5].

All experimental enterprises of the types which before 1862 might have tried for a charter, or risked their shareholders' fortunes without one, naturally registered under the Companies Acts. But, up to 1880, the transformation of old businesses, though steady, was certainly slow. Many, even in the industries specially affected by the movement, clung to their traditional organisation. Robert Stephenson and Co. remained a private firm down to 1886[6]. Samuel Cunliffe Lister only made Manningham Mills into a company in 1889, when he was about

[1] Macrosty, H. W., *The Trust Movement in British Industry* (1907), p. 26.
[2] *D.N.B.*
[3] *R.C. on Depression of Trade*, Q. 1520, 1525, 1591.
[4] Kennedy, J., *History of Steam Navigation*, p. 229.
[5] *R.C. on Depression of Trade*, Q. 668, 407. Cp. below, p. 311–12.
[6] Warren, *A Century of Locomotive Building*, p. 417.

to become a Lord[1]. In 1885–6 private firms did the "bulk" of the Birmingham business. There was nothing but private firms in the complex of Bradford trades. There were very few limited companies in Leeds, "and very few in the woollen trade generally." There were none in the jute industry of Dundee; none in the silk industry; few in the Nottingham trades; few in the cutlery trades, though a handful of strong ones in Sheffield steel and armament. There was a group of very large ones in ship-building; but a majority of that business, it was thought, was still in private hands. In the northern section of the cotton area, out of about 110 firms with 870,000 spindles and 40,000 looms in the town of Burnley, there were five public companies "whose shares are bought and sold in the open market," and one or two others "really private partnerships conducted under the form and law of limited liability." In Blackburn and Preston there were "hardly any." It was Oldham and the 'Oldham Limiteds' which provided most of the raw material for discussion of the relations between manufacturing and the free British limited liability law during the decade 1875–85[2].

Here, by 1880, was a really large group of spinning firms started on the joint-stock basis and containing one-seventh of all the spindles in the country. The thing was new. You could already take the temperature of the cotton industry with reasonable accuracy by averaging out the Oldham dividends or the discount on the Oldham shares. For example, the shares of 75 out of 94 mills in and about Oldham stood at a discount in 1885: in 1885–6 only 22 declared any dividend at all and only 6 more than 5 per cent.[3]

There had been many experiments with limited liability in the cotton trade since the 'fifties. The American Civil War and the cotton famine had checked the movement[4]. Only after 1872 did the company system get firmly rooted. "In 1874, owing to the few already in existence paying well, there was quite a mania for new companies, no less than 30 being registered in

[1] Above, p. 88.
[2] R.C. on Depression of Trade, Q. 1581 (Birmingham), Q. 6791 (Bradford), Q. 6331 (Leeds), Q. 5380 (Galashiels and the woollen trade generally), Q. 6207 (Dundee), Q. 7231 (silk), Q. 6601 (Nottingham), Q. 1205, 3438 (Sheffield), Q. 11,911 (shipbuilding), Q. 5595, 5752, 5798, 5810 (the cotton towns).
[3] Ibid. Third Report. App. A, VIII. 310–1. Cp. the discussions in Ellison's Cotton Trade of Great Britain (1886), ch. xi; Jones, B., Cooperative Production (1894), ch. xii.
[4] Watts, J., The Facts of the Cotton Famine (1866), p. 341, gives a list of 44 companies, or projected companies, "all or nearly all" projected since 1859.

two months, all of which, with the exception of two, were formed for building new large mills. The...two...were floated for the purpose of purchasing concerns already in existence.... The formation of these companies was done without the aid of professional floaters. In many cases the shares were subscribed for without even a prospectus being issued, all that was wanted being an application form."[1] "Within a radius of 4 miles from the Oldham Town Hall...are about 32 new cotton mills," the factory inspector reported in 1875[2]. The way in which the Lancashire textile machinists would design and equip a whole mill, an almost standardised unit of production, had been a great help, perhaps a temptation, to the promoters. Hostile critics suggested that promotion was promoted by the machinists, to whom no doubt the equipment of a score of large standardised mills was an attractive proposition. Critics also alleged that the shareholders were "recruited from all over England and even from the continent."[3] There was presumably some truth in this; but there is no doubt that much the greater part of the share capital and practically the whole of the loan capital was raised locally, which does not of necessity mean wisely. The directors, as a class, were certainly not persons from outside. "They are a persevering body of men," said the Oldham apologist of 1885–6, "and a glance at their avocation shows that nine-tenths of them have practically been brought up in the business of cotton-spinning, and not a few [an interesting touch] are to-day engaged as private spinners."[4]

The main interest of the 'Oldham Limiteds' in the history of industrial organisation lies in the extended use which they made of those borrowing powers on which the Companies Acts of the 'sixties had put no restriction, and in the class of people from whom they borrowed. Already in 1866 it was said that most of the early ones had "gone upon the borrowing principle."[5] In 1885–6 their capital of nearly £7,000,000 was divided almost exactly between shares and loans (£3,456,000 shares and £3,435,000 loans). Something like half of it was furnished by the "working classes in the immediate vicinity," mainly by

[1] Kidger, J., of Oldham, in *R.C. on Depression of Trade*, App. A, VIII. 308.
[2] *Report* (1876, XVI. 61).
[3] *R.C. on Depression of Trade*, Q. 5553 (a witness from Preston); and see Q. 5508.
[4] Kidger, J., as above. For the capital see evidence of co-operators before the *R.C. on Labour* (1893–4, XXXIX. part 1), Q. 1109 *sqq.*
[5] Watts, *op. cit.* p. 341.

way of loan[1]. This loan capital was subscribed in very small amounts at rates of interest which varied with the market conditions, not at a long period guaranteed rate like the later debentures. In 1874–5 the rate had been 5 per cent.: in 1877–9 it was as much as 6 per cent.: in 1885–6 it was down to 4 per cent.[2] It was a convenient form of deposit interest. Some trifling part of the share capital, possibly 5 per cent., came from the cotton operatives themselves[3]. Most of the loan holders in 1885, according to James Mawdsley, the Spinners' Secretary, were "small shop-keepers, publicans, and what I may call the odd hands about the mill—lodge-keepers, over-lookers, mechanics, and the people who work in the large machine shops of Oldham."[4] These people also held shares, but a much smaller proportion of the shares than of the loans. The circle of credit is curious. The textile machinist equips the mills, giving credit to the companies. The companies, when share capital runs short, raise money to pay him from the men who made the machines or from shop-keepers and publicans whose business depends on their successful working—an interesting if risky experiment in industrial democracy. (The money, it may be added, had been accumulated largely in the co-operative stores and was rendered available when they paid their 'divis.'[5]) But let the Oldham apologist of 1885–6 again be heard and his grammar and metaphors pardoned. "Private firms had not kept pace with the times, and the formation of Oldham Companies stepped into the breach and took the lead, and up to now have not been displaced.... Out of the whole of the companies formed in Oldham for the purpose of spinning cotton, only three have been in chancery, two of them were taken out by arrangement with the creditors, and the other one proceedings are now pending"[6]—a creditable record after six years of slack trade.

Hitherto the representative industrial joint-stock company had been in a double sense aristocratic. A relatively small number of dominant firms in dominant industrial groups had adopted limited liability. Aristocratic motives had usually influenced the adoption—motives of safety, of permanence, of

---

[1] *R.C. on Labour*, as above, Q. 1138 and figures in *R.C. on Depression*, App. A, VIII.

[2] Oldham evidence of 1885–6, *R.C. on Depression of Trade*, Q. 4334.

[3] *Ibid.* Q. 1141, 1180; where the cotton operatives' share is estimated at 7½ per cent.     [4] *R.C. on Depression of Trade*, Q. 5134.

[5] *R.C. on Labour*, Q. 1138.     [6] Kidger, J., as above.

family. In the Oldham area alone limited liability had prevailed in rank and file businesses and had attracted a democratic investing public. It will not be forgotten that in cotton-spinning rank and file businesses had long ceased to be small.

The Oldham investing public was democratic; but limited liability had as yet done very little to justify one hope of the 'fifties—that it would help to develop a type of large-scale industrial organisation in which worker and capitalist should be one, pure co-operative industry as then conceived[1]. It might even be maintained that the Oldham of 1885-6 had justified a cynical forecast of the individualists, made nearly a generation earlier. Arguing for limited liability and discussing the prospects of a very free law, the *Economist* had written in 1854: "Co-operative societies may be formed; attempts will be made to set up workmen against employers; some philanthropists will advance their £100 or their £1000, certain that more they cannot lose....But these will be momentary delusions, soon dispelled....At present numerous bodies of workmen believe that they will gain much by the change: only by putting their plans into execution can they be undeceived, and to give them the benefit of experience is the one reason why the law should be altered."[2] Workmen with this faith were specially numerous about Oldham. Rochdale of the Pioneers lies within what came to be the territory of the Oldham Limiteds, and the Oldham Industrial Co-operative Society was one of the earliest founded. When limited liability became easy to get, the workmen of Oldham had their experience. Some were disappointed, as the individualists had anticipated. Many were well satisfied with the various, if rather unexpected, results of the experiment.

So early as 1858, the Oldham Building and Manufacturing Society, promoted by co-operators, was registered as a joint-stock company under the old law, with calls on shares of 3d., and directors' fees of 6d. a week[3]. It tried weaving and did not do well. Re-organised as the Sun Mill Company for spinning and

---

[1] The hope, among others, of John Mill. Cp. *Principles*, Bk iv. ch. v, § 5. In 1860 "the working-class imagination was a little dazzled by the prospect of starting Joint Stock Companies under the Limited Liability Law." Redfern, P., *The Story of the Co-operative Wholesale Society* (1913), p. 17.

[2] *Economist*, July 1, 1854.

[3] It was not the first co-operative cotton mill. That was at Bacup, founded in 1850. From the start only a minority of the workers in the Bacup mill were shareholders; in 1851 thirteen or fourteen out of fifty-three. Ludlow, J. M., *Christian Socialist*, ii. 277 *sq.* in Jones, B., *Co-operative Production*, i. 253.

weaving in 1862–3, it did much better but ceased to be in the full sense co-operative. Shareholders might still be wage-earners, but in 1867 only four of them were wage-earners of the company. There were experiments in profit-sharing, but these never included the regular operatives, only the managers and over-lookers. By about 1870 the company had settled down into something very like the 'limiteds' for which it had paved the way[1]. A few of these grew out of similar workmen's experiments in industrial organisation; but the promoting and organising functions passed a good deal out of true working-class hands. Perhaps an organising 'proletarian' became a 'capitalist,' a transformation very familiar in Lancashire at all times. Even lending to the Limiteds became rare among those who worked in them, as has been seen, and shareholding by a company's employees still rarer. The thrifty cotton operatives, and there were many, put their savings into banks and building societies, cottage property and co-operative stores, rather than into the mill companies which paid their wages. Like the sensible small capitalists that they were, they spread their risks. Yet if the Oldham Limiteds had not been got by small capitalism out of co-operation, they might never have had their unique popular features, nor perhaps some of their common popular failings. They helped to forge that double-edged economic tool, the industrial share of small denomination[2].

Of experiments in pure co-operative industry, between the 'fifties and the 'eighties, all that need be said here is this—however deep the interest which they stirred in men of good will unwarped by dogmatic individualism, however moving their ambitions and failures and their tiny successes, however great their possible value for a future not even yet revealed; in a map of industrial Britain drawn on the very largest scale they would hardly be visible at any date; as contributors to the

---

[1] Marcroft, W., *The Sun Mill Company Limited; its Commercial and Social History* (1877). Jones, B., *op. cit.* 1. 282 *sqq.* Webb, Beatrice, *The Co-operative Movement* (1891), p. 129. Article "Cooperation (Partial, Oldham Limited Companies)" in *Dic. Pol. Econ.* (1894).

[2] The very small share appeared before 1858. In the *Companies Return of 1864* covering the period since 1855 the £10 share is perhaps the commonest. The £1 share is fairly common. An unsuccessful mining project of 1856 has 5s. shares. A few newspaper projects have 10s. shares. The Plumstead and Woolwich Co-op. Provisions of 1861 has 5s. shares. Of about 2000 companies registered before 1862 there were 11 which proposed shares under £1. The Oldham Building and Manufacturing Company of 1858 had £5 shares but, as has been seen, 3d. calls.

aggregate welfare of the Britain of 1885–6 they were negligible. Even six years later, a keen co-operator could enumerate only eight manufacturing societies in the whole country which were co-operative in what he reckoned the true sense, that is, societies of "working men employing themselves in their own industries"; and of these some were quite new[1].

As with the hand-workers so with the directors of industry. They often came together to fight, not infrequently to sell; but there was not yet among them much co-operation for the actual business of production. Chambers of Commerce and trade Associations had multiplied, especially since 1860; but the Chambers, true to their title, were always more concerned with dealing than with making. Mixed bodies, often ineffective, they seldom discussed industrial policies and never executed them. In a number of industries and districts, the growth of trade unionism had turned Adam Smith's "tacit, but constant and uniform, combination [of masters] not to raise the wages of labour"[2] into something more vocal and organic, the trade Association. Besides handling questions of wages and hours, these Associations might collect statistics, discuss forms of contract, or direct parliamentary business when the trade's interests clashed, perhaps with railway interests, or perhaps with national policy. There was also a little overt price-fixing by Associations; and informal price-fixing was on the increase inside and outside them. But the imperfect evidence as yet available suggests that, at any rate during the generally prosperous and dynamic third quarter of the nineteenth century, there was rather less co-operation among 'capitalist' producers than there had been in the more difficult first and second quarters. Having secured from the state that free and open competition which theory and interest recommended, they wished, in the slang of the 'sixties, to 'paddle their own canoes.' Organised combinations of employers, a Royal Commission reported in 1869, were "comparatively very few in number," and, so far as the

---

[1] *R.C. on Labour* (1892, XXXIX. part 1). Evidence before the Whole Commission. Greenwood, J. of the Hebden Bridge Fustian Society, Q. 959, and see App. XXVIII. For the successes of consumers' co-operation in distribution and its relations to industrial organisation see below, p. 308 *sqq.* It need hardly be said that Greenwood's definition of 'true' co-operation was disputed by other co-operators, *e.g.* by Benjamin Jones, *op. cit.* II. 775.

[2] *Wealth of Nations* (ed. Cannan), I. 68.

Commission had learnt, absolutely voluntary in character[1]. The Commission was not perfectly informed, but there was certainly no great love of association among the employers. Many of their spokesmen asserted with apparent sincerity, like the spokesman of the Clyde Shipbuilders and Engineers' Association, that their organisations were "entirely defensive" and "would cease if the workmen's unions were to cease."[2] Among themselves they were ready for a perpetual 'fighting trade.' Similarly the Midland Flint Glass Manufacturers had formed an Association "with reluctance" in 1858, to deal with a strike. Ten years later only half even of the local firms belonged to it[3].

Adam Smith's "tacit but constant...combinations" were naturally most widespread and efficient in old industries, nowhere more so than in agriculture. Some ceased to be tacit long before 1850. The London Master Printers, whose compositors had a union running back at least to 1801, had possessed a society from 1836 to 1849. It emerged as a regular Association in 1854-5 *vis-à-vis* the very strong and well-organised London Compositors' Society[4]. "All the large builders"[5] had been organised into the very respectable London Master Builders' Association since 1839. It may be supposed that Superior Dosset Forsyte was a member. It had benevolent funds and other disinterested activities. In 1867 it accepted through its Secretary the description of "a club of gentlemen belonging to your profession."[6] Probably like the National Association of Master Builders of 1877-8 it had the rule "no speculative builders...admitted."[7] Certainly its membership was small. It claimed that as an Association it never touched strikes, not wishing to interfere with the free action of its members; but

[1] R.C. on *Trade Unions and other Associations, Final Report* (1865-9, XXXI. 235), p. xvi. There is some contradiction in the Report which says further on (p. li) "that employers...in many departments of industry have entered into very powerful...associations"; and admits (p. xlix) that "a few great employers ...could in fact always make arrangements among themselves...without forming any definite association."

[2] *Ibid.* Q. 17,446.

[3] *Ibid.* Q. 18,305. Cp. the evidence of Sir Hugh Bell before the R.C. on *Labour* (1892, XXXIV.), Q. 1530.

[4] R.C. on *Trade Unions*, as above, Q. 19,481 *sqq.* (the Masters' Sec.). For the Compositors' early history Webb, S. and B., *History of Trade Unionism* (ed. 1902), p. 20 n., 24 n.

[5] R.C. on *Trade Unions*, Q. 340.

[6] *Ibid.* Q. 2754; the phrase was Tom Hughes'.

[7] See account in R.C. on *Labour* (1892, XXXVI. part 3), Digest of Evidence, p. 48.

working men said "they are organised to try to keep down wages"; and "they" admitted that in wage-crises the Association convened a trade meeting[1].

Long before 1880, probably long before 1850, and at various points all over the country, groups of master builders, speculative or not, had made arrangements with the men—more or less formal: more or less well observed—about wages and conditions of work. These were usually embodied in signed 'working rules.' Of the Associations and agreements there can often be no memorial, but they certainly existed. The General Builders' Association of 1865, not the first of its kind, was based on some eighty local associations, mainly in the North and West with a few in Scotland. It was interested in the terms of building contracts, the relations of builder and architect, and the settlement of trade disputes by working rules and arbitration. The Londoners, whose respectable Association would not at that time sign any treaty with the men, never joined it, and it had not a very long life. But its cells, the "tacit" or plain-speaking masters' combinations, had; or if they died, they rose again. In the labour discussions of the 'eighties a local masters' association is assumed[2].

There was no doubt a great deal of tacit price-fixing by masters in certain trades. The prices of bread and beer were almost as uniform locally in Victorian times as they had been in the years when the Assizes of Bread and Ale were still 'set'; but the processes of formal or informal setting by brewers and bakers are nowhere recorded. Now and again, in some industry or other, a price arrangement among producers is accidentally but clearly indicated in the full day of free and open competition. It is probably fair to assume that there were several hidden for each one disclosed. The salt industry furnishes one such accidental disclosure. There had been price-fixing associations in the first quarter of the century in this industry based on a local monopoly[3]. Many years later comes the evidence that its subsequent history, as might have been expected, witnessed

---

[1] *R.C. on Labour*, Q. 338 *sqq.* (George Potter for the men); Q. 2583, 2606 (the Association's admissions). And for the relations of the two sides, "The Strike and Lockout of 1859–60" in *Trades Societies and Strikes Report* (1860). Cp. Postgate, R. W., *The Builders' Story*, p. 171–2.

[2] For the Assoc. of 1865, *R.C. on Trade Unions*, Q. 2951 *sqq.*; for local agreements, *ibid.* Q. 190 (Applegarth, of the Amalgamated Carpenters and Joiners). And see Webb, *op. cit.* p. 209; Postgate, *op. cit.* p. 214.

[3] See vol. I. p. 200.

alternations of gentlemen's agreements and 'fighting trade.' "Implacable competition," said the *Salt Circular* for 1887, "has brought prices below all record,...the principle of association has been violated again and again, and with more disastrous results than ever yet known."[1] The polite phrase "the principle of association" needs no comment. The upshot of this last and worst spell of fighting trade was that Salt Union which is reckoned among the earliest of the late nineteenth-century industrial combinations. It was only a new device, made easier by limited liability, for handling an old problem.

Railway officials called upon to justify their rate agreements in the 'seventies and 'eighties used to argue that "really almost all traders make similar arrangements about prices." One of them in 1872 quoted ironmasters, coal-owners, "the china men," and the steam packet companies. Another, in 1882, said it was "perfectly notorious" that this was "the practice of nearly all the main trades of the country." To those quoted ten years earlier he added copper-smelters and screw-makers. A third mentioned tinplates, files, glass, nails and "others," and spoke of "a universal practice of endeavouring (how far it succeeds or not is another matter) to agree upon prices." He was defending the principle: as he was a man of wide business experience his reservation is significant[2].

The fixing of prices, or at least the determining of what was "to be deemed the current price," was recognised in a draft report of the Royal Commission of 1867–9 as one of the purposes of associations "among certain classes of employers, the iron and coal producers especially."[3] Price-fixing was no new thing in the iron trade. The witnesses of the 'sixties explained vaguely, but well within the truth, that the quarterly meetings of South Staffordshire ironmasters to fix the prices of marked bars "dated back forty or fifty years." The Association had no rules, however, until 1864[4]. Besides price-fixing, it did statistical and parliamentary work like other associations. The North

---

[1] Quoted from *The Times*, September 24, 1888, in Macrosty, *The Trust Movement in British Industry*, p. 181.

[2] *S.C. on Railway Amalgamations*, 1872 (XIII), Q. 148. W. Cawkwell of the L.N.W.R. *S.C. on Railway Rates and Fares*, 1882 (XIII), Q. 3892. Jas. Grierson of the G.W.R., Q. 3893, a question, in the form of a statement, by the experienced Sir Ed. Watkin. Cp. Cleveland-Stephens, *English Railways* (1915), p. 264.

[3] *R.C. on Trade Unions*, p. xcix.

[4] *Ibid*. Q. 9829. See vol. I. p. 204, based on Ashton, *Iron and Steel and the Industrial Revolution*, ch. 7, "Combinations of Capitalists."

Staffordshire masters had an Association modelled on it, but less effective as a price-fixer. They merely "endeavoured to get as near as possible to the South Staffordshire price," which itself, as one of them explained in 1867, was "really the price of a few firms in South Staffordshire, all the others, in reality, selling much under that price."[1] Like the South Staffordshire Association, the Cleveland Ironmasters' Association and the North of England Iron Manufacturers' Association took definite form in the early 'sixties. The former dealt with pig iron, the latter with manufactured iron. In 1867 they had a common secretary, who had previously served the South Staffordshire Association; and the same firm would often belong to both[2]. Although the secretary stated that they were formed for "regulating prices and the terms for selling iron," he was emphatic that there was "no such machinery for fixing prices in the North"[3] as in South Staffordshire. The action of the two Associations, so far as prices were concerned, was in fact very accurately described in the draft report of the Royal Commission as determining what are to be "deemed the current prices." Such current prices were announced at the close of the meetings, but producers were not bound by them. The Steam Coal Association of Tyneside did much the same sort of thing[4]. So far, but no further, had formal price-fixing co-operation progressed in the 'heavy' trades during the third quarter of the century.

Yet there was memory of more radical policies both in Staffordshire and on the Northern Coalfield. The 'limitation of the vend' of North Country coal, the most conspicuous output and price-controlling combination of the early nineteenth century, had only broken down in 1845. Its breakdown was due to internal difficulties over rationing. There was a rumour of renewal in 1850, but nothing came of it; for as G. R. Porter noted in that year, "the facilities for competition on the part of owners of inland coal-fields are far greater now than they were in 1845, while through the extension of railways these facilities are being continually augmented."[5] Similar forces were at work

---

[1] R.C. on Trade Unions, Q. 10,532. For the relative inefficiency of price control in S. Staffs see also R.C. on Labour (1892, XXXVI. part 2), Group A, Q. 15,486: "at one time it exercised a controlling influence on selling prices."

[2] R.C. on Trade Unions, Q. 9391 sqq., his evidence; Q. 9414, a memorandum which he put in.

[3] Ibid. Q. 9551.     [4] Ibid. Q. 17,777 sqq., evidence of Palmer, C. M.

[5] Progress of the Nation, p. 283-4. And see vol. I. p. 202.

in the iron trade. Regulation of the output of iron had been discussed a good deal and practised a little before 1830. In 1839 the Staffordshire masters—masters of the trade, as they supposed, in every sense—had agreed to reduce the make by 20 per cent. for six months, to maintain prices. But their restriction was accompanied by increases in other districts, particularly in Scotland, which drove the aggregate British make up instead of down[1]. Railway building at home soon rectified the price position. After 1850, for five-and-twenty years, with the markets of the world at their feet and prices generally good, Britain's primary producers had little need even to consider such extreme defensive policies. Limitation of output to keep up price was a charge brought against bricklayers and some other trade unionists. As a policy for manufacturers it became, in the 'sixties and 'seventies, a curious and, to the individualist philosopher, almost an indecent memory.

But the abrupt price fall of the late 'seventies led to the revival of this old policy—and again its fallibility was illustrated. When the 1880 recovery from the disastrously low pig iron prices of 1878–9 proved only temporary, negotiations began between the Cleveland and the Scottish masters. In the autumn of 1881 a 12½ per cent. reduction of output was agreed on for six months. It was continued for a second six months, and then broke down, because the strongest Scottish firm found that it could sell more iron than it was making. Cleveland continued its experiments. Early in 1884, with prices lower than ever, eighteen blast furnaces were shut down by agreement, the owners being compensated by the Association—a new device for spreading losses. Two years later, prices having fallen yet further, Scotland was ready to co-operate again and there was talk of a national reduction of output. But before agreement had been reached, a trade revival took off accumulated stocks and then sent prices slowly upward. A general 'limitation of the vend' of iron was not again discussed for many years[2].

Between 1871 and 1884 Britain's share of the world's known iron output fell from 53·2 to 38·5 per cent. The fall was most

---

[1] Vol. I. p. 205, based on Scrivenor, *History of the Iron Trade*, p. 290.

[2] Macrosty, *op. cit.* p. 57–60. No. 3 Cleveland pig iron averaged for the fourth quarter of 1879, 36s. 8d.; of 1880, 40s. 5d.; of 1881, 38s. 3d.; of 1882, 43s. 6d.; of 1883, 38s. 3d.; of 1884, 36s.; of 1885, 32s. 3d.; of 1886, 30s. 4d. Then the rise began to 44s. 11d. in 1889. *Stat. of Iron and Steel* (*Nat. Fed. of Iron and Steel Man.*), 1926, p. 15. Cp. Lowthian Bell's Memorandum for the *R.C. on Depression of Trade*, II. 323.

rapid after 1877, with the development of the open-hearth and basic processes and the extension of steel-making in America, Germany, France and Belgium. While rails had been of iron, that is till the late 'seventies, Britain had almost a monopoly of the export trade in them. Now Belgium and Germany had steel rails to sell[1]. The low prices of the early 'eighties led to an international 'fighting trade'; that in its turn to a thing unprecedented in British industrial history, indeed unprecedented in the industrial history of the modern world—an international market-sharing agreement. With the experience gained in their various Associations to help them, all the British makers of steel rails except one came together at the end of 1883. "It was decided to endeavour to associate the Belgians and the Germans with us as being the only two countries that exported rails."[2] All the Belgians came in and all the Germans but two. The upshot was an assignment of 66 per cent. of the export trade to Britain—a percentage slightly reduced later—27 per cent. to Germany and 7 per cent. to Belgium. The price was fixed from England " at very much what we considered the cost price would be at the least favoured works "—in economists' jargon, at the marginal price—and the different works were given quota according to their "assessed capabilities."[3] The thing did not work well either nationally or internationally and in April of 1886 it was dissolved; but the age of free and unrestricted competition had closed with this novel experiment in treaty-making by associated manufacturers, and this rationing of producers. It was less than forty years since the coal 'vend' had broken down.

Formal, if always voluntary, associations of producers had certainly made most progress before the 'eighties in the heavy basic industries. Besides those already mentioned, there was now a British Iron Trade Association which attempted to watch, without directing, the course of the whole industry. Parallel to it in the coal trade of the 'eighties was the Mining Association of Great Britain, with its six or eight local Associations on the principal coalfields. These also had no real directing power. Higher up the metallurgical scale were the Association of Tinplate Manufacturers and the Wire Trade Association, among others. Papermakers, English and Scottish;

---

[1] Belgian iron had appeared on the British market before this. Below, p. 248.
[2] Smith, J. T. of Barrow, *R.C. on Depression of Trade*, Q. 2271
[3] *Ibid*. Q. 2284.

Sugar-refiners; Alkali Manufacturers; Leather Manufacturers in Leeds and Bermondsey; and the powerful Master Cotton Spinners' Association of Oldham, which spoke for the owners of more than a quarter of the British cotton spindles, were among the other important organisations which were active enough to reply to a circular from the Royal Commission on the Depression of Trade and Industry in 1885–6 asking for their views on the economic health of the country[1].

Many of these Associations had little more to do with concrete industrial policies than the Chambers of Commerce, though all might serve as rallying-points for employers in times of trade dispute. In many places, especially in those dominated by a single trade, like Bradford, the Chamber did the statistical, parliamentary, and other work natural to a trade Association. No doubt meetings of either type of organisation gave opportunities for unofficial discussion of prices and labour, and perhaps even output. But the strongest Associations had no coercive power, and the weaker little value. The Secretary of the Alkali Manufacturers' Association informed the Commission of 1885 that he could tell them nothing because his members only met once a year; except, he added, "on occasions of urgency."[2] A request from a Royal Commission was evidently not such, and he did not explain what kind of urgency would have been held to justify a special meeting. Perhaps a strike or a new Alkali Act. The President of the Tinplate Manufacturers made a double confession of industrial impotence on behalf of his Association—"our wages are controlled not by supply and demand but by a trades union": "the great cause of depression in our trade is over-production, for which we are ourselves to blame."[3]

Several Associations spoke of over-production, actual or potential, national or international. It was not the business of the few of them which had tried to deal with the problem by policies of their own to explain those policies. The cure ordinarily suggested or implied was not associated action, except perhaps external action against the railways, or the rates, or the

[1] The total number of Associations replying was only 26, if the Mining Assoc. be taken as one. This includes such commercial organisations as the Linen Merchants' Assoc., the Flax Supply Assoc., the Nottingham Merchants' Assoc. and the Rye District Commercial Assoc., also two Builders' Assoc. and the General Shipowners' Society. *R.C. on Depression of Trade*, I. 114 *sqq.*, II. 409 *sqq.*

[2] Muspratt, E. K., to the Commission, September 17, 1885; *Report*, I. 115.

[3] *Report*, I. 119. And see below, p. 169.

income tax, or internal action against the trade unions, but individual reduction of costs, as put clearly, if with an interjected economic fallacy, by the Oldham Spinners—"there can be no doubt that our trade is suffering very greatly from over-production, but it is not that we are producing more than the world really requires, but that we are producing more than the world can really afford to pay for, and this points to the importance of lessening the cost of production to the last possible degree."[1] Here spoke the organ of a highly competitive individualist industrial group. So individualist and so competitive were many other such groups, that they had not recognised even the need for regular collection and dissemination of industrial facts, or for any standing organisation to handle labour questions. They had no Associations at all.

This indifference is to be explained in some measure by the still partial and local development of trade unionism. After the extension of the franchise in 1867 and the Trade Union Commission of 1867–9, legislation, at first haltingly and then decidedly in favour of the unions, had culminated in the replacement of the old unequal law of Master and Servant by the Employers and Workmen Act of 1875 (38 and 39 Vict. c. 90) and in Mundella's Trade Union Act Amendment Act of 1876 (39 and 40 Vict. c. 22). It was held in official quarters during the 'eighties that "every legal grievance of which the union complained" had been removed[2]. Most trade union leaders of the day would have agreed. They were now "liberated from the last vestiges of the criminal laws specially appertaining to labour," as George Howell said[3]. Some trade union critics maintained later that the unions had not only been given a free field, but had been privileged. However, more than ten years of free opportunity, and possibly some privilege were needed before the open land could be occupied. Besides, those had been years of shocking bad trade. The Unions' statistics of unemployment benefit, whose value as industrial barometers was just beginning to be recognised outside trade union circles, showed it. The Amalgamated Society of Engineers had an

[1] *Report*, II. 427.
[2] *Stat. Tables and Report on Trade Unions*, 1887 (LXXXIX. 715), p. 9. By Giffen and Burnett; the first of the annual Trade Union Reports of the Chief Labour Correspondent of the Board of Trade (Burnett).
[3] At the T.U. Congress of 1875; Webb, *op. cit.* p. 276

unemployment figure of 13·3 in 1879; the London Compositors one of 14·3; the Boilermakers and Iron Shipbuilders of 20·4; and the Ironfounders of 22·3. From 1884 to 1886 the Boilermakers' figure was continuously above 20·0, reaching 22·3 in 1885[1]. It was no time for expansion or difficult experiments. Some of the strongest societies were barely holding their own; others, once strong, had lost members and money wholesale.

It is probable that in the early 'forties, when the hopes of 1832–4 had died and missionary spirits had turned from the cause of the Union to the cause of the Charter, not more than 100,000 wage-earners were full members of trade societies, in spite of the strong union tradition in the old crafts and the resolute attempts to transplant it into new or revolutionised industries[2]. Law was unequal. Employers were hostile. Wage-earners were poor. Unions were born and died in dreary cycle. A Staffordshire employer had known "three sets of unions" in the iron industry before 1867[3]. There had been "scores of unions" in the Ayrshire coal-mines before 1886, Keir Hardie once said[4]. All had failed. How many trade unionists there were in 1867–9 the Commissioners of Inquiry of those years did not venture to calculate. But when drawing conclusions from the evidence, they unfortunately quoted a guess made by an ardent official of the London Operative Tailors, who had said that "there might be more but not less" than 860,000[5]. They would have done better to trust another contemporary trade union estimate that "there were never at any time more than a quarter of a million."[6] With more stable conditions, better organising methods, and reduced risks of legal embarrassment or death from a planned attack by employers, the unions of the 'seventies and 'eighties had more continuous lives than their predecessors; though there was still mortality among them. There is no doubt that aggregate membership moved up very rapidly during the good trade of the early 'seventies; and it seems probable that the formation of new unions may have balanced loss of membership in some old ones between 1876

[1] The figures which started modern statistical study of unemployment, first made public in the *Report* of 1887.

[2] Vol. I. p. 593–4.      [3] *R.C. on Trade Unions*, Q. 9839.

[4] *R.C. on Labour*, Group A, Q. 12,951.

[5] Druitt, G., Q. 18,222.

[6] Macdonald, W., *The True Story of Trades Unions contrasted with the caricatures and fallacies of the pretended economists* (1867), quoted in Postgate, R. W., *The Builders' History*, p. 205 n.

and 1886. But in 1886 no one knew to a quarter of a million how many trade unionists there were in Britain. When one government official suggested a probable figure of "over 600,000," another, better informed, countered with 1,000,000 as "not...an exaggerated estimate." The higher figure was certainly the more nearly correct; it may perhaps not have been quite high enough[1].

The big battalions of the movement, some of them thinned by the casualties of trade depression, were to be found in a limited group of industries—building, engineering and certain allied trades, coal-mining, the cotton manufacture. But some of the best bits of organisation and most complete triumphs of trade unionism were outside this group; such as the ancient society of the London Compositors with its 6600 members and virtual monopoly in important sections of the trade; the London Bookbinders and Goldbeaters with proved pedigrees of over a century; the Journeymen Hatters on whose behalf a more august claim has been put forward[2]; or the small exclusive and masterful unions, new on old foundations, in certain Sheffield trades, with their obvious 'gild' merits and defects. It was from Sheffield that these unions reported frankly in 1867-9, some that they had stopped taking apprentices because trade was bad; some that only members' sons were ever admitted apprentice; all that limitation of apprentices was a matter of course[3]. The Commissioners, who disliked limitation of apprentices, made no comment—probably because they were obsessed with the greater societies, not because they recognised the truth that these Sickle and Hook Forgers, Pen- and Pocket-Knife Blade-Forgers, Steel Fork Forgers, and members of the Work Board Branch of the Scissor Trade were on the border-line between the old fashioned independent craftsman and the wage earner. They could regulate apprenticeship because the apprentices

[1] The 600,000 was Giffen's figure (*Report* of 1887) based on the reputed 630,000 represented at the previous Trade Union Congress. The Chief Registrar of Friendly Societies (*Report*, 1887, LXXVI) pointed out that these figures were "far from including even all the largest" societies, and guessed 1,000,000. After the great Trade Union revival of 1886-91 Mr and Mrs Webb estimated the figure at 1,471,000 for 1892; *op. cit.* p. 415.

[2] See Unwin, G., *Industrial Organisation in the 16th and 17th Centuries* (1904), p. 215, where a continuous history from the seventeenth century is, with great probability, suggested. The facts about the other societies are in the *Report* of 1887.

[3] *R.C. on Trade Unions, Final Report* (1868-9, XXXI. 235), *App.* of T.U.'s which replied to a circular from the Commission.

really were theirs, not 'factory apprentices' of some great firm. They and their lads took jobs by the piece, in the factory or out of it[1].

The trade-unionist employer was well known in other industries, for sub-contract in one or other of its innumerable forms was common[2]; but he was slowly becoming rarer.

Down to about 1850, the masons, at that time the most powerful group in the building trades, of which they were the conscious aristocracy, still permitted 'operative masters' in their lodges. But the arrangement had become unnatural and it died out[3]. In all England, and even in the large stone-built towns of Scotland, masons were typical, if high-grade, wage earners. In England a mason rarely became a 'builder.'[4] In districts where he might do so, such as the West Riding or Wales, either he would avoid the lodge or there would probably be no lodge. Out of a loose federation of lodges had already been built up the Operative Stonemasons' Union, whose membership passed 9000 in 1854 and 18,000 in 1868 and 1872; touched its maximum, 27,188, in 1877; but fell away to below 13,000 in 1880, never to recover. The Scottish Masons' Society was still more unfortunate. It had raised its membership to nearly 14,000 by 1877. Next year it lost nearly all its funds in the failure of the Glasgow Bank. By the middle 'eighties its numbers were down to 3000 and less[5].

Trade depression, strikes on a falling market, the relative decline in the importance of masons' work, and defects of leadership were the proximate causes of decay. But defects of organisation had a full share. Even throughout the long fighting secretaryship of Richard Harnott (1847–72) the English masons had a shifting seat of government and no proper central organisation. They only agreed to a London office in 1883. Meanwhile, for lack of any central policy, "provincial lodges fought uselessly on their own funds or accepted defeat as they chose"[6]; and their membership fell away.

[1] For the term 'factory apprentice' see vol. I. p. 177. And see above, p. 129, for the persistence of this semi-independence.

[2] The "practically ubiquitous" of Schloss, D. F., *Methods of Industrial Remuneration* (1892), p. 120, suggests, however, rather more than there was. See above, p. 128.

[3] Postgate, *The Builders' History*, p. 150. Cp. vol. I. p. 595.

[4] Foremen, and so embryo builders, usually came from among the carpenters; above, p. 130.

[5] Figures from Postgate and the *Report of* 1887.

[6] Postgate, *op. cit.* p. 304.

The younger but far better organised Amalgamated Society of Carpenters and Joiners actually increased its membership in the early 'eighties—but partly at the expense of a rival and older carpenters' society. Founded in 1861, and built up by Robert Applegarth, secretary 1862–71, on an effective central organisation, substantial contributions from members, high Friendly Society benefits, no Owenite nonsense, and the policy of "doing all we can to extend"[1] friendly agreement between employers and employed, the A.S.C.J. had been, with a few reservations, the model union of the Commissioners of 1867–9. Applegarth left it with a membership of 11,000, which rose to 16,000 in 1876, and to a temporary maximum of nearly 29,000 in 1885. Although its rival, the General Union of Carpenters, fell from 11,000 in 1876 to under 2000 in 1883–5, there remained a net increase of trade union carpenters in those difficult years[2].

Conflict of unions inside the same craft was a common and enervating weakness of building trade unionism. Like the strong local and lodge feeling, the strong craft feeling, and the jealousy between the crafts—all equally common—it was natural enough in trades which had always existed everywhere, usually with some local society, and had each begun its modern inter-lodge organisation from several different geographical points. The bricklayers had two central English Societies from an early date, the London Order and the Manchester Unity[3]. Many local societies were not affiliated to either. There were several more or less competitive general societies among painters and plumbers: there were at least a dozen distinct painters' societies in London alone[4]. Where societies were primarily local, efficiency was impaired. The painters could not even get an arranged scale of pay for London. Where societies originally local aspired to national character, they were likely to gain it, if at all, only over the bodies of fellow societies. Jungle

---

[1] Applegarth to the *R.C. on Trade Unions* in 1867, Q. 191. For his life, Webb, *History of Trade Unionism*, p. 219 n. and *passim*, and Postgate, p. 456. He died only a few years ago.

[2] Figures from Postgate and the *Report of* 1887.

[3] Postgate, *op. cit.* p. 140, 222, 225. These are the early names: there were changes later, but the two main head-quarters remained.

[4] "I think there are about 12 or 14": there "may be eighteen." Painters' witness before the *R.C. on Labour*, Group C, Q. 19,144; for plumbers, among whom there was only one really strong English society and one Scottish, Q. 19,178.

law broke out among brethren—Amalgamated against General, Order against Unity. "We used Prussian methods on them" an old official of the Amalgamated Carpenters once said to an inquirer[1].

Craft pride led to inter-craft jealousy and, at its worst, to interminable disputes about 'overlap.' The old unchanged technique of the trades led each to regard certain jobs as its inalienable right. At the height of their power, the Operative Masons had been resolute to keep 'brickeys' in their place[2], just as barristers meant to keep solicitors. Later, Manchester bricklayers often struck to keep labourers and, by a turn of the wheel, masons off bricklayers' work. They had a ten years Trojan War with the plasterers to retain the monopoly of terracotta work—and lost it[3]. As the wooden shipwrights' trade declined, the Amalgamated Carpenters tried to stop the shipwrights' "endeavours to travel along the vessel" to their work[4]. Meanwhile the Amalgamated Engineers resented the growing activity of plumbers on iron and steel ships, as the liners acquired the sanitary conveniences of a house[5]. The extreme case is an 1877 strike of plumbers in the Potteries, which failed because a rival plumbers' society took on the jobs[6]. These enervating squabbles led to a scheme for a national federation of building trades unions drafted by Edwin Coulson, the strong man of the London Bricklayers, in 1880. Nothing came of it; and the building unions went on into the 'eighties still strong in numbers, as trade union strength then went, but striking against employers and bickering among themselves on the falling market. Their aggregate membership in 1885–6 was something like 100,000, out of a body of perhaps 775,000 building craftsmen in Great Britain[7].

It is to be noted that the associated master-builders of the

---

[1] To Mr Postgate, *op. cit.* p. 308 n.

[2] Postgate, p. 300.

[3] Postgate, *op. cit. passim*; the first full study of any group of associated unions.

[4] *R.C. on Labour*, F. Chandler of the A.S.C.J., Group A, Q. 22,011. Cp. A. Wilkie of the Associated Shipwrights, Q. 21,389 *sqq.*: the shipwrights had only just lost their old organisation; "till recently...the bulk of our apprentices used to be indentured," Q. 21,462.

[5] *Ibid.*, Group A, Q. 26,056 (Evidence from the Wear).

[6] Postgate, p. 300.

[7] The estimate for 1885–6 is based on Postgate and the *Report of* 1887. Mr and Mrs Webb estimated the membership of the same group of unions in 1892 at 120,000. Their table, *op. cit.* p. 420, deals also with the furniture trades, here excluded. The estimate for the whole body of craftsmen is based on the census of 1881 when the figure was 761,000: above, p. 120.

late 'eighties were of opinion that the amount of building work, particularly of bricklaying, done in an hour had been approximately halved during thirty years of fairly effective trade unionism[1]. Their opinion is not a proof; for they gave no statistics and had the cumulated bias of the employer, often of the self-made employer who has risen by abnormally hard work, and of the *laudator temporis acti*. The unions would have admitted some decline and been proud of it, for they had always set their faces against "chasing," "bell-horsing," piecework, and other speeding-up devices. They maintained that work was better done and that workers were not worked out[2]. They could easily have illustrated the scamping and ill-health that had often gone with speed. No balance can be set between this un-measured slackening of the average pace of production and its technical and social counter-weights.

When Applegarth was working at the organisation of the Amalgamated Carpenters he took as his model the greatest piece of amalgamation which the trade union movement had then known, the Amalgamated Society of Engineers. "I lent him our books" said William Allan, the Engineers' Secretary[3]. The Engineers had proved their strength, and won the grateful admiration of the building trades and the whole world of labour, by subscribing £3000 when the London builders were locked out in 1859–60 because they would not sign a document, or give a verbal promise, renouncing trade unionism[4]. The A.S.E. had been created, appropriately enough, in the year of the Great Exhibition and its victorious engines, out of 121 distinct societies or branches of unions connected with the risen engineering industry. Naturally such an amalgamation was not complete. Two strong old unions, the Steam-Engine Makers founded in 1824 and the United Machine Workers of 1844, never came in. The Pattern Makers formed their own union in 1872 because they thought no general society could safeguard their special interests. There were several Smiths' societies, and a few others. But the A.S.E. gathered in most of the trade. Starting with nearly 12,000 members and surviving a great lock-out early in 1852—a reply to attacks on employment of 'illegal' men, piecework, and overtime—it grew fast,

---

[1] *R.C. on Labour*, Group C, Q. 32,216: Bird, S. G. of the Central Assoc. of Master Builders.

[2] Evidence on these points was specially abundant in 1867–9.

[3] *R.C. on Trade Unions*, 1867–9, Q. 1023.

[4] *Trades Soc. and Strikes* (1860), Article on the lock-out; Webb, *op. cit.* p. 210–12.

without further serious fighting, until it had over 33,000 members in its 312 branches in 1868[1]. It came through the depression of the 'seventies with a surprisingly low maximum unemployment figure, a hardly perceptible drop in standard wages, and only a small drop in membership. This was soon recovered, and the membership had reached 52,000 in 1886. Nothing illustrates more clearly the relatively easy task of a recruiter for the A.S.E. Engineering as a whole was so buoyant, in this age of the engineer, that it rode easily over the waves of trade cycles and price vicissitudes.

Under William Allan (secretary 1851–74) the society was built up on the principles which Applegarth borrowed—substantial and regular contributions of a shilling a week or more; generous superannuation, funeral, and other allowances; as few strikes as possible that these funds should not be dissipated; and, as a natural consequence, a high level of skill and earning power among the members. His successor, John Burnett (secretary 1875–86) carried on this safe policy, although he had come to the front as leader of a notable strike on the North-East coast which won the nine hours day in 1872. It was he who, having resigned his office to become the first Labour Correspondent to the Board of Trade, reported of trade unions generally in 1886 that "although strikes have of course not yet been entirely superseded" yet "there is a gradual tendency in that direction."[2]

Reluctance to strike and lack of interest in Utopia had not implied acceptance of an employers' standpoint on work and wages. Like their predecessors the millwrights, the Amalgamated Engineers aimed at high time-rates and none of that payment by results, that 'engineers economy,' whose partial introduction about the years 1815–25 had been intended both to break the millwrights and help scientific management[3]. We have "a very decided objection to piecework," Allan said in 1867, because it leads to "sweating."[4] He meant speeding up, followed, as it had often been, by a reduction in the piece-rate when the maximum working speed had been ascertained. Like

---

[1] Statistics in 1867–9 *Final Report*, p. 283; *Report of 1887*, p. 30 *sqq.* For the other unions, see also *R.C. on Labour*, Group A, Q. 22,353 *sqq.* (Pattern Makers); *Report on Trade Unions for* 1901, p. 18. For the lock-out, Thomas Hughes in *Trades Societies and Strikes*, p. 169 *sqq.*; Nasmyth, *Autobiography*, p. 298, an employer's point of view; Webb, *op. cit.* p. 195 sqq.

[2] *Report of* 1887, p. 9. For Allan and Burnett, Webb, *op. cit.* p. 216 n., 300

[3] Vol. I. p. 207.     [4] *R.C. on Trade Unions*, Q. 638, 672.

the millwrights again, the Engineers wanted to control admission to their trade. Allan was very plain. "What is your object in limiting...apprentices?" "To keep the wages up: no question about it."[1] They had taken their part in agitations and occasional strikes for a shorter working day. As in some districts the standard week was already down to 57 hours in 1851, the question was not urgent everywhere. By 1872 the 54-hour week had been secured generally, and with that the leaders, who had not been very active in securing it, were content[2]. Whether a more combative policy, on this and other issues, might have won more for the men between 1851 and 1874 is uncertain: the avoidance of too much combat in the decade following 1874 was undoubtedly wise.

The Engineers' nearest industrial neighbours, the Boiler-makers, more specialised and so hit much harder by trade depression, were struggling with unemployment and loss of numbers in the 'eighties, but remained a strong force and included nearly all the trade. Their recent rise had been easy and quick. Founded in Lancashire under William IV, this union of the men who made things out of iron plates had expanded until the ship-building element in it had swamped the true boiler-makers. The decade 1872–82 was its great era of expansion: the law was becoming friendly and the wooden ship was dying. From a membership of 7000 in 1870, it had reached 28,000 in 1883. Seeing that 20·0 per cent. of the members were unemployed in 1884 and 22·3 in 1885, it is creditable both to the leaders and to the loyalty of the rank and file that the membership had not fallen below 26,800 in 1886. Probably there were a good many nominal members and heavy arrears of contributions. The society was national, of the amalgamated type, with 212 branches and good benefits. Like the Engineers, its members had enjoyed the 54-hour week since 1872. Its leaders were now nursing their financial wounds and steering a judicious unprovocative course. Robert Knight, their secretary, was one of the state's most trusted consulting industrial experts[3].

[1] Q. 927.
[2] There is a summary of hours' history in the *Report of* 1887, p. 30: in 1851–61 hours varied locally from 57 to 63. From 1872–9 Scotland had a 51-hour week, which it lost later. See below, p. 449.
[3] *Report of* 1887, p. 10, 22, 30. Knight's evidence before *R.C. on Depression of Trade*, Q. 14,733 *sqq.*; before *R.C. on Labour*, Group A, Q. 20,680 *sqq.* He 'supposed' that the Union included 95 per cent. of the men, Q. 20,725.

Among the iron-workers who were not engineers or boiler-makers, the unions, with the exception of the Friendly Society of Ironfounders, had hitherto been either local or rather short-lived or both. The experience of the employer of the 'sixties who had known three sets of unions remained typical. At the close of the century no important society except the Iron-founders was credited with a continuous history which went earlier than 1880; although the Associated Iron and Steel Workers, never very large, carried on the functions of a similar society which started in 1862, and the Cleveland Blastfurnace-men established in 1881–2 a small association which later became national[1]. Constant technical revolutions; transfer-ences of the industrial centre of gravity; the isolation of some of the greatest iron works and the resultant survival of so-called patriarchal relations; sharp alternations of prosperity and adversity; and, perhaps most important of all, the widespread existence of sub-employment, by puddlers, rollers, steel-makers and the rest, all tended to hamper local trade union activity and to make national activity almost impossible. Here the trade unionist employer had been very much at home. "Every puddler is a contractor; and they would like to pay their under-hands by the ton, but the under-hands will not have it." That concise summary comes from a district where unionism was fairly strong and from the year 1891[2]. The "under-hands" had only recently become assertive. It illus-trates the divisions so adverse to anything like what came to be called later 'industrial' as opposed to 'craft' unionism, and so hampering to unionism of any sort.

The Ironfounders, belonging to an old section of the industry which existed everywhere and whose essentials had not changed for a century, were in a totally different position. Their Friendly Society dated from a year (1809) in which every wise trade union had underlined its 'friendly' character. Its principal work had always been on the friendly rather than on the in-dustrial side. It had over 70 branches and over 7000 members in the late 'fifties; over 100 branches and nearly 10,000 mem-bers in 1868; 12,300 members in 1875 and 12,400 in 1885. The unemployment of the 'seventies had nearly ruined it with out-of-work pay. By 1880 its splendid reserve of over £60,000 was

---

[1] *Report on Trade Unions*, 1901, p. 18; *R.C. on Labour*, Group A, Q. 13,960 (Nat. Assoc. of Blastfurnacemen), Q. 15,301 (Assoc. Iron and Steel Workers).

[2] It was made by Ed. Trow before the *R.C. on Labour*, Group A, Q. 15,329, and refers to the N.E. Coast.

gone, and in the early 'eighties it was hardly in a position to perform the traditional friendly functions. The corresponding Scottish society, however, the Associated Iron Moulders of Scotland, was growing while the English society was stationary. It added 1000 to its membership between 1880 and 1885, when the total stood at 5600[1].

There were other effective metal-working unions, as the Sheffield trades show, but not one of them was large or of national importance.

No industry had registered more clearly than coal-mining the ebb and flow of the tides of trade unionism, or the difficulty with which the union was becoming part of the recognised industrial organisation of the country. On every coalfield at least a second and third, if not Keir Hardie's nineteenth and twentieth, attempt was needed to give unionism vitality and permanence. With the flow and ebb of local life goes the rise and fall of the national union ideal. Sometimes a measure of continuity can be traced behind a series of apparent new beginnings. Sometimes a local federation, important for a time in the life of a whole coalfield, disappears, leaving at most some pit clubs of little general significance, yet continuous. But such continuity of mere existence often only underlines the discontinuity of effective power[2]. The era begins at a time of dead water.

"At the close of 1855, it might be said that union among the miners in the whole country had almost died out."[3] Then came local revivals connected, among other things, with a Yorkshire fight for the introduction of miners' 'checkweighmen' to prevent abuses in the system of paying earnings by weight. Then also came Alexander Macdonald and his great scheme, itself a revival, for a National Miners' Union. It has been suggested that by the end of the 'sixties there were actually two hundred thousand miners 'in union.'[4] Through their political friends,

[1] Statistics in *R.C. on Trade Unions*, 1867–9, *Final Report*, p. 306, and in *Report* of 1887. For this and many other unions see the membership statistics 1850–90 in Webb, *op. cit.* p. 491–5. The Ironfounders have the most exact records of any society.

[2] Webb's *History* and Welbourne's *Miners' Unions of Northumberland and Durham* give the general story. And see vol. I. p. 217–18, 597.

[3] Alexander Macdonald, quoted in Webb, *op. cit.* p. 285.

[4] Webb, *op. cit.* p. 292. No authority given. The figure seems most improbable. The census of 1871 gives a maximum of about 350,000 coal-miners in Britain, a figure which includes most of the 'miners undefined' and all the boys and lads: 1873, LXXI. part 2 (England and Wales), LXXIII. (Scotland).

they were already a force in Parliament and had influenced legislation in 1860 and 1872[1]. The two hundred thousand level, if ever attained, was soon lost when prices broke and trade collapsed after 1873. The national ideal as an effective force was lost with it. By 1880 "the Lancashire and Midland...organisations...had either collapsed altogether, or had dissolved into isolated clubs, incapable of combined action."[2] In the single year 1878 the Durham men had paid away £54,000 in unemployment benefit[3]. In the years from 1875 to 1880, the Northumberland and Durham unions, the two strongest and the only two with continuous numerical histories, had fallen from an aggregate membership of nearly 56,000 to not quite 41,000. Both recovered a little during the next five years, so that the aggregate stood at 48,000 in 1885[4]. Probably this represented about half the enrolled coal-miners of Great Britain at that date, and the Durham union alone, with its 35,000 members, a full third. Lancashire was reorganising its Federation in 1882–5, but rapid recruitment only began in the final year. The Yorkshire Federation had at this time only about 8000 members. None of the Scottish, Welsh, or Midland areas had organisations which were numerically strong, though in nearly all of them during 1885, and still more during 1886, there was great activity in propaganda and enrolment[5].

In spite of the fall in numbers since 1875, the coal-miners' unions of the middle 'eighties contained about a quarter of the available men in the whole trade[6]. Where they were strongest, in Northumberland and Durham, the proportion was far higher. Built up rapidly on older foundations, during the politically and economically prosperous decade which followed the Reform Bill of 1867 and witnessed the freeing of trade unionism from the shackles of the old law, the Northumberland union had stood effectively in the way of any reintroduction by employers of that ancient fetter of the North-Country pitman, the yearly

---

[1] The Mines Acts, 23 and 24 Vict. c. 151 and 35 and 36 Vict. c. 76. See below, p. 420.

[2] Webb, *op. cit.* p. 372.

[3] Welbourne, *op. cit.* p. 194.

[4] *R. of Chief Registrar of Friendly Societies*, 1887, p. 63.

[5] The annual *Reports* and evidence before *R.C. on Labour*, Group A (given in 1891) are the main sources. The evidence of 1891, given by district officials, is particularly valuable.

[6] The *Survey of Industrial Relations* (1926) accepts the figures 434,000 (1881) and 595,000 (1891) for 'coal and shale' miners in Britain. The shale miners were only a few thousands but there were many lads.

bond. The Durham union had prepared a last fight against the bond in 1872, only to find that it was forcing an open door. Coal was at impossible prices. Miners were coming in from Lancashire and the Forest of Dean. The coal-owners were very ready to pay for willing work in cash and concessions. "The most pleasant and amicable feeling prevailed on both sides at the meetings of 1872"; and the men got fortnightly agreements and 20 per cent. on wages[1].

Their strength and moderation and the national position acquired by their leaders carried these two unions through the bad years that followed, when for a decade (1878–87) the average export price of British coal was all but 30 per cent. lower than it had been in the decade of prosperity. They did not get through without strikes, nor without the frank and uncompelled acceptance by their leaders of the principle of a sliding scale: 'that wages should be based on the selling price of coal.'[2] This acceptance was condemned at the time, and has been condemned since, as a compromise with the commercial doctrines of the coal-owners and a potential abandonment of the miners' standard of life; but there can be very little doubt that, like the engineers' no-strike policy, it helped to give the North-Country miners' unions complete uncriticised recognition, and an accepted place in the industrial organisation of the country. The sliding-scale in fact yielded a 'living' wage. Policy could be changed to meet fresh conditions. The local and national status of the unions were things established[3].

Where unionism was strong among the coal-miners, as on the North-East Coast, it was usually strong among the much smaller trade of the iron-miners. It was strong, too, among the quarrymen, especially the slate quarrymen of Wales. But among the tin, lead, and copper-miners it was—so far as can be ascertained—"absolutely unknown."[4]

---

[1] Welbourne, *op. cit.* p. 71, 114, 151 and *passim*. For the bond see vol. 1. p. 217. Abandoned in 1844, it had been revived in Durham. An attempt to revive it in Northumberland in 1862 was fought successfully. In Durham it survived to 1872, as above.

[2] From an 1879 circular of the Northumberland Miners' Executive, quoted in Webb, *op. cit.* p. 325.

[3] The points are touched on, not without some confusion of thought, in Webb, *op. cit.* p. 324–5.

[4] Webb, *op. cit.* p. 421. For its complete absence from Cornwall see Price, L. L., "West Barbary or Notes on the System of Work and Wages in the Cornish Mines," *S.J.* 1888, p. 494.

In public estimation, and in the national position won by their leaders, the Cotton Spinners ranked with the miners and engineers, although their union had less than 17,000 members in 1885[1]. But then they were 17,000 out of a possible 20,000 at most. They were one of the dominant male groups in an industry full of women and children. Like the puddlers, they were wage-earning employers who hired their own piecers, 'big' and 'little,' from whom their successors were recruited. But piecers could not all succeed to spinners' work, because they outnumbered the spinners by more than two to one. A federation of local societies, each with its own rules and funds, the Association dated officially from 1853. It had enlisted a great majority of the trade by the 'sixties. Although in some places spinners maintained that, so late as 1881, mill-owners "would not listen to reason,"[2] in most there had been a growing friendliness ever since the common sufferings of the cotton famine. Up to the famine, "a majority" of masters would not even deal with a trade union[3]. In the democratic air of the Oldham 'province' the mill-owner was melting away into anonymity, and the spinner was as good a man as the machinist who put up money to help him to spin. Even in aristocratic Preston, employers were realising that the union committee was "a committee of conciliation and not...a paid body of agitators."[4] Within a very few years, the Spinners' Secretary would be explaining that over the whole area with which his Association dealt, there was not "the slightest trouble or friction" with employers[5]. More completely perhaps than any other union, the cotton spinners were a regularly working part of the industrial machinery of the country.

There were many more cotton unions, and their aggregate membership was far greater than that of the spinners, but they were still in the unfederated stage, or only just passing out of it. Except among certain specialists, and in places where the

[1] There were no spinners in Parliament, with Thomas Burt and the other early miner M.P.'s, but James Mawdsley, the Spinners' Secretary, had a national position.

[2] Cowell, J., spinner, of Preston, before the *R.C. on Labour*, Group C, Q. 4750.

[3] Evidence of Henderson, Jas., Factory Inspector, given in Nov. 1891 and referring to "thirty years ago." *R.C. on Labour*, Group C, Q. 7309. He added, "all this is now changed."

[4] Cowell, J., Q. 4751.

[5] *R.C. on Labour* (evidence taken in 1891), Q. 721. Spinners' history is in Webb, *op. cit.*; the fullest discussion of spinners' function in Webb, *Industrial Democracy* (1897), *passim*.

trade union spirit was particularly strong, they had, as yet, nothing like the spinners' control of the situation. A dozen or more local associations of power-loom overlookers, each with a few score or a few hundred members, safeguarded the interests of this aristocratic group. There were some efficient societies among bleachers, dyers, and calico-printers, with an aggregate membership which perhaps approached 10,000. Much more important were the local societies of weavers, cardroom operatives, and 'beamers' and 'twisters'; for all these, whose total membership may have been 80,000, admitted women—indeed contained a considerable majority of women. And these women, not less than 50,000, formed the only important group of women trade unionists in the kingdom[1].

Many of the strongest power-loom weavers' societies dated from the 'fifties, from the time of the final victory of the machine whose name they bore, and the established predominance of the woman weaver. Padiham and District, 1850; Blackburn and District, 1854; Chorley and District, 1855; Accrington and District, 1856; and so on. Some had taken over half-official agreements which were in existence before there was any permanent union. The Burnley and District Society, for example, which dated nominally only from 1870, worked on a 'local list' of weaving prices which was never revised in essentials during the forty years 1843–83, though percentages might be added or subtracted[2]. All the societies had admitted women from an early date, and the number of women members had grown with the decline of male weaving. There had just been formed (in 1884) the Northern Counties Amalgamated Association of Weavers; but the active life of the movement was in the twenty-five districts, with their local specialities and lists[3].

So too with the Card and Blowing Room societies. They were, as a group, a good deal younger than the weavers' societies and very much weaker. Two only, those of Bolton and Stockport, dated from the 'fifties: three more from the 'sixties. Although most of them allowed the women who span at the throstles and ring-frames to join—James Mawdsley's spinners

---

[1] Figures from *Report of* 1887 and subsequent *Reports* (that of 1901 has been used). Cp. estimates in Webb, *History*, p. 413, 423, 492 *sqq.*

[2] *R.C. on Labour*, Group C, Q. 1084–6.

[3] Association was in the air in 1884–6 (Webb, *History*, p. 422) but its importance is for a later period.

all tended mules—they had not as yet succeeded in enlisting an important proportion of the workers anywhere, except at Oldham, and even there the large numbers were a new thing. As for the unions among the 'beamers' and 'twisters'—people who prepare the weavers' beams for the loom and 'twist in' the ends of the new warp threads—they could not be large because their trades are small, and though they admitted women they only contained a handful. The cardroom people were just working out an amalgamation of their district societies. It was completed in 1886. The others had not arrived at this stage, and it was not likely that they ever would[1].

Throughout all the other textile trades, unionism was extraordinarily weak. There were a few old-established friendly societies of overlookers and other managing people; a few discouraged organisations among hand-workers—Midland knitters, Macclesfield silk-weavers, or the tiny remnant of cotton hand-loom weavers at Bolton[2]; some isolated local societies among general factory workers; and a few ambitious, but still weakly, beginnings, like the West Riding General Union of Weavers and Textile Workers of 1881. Scattered, sectional, poor in funds, their membership all told can hardly have exceeded that of the cotton cardroom workers. Great industrial diversity even inside particular industries, as in wool; late and incomplete revolutionising of technique, as in silk; geographical division; predominance of women and child workers; low pay for nearly all—these seem the main causes. To them add the stubborn local feeling of the West Riding: Guiseley did not work with Pudsey, and Birstall followed not Ossett.

Among the clothing trades of all kinds unionism was weaker still. Only a few of the tailors were in the Amalgamated or the Scottish Societies. A union which was to become very strong had been formed among the machine boot-makers in 1874; but in 1886 its membership had not passed 14,000. This, with a few old craft societies among shoe-makers, hatters, glovers and the like completes the scanty list.

The potters' unions were specialised, small, and independent[3]. The miscellaneous metal, leather, and wood-working

---

[1] *Reports* on Trade Unions and Webb, *op. cit.* as above.

[2] The Bolton Hand-loom Weavers still had 24 members in 1898, but were dissolved about the end of 1899: *Report of* 1901, p. 47. Cp. above, p. 81.

[3] Warburton, W. H., *Trade Union Organisation in the North Staffordshire Potteries* (1931), p. 168 *sqq.*

trades contained hundreds of unions, a few strong locally, like some of those at Sheffield, but mostly weak; though their aggregate membership was considerable. They were seldom representative of their trades, though most trades in the groups were represented by unions. There were at least a score of small societies in the brass and copper trades, besides the five thousand or so of the Amalgamated Brass Workers. Struggling little societies of tin-plate workers, braziers, and workers in precious metals were scattered about the country[1]. Twenty distinct unions catered for the needs of a few thousand coopers. A hundred or more of the very old shipwrights' societies had recently (1882) come together as the Associated Shipwrights; but a number were still standing out. Most shipwrights were in union locally; they always had been[2].

So were very many, if not most, printers. Besides the powerful London Compositors, the Typographical Association, founded in Sheffield in 1849 but with headquarters at Manchester since 1865, together with some smaller kindred societies, covered a great part of the trade. Yet the Lithographic Printers of 1879, strong in the 'provinces,' were weak in London: "so many shops...are up mysterious back places and courts and such-like that we cannot get at them," an official of the union once said[3]. The explanation deserves to be borne in mind; for it was true of many London trades, and it helps to account for the weakness and provincialism of many London trade societies.

Outside the skilled trades and the manufactures, unionism was still almost unknown. There were a handful of weak societies of builders' and general labourers. London stevedores and watermen, with a few other riverside groups, had local organisations. But the Amalgamated Society of Railway Ser-

---

[1] Up to 1887 tin-plate unionism was intermittent, in spite of the power which employers attributed to it (above, p. 152). Jones, J. H., *The Tin-plate Industry* (1914), p. 178.

[2] Evidence of Wilkie, A., of the shipwrights, *R.C. on Labour*, Group A, Q. 21,389 *sqq.* Cp. vol. I. p. 201, 212–13.

[3] Kelley, G. D. before *R.C. on Labour*, Group C, Q. 22,693. The evidence for the Typographical Assoc., London Compositors and Scottish Typographical Assoc. is also full and very valuable, both for history and function. In spite of the strength of the London Compositors, more than half the government-contract printing shops in 1891 were non-unionist; Bowerman, C. W., Q. 23,031. For the small printing shop, see above, p. 119, n. 1. Jones, Benjamin, in 1894 (*Co-operative Production*, II. 572) explained the absence of co-operation in printing by "the comparative ease with which a pushing man can become a small master."

vants, which had started with over 17,000 members in 1871–2, had fallen to 6300 by 1882 and was only slowly recovering, though its funds were better than its numbers. The first reasonably durable society ever formed among road transport workers was the Edinburgh and Leith Cabdrivers' Union of 1885. It was neither very large nor at all rich[1].

The case of the cotton spinners shows how slowly the most inclusive and best managed of unions were winning a fully recognised position, although the situation of the late 'fifties, when a majority of the employers in the cotton industry would not deal with a union at all, was a thing of the past. That ill-managed and not representative societies should win a recognised place was not to be expected. Yet, whether representative or not, ill managed or well, their importance at crises was often out of proportion to their numerical strength or their degree of formal recognition. For John Burnett's claim that they contained "the flower of their respective trades," if possibly biased, was probably true[2]; and their aims were the natural aims of every wage-earner.

That policy of persuasion and restraint which their most prominent leaders had pursued for over twenty years, combined with the old traditions of trade club and gild, had given prominence to their friendly society functions. Funeral benefit was the most universal of all: £10 to £12 was an ordinary figure for a member's funeral, and half as much for that of a member's wife. All strong unions gave sick pay, compensation for injury when the trade was risky, and superannuation pay. A few helped widows and orphans. The more strictly industrial strike pay, unemployment pay, and travel pay were less universal than funeral benefit, though they were the main items of expenditure in the greater societies. Strike pay might be as high as £1 a week. The more usual 10s. to 15s. might be supplemented by special levies or sympathetic contributions. Unemployment pay was never more than 10s. a week: so strong a union as the Boilermakers offered only 8s. It was never guaranteed indefinitely. Small as it was, small as the aggregate outlay from all trade union funds in a bad year can have been if

[1] Alcock, G. W., *Fifty Years of Railway Trade Unionism* (1922), p. 625. Evidence on transport and waterside unions before *R.C. on Labour*, Group B (1892, xxxv), *passim*. For the Edinburgh cabmen, *Report on Trade Unions of* 1901, p. 65. There had been ephemeral unions among London cabmen before 1886; see *e.g.* Webb, *History*, p. 355.

[2] *Report of* 1887, p. 14.

set beside the figures of the poor-rate, the friends of the unions did well to call public attention to the national utility of this growing system of co-operative insurance against the most grievous risk of the wage-earner's active life. It was not so long since respectable Scottish masons had been obliged to meet seasonal unemployment, 'when every other resource had failed them,' by public begging[1].

The local and national organisations in which many trade unionists now came together, Trades Councils and Trade Union Congresses, were not as yet fully representative and had no regular functions in national industry. Permanent Councils had not existed before the late 'fifties[2]. But there had often been inter-union committees in times of crisis, and it was usually a crisis which led to permanent organisation—to be ready for the next. Such organisations, being new and voluntary, were never inclusive. A quarrel in the printing trade, for example, threw up the Association of Organised Trades of Sheffield in 1858. Two years later, twenty-two out of the no less than fifty-five unions of the Sheffield area were affiliated[3]. The troubles in the building trades in 1859–60 led to the creation of the London Trades Council, from which in its early days most of the greater societies stood aloof. At that time there were only five permanent councils. Their numbers and strength grew slowly during the next twenty years, but at least they existed in most important centres during the early 'eighties. Yet they were often weak, and only some quite small proportion of the trade unionists in the country was even nominally represented in them[4].

The first Congress was called together, in 1868, by the Manchester and Salford Council as a publicity organisation in the anticipated fight over trade union law; and publicity remained the principal function of these necessarily short annual gatherings. In order to enlighten the "profound ignorance which prevails in the public mind" they were to "assume the character of the Annual Meetings of the Social Science

[1] Vol. I. p. 585–6 (referring to the 'forties). The 'friends of the unions' referred to are George Howell in his *Conflicts of Capital and Labour* (1878), p. 154–5 and *passim*, and John Burnett, in the *Report of* 1887. The illustrative figures in the text are taken from these two sources.

[2] See the full note in Webb, *History*, p. 225–6.

[3] *Report on Trades Societies and Strikes* (1860), p. 565–6.

[4] For their relative insignificance even in the early 'nineties see Webb, *History*, p. 466.

Association."[1] So the original summons said; and so they did. A trade union historian has written that Congress met "to talk about every subject under the sun except Trade Union Policy"[2]: a recent president has spoken with respect of how in those early days it "gave more attention than it does to-day to the consideration of fundamental principles of economic organisation and industrial development."[3] Most Congresses of all kinds have futile aspects, but may nevertheless have educational value. This Congress did not seek to direct trade union policy, and need not be blamed for failure to do so.

From time to time during nearly three generations, the state, conscious of friction in industrial affairs, had tried to furnish legal facilities for the settlement of industrial differences. There was the Act of 1800 'for settling disputes that may arise between masters and workmen engaged in the cotton manufacture in that part of Great Britain called England' (39 and 40 Geo. III, c. 90). There was the general Act of 1825 (5 Geo. IV, c. 96), a pendant to the Combination Law controversy of 1824–5. Under it the Justices of the Peace, on appeal from the contending parties, might appoint mixed panels of masters and men, from which the parties would choose referees. If no settlement were reached, the Justices might give a final award. No master manufacturer was to sit on the bench when such an award was given. Nothing could be fairer or more well-meaning. Nor was anything ever much less effective, though very occasionally, in the 'forties and 'fifties, a puzzled London police magistrate had to decide whether or not a piece of Spitalfields velvet was well made[4]. The law was still there, with its working parts intact, in the 'eighties. "It is, I presume, but seldom appealed to," Stanley Jevons wrote in 1882[5]. He was right.

Revived interest in industrial questions during the 'sixties had produced other ineffective laws. That known as Lord St

---

[1] Printed in Webb, *op. cit.* App. III.

[2] Milne-Bailey, W., *Trade Union Documents* (1929), p. 25.

[3] *Ibid.* p. 75. The President's Address for 1926.

[4] Hamill, J., Police Magistrate, before the *S.C. on Masters and Operatives*, 1856 (XIII. 1), Q. 2318 *sqq.*

[5] *The State in Relation to Labour*, p. 156. There is a comprehensive summary of legal history, and of arbitration history generally, in a memorandum of the *R.C. on Labour* (1892, XXXVI. part 5); and cp. Lord Amulree, *Industrial Arbitration in Great Britain* (1929).

Leonard's Act of 1867 (30 and 31 Vict. c. 105) was intended to promote "equitable councils of conciliation," with a half-memory of the French *conseils des prud'hommes*. It was an enabling act and a dead letter. Its successor of 1872 (35 and 36 Vict. c. 46), known as Mr Mundella's, "to make further provision for arbitration between masters and workmen," was never once used[1].

Goodwill had not spent itself entirely on vain laws "with the taint of the Justice of the Peace about them."[2] Though no trade of importance had ever gone regularly to the courts, there had been a number of private experiments in arbitration which had, in fact, inspired those who framed the later ineffective laws. The laws were meant to help on a movement which already had a history. The notion of a 'Board of Trade,' to fix wages, had been dear to the suffering hand-loomers and their friends in the 'thirties and 'forties[3]. In the 'thirties there was a short-lived committee of conciliation in the Potteries, and from 1851 it was customary to insert an arbitration-clause in the yearly contract of service between the potter and his employer[4]. Up and down the country, disputes had occasionally been referred to trusted local men as arbitrators. Between 1845 and the early 'sixties, the wage-earners' National Association of United Trades did valuable conciliatory work in many places, London especially[5]. In 1849 a silk trade arbitration board had been set up at Macclesfield, in imitation of the *conseils des prud'hommes*; but it broke up in four years, being said to have driven trade out of the town, as perhaps, with its strict insistence on standard weaving rates, it had[6]. In the printing trade there appear to have been small local committees very much earlier; but an attempt to create a regular court of arbitration, with a barrister as umpire, failed about the time that the Macclesfield board broke down[7]. It was in 1860 and at Nottingham, after a period

[1] Mundella, A. J. and Howell, G., "Industrial Association," in *Reign of Queen Victoria* (ed. Humphry Ward, 1887), vol. II.

[2] Jevons, *op. cit.* p. 167.  [3] Vol. I. p. 552.

[4] Owen, H., *The Staffordshire Potter* (1901), p. 114. Evidence of M. D. Hollins, employer, and W. Maitland, potter, before *S.C. on Masters and Operatives*, 1856, Q. 2386 *sqq.*, 2557 *sqq.* Warburton, *op. cit.* p. 67, 142.

[5] For its general history see Webb, *History of Trade Unionism*, p. 168-9; for its special conciliatory work evidence of T. Winters, Sec. and E. Humphries, of the Committee, in 1856, Q. 1 *sqq.*, 512 *sqq.*

[6] Evidence of S. Higginbotham, its promoter, in 1856; Q. 1890 *sqq.*

[7] Evidence of J. Avent, compositor, Q. 2715 *sqq.* Cp. Crompton, H. C., *Industrial Conciliation* (1876), p. 130-1.

of wearing industrial friction, strikes, lock-outs and bitterness, that Mundella, a manufacturer, managed to establish the Board of Arbitration and Conciliation for the Hosiery and Glove Trade, an elective body of twenty-one with secretaries for employers and employed. Disputes of all kinds were to be tackled first by the secretaries; next by a committee; only in the last resort by the whole board[1]. For some twenty years the system worked fairly well. In the 'seventies it controlled the knitting piece-rates for some 6000 separate articles[2]. The Board was much discussed and a good deal imitated. But in the 'eighties it was breaking down. The industry had changed greatly. Some employers had shown themselves hostile: naturally workpeople had not always been satisfied. In 1884, a strike which the Board failed to avert left bitter memories, and the machinery fell into disuse[3]. Unionism was weak in the hosiery trade and the system was thereby handicapped. But the method of settlement through the officials of associations of wage earners and employers had been taken over meanwhile by some better organised industries, and was bearing fruit in the 'eighties, especially in Lancashire[4].

Four years after Mundella's board started, Rupert Kettle, the County Court Judge of Worcestershire, attended a meeting called by the Mayor of Wolverhampton to settle a building strike[5]. He suggested permanent arbitration arrangements, and drafted a scheme for settling disputes by a joint board with an umpire or referee. The acceptance of arbitration became part of the wage contract. Master builders and carpenters agreed. Next year a conciliation clause was added which, as Kettle said later, was more useful than the arbitration clause. Soon the plasterers and bricklayers came in. The masons, relying on their strength to get what they wanted, stood out[6]. The system was imitated elsewhere, in the building trade and in other trades. Kettle was called on to arbitrate both by those who did,

[1] Mundella, *op. cit.* Price, L. L., *Industrial Peace* (1887), p. 43. Cp. Wright, C. D., *Industrial Conciliation and Arbitration* (1881: Boston); Weeks, J. D., *Labor Differences and their Settlement* (1886: New York).

[2] Compton, *op. cit.* p. 39.

[3] The memorandum for the *R.C. on Labour*, as above.

[4] See *e.g.* the account of how minor difficulties were settled by the "practical committee" of the Card and Blowing Room Operatives, *R.C. on Labour*, Group C, Q. 115.

[5] Kettle, *Strikes and Arbitration* (1866) and his evidence (Q. 6985 *sqq.*) before *R.C. on Trade Unions*, 1867–9.

[6] Crompton, *op. cit.* p. 112 *sqq.*

and those who did not, adopt his particular system. In 1880 this "prince of arbitrators" was knighted. Although, some years before, the bricklayers of his home area had rejected an award and withdrawn, there were important centres in the late 'eighties where arbitration was the rule in all branches of the building trade. At Liverpool the court—equal numbers of masters and men, with an umpire if required—had functioned from 1874 almost without a hitch[1].

While Kettle was showing what his method could achieve, boards more or less on Mundella's lines were set up, in 1868, in the Leicester and Derby hosiery and in the Nottingham lace trades, and in the Potteries. The last merely developed existing arrangements. "Long before we had our board," an employer wrote in 1876, "we settled our disputes on the same principle, by fixing on two workmen and two masters, and I never remember a single failure."[2] Failures came later. In the 'eighties the Leicester board went the way of Mundella's hosiery board; and stresses were developing in the Potteries board which led to its disintegration in 1891–2[3].

Early in 1869, iron-workers from the Middlesbrough district had appeared at Nottingham to study Mundella's methods. Within a few weeks (on March 22, 1869) the most famous and successful of the boards of conciliation and arbitration had come into existence—the North of England Iron and Steel, under the chairmanship of David Dale[4]. Its creation was something of a feat. The industry was young, without traditions, and without regular unionism. Men had come in from all quarters. They were sturdy, illiterate and well paid. They proved, however, "at least as ready" for the experiment as their employers[5]. Perhaps, without much book learning or very long experience, they had grasped the essentially fluctuating character of an industry which turns out 'production goods,' whose members are therefore well-advised not to fight as they ride those waves of the trade cycle which are always steepest in such industries. True, the Board had the good fortune to start with a rise of 6d.

---

[1] *R.C. on Labour*, Group C, Q. 18,473 *sqq.*

[2] A correspondent of Crompton, *op. cit.* p. 121. Cp. Warburton, *op. cit.* p. 150.

[3] The memorandum of the *R.C. on Labour*; Warburton, *op. cit.* p. 159 *sqq.*

[4] See evidence of W. Whitwell, employer, and Ed. Trow, ironworker, before *R.C. on Labour*, Group A, Q. 14,997 *sqq.*, 15,159 *sqq.*, on its working; Samuelson, B., paper before *British Iron Trade Assoc.* 1876, for its early history; Price, *op. cit.*, for the 'eighties.

[5] Whitwell, as above.

a ton in puddlers' wages. Within four years, in the boom of the early 'seventies, another 4*s*. 9*d*. was added. This was easy arbitration. But in 1891, leaders from both sides could report with justifiable satisfaction that only a few short stoppages of work owing to disputes had ever occurred, and then only "under circumstances of special irritation or excitement"[1]; although puddlers' wages had moved from the 8*s*. a ton of 1868, through the 13*s*. 3*d*. of 1873, to a nadir of 6*s*. 3*d*. in the later dark years. The conciliation of all sorts of minor and local disputes was done throughout by a standing joint committee. Great wage decisions went to arbitrators with an umpire behind them—Rupert Kettle or Tom Hughes from outside, Joseph Pease or Spence Watson from nearer home.

"Arbitration in the coal trade," Henry Crompton wrote in 1876, "is an accomplished fact, as far as England and Wales are concerned. As yet, however...no permanent board...has been adopted."[2] In Durham and Northumberland joint committees of owners and miners with an outside chairman were set up in 1872–3. These committees were soon dealing with some hundreds of particular and local issues yearly. Their decisions were "scarcely ever disputed" throughout the period[3]. For the settlement of general wage questions, however, *ad hoc* arbitration tribunals were created from time to time. The chief dangers of this system were already apparent by 1876. It tended to stimulate a "refined advocacy,"[4] with bad psychological effects on both sides; and the frequent recurrence of full-dress arbitrations—one was concluded in Durham during November 1874: another begun in April 1875—was unsettling to the industrial atmosphere. Why all this trouble for a five months' agreement? Why reverence the majesty of a law so little durable? Agreements could scarcely hope to be durable in the fierce price fluctuation of the 'seventies; but, as a result of such questionings, there was no general arbitration in Durham after 1882[5].

Gradually, during the late 'seventies, with or without formal arbitration, but of necessity through the preliminary work of some joint committee, in Durham and Northumberland and on many other English and Welsh coalfields sliding scales were

---

[1] Whitwell, as above.
[2] *Op. cit.* p. 68.
[3] Memo. for *R.C. on Labour* and evidence before Group A, Q. 1 *sqq.*
[4] Crompton, *op. cit.* p. 71.
[5] *R.C. on Labour*, Group A, Q. 1716 and cp. Price, *op. cit.*

adopted, under which wages shifted with prices; but the mere sliding-scale committees, such for example as that of South Wales and Monmouthshire, had not the organic character of the general-purposes joint committee of Durham and Northumberland. In itself the principle of the sliding scale was hardly a bond of union. Miners' leaders in Yorkshire and Lancashire never accepted it, though there was a short-lived West Yorkshire sliding-scale agreement in 1880. Several of the other agreements were terminated before 1885-6, and a campaign against the principle, based on the view that some 'living wage' minimum should be a first charge on industry, was carried on by the Miners' Federation in the years that followed[1].

In the South Staffordshire iron industry a conciliation board was started in 1872, and re-started in 1876 with Joseph Chamberlain as chairman. It failed the first time because, on the men's side, it represented only those who were in union, and the union was not strong. Employers who accepted its decisions found that not all their men did. The second time it did better, trying to get on to North of England lines. "We struggled on," the men's secretary said long afterwards, "but it was not growing strong enough."[2] In the 'eighties it was still struggling, but not to the satisfaction of either side. The standing committee arranged "hundreds of cases"[3]; but now it was the men who were complaining of non-observance of decisions by firms outside the forty-two who subscribed to the board[4]. In 1886 it was just changing its name from the South Staffordshire to the Midland Iron and Steel Board. In fact it had little to do with steel and never thoroughly controlled even the puddled iron.

It is not surprising that the success of the North of England board should have led to its imitation in the small associated industries of the Cleveland ironstone miners (1873) and the Cleveland and Cumberland blastfurnacemen (1879-80). Of these the miners' board had worked best. Its problems were relatively simple, for iron-mining has not the shattering variety

---

[1] The sliding scale is discussed fully, from the 'living-wage' point of view, in Webb, *History*, p. 323-7; a list of all known sliding-scale agreements is in App. II. p. 484-6. See also Munro, J. E. C., "Sliding Scales in the Coal Industry" (1885: a Brit. Assoc. paper); "Sliding Scales in...Coal and Iron... 1885 to 1889" (*Manchester Stat. Soc.* 1889).

[2] *R.C. on Labour*, Group A, Q. 15,615 (Wm. Ancott). Compare the contemporary account in Crompton, *op. cit.* p. 64.

[3] *R.C. on Labour*, Group A, Q. 15,486.     [4] *Ibid.* Q. 15,617.

of coal-mining. More interesting was the attempt, begun in 1875, to adapt the machinery of conciliation and arbitration to the young and changing factory boot and shoe industry of Leicester. It was natural that the attempt should be made in that area; perhaps equally natural that it should not be an entire success in that trade at that time. The board was not continuously active nor always able to avert strikes. At the end of the 'eighties, though still in existence, it was reported to be only "on the whole" successful[1].

Behind the standard thought of the third quarter of the nineteenth century lay mechanical conceptions of the industrial world. It was a concourse of competing and clashing atoms. The law ought to equalise opportunity for atoms; no more. All atoms of capital should have equal access to the conveniences of limited liability. The more complex and heavier atoms of business organisation, the firms, were to have all markets opened to them—so far as might be—and were to be exposed to clashes from all. Atoms of labour were to be free to come together unhindered. It was hardly anticipated, as it had been by sanguine atomists of the first quarter of the century, that, if set quite free, they would perceive that it would be inexpedient to come together[2]. The full atomic chaos had never existed as pictured, nor had standard thought been universal. There were always protestants and co-operators. But it was to some such conception that those average minds tended whose workings mostly determine social activity. The best of them had thought about reducing friction between the sorts of atoms; hence the arbitration and conciliation. Prophets and poets had taught righteousness and honest workmanship, or had dreamed of a new world, of lands East of the sun and West of the moon. They had not thought hard and clear about the day after to-morrow. Those among them who had the spirit of the Old Testament, from Thomas Carlyle to Karl Marx, had feared, or looked to, the coming of some terrible or some glorious catastrophe, a Day of the Lord when the elements should melt with fervent heat into a great new thing.

It was among the atoms of labour that the phrase to be 'in union' had first gained a half-sacred meaning: indeed it had

---

[1] In the memorandum for the *R.C. on Labour*.
[2] The well-known view of Francis Place, among others.

religious associations[1]. The honesty of those business-man atoms who had protested that union for them was only a tiresome necessity need not be disputed[2]. Very slowly, and first from the other side, their union also came to be viewed, not indeed as sacred, but at least as a thing highly convenient socially, rather than as a mere fighting device. "Is the tendency of the employers to become organised?" a trade union leader was asked in 1891. "Yes." "And you thoroughly approve of it?" "Just so."[3] Such approval was recent and perhaps not usual, but very genuine. The atoms were grouping themselves, and small new things were coming, without catastrophe so far.

How the entire freedom of capital to flow and combine, while limiting its risks, might affect industrial organisation was very imperfectly pictured in the 'eighties, either by savers, capital handlers, or thinkers. The weakness of the joint-stock in industry had been debated far more than its future. In 1877 the Master of the Rolls, no doubt a conservative critic, had pronounced it unsuitable for manufactures and had advocated the partnership *en commandite* as an alternative[4]. Before the Depression Commissioners of 1885–6 it was definitely on its trial. In what ways the newly 'limited' family businesses might evolve was not much considered. Businesses had expanded, absorbed one another, run together, in the simple partnership age. Karl Marx had made of their inevitable expansion an historic dogma and a forecast. The facilities for expansions and absorptions were now greatly increased, as was being demonstrated in America. But when a general running together began in Britain, under limited liability law, about a dozen years later, it came unexpected by standard British opinion. If the economists had foreseen it, they had not distinctly foretold it.

[1] *E.g.* "Thus may we abide in union with each other, in the Lord" from John Newton's benediction hymn. Evangelical hymnology is never irrelevant to nineteenth-century labour history.

[2] Above, p. 146.

[3] *R.C. on Labour*, Group C, Q. 634–5 (Geo. Silk of the Card and Blowing Room Operatives).

[4] *S.C. on the Operation of the Companies Acts of 1862 and 1867; 1877* (VIII. 419), evidence of Sir G. Jessel, Q. 2225 *sqq.* He allowed that it might be appropriate for 'limiting' a family business.

CHAPTER V

COMMUNICATIONS

HAVING conquered Britain by the early 'fifties, the railway consolidated and extended its conquest during the next generation, without any thorough-going change in weapons or tactics. Though the iron road had turned to steel, the engine which dragged Gladstone to face Parnell in 1886 was nearer in type to those which had dragged him, a Peelite unattached, forty years earlier than to the high-bellied bull-necked monsters of forty years later[1]. So good were the best early engines, and so permanent the way, that maximum journey-speeds went up very little between the 'forties and the 'eighties, though far more trains touched the maximum at the end. In 1845 the best expresses on the London and North-Western averaged 37 miles an hour[2]. In 1854, on the young North-Eastern, 37 to 41 is said to have been express speed[3]. In 1865-6 expresses in general were credited with "about 40"; but a more exact measurement of the quickest runs on various lines yielded only $36\frac{1}{2}$[4]. In 1871 a still more exact measurement of 250 distinct expresses gave $37\frac{2}{8}$. By 1883 as many as 407 trains averaged $41\frac{3}{8}$[5]. The best practice of the 'forties had been slightly improved on and much extended. The improved service had been put within everyone's reach on most lines since the Midland Railway announced on May 19, 1872, that in future third-class passengers would be carried on all its trains[6]. But there was no technical revolution at all.

So also with amenities. The open 'thirds' of the early days died out. Seats were softened. But when in 1874 the Midland, always spirited, imported from Detroit an experimental 'American train' whose coaches were not cut up into compartments, its reception was mixed. English travellers, especially

---

[1] Above, p. 76. But there were experiments with compound engines from 1881.

[2] *R.C. on Railways*, 1867 (XXXVIII. part I), p. liii.

[3] Tomlinson, W. W., *The North-Eastern Railway* (1914), p. 545.

[4] *R.C. on Railways*, p. lviii.

[5] Willock, H. B., "English Express Trains in 1871 and...1883," *S.J.* 1884, p. 259.

[6] Stretton, C. E., *The History of the Midland Railway* (1901), p. 201. The Great Western did not put 'thirds' on all expresses till 1890. Sekon, G. A., *A History of the Great Western. Railway* (1895), p. 278.

Manchester travellers, "expressed a preference for the ordinary compartment vehicle"[1]: no revolution for them. The train was taken off and used in bits. The Midland persevered cautiously. It was accustoming first-class passengers to dining cars in the early 'eighties. First-class sleeping cars, which formed part of the experiment of 1874 and had been started on the East Coast route to Scotland a year earlier, seem to have been accepted from the start.

In 1848, although there was still plenty of railway work in hand, railway promotion was stagnant—not unnaturally, after the fever of the past three years. Nearly 1200 miles of line were opened and only 330 were authorised. Altogether 4646 miles were open for traffic in Britain at the end of the year[2]. The network seemed dense and complete, and the recently appointed Commissioners of Railways were pointing out that probably a great part of the 7000 odd miles of line, authorised but not yet made, never would be made. Why should it be, some people asked[3]. Since February 14, 1848, when the Caledonian was opened, there were even alternative railway routes to Scotland. There had already been racing on them. John Russell's Budget speech of 1848 had been put through to Glasgow at a journey-speed of nearly 46 miles an hour[4].

The 12,000 mile long railway system, which would have existed had all the lines authorised by 1848 been built, was not in fact reached for nearly twenty years, with the aid of a number of new trunk lines in England, railway systems for Wales and the Highlands, and a great number of branch lines, link lines, and short competitive stretches everywhere except in Wales and the Highlands. The total open mileage of British railways was:

| | | | | | |
|---|---|---|---|---|---|
| 1848 (Dec. 31) | 4,646 | | 1870 | ... ... | 13,562 |
| 1858 ... | ... 8,354 | | 1886 | ... ... | 16,700 |

For the whole United Kingdom—British figures are not to be had—the number of passengers carried on the growing mileage,

---

[1] Stretton, *op. cit.* p. 206.

[2] Lardner, D., *Railway Economy* (1850), p. 54–5.

[3] An Act of 1850 (13 and 14 Vict. c. 83) was expressly designed to authorise the abandonment of Railways and the Dissolution of Railway Companies. Some 2000 miles were abandoned without authorisation. Cleveland-Stevens, E., *English Railways, their Development and their Relation to the State* (1915), p. 179.

[4] Tomlinson, *op. cit.* p. 486.

exclusive of season-ticket holders, increased nearly tenfold between 1850 and 1885, and the weight of goods and minerals nearly threefold between 1860—there are no figures for 1850—and 1885. No doubt the British ratios were much the same[1].

Of new trunk lines, the Great Northern was ready for its trial trip by August, 1850, in time to take part in the Great Exhibition rate war of 1851, when return fares, Yorkshire to London, fell to 5s.[2] It never got to York as had originally been planned. Its main line ended, as a standing jest said, "in a ploughed field four miles North of Doncaster,"[3] the point at which the ownership of the permanent way passed into other hands. The South-Western, which grew out of the London and Southampton, was putting together its long western trunk line by construction and purchase in the 'fifties. The London-Salisbury direct line was opened in 1857. In 1860 Exeter was reached and connection established with some far western lines already built or controlled[4]. All this had been contemplated before 1850. The chief additions to the English trunk line system as then conceived were made by the Midland, always striking out from its North Midland headquarters[5]. In 1867 it first brought goods into St Pancras and passengers through Peak Forest into Manchester. In 1875 goods, and in 1876 passengers, were carried along its second mountain line, the Settle and Carlisle through the High Craven and the Pennines[6]. Except the Settle and Carlisle, no important long lines were put in hand after 1870. The new mileage of 1870–86 was almost all branch, link, or local. Great enterprises of construction were of a different kind: in 1886 the Severn Tunnel was opened and the Forth Bridge was building.

The last years of the early railway age had been years of amalgamation and of George Hudson the Railway King. The Midland and the London and North-Western were created by

[1] From the Railway Returns summarised in the *Statistical Abstracts for the U.K.*

[2] See vol. I. p. 392 and the map facing p. 184 below; Grinling, C. H., *The Great Northern Railway* (1898), p. 103, for the rate war.

[3] Acworth, W. M., *The Railways of England* (1889), p. 207. Denison, the first chairman, is said to have made the remark to a shareholder.

[4] Sherrington, C. E. R., *Economics of Rail Transport in Gt. Britain* (1928), I. 42–3.

[5] See vol. I. p. 392–4.

[6] Stretton, *op. cit.* p. 168, 186.

amalgamations in 1843–6. Hudson made the Midland, Carr Glyn and Captain Mark Huish the North-Western. In 1847–8 amalgamation made the Lancashire and Yorkshire, the Manchester Sheffield and Lincolnshire, and that York Newcastle and Berwick from which, within a few years, the North-Eastern was born[1]. This was Hudson's home system; in York he had once been a linen draper. But it was at one of its meetings in 1849 that the question was asked which would make him homeless. Why had certain shares been sold to the company, by Hudson, at a price never touched on the Stock Exchange? His reply started the hunt. Once on the scent they found it rank. He had bought iron at £6. 10s. and sold it to his companies at £12. He had kept for himself shares 'placed at the disposal of the directors,' really to be used for palm-greasing. He had inflated traffic returns and treated capital as revenue; and so forth. For four more years, no longer a Railway King but still an M.P., he remained something of a Dock King, and did good work for Sunderland and the Hartlepools. By 1854 he was with Thackeray's gentleman exiles at Boulogne[2].

The year before, the directors of the York, Newcastle and Berwick, the Yorkshire and North Midland—another Hudson system, which served the triangle Leeds, Hull, Whitby—and the Leeds Northern[3], which skirted the gates of the Yorkshire Dales, having failed to carry an amalgamation bill, had strengthened existing working agreements. On July 31, 1854, their revived amalgamation bill received the royal assent. It established that North-Eastern Company which became, within little more than a decade, a standing British instance of the system of territorial monopoly, which in France had been adopted by the state as the basis of its railway system. After the absorption of the Newcastle and Carlisle (1862), the Stockton and Darlington (1863) and some lesser companies (1857–65), there was not a bit of permanent way between Berwick, the Pennine foot hills, the sea and the Humber which the North-Eastern directors did not control. Hull men did not like the North Eastern in the 'sixties, or subsequently: they said that it cramped them in the interest of more favoured ports farther North. In 1880 they projected a competing line into the York-

[1] See vol. I. p. 390–5.
[2] Tomlinson, *op. cit.* p. 493, 507, 548. The *D.N.B.* He returned to England later and died in 1871.
[3] Until 1851, the Leeds and Thirsk.

shire coalfields. It was opened as the Hull, Barnsley and West Riding in 1885[1].

Another and greater territorial monopoly had been discussed in 1848, when the companies, suffering from trade depression, were trying to reduce their working and fighting costs. A series of conferences was held between representatives of the North-Western, the Great-Western and the South-Western. Complete amalgamation, which would have put nearly all the western side of the country under a single control, was discussed, but no bill was promoted. When special meetings of the share-holders of all three companies had already been summoned to discuss the representatives' proposals, those proposals were abandoned because Carr Glyn and his board stood out for a North-Western predominance in the new company, which the two other parties to the negotiation would not accept[2].

In the years during which the North-Eastern was coming together there was talk of other great amalgamations. One of the plans might have produced, seventy years in advance of the fact, something very like the existing London Midland and Scottish, by an amalgamation of the North-Western, the Mid-land, and the North Staffordshire, which would have controlled a sixth of the mileage then existing in the United Kingdom. Another would have absorbed the Brighton line into the South-Western, a step towards the existing Southern[3]. Neither plan was carried through, although "the most experienced and the most able of the gentlemen connected with the management of the railways," in the early 'fifties, were decidedly favourable to amalgamation, and the notion of "perhaps seven" regulated monopoly areas for Great Britain was already familiar[4]. Railway opinion, however, was not clear about this notion and parliamentary opinion was definitely hostile. "No such engagement can in reason be asked for from Parliament," the Committee of 1853 reported, "nor would it be of any enduring value if it were given."[5] Next year, under the odd working of the Private Bill system, something very like an unregulated

---

[1] For the North-Eastern, Tomlinson, *passim*; for the Hull and Barnsley, Sherrington, *op. cit.* I. 124; for Hull and the N.E.R. at an earlier date, the evidence of H. J. Atkinson, Mayor of Hull, before the *R.C. on Railways*, 1867, Q. 881 *sqq.*

[2] MacDermott, E. T., *History of the Great Western Railway* (1927), I. 307; a fuller account than that in Cleveland-Stevens, *op. cit.* p. 171.

[3] *S.C. on Railway and Canal Bills*, 1852–3 (xxxviii), App. viii; *S.C. on Railway Companies' Amalgamations*, 1872 (xiii. parts 1 and 2), App. A; Cleveland-Stevens, p. 179–80.

[4] *S.C. of 1852–3. Fifth Report*, p. 3, 5.     [5] *Ibid.* p. 6.

monopoly area was given to the North-Eastern, which was never taken from it.

This Act, of July, 1854, sanctioned the only large-scale amalgamation of the 'fifties. In four out of the ten years there was not even a single small amalgamation. With the early 'sixties the movement was resumed. While the North-Eastern was absorbing the Newcastle and Carlisle, and fighting before absorbing the Stockton and Darlington, another almost complete monopoly area came into being in East Anglia by the establishment of the Great Eastern (1862; 25 and 26 Vict. c. 223). Its trunk, the old Eastern Counties, had been for years an ugly duckling of the railway world and a butt for public humour. No one had objected to the attempt made, in 1854, towards greater efficiency of service in a rural area, when the Eastern Counties was allowed to manage two adjacent lines, the Norfolk and the Eastern Union. It was merely a further stage in the end to end combination by which these small railways had themselves been made; the Norfolk, for example, by union of the Yarmouth and Norwich with the Norwich and Brandon. Indeed the bill of 1854 foreshadowed the complete arrangement of 1862 quite distinctly, reference being made in it to ultimate absorption of the two other constituent lines of the future Great Eastern, the East Anglian and the Newmarket. So the consummation of the union stirred no interest except among the shareholders of five unprosperous concerns. The outside world wished them and East Anglia better luck[1].

Large-scale amalgamation, or leasing of the lines of one company to another, went on steadily down to 1866. In 1863 the Great Western added nearly 400 miles to its system by taking over the West Midland and the South Wales; and the North-Eastern, as has been seen, annexed the Stockton and Darlington. Nothing striking happened in 1864; but 1865–6 were great amalgamation years in Scotland, the Caledonian and the North British absorbing many hundred miles of other companies' lines. The financial crisis of 1866 checked this form of enterprise. By 1870 the railway system was all but stabilised. The London and North-Western, in length of line and relations with its neighbours, had become very much what it remained when welded into the London Midland and Scottish of 1923[2].

---

[1] Cleveland-Stevens, *op. cit.* ch. ix, especially p. 221, 225; Tomlinson, *op. cit.* ch. xiv; Acworth, *op, cit.* ch. x; Sherrington, *op. cit.* I. 130–1.

[2] Cleveland-Stevens, *op. cit.* p. 227 (table of amalgamations in the 'sixties), 236–7; Sherrington, *op. cit.* I. 91 (the L.N.W.R.).

Stabilisation was not planned by the railway strategists. In part it just happened; in great part it was imposed on them. In 1867 the Midland, not yet at Carlisle, was dreaming of an amalgamation with the Glasgow and South-Western, which would be useful when it got there. Its dream was only dissipated in the Lords. After that it courted the Great Northern and the Manchester, Sheffield and Lincolnshire. There was always prospect of a revived Scottish alliance, when it should reach Carlisle. So the North-Western manœuvred for position and announced, late in 1871, that it would unite with the Lancashire and Yorkshire. The alliance was most natural. East and West the two companies might be needlessly competitive. North and South they were obviously complementary. For years their relations had been of necessity close, and as a rule amicable. There had been a series of ten-year traffic treaties between them, one of which was just running out. Natural as the alliance might be, it alarmed all adjacent or competitive lines. The fighting chairmen and the general managers who dominated their chairmen began to stir—Edward Watkin, of the Manchester, Sheffield and Lincolnshire and other lines, who spent a restless life in extending and amalgamating companies which rarely paid much to the ordinary shareholder; James Allport, who managed the Midland with patent success from 1853 to 1857, and again from 1860 to 1880[1].

Parliament and the public became uneasy about monopoly. Chambers of Commerce petitioned. A Select Committee of both Houses inquired into the whole matter in 1872. In the marginal analysis of its conclusions occurs the heading—'Amalgamation inevitable; and perhaps desirable.' The attitude thus disclosed raised the hopes of the North-Western projectors, who had withdrawn their bill for the time. But the opinions of nineteenth-century committees and commissions of inquiry were always singularly bad indications of what was likely to happen to particular railway bills. This one was thrown out in 1873. The evidence of opponents was never even called: the preamble, it was said, was not proved. With it was rejected a new bill for the amalgamation of the Midland and the Glasgow and South-Western. This blocked the amalgamation movement finally. Minor absorptions went on. Edward

[1] Watkin's evidence before the *S.C. on Railway Amalgamations*, 1872, Q. 4542*sqq.* Cleveland-Stevens, *op. cit.* p. 233, 239, 241, 296, 309; Jackman, W. T., *Transportation in Modern England*, II. 601; Stretton, *op. cit.* p. 280.

Watkin schemed and negotiated. There were fights and alliances, leases of lines and traffic agreements, but no important change in the railway map before the 'nineties[1].

Since very early days the lease, the alliance, and the traffic agreement had prepared the way for complete amalgamation, or had secured for non-amalgamated companies many of its benefits—for the public, as some argued, all its disadvantages. Even in 1852, the five rail and water routes between Liverpool and Manchester had "more or less a common understanding ...no rivalry exists bearing any analogy to the...competition of private individuals contending in the same trade."[2] At that date the London and North-Western and the Great Northern had a regular agreement about the division of traffic at certain competing points, with an arbitration clause in case of difference. Further East, the Great Northern and the Eastern Counties had an agreement "putting an end to any real competition." These compacts, which the Committee of 1852–3 reported, perhaps slightly exaggerating their real efficiency, were "only examples...of the general tendency"[3]; and of the generality of the tendency throughout the period there can be no doubt. When some change in the railway balance of power was threatened, such as a Midland line to London or to Carlisle, there was sure to be a fight, at least in the parliamentary committee, and perhaps for a time on the permanent ways. But co-operation soon reasserted itself, if never completely. Rate wars were a proved waste and were always dropped. There remained competition for access to bits of territory still unoccupied, and much competition in facilities; for the rest, local and general agreements of all grades up to those hardly distinguishable from amalgamations, like the ten-year treaties between the North-Western and the Lancashire and Yorkshire.

Co-operation had been much encouraged by the early establishment and quick development of the Railway Clearing House. Started in 1842 by "a few of the narrow gauge companies,"[4] in imitation of the Bankers' Clearing House, its

---

[1] See *Report of* 1872; and for the bills of 1873, Cleveland-Stephens, p. 241–2. For (Sir Edward) Watkin and Allport, the *D.N.B.*

[2] *S.C. of* 1853, p. 4. And see vol. I. p. 415, 418.    [3] *Ibid.* p. 4, 5.

[4] *R.C. on Railways*, 1867, p. xviii, with the wrong date 1847 (copied in the *S.C. of* 1872, p. x, and naturally by Cohn, *Englische Eisenbahnpolitik*, I. 262). See Morrison, K., *The Origin and Results of the Clearing System* (1846); the chapter on the Clearing House in Lardner, D., *Railway Economy* (1850); and especially the discussion in Cleveland-Stevens, *op. cit.* p. 173 sqq. The early years of the Clearing House are obscure.

business was to facilitate through traffic and adjust the debts arising from through booking. By 1849 it included "all the railways of the kingdom, except the Great Western, the South-Western, the London, Brighton and South Coast, the South-Eastern and their branches and collateral lines"[1]; that is the broad gauge lines and the lines for which at that time long distance through traffic was impracticable. Within the 'cleared' area, through booking and through movement of waggons were universal. Carr Glyn and Denison, Watkin and Allport, might brief their gladiators for the committee room; but all the time Clearing House clerks in Euston Square and Clearing House agents up and down the country were balancing accounts, tracking consignments and taking the numbers of migrant waggons or tarpaulins, working the railways as an inevitably co-operative group. The system seemed so promising and efficient to Dionysius Lardner, in 1850, that he contemplated the possibility of the Clearing House growing into "an establishment for the maintenance of a general locomotive and carrying stock for the use of all the railways,"[2] a most rational ambition which was never realised.

At that time, as has been seen, a few people, possibly inspired from France, were toying with the notion not of a common rolling stock, but of regulated monopoly areas—"perhaps seven."[3] This was before the North-Eastern had created such an area. The notion revives from time to time in the railway discussions of the next thirty years. Before the Committee of 1872, both Allport and Watkin spoke in favour of what the Report called "districting," how far in the interests of the nation, and how far in those of the Midland or the Manchester, Sheffield and Lincolnshire, is not at this date worth determining. The committee observed curtly that it could not recommend any "attempt to make a new railway map,"[4] and left it at that.

As old as the notion of monopoly areas, though less vigorous, and like it a product of the reaction following the fever of 1845–7, was a suggested "union of all railway property...in one stock."[5] Its main object was to improve the security of shareholders. Neither its detailed working-out nor its implications were ever fully discussed. It remained purely notional.

So for that matter did railway nationalisation proper; but it has a more vivid history. Praised by a handful of experts in

[1] Lardner, p. 153.  [2] Ibid. p. 164.  [3] S.C. Report of 1852–3, p. 5.
[4] Report, p. xli.  [5] Report of 1853, p. 6.

the 'forties, it had been embalmed in the Act of 1844. After twenty-one years, the state might buy up any railway built since the Act[1]. For twenty years, as was natural, there was little talk about the mummy. But Edwin Chadwick, that uncompromising innovator and centraliser, had praised state control of railways before the Statistical Society in 1859; and there were other critics of railway management and monopoly in the early 'sixties. Most remarkable among them was Walter Bagehot, who had taken over the editorship of the *Economist* in 1860[2]. In December, 1864, an article on *The forgotten Act of 1844* revived memory of the repurchase clause[3]. It might be utilised as from October, 1865. Let it be considered, Bagehot argued. "No one would...suggest a wholesale purchase of the English railways. But if it was proved to be desirable it might begin...." He talked of railway monopoly and of the penny post. On January 7, 1865, he resumed under the title *The Advantages that would accrue from an ownership of the railways by the State*. His tentative notion was state ownership and co-ordination of the lines, with terminable leases to commercial working companies. "The present mode of railway management may be described as that in which trading management is at its worst": railway Boards have "many of the defects of Government Boards." Their members are peers and M.P.'s and merchants, everything but practical railway men. "Granting that a State purchase would be exceedingly beneficial, it becomes the plain duty of the Executive Government to *inquire* whether that transfer cannot be effected." Those were his closing words.

Whether the Royal Commission of 1865–7 would have inquired with more sympathy had its sittings not been cut across by a commercial crisis cannot be ascertained; but the probability is that it would not. The policies of repurchase, state control, and leasing were fully laid before it. It heard Chadwick, possibly with some impatience, for that ageing and

[1] Vol. 1. p. 418-19.

[2] Chadwick's paper is in *S.J.* XXII. 381. It has the characteristic title "Results of Different Principles of Legislation and Administration in Europe: of Competition for the Field, as compared with Competition within the Field, of Service"; it deals with regulated monopoly areas for public services. See other critics quoted in Cohn, *op. cit.* 1. 348. They are less important than Bagehot, whom Cohn does not quote.

[3] *Economist*, December 10, 1844. The present editor of the *Economist* agrees that these leading articles must be Bagehot's. They are not signed but the style suggests him. Even if they were not his composition, their policy would be his; but there is no precise record in the office.

omniscient Benthamite was dogmatic and tiresome[1]. It received an able memorandum from Rowland Hill, a commissioner, who finally put in a separate report in favour of the leasing system[2]. George Bidder, the 'calculating boy' become a railway engineer and director, having advocated the amalgamation of all the Irish lines, admitted that his argument applied "in some respects" to England. The state, he thought, might perhaps secure financial control by guaranteeing the prior charges of the railway companies and leaving the management and the common stock free[3]. All this the Commission heard, but its decision was simply "that it is inexpedient at present to subvert the policy which has hitherto been adopted."[4]

Once again, in 1872, advocates of systems approaching nationalisation were given an opportunity. Rowland Hill, now a very old man, was not called, but Captain Tyler, inspector of railways under the Board of Trade, was examined on an important memorandum which he had submitted. He was all for rigid control, though he did not "wish to appear here to advocate state purchase." He finished his evidence, in words much quoted at the time, "and then the question arises at last, whether the State shall manage the railways, or whether the railways shall manage the State."[5] Various business men, especially a Liverpool group, gave evidence in favour of nationalisation, or at least thorough state control. The *Economist* had been writing about "the expediency of inserting new conditions providing for compulsory purchase in the railway amalgamation bills." In discussing a quarrel between traders and the North-Eastern Railway, it had argued that the possession of that monopoly area by the state "would clearly be more advantageous to the public than its possession by a joint-stock company."[6] But in its final report this very strong and most representative joint committee of the Lords and Commons said that there was no "present necessity" to discuss state purchase[7]. The historian may agree with them.

"It is an admitted principle of political economy," Bagehot had written in 1864, "that all monopolies granted by the State ought to be under the superintendence or correction of the

---

[1] *R.C. on Railways*, 1867, Q. 17,179 *sqq.*      [2] *Ibid.* p. cvii.
[3] His evidence is Q. 4213 *sqq.*: the quotation is from Q. 4301.
[4] *Report*, p. xxxvii.
[5] *S.C. on Railway Companies Amalgamation*, Q. 7020.
[6] Title of an article of Feb. 10, 1872, and quotation from one of Oct. 5, 1872
[7] *S.C. on Railway Companies Amalgamation*, p. xxxi.

State."[1] The state, which for good reasons was not willing to buy out the railway monopoly, blundered along into the 'eighties, sometimes assuming that there was no monopoly, at others that all things considered there was rather an efficient one. In this it was probably right. Meanwhile it had exercised a minimum of "superintendence and correction." Ever since Peel threw over Dalhousie in 1845[2], there had been no considered attempt to guide the territorial development of the railway system. Each project was a special case for the investor, the railway barrister, and the private bill committee. There had been no serious attempt to guide technical development, even on the vital question of the gauge. Talk of guidance there had been; but as the committee of 1853 had written, in pathetic helplessness, "what Parliament had...undertaken to settle by general legislation, Parliament, in compliance with the findings of Private Committees...forthwith proceeded to unsettle."[3]

To one matter at least Parliament had given real if limited attention—safety of travel. Since 1842 (5 and 6 Vict. c. 55) the obligation to inspect new lines and forbid their opening for traffic if they proved unsatisfactory had rested with the Board of Trade[4]. Its inspectors were the first and only permanent link between the railways and the state. They had to report on accidents also; but for nearly thirty years they had no compulsory powers. Until the passing of the Regulation of Railways Act of 1871 (34 and 35 Vict. c. 78) they must beg their information from the companies. Still, their reports kept before the public mind and before the companies the need for safety devices of all sorts. How far they influenced railway policy is hard to say; but at least their statistics of accidents, especially the accidents to railway men in the shunting yards, were there for all to read. Not many read, and in the matter of shunting fewer acted. Meanwhile, for the traveller, the British railways became remarkably safe, as compared with those of most other countries, or with most other forms of transport; so the companies always had a case, even when criticising the introduction of a safety device of such obvious merit as the block system.

Long known and advocated, this system was resisted by most of the great railwaymen of the 'sixties. About a fifth of the British mileage was under it in 1870, but that mileage was

<hr />

[1] *Economist*, December 10, 1864.    [2] Vol. I. p. 423.    [3] *Report*, p. 13.
[4] See Cohn, *op. cit.* II. 219*sqq*. Cleveland-Stevens, *op. cit.* p. 76–7. There was an earlier Act dealing with safety, of 1840 (3 and 4 Vict. c. 97).

mainly of the second rank[1]. The North-Eastern, for example, had only 48 miles of line under the 'absolute' block system[2]. However, in 1871 steps were taken by the North-Eastern towards its general introduction. During the 'seventies it made rapid progress almost everywhere. More than a quarter of the North-Western was 'blocked' by 1872, and another fifth was in hand for 'blocking.'[3] So when Lord Buckhurst brought a Bill into the Lords in 1873 to make the system compulsory, critics could argue fairly that he was wasting effort. The Bill never became law. Compulsion was not applied to the outstanding minority of the railway mileage until 1889 (52 and 53 Vict. c. 57). The same Act imposed at length on all passenger trains the fitting of continuous brakes. By that time it was again only a case of whipping in the laggards. At least two well-tested types of continuous brake had been available twelve or fifteen years earlier[4]. Since 1877, Captain Tyler and the Board of Trade had been pressing their use on the companies, after an accident in that year at Morpeth in which their presence would have saved life. They were soon fitted on expresses, and by the mid 'eighties only inferior 'parliamentary' trains, or the small backward lines, were without them. At length the law compelled every one to do what nearly everyone was already doing.

The reluctance of the state, that is to say the statesmen, to prescribe in these technical matters is more explicable than some other of their reluctances. There was always the risk that prescription on the technical side might mean petrification; and it was only the railways, not the state, which could experiment. Among less explicable reluctances is the sustained one to touch railway rates and charges. Quite indefensible at first sight, closer inspection reveals two important lines of defence. First: the economics and ethics of railway charges, nowhere simple, are for geographical reasons especially complex in Britain, as committees and commissions soon found out. Second: since no British railway ever made very large profits, it was never possible to prove a general abuse of monopoly, however loudly particular abuses might be alleged. The initial action of the state, determined by inevitable ignorance married to lack of imagination, had been so primitive and casual that such alle-

[1] *E.g.* the London and Brighton, Cohn, *op. cit.* II. 210.
[2] Tomlinson, *op. cit.* p. 649.
[3] Cawkwell's evidence before the *S.C.* of 1872, Q. 1256 *sqq.*
[4] Sherrington, *op. cit.* I. 239.

gations began very early. In this matter of their charges, the railway companies, it will be recalled, were treated like the canal companies[1]. Short schedules of maximum tolls, to be levied on goods classified in a few rough categories, were inserted in the bills to which they owed their existence. These maxima were so high that they soon became futile, and there was no law against the greatest variety of charges within them. In 1845 the average charge of twenty-two companies for actually moving coal was 1·83$d$. per ton-mile[2]. Many of these companies were entitled by their schedules to charge a toll of 1·5$d$. for letting other people move it—which no one ever did. The 'parliamentary' 1$d$. a mile in a third-class stopping train, fixed in 1844, was below the then existing maxima but was nevertheless fairly high, as was shown in later years when the companies found that they could profitably move people faster and with infinitely greater conveniences at the same price.

No one ever complained of cheap excursion rates far below the penny, to attract those who otherwise might not have travelled at all; but when the companies applied this principle of 'charging what the traffic will bear' to goods, offering, for example, very low rates to consignments which otherwise might have gone by water, there was likely to be complaint from the waterless places, who attributed to railway vice what should have been attributed to Britain's good fortune in being an island with a much indented coastline. It was reckoned that goods charges from three-fifths of the stations in the country were affected by the competition of transport by sea[3]. Must the railways lower all their rates because they were forced unwillingly to keep three-fifths of them competitive with those of the cargo boats?

Supervision and revision of charges, and a public facing of such problems, might have been very suitable functions for the Commissioners of Railways created in August 1846 by 9 and 10 Vict. c. 105, when Parliament was feeling uneasily that the new railway jungle ought to be policed somehow[4]. But although these Commissioners issued some very valuable reports, they were given no executive powers at the start, and had never been given any when they were abolished without discussion in 1851 (by 14 and 15 Vict. c. 64), mainly for economy's sake. Their reporting and statistical functions reverted to the Board

---

[1] Vol. I. p. 414–15.
[2] Graham, W. A., in *S.J.* VIII. 222.
[3] *Report of* 1872, p. xix.
[4] Vol. I. p. 424.

of Trade, whose President, Labouchere, was both their chairman and their executioner. The Commissioners having been abolished just when they were learning their way about the jungle, it was easy and correct to argue, when railway regulation was again being discussed in 1853, that there was "no public department sufficiently educated to take the command."[1] Interest still centred in the problems of amalgamation, of the grant of 'running powers' to one company over the lines of another, and of the control of canals by the railways; but the Committee of 1853 also referred, with a touch of censure, to the "special favour" often shown by the companies "to particular classes of traffic," and suggested that the ordinary courts of law were not well qualified to settle the resulting disputes[2]. Much of the work of the Committee was wasted, but this reference bore fruit in the Act of 1854 (17 and 18 Vict. c. 31) which forbade railway companies "to make or give any undue or unreasonable preference or advantage to or in favour of any particular person or company, or any particular description of traffic." Here were many words to be interpreted by the Court of Common Pleas, to which the jurisdiction was assigned. But the Act was not much used, and the Court was neither very ardent nor very competent to interpret it. It did, however, decide, in the case of Ransome v. the Eastern Counties Railway, that preference given to the traffic of a place—to meet water competition, perhaps—was not "undue or unreasonable," though preference given to a person would have been[3]. And it is probable that the mere existence of the law acted as a deterrent to railway managers, when tempted to favour "particular persons or companies." Little is heard of personal favour after 1854[4].

The railways' toll-schedules, as has been seen, were crude and useless. They said nothing about haulage charges and nothing about charges for loading, unloading, and other terminal services. To meet the crudities of the toll-schedules, the Clearing House worked out an elaborate classification of goods for the use of all the lines—so great a convenience that the Commission of 1865–7 wished the state to adopt it bodily[5].

---

[1] S.C. on Railway and Canal Bills: evidence of Baxter, "an eminent railway solicitor," Q. 3496.　　　　　[2] Ibid. Report, p. 12.

[3] Case quoted in the report of the R.C. on Railways, 1867, p. xlviii.

[4] Hadley, A. T., Railroad Transportation, its History and its Laws (1885), p. 183. Cleveland-Stevens, op. cit. p. 195.

[5] Report, p. lxvii.

Like most of the wishes of that Commission, this was neglected. Twice during the 'sixties, in 1861 and 1866, the companies tried to secure Parliament's approval for the system of 'terminals.'[1] They were prepared to accept classified maxima in return for a statutory recognition of the principle. Twice they failed, and terminals remained an unregulated cause of friction and sometimes of complaint. Though perfectly defensible, provided they are not excessive, they continued to surprise parliamentary committees down to the 'eighties by their mere existence. Charges "alleged to be in excess of the maximum," said a Select Committee of 1882 naively, are defended by reference to "what is called 'terminals.'"[2]

The Committee of 1872, which considered amalgamation "inevitable and perhaps desirable," yet saw no "present necessity" to discuss state purchase or to "make a new railway map," was worried by the question of rates. A new classification on the Clearing House basis, it said, would be good. Equal mileage rates, which had been suggested, would be impracticable and bad. Terminals were hard to regulate: they might cover such varied services. "Undue preference" was a difficult conception; and so on. The one thing that they were quite clear about was that an expert tribunal, not an ordinary court of law, was needed to deal with disputes arising out of railway legislation. Parliament agreed, or half agreed. It passed the Act of 1873, "to make better provision for carrying into effect the Railway and Canal Traffic Act, 1854, and for other purposes connected therewith" (36 and 37 Vict. c. 48), the Act which set up the Railway and Canal Commission of three[3].

The Committee had thought of a strong permanent body with full powers, what Denison of the Great Northern called in the House "a sort of Railway Star Chamber."[4] They only got a five-year Commission, which was prolonged thereafter from year to year until 1888. It did something to prevent "undue preference" and encourage "reasonable facilities." But its life was uncertain. Its powers were limited. In its early years companies could defy it. Its injunctions could only affect the particular case tried, and the future. It could be appealed against, and could be called upon by the higher courts to "state

[1] *Report*, p. xxii.  [2] *S.C. on Railways (Rates and Fares)*, 1882, XIII. 1, p. iii.
[3] The fullest account of the Act is in Cohn, *op. cit.* III. 131 *sqq.* The Commissioners issued annual reports from 1875, *e.g.* 1876, XXI. 275.
[4] Hansard n.s. ccxv. 367, quoted in Cleveland-Stevens, *op. cit.* p. 274.

a case" as to whether a given matter was or was not within its jurisdiction. All this opened doors wide to the trained and well-paid legal forces of the companies. Few cared to fight them—not even the War Office[1].

The British railways of the early 'eighties, if conservative and rather arrogant[2], were neither generally inefficient nor corrupt. Manufacturers and traders criticised them and invested in them impartially. It may be doubted whether there was a comfortable family in the country which did not hold railway shares. So the companies were very strong in face of criticism. However, general prices had been falling for years. Looking about in its *malaise*, the trading community saw some real abuses on the railways; a great many things which it did not understand that looked like abuses; and a government mechanism for checking abuse—real or potential—which was unmistakably inadequate. At all costs traders wanted lower rates or better facilities, or a combination of the two, to meet the needs of the time. They alleged that they got neither, or that the wrong people—importers of foreign goods in bulk, perhaps—got both. Interest was now concentrated on prices; and it is significant that the first important parliamentary committee on railways in the 'eighties, that of 1881–2, was appointed simply to discuss Rates and Fares.

It dealt with most of the old questions—the need for a uniform classification of goods; the supposed evils of railway control of canals; the mystery of the terminals. It suggested that terminals should be recognised but published—what the railways had asked for twenty-one years earlier—and that they should be challengeable before the Commission. It even had the boldness to propose that the select committees which dealt with railway bills should take up this complex question of rates and fares. But its main wish was to see the Commission strengthened, made permanent, and made a Court of Record. Its scope ought to be widened. The right of appeal from its decisions ought to be curtailed[3]. To balance the weight of the

[1] *S.C. on Railway Rates and Fares*, 1882, Q. 5965. For the general history of the Commission, 1874–86, see Hadley, *op. cit.* p. 173 *sqq.* Cleveland-Stevens, *op. cit.* p. 270 *sqq.*

[2] Their arrogance, especially towards the Commission, greatly impressed the American observer, Hadley.

[3] In fact, in the first nine years of its existence (1874–82) the Commission decided 110 cases: there were only 17 appeals: only 6 successful appeals. Hadley, *op. cit.* p. 177.

companies, collective bodies such as Chambers of Commerce, not merely individual traders with a grievance, ought to have the right to appear before it by counsel. The Chambers, it should be noted, had been, and continued to be, active exponents of the traders' grievances. They now had an Association which, although it did not yet include London or Manchester or Liverpool or Edinburgh or Glasgow, could speak for forty-nine industrial communities, headed by Birmingham, Sheffield and Leeds[1]. Nothing was done in 1882. The business world remained uncomfortable and unappeased—prices were still falling—and Birmingham, in the formidable person of Joseph Chamberlain, Birmingham which had no sea facilities and no reverence for vested interests, was at the Board of Trade.

There was a pause; and then, in 1884, Chamberlain tabled a bill to extend the powers of the Commissioners[2]. It was not passed or even discussed; but it seemed so terrible to the boards of directors that a Railway Companies' Association was created to fight it[3]. As a counter-move to this bill, the great companies, acting together, prepared bills of their own for 1885, which interpreted the wishes of the Committee of 1881-2 about railway charges as the railways understood them. The traders rose in opposition: it was said that the object was to raise goods rates all round and legalise preferential treatment of foreign imports. Though this may not have been true, the object certainly was not to lower goods rates, which was what the traders would have wished. Once more railway business was crowded out in Parliament—Gladstone fell in June. The spring of 1886 saw him back with his Home Rule plans, and saw the companies beating up opposition to another Board of Trade bill, Chamberlain's modified and become Mundella's; for Chamberlain had just parted with Gladstone over Home Rule. Two years of political turmoil were to go by before a very different government found time to see a bill through[4]. It was at least evident in 1885-6 that a bill was coming, and that goods rates would not much longer be regulated only by antiquated maximum tolls and a few score of specific decisions in the courts or by the Commission. Railwaymen said that when Government did touch those millions of distinct, empirically determined, rates

[1] See its memorandum in the *Report of* 1882: App. 20, p. 395.
[2] "To amend the Regulation of Railways Acts and for other Purposes," 1884, VI. 333.
[3] See Grinling, *The Great Northern Railway*, p. 369.
[4] The Railway and Canal Traffic Act, 1888 (51 and 52 Vict. c. 25).

—manure from Cavendish to Long Melford; matches from London to Aberdeen—Government would burn its fingers[1]. They were not entirely wrong.

From 1846 to 1882, no Committee or Commission on the railways ever failed to discuss the fortunes of the canals[2]. And all the time the fortunes of the canals declined. After 1852 there was very little change in the mileage of railway-owned or railway-controlled canal, so that the map prepared for the Committee of 1872 represents with substantial accuracy the geographical position as it was throughout the period[3]. In view of all that was said at the time, and has been said since, about the destruction of water transport by railway control, the most remarkable feature of the map is the great network of canals and navigations which never was controlled. It was always possible to go by railway-free canal from London to Gloucester, Birmingham, Leicester, Newark and the Humber basin. The link canals between Trent, Severn and Mersey were in railway hands; but the chief of them, the Trent and Mersey (Grand Trunk), had not been captured by the North Staffordshire Railway but had made it[4], and remained in alliance with it. The canals across the Pennines had also fallen under railway control[5]; but it was never likely that much trade would pass from Yorkshire to Lancashire up 45 locks and down 54, and those not all of a size, once it became possible to send it in two hours by rail, and by railway siding into the works or up to the coal pit. Eastward from the West Riding manufacturing area, the Aire and Calder Navigation was never beaten. It was apparently the only canal which was "still spending large sums on improvements" in 1872[6]. The reason is simple. Its head

---

[1] See the opinions quoted in Grinling, *op. cit.* p. 374, where these years are discussed from the railway side. Cp. Acworth, W. M., *The Railways and the Traders*, 1891, a discussion, also sympathetic to the railways, by the best railway economist in England.

[2] *I.e.* from the *S.C. on Amalgamations of Railways and Canals*, 1846, XIII. 85 to the *S.C. on Railway Rates and Fares* of 1882. There was also a special *S.C. on Canals* in 1883 (XIII. 1). For the early period cp. vol. I. p. 398–9.

[3] See map at www.cambridge.org/9780521101004. The Kennet and Avon Canal was taken over by the Great Western Railway in 1852.

[4] Vol. I. p. 399.

[5] Between 1872 and 1883, however, the Leeds and Liverpool Canal and the Rochdale Canal came out of railway control, by expiry of leases. *S.C. on Canals*, p. 4, and below, p. 200.

[6] *S.C. on Amalgamations*, p. xxi.

offices in Leeds are about a hundred feet above sea-level: coal goes down it, timber and other bulky cargoes come up it, in quantities to this day[1]. On the other side of the Pennines, below most of the locks, the Bridgewater canals, though narrow and antiquated, did continuously good business until absorbed by the Manchester Ship Canal Company in 1887. The Weaver Navigation has always carried coal, salt and chemicals across the Cheshire flats. Squth of Birmingham, the Stourbridge and some other independent canals did well for years: "dividends of 16 and 12 per cent." are even heard of in the boom of 1872[2].

Prosperous canals were exceptional, not because of illicit railway devices, though there were such, but because of the sheer superiority of the railway as a means of transport. Of this there is no better illustration than the Fen Country. No railway ever controlled a furlong of its innumerable waterways, except the Witham Navigation from Boston to Lincoln. Locks were few. The whole of the country was waterish. For centuries, timber, coal and wine had been handled at Lynn and Wisbech, and there was a well-organised distributing trade from the heads of navigation. "By these Navigable Rivers," Defoe had written, "the Merchants of Lynn supply about six Counties wholly, and three Counties in part."[3] The railways came slowly into this 'marshy ground' and they were wide spaced. Yet they won with ease. The coal trade at Cambridge, Peterborough and Ely was soon based on the new railway stations. Cellars at Wisbech were still well stocked, but not now with wine which had come up the Lynn Deeps; and the Cambridge bargee, without whom there could have been no University, was dying out.

Committees and Commissions reiterated the need to keep canals independent of the railways. Almost as often their reports, or the evidence of some thoroughly competent witness, registered the technical inferiority of the average canal. "The railway can always carry cheaper," Donatus O'Brien of the Board of Trade said in 1846[4]. Canals had blackmailed projected railways for fear of their competition, the Committee of

---

[1] Its Secretary, however, complained bitterly of the railways in 1867 (*R.C. on Railways*, Q. 9899 *sqq.*) but then he was also Sec. of the Canal Association and so was bound to complain in any case.

[2] *S.C. on Amalgamations*, as above. The Manchester Ship Canal, which got its first Act in 1885 (48 and 49 Vict. c. 188) falls outside the scope of this volume.

[3] *Tour* (ed. Cole, G. D. H.), I. 73: perhaps a Defoeish exaggeration, but based on fact.

[4] *S.C. on Amalgamations*, Q. 154.

1853 reported[1]. The powerful Committee of 1872 underlined
all occasional canal successes. But its report allowed that canals
could not compete for the long haul, or for valuable cargoes,
though they were efficient carriers of things like London dung.
It was most desirable that they should be kept alive, said the
report. But one could hardly hope to get Parliament "to vote
money (as is done in France) not for the purpose of developing
a profitable traffic, but for the purpose of maintaining a losing
competition with railways."[2] Here the reporters touched the
core. It had never been necessary to ask Parliament to endow
railways. In no country of Europe since the railway was invented had, or have, canals been built by private enterprise[3].
There may be reasons, strategic or commercial-strategic, for
building or remodelling them with public funds; but those
reasons will always be at their weakest in Britain. They were
infinitely weak in Victorian Britain. When the forty-nine
associated Chambers of Commerce memorialised the Committee of 1882 in favour of the canals, they were thinking
vaguely of maintaining that competition with the railways
which had proved so ineffective, and were hoping, it may fairly
be argued, for a cheapness of water transport which only direct
subsidy could create. The Committee merely recommended
that there should be no further control of canals by railways,
an ancient and superfluous piece of advice. Next year yet
another Committee, appointed to discuss canals only, had its
attention called by a Board of Trade witness to that network of
rather unprosperous ones which the railways never had controlled, and to the fact that since 1872 one long and one short
trans-Pennine canal, the Leeds and Liverpool of 144 miles and
the Rochdale of 35, had escaped from the railway grip[4].
Another witness mentioned that the Leeds and Liverpool,
since its freeing in 1874, had reduced its tolls and paid very
good dividends[5]. It crosses the Wigan coalfield between
Liverpool and the hills, so that its plains section is in the same
category as the Aire and Calder and the Bridgewater; and it
can do local short haul traffic along its entire length. Its recent

[1] S.C. on Railway...Bills, p. 11.        [2] S.C. on Amalgamations, p. xxiii.
[3] The late Sir William Acworth, in his last letter to the author, challenged
him to find a single instance. Private enterprise started the Manchester Ship
Canal but public support was required for its completion.
[4] S.C. on Canals, evidence of H. G. Calcraft.
[5] Ibid. Q. 827. Compare Jackman, Transportation in Modern England, II.
661 n. 2.

success was a strong reason for keeping it alive and a proof that, under favourable conditions, inland water transport in Britain still had its uses. It was no proof that public endowment of canals was in the general economic interests of the country.

Technically, the canals retained nearly all their old defects. With very few exceptions, such as the Aire and Calder Navigation, they had merely kept up the original works—with their different widths, their different depths, their locks of all sizes and occasional narrow tunnels[1]. The canal boat, the 'flat,' of one-horse power the wags said, was as standardised and unvarying as the state coach. On the coalfields it still had plenty of short haul work to do. To the quiet basin at Paddington it brought in Middlesex hay for the mews, and it took out London dung; but the term 'Paddington coal' had long since gone out of use[2]. Most of the landward coal rumbled into London by rail east of the Edgeware Road.

Parliamentary committees usually thought it as desirable that canals should unite as that railways should not; but though there were a few amalgamations[3], there was not vitality enough for an amalgamation movement. Apart from a few local groups of business men, investors were no longer interested in canals, and it would have been hard to raise capital for them. In 1855 *Fenn on the Funds* still tabulated in an Appendix twenty-six canals about which the general investor might be supposed to care. They ranged from the Stourbridge with its 12 per cent. dividend, through the Derby with $6\frac{1}{2}$, the Grand Junction and the Birmingham each with 4 (the latter guaranteed by the London and North-Western Railway) to the 10s. of the Wiltshire and Berkshire and the 6s. of the Kennet and Avon. In 1883 the thirteenth edition of *Fenn on the Funds* did not think it necessary to mention any canal except that of Suez.

By the 'eighties, the small impersonal group of the railway companies rivalled the large and varied personal group of the makers of machines as direct employers of labour, though railway work could not compare with agriculture, building, coal-mining or the textile industries. From 65,000 in 1851, the male railway workers of all sorts had grown to 174,000 at the

---

[1] Vol. i. p. 82.                                    [2] Vol. i. p. 283.

[3] *E.g.* the Leeds and Liverpool Canal and the Aire and Calder Navigation jointly acquired the short Bradford Canal in 1878. See the summaries of canal history in *R.C. on Canals and Waterways*, 1908, vol. iv. (Returns for all canals).

census of 1881, a growth in almost exact proportion to that of the railway mileage. The machine makers, employed and employers, were returned as 193,000. Though the railwayman dominated the transport business of the country, they formed only a fraction of the steadily growing mass of what the census officials called labour engaged in conveyance. This mass was quite comparable in size with that of the building trades. It contained 750,000 men and boys against their 761,000. Only agriculture was greater. Almost exactly one working man or lad in every twenty was now a conveyancer of some sort; for road conveyance is by nature extravagant of human effort.

A great part of the road users were always attached to special manufactures and trades, including the railways, as collectors and distributors for them. With the decline of the stage waggon and stage coach, general conveyance by road was localised, left to a few large carrying firms, like Pickfords, to many short distance country carriers, and to the cabmen and 'busmen and the new tramwaymen. Down to 1830, the number of 'hackney carriages' which could be licensed in London had been fixed by statute. A law of that year (1 and 2 Wm. IV, c. 22) had removed all restrictions and their numbers had grown fast. In 1881 there may have been 15,000 London 'cabbies.' The trade was always individualistic, its typical figures the owner-driver and the very small cab-proprietor. In 1892, out of about 3600 London proprietors, 3125 owned less than 5 cabs and only 4 more than 100[1]. Three years later, the single really large firm, a new one, giving evidence before a Home Office Committee, had "close upon 300"; but the other witnesses had 40, 34, and 24 respectively, and employer witnesses are always the big men of their trades[2]. London conditions had been reproduced in other towns with the growth, often long delayed, of demand for the cab that plies for hire, as opposed to the 'fly' hired by arrangement from the local liveryman or publican.

While the cab remained a small man's venture, the omnibus came under associated impersonal capital, international capital even. Omnibus owners had been more substantial men than cab proprietors from the first. After twenty years of experiment following George Shillibeer's first London omnibus venture of 1829[3], various lines of some size had grown up under in-

[1] Booth, C., *Life and Labour of the People in London*, VII. 287.
[2] *H.O. Committee on Cabs*, 1895 (XXXV. 1), Q. 992, 6007, 6251, 7239.
[3] Vol. I. p. 385.

dividual proprietors and private companies—Eagles, Favourites, and the like. The year of Corn Law repeal had seen the first twopenny fare and the first advertisements on the 'buses[1]. About that time the lines were co-operating a little; adjusting their runnings to fit one another; agreeing not to cut fares; jointly approaching the Metropolitan Roads Commission to ask for more granite macadam roads instead of the traditional London flint gravel "which destroyed their horses."[2] In 1855 there appeared from Paris the *Compagnie générale des omnibus de Londres*, a *société en commandite*. It was a product of that flamboyant era of Parisian company promotion which is connected with the names of the brothers Pereire, and which ended in the commercial catastrophes of 1857[3]. Perhaps it was appropriate that the London omnibus business should be organised from Paris, for Shillibeer, though he started life as a British midshipman, had been a Parisian coachbuilder, and had brought both the thing and its name with him to London[4]. Within a year of its foundation the company of 1855 had bought up "perhaps a little over half the carriages [omnibuses] in London; and the other proprietors" were "working in connection with them in associations."[5] In 1858 it became a British Limited Liability Company, with Edwin Chadwick as one of its directors. But it retained its Paris office and many French shareholders. It never lost the position gained at the outset. Indeed it improved on it. By 1877 it owned nearly 8000 horses and handled three-quarters of the metropolitan omnibus traffic[6]. There were smaller companies, and intermittent competition from 'pirate' 'buses; but the first serious rival, the London Road Car Company, only came in 1880–1. Within a few years there would be war between them. As yet the General was supreme, and had merely registered the challenge[7].

If the 'bus and the 'bus company were French, the tram and the tramway company, oddly enough, were American. The

[1] Morse, H. C., *Omnibuses and Cabs* (1902), p. 62.

[2] *S.C. on Metropolitan Turnpike Roads*, 1856 (XIV. 79), Q. 1592. Cp. vol. I. p. 92.

[3] See below, p. 364 *sqq*.

[4] Morse, *op. cit.* p. 11 and the *D.N.B.*

[5] *S.C. on ... Turnpike Roads*, Q. 1447.

[6] *S.C. on Tramways (Use of Mechanical Power)*, 1877 (XVI. 445), iii and Q. 2407 *sqq*.

[7] Morse, *op. cit.* p. 100–1. Tramway evidence before *R.C. on Labour*, Group B, 1892 (XXXVI. part 2), Q. 15,746 *sqq*.

cars themselves for a time were American built[1]. It was odd because British railways were still using horse traction here and there, at the time of the first experiments with 'street cars.'[2] But British railways had been kept out of the streets and American railways had not. So the horse-drawn 'street car' came as a new notion, when an American tried one at Birkenhead, late in the 'fifties. By 1861 experiment had begun in London[3]. But the lines started without any regular authorisation in Bayswater, Westminster, and Kennington used a type of rail objectionable to the general traffic, and were pulled up. There was a halt, and then, in 1868, trams were started under a private Act in Liverpool. They succeeded. Next year London was tried again, but not Bayswater. The new lines, also built under private Acts, were the Mile End and Bow Road, the Kennington and Clapham, and the Vauxhall and Greenwich. The police reported favourably on them: so far from obstructing traffic, they were said to have the effect of shepherding the more wayward traffic towards its right side of the road[4]. This all helped the general encouraging and regulating Tramways Act (33 and 34 Vict. c. 78) which went through Parliament in 1870. It worked slowly. For the next sixteen years the average annual addition to British tramways was forty-five miles[5].

There were only 237 miles all told in 1878, when the tramways of Britain had just about as many horses as the London General Omnibus Company. After that they went ahead rather faster. The figures for 1886 are 779 miles and 23,000 horses. Besides, there were 439 steam tram locomotives, a new thing since 1877, when apparently the only line which really used steam traction was one which can still be seen in the grass by the roadside between Wantage Road Station and Wantage[6]. In the 'eighties, steam trams were mainly used on the steep gradients of the industrial North, where they were made.

Meanwhile the main roads of Britain, very little altered in their lay-out or gradients since Telford died in 1834 and

[1] Booth, *Life and Labour*, VII. 310.

[2] There was occasional horse-traction on the North-Eastern until 1864. Tomlinson, *op. cit.* p. 529.

[3] See the Report of Capt. H. W. Tyler, R.E., in App. to *Return of the Board of Trade under the Tramways Act*, 1870; 1871 (LX. 539).

[4] *Return*, as above, p. 14.

[5] *Tramway Returns*, 1895 (LXV. 1017).

[6] It used steam under a Tramway Order of 1876, *S.C. on Tramways*, 1877, Q. 147. The line may have been pulled up of late: it was there a few years ago.

McAdam in 1836, had been slowly brought up to something approaching McAdam's standard of surface, under a varied and halting administration. The slowness must be stressed. Even the Metropolitan Commission, one of the model authorities of the Early Railway Age, which managed all the chief Middlesex roads out of London, though served by three generations of McAdams, had not half its mileage macadamised with broken granite in 1856[1]. Pressure from omnibus owners had been needed to get it even so far. Its gravel roads had "destroyed their horses."[2] It kept its main toll-gates in the 'fifties and 'sixties, though it had moved some of them farther out of town. Each acted as an automatic terminus for the 'bus line[3]. Other Commissions and Consolidated Turnpike Trusts had done similar work; but the breakdown of the country Trusts before railway competition threatened its continuance[4]. Through two generations, after the opening of the Liverpool and Manchester Railway, the state had no considered policy for their fortification or replacement. So the roads waited on the road authority.

Boroughs, reformed by the Whigs, had full power within their bounds. Each at its own pace macadamised; or left muddy side roads mended with cinders; or paved its streets with local stone, or with the new small squared granite 'sets' from Charnwood Forest, Cornwall or Aberdeen. Sets stood the heavy traffic of the industrial towns, and their use was stimulated by tramway enterprise, since nothing holds rails so well. Just as that enterprise got under weigh, at the close of the 'sixties, the first trials of Val de Travers asphalt, "somewhat after the Paris model," were made in the City[5]. Ten years later came the wood block pavements; but neither system was of general application.

Even in the best days of the Turnpikes most British roads, and all the minor roads, had been kept up or neglected by the parishes, under the general supervision of Quarter Sessions. As Trusts decayed and collapsed, these old resistant cells of the national life revived, with that rating power which they had first used centuries back to maintain their parish churches. The Highways Act of 1835 (5 and 6 Wm. IV, c. 50) had

---

[1] See vol. I. p. 93; and for the position in 1856, *S.C. on Met. Turnpike Roads*, Q. 1593-4.
[2] *Ibid*. Q. 1592.  [3] *Ibid*. Q. 82-9.
[4] Vol. I. p. 94; and Webb, S. and B., *The Story of the King's Highway*, p. 192.
[5] Capt. Tyler's report of 1871, as above.

strengthened them: they might pay surveyors and road-workers from the rates: the old obligation on parishioners to survey the roads in turn gratis was abolished, together with the unpaid Statute Labour[1]. The Act, being a Whig Act, weakened rather than stiffened the county control of Quarter Sessions[2], and did nothing to make the parish a fit custodian for roads of national importance; but then the railways were already beginning to make men think that roads were not of national importance, only for local use. By the 'sixties, this would be the official view[3]. Where traffic was really heavy, you had the borough, except in Greater London. There the Metropolitan Commission is found in 1856 defending its toll-gates as the only practical alternative to "the parishes" and the rates[4]. But at that very time, under the Public Health Act of 1848, the first Boards of Health were being created in urban areas other than boroughs[5]. One of their functions, sanitary in origin, was the care of the highways. Such a Board, in Chelsea, had just taken its roads back from the Metropolitan Commission in 1856[6]. A few years later, an attempt was made under an Act of 1862 (25 and 26 Vict. c. 61) to encourage the creation of Highway Districts out of parishes grouped by the Justices in Quarter Sessions. Some grouping was done, but a number of parishes resisted, especially small urban parishes in the North. As a means of resistance, they 'adopted' the Local Government Act of 1858 (21 and 22 Vict. c. 98), which had reinforced the principles of the Public Health Act of 1848, so becoming 'sanitary authorities' with control of their own highways. The sanitary legislation of the 'seventies based rural sanitation on the Poor Law Union which, as a Rural Sanitary District, was to acquire control of the roads; but the creation of Sanitary Districts went on so slowly that more than 5000 parishes, rural and urban, remained supreme highway authorities until 1894.

Meanwhile the broken Turnpike Trusts were disappearing, not because any minister decreed their abolition, but because

---

[1] Cp. vol. I. p. 401–2.    [2] Webb, *op. cit.* p. 202.

[3] See *S.C. on Turnpike Trusts*, 1864 (IX. 331), p. iii, where the essentially local character of all roads is used to defend the policy of charging their upkeep on the local rates. A witness had explained that the Great North Road was now as local as "an ordinary parish highway."

[4] Before the *S.C. on Met. Turnpike Roads*.

[5] For what follows see the expert discussion of the local government problems involved in Webb, *op. cit.* (forming vol. v of *English Local Government*), ch. ix, on which it is mainly based.

[6] *S.C. on Met. Turnpike Roads*, Q. 825, 1593.

their gates annoyed a travelling people. The annoyance is very perceptible in 1856. It is clamorous by 1864[1]. The Highway Districts which might have removed its cause were not a success. These failing, a Committee of the Commons, regularly reappointed from 1871, took upon itself to kill the Trusts in turn as their leases of life came up for renewal, trusting to the Boroughs and Sanitary Boards to take care of the roads[2]. Tolls ceased in London in 1871; but there were still 854 Trusts in Britain. Ten years later there were 184; by 1887 only 15. The last was snuffed out in 1895 in Anglesey[3].

At the time of the Great Exhibition the electric telegraph was very little more than a railway convenience[4]. There were even important railways which had not made use of it. This was soon remedied. Three years later, eight out of the seventeen London telegraph offices were at the railway stations. This blending of railway and general telegraphy continued down to 1870. By 1854, business was developing and telegraph competition had begun. To the pioneer company, the Electric and International of 1846, had been added the British and Irish Magnetic. Others had been sanctioned or were in prospect[5]. Abroad, except in America, the state had everywhere taken control of the telegraph. In Belgium and Switzerland it was being worked satisfactorily by the Post Office. So obvious a solution attracted not only the more ambitious Post Office officials, flushed with the success of the penny post, but also leading inventors and promoters. Thomas Allan, an electrician who in 1851 had secured an Act authorising a company which was to levy "a uniform rate of charge irrespective of distance,"[6] published his *Reasons for the Government annexing an Electric Telegraph System to the General Post Office* in 1854. His company was still in abeyance: it only got started, as the United Kingdom Telegraph Company, in 1861. In 1856 a Post Office official[7] submitted to the Treasury a detailed plan for a nationalised telegraph system. In 1861 no less a man than J. L. Ricardo, M.P. for Stoke, Chairman of the North

---

[1] *S.C. on Turnpike Trusts*, 1864; evidence, *passim*.

[2] Such a policy was adumbrated by the S.C. of 1864; *Report*, p. iv.

[3] Webb, *op. cit.* p. 222.　　　　[4] Vol. I. p. 395–6.

[5] *Return of all...Telegraph Companies*, 1860 (LXII. 189).　　[6] *Ibid.* p. 14.

[7] Mr Baines. In the *Reports by Mr Scudamore on the proposed transfer to the Post Office...of the Electric Telegraphs throughout the United Kingdom*, 1867–8 (XLI. 555), App. B.

Staffordshire Railway and founder and Chairman of the Electric and International Telegraph Company itself, memorialised My Lords in the same sense[1]. Perhaps if he had not died next year action might have been quicker. His successor in the Electric chair took a different view.

Conceivably Ricardo was influenced by the growing troubles of competition. His company had felt bound to oppose Allan's United Kingdom project, but had been beaten. Besides, there was now the London District Company of 1859 catering for metropolitan business. The natural tendency was for competing offices to grow up thickly where business was dense, and far too sparsely elsewhere. The United Kingdom made its bid for patronage by applying Allan's principle of a uniform charge, as against minimum charges varying from 1s. to 5s. for distance, with all sorts of extras. Though it paid no dividend in its first four years, the United Kingdom posed, not unjustly, as a public benefactor on that account[2]. As for the commercial world, it wanted more uniform and cheaper facilities, and thought that the state, on the analogy of the penny post, should be able to furnish them. A final campaign was started by the Edinburgh Chamber of Commerce in the autumn of 1865.

The then Postmaster-General, Lord Stanley of Alderley, had long believed that his department ought to take over the telegraph[3]. He was glad to have his hand forced, and he set his officials to report. Edwin Chadwick, need it be said, was demonstrating, in memorials to the Treasury and papers for the Royal Society of Arts, that the state, and the state only, could maximise telegraph utility[4]. This time public opinion was unmistakably on his side. Although the Treasury, for very good reasons, did not act in 1866–7[5]; and although the Electric Telegraph Company, under its new chairman Robert Grimston, went down fighting in perhaps less sportsmanlike style than might have been expected[6], the telegraph system was finally

---

[1] Scudamore's *Reports*, App. C.          [2] *Ibid.* p. 87.

[3] See his covering letter to Scudamore's *Reports*. Scudamore was his Assistant Secretary.

[4] For the memorial Scudamore's *Reports*, p. 8; for a paper of Chadwick's, p. 159. For an earlier paper, Wood, H. T., *The History of the Royal Society of Arts*, p. 477.

[5] See below, p. 375, for the commercial crisis of 1866.

[6] Grimston was a noted boxer, swimmer, rider and cricketer. His life was written in 1885 by F. Gale, author of *Echoes from old Cricket Fields*. He produced a pamphlet—*A review of the leading principles involved in the proposed transfer of Electric Telegraphs...from Trading Companies to the State, etc.*, not mentioned by his biographer.

bought for the Post Office at a very high price under 32 and 33 Vict. c. 73 of 1869, and taken over as from January 31, 1870.

The Office had promised the Postmaster great things, not only cheap, uniform, extended facilities but also an efficient personnel and a large profit[1]. When taunted by Grimston with the supposed incapacity of local postmasters to handle the telegraph, it had replied that there were "even institutions at which girls are trained to use it."[2] For about two years all hopes seemed to be fulfilled. The girls learnt their job. The public secured a uniform 1s. rate for twenty words, addresses free; complete separation of railway from general telegraphy, with resulting convenience in the location of telegraph offices; and above all the abolition of what had perhaps done more than anything else to set opinion against the companies, their intelligence department. This had made the supply of news to the provincial press "a thorough monopoly,"[3] and had thrown that press on to Chadwick's side. Newspapers had been forced to take what the intelligence department gave, rarely receiving separate messages because the rates for them were too high. They wanted special rates for their own news-collecting association; and they got them.

The extension of facilities soon absorbed the promised profit —rightly, it may well be argued. Then came compensation for displaced servants of the companies; levellings up of stipends to the old Post Office scale; and, quite unexpectedly, the price and wage rise of the early 'seventies[4]. The ratio of working expenses to receipts, which had been 78¾ in 1871–2, stood at 96⅔ in 1874–5, leaving no proper margin for interest and sinking fund on the telegraph debt. This produced inquiry, reorganisation, and revision of charges. Helped by these, and by the price fall after 1873, the ratio improved slowly. In 1875 the Treasury had urged the Post Office to aim at a ratio of from

---

[1] Scudamore's *Report*, p. 37–8.

[2] Scudamore's supplementary *Report*, a reply to Grimston's pamphlet, p. 133.

[3] *Report on the reorganisation of the Telegraph System of the U.K.*, by Scudamore, 1871 (XXXVII. 703), quoting Q. 1255 of the evidence before the *S.C. on the Telegraph Bill* of 1868.

[4] *Report of the Treasury Committee on the increased cost of telegraph service since the acquisition by the State*, 1875 (XX. 643). And see *S.C. on the Telegraph Department of the Post Office*, 1876 (XIII. 1). The price paid for the telegraphs was too high. Henry Fawcett once said that it ought to have been £7,000,000 instead of £10,500,000 (Buxton, *Finance and Politics, an Historical Study*, II. 50 n.), but this does not explain the deteriorating ratio of working expenses to receipts.

70 to 75. By 1881 the Post Office had achieved 80. Two years later it was only able to show 89·5. For 1884–5 there was no margin. All the same, it introduced the 6d. telegram in 1885, hoping to attract custom by a popular price. Figures showed that it was perfectly solvent, but its telegraph department was not. The letters paid interest and sinking fund for the wires[1].

Fundamental problems in the relations of the state to communications and transport were taking shape. On what principles shall railway rates be controlled? It is the same problem whether the lines are publicly or privately owned, and as yet it was unsolved. Is the public as traveller, or sender of goods and messages, to be served at the expense of the same public as taxpayer? This had been decided in the negative for the time being by the Railway Committee of 1872, without open discussion: the public as taxpayer could not be expected to subsidise the public as canal user, after the French style[2]. Shall one form of transport in the hands of the state subsidise another? This was being solved empirically in the matter of the letter and the telegram. After all there was only one Postmaster General, and he ran his whole concern at a profit. But Treasuries and business critics of departmental methods were uneasy, and rightly so. In the absence of the vulgar bookkeeping test of a profit, how shall the utility and efficiency of particular government enterprises be decided? With a government so little given to economic enterprise as that of late Victorian Britain the question was not very insistent. But, in view of the trend of thought and activity throughout the civilised world in the 'eighties, it deserved diligent consideration.

---

[1] See the *Report* and *Review* in 1886 (XXXVIII. 493 and 499). Buxton, *op. cit.* II. 52 (1888) spoke of the "wretched result" of the whole transaction and of the "appalling deficiency" on the telegraph account.

[2] Above, p. 200.

# CHAPTER VI

## OVERSEAS TRADE AND COMMERCIAL POLICY

RAILWAY building in and outside Britain, hunger in Ireland, growing population and free trade had given an extraordinary impetus to overseas traffic in the late 'forties. The tonnage of shipping entered and cleared from United Kingdom ports in 1844 was 10,300,000, exclusive of the coasting trade and of that between Britain and Ireland. Ten years earlier it had been 6,300,000. Three years later it was 14,300,000. When the worst of the famine and the commercial crisis of 1847 were over, there was a natural set-back; but the upward movement was resumed in the 'fifties—to 24,700,000 in 1860; to 36,600,000 in 1870; to 58,700,000 in 1880. Then came a slackening. Instead of a decade rise of from 50 to 60 per cent. as before, there was one of only 26 per cent., to 74,300,000 in 1890. The acceleration which registered the passage into a new era in the economic history of the world was over.

But the growth in Britain's strength at sea, and in her share of her own and other people's carrying trade, was not over yet, though there had been vicissitudes. In 1847–9, 69 per cent. of the tonnage using United Kingdom ports was British, and in 1850, so far as is known, something not very far below 60 per cent. of the world's 'civilised' ocean-going tonnage[1] was also British. The next decade saw a relative decline. The United States were at the summit of their naval strength. Their whalers were out from Nantucket; their supply ships were beating round the Horn to make the Golden Gate; their clippers were in the Canton river, the Mersey and the Thames. In 1860, United States shipping employed in the foreign trade and the whale fisheries alone[2] was more than half that of the United Kingdom, and nearly half that of the whole British Empire. The proportion of British tonnage in United Kingdom ports

---

[1] *Tables showing the Progress of Merchant Shipping in the United Kingdom and the Principal Maritime Countries*, 1912 (Ed. 6180). These tables are defective for 1850. For a number of countries no figures are available; but several of these, *e.g.* Italy and Greece, had not at that time many 'ocean going' ships.

[2] Excluding coasting, river, and lake shipping.

had fallen from 69 to 56. Some people wondered whether the
repeal of the Navigation Laws had not been over hasty[1]. Next
year the armies were loose in America. In July, 1862, the
*Alabama* was away to raid Northern shipping from Birkenhead.
When all was over, in 1865, Americans were thinking more of
the prairies than of the seas: by 1870 the ratio of British ships
using British ports was back at 68. It increased as steam tonnage grew, to reach its absolute maximum of 73 in 1895. It
had been over 70 then for fifteen years, years during which, in
spite of much slack trade, Britain had a greater share of the
traffic of the high seas than at any time in her history.

In continent after continent that traffic had been fed continuously by new railways; those railways made more often than
not by British capital. When Europe broke into Revolution in
1848, only Belgium had a complete skeleton through railway
system, though Prussia had 1500 miles of line open, and there
was activity in other German states[2]. France had a number of
detached lines and a great unfinished scheme of construction
on hand. In the United States by 1850 there were 9000 miles
of line working, but it was not yet possible to go westward by
rail without break from the Atlantic coast beyond Buffalo[3].
The twenty years from 1850 to 1870 saw Western Europe
supplied with a fairly complete railway system, partly by
private enterprise, partly by state enterprise, partly by some
combination of the two. Spain, to take an illustration from a
slow-moving country, which had not 20 miles of railway in
1850, had 3500 miles by 1870. In Eastern Europe, Russia got
to work seriously after 1860, but in 1880 she had not as much
railway on her huge surface as there was then in the British
Isles. The Turk lagged, yet even he had his 1000 miles of railway before 1890[4].

The people of the United States, interrupted in the conquest
of their continent by civil war, returned to it with insatiable
energy after 1865. The railway map of 1870 shows a relatively
dense network east of the Mississippi and the lower course of

[1] Clapham, J. H., "The last years of the Navigation Laws," *E.H.R.*, July, 1910.
[2] Clapham, J. H., *The Economic Development of France and Germany*, p. 142, 153.
[3] Johnson, E. R., *American Railway Transportation* (1904), p. 24–5, with a map for 1850.
[4] The best summary of construction, mileage, and policies is in the various articles under *Eisenbahnen*, by Cohn and others, in Conrad and Elster, *HWB. der Staatswissenschaften* (Ed. 1909), III. 805–926.

the Missouri; west of that hardly anything, except the single brand-new line reaching out over twenty-five degrees of longitude from Omaha through Utah to the Pacific. There was rather more railway in the United States that year than in all continental Europe—53,000 against 50,000 miles. During the next twenty years 110,000 miles were added, 70,000 of them between 1880 and 1890, mainly in the early years of the decade. If a single national contribution towards the making of the new era had to be selected for its world-wide economic importance, it would probably be this[1].

In Canada there was a similar, but later and as yet much less significant, development: the Canadian mileage in 1890 was still below that of the United Kingdom in 1870. The Argentine Republic and South America generally were later still. The Argentine had only 450 miles of line in 1870, 1400 in 1880, and even in 1890 not yet as much as there had been in Great Britain forty years before; though in the Argentine, as in all new countries, a few pioneering lines driven over virgin soil might have an influence upon world trade out of all proportion to their length.

So, for that matter, might pioneering lines in very old countries, as the Indian railways were showing. These were built on a far-sighted plan. Lord Dalhousie, who would have controlled the geographical development of British railways in the 'forties, had he not been baulked by his chief[2], was able by his minute of 1853 to determine absolutely both the geographical and the administrative development of the railways of India for the next twenty years, and to influence all future development[3]. The Mutiny first delayed and then hastened the completion of his grand design. Nearly 4000 miles were open by 1870; over 9000 by 1880, when there were only 800 miles in all the rest of Asia and they mainly in Ceylon and the Dutch Indies; nearly 17,000 by 1890. Perhaps, in the history of the human spirit, these Indian lines may prove to have been of greater moment than all the mileage of America.

The first Australian railways were opened before 1857 but progress was slow down to 1870, when the whole continent had

[1] Figures and maps in Johnson, *op. cit.* p. 26 *sqq.*
[2] Vol. I. p. 421–3.
[3] Hunter, Sir W. W., *The Indian Empire* (1892), p. 648. "The elaborate minute, drawn up by Lord Dalhousie...substantially represents the railway map of India at the present day."

only a little over 1000 miles of line, in sections running inland
from its sea-coast capitals. There were more than 3500 miles
in 1880, and more than 9000 in 1890. New Zealand, beginning
ten years later than Australia and needing railways less, had
shown relatively greater enterprise: she had 1250 miles open in
1880 and nearly 2000 in 1890. In Africa there had been a little
building at both ends—Egypt, Algiers, the Cape—during the
'sixties and even the 'fifties; but, except for the cotton lines of
the Egyptian delta, the African railways of the 'eighties had not
great international importance. Their total length was not quite
one half that of the Australian lines in 1890.

It has been reckoned that the whole earth, which had not
5000 miles of railway in 1840, had 24,000 miles in 1850;
239,000 miles in 1880; and 386,000 miles in 1890. Of the
386,000 miles, more than two-fifths were in the United States
of America[1].

More important for Britain than the opening of many railways was the opening of the Suez Canal in 1869. Dreamed of
by Frenchmen for centuries; planned and executed by a Frenchman and with French capital; opposed by old English statesmen who remembered Napoleon's Egyptian campaign, and by
younger ones who fancied that it would benefit principally
Levantines and other Mediterranean people, it soon verified the
forecast of a more prescient Englishman made in 1867. France,
Charles Dilke wrote, "will only find it has spent millions in
digging a canal for England's use."[2] Many people had doubted
the use; but English naval and military experts sent to report
early in 1870 said that it was "undeniably a navigable canal for
vessels of considerable draught"; that its success had "probably
far exceeded the most sanguine expectations of its warmest
supporters"; that, contrary to pessimistic expectations, its
Mediterranean entrances need not silt up, nor its maintenance
costs be prohibitive; but that as the "grand highway" between
East and West it was too narrow[3].

Narrow or not, 2,263,300 tons of shipping passed it in 1879.

[1] Conrad and Elster, as above, *s.v. Eisenbahnstatistik.*

[2] *Greater Britain*, p. 569. For early plans see Conrad and Elster, VII. 1048,
*s.v. Suezcanal.* For British opposition see *Cambridge Modern History*, XI. 637;
Clapham, *The Economic Development of France and Germany*, p. 356. French
investors took 52 per cent. of the first capital issue, the Khedive nearly all the
rest. Hobson, C. K., *The Export of British Capital*, p. 129.

[3] *Report on the Suez Canal*, by Capt. Richards, R.N. and Lt.-Col. Clarke,
R.E., *A. and P.* 1870, LXIV. 807.

Of this total 1,752,400 tons were British and only 181,700 French. Dilke could hardly have expected such a sweeping majority. It was France's misfortune that in this decisive decade she was both recovering from a lost war and ill-equipped for iron and steel shipbuilding. For the crowding of the canal with British tonnage owed much to the advent of the iron or steel screw steamer as a general cargo carrier, an advent which the existence of an interoceanic canal debouching in the not too navigable Gulf of Suez had, in its turn, helped to precipitate.

One pessimistic forecast which Dilke shared with most Englishmen miscarried: "it is hard to believe that it can pay."[1] In fact, helped by the screw steamer, it began to pay real dividends in 1875. When Disraeli bought the Khedive's shares in that year he bought them above par[2]. In 1879 the 500 franc share was never quoted below 600. By 1886–7 the original shareholder had received an average dividend of 7½ per cent. for the whole period, and his share was worth a round 2000 francs[3]. Prosperity had permitted that widening and deepening necessary to make the canal the grand highway of commerce. The work was begun systematically in 1884. Early in 1887, arrangements were made to render the passage by night possible. The passing tonnage rose accordingly to 6,783,200 in 1889. Dilke was still right. The British share of the whole was 5,352,900; the French 361,800.

On June 23, 1870, Lord Mayo from his bedroom at Simla had telegraphed in a few minutes to President Grant at Washington, by way of an evening party in Arlington Street, W. Grant had replied in "American idiom."[4] The party was given by the Chairman of the British Indian Telegraph Company to celebrate the successful laying of the last stretch—Gibraltar to Falmouth—of the direct and independent cable from England to Bombay. Very appropriately, de Lesseps of the Suez Canal was at the party. In the five preceding years the problem of the deep sea cable had been solved, after two decades of

[1] Dilke, Sir C. W., loc. cit.

[2] The best account even of the finance is in Monypenny and Buckle, Disraeli, v. 339 sqq. Cp. Jenks, L. H., The Migration of British Capital to 1875 (1927), p. 321, 324; Conrad and Elster, as above.

[3] For the very complicated story of Suez Canal finance see Robino, J., "The statistical story of the Suez Canal," S.J. 1887, p. 495–541.

[4] The Annual Register's Chronicle for June 23, 1870.

experiment and disappointment. The early 'fifties had been the
era of the shallow sea and narrow sea lines—Dublin-Holyhead;
Dover-Calais, a cable which gave no trouble for nine years;
Genoa-Corsica, and the like[1]. The late 'fifties were the era of
heroic, if often careless, experiment in deep water—Cyrus
Field and his Atlantic Telegraph Company; the cable that
snapped; the cable that worked feebly from August 5 to
September 1, 1858, and was then silent; discoveries about the
awkward conformation of the ocean floor and about the be-
haviour of insulated and protected copper wire lying at two
to three thousand fathoms in the globigerina ooze[2]. They were
also the era of a feverish effort made by Lord Derby's government to link India to England after the Mutiny, as a result of
which the Red Sea and Indian Telegraph Company of 1858
received a generous subsidy, and the Treasury itself ordered a
cable for the Falmouth-Gibraltar route, a cable which was never
laid there because the Atlantic had proved "the extreme risk
of failure" in deep waters[3].

The Red Sea and Indian Company—Alexandria, Suez, Sua-
kim, Aden and so to Karachi—reported that its cable line was
"complete through its entire length" on March 14, 1860[4].
It did not remain complete long; and as the company had made
no systematic arrangements for repair, it became derelict. The
situation in 1860–1 was most discouraging. Although lines
stretched "from Norway to the shores of Africa, from Nova
Scotia to the Gulf of Mexico," and "from Great Britain...
eastwards to Constantinople"[5]; out of 11,364 miles of submarine cable laid to date not much more than 3000 were
working[6]. To the Atlantic and Indian failures were to be added,
among others, the English Malta and Corfu and the Dutch
Singapore and Batavia. Soon the blockade runner would super-
sede the cable ship off the coast of the United States. American

---

[1] Cp. Clapham, *The Economic Development of France and Germany*, p. 157.

[2] See the *Report of the Joint Committee of the Board of Trade and the Atlantic
Telegraph Company...Submarine Telegraph Cables*, of April, 1861 (*A. and P.*
1860, LXII. 591): an excellent historical survey with full technical evidence. The
conclusion (p.xxxvi) was that, with sufficient care and forethought, all the failures
might have been avoided.

[3] *Papers on the Falmouth and Gibraltar Cable*, 1860 (LXII), p. 2. Treasury
Minute of November 14, 1859. Cp. *Return of all...Telegraph Cables* and *Return
of Correspondence with the Electric Telegraph Companies* in the same volume.

[4] *Return of Correspondence*, p. 17.

[5] Wilson, G., *The Progress of the Telegraph* (1859), p. 25.

[6] *Report of* 1861, p. v.

enthusiasm and enterprise were diverted for four years, and joint Anglo-American action became impossible.

But the cable ships were out as soon as civil war was over. This time it was the *Great Eastern*, employed by a new company[1]. After a failure in 1865, came the success of July, 1866. Then the broken cable of 1865 was recovered and completed[2]. Thereafter lines were laid rapidly about the earth by land and sea. The longest, carried overland in the late 'sixties, was not American but that of the Northern Telegraph Company of Copenhagen, across the full breadth of the Russian Empire to Vladivostock. Soon after the last link between England and Bombay was completed in 1870, the Northern laid short sea lines from Vladivostock into China and Japan[3].

These were met there by the cables of the Eastern Extension Company, coming from India south about Asia, and branching from Singapore through the Java Sea for Australia. South America was given direct communication with Europe by the Brazilian Company—Lisbon, Madeira, Cape Verde Islands, Pernambuco—in 1874. By the early 'eighties the best of the work was done. The North Atlantic was full of cables. They even crossed one another near Faraday Hill, a telegraphic eminence on the ocean floor. Africa, like Asia, was hung about with them. Mixed land and sea lines threaded the Turkish Empire and the Persian Gulf[4]. Only the Pacific remained virgin, from New Zealand and Japan to the looping inshore cables off the western coasts of South America and Mexico. It was not yet possible to telegraph to Honolulu, Iceland, New Guinea, or Tierra del Fuego. Nearly every other place of real importance not in the heart of China could be reached overland or under sea. The world, on the economist's projection, had shrunk into a single market. The final process of shrinkage had only taken about fifteen years and the greater part of it had been done in less than ten[5].

In the middle of this shrunken world, whispering along its copper wire news about the goods that slid along its lines of iron and steel to the seas, Britain lay now once for all an

---

[1] Above, p. 70.

[2] *Annual Register*, 1865 and 1866.

[3] Conrad and Elster, *op. cit.* VII. 1150, *s.v. Telegraphie*.

[4] In 1860 the Turks had been offered "une ligne sous-marine de Bagdad à Bassorah," *i.e.* up the Tigris (*Return of Correspondence*, No. 425), but that came to nothing.

[5] In 1866–75: see any cable maps of the 'sixties, 'seventies and 'eighties.

'industry state,' and a trade state, a state that lived by the export of its manufactures and could by no possibility feed itself for long in the way to which it was accustomed, nor find appropriate and sufficient raw materials for all its industries at home[1]. Rapidly as the imports of food of every kind had grown since Peel broke down the last serious barriers, the mere mass of the home-raised food supplies still outweighed that of the imports many times. The United Kingdom had, for example, in 1884–6 on an average 10,700,000 head of cattle[2]. She imported in those years an average of 372,000 head, together with 53,000 tons of beef. Beef imports even on this scale were a new thing. In 1872–4 they were only 12,500 tons. But for the most vital import of all, the bread corn, dependence on trade was now absolute. Even in 1850–2 it is possible that something like 25 per cent. of the consumption was imported[3]. During the eight years 1852–9 this proportion did not grow rapidly. Russia was at that time the leading source of supply and the Crimean War cut her off; but for the whole period the proportion imported was not less than 25 per cent. and may have been as much as 30 per cent. For 1860–7 it mounted towards 40 per cent., for 1868–75 towards 50 per cent. By the end of the 'seventies (1876–8) it was certainly over 50 per cent., the best available calculation suggesting more nearly 60 per cent.[4] No doubt the 60 per cent. line was passed in the early 'eighties, though the growth in imports of wheat and flour was not abnormally rapid after 1880. At the very end of the era, the picture of an island population getting from overseas two loaves of bread out of every three that it ate would not be appreciably out of drawing, though it might conceal the fact that few loaves were now made from home-grown wheat unmixed.

The loaves from overseas were mostly American by 1886. Wheat or flour, whenever allowed to come at all, had always

---

[1] Cp. above, p. 22.

[2] The figures were: Britain, 6,500,000; Ireland, 4,200,000. They are put together in the text because the only import figures are those for the United Kingdom and because Irish 'stores,' like Irish butter, were an important element in British consumption. The import of bacon and ham was very great: 372,000 tons in 1884–6.

[3] Above, p. 3.

[4] Lawes and Gilbert, "On the Home Production, Imports, Consumption and Price of Wheat, 1852–3—1879–80," *S.J.* 1880, p. 313 and *J.R.A.S.* 1880, p. 357. The figures are for the United Kingdom, but as Ireland no longer sent wheat to Britain they serve approximately for Britain alone. For Britain the higher alternative should always be taken because Ireland more nearly fed herself.

come in considerable quantities from the northern states of the Union[1]. Sometimes the American proportion had been high. In 1860 it was a full quarter of the wheat and more than two-fifths of the wheaten flour. But the main supplies at that time were European: Russian, North German, Danish, French, with a little from the Turkish Empire—Moldavia, Wallachia, and Egypt. The civil war postponed an American conquest of the British market. When it was over, the old position was not re-established at once. Russia was the most important supplier of wheat, and France of wheaten flour, during the four years 1866–9. But in the single year 1869 the United States sent more wheat than Russia and more flour than France. In the vicissitudes of harvests, Russia was once again the principal purveyor of wheat in 1872. France had fallen out. After that the dominance of the United States was unquestioned. From 1874 onwards, they sent again and again more than half the requirements of the United Kingdom in wheat and flour, whether measured by quantity or by value; and in one year, 1881, very nearly two-thirds. India first appeared as a really important contributor in 1877. She sent no flour, and in her most successful season, that of 1885, only one-sixth of the wheat, or one-seventh of the wheat plus the flour reckoned as grain. Russia made her contribution throughout, as did British North America, Australia, Germany, and many other countries; but this hardly affected the American dominance during the decade which ended in 1886[2].

British policy had however now restored to Europe the right to supply the United Kingdom with the greater part of her bulkiest and most widely used raw material, the one for which—tropical and sub-tropical materials apart—she had longest been dependent on imports: timber[3]. As a result of the huge discriminating duties on foreign timber imposed during the Napoleonic wars, the natural trade with Scandinavia and the Baltic had been crippled in favour of that with British America. The discrimination, though much reduced by Peel and again in 1851, survived until 1860[4]. Before Peel's reduction had taken

[1] Above, p. 3.
[2] Based on the annual trade returns which, for wheat, are very full and satisfactory.
[3] Above, pp. 5, 6, and Vol. I. p. 237-8, etc.
[4] *Customs Tariffs of the U.K.*, 1800–1897; 1897 (C. 8706), p. 290; Buxton, S., *Finance and Politics, an Historical Study* (1855), I. 344-5. Cp. Vol. I. p. 500.

full effect, in 1848, five-eighths of the timber imported was still British. In spite of the reduction of 1851, the American war helped to keep it British. For the four years 1856–9 the British and foreign imports of the timber which was measured by bulk almost precisely balanced[1]. In 1860 the duties were equalised at the nominal figure of 1s. a load on hewn wood and 2s. on sawn. In 1866 this odd irrational survival, without economic or imperial utility, was abolished. Geographical conditions had free play. By 1886 four-fifths of the imports which were measured by bulk were foreign. They were not all European. Besides the tropical woods, there was now a heavy shipping of pitch pine from the gulf ports of the United States, as mid-Victorian ecclesiastical and domestic architecture witness. But the major part of the imports came by the short sea passages from Northern Europe, and still nearly all in sailing ships. There was also now a great trade in pit-props from the lower Biscay coast. The grand total of measured imports stood in 1886 at no less than 5,100,000 loads (approximately tons). A generation earlier (1845–50) a yearly average of 1,870,000 loads had sufficed[2]. In the Britain of the 'eighties, economic life could not have gone on for six months without imported timber, and at certain seasons of the year not for three[3].

Lancashire's dependence on an imported raw material was primitive and inevitable. It helps to explain Lancastrian pacifism. Between 1820 and 1850 it had ceased to be a general dependence upon the world's cotton areas and become a special dependence upon the United States. In 1820 the United States had for the first time sent more than half the British import. In 1820–30 she sent three-quarters. From that time forward no other country had shown capacity to increase the crop in proportion to the growth of the world's demand. For the whole decade 1851–60 the American percentage of the cotton bales landed at British ports was 72; and as the American bale was heavier than others, and the American cotton more valuable than most, the absolute dependence figure was higher. For the year 1860, in which America sent nearly 500,000 more bales than she had ever sent before, and more than she sent again

[1] See a note in *S.J.* 1860, p. 85.
[2] Porter, *Progress of the Nation*, p. 579.
[3] Owing to the closing of the Baltic and White Sea by ice, Britain carries heavy stocks over winter. The spring timber contracts are for 'first open water' delivery.

until 1880, a Lancashire statistician put it as high as 85 per cent.[1]

There was already anxiety among the far-sighted. They had formed in 1857 the Cotton Supply Association, believing "that some dire calamity must inevitably, sooner or later, overtake the cotton manufacture of Lancashire; whose vast super-structure has so long rested on the treacherous foundation of restricted slave labour."[2] Some feared a servile war in America. Probably few anticipated a war of secession. They were being warned by Americans in 1860 that in any event there was little prospect of the American crop continuing to grow at the same rate as the world's demand, "and that as a consequence, the price of cotton would rise to a yet higher standard."[3] The reference was to a rise in prices which, in the case of average 'upland' cotton, was from just over $5\frac{3}{4}d$. a lb. for the decade 1848–57 to just under $6\frac{3}{4}d$. for 1858–60. In 1864 the small quantity of that cotton available was worth $27\frac{1}{2}d$. a lb.[4]

Before the civil war, whose coming "the great mass of traders refused to credit"[5] until it came, the Association, aided by the Foreign Office and the Consular Service, had been collecting information and surveying cotton areas, actual and potential. When war began and the Association's fears were justified, inquiries, cotton seed, judicious advice, and commissioners were sent out broadcast: 500 tons of seed, 1200 gins, and "millions" of pamphlets are recorded by 1866[6]. Naturally India was the chief field of activity. She stood second to America as a source of supply for Lancashire in the 'fifties, and a belief was current that she had a crop equivalent to five or six million American bales[7]. (The European import from all sources whatsoever in 1860 was not the equivalent of five millions; the British not three and a half.) Inquiry showed that the equivalent of two and a half million bales was probably the outside figure for India, including all the cotton worked up

[1] Ellison, T., *The Cotton Trade of Great Britain* (1886), p. 91 and tables in App. Cp. *S.J.* 1862, p. 527 *sqq.* "The great crisis in the history of the Cotton Trade," and *S.J.* 1869, p. 428 *sqq.* "The Cotton Trade, 1862–8, as compared with 1855–61," by Elijah Helm of the Manchester Chamber of Commerce.
[2] Quoted in Watts, J., *The Facts of the Cotton Famine* (1866), p. 402.
[3] *The U.S. Economist* quoted in the 1860 Report of the C.S.A. in Watts, p. 403.
[4] Figures from Ellison. Those given by Neild, in *S.J.* 1861, p. 491, "Prices of Printing Cloth and Upland Cotton, 1812–60," are rather lower but show a similar rise to 1860. Upland cotton had averaged less than 6d. from 1838 to 1858.
[5] Watts, *op. cit.* p. 112.    [6] *Ibid.* p. 404–5.    [7] Ellison, p. 91.

in the country. Though prices doubled and trebled, and though in 1864 two-thirds of the much reduced quantity of cotton used in Britain was Indian, it was never possible to draw anything like the amount required from the East. Nearly 19 per cent. of the British imports had been already Indian in the years 1855–61; in spite of all efforts barely 28 per cent. of a reduced total were Indian in 1862–8[1]. Egypt and Brazil, whose cotton-growing industries were younger and more adaptable, showed greater elasticity of supply; but their total contribution was much less. Altogether, during the four war years 1862–5, the United Kingdom managed to secure a yearly average weight of cotton rather more than half that of 1860 and 1861, two seasons of abnormally heavy imports. The achievement was creditable and significant of the creative power of high prices, for the first of the four years was much the leanest; but the preponderance of rough short-stapled Indian cotton was unwelcome. Lancashire cherished the story of the Methodist spinner who interrupted extempore prayers for cotton with an anguished cry of "but not Surat, O Lord!"

For a few years after the 'famine' and the peace, the Indian supply kept up, while the American recovered and the Egyptian grew slowly. In spite of social revolution with its disturbing economic consequences in the Southern states of the forcibly re-united Union, America was able to send more cotton to Europe in 1871 than she had sent in 1861, although the peak figure of 1860 was not passed until 1879[2]. By 1870 more than half the British consumption was again American. A decade later India had fallen to a very subordinate place and America had re-established her old position, no longer on the "treacherous foundation...of slave labour."[3] During the five years 1880–4 she supplied 74 per cent. of the cotton consumed in Britain. Thanks to American enterprise and railways, to steamers and a fall in general world prices, the standard cotton which had averaged just under $6\frac{3}{4}d.$ a pound in 1858–60 could be grown by freemen and delivered in England in 1880–4 for a minute fraction under 6d. But the problem of the Cotton Growing Association, how to relieve Lancashire, and indeed

[1] Helm in *S.J.* 1869, as above.
[2] Ellison, *op. cit.* p. 91 and tables.
[3] Indian cotton had not ceased to be exported, however, nor did the export fall off appreciably, except during the years 1877–9: it went elsewhere. Indian exports to Europe in 1882 were higher than in any previous year except 1866 and in 1883 higher than in any years except 1866, 1882, 1869 and 1872.

Europe, from undue dependence on a single source of supply, remained unsolved. American cotton being again so plentiful and cheap, the majority had again lost interest in the solution. What with the cotton and the wheat, the United States sent a larger share of the imports of the United Kingdom in 1880–4 than at any earlier date. It came to nearly a quarter of the whole, 23·7 per cent.[1]

The check to the cotton industry in the 'sixties had been registered in the prosperity of the other textiles and their heavy imports of material. For the quinquennium 1860–4, the imports of raw wool leapt up 41 per cent. above the level of 1855–9: 1865–9 was again 41 per cent. above 1855–9. Besides that there were more sheep in Britain in 1868 than in any earlier, or later, year. British flax-growing was almost extinct and not even the lack of cotton could revive it; but the imports of flax, hemp, and jute moved up with those of wool, and the acreage under flax in Ireland, which had averaged 115,000 in 1855–61, stood at 234,000 for 1862–8[2]. Even when the abnormal stimulus was withdrawn, the imports of these textile fibres continued to grow fast, though not so fast. The wool import of 1881–4 was more than double that of 1865–9, and although the flocks of sheep were at their minimum in 1882, they were recovering by 1886. The decline had coincided with a set of the fashions against fabrics made of the long wools which can be grown nowhere better than in England[3], and with the beginnings of the import of frozen mutton[4].

From 95·2 millions of lbs. in 1850–4, the imports of wool had grown to an average of 485·0 millions for 1880–4, of which more than half (264·2 millions) was re-exported. The home supply, including Ireland, may have been as much as 160 millions at the latter date. About a fifth of this was exported, but the balance, together with the skin-wool from slaughter-houses and the home-made shoddy, estimated together at 143 million lbs., met more than half the needs of the industry. Dependence on foreign supplies had almost ceased. Cheap, rough, 'carpet' wools were imported from all kinds of places.

---

[1] There are useful summaries and analyses of imports 1854–84 in *R.C. on Depression of Trade*, 1886, I. 127 *sqq.* The figure quoted is from Supplementary Table 6, p. 193.

[2] Helm in *S.J.* 1869, p. 420, and cp. Watts, *op. cit.* ch. xx.

[3] Lincoln and Leicester wools especially; cp. below, p. 281.

[4] Above, p. 90.

Some alpaca came from South America and mohair from the Levant and the Cape; but since 1850–60 the fine Saxon and Silesian merino wools had been finally replaced by those of Australia, New Zealand, and South Africa. So abundant had the Dominion supplies become that British buyers made hardly any use of the B.A. (Buenos Aires) wool from the river Plate, which now formed an important element of the continental consumption[1].

For technical reasons, it is not easy to compare specific wool prices of the 'eighties with those of earlier years[2]; but it is noticeable that whereas the average price of all cotton imported, as well as the price of a particular standard cotton, was slightly higher in 1880–4 than it had been thirty years before, the average price of wool was definitely lower. Transport from Australasia had greatly improved, and the carcase value of sheep had gone up, allowing that of the 'joint product,' wool, to fall a little, in spite of the world's ravenous demand[3].

No change of importance had occurred in the import of the other chief textile materials, apart from the gross increase in quantity set out below, and the way in which jute had, as it were, taken the pressure off flax and hemp. It is unlikely that supplies of those fibres could have been increased in proportion to the increased demand for sacking. Except in time of war, most of the hemp was Russian; most of the flax Russian and Belgian; all the jute was at all times Indian. Of the wool more than half was re-exported in 1880–4, as has been seen. About a seventh of the cotton; a quarter of the jute—for which Dundee was the depot; and varying proportions of the other fibres were also re-exported[4].

---

[1] The estimates are based on those adopted by the *Bradford Observer* and by the Sec. of the Bradford Chamber of Commerce. Cp. Clapham, J. H., *The Woollen and Worsted Industries*, p. 10, and Senkel, W., "Wollproduktion und Wollhandel im 19ten Jahrhundert," *Zeitschrift für die Gesammte Staatswissenschaft*, 1901; and above, p. 7.

[2] In early years little if any imported wool was 'scoured.' The yield of clean wool from greasy varies; and so on. Hence a lb. of imported wool means different things at different times.

[3] The growing import of scoured wool tells in favour of the argument, as it is more valuable than greasy wool.

[4] For jute, see above, p. 84, and for wool, pp. 7, 223. Silk is omitted from the table of quantities of textile raw materials imported, on p. 225, because of statistical difficulties connected with the returns. It is included in the second table of values. The average annual import of silk—'knubs and waste,' 'raw' and 'thrown'—was under £4,000,000.

*United Kingdom imports in million lbs. annual average*

|        | Cotton | Wool  | Flax  | Hemp  | Jute   |
|--------|--------|-------|-------|-------|--------|
| 1850–4 | 825·6  | 95·2  | 175·5 | 107·6 | 48·4*  |
| 1860–4 | 946·4  | 167·2 | 176·2 | 102·9 | 132·9  |
| 1870–4 | 1524·3 | 307·0 | 265·0 | 132·8 | 420·3  |
| 1880–4 | 1714·7 | 485·0 | 215·7 | 150·6 | 616·3  |

\* Three years only.

Reckoned by value, cotton was by far the most important of the incoming raw materials of all sorts. Its value varied between a third and a quarter of the whole. The timber, though it filled so much tonnage and was so essential, was worth less than the wool. The grouping of the raw material imports by value stood thus:

*Principal Raw Material groups, annual average value
of imports*

| 1880–4 | £ |
|--------|---|
| Total of raw material | 141,000,000 |
| Textile raw material | ⎰84,000,000<br>⎱(Cotton 44,500,000) |
| Timber, all kinds | 16,000,000 |
| Metallic ores and unworked metals | 15,000,000 |
| Hides | 4,000,000 |
| Rubber and gutta-percha | 3,000,000 |
| Paper-making materials | 2,000,000 |

Of the gross £141,000,000 worth of raw material imported, £36,000,000 was re-exported. Of this £36,000,000 no less than £15,000,000 represented the re-export of wool.

Since the first cargo of Spanish hematite was delivered at Hartlepool in 1861[1], the import, which fluctuated greatly, had risen to a maximum of over 3,000,000 tons in 1882–3. There were also occasional, but small, imports of pig iron. The days when England was on the balance an exporter of copper and a great exporter of tin and lead were over[2]. She still exported unwrought copper, but it was mostly smelted from imported ore; and there was besides an import of unwrought copper which averaged 40,000 tons a year. She exported her own lead, but imported nearly three times as much. She exported her own tin, but five times as much came in from the tin isles of

[1] Above, p. 50 n. 2. There were earlier deliveries in S. Wales.
[2] Vol. I. p. 240–1.

the East. Cornwall must suffer that the metallurgical industries might live and compete. In no case could the Duchy have supplied copper enough for the world's cables, which were mostly made in Britain, nor tin enough for the world's tin-cans, made there also[1].

The loss of the ancient British export trade in tin and copper had been much more than outweighed by the growth of the export of coal. That, too, was an old trade which, when it passed 1,000,000 tons in the year of Queen Victoria's accession, had seemed a very great trade. In the early 'fifties it stood at 3–4,000,000 tons. After 1855, although there were some annual fluctuations, there was a smooth steady rise from quinquennium to quinquennium, varying between 22 and 34 per cent., which brought the figure to 20,120,000 for 1880–4 and to 23,500,000 for 1884–6. The value of the exported coal was relatively small, not more than 4 to 5 per cent. of the total of United Kingdom produce exported, but it had a use disproportionate to its money value. By providing bulk cargoes outwards to balance the incoming timber, ores, grains and other bulky raw materials and foodstuffs, it often saved British ships from having to sail half-filled or in ballast, and so kept down transport costs both out and back. There was profit to be made on both voyages and the coal went all over the world, though mainly to Europe and the Mediterranean[2]. Made by coal, launched near coal, loaded with coal, the iron and steel tramps from the North-East coast were keeping British shipping in its high position.

Weighty bulk cargoes of iron and steel in their rougher forms supplemented the coal cargoes. There was nothing smooth in the course of this trade. Being a trade in production goods, it moved by jerks in the years of rapid railway construction and general industrial activity overseas. Also it was liable to interruption from the growth of primary metallurgical industries of the English type abroad, and from the tariffs which usually accompanied that growth.

[1] See above, p. 104, and p. 91. Strictly speaking it was only the tin-plates not the tin-cans which were made there: above, p. 91. The export of tin-plates grew from 116,000 tons in 1870–4 to 257,000 tons in 1880–4, in spite of trade depression.

[2] In 1886, 18,400,000 out of 23,200,000 tons of coal exported went to Europe and the Mediterranean. See Thomas, D. A. (Lord Rhondda), "The Growth and Direction of our Foreign Coal Trade during the last Half-Century," a classical article, in *S.J.* 1903, p. 439–522.

After a period of what then seemed extraordinary expansion, down to 1853[1], came stagnation during the Crimean War; a jerk to a higher level, and stagnation again after the commercial crisis of 1857; and so forward. The greatest jerk occurs after the American Civil War, when railways were being built at speed in many countries, in America itself above all. There

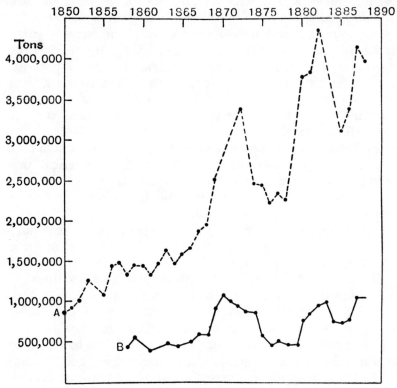

A. Exports of iron and steel, excluding machines, cutlery and hardware.
B. Exports of railway iron and steel.

followed the greatest check of the century, after the world-wide commercial collapse of 1873–4[2]. With 1880 came recovery. American purchases of British railway material revived, for the last time[3]; and although conditions of sale were so difficult that rail-makers were constrained to experiment in market-sharing with their continental rivals[4], the expansion of new markets,

---

[1] Cp. vol. 1. p. 483, and above, p. 8.      [2] See below, p. 381–3.
[3] In 1881 the United States took 294,000 tons: in 1884, 18,000 tons.
[4] Above, p. 151.

particularly within the Empire, raised the aggregate export for 1882 nearly a million tons above the great iron year 1872. And then another check, with a momentary fall below the level of the great year.

If the quantities of the iron and steel exports moved feverishly, their values moved more feverishly still. In values the great year and its successor were never touched. In 1872 pig iron had averaged £5. 1s. 10d. a ton and bars £12. 5s. 0d.; in 1873 pig £5. 17s. 3d. and bars £13. 10s. 0d. The highest yearly average for pig in the 'fifties had been only £3. 19s. 9d. in 1854, a war year, and in the 'sixties £3. 0s. 6d. in 1866, a post-war year. After 1875 the average price was always below £3. In the great exporting year 1882 it was only £2. 9s. 4d.: there was abundance of trade, but, as the saying is, not much fat on it. Hence the rail pool.

As producers of export values, the textile industries held their own, though they were steadily losing that numerical predominance in the industrial life of the country which they had achieved by 1850[1]. At no time could the mineral industries compare with them in the field of export. In 1850 textile yarns and fabrics of all kinds made up 60 per cent. of the exports of United Kingdom produce by value; in 1860 and again in 1870 they were 55 per cent. They still averaged 46 per cent. in 1880–4. Of textile exports the cotton goods formed throughout, except during the years of the American Civil War, fully two-thirds or, in round figures, from 30 to 40 per cent. of all the exports of the United Kingdom. Lancashire's markets were so widespread that losses in one could usually be balanced by gains in others; and its goods were consumption goods which had to be perpetually renewed. There were years of decline, but, with the great exception of 1861–5, they were due primarily to general price movements, which also affected the raw material. Even so, the percentage decline from one year to the next was never so much as six. When middling uplands cotton dropped from $10\frac{9}{16}d.$ a lb. in 1872 to $6\frac{1}{4}d.$ in 1876, the value of the exports fell only from £80,163,000 to £67,633,000; for, in spite of the depression after 1873, the quantities both of yarns and of manufactures exported had gone up somewhat in the interval.

Other textiles were rather less trustworthy as creators of

[1] Above, p. 29. Cp. Bowley, A. L., *England's Foreign Trade in the Nineteenth Century* (1893).

export values. Fashions and tariffs affected them more. Varied as their markets were, they had none to compare in size and permanence with the markets of India and China for cotton. The cotton trade, having come through its "dire calamity" of the 'sixties, showed itself again the backbone of the export trade of Britain, giving to it that cohesion and stability for which backbones exist.

The distribution of the greater or more significant export values in the quinquennium 1880–4 stood thus:

### Annual average values, 1880–4

| | |
|---|---|
| Of all British and Irish produce exported | £234,000,000 |
| Of all yarns and textile fabrics ... ... | £108,000,000 |
| (Of which cotton ... ... ... ... | £76,000,000) |
| Of coal, iron and steel ... ... ... ... | £38,000,000 |
| Of hardware, cutlery and machinery ... ... | £15,000,000 |
| Of articles of clothing ... ... ... ... | £10,500,000 |
| Of foodstuffs ... ... ... ... ... | £10,000,000 |
| Of chemicals and salt ... ... ... ... | £6,200,000 |

Those exports which were classified as going to British Possessions remained an oddly constant proportion of the whole, in spite of the growth of the Indian market and the economic expansion of the Dominions[1]. British Possessions had taken 35·1 per cent. of the exports in 1854; they took 34·5 per cent. in 1880–4. In the interval they had never, for any series of five years, taken more than 33·2 (1860–4) or less than 25·6 (1870–4). It is curious that in the five years of most furious trade and swollen prices the imperial percentage was least. It is not however very significant, because the chief trade fury was American and continental. Imperial trade was throughout valuable and expansive. From coal to the finest manufactures, the Empire absorbed the whole range of British produce. Tariffs checked the absorption very little, though the Dominions had gained complete control of them[2]. But foreign trade proper grew on the whole just as fast as imperial trade, sometimes a little faster, sometimes a little slower.

The United States had lost little of their importance as a market. Between 1830 and 1849 they took 15·7 per cent. of the

---

[1] The matter was investigated by the *R.C. on Depression of Trade*, from the Appendices to whose reports the figures are taken. Cp. Farrer, T. H., *Free Trade and Fair Trade* (3rd ed. 1886), p. 38.

[2] It is no part of the plan of this book to tell the political story of the emancipation of the Dominions: see *Camb. Hist. of the British Empire*, vol. VI (1930), *Canada*; Shann, E., *An Economic History of Australia* (1930).

British exports[1]. From 1850 to 1884 they took 12·6 per cent. But for the Civil War and the collapse in their purchasing power after 1873, there might have been little reduction. Some reduction could hardly have been avoided, because of their growing industrialism and protectionism. But the tariff was not high enough even at the close to divert British trade into indirect channels: the percentage was still 12·2 in 1880–4. British steel rails, though taxed, were going in freely: there was still a good market for fine cottons, linens, woollens and miscellaneous manufactures; for worsted dress-goods and coatings from Bradford an excellent market. America as yet did not make nearly enough of these to satisfy her needs[2].

France was never very accessible to British produce[3]. In every quinquennium, except 1870–4, when she was stocking up after war, she was definitely inferior to Australasia as a market. She took less absolutely; and what she took was cruder—more coal, less manufactures. But the combined market of Belgium, Holland, and the states which became Germany—it is necessary to combine them because so much of the trade of Rotterdam and Antwerp is transit trade for the Rhine—was from 1855 always more important than that of the United States. It never took less than 14·9 of the exports (in 1880–4): in the years of continental trade fury, 1870–4, it almost touched 20·0 per cent. The Belgian and German tariffs were most moderate at that time; the Dutch at all times.

Though never a really important buyer of British produce, France was a leading sharer in the English depot trade, the re-export of foreign and colonial produce, mainly raw materials and 'colonial wares.' This trade had always been valuable. It was most valuable in the 'sixties, when 17·5 per cent. of the imports of the United Kingdom were re-exported. In the late 'fifties, 1855–9, the percentage had been 13·6. Subsequently, on the five or ten years' average, it was always under 16·0. The rise in the 'sixties was connected with the addition to the old depot trade of the heavy new trade in colonial wool. For many years after that trade was established, little or no wool went from Australia to the continent direct[4]. All came under the hammer at the wool exchange in Coleman Street. Indeed it

---

[1] Cp. vol. I. p. 483.
[2] Cp. Cole, A. H., *The American Wool Manufacture* (1926), vol. II. ch. 28.
[3] For the Commercial Treaty of 1860 see below, p. 244–6.
[4] Cp. above, p. 7, 223.

was only at the very end of the period under review that direct shipment began. For 1880–4 the re-export was worth £15,300,000 a year out of a total re-export trade of £64,000,000. It was much the greatest single item in the total. Cotton, which came second, averaged only £5,500,000 and coffee, which came third, not £4,000,000. Rubber had already passed £1,000,000. The importance of the re-exports, not only in Anglo-French commercial relations, but in the whole Channel and North Sea trade, is shown by the proportions of British and Irish produce and of foreign and colonial produce absorbed by the French market and by the Belgian-Dutch-German market in 1880–4. In neither case was this proportion new: it had been much the same since the 'fifties.

*Annual average imports from the United Kingdom,* 1880–4

|  | British and Irish Produce | Foreign and Colonial Produce |
|---|---|---|
| By France | £16,500,000 | £11,900,000 |
| By Belgium-Holland-Germany | £34,000,000 | £25,600,000 |

Most of this re-export trade went up the Thames to London and down it again for the narrow seas.

The early railway age had closed during one of the great swellings of the export trade in men—men mostly self-exported to places where, as they hoped, nature and society would add vastly to their productive value, besides offering them other and higher values. All Europe was affected; for if Europe had less famine it had more revolution than the British Isles. The Californian gold drew all impartially, and it was followed by the gold of Australia. But at that time, and for many years later, the British Isles were the chief source of supply of human export values. In the year of the forty-niners, 300,000 people left United Kingdom ports, 220,000 of them for the United States. For the next five years, 1850–4 inclusive, the average was over 325,000, the United States continuing to take more than 230,000 each year. This flood of emigration was mainly Irish. In 1852, the first complete year for which precise figures exist, 190,000 Irishmen emigrated from the Irish ports alone, and no doubt many thousands more from British ports. The movement into the United States was overwhelmingly Irish; that to Australasia was overwhelmingly British; and 1852, with its 89,000 travellers, still remains the peak year of emigration to Australasia. Judging by the figures of the next eight years, during which 365,000 emigrants went there, nearly three-quarters of whom were British, Britain's share of the emigration in the peak year can hardly have been less than 65,000[1].

Between 1853 and 1880 the aggregate outflow of British subjects from Britain was returned at 2,466,000. The permanent outflow was less. Down to 1876 the returns gave either no figures, or no satisfactory figures, of emigrants who came back. In early years such people were probably few. Most emigrants were very poor. Memories of the outward voyage, which in those days had points in common with the old slavers' 'middle passage,' would be deterrent[2]. But as travelling facilities improved, decent steamers replacing the detestable emigrant ships with advantages which it was "scarcely possible to exaggerate,"[3] there was coming as well as going. It became difficult to distinguish the emigrant proper from the long or short period experimenter in a new country. When the analysis of the immigrants by nationality had been made fairly complete[4], between 1876 and 1880, the difference between gross and net emigration of British subjects had become noticeably great. For the five years 1881–5, a period of renewed heavy outflow but also of quick inflow, more than a quarter must be subtracted from the gross figures. Even so the net emigration from Britain in that short period cannot have been much less than 675,000: the gross figure was 893,000[5].

An important transit business in European emigrants had developed, mainly along the line Hull to Liverpool. Even in the 'fifties Britain passed on Westwards some 35,000 foreign emigrants a year, and 55,000 in the 'seventies. In 1881–5 the annual average had reached 95,000. A new era of migration had begun for all Europe, with the opening up of the world and the social discomfort of those difficult years.

Not that emigration can be treated always, or even usually, as a mere product of distress. It was that in 1846–7, when there was famine in Europe and worse famine in Ireland and the

---

[1] The fullest statistical material is in *Papers relating to Emigration*, 1899 (CVII. 1). Cp. Johnson, S. C., *A Hist. of Emigration from the U.K. to North America* (1913); Carrothers, W. A., *Emigration from the British Isles* (1929).

[2] See Walpole, K. A., "The...movement...to remedy abuses on emigrant vessels...," *T.R.H.S.* 1932; *Gen. Rep. of the Colonial Land and Emigration Commission*, 1842 (XXV. 55).

[3] *R. of Emigration Commission*, 1870 (XVII. 111), p. 3.

[4] In order to distinguish emigrants of British and Irish origin from the continental emigrants who passed through England.

[5] The net emigration from the United Kingdom was 934,000.

Western Isles. It was not, when gold drew eager men to Bendigo and Ballarat. It was, in some degree, in 1869, a year of heavy emigration and dull trade. It certainly was not in 1872–3, years of still heavier emigration. Trade and agriculture were active enough in Britain; but being still more active in America and Australia they drew the capable, ambitious, and reasonably successful, besides some normal percentage of the distressful. Indeed there was some tendency for emigration to fluctuate with the export of capital, and so to coincide with industrial activity, since much capital was exported in the form of British capital goods. In the years 1876–8 there was a very low net emigration. At that time export of capital was stagnant. It is even probable that on the balance there was a net import[1].

The mass of the emigration was individual and unorganised, although official and officious organisations to promote it were always at work, especially in times of gloom. Philanthropic people might help out-of-work ribbon weavers from Coventry, or hand-loom weavers from Ayrshire, to get away from the country. Trade unions often kept emigration funds; but there is no reason to think that they financed very much emigration. The London Female Emigration Society of 1850, the Female Middle Class Emigration Society of 1861, and similar private organisations later, did work of mixed value in a limited field. Poor Law Authorities were empowered to help the destitute to emigrate. They did; but the number helped dwindled to 36 in 1864–5 and, after rising to some hundreds in 1871–5, was down again to 23 in 1878[2]. The only large scale and really important official operations were those carried on by the Colonial Land and Emigration Commissioners between 1847 and 1872. When the Commissioners handed over their remaining functions to the Board of Trade in the latter year, they explained that since 1847 they had selected and assisted 340,000 "government emigrants," of whom perhaps 240,000 would be British[3].

---

[1] See the discussion in Hobson, C. K., *The Export of Capital* (1914), p. 204. Hobson argues in favour of the view that there was an average net yearly import of £6,666,000 for the three years, more money being brought home from foreign investments sold than was freshly invested abroad. See below, p. 235.

[2] Johnson, *op. cit.* p. 59, 72, 81, 89–90, 255, 257.

[3] *Report*, 1873 (XVIII. 295): the last of an annual series. The British proportion is uncertain. It is based on the average proportion of British to Irish emigrants from the United Kingdom throughout the period: *Papers relating to Emigration*, 1899; as above.

For fourteen years before the Commission was wound up it had been running at low pressure. Three-quarters of its work had been done between November, 1847 and the end of 1858. This work was almost entirely Australian, with a little for the Cape and the Falkland Islands. In its most active year, 1854, the Commission had chartered 127 ships and sent 41,000 men women and children to Australia[1]. Its funds came, on Gibbon Wakefield principles, from the sale of Australian land. Of £4,864,000 spent between 1847 and 1870, all but £523,000, which the emigrants themselves found, was drawn from this source. As the colonies became more completely self-governing and more self-conscious, in the later 'sixties, they ceased to vote money from their land revenue, or even, as in the case of South Australia, used money intended to finance emigration for other purposes. That is all matter of Commonwealth history[2]. The historian of Britain has to record that by 1870 assisted emigration was out of fashion. The Commissioners themselves were reflecting most sensibly that, had government funds been available, emigrants and their friends would never have raised the £15,000,000 or so spent up to date on transatlantic migration[3]. The Commissioners were ripening for abolition; but they had done good work in their time, and had believed in it[4].

The export of men had always been connected, but in intricate and varying ways, with the export of British capital. The export of capital in its turn was linked with the export of capital goods; but was far from identical with it. Some capital emigrants took with them, usually not in the form of goods. Small as individual takings normally were, the aggregate must have been considerable. When British manufacturers were spreading the new industrialism in Europe, during the early years of the century, they had often taken their skilled men and their money too. Railway building on the continent in the great days of Thomas Brassey and Morton Peto (1840–70) involved heavy exports of capital and migrations of labour and directing

---

[1] *Report*, 1854–5 (XVII. 1), *Report*, 1873, p. 81 and Johnson, *op. cit.* p. 234.

[2] See Shann, E., *The Economic History of Australia*, esp. ch. IX, "Free Colonies and Assisted Migration." Cp. the criticism of colonial policies in *Report*, 1870 (XVII. 111), p. 3.

[3] *Report*, 1870, p. 3.

[4] So had John Stuart Mill. In all the editions of his *Principles of Political Economy* the passage in praise of Wakefield and of colonisation as a "national undertaking" stood; book V. ch. 11. § 14.

personnel, large at first though soon dwindling; but very little permanent emigration[1]. Railway building in India also involved migration of skilled men and a little permanent emigration. There were those who served the East Indian Railway from father to son[2]; but India was a land already full of men who understood clerical work and of others who could learn machines. It was principally in America and the Dominions that capital export brought men, accompanied men, and followed men—though distress emigration might have a very scanty accompaniment of capital. The export of capital, so far as is known, was at its peak in 1872. The estimate for that year is £83,500,000. Emigration was at its peak, for that decade, in 1872 and 1873, having begun to move up in the slack trade years 1867-9 when capital exports were low. The net emigration was very low in 1876-8; and in those years the estimated export of capital account shows a small adverse balance, as has been seen. Britain, the estimate suggests, had rather less than nothing for foreign investment when the necessary steps had been taken to adjust a trade balance upset by the disastrous harvests of the late 'seventies and by the blocking of export channels by war, the growth of foreign industries, tariffs and the depreciation of silver[3]. In effect, she had to sell a trifle of her foreign investments to pay her way. Something similar had happened, though the facts are more obscure, in 1847-8, when famine called for abnormal imports and revolution shut European markets. It was not to happen again until after 1914. In 1879 and 1880 the heavy flow of men was resumed. It might be called a distress flow, though it was not of the old tragic sort. They were building 10,000 miles of railway a year in the United States and wanted men. Meanwhile the capital position was being readjusted. From 1881, the country was at least able to keep the greater part of the earnings of its foreign investments abroad for fresh investment[4]. More it was not in a position to do at

[1] Brassey's enterprises are tabulated (after Sir A. Helps, *Life of Thomas Brassey*) in Jenks, L. H., *The Migration of British Capital to 1875* (1927), App. p. 419.      [2] Cp. Kipling, Rudyard, *Among the Railway Folk*.

[3] The estimates are those of Hobson, *op. cit.* Cp. throughout Jenks, *op. cit.*, where it is argued that the adverse balance continued to 1880 (p. 414). For tariffs and silver see below, p. 249, 339.

[4] A mere statistical statement of the position: from 1881 to 1911 the fresh investment abroad is estimated not quite to have equalled the yield of existing foreign investments. Actually much of that yield was of course brought home by individuals, and new investments, slightly less in amount than the annual yield of the old ones, were made by other individuals.

this time. Emigration meanwhile reached another peak in 1883, to slide down again with the American crash of May 1884.

The link between the export of capital and the export of capital goods was not always strong or direct. No doubt the £163,000,000 worth of railroad iron of all sorts and the many locomotives exported in the thirty years 1856–85 were mostly associated with railway investment overseas. In one case, that of the Indian railways, it is known that a third of all the capital raised for them down to the 'eighties was spent on British rails and their carriage to the East[1]. But in the triangular workings of foreign trade, rails and other capital goods might go to countries in which the British investor was not interested. And such goods go largely to all countries in the ordinary way of trade, together with consumption goods like textiles, to pay for food and raw materials, even when no fresh investment is being made.

At least half the foreign investments were always in government securities. If these went directly in British goods at all— and the trade triangle might easily so work that a loan in America would show in the returns as an extra export of cotton piece goods to the East—they might go in Armstrong's guns, saddlery, uniform cloth, or luxuries for foreign potentates: consumption goods and destruction goods. Some part of the Egyptian debt was no doubt represented by a gilded locomotive, decorated to the design of the Slade Professor of Fine Art at Cambridge, which Robert Stephenson & Co. built for Said Pasha in 1862. A more workmanlike engine which they built for the Danish State Railways in 1868 may well have reflected British investment in the Danish 5 per cents. of 1864[2]; for governments sometimes buy genuine capital goods with their borrowed money. All that can be stated with perfect accuracy are the economic commonplaces that British foreign investment was covered, over a period of years, by British exports of goods and miscellaneous shipping and commercial services; that the goods were sometimes connected directly with the investment, but much more often not; and that, as many of the services were rendered overseas by ships, banks, and domiciled trading Britons, payment for them might be reinvested there and would not affect British trade returns, unless and until profits from it began to come back in the form of imports.

[1] Worked out by Jenks, *op. cit.* p. 227.

[2] For these locomotives see Warren, J. G. H., *A century of locomotive building* (1923), p. 411, 413.

The net addition to the stock of British capital invested overseas between the early 'fifties and the middle 'eighties was
round about £1,000,000,000. By the latter date, with the growth
of statistical material and method, estimation was not liable to
very serious error, when in skilled hands. Sir Robert Giffen,
in 1885, reckoned the total of United Kingdom capital invested
abroad at £1,302,000,000. (For comparison, it may be noted
that he estimated the capital invested at home to be seven times
as much.) What the amount was in the early 'fifties is not known.
Estimates have varied between £200,000,000 and more than
£400,000,000. As the tendency of inquiry has been to reduce
them, it may be wise to adopt a speculative maximum of
£300,000,000. Whatever figure is accepted stands for the value
of the investments immediately before tolerably accurate trade
statistics begin, with the abandonment of the old 'official'
values of imports in 1854[1].

By that time the pause in the outflow of capital which had
occurred at the end of the early railway age was over. The
Californian and the Australian gold were coming in. Europe
was calm. In England the sharp upward movement of wholesale prices was under weigh which would set the average level of
1856–70 25 per cent. above that of 1849–51[2]. In 1852 Thomas
Brassey had taken contracts for 264 miles of French railway.
A little later there was at least one English director on the
board of nineteen different French companies[3]. Contractors,
the great contractors, were ceasing to be called in by companies. They were devising railway schemes for Europe and
arranging for companies to be born to finance them. Into the
American railways however investors put their money direct.
Brassey did not work in the United States, though with Peto
and Betts he was engaged in the disastrous business of the
Canadian Grand Trunk; but it was believed in 1857 that
£80,000,000 of American railroad stock was held in England[4].

[1] Facts and discussions in Seyd, E., *Journal of the Society of Arts*, XXIV.
309 (1875); Nash, R. L., *A short inquiry into the profitable nature of our investments* (1880); Giffen, Sir R., *The Growth of Capital* (1885); *The Excess of
Imports (Essays in Finance, First Series)*; Bowley, A. L., *England's Foreign Trade*;
Stamp, Sir J. C., *British Incomes and Property* (with criticism of Giffen); Hobson,
*op. cit.*; Jenks, *op. cit.* All the calculations depend on the accuracy of the trade
statistics. After the abandonment of official values of imports in 1854, values
computed according to a plan introduced by James Wilson were employed
until 1870. From 1870 import values are those declared by merchants, as export
values had long been. (See Bourne, *S.J.* 1871; Giffen, *S.J.* 1882.) So estimates
which aim at a high degree of accuracy do not go back beyond 1870.

[2] See the price diagram, p. 378, below.   [3] Jenks, p. 165.   [4] Hobson, p. 128.

Early misadventures in America had been forgotten. Besides railways and the federal securities of the United States, those of a dozen of the constituent states were regularly quoted in London, together with issues of Brazil, Buenos Ayres, Cuba, Chili, Granada, Ecuador, Mexico, Peru, Venezuela and Guatemala[1]. All the while investment went on within the Empire and in European securities, particularly French and Spanish. Between 1855 and 1865 came such enterprises for the spread of industrial civilisation as the various continental gas companies and the water-works of Amsterdam and Berlin[2]. And there were mines of all sorts everywhere.

The world-wide commercial crisis of 1857[3] was specially destructive in the United States. Before investors had completely recovered confidence, the outbreak of the War of Secession led to a scramble to get rid of American securities. Investing England distrusted the North; with the help of investing France it found £3,000,000 for the South—and lost every penny. Its savings had been diverted more and more towards India, especially towards Dalhousie's Indian railways, since 1857. The railways were being built with a government guarantee of interest to the companies, and the security was attractive from every point of view; it was imperial, trade-making, and secure. Apart from the railways, the government of India was a constant and heavy borrower. By 1870 the colonial stocks proper ordinarily listed came to upwards of £45,000,000[4], nearly all of which was held in the United Kingdom. Ten years later, the colonial government securities mainly held in the United Kingdom were put at £98,000,000; the Indian government and railway securities similarly held at £196,000,000[5].

Confidence in the United States soon came back after 1865. Securities of the states were no longer in favour[6], but those of the Union and the new railway network more than replaced

---

[1] The securities quoted in the *Economist* are taken as those in which dealings were really current. The years are 1853–7. Guatemala appears in January, 1857.

[2] The enterprises which Herbert Spencer cited in controversy with Matthew Arnold to prove that England was not poor in ideas. Cp. Sombart, W., *Händler und Helden* (1915), p. 10, where the case is quoted as an illustration of England's *Krämergeist*.

[3] Below, p. 368 sqq.

[4] *Economist*, January 8, 1870.

[5] Nash, *op. cit.* chs. 2 and 3.

[6] Those of Pennsylvania, Virginia and Massachusetts were however still regularly listed in 1870.

them. By 1869 foreigners, and for this purpose most foreigners were British, were believed to have nearly £300,000,000 invested in the country[1]: 300,000 tons of railway iron were shipped there that year.

During the decade which ended in the second world-wide crisis, of 1873, borrowing by governments and borrowing for railways, to quote only the pre-eminent groups of borrowers, were constant and furious. There was greedy blind capital to spare for everyone. France had become a great lender under the Second Empire. Perhaps she had £500,000,000 abroad to Britain's £800,000,000 by 1870[2]. Paris rivalled London as a place of emission. The less reputable borrowing nations could play one off against the other and float their loans simultaneously in both. The Ottoman debt and the Egyptian debt, heavy with misgovernment and the future, took their modern form in these years. Brassey signed a contract for the Central Argentine Railway in 1864, and one for the Callao Docks in 1870. In 1868, the Association of Foreign Bondholders came into existence to watch doubtful foreign governments and keep the home government sensitive to bondholding opinion[3].

Climax came after the Prussian War. Helped by London, Amsterdam, and the sale of some of her £500,000,000 invested abroad, France easily paid Bismarck. Britain took a good deal of what she had to sell. American railways were being built faster than ever. The new Germany, victorious and enriched, was full of ordered, with some disordered, activity. The canal was open. The cables were being laid. India and the colonies were borrowing handsomely. As a Dominion, Canada was taking far more than she had taken when disunited[4]. Most of the borrowers were sound and honourable. Britain came through the financial bad weather of 1873 better than any of her neigh-

---

[1] Wells, D. A., *Report of the Special Commissioner of Revenue*, 1869, p. xxvii, quoted in Hobson, *op. cit.* p. 133.

[2] For France see Say, J. B. L., *Rapport...sur le paiement de l'indemnité de guerre* (reprinted in his *Finances de la France*, vol. I); Giffen, *The Cost of the Franco-German War* (*Essays in Finance, First Series*); O'Farrell, H. H., *The Franco-German War Indemnity* (1913). The rough estimate for Britain is based on Giffen, *The Growth of Capital*.

[3] See in general the *S.C. on Loans to Foreign States*, 1875, XI. For the Association of Foreign Bondholders and its Council see the evidence of Hyde Clarke its secretary, Q. 607 *sqq.* Cp. Feis, H., *Europe the World's Banker* (1930), p. 113–14.

[4] For her comparatively small borrowings before 1867 see Jenks, *op. cit.* p. 205–6.

bours: she had experience of that kind of thing. But when she was going over the broken spars and split sails in 1874–5, it was said that there were £76,000,000 of foreign loans in default, besides £165,000,000 of doubtful Spanish debt, of which a third was held "in this country."[1] The worst was a series of loans of the nominal value of £10,000,000 floated down devious and muddy channels by Honduras, Santo Domingo, Costa Rica, and Paraguay; on the whole of which, "with one unimportant exception," no interest had been paid except out of the original capital[2].

For ten years after 1875 the export of capital was slack, as has been seen. Investments overseas increased steadily, except in 1876–8; but it is probable that the investment of 1876–86 was not so great as that of 1872–3; and it is certain that this investment of 1876–86 was very much less than the total income from capital overseas during that period[3].

The ordinary Englishman was worrying about the balance of trade in the late 'seventies as he had not done for many generations. He was alarmed at the steadily growing 'adverse' balance, the arithmetical excess of imports over exports; and there was much wild abuse of statistics. Few men were so simple as the politician from the antipodes of twenty years later who supposed that this balance was paid in "golden sovereigns"[4]; but many fancied that it must be met by heavy sales of securities. Statistical science, in the person of Sir Robert Giffen, a little bewildered to find its "special study so little advanced," asserted roundly in 1882 that there was "no question at all of the nation bringing home capital in recent years,"[5] and proceeded to give such statistical precision as is possible to the facts of the trade balance; to show how—arithmetical misconceptions apart—the excess imports represent mainly earnings of investments and earnings of shipping, with earnings of banking, insurance and commercial service generally[6]. Giffen

---

[1] S.C. on Loans to Foreign States, Q. 5950.

[2] Ibid. p. xlv. Jenks makes far too much of the scabrous and picturesque story of these loans. They were not really representative of the foreign investment of the period and were trifling in amount: see below, p. 323 n. 4.

[3] Hobson, op. cit. p. 204, makes it not much more than a quarter.

[4] R. J. Seddon, Prime Minister of New Zealand, in 1903.

[5] "The Use of Import and Export Statistics," S.J. 1882, reprinted in Essays in Finance (Second Series) in which the quotations occur on p. 135, 195.

[6] Giffen only gave precision to the argument of the Economist of 1851, quoted above, p. 10. He was criticising semi-popular discussions, e.g. in The

did not point out that there had in fact been a sudden and quite abnormal excess of imports in 1876–8. Such an excess was not approached again until 1891–3[1]. If his "recent years" went back to the former triennium, as presumably they did, though there was indeed no question of bringing home large amounts of capital annually, there was probably a little bringing home as has been shown; and his estimate of the amount invested abroad "in recent years," if intended as a net estimate, was almost certainly too sanguine. Clumsily, ignorantly, and with much misunderstanding, the balance of trade controversialists were pointing to a real change in Britain's international position. "The export of a capital surplus was over. Her further investments were to come for a generation from the accruing profits of those which had already been made."[2]

John Stuart Mill, the economist of the age, died in 1873. Through seven editions in his lifetime and others after his death, his *Principles of Political Economy* reiterated his satisfaction that it was now hardly necessary, "at least in our own country," to do more than state without much argument the falsity of the "doctrine of Protection to Native Industry."[3] "The importation of foreign commodities, in the common course of traffic, never takes place except when it is, economically speaking, a national good." Even speaking politically, and considering war risks, the conclusion is the same: the more sources of food a nation draws on the safer it is. "It is ridiculous to found a general system of policy on so improbable a danger as that of being at war with all the nations of the world at once; or to suppose that, even if inferior at sea, a whole country could be blockaded like a town." (It will be noted that "a country" is an island, cosmopolitan as Mill conceived himself to be.) One exception he made, which became notorious as the case of the infant industry, the industry which government, "especially in a young and rising nation," may with reason protect "temporarily," provided that the industry is "in itself perfectly

*Quarterly Review*, July, 1881 and the *Nineteenth Century*, August, 1881 (Sir E. Sullivan). For more serious discussion see Bourne, S., "The growing preponderance of imports," *S.J.* 1877; Newmarch, "On the Progress of the Foreign Trade of the United Kingdom," *S.J.* 1878; Seyd, E., *The Decline of Prosperity* (1879).

[1] The average annual excess in 1876–8 was £128,000,000: in 1874–5 it had been £81,000,000: for 1879–88 it was £101,000,000.

[2] Jenks, *op. cit.* p. 333. Cp. n. 3 to p. 235, above.    [3] Book v. ch. 10, § 1.

suitable to the circumstances of the country." List and his national political economy of productive forces, as opposed to exchange values, Mill always ignored. It is not apparent that he realised how large a concession he had made to national economics, false and less false. Many nations feel young at times and claim the privileges of youth.

No one supposed, however, that Great Britain was "young and rising" in 1850–86. She was old, risen, yet still rising. The exception did not apply. It was only a matter for debate in the schools. Successive chancellors of the exchequer—Gladstone and again Gladstone and shadows of Gladstone like Northcote —had the rather simple task of pulling down surviving tolls on the entry of foreign commodities, when our expanding revenue or economies in the spending departments made the abandonment of receipts from them easy. As a great number of the tolls surviving in 1850–2 brought in no revenue, they could be abandoned with a superb gesture of freedom. In this way the home producers of "bandstring twist," blacking, "cat-lings,"[1] and many other things, were exposed to a not very shrewd blast of competition by Gladstone in 1853.

The only raw materials of importance on which duties re-mained in 1852 were timber, copper, lead and tin. The duties on all four were by this time trifling[2]. The timber duties worked out at 2 per cent. *ad valorem* and upwards. They alone survived the budget of 1853, low but very intricate. Teak, shovel hilts, and most tree-nails were free, and there was a preference for British timber throughout the schedules. The preference went in 1860 and the duties in 1866, as has been seen[3]. No doubt they would have gone earlier had not the vast import of timber made even 1s. or 2s. a load yield a revenue which chancellors could not lightly abandon.

After the controversies and suspensions of the famine years, the corn duty had settled down, as from February 1, 1849, at 1s. a quarter; that on flour at 4½d. a cwt.[4] These so-called registration duties Gladstone did not touch, either in 1853 or in 1860: they were a legacy from his great chief. But after twenty years, he allowed Robert Lowe, then serving under him at the exchequer, to abandon them by 32 and 33 Vict. c. 14,

---

[1] *I.e.* catgut strings, as for violins.
[2] *Customs Tariff of the United Kingdom from* 1800 *to* 1897, Section 1845–6 to 1852–3.
[3] Above, p. 220.     [4] See vol. 1. p. 498.

the budget Act of 1869[1]. With the corn duties proper went duties on rice, sago, tapioca and vermicelli. The imports of all were growing yearly: revenue lost an expanding source of easily raised money, the immediate loss being £900,000. Lowe was giving taxes away right and left that year, and the economic impropriety of this sole surviving tax on "raw material in its very rawest state" annoyed him. But abolition did not increase the English depot trade in corn, as he had hoped; and a political thinker who had not the least hankering after protection wrote in 1888—"it is pretty certain that if the duty were still in existence, it would now be retained."[2]

A few food duties besides that on corn escaped Gladstone's axe in 1853. He cut away those taxes on foreign imported fish which recalled an ancient rivalry with the Dutch in the fisheries; also duties on cider, because when made at home it paid no excise, and on honey. But he left small duties on raw fruit and eggs, with those on the agricultural manufactures butter and cheese, biscuit, and bread[3]. The complex preferential duties on sugar he did not touch. They had been fixed for six years in the interest of the West Indies, after a fight between Lord George Bentinck and the Whigs in 1848[4]. Next year, however, when financing the Crimean War, he carried through the equalisation of duties on foreign and colonial sugar which the Whigs had planned; but wanting revenue, he equalised rather by raising the colonial duty than by lowering the foreign[5]. For the next twenty years, while nearly all the surviving odds and ends of food duties were abolished, mainly in 1860, those on sugar and all sugary things remained an important source of revenue. They were reduced as opportunity offered, in the interests of the consumer, but they were never made very simple. There was much advocacy of their abolition. Finally Stafford Northcote abolished them in 1874, immediately after his chief, Disraeli, had expressed the opinion that the number of distinct sources of revenue was unwisely small[6]. For over

---

[1] In 1864 (by 27 and 28 Vict. c. 18) the 1s. a quarter had been changed into the nearly equivalent 3d. a cwt.

[2] Buxton, S., *Finance and Politics, an Historical Study*, II. 93.

[3] He also left the duty on hops, as there was a, not quite equivalent, excise on home-grown hops.

[4] Vol. I. p. 499.

[5] The duties were intricate: see *Customs Tariff of the U.K.* p. 219–20 and Buxton, *op. cit.* I. 152.

[6] Speech at Newport Pagnell, February 4, 1874, quoted in Buxton, II. 187 n.

a quarter of a century the United Kingdom consumed untaxed sugar.

The duties on manufactures which survived 1853 had for the most part no perceptible protective quality. Foreign china, earthenware, flint glass, or manufactures of bronze cannot have been excluded by a levy of 10s. on the hundredweight; nor cotton gloves by one of 3d. a dozen pairs; not even grand pianos by £3 each; nor "accordions, commonly called Chinese" by 1s. on "the hundred notes."[1] Ordinary cottons and woollens and all 'half-manufactures' such as yarns were free. Machinery, cutlery, and iron and steel manufactures paid 2s. 6d. a hundredweight. Such obstacles to trade may occasionally have diverted an order into home channels, but not often. More serious were the duties on luxuries like lace, cambric handkerchiefs, carpets (6d. a square yard) and shawls. That on paper, at 2½d. a lb., was no doubt definitely protective for all the common sorts. So were, and were meant to be, the long untouched series of silk duties—turbans 3s. each; dresses 30s. each; plain silk ribbons 6d. a lb.; with many more specific rates; and on all silks, not otherwise specified, 15 per cent. *ad valorem*.

As the world's trade lines lay in the 'fifties, the protective or possibly protective British duties interfered almost exclusively with that section which ran from Paris to London. Hence the importance of the Anglo-French treaty of 1860, the 'Cobden' treaty, combined with the budget policy of that year. How far the treaty made the policy or the policy the treaty, or to which side or to which persons the greater credit is to be assigned for the agreement, need not be discussed here[2]. Treaty and policy together, when the policy had been rounded off by the budget of 1861[3], put the United Kingdom into a position which no kingdom had occupied before since kings first took presents from visiting merchants or blackmailed the caravans. From October 1, 1861, when the paper duties ran out, no foreign manufacture whatever appeared in the British tariff except flour, alcoholic drinks, manufactured tobacco and sugar, gold and

---

[1] *Customs Tariff of the U.K.* p. 826.

[2] The points are fully discussed in Dunham, A. L., *The Anglo-French Treaty of Commerce of* 1860 (*University of Michigan*, 1830). Cp. the older accounts in Morley, J., *Life of Richard Cobden*, ch. XI–XIV and *Life of Gladstone*, II. 18 *sqq.*

[3] Which abolished the paper duties (24 Vict. c. 20). The great budget Act of 1860 was 23 and 24 Vict. c. 110. For the paper duties, custom and excise, see Buxton, *op. cit.* I. 259–68. In the political cant of the day they were the "taxes on knowledge." At most, they were only lightly protective.

silver plate, playing cards and dice. It is true that "ships with all their tackle...built of wood" paid 1s. a ton for admission to the British register; but that really was a fee and was levied on colonial as well as on foreign ships. Flour was no longer taxed after 1869, nor sugar after 1874. The ship registration fee had gone in 1866. Gold and silver plate were not free until 1890. Except for these, all the classic luxuries of the ages could come in freely, purple and fine linen, carpets of Ispahan, silk and cloth of gold, "and broideries of intricate design and printed hangings in enormous bales." The dice, those wicked dice, had paid a guinea a pair. They were freed, as it happened, when a Derby was prime minister and in the year of the second Reform Bill which gave the artisan his vote, by 30 and 31 Vict. c. 82. Remained the playing cards.

An Anglo-French commercial treaty meant reductions and reorganisations of the duties on wines and spirits. So it had been in 1786, and so it was again. This was what Britain really gave, revenue; and with it a promise not to prohibit or tax the export of coal. Had there been no negotiations, she would probably not have modified her wine-duties at that time, or exactly in the way she did; nor would she have made promises about coal. Also she might perhaps have retained some of the duties on luxury manufactures; but their abolition was in the direct line of a policy to which she was already committed. So was the unhindered export of the coal[1]. The pledge not to interfere with the export however had a political, rather than an economic implication, an implication which, in the year after the volunteer movement, some parties disliked[2].

France gave in return a great deal more than her protectionists approved. She abandoned the antiquated policy of prohibition, which had affected many of the finer British manufactures, and pledged herself not to levy on any of them—fine or coarse—more than 30 per cent. *ad valorem*. In the tariff

[1] Sir T. H. Farrer (later Lord Farrer), who was Assistant Secretary to the Board of Trade in 1860 and Secretary from 1865 to 1886, always maintained that "what we did was, with one doubtful exception, what we should have done, and ought to have done, had France made no relaxation in her duties" (*Free Trade versus Fair Trade*, p. 278). The exception was the wine duties, which gave "some advantage to French wines over the wines of other countries"; led to retaliation by Spain; and were eventually modified so as to admit the heavier peninsular wines at the same rates as the French—but not till 1886, by 49 and 50 Vict. c. 41.

[2] Among them the Prince Consort, who thought that we were 'giving the Emperor our coals and iron,' *Life*, v. 13, 23.

finally adopted the average was a good deal less; but it was at least as high as those protective silk duties which Britain had abandoned completely. As industrialism had made great progress in France since 1848, and as in many fine manufactures she equalled or excelled Britain, the result of the treaty was less remarkable than some had hoped and others have suggested[1]. There was a satisfactory expansion of trade, but part of it—it is impossible to say how much—would have come in any case. A large prompt increase in the export of British woollens balanced a corresponding increase in the import of French silks and Paris wares. In time, a substantial export of the finer British cottons grew up; but in 1868–9 cotton exports to France were worth little more than those to Holland, and less than those to Syria and Palestine. Though more French wines and brandies came in, the English did not become heavy claret drinkers. Whiskey, for years a favourite navvies' drink, was now coming into fashion, like the Highlands. France hardly increased her consumption of British iron and steel. In short, the direct trade between the two countries was not revolutionised. Exports of British produce averaged £6,000,000 in 1855–9. In 1860 they were £5,000,000. For 1861–4 they averaged £8,700,000 and for 1866–70, £11,000,000. To this must be added the re-export trade to France, which in the late 'sixties was actually greater than the direct trade, because of France's huge takings of colonial wool. The wool and the coal paid for an important part of Britain's very heavy French imports[2].

The 'Cobden' treaty was denounced in 1872, when France, fallen into that post-bellum mood in which the non-economic arguments for protection always have most power[3], was turning back towards an inherited and only half-interrupted system of full tariffs. It had been the first of a famous series of commercial treaties negotiated in a free trade spirit, which usually contained the most favoured nation clause. Britain alone con-

---

[1] *E.g.* Buxton, *op. cit.* I. 236.

[2] United Kingdom imports from France, 1866–70, averaged £35,000,000 a year; exports of British produce to France £11,000,000; and exports of foreign and colonial produce (mainly wool) £12,000,000. The imports contain freight charges, the exports do not. But freight would not nearly account for the difference. In the trade triangle, Britain was paying France by exporting to some third country.

[3] The mood of nationalism at war, convinced "dass alle internationalen Wirtschaftsbeziehungen ein notwendiges Übel sind, das wir so klein wie möglich machen sollen." Sombart, *Händler und Helden* (1915), p. 133.

cluded eight major treaties of this type in the 'sixties[1]. There were many more among the European powers, a whole network of them. The clause so worked as to extend any negotiated tariff concession to the whole group of 'most favoured' nations[2]. Side by side with treaty-made concessions, there was much autonomous lowering of duties as in Britain, though nowhere with such complete free-trading logic. War made France pause. In 1879 falling prices, gathering agrarian competition from overseas, and a need for revenue made Bismarck pause. Everywhere the economic protectionism of the natural man, and the political protectionism of the statesman thinking in terms of war-risk, asserted themselves: surely Bismarck knew! Even if started for agrarian reasons, as a war food-insurance fee perhaps, an upward tariff movement never missed manufactures. Russia, whose trade had not got very free, began such an upward movement in 1881; France in 1882. Italy, Austria-Hungary, and others were also moving. Yet the work done in Europe during this short era of falling tariffs and commercial treaties had not been completely undone by 1885-6. Prohibition as a habit was dead. Duties, a cautious commentator wrote, were "on the whole lower than before 1860."[3]

That was in Europe. The United States came out of their Civil War with a war tariff, high and unsystematic. During the free trade years, the directors of their policy had no sympathy with a creed which in America had been professed principally by slave-owning agrarian Southerners—'rebels.' Through fluctuating policies, which fluctuated little on the main issue, they had built up, by the 'eighties, a tariff wall such as Europe did not know[4]. The European mind had not yet conceived of a system under which cotton yarn paid 5d. a lb. and 20 per cent. *ad valorem*, or bituminous coal 3s. 1½d. a ton. That some fantastic impositions on fine manufactures accompanied these fiscal extravagances lower down the scale need not be said. Duties as a whole ranged from 35 to 100 per cent. *ad valorem*. Yet many manufactures, fine and coarse, still got over the wall.

In America and other continents, the British dominions,

---

[1] See the list in Levi, *History of British Commerce*, p. 511. The most-favoured nation clause has a heavy literature of its own, *e.g.* Schraut, *System der Handelsverträge und der Meistbegünstigung* (1886); Glier, *Die Meistbegünstigungsklausel* (1905).

[2] See the eloquent passage in Morley's *Cobden*, II. 342-5.

[3] Farrer, *op. cit.* (ed. of 1886), p. 61.

[4] See Taussig, F. W., *The tariff history of the United States.*

those "young and rising nations," were doing what Mill had almost encouraged them to do, taking care of their infants. Across that undefended line, Canada had the example of her southern neighbour. The Canadian tariff of 1879 was decidedly higher than the French or Italian, much higher than the German, very much higher than the Belgian or Dutch. Like the United States, Canada taxed bituminous coal heavily. Unlike the United States, she taxed anthracite coal rather more heavily. On typical British products, such as steel rails cottons and woollens, she levied duties which worked out at from 15 to 30 per cent. Australasian tariffs, with the sole exception of that of New South Wales, were also moving upwards in the 'seventies and early 'eighties[1].

Meanwhile the growing industrialism of the whole civilised world, with the absence of any obstacle to the entry of foreign produce into the British market, was producing its natural result. British imports contained a somewhat increased percentage of manufactured and part-manufactured goods. In the circumstances, the percentage increase over a quarter of a century was remarkably slow. It was[2]:

| | Percentage of imports fully manufactured | Value million £ | Percentage fully manufactured and part manufactured | Value million £ |
|---|---|---|---|---|
| 1855-9 | 6 | 10 | 14 | 24 |
| 1865-9 | 9 | 27 | 17 | 48 |
| 1875-9 | 13 | 48 | 20 | 75 |
| 1880-4 | 13 | 55 | 20 | 83 |

There is an upward jerk in the 'sixties. At the same time the finished manufactures become more than half of the total. The duties on the fine old luxury goods from abroad, which could always compete in an open field[3], have gone. A little later, competition begins to be felt in the home market for straightforward products of modern metallurgy. Even in the 'fifties, rail contracts in Spain had been lost to Belgium[4]. By 1867 an ironmaster is lamenting that the Belgians have "superseded us everywhere." They have sent iron to America and have even

---

[1] All the tariffs of the period are conveniently summarised in Farrer, *op. cit.*
[2] Based on the value figures compiled for the *R.C. on Depression of Trade*, I. 130.
[3] Above, p. 16–17.
[4] Jenks, *Migration of British Capital*, p. 192.

secured an order from St Thomas' Hospital "for what are called girders."[1] It was the fault of a trade union, he said: but that is as it may be. Next year the import returns included for the first time a distinct heading for 'iron and steel wrought or manufactured.' Ih 1868–9 the amount averaged £400,000. In 1875–9 it averaged £1,700,000 and in 1880–4, £2,600,000. Throughout the whole period, the silk and fine wool fabrics, mainly French, varied between about a third and about two-fifths of all the imported manufactures, by value. France also sent a varied selection of unspecified luxuries, and from £1,000,000 to £2,000,000 worth of gloves. Towards the close there was growing import of a most miscellaneous kind from Germany—some of the silk; much of the steel; masses of toys of every kind, including nearly all the lead soldiers of the nurseries; all the best chemicals and appliances of the laboratories; all the lead pencils worth using; with cheap and sometimes nasty imitations of British cutlery and other wares, which gave weight to the half-informed sneer of the middle 'eighties about things 'made in Germany.'[2]

It was most natural that after the trade collapse of the early 'seventies, and during the continued puzzling commercial and industrial difficulties which followed, plain men should begin to put the question—is it 'fair' to keep open market for nations who are closing theirs? Some of the plain men made much of the less desirable element in the imports, which in fact was trifling. Others put further questions, of varying relevance to the problems of commercial policy. Was it proper to call free imports 'free trade'? Had Cobden and Peel proved good prophets? Had it been sound politics so to arrange our tariffs as to exclude imperial preference? Did not various nations flourish under varied forms of protection? Was Bismarck a fool? Were we alone wise? Questions all well suited to the pamphlet, the platform, and the evening press; and many of them well worth the asking. They were mixed up with those doubts about the balance of trade which were disturbing the public mind in the

[1] *R.C. on Trade Unions* (1868–9, xxxix), Q. 10,696: a witness from N. Staffordshire.

[2] The consular reports and those prepared for the *R.C. on Depression of Trade* are summarised in Farrer, *op. cit.* p. 161–6. The most important is Strachey's *Report on the effect of the German Tariff* (c. 4530) of 1885. By the Merchandise Marks Act of 1887 (50 and 51 Vict. c. 28) things 'made in Germany,' or anywhere else, had to be so labelled. The label was made the title of a popular book (by E. E. Williams) in 1896.

late 'seventies[1]. The 'fair trade' controversy and the balance of trade controversy "ran very much into each other."[2]

The questioners came together into a Fair Trade League in 1881[3]. Their scheme was not fully worked out at first and they never had to apply it. It did not at this time deflect British policy. For 'fairness,' it demanded at the outset a moderate import duty on foreign manufactures, to be removed from the goods of any country so soon as that country agreed to admit British manufactures free. For the Empire's sake, it demanded a lowering or abolition of duties on empire tea, coffee, fruit, tobacco and wine; and, though less decidedly, a light general tax on all foodstuffs coming from foreign countries. How dominion tariffs on British manufactures were to be dealt with was not declared. Nor were the implications of the proposed crude form of retaliation investigated. Yet, according to a recognised political tradition, for several years the country was represented by convinced Fair Traders and by politicians speculating in Fair Trade as dying for lack of what, in due course, if called in, they would prescribe. "Your iron industry is dead, dead as mutton; your coal industries...are languishing. Your silk industry is dead, assassinated by the foreigner. Your woollen industry is in *articulo mortis*, gasping, struggling. Your cotton industry is seriously sick." So Randolph Churchill in 1884[4]. He pressed for a Commission of inquiry into the very real trade depression thus garishly delineated. The Minority Report of that Commission gave the later form of the Fair Trade proposals—a 10 to 15 per cent. tariff "upon all manufactures imported from foreign countries," and similar duties "upon those articles of food which India and the Colonies are able to produce," when sent from foreign countries. The duties on manufactures were now treated as at least semi-permanent, because we might "be unable to alter the protectionist policy of other nations."[5]

[1] Above, p. 240.

[2] Giffen, *The Use of Import and Export Statistics (Essays in Finance, Second Series)*, p. 132.

[3] The movement is generally dated from the issue in 1879 of *The Policy of Self-Help. Suggestions towards the Consolidation of the Empire and the Defence of its Industries and Commerce. Two letters by...*(W. Farrer Eckroyd).

[4] Churchill, W. S., *Lord Randolph Churchill* (1906), I. 291: speech at Blackpool, January 24, 1884.

[5] *R.C. on Depression of Trade. Final Report*, p. lxv *sqq.* Minority Report signed by Farrer Eckroyd, P. A. Muntz, Nevile Lubbock. Lord Dunraven also signed but with the reservation that he 'objected to protection.'

When the Minority and Majority Reports had been weighed, Randolph Churchill stopped speculating in Fair Trade. The movement seemed to die. Joseph Chamberlain, munitioned by the Board of Trade, had shot at it dangerously. The League and the name he helped to snuff out: years afterwards the spirit entered into him. For its strength lay less in its economics, though they were not negligible[1], than in its sense of a changing world and in its nationalism. Sampson Lloyd, its parliamentary leader, knew this when he translated and published, for the first time in English, Friedrich List's *National System of Political Economy*. That was in 1885[2].

---

[1] The Minority Report of 1886 deals scientifically, for example, with the creation of surplus productive power in protected countries and resulting competition and 'dumping' in neutral and open markets.

[2] For the Fair Trade movement generally see the Publications of the Fair Trade League. Farrer, *Free Trade versus Fair Trade*, though controversial, quotes Fair Trade writers verbatim. There is no good narrative in English. See Fuchs, C. J., *Die Handelspolitik Englands und seine Kolonien* (1893), p. 157 *sqq.* and Halévy, E., *Histoire du peuple anglais. Epilogue* (1926), p. 272–5.

# CHAPTER VII

## AGRICULTURE

D URING the first decade of the reformed Poor Law, anxious publicists had believed that men were redundant in rural Britain. They were probably right, as things then were. Forty years later the spectre was rural depopulation, not re-dundance. But careful inquiry in the 'eighties, applied to the fifteen most agricultural English counties, showed that between 1851 and 1881 there had been a decline of only 1 per cent., on one definition of the word rural, and of 2·1 per cent. on another. In an absolutely rural county such as Huntingdon, with no town of even 5000 inhabitants, there had, it is true, been a decline of 11·8 per cent.; but even in Huntingdon the popu-lation of 1881 was almost precisely what it had been in the year after the Poor Law was reformed. The new conditions of free-dom, mobility, and a partly mechanised and less arable agri-culture had done no more than lop off an intervening growth. Much the same was true of the other counties of maximum rusticity. One way and another, by agriculture and the occu-pations immediately dependent on it, the land was still carrying approximately the head of men that had once been too big, and carrying them in much greater comfort. They only seemed fewer when set against the multitudes of the streets. But the streets and the new worlds had apparently got hold of the best stocks. How else, the inquirer wrote, could you explain the now certain fact that there was more idiocy on the land[1]?

While the rural population proper remained about stationary, it was arguable, and was in fact being argued in the 'eighties, that the number of landowners was still "progressively dwind-ling"[2]; through the automatic working of the tradition of pur-chase by great proprietors, of family settlements which hindered sales, and of the law of primogeniture in cases of intestacy[3]. Down to 1870 no one knew with precision how the land of

[1] Ogle, Dr W., "The alleged depopulation of the rural districts of England," *S.J.* LII (1889), 205.

[2] Brodrick, Hon. G. C., *English Land and English Landlords* (1881), p. 111.

[3] The direct effect of the Law of Primogeniture was small, as nearly all landed estates descended under settlements and wills. See Kenny, C. S., *An Essay on...Primogeniture* (1878); Williams, J., *Real Property*; Pollock, Sir F., *The Land Laws* (1883), esp. p. 179–80. It was generally held that "a much larger

Britain was owned. An attempt made to ascertain the facts, in 1871–3, led to the issue of what contemporaries called " The New Domesday Book[1]." Those who compiled it only claimed that it was "proximately accurate": those who used it doubted even that. It was at best, they said, not "a perfect record of owners" but "an imperfect record of estates."[2] In it, *exempli gratia*, the Duke of Buccleuch counted as fourteen landowners because he owned in fourteen counties. But even the Book yielded the remarkable conclusion that about a quarter of the land of the United Kingdom was owned by 1200 persons, and about a half by 7400. One critic felt certain that, when allowance had been made for its errors, it showed that in England and Wales not more than 4000 proprietors owned about four-sevenths of the area reported on, which was the area assessed to rates[3]. It was pointed out further that the apparent dispersion of ownership in the remaining three-sevenths, or one-half, or whatever it might be, was connected as much with suburban freehold plots as with the properties of lesser gentlemen and 'yeomen.' The experiment of a New Domesday Book was not repeated, so the question whether or not the number of landowners was "progressively dwindling" down to the 'eighties cannot be answered. That the concentration of rural ownership was at least unweakened, and was excessive, is sure.

Various attempts had been made by the good sense of conveyancers and their clients, and by the law, to reduce the restrictive pressure of the older sort of family settlement and facilitate transference of family property. At law, down to 1856, the tenant for life under a settlement could not give a lease to run beyond his own lifetime, unless definitely empowered to do so by his settlement. Often he was empowered; and when he was not, relief might be secured by private Act of Parliament. In 1856 this relief was generalised (19 and 20 Vict. c. 120). Later, the Settled Estates Act of 1877 (40 and 41 Vict. c. 18) reversed the old presumption of law—leases might be granted unless forbidden in the settlement. To overcome the difficulties

---

area" was "under settlement than at the free disposal of individual landlords"; Brodrick, *op. cit.* p. 100. Under a strict settlement, of course, the 'owner' was properly only a life tenant who could not sell.

[1] *Return of Owners of Land*, 1874 (LXXII. parts 1, 2, 3) and the summary *Return* of 1876 (LXXX). It was made at the request of the House of Lords to disprove the popular view that there were not very many thousand landowners in Britain. It was hardly successful.

[2] Brodrick, *op. cit.* p. 163.      [3] *Ibid.* p. 165.

of sale by the tenant for life, the average settlement had long included clauses authorising the trustees to sell at his request and use the proceeds for discharging mortgages, or in other ways; though landed opinion always frowned on such impairings of the estate. For Scotland, the heir of entail had been given power to disentail in 1848. Finally, but only in 1882, Lord Cairns' Settled Land Act (45 and 46 Vict. c. 38) gave English tenants for life "as large and effectual powers of using the land to the best advantage as are compatible with settlements existing at all."[1]

Changes in custom had usually preceded changes in law. But neither had yet transformed the essentials. Tenants for life got free power to lease; but yearly tenancy remained the normal arrangement, though Scotland kept her nineteen-year leases[2]. In England, possibly through inertia, both owner and farmer usually preferred the short tenure. It was compatible with either a patriarchal or a commercial relationship. In Wales "hereditary succession [of farmers] prevailed on most large estates."[3] In what the eighteenth century would have called the improved parts of England, farming families moved about a good deal as profit directed. Thanks to the easing of settlements and to the ordinary ruins or extinctions of families, great and small, land came rather freely into the market. Estates were always being acquired or built up by new men, even by the newest, like Sir Roger Scatcherd of Boxall Hall, "whilom a drunken stone mason," now (1858) a great contractor[4]. A French observer in the early 'fifties, wishing to correct his countrymen's "erroneous impression...that landed property in England does not change hands," had pointed out that "properties of fifty to five hundred acres...in fact are sold every day."[5] He quoted typical advertisements for the guidance of the French. Yet in spite of the advertisements and of Sir Roger Scatcherd, Buccleuch still counted as fourteen landlords and the land was not effectively mobilised. If Sir Roger's estate were big enough, and he had sons, there would probably be a conveyancer and a settlement to 'make an eldest son.' Twenty-five years later, however, the law was preparing for a time when, given sufficient provocation, the land might begin

[1] Pollock, *op. cit.* p. 192. The Scottish Act is 11 and 12 Vict. c. 36.
[2] See vol. I. p. 109.
[3] *R.C. on Land in Wales and Monmouth*, 1896 (xxxiv), p. 291.
[4] Trollope, Anthony, *Doctor Thorne*, ch. 9.
[5] Lavergne, L. G. de, *The Rural Economy of England, Scotland and Ireland* (Eng. trans. 1855), p. 94-5.

to move faster. There was a foretaste of the provocation so early as 1853. Gladstone, stopping a gap in the fiscal system left unwillingly by Pitt, placed beside Pitt's legacy duty on personal property a small 'succession' duty on real property—the first new tax levied since Waterloo. Pitt had only proposed to tax collateral, not direct, succession to land; but Fox had fought èven this on the ground that the principle would "enable the state to seize upon the whole property of the country."[1] There certainly was some such possibility latent in 'death duties.'

Custom again showed the way to law in regulation of the dealings between landlord and farmer. At common law, an outgoing tenant had no right to any particular notice, and could claim nothing attached to the land but the *emblements*, the growing crops or their value. When the typical farmer was a small open-field husbandman, not given to sinking capital in the land, this may not have been unjust. It was long since even small farmers in England had sunk capital in building their own houses; though in out-of-the-way districts they might have had very little capital assistance from their landlord. In eighteenth-century, and to some extent in nineteenth-century, Scotland and Wales they had built houses, such as they were. Tenant-built 'black houses' in the Hebrides long survived 1850 and 1885. The original Scottish leases had been designed to encourage tenants who sank capital in gathering up the stones, doing rough drainage, or running up a dry-stone house: the improvement was given nineteen years in which to exhaust itself. The strong nineteenth-century farmer, in Scotland Wales or England, always had a house provided, and so had no claim under that head; but he too had sometimes done all the draining, and had generally done part of it. He might also have stubbed wastes, or marled, or limed, or fenced, or used expensive and unexhausted 'artificials.'[2]

From these different sources—the primitive conviction of old-fashioned cultivators that they had done something for which they might claim compensation on quittance; and the calculated wish of intelligent landlords to attract farmers who would do something to deserve it—there had grown up 'tenant

[1] See Buxton, S., *Finance and Politics*, I. 114, 117; II. 292 for the parliamentary history. Fox's speech was May 26, 1796.

[2] On the law see Clifford, F., "The Agricultural Holdings Act," *J.R.A.S.* 1876, p. 129. For Wales, *R.C. on Land in Wales*, p. 576 *sqq.*, 690 *sqq.* For the Hebrides, below, p. 506. On drainage, etc., by the farmer see vol. I. p. 460-1, and Squarey, E. P., "Farm Capital," *J.R.A.S.* 1878, p. 167.

right' customs of different kinds in various parts of England and Wales, long before 1850. Caird found them "fully recognised" in that year amid backward conditions in Surrey, Sussex, the Weald of Kent and part of the West Riding, and among progressive conditions in North Nottingham and Lincolnshire[1]. Had he been into Wales, he might have added the moderately progressive Glamorgan and the rather primitive Brecon[2]. During the great transformation of Lincolnshire agriculture, enlightened owners like the Yarboroughs and the Chaplins, by guaranteeing compensation for unexhausted improvements, had secured what Scottish landlords had secured by the long lease[3]. As a Scot, Caird preferred the lease. He could not deny the merit of the Lincolnshire system; but he made much of the bad farming, stupidity and chicane connected with tenant right in Surrey and the Weald. Farmers "worked up to a quitting" and tried to get a good valuation on bad manure[4]. But a rogue can spoil any system. He can let a farm down in the later years of a long lease; and Caird himself was to argue in 1878 that the Scottish system needed, among other things, "some equitable rules to secure continuance of the tenant's interest in good farming to the close of the lease."[5]

By that time England had put the Lincolnshire custom tentatively into the law. The Agricultural Holdings Act of 1875 (38 and 39 Vict. c. 92) reversed "a presumption of law in existence for centuries past,"[6] by legalising compensation for tenants' improvements and fixtures and regulating the notice to quit. But it was a permissive Act. Farmers could contract out of the whole or any part of it, or they could contract for more than it gave, if local custom sanctioned more. The Act was adopted "in whole or in part on many estates."[7] Where not adopted formally it was not without influence as a model. Eight years later, when depression had come, tenants, or those who spoke for them, decided that this was not enough. The Agricultural Holdings Act (England) of 1883 (46 and 47 Vict. c. 61), a contemporary grumbled, showed that Parliament no longer trusted farmers to take care of themselves, and made com-

---

[1] Caird, J., *English Agriculture in 1850 and 1851*, p. 505 and *passim*.

[2] *R.C. on Agriculture*, 1882 (XIV; also 1881, XV–XVII); Doyle's report on Wales based on Q. 32,260; 65,808; 65,873. Cp. Little, W., "The Agriculture of Glamorgan," *J.R.A.S.* 1885, p. 165.

[3] For the Lincolnshire custom see Caird, p. 194.    [4] *Ibid.* p. 119.

[5] *The Landed Interest*, p. 71.    [6] Clifford, *op. cit.* p. 129.

[7] Clifford, F., "The Agricultural Holdings Act, 1883," *J.R.A.S.* 1884, p. 2.

pensation compulsory[1]. It was a cumbrous Act and was to require much interpretation and amendment. But it marked an important turning point in the history of the Land Laws.

Very soon political events would shake the social economic system of which those laws had been an expression. The country labourer would get his vote. The County Council would take over local government. Wise and popular resident landowners would continue to work for their county through its Council, but where landlords were not popular their power in local government would dwindle or cease. In South Wales, to take the extreme case, the County Council Act of 1887 "smote the whole class beyond recovery."[2]

From one vexation of his father and grandfather the mid-Victorian cultivator in England and Wales had been freed completely by the Reform Bill Whigs—payment of tithe in kind, or bargainings about the *modus* in money or corn, when that had replaced the actual taking of the tenth sheaf or tenth pail of milk, as in fact it generally had[3]. After 1850 there could be only family traditions of that "horrid greediness" in exacting tithe which according to Arthur Young was "the disgrace of England"[4] in 1792, and which, it is to be feared, had not become much less disgraceful in Cobbett's time. The Whig Law of 1836 (6 and 7 Wm. IV, c. 71) had been in good working order since 1840, and the tithe barn was becoming a matter for anti-quarians instead of a centre of rather indecent clerical activity. The law had created a nationalised *modus*, a general commutation, whose history and economics are a complex thing apart. Caird believed that the removal of the liability to hand over part of the produce to tithe-owners had done good by encouraging farmers to break up sheep-walk for corn[5]. Perhaps

---

[1] Clifford, F., *op. cit.* p. 1. Cp. Pollock, *The Land Laws*, p. 154.

[2] Vaughan, H. M., *The South Wales Squires* (1926), p. 3.

[3] The Scottish *teinds* were quite different. Since the Reformation and the tithe-commutation of 1627–33 the clergy had no direct interest in levying them. They were in effect a levy on the rentals of the heritors (landowners). Scottish agrarian economists attributed a good part of the agricultural progress of Scotland in the eighteenth century to the absence of the vexatious tithe system of England and France. Anderson, J., *Essays relating to Agriculture* (1796), III. 157. For the general history see Cormack, A. A., *Teinds and Agriculture, an Historical Survey* (1930). For English tithe see Venn, J. A., *Foundations of Agricultural Economics* (1923), ch. 5, on which this section is based.

[4] *Travels in France* (ed. Maxwell), p. 332.

[5] *English Agriculture in* 1850 *and* 1851, p. 80. Venn's endorsement of this view (*op. cit.* p. 118) is open to question.

he was right; but after all plenty of the breaking up was done before 1836, and done at least as quickly as was wholesome. Moreover down-fed lambs and wool were tithable. Whether correct or not, his belief appears to have not much importance in the general economic history of the country. Nor has the tithe rent-charge itself, in the period from 1836 to 1886. Based on a seven-year average of the prices of the three principal grains, it fluctuated very little about par, that is the value of tithe as estimated in the 'thirties. Its lowest and highest were just over 10 per cent. below par in 1854, and nearly 13 per cent. above in 1874. In 1886 it fell to nearly 13 per cent. below[1]. After that a continuous fall created a new situation. Throughout the fifty years, £4,000,000 was about the figure of total tithe-rent charge at par. It was probably near to a tenth of the rental of lands in England and Wales in 1836–40. When it came back to par in 1883, after the rise of the 'seventies, it was only about one-twelfth of a rental also falling[2]. How it was divided between the Church, the Colleges, and the lay impropriator, is a matter for specialised histories. Always to economists a tax on rent, whatever it might seem to farmers, it had now assumed that character definitely, although by agreement the tenant very often paid it[3]. Neither its existence nor its apportionment affected the tenant's daily life as the tithe in kind had, though he might have politico-religious grievances about the way in which it was spent, especially if he were a Welshman.

Not much vexed by tithe, the mid-Victorian farmer was very little vexed by problems of open field and common, or by those of their enclosure. There was no county of England or Wales except Leicestershire in which enclosing was not done by Act of Parliament after 1850; but apart from some big enclosures of hill-common in Wales and the North-West, like the 16,036 acres at Llandewi-Brefi in Cardigan in 1863 or the 7637 acres of Ennerdale in 1864, it was a clearing up of scraps, with an

---

[1] The tithe-table is reproduced in the *Dict. Pol. Econ.* s.v.

[2] Cp. Caird, *The Landed Interest*, p. 132–3. Caird's contention that the land rental of England had risen 50 per cent. in the period 1836–78 is not borne out by the figures in Stamp, Sir J. C., *British Incomes and Property* (1927 ed.), p. 36 and *passim*. Probably 30 per cent. would be nearer the mark. Stamp's figures, based on the Income Tax, begin in 1842–3.

[3] It was only by the Tithe Act of 1891 (54 and 55 Vict. c. 8) that the liability to pay tithe rent charge was finally put on the owner, any contract to the contrary between owner and tenant notwithstanding. Cp. Venn, *Foundations of Agricultural Economics*, p. 121.

occasional and rare parish[1]. A writer on Hertfordshire in the *Journal of the Royal Agricultural Society* for 1864 was puzzled and shocked to find that all the fields of Baldock and Clothall still lay open[2]. The Enclosure Commissioners reported in 1878 that nearly 600,000 acres, the equivalent of a fair-sized county, had been dealt with since the General Enclosure Act of 1845; but of this nearly a quarter was done before the end of 1850[3], and the rest was mostly in the Ennerdale group. There were over 30,000 acres in Cardiganshire alone, and over 22,000 in Westmorland. It is worth noting that towards the very end of the age of enclosure there were still proved abuses on the unstinted hill-commons. In Westmorland, in 1868, Sunday was "often the favourite day for a quiet dogging of the neighbours' sheep," to make more room for your own. Monmouthshire hill farmers in 1870 were selecting shepherds and sheep for their fighting qualities. Some combative little breeds were as good as dogs in pushing weaker sorts off the best ground[4].

The decade 1865–75 marked the end of the enclosure age because there was not much left to enclose and because a crowded urbanised society, well fed from overseas, had come— naturally and rightly—to think of common, not as cattle ground, still less as potential corn-field, but as 'open-space.' The organised movement for preservation began in London. For ten years the Commons Preservation Society worked. In 1876 Parliament legislated for the first time about commons in general on the assumption that their destiny was not enclosure. With that common-land passed out of agricultural into social history[5].

Enclosure being done, what had been the ultimate fate of the cultivating owner, the 'yeoman,' who moves in close company with commons and open fields through history, in closer through

---

[1] *Return of Inclosure Acts*, 1914 (Cd. 399).

[2] *J.R.A.S.* 1864, p. 301. These were the fields which helped Frederick Seebohm to recreate the English Village Community. The last 'commonable fields,' of a different sort, to be enclosed in Wales were 50 acres at Llyswere in 1856 and 105 acres at Bronllys in 1860. Both places are in Brecknock. Bowen, Ivor, *The Great Enclosure of Common Lands in Wales* (1914), App.

[3] Between 130,000 and 140,000 acres. The *Return* of 1914 gives the acreages and years. Cp. vol. i. p. 454.

[4] *J.R.A.S.* 1868, p. 14, Westmorland; 1870, p. 289, Monmouth. Cp. Vol. i. p. 107.

[5] The Metropolitan Commons Act of 1866 (29 and 30 Vict. c. 122) had stopped enclosure within the London police area. The Act of 1876 is 39 and 40 Vict. c. 56.

legend? The probability is that his numbers and the area under his control did not change much, on the balance, between Victoria's accession and her jubilee. If there was any change, it was slightly downwards. Every one knew that he could be found rather easily in Cumberland, Westmorland, the Yorkshire Dales, the Isle of Axholme and the Fens, and with a little search in most places[1]. He was often bought out; but small men also bought land to work it, and farmers of all sorts bought occasionally. In the early 'nineties, about 4 per cent. of landholders owned part of the land which they worked, besides those who owned it all[2]. Wales with its "leech-craving" for land, as the drafter of an official document once put it in non-official style[3], shows both buying and selling at work. The occupying freeholders of the 'nineties turned out to be of "very recent origin."[4] Some had bought crown land on enclosure: there were many such in Cardigan, where so much had been recently enclosed. Others had acquired a sort of freehold in the good old way by squatting on crown land before enclosure, cribbing little crofts from it, and turning out a few sheep. Sitting tenants had bought and mortgaged to get security, in a society where news of occasional evictions ran angrily across the hills[5]. Welshmen challenged the statement of a Saxon assistant-commissioner who said in 1881 that "the half-starved proprietor of 10 or 20 acres" was "perpetually trying to persuade the larger owner to buy his bit of land"[6]; but such things happened. Lord Penrhyn told how he had himself bought out from 25 to 30 small men at their request[7]. When exact inquiry was at length made, in 1887 and subsequent years, it was found that from 10 to 12 per cent. of the cultivated land of Wales was occupied by its owner, nearly always a small man[8].

For Great Britain the same inquiries gave between 14 and 15 per cent.; for England between 15 and 16; for Scotland just

---

[1] The reports on the *Employment of Children* of 1867–9 noted that the numerous 'statesmen' in Cumberland and Westmorland were a bar to education: they kept their children at home to work (1868–9, XIII. 142).

[2] Curtler, W. H. R., *The Enclosure and Redistribution of our Land* (1920), p. 240.

[3] *R.C. on Land in Wales*, p. 313.                          *Ibid.* p. 291.

[5] *Ibid.* p. 549 *sqq.*, 576 *sqq.*

[6] *R.C. on Agriculture*; Doyle, A., Q. 32,050.

[7] *Ibid.* Lord Penrhyn's evidence, Q. 7350–8.

[8] The figures are from the annual agricultural statistics: *e.g.* in 1891 the Welsh figure was 11·6. The statistics deal with cultivated land "owned and occupied" by the same person.

over 12. In England certainly not all of this was yeoman land. A squire who cultivated a home farm, or who was forced by agricultural depression to cultivate an outlying farm through a bailiff, "owned and occupied" the land as much as any fenman or dalesman. The high proportion of occupying owners returned in 1887–8 in some counties not known to have been abnormally rich in yeomen, and known to have been hard hit by depression, suggests a good deal of this kind of owner-occupancy. Essex is in that group. It has always had its yeomen[1]. There may well have been 12 or even 15 per cent. of the cultivated area in their hands. But it is hard to believe that there was over 21 per cent. which is the figure for "land owned and occupied" in Essex in 1887. There were a good many farms without farmers on the Essex clays just then. As Cumberland and Lincolnshire, counties certainly rich in yeomen, had only 15 and 16 per cent. respectively of owner-occupied land, and as Lincolnshire like Essex would have a good many farms in hand, Cumberland few or none, it is unlikely that any county figure above 15 can represent nothing but working owner-occupiers. The aggregate English figure for their land must be somewhat lower, probably not above 12[2].

The nests of small owners in the Lincoln flats deserve particular notice. Everyone interested in such things had heard of the Isle of Axholme in the North-West, where, favoured by a soil good for all kinds of specialised crops, small men in the 'eighties still owned and tilled the strips of some surviving open fields[3]. Others were less widely known, such as Hogsthorpe in the marsh below Tennyson's wolds, where half the occupiers of twenty acres or less were owners, or Wrangle between the East Fen and the Wash, where the proportion was two-thirds[4]. At Cowbit, where the skating is, South of Spalding, almost everyone was a freeholder in the 'sixties[5]. None of these facts prove that Lincolnshire was a county, or Britain a country, of small owners; only that such people in fair numbers had survived, or

[1] Cp. vol. I. p. 101, 104.
[2] In 1913, when agricultural prices were fairly good and few farms would be in hand, the figure was 10·7. So 10–12 cannot be far out for the twenty-five years from 1887.
[3] Axholme is described and pictured in Slater, G., *The English Peasantry and the Enclosure of Common Fields* (1907) and in Venn, *op. cit.*
[4] See Major P. G. Craigie's classical paper "Agricultural Holdings in England and Abroad," *S.J.* 1887, p. 86 *sqq.*
[5] *R. on Children in Agriculture*, 1867–8, XVII. 74.

come into existence, side by side with Buccleuch and Sir Aylmer Aylmer[1]. They formed a much larger proportion of the land-owners than their acres did of the land, because their holdings were so small. It will be observed that they were most numerous in districts where the hunting was not good, where air and water were rather bad, and where Sir Aylmer could not have inherited nor Sir Roger Scatcherd laid out a properly undulating park. It must be added that their situation in Lincolnshire, as in Wales, during the gloomy 'eighties was said to be "deplorable."[2]

Until those years of trouble, it was the universal opinion that the tendency still was for the average British holding, normally of course a tenant-farmer's holding, to grow. In the 'sixties farms were said to be getting bigger with the more extended use of machinery in Oxford and Berkshire; and the tendency, it was reported, "has been and is toward consolidation" in Westmorland[3]. A commissioner who had conducted inquiries in various districts from Cornwall to Cambridge, during the early 'nineties, reported that in all of them, from the 'forties to "within ten years...the tendency to amalgamate farms was universal."[4] In Wales there was a good deal of consolidation between 1865 and 1875. It was mostly on "arable lowland farms where machinery could be used," as in the Vale of Clwyd; but land-agents sometimes allowed the mean dwellings on little upland holdings to fall into decay, because in no way could the holding be made to yield a decent living[5]. At that time they saw in consolidation the only hope of progress, just as Scottish agents had when they cleared estates over-crowded with crofters and cottars. "Every Welsh farmer and every Welsh labourer" called down on them the curse reserved for him who lays field to field[6]. But even after "the most reprehensible...evictions" —the reference is to political evictions, but would apply to economic ones—the farms always let easily, to Welshmen[7]. So land-hungry were the Welsh. The English and the Scots were just as ready to risk the curse. They had longer experience of the business; and cursing, if it came, came fainter across the wider gap between farmer and labourer.

[1] See Tennyson, *Aylmer's Field*.
[2] *R.C. on Agricultural Depression*, 1882, p. 10.
[3] Oxon and Berks, *R. on Children in Agriculture*, 1867–8, XVII. 10; Westmorland, *J.R.A.S.* 1868, p. 8.
[4] *R.C. on Labour*, 1893–4, XXXV. 13.     [5] *R.C. on Land in Wales*, p. 347.
[6] *Ibid.* p. 357.                         [7] *Ibid.* p. 314.

No doubt consolidation was going on more or less everywhere from 1850 to 1880. But the statistical evidence shows odd features and suggests the coexistence of consolidation and sub-division. The first oddity is that the number of people who returned themselves at census time as 'farmers and graziers' in England and Wales did not decline at all. There were 249,431 in 1851. In 1881 there were 233,943. In the former year the figure included retired farmers and graziers: in the latter it did not. An expert estimate for the retired of 1881 brought the two figures within 350 of one another[1]. Some land had been brought under cultivation in the interval, but not enough to add much to the average holding of nearly a quarter of a million farmers. Moreover a good deal had been lost to the towns and railways. So far as these figures go, there might have been no increase in the size of farms and no consolidation at all.

At the census of 1851 'farmers and graziers' were asked to make returns of the acreage which they farmed. They did so almost universally[2]. The returns covered 24,700,000 acres of cultivated land in England and Wales and gave an average farm of 111 acres. Only 7656 farms of under 5 acres were returned. Nearly 50 per cent. more of these small holdings were returned in Scotland, even though large numbers of crofters and cottars are known to have been omitted. For Scotland it is expressly stated that many of the small farmers had other occupations. It is evident that innumerable holders of small plots in England—butchers, carters, cowkeepers, market-gardeners, miscellaneous persons with a paddock or a hay-field—did not make returns because they did not picture themselves as farmers. When holdings not farmers came to be enumerated, in 1885, it appeared that there were 136,000 holdings under 5 acres in England and Wales against the reputed 7656 of 1851. The Scottish figure meanwhile had barely doubled, a change which a full return of crofters and some increase in the butcher-carter group would amply explain. Owing to the omission of these people in the English return of 1851, the 'average farm' of 111 acres in that year was much less of a statistical abstraction than the 'average English holding' of 60 acres in 1885. What looks at first sight like a huge increase of very small cultivators in the interval was mainly, there can be no sort of doubt, an increase in returns relating to miscellaneous holders of pad-

[1] Dr Ogle's paper on rural depopulation, as above, *S.J.* 1889, p. 219.
[2] *Occupations*, etc. I. 450 *sqq.* (England and Wales); II. 1025 *sqq.* (Scotland).

docks and accommodation-land. And the holdings of these people were by-products of urbanisation.

The upshot of the 1851 figures for England and Wales, omitting those referring to less than 5 acres, was:

| Size | No. of farms | Acreage of group | Percentage of total acreage re- ported on |
|---|---|---|---|
| (i)   5– 49 acres | 90,100 | 2,122,800 | 8·6 |
| (ii)  50– 99 acres | 44,600 | 3,206,500 | 13·0 |
| (iii) 100–299 acres | 64,200 | 11,015,800 | 44·6 |
| (iv) 300–499 acres | 11,600 | 4,360,900 | 17·6 |
| (v) 500–999 acres | 4,300 | 2,841,000 | 11·5 |
| (vi) 1000 acres and upwards | 771 | 1,112,300 | 4·5 |

The holdings figures of 1885 were not classified in precisely the same way. Instead of 5–49 acres the group is 'above 5 but not exceeding 50 acres,' and so on; the farm or holding of exactly 50 or 100 acres falls into a lower group in 1885 than in 1851, so slightly swelling the lower groups. This, among other things, prevents very exact comparisons. But the figures for 1885 are important, even apart from comparison[1]. They cover 27,700,000 acres in England and Wales against the 24,700,000 of 1851.

| Size | No. of holdings | Acreage of group | Percentage of total acreage re- ported on |
|---|---|---|---|
| (i)   Above 5–50 acres | 200,100 | 3,888,700 | 14·0 |
| (ii)  51–100 acres | 54,900 | 4,021,000 | 14·5 |
| (iii) 101–300 acres | 67,000 | 11,519,400 | 41·6 |
| (iv) 301–500 acres | 11,800 | 4,472,300 | 16·1 |
| (v) 501–1000 acres | 4,200 | 2,737,600 | 9·9 |
| (vi) Above 1000 acres | 573 | 745,500 | 2·7 |

Evidently a great number of holdings between 5 and 20 acres were returned by persons whose predecessors or equivalents in 1851 would not have called themselves farmers. There is room for this, for there were over 126,000 holdings in that group[2]. From 50 acres upwards the tables are curiously similar. The extra 3,000,000 acres reported on in 1885 are mostly absorbed in the lowest groups, up to 20 acres. The excluded group, below 5 acres, accounts for 331,000 of them, whereas in 1851 it was almost empty. For true farming, the areas are nearly identical, and the figures show little trace of concentration;

[1] Used in Craigie's article, as above.
[2] The returns go into greater detail than the table given above, so the holdings of 5–20 acres can be separated out.

though 600,000 more acres are now in holdings from 100 to 500. The apparent decline in the highest groups and the un-expected increase between 50 and 100, *i.e.* in the farms which a family can work, are explicable in part by a simple hypothesis. Farmers are not confined to one holding. This fact was con-spicuous in the 'eighties, when competent men in depressed arable areas who could keep their heads above water were taking over holdings from those who could not[1].

In 1851 such men would presumably return all the land they occupied, as they were asked to do. It would appear as a very large farm. Their more numerous successors would be split up, like Buccleuch, into several holders; for the basis was the holding not the man. A second partial explanation of the in-crease between 50 and 100 is that concentration in a district of small holdings—Wales, for instance—would show its results low down the scale: little hill farms under 50 acres had been thrown together. When these things are taken into account, the figures become compatible with a certain amount of concen-tration, if not with so much as the general descriptions would suggest. But all conclusions from statistical series with different bases are somewhat uncertain[2].

Figures continued to be collected on the 1851 base, but they were not again published in full. The census officials of 1861 did not think it necessary "to abstract all the information."[3] They did, however, abstract the number and sizes of farms in ten thoroughly representative counties, East and West, arable and pastoral[4]. The lower parts of their table are unsatisfactory, the upper instructive. The latter are as follows:

### Farms in Ten Representative Counties

| Size | Number | |
| --- | --- | --- |
| | 1851 | 1861 |
| 100–299 acres | 15,900 | 14,700 |
| 300–499 acres | 3,200 | 3,400 |
| 500–999 acres | 1,529 | 1,582 |
| 1000 acres and upwards | 323 | 308 |

[1] Cp. Hall, A. D., *A Pilgrimage of British Farming* (1913), p. 42–3.

[2] There are also the uncertainties of statistical collection and compilation which cannot be discussed here.

[3] On the ground that "there is now some prospect that England as well as Ireland will enjoy...agricultural statistics." *Census of* 1861: *General Report* (1863, LIII, part 1), p. 29.

[4] Bucks, Cambs, Cheshire, Cumberland, Lincoln, Norfolk, Shropshire, Sussex, Wilts, the North Riding. The absence of Wales is the only defect, but this does not affect the comparison with 1851.

Here is evidence of definite but limited concentration. The reputed decline in giant farms is curious; but in so small a group it may be due to some accident of times or personalities. Not every one can farm a thousand acres, and those who can do not always get the chance.

In the census of 1871 appeared the figures for a different group of counties, seventeen this time, with about a third of the cultivated acreage of England and Wales. They were the big farm counties, for their average farm in 1851 had been of 143 acres against 111 for the country as a whole. By 1871 this figure had grown only to 152, a bare 6 per cent. in twenty years. This is decisive as to the slowness and limited nature of the concentration[1].

In the 'eighties, Dr Ogle consulted the unpublished census books of a single, small, purely agricultural and primarily arable county, Huntingdon, for the whole period 1851–81. He found the same consolidation of moderate-sized into large farms as the 1861 figures suggest for a wider area. The decline in Huntingdon was almost entirely in the groups 50–99 and 100–299 acres. There had been concurrently some breaking up of land into parcels. Huntingdon in 1851 had 296 'farms' of 5–49 acres: in 1881 she had 334. Ogle argued that some of these might "very probably be held in connection with other businesses,"[2] others by market gardeners who returned themselves as farmers, in spite of census instructions to the contrary. (They were to appear among the multitudinous small holdings of the agricultural returns.) Concentration there had been; but the number of census 'farmers' was kept near to the old figure by this growing class, although in Huntingdon, with its low urbanisation, there was a fall in these census 'farmers' from 1066 to 967 in the thirty years, even after allowance had been made for the change of census practice about farmers who had retired.

Through the minor uncertainties of all the figures, some certain facts show clear. Concentration had been going on far more slowly during this generation of maximum non-interference with the natural working of economic forces than almost any of the general references would suggest. And it had been accompanied by an incipient disintegration.

[1] *Census of* 1871 (1873, LXXI. part 2). The list includes no county S.W. of Hampshire and no county in the Western tier except Cumberland and Westmorland. It also excludes Yorkshire.

[2] *S.J.* as above, 1889, p. 220. He was no doubt right. We are dealing with what was called above 'the butcher-carter group.'

"In running my eye over the account which I wrote of...
agriculture in 1850," James Caird said in 1878, "I find
descriptions of good farming in nearly every part of the country,
the details of which differ very little from the practice of the
present day....The change has been not in any considerable
progress beyond what was then the best, but in a general upheaval of the middling and the worst."[1] Neither the inconsiderable progress beyond the best of 1850, nor the generality
of the upheaval, nor its height, are easy to estimate. It is evident
that the ground had not been cleared for improvement, cleared
in the literal sense, to anything like the extent which the best
farmers of the early 'fifties would have wished. Common, it is
true, had been cut to a minimum, but not hedgerows. To make
room for more mechanical agriculture; to preserve the powers
of the soil for the crops instead of spending them on thorn and
hedgerow elm; and to let in light and air both for crops and
cattle, the best farmers had been great grubbers of hedges. The
work had often accompanied consolidation of farms. "All
practical men," in Berkshire in 1860, were "agreed...that
hedgerows are a great bar to agricultural improvement."[2] By
1861 in Yorkshire they were said only to survive in their ancient
"wild luxuriance" on the land of a few non-improving owners;
but the "woodland" farmers of North Hampshire who won
reformers' praise by grubbing them sound like a minority; and
the reformers of 1866 were complaining of the fourteen foot
"ox-fences" of the Leicestershire grazing country, with their
superfluous timber[3]. These fences had been prized for their
shelter, but good farmers no longer exposed the beasts to
weather bad enough to require them. Arable farming was at its
best in districts newly enclosed from open field, sheep-run, and
fen—the Lothians, the East Riding, Lincoln and Cambridge.
There fields were big, hedgerows few and small; but in all old-
enclosed districts there can be little doubt that hedgerows remained—as they still remain—very much more numerous and
bigger than maximum agricultural efficiency would require.
After Caird's report of 1878 came bad years in which the hedges
were apt to stay and grow: grubbing and plashing cost money.

The leading hedge-grubbers were usually advocates of the
brand-new system of steam cultivation. Agricultural literature

---

[1] *The Landed Interest*, p. 28.
[2] *J.R.A.S.* 1860, p. 3, Spearing, J. B., "On the Agriculture of Berkshire."
[3] *Ibid.* 1861, p. 92 (Yorks), p. 266 (Hants); 1866, p. 300 (Leicester).

during the 'sixties is full of it—the various methods; the costs; the soils and surfaces fitted for it; the size of farm which could carry its own steam tackle; the difficulties of hiring tackle. Actual progress was slow. There were only five sets of tackle even in East Lothian in 1865. Two years later, when committees of the Royal Agricultural Society made a full inquiry, they estimated that there might be 200,000 acres of steam-tilled land in the Kingdom. They maintained that its extension required, apart from mechanical improvements in the tackle and less folly in handling it, the introduction of a normal 30–40 acre field, greater freedom of cropping, the establishment of tenant-right, and more co-operation between tenant and landlord in getting rid of the hedgerows[1]. There is no estimate of progress for the next decade. Progress there was, but not so rapid as it might have been; for the committees' conditions were very imperfectly fulfilled. Soil and surface limit steam cultivation in Britain, but the human limitations were more decisive.

Yet there had been a great increase in the use of agricultural machinery. It was needed. There were still in the early 'fifties whole districts with the most antiquated implements and completely unmechanised[2]. In the Sussex Weald, ox-tillage, cumbrous ploughs, unchallenged flails, and cows which were bad milkers because they sprang from a "working race," recalled to a Frenchman one of his own "second-rate provinces"—at a time when some methods in a first-rate French province suggested to another Frenchman those of the thirteenth century[3]. In 1861 it was said that the Isle of Wight was "a century behindhand in practical agriculture"[4]: if this was true, the Island also was dangerously near to the Middle Ages.

In the next twenty years, however, the locomotive steam threshing machine penetrated almost everywhere[5]: its victory over the flail and the flail's successor, the rude hand or horse-driven thresher, was probably the most important change of the period. The victory was not yet complete. The flail was common enough on Welsh upland farms into the 'nineties. Indeed

---

[1] *J.R.A.S.* 1865, p. 102 (East Lothian); 1867 (reports of committees); 1868, p. 274 (Huntingdon).

[2] Vol. I. p. 461.

[3] Lavergne, *op. cit.* for Sussex; for the French province and the thirteenth century Delisle, L., *La classe agricole...en Normandie au moyen âge* (1851), p. xl.

[4] *J.R.A.S.* 1861, p. 359.

[5] Caird, *The Landed Interest*, p. 27.

at that time the plough was the only Welsh implement quite universally improved. The majority of Welsh farmers sowed broadcast, except for turnips, which not all of them grew. These were drilled[1]. In England, the leisurely adoption of new machines and implements can be traced in the series of prize essays on county agriculture issued by the Royal Agricultural Society. Neither the reaping nor the mowing machine was used "to that extent which it deserves" in Berkshire in 1860. Machines for cutting fodder and pulping roots were recent and "only partially adopted" by Nottingham farmers in 1861. By that year the scythe, which had driven out the sickle on the East Riding wolds before 1850, was "giving way to the reaping machine"; but in 1864 the sickle was still much used in Hertfordshire, the reaping machine apparently very little. From the Lothians, on whose big farms a fixed steam-engine for threshing and other work had long been "all but universal," it was reported in 1865 that the English type of peripatetic steam threshing machine was now "often found convenient." The most patriotic Scottish farmers had abandoned Bell's reaper: it was left to "rot in corners" now that varieties of more or less American ancestry were available[2].

The scythe was still usual for mowing hay in Leicestershire in 1866, though threshing was generally done by the hired machine. Worcestershire in 1867 was backward: there was much of the old high ridging of arable land on which reaping machinery was out of place. Mowers and reapers were known and the drill was almost universal; but in general the implements were old-fashioned, as were the buildings. In the fens of Huntingdon the scythe had driven out the sickle and the hook by 1868; but the fen arable was said to be mostly too soft to carry reaping machines. Middlesex, two-thirds of which was meadow land, was as backward as it had been in the 'forties. Then, the first man to use a rude threshing machine had been abused for robbing labourers of work: now, in 1869, there was not so much machine mowing "as you might expect," because the casual mowers who came in for the Middlesex hay-making were jealous of it[3]. It is true that Caird in 1878 spoke of the "general"

[1] R.C. on Land in Wales, p. 726-7.

[2] J.R.A.S. 1860, p. 22 (Berks); 1861, p. 165 (Notts), p. 103 (Yorks); 1864, p. 299 (Herts); 1865, p. 102 (East Lothian). For Bell's reaper, above, p. 13.

[3] Ibid. 1866, p. 296, 300 (Leicester); 1867, p. 450 sqq. (Worcester); 1868, p. 270 (Huntingdon); 1869, p. 9 sqq. (Middlesex). For Middlesex, cp. vol. I. p. 462.

introduction of reaping machinery as "the most striking feature" of the previous twenty years[1]; but general must not be read universal. Nor had Caird been on another comprehensive tour.

It was mainly of the Eastern corn-lands that men thought when they tried to gauge progress. Kentish fruit and hop-growing, in which machines had no place, seem to have been resting more than was wise on an old and merited reputation. There was, at any rate, still far too much grazing and mowing of the orchards in 1877[2]. Among the little milk and pasture farms of the North-West, the South-West, and the Welsh marches could be found plenty of bad casual farming, with an un-instructed reliance on the Western rain, which kept the pastures green, and on uncritical towns which took the milk, meat and cheese as they were. And so to Wales, with its primitive sur-vivals and short stock of machinery. In Scotland there was a still wider gap—between the mechanical farm of the Lothians and the Skye croft with its *caschrom*, the foot-plough of primitive agriculture. But even in a westward shire like Stafford, in which the small and rather old-fashioned grazing farm was common, solid work had been accomplished since 1850 where it was most needed, in land drainage. Not a possible maximum amount, but nearly all that was absolutely essential, had been done by 1870[3]. This was probably true of most counties, though there was still too much old undrained pasture[4]. On the strong arable lands of Huntingdon, drainage was said to have doubled the yield in the twenty years before 1868. It had "worked wonders for the clay in Sheppey."[5] Similar evidence could be collected from most clay districts. It is true that an expert told a Committee of the Lords in 1873 that out of twenty million acres which needed drainage in England and Wales only three were yet drained. But 'need' is not an exact word; the expert was engineer to a drainage company; and both his figures were disputed by James Caird. Caird put the first at ten millions or rather more, not for England and Wales but for Britain; and allowed that four or five might not be too high for the second. He noted that in "scarcely any case...more than half of any

[1] *The Landed Interest*, p. 16.
[2] *J.R.A.S.* 1877, p. 97.
[3] *Ibid.* 1869, p. 263 *sqq.* There was good farming in Stafford in 1850. Vol. I. p. 460. For western farming, generally about 1850, see vol. I. p. 460-5. It changed slowly.
[4] *J.R.A.S.* 1868, p. 266 (Hunts).
[5] The *R.A.S. Report* of 1878, p. 316.

estate required" drainage, and that great stretches of chalk did not require it at all. He might have added some other soils[1]. His evidence is weighty. In 1850–1 he had reported an almost universal backwardness in the business. Since then, as an Enclosure Commissioner, he had supervised it. For, by what seemed a great anomaly to the Lords' Committee of 1873, "private transactions" in drainage and the financing of improvements had been "committed to the control of a Government officer."[2] The control originated with Peel's Act of 1846 (9 and 10 Vict. c. 101) and its £2,000,000 of government money to be advanced in drainage loans to landlords shaken by Free Trade[3]. The Whigs had added another £2,000,000 in 1850[4]. In the interval two important drainage and improvement companies had secured Acts, so that the work might be carried on when the Treasury grants were exhausted. Two others followed, in 1853 and 1856[5]. Interest and sinking fund on improvement loans, whether payable to the exchequer or to a company, could be so charged on estates as to take priority of existing mortgages. Supervision of some kind was therefore necessary, and it had been entrusted to the Enclosure Commissioners. "On the whole the drainage under Government inspection has been very well done," a grudging agricultural writer felt bound to admit in 1869[6].

There was a great deal done in which neither the government nor the companies had any hand. Farmers and landlords had begun the work before 1846 without external assistance, and they continued to help themselves, dividing the burden in various ways. At least the farmer carted the pipes: he might do much more[7]. Whether more had been spent in drainage without Government inspection than with it before 1873 Caird doubted: five years later, he had no doubt that in improvements generally landowners in Britain had spent "a much larger sum...from

[1] *S.C. of H. of L. on Improvement of Land*, 1873 (VI. 1), p. iii and Q. 830 for the expert (Bailey Denton); p. iii and Q. 4125–6 for Caird. Cp. his *Landed Interest*, p. 82–3.
[2] *S.C. of H. of L.* p. vii.          [3] Vol. I. p. 460 n. 3.
[4] By 13 and 14 Vict. c. 31.
[5] There was another in 1860. The companies were: The West of England and S. Wales (1848), The General Land D. and I. Coy. (1849), The Lands Improvement Coy. (1853), The Scottish D. and I. Coy. (1856) and the Land Loan and Enfranchisement Coy. (1860). *S.C. of H. of L.* 1873, App. A.
[6] Evershed, H., in *J.R.A.S.* 1869, p. 306, referring to Stafford.
[7] Cp. vol. I. p. 460; Lavergne, *op. cit.* p. 263; *J.R.A.S.* 1868, p. 25 (Lord Lonsdale deep drains 10,000 acres).

their own resources" than had been advanced to them by the state and the companies[1]. The advances had amounted to £12,000,000 in thirty years, of which upwards of £9,000,000 had gone in drainage. Advances made by the state (£4,000,000) had been largely repaid; many of those made by the companies had still long periods to run[2]. After 1878, though the work of drainage did not stop, the saddling of estates with heavy liabilities for it did; and the whole movement slackened as prices and rents fell away. But plenty of dry land with healthier crops and cattle testified to the good work done.

Much experience had been gained, and the technique of drainage had changed a good deal, since machines for making drain-pipes had first come into general use in the 'forties[3]. The early pipes, as advocated by Josiah Parkes, had been only 1 inch or 1½ inches bore. By the 'seventies none were under 2 inches and some were 5 or 6 inches. Many of the old drains had been remade deeper and with these bigger pipes[4]. It had been shown that there was such a thing as overdrainage on gravel or sand— a discovery which should not have been necessary—and that the proper amount of drainage for pasture land on various soils was not easy to determine[5]. Landlords had often felt that there was too much speculation in the system by which they paid a normal 7 per cent. for 25 years to a company, as interest and sinking fund, and got 5 per cent. on the outlay as extra rent, ostensibly for ever[6]. They felt it more sharply when rents fell before liabilities were cleared off. This experience also they bought.

Scientific manuring had hardly kept pace with scientific drainage. Léonce de Lavergne in 1854 said that most English farmers were "already familiar with the technical terms. They talk of ammonia and phosphates like professed chemists."[7] Perhaps he had not talked with very many, nor studied average practice closely. Phosphates and ammonia were known: all kinds of manures had been tried; and there was just then a rage among the progressive for guano. It came in at the rate of about

---

[1] *The Landed Interest*, p. 87.

[2] *Ibid.* p. 83. The General Land D. and I. Coy. (Bailey Denton's company) advanced £2,000,000 between 1857 and 1871. *S.C. of H. of L.* 1873, App. F.

[3] Vol. I. p. 458–61.

[4] *S.C. of H. of L.* Q. 4186 (Caird); *J.R.A.S.* 1868, p. 266.

[5] *Ibid.* p. iv; Lavergne, *op. cit.* p. 183 n.

[6] *S.C. of H. of L.* p. v. These were the normal rates.

[7] *Op. cit.* p. 220.

300,000 tons a year—enough to give a good average dressing to 2,000,000 acres[1]. But that left a great deal of land undressed. The 'antiquated farmer' whom Caird had found everywhere in 1850–1, who did not even make intelligent use of his farmyard muck, had still to be taught 'artificials.' He was a stubborn suspicious pupil. Even up-to-date men had their suspicions of chemistry. Caird was still preaching to them in 1878 that a cwt. of nitrate of soda was worth "fifty times its weight in farmyard manure" and could be applied "at one-fifth of the labour." Lawes' Rothamsted demonstration of this had "been before the country for more than thirty years," and yet it was "only beginning to be generally recognised."[2] While the use of nitrates was growing slowly, there had been a recent heavy fall in that of guano. Imports for 1874–8 were barely half what they had been in 1854–8. This was not surprising, for the average price at the ports in 1874–8 was £11 a ton, as against just over £9 ten years earlier[3]. Imported nitrate was coming down; but whatever its merits, it seemed dear to the ordinary farmer at £14 or even at £12. 10s. a ton, plus cost of carriage from the ports[4]. He figured out his farmyard manure at much less than 5s.; and as times got harder after 1876, he was tempted to economise on manures which meant cash outlay. Guano imports dropped abruptly—by 100,000 tons—in 1879 and never recovered. By 1887 they were negligible.

What the course of consumption of the home-made phosphates was there is no means of determining. Superphosphate of lime had become "the most largely used artificial manure" by the late 'seventies[5]. It had to a great extent superseded the phosphatic manures made from bones; and apparently it was replacing guano. It was relatively cheap and wise men used it freely. How freely it, or any of the artificials, was used below the levels of 'high-class' farm management is not known. Everyone had heard of superphosphate and probably most had tried it. But how often and how much?

[1] The average import in 1854–8 was 298,000 tons. Guano dressings ran from 2 to 4 cwts. an acre. Clarke, J. A., R.A.S. Report of 1878, p. 357. For the early days of guano, see vol. I. p. 456.

[2] The Landed Interest, p. 22.

[3] 'Computed real values' from the Trade Returns: similar computations for 1854–8 are not available.

[4] The price at the ports averaged £14 in 1867–76 and £12. 10s. in 1877–86.

[5] Clarke, Practical Farming in R.A.S. Report, p. 357. Clarke is speaking of 'high class' farming.

The cropping of the soil of Britain was in no essential way changed between 1850 and 1886. Even during the last struggle for self-sufficiency in bread-corn, between 1830 and 1846, the land of England and Wales appears to have been divided not very unevenly between arable and permanent pasture, a situation which seemed remarkable to the European visitor: "nearly half the cultivated soil has been maintained in permanent grass," Lavergne wrote with surprise but apparent admiration[1]. He was following, for lack of statistics, Caird's estimate made three years earlier[2]. Caird may have somewhat overestimated the permanent pasture; for when the first statistics were compiled in the late 'sixties, it appeared that it was then only about 43 per cent. of the whole cultivated area[3]. From 1870 the proportion rose, but slowly. It did not reach Caird's 1851 estimate until 1882, and the pasture exceeded the arable for the first time in 1883. In 1886, although the wheat area had been heavily reduced, pasture was still only 52·0 per cent. of the whole as against Caird's assumed 49·2 for 1851[4].

Even before 1850 crop rotations had become generally elastic. They became more elastic in the next generation. Strict 'Norfolk' four-course husbandry was maintained in many districts, especially in the East, with little change, except that to avoid 'clover sickness' red clover was now never grown oftener than one year in eight. There were various standard five-course shifts. But land in Britain varies so greatly, even on single farms, and heavy land in particular needs such different treatment in different localities and years, that much is heard of farming "as the seasons direct," of farming on "no regular system," or of farmers "having systems of their own."[5] Individual practice varied about varying local standards. Clayland men in Stafford, with an eye to cattle and dairying, used a five- or six-course shift with two or three successive years of seeds in the middle[6]. Cornwall had something similar but cruder with a trace of ancient 'outfield' agriculture in it[7].

[1] Lavergne, op. cit. p. 51.
[2] In English Agriculture in 1850 and 1851, p. 522. The basis is the rough assumption that the cultivated land is two-thirds pasture in the West, and one-third in the East.
[3] Venn, J. A., Foundations of Agricultural Economics, p. 381.
[4] These figures, taken from Venn, apply like Caird's to England and Wales, not to Britain.
[5] J.R.A.S. 1860, p. 15 (Berks); 1861, p. 274 (Hants); 1867, p. 450 (Worcester).
[6] Ibid. 1869, p. 272.
[7] Clarke, Practical Farming, as above, p. 329. Cp. vol. I. p. 24.

On heavy Hampshire land a "sort of double three-field system was sometimes found."[1] The standard Lothian shift was a very different six-course—seeds; oats; potatoes or beans; wheat; turnips; barley[2]. When applied to England, as it often was, a second wheat would be inserted somewhere[3]. The usual course in Aberdeen, which lived mainly by cattle feeding, was—seeds; seeds; oats; roots; barley[4]. Wheat was rare in these Scottish rotations. This helps to explain why, when crop statistics began to be collected (1866–7), 90 per cent. of the wheat of the United Kingdom was found to be English[5]. It explains also Scotland's greater resisting power for the crisis to come, which would be predominantly, though not entirely, a crisis of wheat.

Careful landlords always inserted some cropping conditions in the agreements with their farmers, and this was sometimes a farmers' grievance. But there is so much variety of cropping recorded[6] that interference with a good cultivator's liberty of action cannot often have been serious. Bad cultivators needed interference and hardly got enough. The system was certainly good on the average for agriculture and the land, the more so as breaches of the agreement were usually winked at, if within reason, especially in bad times[7]. In very bad times even unreasonable breaches had to be tolerated. In the 'eighties some discouraged farmers on the clays were falling back, just to save money, into that primitive three-course agriculture, with its recurring fallow, from which it had been a main object of agrarian reform and landlords' restriction to extricate them during a hundred years and more[8].

With its 40–50 per cent. of permanent pasture and its established connection between arable farming and the rearing of flocks and herds, the Britain of the 'fifties probably carried a bigger head of livestock in proportion to its area than any part

---

[1] *J.R.A.S.* 1861, p. 273.    [2] *Ibid.* 1871, p. 168.
[3] *Ibid.* 1860, p. 264 (Tuckett, P. D., "On the modifications of the four-course rotation"); Clarke, *op. cit.* p. 339 (Warwick); p. 350 (North Riding).
[4] *J.R.A.S.* 1871, p. 192.
[5] *S.J.* xxxi (1868), 140. Caird, "On the Agricultural Statistics of the U.K." Ireland by this time was important only as a producer of oats, potatoes, cattle and dairy produce. Her wheat export of the early nineteenth century (vol. i. p. 134) had ceased.
[6] Besides the cases quoted see Clarke, *op. cit.* ch. 6, a summary of cropping county by county based on the agricultural statistics of the previous decade.
[7] *R.C. on Labour*, 1893–4 (xxxv), p. 55, 75; evidence from Beds, Sussex, Hants.
[8] *Ibid.* p. 103 (Notts). An occasional fallow on clay may still be good farming.

of Europe. The number and quality of the sheep was what most impressed Lavergne in 1851–2. He believed that the United Kingdom kept as many sheep as France, and far better, on three-fifths of France's area[1]. This was the more remarkable, because there were few in Ireland and, in proportion to area, not very many in Scotland. He supposed that there were 30,000,000 in England and Wales and about 4,000,000 in Scotland. His figure was certainly a few millions too high; for the agricultural returns of 1867–79 showed that the total for Britain fluctuated between 28,000,000 and 30,000,000. In the early 'eighties, the range was between 24,300,000 and 26,500,000. Anything above 28,000,000 was exceptional; and that figure, which was returned in 1867 after a spell of unusually high wool prices, may be taken as a full normal head for the country[2].

It was sometimes argued during the 'seventies and 'eighties that the extension of Highland deer forests since 1850 had seriously curtailed the British flocks: once the sheep had eaten up the crofters, now the unthrifty deer had driven out the sheep. They had; but very careful calculations made in 1873 and again in 1884 showed that the maximum of evicted sheep could not exceed 400,000 and that the real figure was probably very much less, as these calculations required every forest, if cleared of deer, to carry its full potential stock of sheep[3]. In fact, important as the mountain flocks were in Scotland, England and Wales, they were far less important than those of the arable districts. There were always over 1,000,000 sheep in Northumberland, many of them on the Cheviots and the backside of the Pennines, but there were also over 1,000,000 in Lincolnshire, where the plough had been run through nearly every acre of wold sheepwalk before 1850; and there were 1,000,000 more in Kent. Sussex with its downs had not half as many. In no country at any time has the combination of arable farming and sheep-farming been so successfully carried out as in nineteenth-century Britain. The difficulties of the years after 1878 did not impair it.

Lavergne held that Britain excelled France less in cattle than in sheep, but that there was still "a sensible difference"[4] in

---

[1] Lavergne, *op. cit.* p. 14.

[2] The estimate for 1809 had been 19,000,000. *Lord's Report on the Wool Trade* (1828), p. 74.

[3] *Inquiry into the condition of the Crofters and Cottars in the Highlands and Islands*, 1884 (XXXII), p. 86 *sqq.*

[4] *Op. cit.* p. 31.

her favour both in quality and in numbers related to area. The figure of about 6,000,000 head of cattle which he accepted was probably correct; for it was the figure about which the recorded number fluctuated from 1867 to 1883, when a slow and intermittent rise began. "The consumption of milk under every form" by the English seemed to him "enormous." He thought that "their habits in this respect were those of past ages," and he quoted from Julius Caesar a sentence familiar to English schoolboys. "The quantities of butter and cheese manufactured," he added, "exceed all belief." He reckoned that the English farmers sold twice as much milk as the French and got twice the French price for it. "Not content" with all this, the English imported yet more butter and cheese[1]. He did not note that while the English had not milked their sheep for a very long time, and "lilting at the yow milking" had gone out in Scotland, sheep's milk was still regularly used in Wales. Twenty years later that use was declining: forty years later it would be extinct[2]. Unlike Lavergne's compatriots of Roquefort, these cheese-eating English had forgotten how to make ewe's milk cheese[3].

British superiority in cattle had been the result of concentration on milk and meat and deliberate neglect of ox-power. Even in 1878 ox-teams were still "employed to a small extent in Wiltshire, Devonshire, Cornwall, Sussex, and some other counties." A writer on practical agriculture had a few words to say about their feeding and management; but he added that "the exigencies of the meat supply and the ability of modern feeding processes to mature cattle of refined breeds into two-year-old beef" left no place for the draft ox[4]. It had been an anachronism since 1800 at least. All modern types of cattle: the short-horn now spread over the whole country[5], the Hereford, the Devon, the 'Alderney,' the Aberdeen-Angus and the rest were beef or milk makers, or both. Every year increased the

[1] Lavergne, *op. cit.* p. 34-5.
[2] *R.C. on Land in Wales*, p. 606, Q. 259, 359. The decline from 1875 is noted. By 1895 the practice was extinct.
[3] For the history and economics of Roquefort cheese, see Brunhes, *Géog. humaine de la France*, II. 501 *sqq.* The Roquefort caves which are held responsible for the quality may have no equivalent in Britain, although the island has its fair share of limestone caverns.
[4] Clarke, *op. cit.* p. 362-3.
[5] By the 'seventies the long-horn was "confined to a few amateur farmers in the midland counties"—*Ibid.* p. 277. Bakewell's long-horns had almost disappeared from Leicestershire by 1866, *J.R.A.S.* 1866, p. 328.

importance of meat and dairy produce as against grain crops, and that long before the great fall in grain prices. Caird thought that meat and dairy produce had "risen 50 per cent." in price between 1850 and 1867[1]. For wholesale prices 40 per cent. is probably nearer the mark[2]; but even 40 per cent. in seventeen years was encouraging to the farmer and his landlord. If the herds did not increase much in number, their care and management improved. Though at the end of the 'seventies there was still too much tying of cows and bullocks by the neck in "semi-open sheds or hovels,"[3] and too much herding of bullocks for the winter in open yards, the decently arranged milking stalls and the covered or part-covered yards which for years had been recommended[4] were to be found on an increasing number of well-managed estates.

Yard building, like cottage building and most drainage, was landlord's business. What proportion of the increasing rent-roll of the years between 1851–2 and 1878–9 was really interest on such new capital expenditure cannot be ascertained; but the proportion on many estates, perhaps on most, must have been very great. The cash increase in rents between these dates was impressive. For all Britain the income from Lands under Schedule A of the Income Tax[5] rose by nearly 28 per cent.—from £47,000,000 to £60,000,000. For Scotland the rise was 41 per cent.; for England and Wales 25. It was greater in the more pastoral West than in the ploughed East, greatest of all in green and land-hungry Wales. In the second half of the period alone (1864–5 to 1878–9) the rise for the six westernmost Welsh counties was 21·1 per cent.[6] For England and Wales, including those counties, it was 11·4 per cent. There must have been wide areas in the English arable East where the rise over the whole period 1851–2 to 1878–9 was well under 20 per cent.[7]; and it was on these arable lands, especially the clays, that most

---

[1] In *S.J.* XXXI. 141.

[2] Based on the price-currents of the *Economist* which there is not space to analyse here.

[3] Clarke, *op. cit.* p. 232.

[4] The *J.R.A.S. passim, e.g.* 1865, p. 88; 1866, p. 326.

[5] For the complex details of tithe and rent-charges see Stamp, *British Incomes and Property*, p. 41 *sqq.*, and books there quoted. The figure never quite touched £60,000,000 but was above £59,500,000 from 1876–7 to 1879–80.

[6] See the very interesting calculations in *R.C. on Land in Wales*, p. 469.

[7] In the five English counties whose climatic and agrarian conditions most nearly resembled those of West Wales—Cumberland, Westmorland, Cheshire, Devon, Cornwall—the rise from 1864–5 to 1878–9 was 17·2 per cent. *Ibid.*

landlord's capital had been expended. The increase there in pure rent, that is in the purchasing power of the payments for fertility and site value, may quite well have been negative, for prices were rising; but as it is not easy to set out a mid-Victorian clay soil landlord's cost of living index, the point must remain obscure. There is no doubt that landlords as a class felt comfortable, or that rents and land values continued to rise, until the end of the 'seventies. The figure for Schedule A, Lands, was indeed a trifle higher in 1879–80 than in 1878–9. After that it fell yearly until the end of the century—and beyond it.

"Times have been," a witness told the Royal Commission on Agriculture in 1881, "when there has been a very bad crop of wheat that prices have risen."[1] But it was not so in those disastrous wet years of the late 'seventies which lead in the great agricultural depression. Farmers had lost much working capital and the land was "four years to the bad, suffering from weeds and reduced manure."[2] James Caird put the price point to the Commissioners statistically. He took five bad harvest years between 1852 and 1862. With these he compared the five crescendo years of bad harvests in the 'seventies—1873, 1875, 1876, 1877 and 1879. For the early group he reckoned that wheat yielded on an average 24 bushels to the acre and fetched 61s. 1d. a quarter. For the late group the yield was 19 bushels and the price 49s. 10d.[3] If he had left out 1873, when wheat averaged 58s. 8d. and 1877, when the Russo-Turkish War drove it for a few months above 60s., he could have shown a still more disastrous price figure. For 1879, the year of the worst harvest of the century, the average was 43s. 10d. and it was 44s. 4d. for 1880. For a couple of years it held and then broke away again. It was 31s. in 1886 and 32s. 6d. in 1887. The other grains fell with wheat, but not quite so fast. The average price of wheat in the four years 1884–7 was 35 per cent. lower than it had been in 1874–7; that of oats was 31 per cent. lower and that of barley 28 per cent. lower.

Down to 1877 the index number of grain prices had remained very steady for successive groups of years, though there were steep monthly and yearly fluctuations. For 1867–77 it was

---

[1] *R.C. on Agriculture*, 1882 (XIV *sqq.*), Q. 34,682.
[2] Lord Randolph Churchill to his Mother, March 21, 1880; Churchill, W. S., *Lord Randolph Churchill* (1906), I. 117.
[3] *R.C. on Agriculture*, Q. 62,647.

only a trifle over 2 per cent. lower than it had been in the so-called hungry 'forties (1838–47)[1]. The lowest intervening figure for a group of years of any length had been in 1858–66, and that was only 9 per cent. below 1867–77. Each decade had seen some international dislocation which favoured the British farmer—a Crimean War, an American Civil War, a Russo-Turkish War—and until the late 'seventies these dislocations, helped by the quick growth of population and the relatively backward state of transport, allowed increasing dependence on foreign grain supplies to accompany a reasonably well-sustained level of prices and of the acreage under corn. Only about a fifth of the barley and less than a sixth of the oats available for consumption were imported in the late 'seventies; but for wheat the proportion had risen from 26·5 per cent. for the years 1852–9 to just over 48 per cent. for 1868–75[2]. The bad harvests of the late 'seventies drove it up first to nearly 60 and then to nearly 70 per cent. It never came down permanently; and the price of British wheat was slipping towards thirty shillings. American railways and British cargo steamers had done their work well for the consumer.

Caird reckoned in 1878 that there was no foreign competition at all with nearly one-fifth, by value, of the staple products of British agriculture. No effective competition with that fifth developed during the next seven or eight years. Taken together these products—milk, hay, and straw sold for town consumption—were twice as important as barley, and their importance, compared with wheat, was as 3 to 4. There had long been foreign competition in the beef market, and active foreign competition in the markets for 'hog-products,' butter, and cheese. But even in 1885, the imported beef was only about 9 per cent. of the total consumption by weight: no doubt less by value; and the imported mutton was between 7 and 8 per cent.[3] The movement of the index number for meat and butter reflects the situation. In the late 'sixties it had varied between 30 and 45 per cent. above the level of 1850–1[4]. It ran up to 60 per

[1] It is to be borne in mind however that general prices had risen so that grain had not retained its comparative position. See the diagram on p. 378, below, and cp. Layton, Sir W. T., *Prices in the Nineteenth Century*.

[2] Caird, *The Landed Interest*, p. 14; Lawes, J. B. and Gilbert, J. H., "On the Home Produce, Importation, Consumption and Price of Wheat, 1852–3 to 1879–80," *J.R.A.S.* 1880, p. 337: also in *S.J.* XLIII (1880), 313.

[3] Sauerbeck, A., in *S.J.* XLIX (1886), 606.

[4] *Ibid.* and also *S.J.* LVI (1893), 220.

cent. above 1850–1 in 1873, an abnormal year in every way; but the subsequent fall never took it, in that generation, below the level of the late 'sixties; and it only got down to that level in 1885. Taking decade averages, the index number for 1878–87 is only 5 per cent. below that of 1868–77. For milk, hay, and straw there are no trustworthy index numbers, but it is likely that they would show no serious fall[1].

Wool prices had a peculiarly disastrous history. Driven over-high by the cotton famine[2], and again by the trade boom of the early 'seventies, more was expected of them than they could maintain. By 1885–6 they were about half what they had been in 1873–4. Everything was against them—the gold position, slack consumption, cheapening transport, changing fashions. The last dragged down abnormally the prices of the long Lincoln and Leicester wools. One standard Lincoln grade, a staple raw material for Bradford, which could be had for 10$d$. a lb. in 1883–6 had fetched 22$\frac{3}{4}d$. in 1873–4. For the whole period 1850–80 its price had averaged 18$\frac{3}{4}d$. Farmers were left bewildered: there seemed to be neither precedent nor reason for these things. They meant black ruin on many of the great corn and wool farms of the Lincoln wolds[3].

The Commissioners of 1881–2 were misled by the belief that depression was primarily a matter of weather, of a quite abnormal cycle of lean dripping years. European experts "all agreed," they said, "in ascribing it mainly to...unfavourable seasons." English counties' fortunes had varied with their weather. Yorkshire had got off better than many because "the rainfall having been less than in the Midland counties, the crops did not suffer so much." Foreign competition the Commissioners allowed to be a true cause for Caird's dilemma of the

---

[1] Milk fell hardly at all. There are no comprehensive figures for the three years 1868–70, but on the assumption that they were not higher than those of 1871 the index number for 1868–77 would be 135·4: for 1878–87 it was 131·6. (The base year, 100, is 1900.) For the seven years 1871–7 it was 141·7. Probably the price was rather lower in 1868–70 than in 1871. *B. of T. Return on Wholesale and Retail Prices of* 1903 (Cmd. 321). These returns start with 1871; but some milk prices from the books of London hospitals given on p. 137 make it certain that prices in 1868–70 were at least not above those of 1871.

[2] Above, p. 223.

[3] Sauerbeck, in *S.J.* 1886, and the *Return of Wholesale and Retail Prices*, as above. The *Return* unfortunately exaggerates the wool situation because it is based almost entirely on Lincoln prices, and Lincoln wools had suffered most owing to changes of fashion. There is no means of correcting it, short of an elaborate inquiry.

reduced crop and the unrisen price; but they tended to over-
look its importance. Whilst noting that the only part of the
continent which had suffered little was the dairy country of
Denmark, and that Cheshire had not suffered "to anything like
the same extent as many counties,"[1] they did not underline
what was already clear, that beyond the weather, and apart
from that shift in the purchasing power of gold which they
neither apprehended nor discussed, lay the question of corn
transport; behind that, for the future, the new methods of trans-
porting meat and wool[2]. So recently as 1878, Caird had thought
that the British farmer might "rest content" with the "natural
protection" of distance[3]; but distance had ceased to protect
corn and would soon cease to protect meat. The age, as it was
fond of saying, was engaged in annihilating distance.

Assistant Commissioners' reports in 1881–2[4] show that where-
ever wheat and arable were subordinate, or towns near and
large, there no evidence of really serious distress was to be
found; none in Cheshire, Lancashire, Cumberland, Westmorland, Northumberland or Durham; little in Kent, West Somerset, Devon or Cornwall; little among the Welsh hill farmers,
though cold rains had brought some "disastrous" losses of
sheep. While landlords in Eastern England were abating rents
and losing tenants, Lord Penrhyn explained that on his Carnarvon estates there were no arrears and no farms unlet[5]. Indeed it became almost a Welsh national grievance subsequently
that, in the six westernmost counties, rents, measured by
Schedule A of the Income Tax, fell very little after 1878–9,
remaining in 1893–4 no less than 18·5 per cent. above the level
of 1864–5, though 2·1 per cent. below that of 1878–9. In the
seven easterly counties there was a fall after 1878–9 very nearly
to the level of 1864–5. English rents on the same basis, after a
rise and fall, showed a net reduction of 15·2 per cent. over the
twenty-nine years 1864–5 to 1893–4[6].

The actual fall, in England and Wales together, from 1878–9
to 1893–4 was 22·6 per cent.[7] In Scotland it was 18·5 per cent.

---

[1] *Report*, p. 12 (Europe and Denmark), 9 (Yorks and Cheshire).
[2] Above, p. 91, 224.          [3] *The Landed Interest*, p. 5, 7.
[4] They are summarised in the general *Report*, p. 9–10.
[5] *R.C. on Agriculture*, Q. 7467.          [6] *R.C. on Land in Wales*, p. 469.
[7] The *R.C. on Land in Wales* gives the English fall, 1878–9 to 1893–4, without
Wales, as 23·7. In the five English counties least affected by the depression—
Cumberland, Westmorland, Cheshire, Devon and Cornwall—the fall was only
10·5 per cent. *Ibid.* The other figures used here are from Stamp, *op. cit.* p. 49.

Scotland had a greater area of westerly conditions and much less wheat. In the English counties most affected, the fall was far more than 22·6 per cent.; for some landlords of the West got off easily as has been seen. An English corporation which at that time held land in thirteen counties, nearly all of which had to meet the full shock of falling prices, may serve as an illustration. Its net receipts from its estates fell by 38·9 per cent. between 1878–9 and 1893–4[1]. The fall of rents was greatest precisely in those areas where the rise since 1851–2 had been least, and where, as on the clays, there was a maximum interest element in it. A certain bitterness was natural among landowners who were criticised for taking an 'unearned increment,' or an excessive price, for the economists' 'natural and indestructible properties of the soil.' Such criticism there had always been; but never such a volume of it as in the 'eighties[2].

How desperate the position seemed to farmers, before there had been time for adjustment of rents, was shown by the inquiries of 1881–2. Rents, it is to be borne in mind, had been rising all through the lean years from 1875 to 1879. An increased rent at least on every change of tenancy had come to be assumed. A good deal of land had been bought by those who cultivated it, at the inflated prices which such rents implied. In Wales land had risen to an "absurd value."[3] Wales, as has been seen, was a relatively fortunate area. So were the English North-West and South-West. But in the counties of the Welsh marches and the West Midlands the situation was worse by the end of 1881 than at any time "within the memory of this generation."[4] In the East Midlands and East Anglia it was worse still, worst of all, it was said, in Huntingdon, which is all clay with an edging of fen; in Cambridge with its fen, gault, and chalk; and in Essex, where a little hilly chalk in the North-West soon leads down to long stretches of the London clay[5]. North and South, no county had escaped.

By 1880 the years of rising rents were over. There were arrears, abatements, remissions. As tenants died or threw up their land, a new scale began to establish itself. Some land

---

[1] These are the figures for King's College, Cambridge, as given in its 'Mundum' Books.

[2] The age of Chamberlain radicalism and of Henry George's *Progress and Poverty*. See below, p. 483 *sqq.*

[3] Colonel Hughes before the *R.C. on Land in Wales*, p. 468.

[4] Assistant Commissioner Doyle to *R.C. on Agriculture*, p. 9.

[5] *Ibid.* p. 10.

went right out of cultivation, 'tumbled down' to grass, or even to thistles and thorns. Of this there was not a great deal; off the clays very little. The cultivated area of Britain did not decline. But there was enough to be talked about; and for the years 1879–85 there were on the average 133,000 more acres of 'bare-fallow or uncropped arable' than there had been in 1874–8. Expensive drainage operations slackened off. A census of farmsteads and cottages rebuilt would not contain many entries for the decade 1878–88. From 1879, the *Journal of the Royal Agricultural Society* began to fill with papers on Dutch or Danish dairy practice and on the best and most economical methods of laying land down to grass. Whether laid down or 'tumbled down,' a million and a half acres, 10·5 per cent., were added to the permanent pasture of Britain between 1879 and 1887. Arable farmers were tempted to economise on 'artificials'; on the trimming and plashing of hedges; on the cleaning of ditches and water-courses; on hoeing and thistle-spudding; on deep expensive ploughing or on those repeated workings of the land which make the perfect seed-bed. Those who came best through the troubles had a sense of the market and knew how to farm light, to skim the land without too much risk to its 'indestructible' qualities. A few such men came through very well indeed, sometimes taking on farm after farm from less adaptable men who were going to the wall[1].

Farmer and land-agent witnesses, setting out their troubles before the Commissioners and Assistant Commissioners of 1881–2, had much to tell about a reputed decline in the quality of agricultural labour[2]. There was less willingness, less persistence, and so less skill, they said. Education and the Act of 1870 were blamed for this, and for its alleged cause, the growing social and political self-consciousness of a class not supposed liable to distracting discontents. Farmers had learnt no historical generalisations about the coming of discontent and revolution, not when circumstances are worsening, but when they are on the mend, though too slowly; so all this seemed to them most unreasonable. For every one agreed in 1881–2 that the labourer, whether his skill were declining or not, was "never in

---

[1] There were such episodes in the hardest-hit parts of Lincolnshire, for example (private information).

[2] *E.g.* Q. 34,066; 34,523. For the other side of the picture see W. C. Little's Report to the *R.C. on Labour* (1893–4, XXVII. part 2), p. 44.

a better position."[1] Ten years later, when depression had done
all its work, the evidence was still more general and emphatic.
The labourer's condition had "greatly improved...he dresses
better, eats more butchers' meat, he travels more, he reads more,
he drinks less."[2] Between the inquiries of 1867 and those of
the years 1891–2 "a quiet economic revolution...with little aid
from legislation" had "transferred to the labourer from one-
fourth to one-third of that profit which the landowners and
farmers then received."[3] The calculation must not be pressed;
but it pointed towards a real transfer and dated it with fair
accuracy. A foreign student of British economic conditions had
just published a table of the estimated purchasing power of
agricultural day-wages in terms of wheat. He suggested that
whereas an average day's work in the 'forties yielded 16 lbs.
of wheat, and in the 'fifties 17, it was worth 23 lbs. in the
'seventies and 30 in the 'eighties[4]. Men do not chew wheat.
Millers' and bakers' pay had not fallen. A bread calculation
is therefore not quite so favourable to the labourer, and it cannot be made so precise. But it suggests that, on the average, in
the 'eighties he could get three four-pound loaves for every
two that his father had in the 'fifties. In so far as he lived on
bread, he was 50 per cent. better off[5].

The general course of his cash earnings, weekly, harvest and
miscellaneous, together with the estimated money value of his
allowances in kind—a small item—had been as set out below[6].
The curve shows these earnings for the year as percentages of
those of 1892. It masks the varying movements of the counties

[1] R.C. on Agriculture, 1882, p. 22 and Q. 4791.
[2] C. M. Chapman, Assistant Commissioner, 1893–4, XXXV. 44.
[3] Little's Report, p. 2.
[4] Steffen, G., in the Nineteenth Century, quoted in Little, p. 161. Steffen's
fuller discussion is in his Studien zur Geschichte der Englischen Lohnarbeiter,
vol. III (1905).
[5] Bread prices for the whole country are not available. In London the average
price fell nearly 24 per cent. between the decades 1850–9 and 1880–9. See
below, p. 460. Earnings averaged over all the years of the two decades in the
same way rose also by nearly 24 per cent. The statement in the text is a fair
rough result.
[6] In the diagram on p. 286, based on Bowley, A. L., in S.J. 1898 and 1899.
The figures for many of the years are statistical interpolations. It will be seen that
a curve drawn through those years for which information is fullest would have
the same general character. So would a curve based simply on weekly money
wages, as in Bowley's Wages in the United Kingdom (1900). For "there is no
reason to think that the ratio of wages to earnings changed to any great extent
on the average since Arthur Young's time," S.J. 1899, p. 556.

to give a generalised national picture. But this masking of county differences is not important; for since labour had become more mobile the counties moved more nearly in step. Their wage levels differed, often widely; but there was no great risk of wage stagnation or fall in one coinciding with wage rise or stagnation in another. Movements at any one time tended to be in one direction.

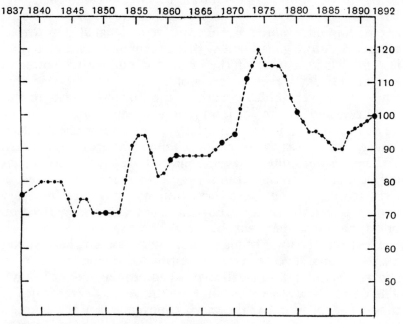

Agricultural earnings in England and Wales, expressed as percentages of the earnings of 1892. (After Bowley.)

The larger mark ● denotes years for which information is most complete.

The long depression, it is seen, brought a sharp fall in money earnings, just as the short depression which followed the repeal of the corn laws had brought a fall, though a slight one. To the labourer, whose peak wage of the 'seventies had been nothing magnificent, this fall might well seem unmerited and monstrous, although prices fell further. Perhaps he did sometimes work grudgingly, as the farmers said. In the areas from which evidence mostly comes, he had just been beaten in a wage-fight and he was looking to redress through his new vote and what people were telling him it would bring. Yet when earnings touched bottom, in 1886–7, they were still as high as they had been in the late 'sixties and nearly 27 per cent. higher than in the years about 1850. From 1887 recovery began. It was odd that its start coincided with the labourer's early use of his vote and with Victoria's jubilee: they were only coincidences.

In Scotland, the course of earnings, which is less well known than that for England and Wales, was similar but more favourable to the labourer. Comprehensive Scottish figures for the years about 1850, comparable with those which Caird collected in England, are lacking. But all the evidence suggests that the claim made in 1892 that Scottish earnings had risen 50 per cent. in the previous forty years was approximately correct—perhaps an understatement if the exact years 1852 and 1892 are taken[1]. (English wages, as the curve indicates, had risen 41 per cent. in the same period.) Nor had Scottish earnings during the 'eighties fallen quite so far as English from their summit of the 'seventies. Scotland's small wheat area helped both farmer and labourer when the crisis came.

The provision of adequate cottage gardens, allotments, potato patches and the like had become more general since 1850; but how much more general it is hard to say. The gardenless cottage was far from extinct in 1867. Sometimes whole villages, 'open villages,' like Docking in Norfolk and similar places in arable and late enclosed districts, were made up of very little else[2]. Sometimes a whole county was said to show an unusual number of them: Devon was such a county[3]. But the impression left by the inquiries of that year is reasonably satisfactory; and though there is not evidence of marked improvement in those areas where the garden position had been worst a generation earlier[4], there are many counties where it is said to be definitely good, counties so far apart as Hampshire, Hereford, North Lancashire and Yorkshire. In Yorkshire the garden was almost universal and was often accompanied—as it sometimes was in

---

[1] The claim is in the Report on Scotland of R. Hunter-Pringle and E. Wilkinson to the *R.C. on Labour*, 1893–4, XXXVI. 33. Scottish figures are "not so discursive nor so complete" as the English; Bowley, *S.J.* 1899, p. 140. The interpolated figure which Bowley accepts for 1852 is 60 against the basic 100 of 1892, or a rise of 66·6. In the depression of the 'eighties his lowest Scottish figure is 93 against the English 90.

[2] *R. on Employment of Children...in Agriculture*, 1867–8 (XVII), p. 35 (Docking) and *passim*.

[3] *Ibid.* vol. II (1868–9, XIII): Report of E. Portman on Hants, Devon and Cornwall.

[4] Cp. vol. I. p. 467–8.

Cheshire and Shropshire—by a 'cow-gate,' the right of grazing your cow in the lanes and by-places[1].

The allotment or potato patch had been adopted experimentally between 1820 and 1850 by landlords, farmers and parsons as a social palliative, especially in those districts where gardens were most scarce and the old poor law had been most abused. Parliament in the early 'forties had left the work in the hands of the men who had begun it, after playing with the idea of bringing it under government supervision[2]. Progress was intermittent and slow. A Berkshire report of 1860 speaks of retrogression except in the neighbourhood of towns[3]. The Commissioners of 1867-8 were convinced that there had been a considerable general advance since 1843; but though they could quote instances they could not gauge the movement. They noted with regret that the only public method of providing allotments, by the setting aside of land newly enclosed under the General Enclosure Act of 1845, had yielded no more than 2119 acres in twenty-two years[4]. The Commissioners of 1881 listened to discouraging evidence. One witness spoke of the disappearance of allotments in many counties, and Joseph Arch, the labourers' leader, offered an explanation when he complained of the exorbitant rents often asked for them by farmers and others[5]. Of this there is much good evidence[6]. It was Arch's ambition to see the labourer pass from allotment-holder into peasant-proprietor. Next year his parliamentary sympathiser, Jesse Collings, tried to help the cause by his Extension of Allotments Act (45 and 46 Vict. c. 80).

That Act did not work well and yet, when allotments and cottage gardens of fair size were first counted in 1886, the confessedly imperfect results were most encouraging[7]. The tide

---

[1] *Report*, as above, vol. I. p. 105 (Yorks); vol. II. 27 (Cheshire and Salop), 30 (Hants), 60 (Hereford), 154 (N. Lancs). The *R.C. on Labour* (1893-4, XXVII. part 2, p. 128) summarises the garden position for six sample districts, in Lincs, Cambs, Wilts, Worcester, Somerset, Essex. Nearly 20 per cent. of the cottages had only tiny gardens and 11·5 per cent. had none. But the cottager with no, or an inadequate, garden might have an allotment.

[2] Vol. I. p. 473-4.　　　　[3] *J.R.A.S.* 1860, p. 44.

[4] *Report of* 1867-8, as above, vol. I. p. xli-li.

[5] *R.C. on Agriculture*, Q. 59,303; 54,463-4 (Arch). These replies are quoted in Curtler, W. H. R., *The Enclosure and Redistribution of our Land* (1920), p. 280-2.

[6] Arch, Joseph. *The Story of the Life of Joseph Arch* (1898), p. 343; Heath, F. G., *Peasant Life in the West of England* (1872), p. 149; Stubbs, C. W., *The Land and the Labourers* (1891), p. 45.

[7] See the discussion by Major Craigie, "Agricultural Holdings in England and Abroad," *S.J.* 1887, p. 86 *sqq.* and Curtler, *op. cit.* p. 283.

had been flooding quietly while good men in a hurry were crying that there was no motion and some observers were unable to detect any. It appeared that there were in England and Wales 389,000 detached allotments, mostly within half a mile of the homes of those who worked them; 257,000 gardens of an eighth of an acre and upwards attached to cottages (those below an eighth of an acre were not reported); 93,000 field potato plots; and 9400 'cow-gates.' These figures excluded the gardens and allotments provided by railway companies for railway workers; but no doubt some considerable proportion of those included would be held by men who were no more agriculturalists than they. Yet even with a generous allowance for such men, it is evident that there were allotments, fair-sized gardens, and potato patches enough to serve most of the 580–600,000 agricultural labourers of twenty years old and upwards in England and Wales. Gardens and allotments might have been bigger and better and cheaper; they could not with advantage have been much more numerous. This was confirmed a few years later when it appeared that in most English rural Poor Law Unions the allotment supply approximately met the demand; that in none of the sample Unions reported on were there more than 14·6 inhabitants per allotment; and that in the most favoured Union there were only 5·3. The figures include small country towns and exclude gardens[1].

In Wales the allotment was not popular; but the field potato patch was, and it was found everywhere[2].

The Scottish figures for 1886 suggest at first sight a rather less satisfactory situation. There were only 46,500 allotments, good gardens, potato patches or cow-gates among some 70,000 labourers and shepherds of twenty years old and upwards. But living-in on small farms, or boarding with married men on large ones, were commoner practices in Scotland than in England, and the bothy system was not yet extinct; so there was less demand for allotments and gardens. The Scottish married labourer normally had his kale-yard or potato patch, though sometimes he preferred an allowance of potatoes to the toil of growing them[3].

Boarding unmarried labourers with a foreman or other leading hand was known also in England, being commonest in Notting-

---

[1] Little's Report to the *R.C. on Labour*, p. 134.

[2] Report on Wales (1893–4, XXXVI), p. 25.

[3] Report on Scotland (1893–4, XXXVI), p. 14, 27–8. For the bothy system, below, p. 511.

ham and Lincoln, where to a great degree it had replaced living-in[1]. Big modern cottages had been provided for foremen to facilitate the arrangement. Only the largest farmer could require them, so the system can nowhere be described as general. Perhaps it accentuated the gap between farmer and labourer, but it did not create it; and it saved many a young labourer the long tramp to his work which had been common before housing was adjusted to the various types of nineteenth-century farm. Side by side with it might be found, if not always any living-in, at least the meal shared by a small farmer with his man. Such habits never died out altogether even in the East: living-in was by no means extinct in Kent in 1867[2]. In the North-West they remained common[3]. But they were declining every-where, even in Wales. At the census of 1861 there were Welsh counties in which more labourers lived in than out. By 1870 the decline of living-in is registered for Monmouth. By 1881 it was only possible to say of Wales that living-in was "much more general...than in England." That it might easily be[4].

Sharing meals is a good democratic habit; but the historian who has personal knowledge of living-in as practised at a later date in the English North-West and in Wales, or in France or in Switzerland, will not waste much sentiment over its decline.

Living-in, boarding, and the bothy system had been Scot-land's solution of the labour problem where population was thin and farms big. In England, the Fens and the districts round about them, having the proletariat of small country towns and open villages to draw on, had supplemented boarding by the gang system[5]. As steam drainage made the fenland safe and firm, in the 'forties and 'fifties[6], those "immense bowling greens separated by ditches" which had delighted Cobbett were turned up black and put under wheat and potatoes. There were farms among them but no cottages, except a few bad ones used by horse and cattle men. The Norfolk sands above the Fen, Lincoln Heath, and the Lincoln Wolds had also been won for cropping

---

[1] *J.R.A.S.* 1861, p. 162 (Notts); *R. on Children in Agriculture*, 1867, p. 75 (Lincs).

[2] *R. on Children in Agriculture*, 1868–9 (XIII), E. Stanhope's Report, p. 26.

[3] Personal knowledge, for Lincolnshire; *R.C. on Labour*, A. W. Fox's Report, p. 6 for Cumberland and N. Lancs.

[4] *R.C. on Land in Wales*, p. 149 for 1861; *J.R.A.S.* 1870, p. 294 for Monmouth; *R.C. on Agriculture*, Q. 65,697 for 1881.

[5] Vol. 1. p. 468–9.

[6] Vol. 1. p. 445.

in the nineteenth century. The working of the close and open village system had delayed their appropriate equipment with cottages. And so from Castle Acre among the heaths and warrens of West Norfolk, from Chatteris, the Deepings and Spalding in the Fens; as from Louth, Caistor and Ludford, under the Wolds, the gang-master led out draggled troops of women and children to weed and pick stones and hoe. In Louth there was a little Irish colony which fed the gangs: elsewhere they were English[1].

The system hardly existed outside these newly won districts; and in them it often declined when the winning was finished; when "twitch had been almost eradicated and other weeds reduced to a minimum."[2] In the greater part of the country it was completely unknown. Because of the transition to arable in the fens, where the system was at its worst, it appears to have grown between 1850 and 1865; although at the same time provision of more cottages by such good landlords as Lord Yarborough, coincident with the final cleaning of the land, was cutting at its roots on the Lincoln Wolds[3]. Besides what came to be known as the public gangs, which included 6–7000 people in the 'sixties, private gangs organised by large farmers and put under their nominees were common in these same areas. The Commissioners of the 'sixties believed that they contained many more people than the public gangs; but the point was controverted and never decided. Even if they did, the gang population at its height was only a fraction of the rural population of a few counties. It was recruited very far down the social scale. The public gang-master was normally the type of man whom no respectable farmer would take on to his permanent staff[4]. Members of the permanent staff did not wish their wives and children to work under such people, and were not forced by need to let them do so. The wife of the regular labourer does not go to work, the Commissioners say, and the children "are

---

[1] *Sixth Report on Children's Employment (Agricultural Gangs)*, 1867, XVI. 67, p. v, vi, vii, 6 (the Louth Irish), etc. See also Hasbach, W., *A History of the English Agricultural Labourer* (Eng. trans. 1908), ch. IV.

[2] *Report*, p. vi. Besides the districts referred to, *i.e.* Lincoln, Hunts, Cambs, and Norfolk, there were gangs, public or private, in Suffolk and Notts and a few in Northants, Beds, Bucks, Leicester and Rutland, generally also on newly won ground. *Ibid.* p. v and 1870, XIII (Index vol. to the *Children's Employment Commission*). The list of counties in the Report is not quite complete.

[3] *Ibid.* p. vi.

[4] *Ibid.* p. xi.

kept longer at school."[1] That is in Lincolnshire, where nearly a quarter of the gang population was enumerated.

Legislative control of this cheap, dangerous, and slavish system was a by-product of the factory and education movements of the 'sixties. The Gangs Act of 1868 (30 and 31 Vict. c. 130) forbade the employment of children under eight, regulated the working relations of men and women, and established licences for gang-masters. As it affected public gangs only, its first effect was to encourage private ones[2]. These, in so far as they relied on the work of very young children, were crippled in their turn by the successive education acts of the 'seventies. They had always been less liable to abuse than the public gangs. Meanwhile the housing position was improving a little; no more land was being cleared for the plough and cleaned after it; demand for gang work slackened. By the end of the 'eighties gangs were said to be "gradually dying out" in the Fens, though there were several about Swaffham, and no doubt at other points[3]. A few sad droves of women stone-pickers could be found on the Lincoln Wolds[4]; and some sort of temporary gang organisation was necessary for potato lifting, fruit picking, and hop-picking, as it still is. But these shrunken and regulated survivals from a harder unregulated time themselves showed that life on the soil was becoming more tolerable for those nearest to it, if more difficult for some others.

It is not easy to show any direct link between the improved position of the agricultural labourer of the middle 'eighties and the Labourers' Unions of the previous decade. The working of impersonal forces would account for all, or nearly all, of that improvement. True, without the Unions the wage peak of the 'seventies might not everywhere have been won; but then it was lost again. Certainly the Unions helped to educate labourers, politicians, and the public. This education bore fruit later. They also educated farmers—in the use of machinery; which proved good for labour in the end, though not for particular labourers at the time. Possibly they hastened the Reform Bill of 1884;

---

[1] *Report*, p. vi.

[2] As shown by the later inquiries of the same series as that of 1867. See 1870, XIII, *s.v.* Gangs.

[3] *R.C. on Labour*, 1893-4, XXXV. Chapman's Report, p. 22; Fox's Report, p. 9.

[4] And probably elsewhere: it is on the Lincoln Wolds that the author has seen them.

but even if they did, in economic fields reform bills work like delayed-action mines, and do not always blow up what they should.

There were strikes before the Unions. When food prices were running up in the summer of 1867[1], the strike of twenty-eight labourers at Gawcott, Bucks, a strike for 12s. a week in place of 10s., caught the attention of the London press and of a sympathising public, now reasonably well-informed about rural wages, cottages and gangs[2]. Money flowed into Gawcott: Karl Marx in London read about it: the strike found its way into *Das Kapital*[3]. Next year the Rev. Edward Girdlestone told the British Association that, to his mind, the only way of bettering the labourers' condition was the formation of a national Union. Girdlestone was working in a particularly stagnant North Devon parish, where wages were low, cottages bad, and farmers savagely hard-fisted[4]. He was trying to speed up the mills of God, grinding slowly just then in the labourers' interest, by organised migration and emigration. Soon, news of the Trade Union inquiry of 1867–9 and of the Trade Union legislation of 1870–1 got through to the villages, where 1830 and 1834 were not forgotten and the Union Workhouse stood gaunt, the reminder of what society had to offer. Food was cheap in 1869–70, but from the harvest of 1870 prices moved up again, and not food prices only. For three years British wheat stood above 55s. and in the fourth, 1873–4, above 60s. Bread in London was dearer on the average in 1872 than it had been in any year since the Crimean War except 1867.

Quite early in 1871 a labourers' union was started at Leintwardine in Hereford, "and it was backed up by the rector." "It spread over six counties in a very short time." "No sooner had this Union caught on than wages in Hereford rose on an average two shillings a week, and all over the six counties there was improvement."[5] Like Canon Girdlestone, these men of the

---

[1] Wheat was above 60s. throughout the year, except for a couple of weeks in February, and reached 73s. 8d. early in 1868. Potatoes were also very dear.

[2] See *e.g.* the *Economist*, July 27, 1867.

[3] Hasbach, *op. cit.* p. 276 n., learnt of it from Marx.

[4] Heath, F. G., *The English Peasantry* (1874), p. 189. Girdlestone had come from a Lancashire parish where the labourers were "well paid, well housed... well cared for."

[5] Arch, *op. cit.* p. 110–11. See also his evidence before the *R.C. on Agriculture*, 1881, Q. 58,371 *sqq.* Cp. Clayden, A., *The Revolt of the Field* (1874); Heath, F. G., *Peasant Life in the West of England* (1872); Clifford, F., *The Agricultural Lock-out of* 1874 (1875); Hasbach, *op. cit.* p. 276–7; Webb, S. and B., *History of Trade Unionism*, p. 314–19.

South-West believed in betterment by increased mobility. "Emigration, migration, but not strikes" was their motto[1]. They helped their members to move into high-wage areas like Stafford, Lancashire and Yorkshire; and they organised a little emigration to America. Their Union was already full-grown when, in February, 1872, some men of Wellesbourne, on the Avon above Stratford, tramped North to Barford to ask Joseph Arch, a Methodist lay-preacher, ditcher and hedger, who had been an organiser of piece-work jobs for farmers while still in his teens[2], to come and address a meeting and start a Union. Warwickshire men dated the whole movement from the wet night of February 7, "when Arch beneath the Wellesbourne tree" so wrought on them that they "enrolled between two and three hundred members that night."[3]

They were on strike at Wellesbourne in March. Helped by bourgeois sympathy, including that of John Stuart Mill, and some bourgeois money, unionism spread fast[4]. Arch claimed "nearly fifty thousand enrolled members" by May. There were strikes or talk of strikes from Dorset to Norfolk. The demand for labour was brisk and wages in every trade were rising, so that the men very often got at least some part of what they asked. Arch believed in migration. Back in the 'forties, while wandering at his trade, he had compared the cottages and gardens of Eastern Wales to their advantage with those of Warwickshire[5]. But he was a fighter of Cobbett's breed, though, unlike Cobbett, he fought with biting Old Testament weapons, prophesying to valleys of dry bones and wielding the sword of the Lord and of Gideon. He never relied on migration alone; and when Girdlestone urged compromise, pointing out that Warwick was already much better off than Devon, Arch's only conclusion was that Devon needed a good fighting Union. So he and his followers sang:

> The farm labourers of South Warwickshire
> Have not had a rise for many a year,
> Although bread has often been dear,
> But now they've found a Union[6].

---

[1] Arch, *op. cit.* p. 110.

[2] With "men working under me," *op. cit.* p. 40.

[3] Arch, *op. cit.* p. 73. The line "When Arch beneath the Wellesbourne tree" comes from a Union song.

[4] Heath, *The English Peasantry*, p. 197 *sqq.* There was active support from the *Daily News* and other Liberal journals.

[5] Arch, *op. cit.* p. 43.          [6] Arch, *op. cit.* p. 87.

In 1873–4, when at the height of its strength, Arch's Union, the National, claimed a membership of 100,000 and branches in every English county except Cumberland, Westmorland, Yorkshire, Lancashire, Cheshire and Cornwall. The other chief organisation, the Federal, was something of a competitor. Even if Unionism could show a few cells in the North, it had not really touched the high-wage territory across the Trent, though the Federal had a strong footing in Lincolnshire[1]. In the East it had called out counter-organisation among farmers, beginning with the Association for Cambridgeshire and West Suffolk started at Newmarket in October-November, 1872. In April of 1873 the associated farmers of the Sudbury district locked out their Union men, and won[2]. There was friction, striking, farmers' stupid attacks on 'agitators,' labourers' crude abuse of farmers, and some persecution of non-unionists, up and down the Eastern counties all that year. In March of 1874 the Newmarket farmers followed the lead of Sudbury, and replied to a demand for a 14s. wage and a 54-hour week by a lock-out of Union men[3]. Before the end of the month the lock-out had affected nine counties and some thousands of men[4]. By July, for it was a long fight, the National Union had made grants to locked-out members in a dozen counties, but had spent four-fifths of its money in three, Cambridge, Suffolk and Essex. At the end of July it gave in, withdrew the grants, and resolved "to place migration and emigration at the disposal of the labourers, or the alternative of depending wholly on their own resources."[5] The Federal Union did much the same.

What with volunteer labour, surplus non-agricultural or non-union labour which was available almost everywhere, Irish labour, and machinery, the East Anglian farmers had come through well and were facing the harvest with confidence. "In-

---

[1] Clifford, op. cit. p. 17, 20. The Lincolnshire League, like some other County Unions, was affiliated to the Federal.

[2] Ibid. p. 9–11.

[3] The Agricultural Lock-out of 1874, of which Clifford wrote the story in letters to the Times. And see Bishop Fraser's letter to the Times, April 2, 1874.

[4] The total number thrown out before the struggle was over is uncertain. It seems to have been from 6000 to 10,000. The National Union claimed 3100 members locked out and the Federal 2500, and there were others. But the rival Union leaders accused one another of exaggeration. Clifford, op. cit. p. 21–2 and Hasbach, op. cit. p. 285.

[5] Quoted in Clifford, p. 146. Money had been received from industrial Unions, e.g. the A.S.E., as well as from bourgeois sympathisers; but the supply could not be maintained.

stead of employing twenty-six men," a representative Suffolk
farmer said just before harvest, "I am doing with seventeen
and my work was never more forward."[1]  Observers noted that
"the machine makers are not without hopes of perfecting a
machine for tying up the corn in the wake of the reapers, which
would indeed be a valuable ally to the farmer."[2]  There was
discouragement and dissension in the Unions, and their numbers
fell off; but Arch still claimed 60,000 in his at the end of 1875.
Then came the black years, and the most that he could claim in
May 1879 was "some twenty-three thousand."[3]  Farmers had
begun to cut wages and turn off men, and would continue to do
both. The Unions almost vanished away[4].

Arch threw himself into the franchise fight and, when the
franchise had been won, into the new democratic politics of
the country-side. At the election of 1885, in *A Word of Council
to the New Electors*, he spoke of "men turned out to starve while
the land by millions of acres is lying starving under your eyes
for want of labour." Men had been turned out. By 1885–6 wages
had fallen back to somewhere about the level at which they had
stood when he went to "the Wellesbourne tree." But if some
land was "starving...for want of labour" that was hardly the
farmers' fault, or the landlords', with wheat at 32s. a quarter or
less; and wheat at 32s. or less meant bread about 25 per cent.
cheaper than it had been in 1871–5 when the Unions were most
active. Bread prices still ruled country budgets, so this was no
small matter. Cheese also was cheaper; tea and sugar much
cheaper; bacon at least no dearer. And so the labourer of the
late 'eighties 'dressed better, ate more butchers' meat, travelled
more, read more.'[5] There was a little surplus now for these
things; but it cannot be said that the Unions had done much to
make it. Perhaps by instilling hope and strengthening self-
respect, they were in part responsible for that other generali-
sation about the village labourer—"he drinks less." If so, they
share responsibility with the chapel, the school, the allotment,
the friendly society, the new cottage, the cricket club, with
each and every thing that eased the cramped tedium of village
life or revealed what lies beyond.

---

[1] Clifford, p. 179. A sample statement out of many.
[2] *Ibid.* p. 65.                    [3] Arch, *op. cit.* p. 254, 333.
[4] At the end of the 'eighties they were very weak and existed only in 6 out
of 38 districts inquired into by the *R.C. on Labour* (Little's Report, p.146).
[5] Quoted above, p. 285.

# CHAPTER VIII

## THE ORGANISATION OF COMMERCE

THE main features of the commercial organisation of Britain, as it existed in the later nineteenth century, were hewn in the rough even before the railway age. Few institutions of new type, few entirely novel practices, grew up in the three decades after 1850. Important modifications there were, no doubt. Writing in 1905, George Joachim Goschen could even refer to the "fundamental change wrought by the transfer of an enormous proportion of our industry and commerce from private individuals to public companies" between 1850 and 1885[1]. But this was only a change of balance, not to be over-rated. Well informed and cautious as Goschen was, there is more than a spice of exaggeration in his "fundamental" and his "enormous." As to changes of method—it is probable that after at most a morning's talk with Goschen in 1885, David Ricardo or Nathan Rothschild would have been able to operate in the City or at Liverpool with ease, though some of their slower witted contemporaries might have been bewildered by the pace, and by certain unfamiliar customs or instruments.

In the country, institutions and methods already moribund in the 'twenties had gone a step or two nearer the grave[2]. The travelling tinker or pedlar had been driven North and West and had lost ground every decade. The fairs, except the horse and cattle fairs, were fast dropping the remnants of their economic importance[3]. On corn or cattle market day in a country town farmers sold to dealers and dealers to the public; but only in outlying districts would there be much of the old-style direct trade in foodstuffs between country producers and town consumers[4]. Market selling was passing more and more into the hands of professionals, resident or migratory. In the

---

[1] *Essays and Addresses*, p. 7, referring to an address given in 1885. Cp. p. 138, above, and p. 311, below.

[2] Cp. vol. I. p. 220-5.

[3] Though there are men living in Cambridgeshire who can remember the farmers waiting for Sturbridge Fair to replace things lost or damaged.

[4] It survived most vigorously in Wales, *e.g.* Cardigan market day, even after 1900.

towns of the industrial North, the great market halls[1] were just shopping places for the multitude; though some of the stalls would be held by producers. All industrial or agricultural villages of any size had their shops of various kinds. The railway, the penny post and the telegraph had brought them within easy reach of urban influences, and had helped to assimilate their business methods to those of the towns.

Quick communications had extinguished a few trades and traders. Long-distance cattle-droving, to take an obvious instance, was extinct; though so late as 1847 some cattle had still been driven " 120 miles or more " to market[2]. Bullocks or dead meat could go from Aberdeen to London by rail or steamer. But if the long trading chains of personal links, by which the country had once been attached to the metropolis and the greater towns[3], had often been shortened, by elimination of middlemen of one sort and another, the greater dependence of the island on imported foodstuffs had added to the weight of central markets and metropolitan dealers, and required fresh middlemen's work in distribution. At the same time, the growing size and intricacy of commercial operations of all kinds had called for additional specialisation, and so perhaps for new links in the commercial chains.

The readjustment of the internal grain trade after the repeal of the Corn Laws, and of the London coal trade after the making of the railways, illustrate these various tendencies. During the last years of the Corn Laws, when the complete cessation of export had simplified a trade now become strictly insular, most of the British wheat had been sold direct to the miller. Small millers would buy only locally, but some of the larger ones employed factors to buy over wide areas, and might resell as merchants what they did not themselves grind. Good quality barley went for the most part straight to local maltsters; the rest, with the farmers' surplus of oats and beans, came into dealers' hands, for local or distant distribution. Great quantities of these and a fair, but smaller, quantity of wheat were handled in Mark Lane. The factors sometimes sold 'growers corn' from the home counties, as the growers' agents; more often the

---

[1] Vol. I. p. 226. The older halls were of course continuously enlarged or remodelled between 1830 and 1880.

[2] *S.C. to inquire into the Necessity of the removal of Smithfield Market as a nuisance in the centre of the British Metropolis*, 1847 (VIII. 275), Q. 969.

[3] Vol. I. p. 219.

corn sold had been bought from the grower outright by London and country dealers. Millers and secondary dealers were the chief purchasers. In Mark Lane were to be found also a small group of jobbers, who bought to resell and "take advantage of momentary changes of the market"—market operators in later commercial speech. The various groups might overlap at almost any point. Meanwhile merchants, many of whom were outside the domestic corn trade, carried on intermittent and necessarily speculative dealings in foreign grain, which could be warehoused in London at times when it might not be sold there, or could be resold in cargoes and parcels for overseas consumption while still on shipboard. Some of these merchants were connected with the Baltic Coffee House, where a business club of the usual English sort had taken shape in 1823, to introduce order into the rather disorderly Russian trade, particularly the trade in tallow[1].

When the world was being searched for grain at the time of the Irish famine, the general merchants—Russian, East Indian, American, whatever it might be—necessarily did most of the work, because no group of specialised foreign corn merchants existed. When the collapse came, in a list of 460 failures which occurred between August, 1847, and August, 1848, only twenty-six of the bankrupts were definitely described as corn merchants, although corn dealing had helped to bring down far more than that[2].

The general merchant did not cease handling grain when the import trade became a regular and fast growing thing. But the growth gave scope for more specialists—merchants, brokers, jobbers—who took part in the London dealings and, from London, in the direction of cargoes to other ports according to their needs. Throughout the period London remained the chief consumer and distributor of foreign grain; though with the increased importance of American supplies, from 1867–70 onwards, Liverpool grew into a serious rival, particularly in the wheat trade; and Hull was always powerful. The Baltic became the headquarters of the larger and more speculative transactions, purchases of cargoes afloat and sales and resales of grain for

[1] Vol. I. p. 231, 232–3, 303–5 (the old corn trade). Torrens, R., *Essay on the External Corn Trade* (1815), says nothing of value about organisation. For the history of the Baltic, Findlay, J. A., *The Baltic Exchange* (1927). Thomas Tooke, the historian of prices, was on the first committee. The rules are of April 22, 1823; p. 14.

[2] The list is in Evans, D. M., *The Commercial Crisis of 1847–8*, App. p. lxix *sqq.*

future shipment. Its Russian and North German connections had attracted merchants from abroad, especially Greeks familiar with the South Russian, Danubian, and Mediterranean grain trades. Among the Tookes and Thorntons and Todds of the old Baltic firms moved Rallis, Rodocanachis and Schroeders[1]. The cutting of the Suez Canal and the laying of the world's cables gave scope for master minds at the Baltic, whose committee in 1857 had not inappropriately taken quarters in the South Sea House. Hitherto the trade had all been done in sailing ships. The set of the wind in the Channel was a regular item of the market reports down to the 'seventies: it affected all dealings on the Baltic. Now a change was in sight.

The Corn Exchanges in Mark Lane provided the link between the insular and the international corn trades[2]. Unlike the Baltic they had, and still have, their stands and samples like any provincial exchange. There had never been auctions: it was the quiet private dealing of factors, some farmers, merchants and millers about the stands. It had always been a 'spot' trade, and a 'spot' trade it remained when the foreign corn got regularly into it. As the personnel of the Baltic and the Exchanges overlapped, and as duty-paid foreign corn had been sold in Mark Lane under the Corn Laws, this easily happened. The bulk of the buying to resell and the professional operating tended to concentrate at the Baltic. Cargoes first handled on the Baltic might be resold on, or near, arrival at the Corn Exchange; but the chief business there was in parcels of grain actually arrived. As the import trade grew, all the foreign grains could be sampled side by side with Essex wheat and Norfolk barley. Through the dealers on the Exchange they passed out into the country, to local dealers and millers, as the use of foreign grain spread from the greater to the smaller centres of population.

The whole story might have furnished Herbert Spencer, the philosopher of the age, with apt instances of his favourite 'differentiation and integration' of social organisms and functions, had he concerned himself with the contemporary evolution of

---

[1] Findlay, *op. cit.* p. 17–21. For the growing importance of America, see *e.g. Economist*, March 12, 1870 (Commercial Review of 1869).

[2] Vol. I. p. 303–5. Dowling, S. W., *The Exchanges of London* (1929), p. 180. The second exchange in Mark Lane was started in 1828: it was the headquarters of the seed trade. The old exchange was rebuilt in 1881.

the corn trade as much as with those primitive Lepchas and Todas whom he had never seen[1].

Changes in the coal trade of London and the South were determined mainly by the simple facts that whereas in 1850 only 55,000 tons of coal came into London by rail, in 1860 the figure was 1,500,000; in 1870, 3,500,000; 6,200,000 in 1880; and 7,250,000 in 1886. The sea-borne supply, which was 3,500,000 tons in 1850 and 3,600,000 in 1860, fell to a minimum of 2,500,000 in 1872, rising again to 4,740,000 in 1886[2]. The early nineteenth century coal code, which stereotyped antiquated differences of commercial function, both on the Tyne and the Thames, had been abandoned in 1831[3]. In the mid-'forties, the North-East Coast 'committee of the vend,' which had regulated prices by the regulation of output, had broken down. Thereafter it was "practically an open fighting trade"[4]—free and unrestricted competition. If local associations of owners gave price rulings, as they sometimes did, they "had no means of enforcing the rules at all," so that they were not "in fact carried out...at least...not entirely."[5]

Since the elimination of superfluous intermediaries on Tyne-side, and the inauguration of a permanent "fighting trade," the bulk of the coal had been shipped by, or on behalf of, the coal-owners[6]. But it was not shipped to the order of London merchants. They bought on the London Coal Exchange through factors acting for the owners. (The Exchange had provided itself with a new building opened by the Prince Consort in 1849[7].) The greater merchants in the 'sixties and 'seventies sold for the most part directly to the consumer, manufacturing or domestic, not as at an earlier time mainly to 'second merchants.'[8] There was, however, a class of 'second merchants,' now generally called coal-dealers, who bought from the principals at the wharf or in the railway yard, "took the coals home to their own place and sold...as little as 14 lbs. sometimes," as a principal put it[9].

---

[1] Spencer, *Principles of Sociology, passim.*

[2] The figures are summarised down to 1870 in *S.C. on the Causes of the Present Dearness and Scarcity of Coal*, 1873 (x. 1), App. 1. There are annual returns.

[3] Vol. i. p. 233–6.

[4] George Elliot before the *S.C. of* 1873, Q. 7518. Cp. above, p. 149.

[5] *Ibid.* R. Tennant, speaking for the West Riding, Q. 2657.

[6] *Ibid.* Evidence of Sydney Cockerell, London coal merchant, Q. 7190.

[7] Dowling, *op. cit.* p. 129.    [8] Vol. i. p. 235.    [9] R. Cory, Q. 7136.

Such dealers frequented the yards more than the wharves; for the poor now consumed chiefly the 'inland coal' from Derbyshire and Yorkshire, not the 'best Wallsend,' with its old reputation and higher price[1].

Apart from points of quality, the inland coal was more economical to handle. There were no lighterage charges and less loss on the small coal through breakage in loadings and unloadings. When first it came, in the 'fifties, the inland coal had been consigned for sale like that sent by sea, but the selling of it was less formal and regular. It "is not sold in the London market in the same way as the sea-borne coal; therefore it is more difficult to get at the price."[2] Consignment for sale continued into the 'seventies and later, but purchase direct from the pit was increasing all the time. "We buy all we can direct": it is "loaded into our trucks at the pits' mouth," witnesses connected with this trade said in the early 'seventies[3]. Whether carried on in this way far from London, or by the small man in the station-yards, the dealings in 'inland coal' were particularly competitive. They helped to give the whole trade its fighting character. Though the air was full of rumours about an unscrupulous group of inland coal-dealers, described as the Forty Thieves, neither on the coalfields nor among the Londoners could a naturally suspicious Committee of Inquiry find any evidence of rings or combinations during the price inflation of 1873[4]. The Forty Thieves if they existed were individualistic bandits. And although the declaring of current prices, or nominal fixings of price, by coal-owners' associations made some little progress during the next decade, there was no change in essentials[5].

The farther it was removed from London towards the coalfields, the simpler the trade had always been, until on the fields themselves even domestic consumers able to buy in cart-loads could do so direct from the pit[6].

In the other primary metropolitan supply trades, milk, meat, and fish, there had again been both shortenings and lengthenings of the chain between ultimate producer and consumer, but mainly shortenings. On the eve of the railway age all the milk used in London came from an area with a twenty mile radius,

---

[1] Cory, Q. 7150.  [2] Cory, Q. 7151.  [3] Cockerell, Q. 7245, 7178.
[4] S.C. of 1873: Report, p. x.  [5] Above, p. 149.
[6] Memories of the 'eighties of a home four miles from the pits where coal was delivered at 12s. 6d. a ton.

THE ORGANISATION OF COMMERCE

and very little of it from points on the outer fifteen miles. The bulk was provided by urban and suburban cowkeepers, mostly small, many of whom delivered their own milk, others selling to milk-dealers and dairymen[1]. By 1878 the "market for milk in London" affected "farms a hundred and fifty miles away"[2]; but the change from a local to a semi-national market had been slow, and in 1878 was by no means complete. The railways had not transformed the trade so quickly as had been anticipated[3]. At first they took no interest in it. Milk transport and milk cooling were not understood. Rail-borne milk was supposed to be inferior, and probably it was[4]. Like rail-borne coal, it went chiefly to the poor. But disease began to ravage the London cow-houses. Foot and mouth disease had been recurrent since 1839. The arrival of *Rinderpest* in 1865 led to the death or slaughter within a few months of four-fifths of the cows in London[5]. Milk-dealers were driven farther afield. Railway handling improved. Milk transport was mastered. The normal unit in the dairying business grew; "and by 1870 the trade was fairly started" on the lines upon which it was running in the late 'eighties[6]. Considerable companies were building up large scale buying and delivery organisations. This did not, however, carry with it the quick extinction of small-scale cowkeeping and dairying. After 1870 these trades fell into the hands of immigrant Welshmen who knew a good deal about cattle, little about anything else, and lived hard. In the 'eighties, their small businesses were numerous in poor neighbourhoods, particularly in Whitechapel. At the close of the decade, when the new County Council took over control, there were still nearly 700 licensed cow-houses in London proper; and at the census of 1891, in the whole metropolitan milk selling business, the employed were to the employers only as five to one[7].

The meat trade had been but little simplified, although long-distance cattle-droving had been cut out. Farmers and graziers

[1] Vol. I. p. 227–8. Cp. Pinchbeck, J., *Women Workers and the Industrial Revolution* (1930), p. 299.

[2] *R.A.S. Reports, Dairy Farming*, p. 670.

[3] Cp. the anticipations referred to in vol. I. p. 228.

[4] See the historical notes in Booth, C., *Life and Labour of the People in London*, VII. 173.

[5] *R. on the Origin and Nature...of the Cattle Plague*, 1866 (XXII). For the first observation of 'mouth and foot disease,' Q. 378.

[6] Booth, *op. cit.* VII. 177.

[7] Booth, as above. Note the scepticism of the census-takers of 1891 about the statistics of employers and employed discussed above, p. 120 n. 1.

might send their beasts to London for sale, or might sell outright to cattle jobbers[1]. Arrived in London, the beasts no
longer made the City "almost impassable"[2] on a Monday on
their way to Smithfield: bulls no longer got into City china
shops: "that sink of cruelty, drunkenness and filth, the cattle
market—where every other building was either a slaughter-
house, a gin-palace, or a pawn-broker's shop,"[3] had been
cleaned out since the opening of the Metropolitan Market at
Islington in 1855, and of the Foreign Cattle Market at Deptford
in 1872[4]. But this had not simplified the trade. The specialist
commission salesman grew in importance with the growth of
business. By the early 'sixties, men with foreign names were
selling beasts for graziers in Schleswig-Holstein or for jobbers
in Berlin[5]. About the new markets were grouped licensed
slaughterers and carcass butchers, just as they had formerly
been about Smithfield, the former killing for the latter or for
retail butchers who did not themselves slaughter. Some carcass
butchers had their own shops in Smithfield, but usually they
sold through yet another group of specialists, the commission
meat salesman[6]. More and more dead meat came up from
the country[7]. The average retail butcher was no longer a killer
but a purveyor of meat killed inside or outside London. In the
'forties and 'fifties he had very commonly killed at least the
calves at the back of his shop; and there were private or commission slaughter-houses all over London. Since that date their
number had declined greatly. There were still more than 1500
in the metropolitan area in 1873. When the County Council
began to deal with them, fifteen years later, they had fallen to
about 700[8]. Control, country killing, and frozen meat would
carry forward the reduction and the concentration.

[1] For jobbers; evidence before the *Smithfield C. of* 1847, Q. 1244; for a bullock
in a linen-draper's shop in High Holborn, Q. 1496.

[2] Vol. I. p. 226.

[3] Dumaurier, G., *Peter Ibbetson*, p. 65—obviously from personal reminiscence
of London in 1851–6. Fully confirmed by the *Smithfield C. of* 1847—"a scene
of great confusion and unnecessary cruelty": Q. 26—and by a second of 1849
(XIX. 247).

[4] Booth, *op. cit.* VII. 190–1.

[5] *E.g.* H. Gebhardt, who sold for the graziers referred to and for jobbers in
Magdeburg and Berlin. *R. on Cattle Plague*, Q. 2031 *sqq.*

[6] The witnesses before the committees of 1847 and 1849 describe an organisation of trade almost identical with that described by Charles Booth's
workers forty years later.

[7] The amount was called "astonishing" by a witness even in 1847: Q. 2075.

[8] Booth, *op. cit.* VII. 202.

Fish dealing was not greatly changed, but all its processes had been speeded up. Billingsgate, a wretched place of wooden sheds until the late 'forties[1], had been cleansed, twice rebuilt, and once enlarged before 1875. Fish brought to London by water was usually handled and sold at auction by the fish-carrying companies which had replaced the cutter-owners of the early nineteenth century. Their steam carriers collected from the fleets at sea. Fish brought by rail, the amount of which in the 'eighties was about twice that of the fish brought by water, was consigned by collecting companies and dealers in the fishing ports to Billingsgate commission salesmen, who sold mainly by private contract. Speed had provided work for a new, or newly grown, type of Billingsgate middleman, called in the slang of the day a 'bummaree.' The ice-filled 'trunks,' hurriedly despatched, contained fish of all sizes and sometimes of various sorts. The retailer usually did not want it like that, nor did he always want a trunk full. The bummaree therefore bought, sorted, and resold to the retailers, so becoming an operator and risk-bearer in a market which was already a by-word among economists for its hour-to-hour uncertainties and fluctuations. Thence to the fishmonger, still normally a man with a handful of employees, not yet a limited company[2].

In the general domestic trade of the country, there were forces obviously at work tending to the elimination of intermediaries between producer and consumer; but their working was much delayed and in various ways diverted or even counteracted. The clothing trades show them in operation effectively, though not uniformly. With the disappearance of the true domestic clothier in the woollen industry, for example, the old-fashioned type of Yorkshire home-trade woollen merchant, who came between the producer and the big wholesale metropolitan distributing or exporting houses, certainly declined. The metropolitan wholesaler, or his equivalent in other towns of the first rank, could not deal with a multitude of small clothiers in the heavy woollen district: a limited group of mill-owners was accessible to him. The rise of ready-made clothing factories led

---

[1] Cp. vol. I. p. 226.

[2] Booth, *op. cit.* VII. 207 *sqq.*, on which this paragraph is based, for the situation in the 'eighties. For fishing-boats and carriers, above, p. 72 *sqq.* The ratio of employers to employed in London fish-dealing was given as 1 : 4. The word bummaree is not in the Ministry of Labour's 1927 *Dictionary of Occupational Terms.*

to still more drastic elimination. They might buy in bulk from the mills and cut out the merchant entirely. Towards the close of the period, they were beginning to practise elimination on the other side—by opening their own retail shops; but as yet this was rare. Quite apart from the fall of the Yorkshire domestic clothier and the rise of the clothing factories, the forces of elimination were at work. A principal from St Paul's Churchyard indicated some of their lines of operation in evidence given in 1885. His firm dealt in everything except boots—silks, linens, cottons, woollens, knitted goods, ribbons, gloves. Twenty-five years ago, he said, "everybody, that is to say all retailers and shippers, had to obtain their goods" through them. Now, both retailers and shippers often went direct to the manufacturer or the manufacturer to them[1].

Why this had happened, particularly since the price-fall of the 'seventies, was explained concisely by a manufacturing witness from Preston: "our business was so exceedingly bare that we had to leave the merchant out and go beyond him."[2] The merchant whom they had left out was a shipping, not a home merchant, but the principle was the same. The witness added, however, that his firm's action was exceptional.

The tendency for the manufacturer to get more often into touch with the retailer was not confined to the clothing trades. One way in which it manifested itself was indeed uncommon, if not unknown, in those trades, that of the agency. Just when the agency system began is not yet clear; but the normal arrangements down to the 'fifties at least did not include it. This system, in which large manufacturers of goods in universal and regular demand kept agencies in all important towns and populous districts, was said in 1878 to have sprung up in "comparatively recent times." Its effect had been to curtail, but not abolish, the operations of the local wholesale dealers and factors, and to reduce the number of bagmen on the road[3].

The hardware and light metal industries of the West Mid-

---

[1] *R.C. on Depression of Trade*, Q. 4070. For the clothiers and the clothing factories, above, p. 118 and p. 92. At the end of the period the makers of clothing began to call themselves clothiers, the clothier proper having died out. There are no exact records of the decline of the Yorkshire home-trade merchants. They were numerous early in the century, rare towards its close; and the reasons are obvious. Cp. Clapham, J. H., *The Woollen and Worsted Industries* (1907), p. 162 *sqq.* based on personal knowledge and information.

[2] *Ibid.* Q. 5673.

[3] More information is needed on this question. The quotation is from Moffat, *The Economy of Consumption* (1878), p. 137. Allen, G. C., "Methods of Indus-

lands became homes of the agency system because of their standardised products; but not until they had reached the factory stage. A few, such as the manufacture of steel pens and of screws, had reached it in or before the 'sixties. Agencies for known brands of these things appeared early. A large number of Midland industries however, especially those which turned out light brassware and fittings, remained into the 'eighties at that stage of development in which a factor dominated and directed, with varying degrees of completeness, a group of small producers, through his control of capital and his knowledge of markets[1]. He would sell, as his predecessors since the eighteenth century had sold, to wholesalers or shipping merchants, sometimes to retailers. In the later 'eighties, owing to growth in the size and strength of the producing firms and to the progress of factory conditions, the factors of this type were in danger of "being reduced to the position of mere wholesale merchants."[2] In those light-metal trades which were now dominated by a few great manufacturing concerns, even the wholesale merchant was finding his sphere contracted in the home market, by extensions of the agency system or by manufacturers sending out their own travellers. This was a natural development, because the large manufacturers had frequently started as factors and so were familiar with distributive business. On the average of the West Midland trades, it would appear, the chain between producer and consumer had been shortened a little; in some of them a good deal. There might only be one shopkeeper between the factory and the user. There had seldom, if ever, been more than that in the steel-pen industry, since Joseph Gillott himself first made pens of steel and sold them to a local stationer for a shilling each[3]. His successors and competitors—he died in 1873—merely sold to more and more distant stationers, 'agents for so-and-so's steel pens.' But this was an exceptional trade, so young and personal that the factor or merchant, having never existed in it, had not to be eliminated. However it seems

trial Organisation in the West Midlands 1860–1927," *E.J.* (*Hist.*), 1929, p. 551, states that, in this area, the factor had "lost his dominating position"..."by the end of the century," owing to the development of the agency system.

[1] For the factor, vol. I. p. 255–6, and above, p. 126.

[2] Allen, *E.J.* (*Hist.*) as above, p. 551.

[3] See the *D.N.B.* Gillott was not the first to make them. They are heard of in 1809–10. There were twelve makers in Birmingham in 1849. See *Birmingham and the Midland Hardware District* (1866), p. 633 *sqq.* For the later history, Allen, *The Industrial Development of Birmingham and the Black Country*, 1860–1927 (1929).

not unlikely that it may have furnished an object lesson in elimination to other Birmingham factory industries.

General elimination of intermediaries between producer and consumer, or even between producer and retailer, was excluded by the growing variety of both production and consumption at home, even if the exotic sources of so much food and raw material are overlooked. As one door was shut in the middle-man's face another often opened on his left hand. Producers of coal and iron, of some kinds of food, or of other primary goods, might establish direct relations with the larger, more corporate type of consumer—the gas company, the shipyard, the hospital —or even with the domestic consumer at their doors. Producers of standardised, and of what were coming to be called pro-prietary manufactured articles, like the pens, might supply re-tailers direct. But most of the consumers were domestic yet remote from the producers' doors: retailers seldom dealt in nothing but standardised or proprietary articles. In a thoroughly urbanised society, only a shrinking minority of families could get coal from the pit or milk from the farm. So for some of his requirements every retailer, and some retailers for all, must rely on the wholesaler, whoever he might be— warehouseman of St Paul's Churchyard; wholesale grocer, stationer, draper, chemist; iron merchant; cheese factor; carcass butcher; bum-maree at Billingsgate.

Within sharply defined limits of occupation and geography, the co-operative movement, since the 'forties, had not so much shortened the chain between ultimate producer and consumer as put the control of an important section of it into the con-sumer's hands. By the close of the 'eighties, after two decades of conspicuous co-operative expansion, there were parts of Lancashire, the West Riding and Durham in which each man, woman and child spent on the average £5 a year at Co-operative Stores[1]. The figure for the whole country was 15s. 8d., weak-ness of co-operation in London, the South, and the rural districts being a principal explanation of the difference. For the years 1876–82, the figure had been 10s. 4d. and the average sales of British Co-operative Societies about £15,000,000. In 1863, the year of the foundation of the North of England Co-operative

[1] See the maps in the second (1892) edition of Potter, B. (Mrs Sidney Webb), *The Co-operative Movement in Great Britain*, giving expenditure at the Stores in £ per 100 of the population of the parliamentary constituencies.

Wholesale Society, an event which marks the opening of the second era of the movement[1], the sales had reached what co-operators rightly considered the fine level of £2,500,000[2]. That was less than 2s. per head of the population. In the middle of the 'eighties, statisticians believed that the total income of the wage-earners of Great Britain was about £480,000,000[3]. The average annual sales of the Co-operative Stores for 1883-7 were £20,000,000[4]. They did not sell houses[5], beer, or some other goods of less importance in the workman's budget. But they did handle things of which the aggregate wage-earners' purchases may have been so much as £350,000,000, and can hardly have been less than £300,000,000. In short, they had still to occupy some 94 per cent. of those fields of wage-earners' consumption which were their promised land; although here and there, in their native industrial territory, they had already occupied perhaps 50 per cent. of it.

From the beginning their trade had been based on provisions, and their first enemy had been the private grocer. With bakers there had been less friction: the wife did the baking in old co-operative territory, and the stores sold her flour. When the Wholesale Society began operations, it also was mainly a provision merchant, as was its colleague, the Scottish Wholesale of 1868. "During its first ten years" (1864-74) the Wholesale "grew fat on butter."[6] Irish butter, with a very little French and Danish butter, made up a third of its trade. When it decided to manufacture for itself, it began with biscuits and sweets. From provisions, the Stores and the Wholesale had passed to drapery, soap, boots and other articles of standard domestic consumption. Some goods regularly sold by Stores, of which coal was perhaps the most important, did not pass through the Wholesales[7]. For those things which the Whole-

---

[1] Or third era, taking the Owenite movement as the first: vol. I. p. 315, 599.
[2] Redfern, P., The Story of the Co-operative Wholesale Society (1913), p. 73.
[3] Giffen, Essays in Finance, Second Series, p. 463, with a deduction for Ireland.
[4] These are the sales as given by Mrs Webb, p. 251, on which the maps quoted above are based. The share of the Stores in wage-earners' expenditure is discussed by Mrs Webb on p. 234-5.
[5] Societies did help members to buy their own houses, but houses do not appear in the sales figures used here.
[6] Redfern, op. cit. p. 95.
[7] Co-operative coal-mining enterprises were without exception disastrous. The Wholesale lost money in them in the 'seventies. See the chapter (XXI) on "Colliery Failures" in Jones, B., Co-operative Production. Cp. Redfern, op. cit. p. 108. The Wholesale did not start a regular coal trade until 1891. Ibid. p. 138.

sales neither handled nor produced, and for things which they did handle but which the local co-operators did not appreciate, or preferred to procure locally, Store buyers went into the open market. Although all the capital of the Wholesales was held by the Stores, at the start there were many Stores not affiliated to them, and there were always some. These bought everything in open market like private retailers. There might at any time be local committee-men in affiliated societies who had no intention of buying only what the Wholesales chose to stock. In early Wholesale days (1869) there had even been a secession of such open-market men from the Rochdale Pioneers[1]. But when, at the close of the period, retail sales averaged £20,000,000, those of the two Wholesales were £7,500,000. As they sold only to the Stores, and as the Stores' sales figure includes profit and working expenses, it would appear that by this time the Wholesales supplied about half the Stores' needs.

The co-operating consumer had long ceased to sell his provisions across the counter to himself, as the Rochdale Pioneers did in the 'forties. But his committee controlled buying and selling policy, and superintended the managers and whatever assistants or buyers the size of the Store might require. The Wholesale necessarily employed experts at both ends from an early date—its sales were £1,153,000 by 1872—but, as it was made at Manchester by the federated Stores of the cotton towns and was governed by federal representatives, selling needed little 'salesmanship,' that dubious exercise of competitive commerce. For buying, on the other hand, all appropriate commercial qualities were required. There is no reason to suppose that they were lacking in the buyers from Lancashire and Yorkshire, or in the committee men who directed them. Yet an honourable dislike of the higgling of the market, and all the anti-social activities which sometimes go with it, was part of the co-operative faith inherited from Robert Owen. It drove the two Wholesales to reach out towards the ultimate producer— in 1882 they co-operated for the first time in shipping tea direct from China[2]—and to make all they could in their own factories. There had to be some higgling at the last, whether over goods which Stores bought on the open market, over raw materials bought for Wholesale factories, or over tea bought in China. But right along the co-operative chain, up to the jarring higgle

---

[1] Redfern, op. cit. p. 34.
[2] Ibid. p. 121.

of the open market purchase, buyers were salaried agents of the associated consumers.

Familiar marks distinguished the developed and legalised industrial co-operative society from the joint-stock company[1]— the limitation (to £200) of the shares in it which any one person might hold; the fixed and moderate return on them which kept their value stable; the equality of all shareholders in control, whatever the size of their holding; the share list always open to new members, and the small denomination of the shares, which made membership very easy; the 'divi,' proportioned not to shares held, but to purchases made; and reliance on the unpaid directing work of members whose co-operation was a lively faith. Many of these marks were lacking in the 'bourgeois' supply associations of the 'sixties which were registered under the Joint Stock Companies Act of 1862. But there was enough similarity in methods and aims between them and the working-class organisations to rouse a common enemy. A new trade journal, the *Grocer*, which tried to start a boycott of wholesale firms who supplied industrial co-operative stores, addressed the promoters of the Civil Service Supply as "two and sixpenny shareholders" and "Post Office and Piccadilly puppies."[2] The expanding population and trade of the country happily found employment for stores of both kinds, and also for grocers, some of whose trade methods, it is generally believed, were quickened and cleansed by the provocative competition of consumers' associations[3].

In spite of such competition, the adoption of a joint-stock or limited liability in the distributing trades, wholesale or retail, had been slow and rare. Before the 'sixties, companies for such things as coal or fish dealing had been projected but had never succeeded. There had been colonising and manufacturing companies which proposed to do wholesale trading, and sometimes did it[4]. Of the old imperial trading companies, the Hudson's

---

[1] See *e.g. Dictionary of Political Economy*, *s.v.* Co-operation.

[2] Quoted in Redfern, *op. cit.* p. 42–3.

[3] The evidence for adulteration and other undesirable practices in the grocery trade of the early nineteenth century is overwhelming (see *e.g. S.C. on the Adulteration of Food and Drugs*, 1856, VIII). How general it was is hard to determine. So is the extent to which improvement was due to co-operative competition.

[4] For projects and failures see the lists in English, H., *A Complete View of the Joint-Stock Companies formed during the years 1824 and 1825* (1827): *S.C. on Joint-Stock Companies*, 1844 (VII. 1), App. IV, the promotions of 1834–6: the *J.S.C. Returns* of 1853 (1856, LXV. 597 and 611).

Bay remained in active business, but it was in a special category. It was no more the habit of East India merchants or City warehousemen than of West End shopkeepers to make use of the developing law of limited liability. Among the mercantile firms proper which went down in the crisis of 1857–8 there was not a single joint-stock company[1]. But after the Act of 1862, the slow change began whose effects impressed Goschen so much twenty years later that he even exaggerated them[2]. Most progress was made amongst the warehouses, least among the specialised merchants and shippers and the whole body of retailers. For a number of years after its establishment in 1864, the Fore Street Warehouse, the earliest successful public joint-stock distributive concern[3], was also the only such concern whose shares were regularly quoted in the Stock Exchange list of miscellaneous securities. During the 'seventies, the forces which were at work to bring about the transformation of private firms into limited companies gathered power in the field of distribution. In 1885 it was said that "a great many" of the City warehouses had adopted limited liability. But few had done so before 1880, and there was rarely full publicity or the quotation of shares[4]. Similar transformations of ordinary partnerships into private companies had occurred sporadically all over the field of distribution; but the company was not dominant, or even at all conspicuous, in any other part of it. The typical merchants' firm of the 'eighties was a pure family concern or private partnership, and so was the typical shop, from Bond Street to the Old Kent Road and from John o' Groats to Lands End. True, the Master of the Rolls told a parliamentary committee in 1877 that he had actually known a case "where a chandler's shop was turned into a limited company"; but his surprise shows what an oddity it seemed[5].

The shrinkage of the commercial world into a single market under pressure of steam and electricity necessarily altered the working of overseas trade, but can hardly be said to have shifted the bases of its organisation. The middleman's functions were

[1] Lists in Evans, D. M., *The History of the Commercial Crisis*, 1857–8, p. 52 *sqq.*

[2] Above, p. 297.

[3] See the *Return of all J.S.C. formed or registered since 18 and 19 Vict. c.* 133 of 1864 (LVIII. 291).

[4] *R.C. on Depression of Trade*, Q. 668, 4100.

[5] *S.C. on the Operation of the Companies Acts*, 1877 (VIII. 419), Q. 2225.

more often modified than abolished; though particular middle-men, too rigid to conform, together with some redundant types, no doubt disappeared. In the old commercial practice, heavy stocks were carried because they could only be renewed slowly and at long intervals[1]. The merchant was generally thinking of markets both distant and future. His methods could be leisurely. Under the new conditions of lighter, faster renewed, stocks and swift decisions, "the old-fashioned merchants...suffer or are extinguished" as an exceptionally well-informed contemporary put it in 1880[2]. But the mercantile function survived. As much skill was needed, probably more, to operate in markets which, though distant, were all telegraphically present, as in those both distant and future; and because the world market of to-day lay all before your eye, as it had never been before your father's, you were not free to neglect its probable position next month or even next season.

In the export trade, fresh facilities for quick intercourse and the spread of British firms and agencies over all the world had greatly reduced the practice of 'adventuring' by merchants—the term was quite extinct—and still more the practice of consignment for sale by manufacturers. Both had been decaying on the shorter trade routes even in the 'thirties[3]. The old-fashioned adventuring merchant had sent cargoes of suitable goods to markets where he hoped to find outlets. It is the method of all primitive trade, and it survived in branches of trade where conditions among the consumers were primitive. Much grey cotton cloth, to take an outstanding instance, was bought by merchants and consigned, 'adventured,' to the tropics[4]. In consignment by the manufacturer, the shipping merchant had taken goods from their maker or from some factor; made a percentage advance against them; and shipped them against orders or as an adventure, settling accounts only when they were sold. The method had never been liked or much practised by strong manufacturers in the nineteenth

---

[1] On the reduced need to carry stocks see evidence of G. Lord before *R.C. on Depression of Trade*, Q. 5278: he thought the effects of the Suez Canal, electricity and steam, were so to speak worked off by 1885. The new equilibrium was established.

[2] Farrer, *Free Trade and Fair Trade*, p. 191.

[3] Vol. I. p. 255–6.

[4] Consignment still "prevailed to an important extent for certain markets" down to 1914. *Economic Advisory Council: Report on the Cotton Industry*, 1930 (Cmd. 3615), p. 14.

century: they preferred working to the merchants' order[1]. Now, working to order dominated the export trade. The merchant consigning goods to remote or primitive markets gave orders to the manufacturer, carrying all risks himself. For many markets, he himself would receive orders from overseas, from a branch or agent or correspondent. There might be an element of adventure in the orders which he received: his Bombay house when ordering would not be certain of sales in Afghanistan. But it was not the old, pure, adventuring procedure.

Strong manufacturers might take orders from overseas direct. This was not a new thing. Wedgwood had done it and so had Boulton and Watt. It was a natural thing in trades where the manufacturer had a world-wide repute and made goods of high unit value and more or less specialised use—a table service for Catherine the Great or a steam engine for the Creusot works. The overseas consumer of such things knew what he wanted before manufacture began. Consumption of this class had much increased since 1850; although it did not form a very large part of the aggregate overseas consumption of British goods. Locomotives, liners, warships, large stationary steam-engines and teams of textile machinery fall into it. Outside manufacturing, the coal trade furnishes parallels. Coal consumers overseas included railways, gas-works and governments, who knew their exact requirements in advance and bought in bulk direct. Intermediaries of various kinds there might be in some of these trades, but there was not much room for the merchant proper.

Even in the textile trades, as has been seen, easy intercourse and hard times had provoked a few manufacturers to "leave the merchant out"; but this was admittedly exceptional[2]. Instances could no doubt be found in other trades than those in goods of high unit value and specialised use; but they too would be exceptional. The mass of the textiles, clothing, light metal goods and miscellaneous manufactures of every kind, from "bags, empty" to "stationery, other than paper"—to cull two entries from early and late in the official list—went through the hands of the export merchant, the shipper, as Lancashire called him to distinguish him from the home merchant[3]. As textiles and

---

[1] See vol. I. p. 256.    [2] Above, p. 306.

[3] This remained true many years later. "It would be incorrect to say that the whole of the export business in cotton yarns and goods was in the hands of 'shippers'; there are some houses which manage their own marketing abroad, but these are exceptions." Chapman, *The Lancashire Cotton Industry* (1904), p. 138.

clothing alone were worth more than all the rest of the exports put together, and as light metal goods and the miscellaneous manufactures were steadily increasing in importance, there was no general prospect of the shipper being left out. No doubt he handled a smaller share of the British exports in 1885–7 than in 1850–3, but probably not very much smaller.

In the import trades there had been a decline, and in some cases a complete disappearance, of the system of consignment so characteristic of the early nineteenth century—the system by which "merchants and planters in all parts of the world" consigned produce for sale in this country and "drew [bills] in anticipation of the value immediately,"[1] the British merchant or broker, as consignee, making advances to them in anticipation of sale by accepting their bills up to two-thirds or three-quarters of the probable value of the consignment. In the old, slow, pre-railway and pre-steamship age, he "frequently kept the goods for months or even years."[2] The system was most prevalent in the longest trades, East and West Indian and Australasian, but was at that time quite common on the comparatively short North Atlantic route. Down to the laying of the cables, the imports of cotton into Liverpool "were chiefly received on consignment by merchants"[3] from American merchants or planters, in the old way, the Liverpool merchant taking only a small commission which he shared with the broker who sold for him. He might buy in America, either through his own house or a correspondent; but consignment predominated.

The cables soon changed the whole position. "Firm offers of cotton were cabled from the other side, either by branch houses or agents of Liverpool firms, or by independent sellers."[4] The selling of consigned cotton on commission had ceased altogether some time before 1886, when this account was written. Incidentally, there had been a little shedding of superfluous middlemen from the cotton trade, though from the point of view of changes in legal ownership the disappearance of consigned planters' cotton from the Liverpool market meant a lengthening of the commercial chain. The middlemen shed were commission merchants and brokers. The former either became importing merchants or disappeared; and so did some

[1] Quoted in vol. I. p. 256 from the 1823 *Report on the Law of Agents and Factors*, p. 11.
[2] *Ibid.* p. 7.
[3] Ellison, *The Cotton Trade*, p. 279.
[4] *Ibid.* p. 280.

of the brokers. For at least twenty years before the War of Secession and the cables, all cotton handled by the merchant—whether as owner or consignee—was sold through his selling broker to a buying broker who acted for the spinner; and the few powerful spinners who imported cotton themselves employed brokers[1]. The cables facilitated this spinner-importing. They did more than that, by producing a fusion of the broker and merchant classes and the appearance of a hybrid type known for a time as a broker-merchant, a man who both imported and sold. Many of the strongest importing merchants continued to employ brokers, finding the brokers' expert knowledge valuable in a specialising market, and being in a position to pay for it because of their large transactions. But by 1886 not "any important portion"[2] of the cotton paid a double brokerage. Handling costs had been considerably reduced since about 1870[3], when the new era effectively began, apart from reductions in the cost of ocean carriage.

Though the course of events is not so well known in the grain trade, there is no doubt that the telegraph, first between England and the Continent and then between England and America, helped to kill the consignment system there also. That system had been extensively used, especially in the Anglo-Irish grain trade[4], during the 'twenties, at a time when the foreign grain trade was intermittent and necessarily rather speculative. As the foreign trade for home consumption settled down into a permanency after 1846, out-and-out purchase in the grain shipping ports appears to have increased rapidly. The dealings in cargoes afloat, which were in regular operation by 1851–3, presuppose it[5]. It was easy for importing firms to keep branches or agents in the grain-shipping ports of Northern Europe, such as Rotterdam and the Baltic towns, where there was an old and well-developed tradition of corn-dealing. Linkage by cable with London came during the 'fifties. The Irish trade declined

---

[1] The arrangements here described were typical of the period 1840–60. Ellison, *op. cit.* p. 181.

[2] *Ibid.* p. 280.

[3] Since "a dozen or fifteen years ago"; Ellison in 1886.

[4] Vol. I. p. 259–60.

[5] In the market reports of the *Economist* during the 'forties references to cargo dealings are rare. They remain rare in 1850. By 1853 they are regular. Their omission does not prove their non-existence. They certainly existed earlier but they could only become regular when the regular import was thoroughly established.

both relatively and absolutely after the famine and, with the telegraph, became less international in character. Consignment no doubt lingered in the more remote branches of the trade, such as those of the Barbary coast and the Black Sea; but by the time that American dominance set in, towards the close of the 'sixties, the course of European business was already quick, free, and modern. The market had changed gradually, instead of being abruptly transformed by the Atlantic cables like the cotton market. Those cables merely linked to it a fresh, powerful, and ultimately dominant, reservoir of supply.

In the tropical, sub-tropical, and Australasian trades old methods of business naturally persisted; longest of all in the wool trade. Here the nature of the commodity was a conservative force. Wool is never sold till it has been sampled. Cargo dealings would have been too risky and were never tried. In the early days of Australian wool growing the consignment system had been the only possible one: McArthur and his imitators shipped their wool in hope. It remained the natural one after the establishment of regular colonial wool auctions in 1835. The whole ritual of the wool exchange was based on it. Dealings were not just in wool of a recognised sort, like middling uplands American cotton, but in so-and-so's wool known by its brand. When strong commercial and banking firms with London connections grew up in Australia, the squatters entrusted to them all the technical work of wool-shipping and insurance, securing from them, at a price, heavy advances against the shipments. But the wool remained the producer's property until it came under the hammer in Coleman Street, to be bought through buying brokers by wool merchants and the larger manufacturers. It was consigned to members of the small group of London selling brokers[1].

Down to the 'seventies, very little was handled in any other way, and to the end of the period not very much. There had been some local selling from an early date. This increased with the establishment of regular auctions in Australia. The buyers were scourers, speculators, mercantile houses, or, as communications improved, representatives of English wool merchants[2]. But as the scourers, speculators, and Australian mer-

---

[1] See Clapham, *The Woollen and Worsted Industries* (1907), p. 90–3. For the origin of financing by the banks in the 'sixties, Shann, *Economic History of Australia*, p. 299–300. For the wool trade generally, above, p. 6.

[2] Senkel, *Wollproduktion und Wollhandel im 19ten Jahrhundert*, p. 74.

chants eventually consigned their purchases to London in the
ordinary way, it was only the buying on English account which
altered the course of trade and side-tracked the London auctions.
From about 1870, Continental and American buyers had become important at the auctions in Australia, at which however
only 32 per cent. of the clip was sold even in 1885–6[1]. It is
evident, therefore, that when the foreign purchases, and those
of wool subsequently consigned to London by an Australian
buyer, have been deducted, the proportion of the wool shipped
to England which did not go through Coleman Street remained inconsiderable.

Writing in 1840 about the commercial speculations of 1825,
Thomas Tooke referred to one feature "which, although of not
uncommon manifestation in the stock and share markets, has
been of very rare occurrence in the markets for produce. There
were some few articles, almost exclusively spices, which were
the subject of successive purchases at advancing prices, without
any intermediate delivery of the article."[2] This mania, he noted,
did not at that time affect "in the slightest degree"[3] either the
corn or the provision markets. It probably brought about the
state of things which worried critics of the organised markets in
futures of the late nineteenth century—the aggregate selling of
much larger amounts of spices than could possibly be delivered
to consumers[4]. Apparently these speculators had bought and
sold spices in the abstract so to speak, not particular cargoes or
parcels after the fashion already known in Mark Lane and
Mincing Lane. Successive purchases of the wheat on board the
good ship *Arethusa* bound from Odessa to Falmouth for orders
were a different matter. "In Mincing Lane when cargoes of
sugar were sold one cargo would change hands four or five
times."[5] No one concerned in such transactions could be left
'short' at the finish, as a stock jobber might who had sold more
stock 'for time' than he could easily lay his hands on. It would

---

[1] Senkel, *op. cit.* p. 75.

[2] *History of Prices*, III. 159: quoted also in Emery, H. C., *Speculation on the
Stock and Produce Exchanges of the United States (Columbia Studies*, 1896, II),
p. 34 n.

[3] III. 167 n.

[4] Cp. *British Association Committee, Report on Future Dealings in Raw Produce*,
1900, p. 6–7.

[5] Goschen, *Essays and Addresses*, p. 201, referring to the middle of the century,
but descriptive of the practice, which was older.

appear that successive sales without delivery of the goods had occurred to Tooke's knowledge, even though very rarely, in other produce markets before 1840. His suggestion that they were outside any reasonable course of trading was perhaps over-done. In the 'arrivals' business, there was certainly plenty of sale without delivery of goods or of documents, during the 'forties, and probably earlier. "It is well known to be a common practice of the first merchants," John Francis wrote in 1849 when defending Stock Exchange methods, "to buy goods for arrival without the slightest intention of receiving them, and directly a profit can be gained or too great loss averted, they are resold without even the bill of lading having been visible to the buyer."[1] The reference to bills of lading suggests trans-actions in particular cargoes and parcels; but the description does not exclude more speculative dealings.

By 1849-50 dealings in 'arrivals' were common on both sides of the Atlantic. New York dealt in grain to arrive from the West and in cotton to arrive from the South[2]. The markets were there before either the European sea-cables or the oceanic cables were laid, though New York was kept sensitive by English de-mand news, brought by steamer to Halifax and telegraphed on. But the international cables were needed for market perfection. Before they were laid, we are told, Liverpool was slow to imitate New York 'arrival' methods[3]. She was not very familiar with them; but "the first merchants" of London had nothing to learn. There was however an outburst of pure speculation in East Indian cotton arrivals at Liverpool in 1857, stimulated—among other things—by the partial establishment of telegraphic communication with the East. During the War of Secession everyone who touched cotton was bound to be a gambler. Men bought and sold it not only 'to arrive,' but for shipment months ahead. In peace, the Atlantic cables gave regularity and per-manence to such transactions. Sales began to be made in agreed grades. Future prices lost their purely speculative war-time character, and acquired a calculable relation to spot prices. By 1869-71, the Liverpool Cotton Brokers' Association, when regulating arrivals business, dealt with a type of general con-tract for delivery of "American, basis of middling, from any

---

[1] *Chronicles and Characters of the Stock Exchange*, p. 82.
[2] Emery, *op. cit.* p. 35: Dumbell, S., "The Origin of Cotton Futures," *E.J.* (*Hist.*), 1927, p. 259 *sqq.*
[3] Dumbell, *op. cit.*

port, Oct.-Nov. shipment." Here is the pure future transaction in cotton in the abstract, divorced from specific consignments, or even from "ship named," a phrase which occurs in other contract types of the same date[1].

These general contracts gave openings for the outside speculator, and were much disliked by conservative merchants for that reason. But regular dealers who bought by telegraph were selling futures as a hedge against price fluctuations; and spinners were already discovering that by buying for remote delivery they too could safeguard themselves. New York had the whole business in futures at work by 1870, with options and margins, but still had to defend it as an innovation[2]. After that it grew swiftly on both sides. Futures passed from hand to hand, and far more cotton was bought and sold than America and India ever grew. There were bulls and bears and shorts. Liverpool brokers started a Clearing House in 1876, "to unravel the tangles of purchases and sales which arrivals frequently found awaiting them,"[3] and straighten out differences. Merchants followed with a rival Exchange. The two came together into a Cotton Association, from which sprang in 1882 a Settlement Association, "to promote a system of periodical cash settlements in the Liverpool cotton market."[4] Although the fixed-date settlements were not at first used by all dealers[5], their establishment was the last important step towards the creation of an organised futures market in standard grades of cotton, precisely comparable in its working with the Stock Exchange markets for standard securities.

The evolution of future dealings in the New York cotton market had been affected by parallel developments in the wheat market at Chicago. Chicago might have influenced Liverpool and London direct. But there is no definite evidence that it did. The Liverpool Corn Trade Association has always maintained that it was not any tenderness for the pure speculator,

---

[1] As in "Charleston, ship named, not below good ordinary." An Indian cotton contract might be for "Dhollerah, fair new merchants, Cape or Canal, May-June shipment": Dumbell, p. 264 n., from the *Liverpool Mercury* of 1870. The possibility of 'Canal' within a year of its opening is significant.

[2] Dumbell (p. 266–7) quotes a New York broker's circular of June 1870, which explains the uses of futures, and argues that "the system has been denounced by superficial observers only because it is new": future contracts are made daily "by parties of the highest respectability."

[3] Chapman, *op. cit.* p. 124.

[4] Rule 4. The rules are given in Ellison, *op. cit.* p. 294.

[5] *Ibid.* p. 296.

or any wish to rival Chicago, which led to the institution of an organised futures market in wheat at Liverpool in November, 1883[1]. The wheat which was selected as the basis for future delivery contracts was in fact not a Chicago sort but Californian, at that time in large and constant supply[2]. Imports were always growing. It was desirable that stocks should be carried and the price curve be kept as smooth as circumstances would permit. The value of future dealings for smoothing cotton price curves and giving security to the serious merchant, who used futures for hedging, was becoming generally recognised. These were the utilities which the Association proposed to confer on the Liverpool wheat market. It was imitated by the London Produce Exchange, which started organised future dealings in wheat and maize in 1888[3]. So the period closes with the system on its trial.

It was only by careful grading and classifications that cotton or grain could be given something approaching to the absolute uniformity, the capacity of every parcel sold to meet the needs of any buyer who desires that amount of the article, which stocks and shares have by nature. Close definition of the goods to be delivered in future contracts, and provision for arbitration and adjustments when it came to actual delivery, were essentials for successful working of future markets with which Capel Court had never been troubled. One £100 of 3 per cents. had always been just like any other, and no buyer had ever challenged it on delivery. But few commodities besides stocks and shares and grain are even approximately uniform, as the organisation of the wool trade shows; and there was certainly no bias in the British mercantile community towards the application of uniform treatment to things of doubtful uniformity: very much the reverse. These new, exact, speculative and suspected practices in certain Liverpool and London produce markets were in no way representative of the British commerce of the 'eighties. Much more typical was the state of things in the oldest, bulkiest, and most varied of the great import trades, timber. Some timber was bought by the ton; some by the load; much by

---

[1] See *Liverpool Grain Futures: Operator's Guide* (1929), p. 7. Information has also been supplied by the present Secretary of the Association, Mr F. W. G. Urquhart.

[2] Broomhall, G. J. S. and Hubback, J. H., *Corn Trade Memories* (1930), p. 34.

[3] Sonndorfer, R., *Die Technik des Welthandels* (ed. 1905), II. 30. The futures market in London never became very important: Dowling, S. W., *The Exchanges of London*, p. 183.

the Petersburg 'standard'; some by other 'standards.' When partially worked, it might be bought by 'feet run,' by fathom, bundle, or square foot; by the thousand (barrel staves) or by the piece (spars). It was contracted for by importers, f.o.b. at the world's timber ports, or c.i.f. delivered in Britain. Though sometimes sold 'to arrive,' it was oftener sold 'ex ship.' These were the larger dealers' sales. It went to inland dealers, or into consumption, partly by auction at London and Liverpool, mainly by private sale after a spell in the importer's timber-yard in the old obvious way. There were no novelties and no speculative refinements[1].

The nature of stocks and shares and the fact that, early in the eighteenth century, the Bank of England closed its government stock books for six weeks every quarter, during which no transfer of stock could take place, had produced time bargains in Change Alley, in the teeth of public opinion and the law, before there was an organised Stock Exchange[2]. Men sold stock which they had not yet got "for the opening" of the Bank's books, trusting to get it in the meantime. This they did quite naturally. As naturally, periodic settlements of business in stock grew up. Operators might, and when it suited them did, accept and deliver not stock but price differences, in defiance of the clauses in Sir John Barnard's Act[3] against time bargains in consols and against "all wagers, puts and refusals." "One hundred and sixteen years have passed, the act is still in force, and speculative bargains have not only increased, but form the chief business of the Stock Exchange," John Francis wrote in 1849[4]. The Act was repealed, as long obsolete, in 1868 (by 30 and 31 Vict. c. 59), but Stock Exchange men looked back with complacency on their habit of defying the law, and persisted in it. "We disregarded for years and years Sir John Barnard's Act," the Chairman of the Committee said in 1875, "and we are now disregarding Mr Leeman's Act,"[5] an Act of 1867 which had tried

---

[1] The methods of dealing are summarised, with a continental dismay at this insular chaos, in Sonndorfer, *op. cit.* II. 252. Some information comes direct from a firm of timber importers.

[2] Francis, J., *Chronicles and Characters of the Stock Exchange* (1849), p. 80-1. Cp. vol. I. p. 301-3.

[3] 7 Geo. II, c. 8.

[4] *Op. cit.* p. 81. Cp. Duguid, C., *The Story of the Stock Exchange* (1901), p. 188-9.

[5] *S.C. on Foreign Loans*, Q. 477.

to regulate dealings in bank shares by prescribing that in every sale the serial numbers of the shares sold should be specified. All that the law could do was to say that contracts of certain kinds would not be upheld in the courts. The Stock Exchange had its own methods for insuring that members should honour all types of contract of which the society as a whole approved. Time contracts for government stock had gone on in spite of Sir John Barnard, and dealings in bank shares, the numbers of which were not given, went on in spite of Mr Leeman, because they suited the habits of the society.

All essentials of Stock Exchange organisation existed before 1850. The next generation saw a vast extension of dealings, but only secondary changes in the structure and methods of the dealing groups. The Committee, started in 1802 as a "domestic tribunal for the regulation of business entirely limited to English stocks,"[1] by the 'fifties had become a public, even an international, body in consequence of the growth of foreign investment after Waterloo. Its strength lay in its power to authorise official quotation of, and grant or refuse settlements in, new stocks and classes of stock. Without quotation no real market; without settlements no organised or speculative dealings. Our power has brought us "into touch with Ambassadors," the Chairman said in 1875[2], as it obviously would. They had allowed quotation of £15,000,000 of Peruvian loans because there were laws to sanction it. They had refused quotation of another £22,000,000 because they questioned the validity of a Peruvian Presidential Decree[3]. That some very doubtful but relatively insignificant South American issues had secured quotation since 1867, the outcome of which was the inquiry at which these facts were put in evidence[4], is only a further illustration of the Committee's international power and responsibility.

Broking and jobbing had been distinct businesses from the first. In 1850 the distinction was old and clear, and the groups of brokers and jobbers were sharply differentiated, not however

---

[1] S.C. on Foreign Loans, Q. 468. Evidence of the Chairman, Samuel Herman de Zoete, a name admirably symbolic of the Stock Exchange with its blend of England, Holland, Germany and Judaea.

[2] Ibid. In Q. 468 de Zoete gave a history of the Committee.

[3] Ibid. Q. 5476 (de Zoete again).

[4] See the Report of 1875 which sets out the whole story of these loans (cp. above, p. 240). The total sum involved was £10,000,000 nominal in eight years, only part of which was taken by the general public. During that period nearly £400,000,000 of new foreign loans had secured quotation. Q. 5527-8.

by rule but by function[1]. The broker bought or sold anything for his clients. The jobber was a specialist dealer in certain stocks or groups of stocks, always ready to make a price in any one of them, *i.e.* to quote his buying and selling figures to a broker. He might solicit business from the brokers. "I look upon a broker and a jobber as totally distinct," the experienced government broker told a Royal Commission in 1877[2]. When cross-examined, he admitted that though normally the distinction was one of persons it might on occasion be only one of function: a broker with special knowledge of some group of securities might himself deal in them and so become a "jobbing broker." But this was very rare and, by 1877 at any rate, no broker was "allowed to stand in the market and make prices as a dealer."[3] Since all the members of both groups were members of the Exchange on precisely the same footing, it was technically legitimate to pass from one group to the other, but such transfers were rare. Public opinion on the Exchange was against them and they were not easy to make[4]. Occasionally a broker who found his business unprofitable would drop it and take to jobbing. The reverse process was however unknown—at least to the government broker of the 'sixties and 'seventies[5]. For everyday purposes the groups were, as he said, "totally distinct."

Some experts in the 'seventies drew a distinction between the jobber proper and the dealer. The former was never a holder of stock if he could help it. He was "pretty well always even,"[6] that is he had agreed to sell as much as he had undertaken to buy, and looked to the price difference, the jobber's 'turn,' for his living. The dealer was more of a merchant and took bigger risks. He would buy large blocks of some security and job them off piecemeal, for he was necessarily a jobber. Through him the Stock Exchange was linked to that promotion of companies and flotation of loans upon which it depended for the expansion of its activities, but which was not properly stock-brokers' business.

---

[1] Francis, *op. cit. passim* and esp. p. 325.

[2] *R.C. on the London Stock Exchange*, 1878 (XIX. 265), Q. 467. Although this Commission had no compulsory powers the evidence given before it gives a full account of Stock Exchange organisation and practice.

[3] Evidence of the Secretary, Q. 347.

[4] *Ibid.* Q. 345.

[5] Evidence of J. H. Daniell, Government Broker, Q. 492, 709, etc.

[6] Evidence of L. L. Cohen, Q. 2817. He elaborated the distinction between jobber and dealer.

How that business had expanded the growing membership of the Exchange suggests without in any way measuring. When it started in Capel Court in 1802, there had been already upwards of 500 members[1]. Foreign loans, railways, and joint-stock enterprise generally had found work for more than another 300 by 1850–1, when the membership stood at 864. More loans, more railways, and the joint-stock companies legislation of 1855–62 raised it to 1100 by 1864. Yet more foreign loans, of which over £400,000,000 worth were listed between 1865 and 1875, and the slow introduction of the public joint-stock company into most fields of economic activity, lifted it once more, to above 2000 by 1877[2]; and the growth did not stop there. Meanwhile provincial exchanges had come into being, at Glasgow, Liverpool and Manchester. Some business was done on them in local securities, not handled in London; but as these new exchanges contained no jobbers[3], the general investment or speculative business was passed on to the jobbers of Capel Court, so further swelling their work and numbers.

The growth of limited liability companies after 1855 threatened to bring about one somewhat important change in Stock Exchange practice, but the threat came to nothing. Dealing in the shares of a projected public company before allotment to the whole subscribing public was a practice as liable to abuse as it was difficult to avoid[4]. Certain sections of the new legislation tended to encourage it. Before the Acts of 1860 and 1862, and especially in the Railway Mania, 'stags' had secured allotments of shares without making any deposit and had proceeded to trade in them. Under the new law, the investing applicant for shares had to make a substantial deposit. To attract him, nothing was more useful than some well-advertised dealings in the embryo shares at a premium. A series of unsavoury episodes connected with such dealings led the Committee of the Stock Exchange, in 1864, to refuse to recognise them as valid. But within a short time the decision was reversed[5]. The dealings had continued because company promoters and certain sections of the public liked them. They had merely been withdrawn from Stock

---

[1] Vol. I. p. 301.

[2] The later figures are from the *Report of the R.C.* p. 5, the earlier from Duguid, *op. cit.* p. 94, 159.

[3] The Secretary of the Stock Exchange said in 1877 that they had no "dealers or middlemen"; Q. 285.

[4] See Duguid, *op. cit.* p. 128, 149, 192–4.

[5] Duguid, *op. cit.* p. 193.

Exchange control. Fear of losing business, combined with the defensible conviction that if the thing was to be done it had better be done on the open Exchange, led the Committee to go back on its ruling in 1865. Thirteen years later a rather unusually ineffective Royal Commission suggested that these dealings should again be stopped[1]; but neither Parliament nor the Committee paid any attention. Though the new era in company history did not modify Stock Exchange practice in any important way, the flood of business which came with it led to the development of a fresh organ of which the 1878 Commissioners decidedly approved, the Clearing House of 1873. A proposal to clear stocks, much as bankers cleared cheques, and so to avoid the passing of tickets from hand to hand, had been made so early as 1851, but nothing had come of it. It was very characteristic of British business methods that the Clearing House of 1873, called after its founder Humphrey's House, was a private organisation within a private organisation. People joined or not as they liked, though the thing was so convenient that membership grew fast. It was not until 1880 that the organisation was taken over by a Settlement Department under the central Committee of the Exchange[2].

One of the suggestions of the Commission of 1878 was that the Stock Exchange should increase its standing, and the binding power of its by-laws, by securing incorporation from Parliament. There was a recent precedent in the Act of 1871 (34 Vict. c. 21) by which an even older private commercial organisation, Lloyd's, had become a body corporate, mainly in order to give full authority to its rules[3]. Lloyd's, and marine insurance generally, had lost something of their former importance during the Great Peace and the stagnation of shipping down to the 'forties. In 1843 Lloyd's had not half as many subscribers as in 1815. Among a crop of new marine insurance companies which sprang up in the 'forties, "only one had so long a life as three years."[4] But wars and revolutions in shipping made risks after 1850. With risks the business revived. Lloyd's became a more specialised society each decade, more exclusively a society of

---

[1] *Report*, p. 19. No one of the seven principal suggestions made by the Commission was ever put into a law or a by-law.

[2] Duguid, *op. cit.* p. 255–6 and references in the 1878 *Report*.

[3] Cp. vol. I. p. 288–91 and Wright, C. and Fayle, C. E., *A History of Lloyd's* (1928), one of the few first-rate specialised commercial histories in existence.

[4] Wright and Fayle, *op. cit.* p. 364.

underwriters; and with specialisation and incorporation its efficiency grew[1]. Its network of agencies spread over the whole earth. From 1869 it was developing its system of signal stations. It was always interested in life-boats. Yet in spite of all this, for the prime business of marine underwriting it was "scarcely more than a supplementary market" during the 'seventies and 'eighties[2]. To a small group of old joint-stock marine insurance companies in London and Liverpool, which had survived into the second half of the century[3], had been added a number of well-managed new ones since 1860. There was already a certain amount of mutual insurance among shipowners; and internal insurance by the stronger shipping lines would follow. But the reformed Lloyd's of the 'eighties contained 'Gentlemen Under-writers'[4] who, besides showing fresh enterprise in marine work, were experimenting or preparing to experiment with ancient risks hitherto regarded as beyond insurance—burglary, earthquake, hurricane—and with fresh risks created by fresh circumstance, such as reinsurance for fire companies, or insurance against the newly devised employers' liability[5]. Lloyd's became a sort of laboratory in which the limits—they proved hard to find—and the very clear benefits of the principle of insurance could be tried out, so that there might be greater security in an economic world whose chances and risks might be increased by man's ingenuity, unless counteracted by more ingenuity. The speculative insurer at Lloyd's smoothed out the risk curves of life like the speculative dealer in cotton futures at Liverpool, only with more certainty and with deliberate intent. And this he did not for Britain only, but for the world.

Meanwhile the ancient risks of property at sea, the first with which civilised man had dealt by way of insurance, had been almost completely covered by private underwriting, company underwriting, and the subsidiary methods. The uninsured hull or the uninsured cargo, exceedingly common in the eighteenth century and by no means rare during the first half of the nine-

[1] Originally it contained a number of members with shipping interests who were not professional underwriters or had ceased to underwrite. Apparently the proportion grew between 1815 and 1847, when there were only 185 under-writing to 621 non-underwriting members: by 1870 the ratio was 401 to 216. Wright and Fayle, *op. cit.*

[2] *Ibid.* p. 429.

[3] Vol. I. p. 288–91.

[4] The title adopted at the foundation of the Club.

[5] Wright and Fayle, *op. cit.* p. 431–2.

teenth, was now a discreditable exception among small obscure coasters or on the by-roads of the seas. 'A 1 at Lloyd's' had become part of the English language. Fraud in the insurance, or over-insurance, of a ship deliberately cast away[1] was probably more common than neglect of the obvious precaution of taking out a policy; though there might be cheese-paring under-insurance by impecunious owners. It was assumed as a matter of course that every shipwreck would have its repercussions at Lloyd's, or somewhere in the underwriting world.

Probably, by the 'eighties, commercial insurance against fire had become no less general than commercial insurance against the risks of the sea. But there were always some uninsured private dwellings and uninsured farming stock; though even by 1850 the insurance of houses was in a totally different position from what it had been when Adam Smith guessed that "nineteen houses in twenty or rather, perhaps, ninety-nine in a hundred were not insured against fire."[2] A record taken of the fires in London during a whole year in the early 'fifties showed that less than 18 per cent. of the buildings damaged or destroyed, but 40 per cent. of the contents of those buildings, were uninsured[3]. How far insurance policies, where they had been taken out, covered the risks, the record did not show; but it is known that insurance up to two-thirds of the value was a common practice[4]. London was the original home of fire insurance and the headquarters of the strongest companies, and so had a high proportion of insured property. But there were many strong country, and some strong Scottish, offices. More-over the London offices, especially the oldest and most famous —the Sun, the Phoenix, and the Royal Exchange—did a great deal of country and Scottish business[5]. Even allowing for a crowd of uninsured cottages, and for the fact that in 1862 nearly all those people whose destructible property was worth less

[1] For which see Kipling, Rudyard, *Bread upon the Waters.*
[2] Quoted and discussed in vol. I. p. 284-5.
[3] *The Assurance Magazine,* 1854, quoted in Walford, C., *The Insurance Cyclopaedia,* v. 501.
[4] *Report* (revised) *on Fire Insurance Duties,* by George Coode, *A. and P.* 1863 (xxvi. 27), p. 25. The original report (of 1856) contained errors which were pointed out by Brown, S., "On the Progress of Fire Insurance in Great Britain as compared with other Countries," *S.J.* 1857, p. 135 *sqq.*
[5] Vol. I. p. 284. Cp. Walford, *op. cit.* III. 424. This fact makes the figures for England and Wales as against Scotland, given in Coode's *Report,* p. 36, of no value as a basis for the comparative amounts of insurance in North and South Britain.

than £300 were believed to be still uninsured, it is likely that, instead of Adam Smith's hypothetical nineteen in twenty or ninety-nine in a hundred houses not insured, ten in twenty would be a considerable overstatement. For in 1857 it was estimated that nearly half the total value of buildings and their contents was covered by insurance[1]. It has been seen that buildings were much more regularly insured than their contents; and the uninsured people with destructible property worth less than £300 were not normally owners of houses.

It was maintained, during the 'fifties and 'sixties, that the survival of a percentage tax on fire insurance policies, an ancient duty which had been doubled during the French wars and never lowered since, was a formidable handicap on the growth of a precaution socially necessary, and on a business of much public utility. 'The tax on prudence' was its nickname. As a result of it, so the companies and their friends argued[2], many large estates and great quantities of merchandise were left uncovered, and policies were taken out for sums much less in proportion to the value of the insured properties than was 'natural.' As the tax was 3s. for every £100 insured, a crushing percentage addition to an ordinary house-insurance premium, the argument cannot be disregarded[3]. It was enforced in practical politics by the domestic or commercial insurers' grievance that policies on farming stock had been exempt from duty since 1853. But the history of fire insurance under the tax suggests that the ill effects of this handicap on prudence and enterprise were less than the companies wished Parliament to believe.

By the end of the 'sixties, the tax, much criticised in and out of Parliament, was ripe for repeal. In 1863 it had produced £1,630,000, excluding the small sum collected in Ireland. Next year Gladstone halved the duty on insurances of stock in trade. The duty on houses was halved in 1866. Yet the halved duty produced more than £1,000,000 in 1868, the year before Robert Lowe decided to abandon altogether this "sort of penalty on providence."[4] With it went a series of official figures, by which

---

[1] Brown in *S.J.* as above.

[2] *E.g. The Assurance Magazine* as above. For the parliamentary assaults on the duty see Buxton, *Finance and Politics*, I. 333.

[3] The companies would insure first-class London house property at 1s. 6d. per £100, apart from the tax. The minimum for agricultural insurance was 5s.; on good warehouse sheds, 12s.; on theatres, "when insurable at all," £5. So on big risks the duty was no great burden. Coode's *Report*, p. 16.

[4] Buxton, *op. cit.* I. 333; II. 91.

the growth of fire insurance and the relative importance of the various companies can be gauged conveniently, if not with perfect accuracy[1]. The amount of duty paid in Britain in 1805 had corresponded to an insured value of about £260,000,000; in 1831 to one of about £500,000,000; in 1851 to about £800,000,000, to which must be added nearly £60,000,000 of agricultural insurance now exempt from duty. By the end of 1862 the two figures had risen to over £1100,000,000 and £75,000,000. In 1868 the agricultural figure had not increased, but the general figure had risen to upwards of £1500,000,000. The course of the two series does not suggest that freedom from duty, or liability to duty, had much to do with the growth of the insurance habit; though the elasticity of the yield when the duty was halved may imply a certain response to lower taxation, not merely a contemporary growth in the amount of property requiring insurance. In any case, considering the immense figure, the official adviser of the government, who had asserted in 1863 that "the limits of possible insurance have been nearly reached,"[2] cannot have been seriously in error; though his "possible" has to be interpreted by the insurance and building habits of the time, according to which many theatres were not "insurable at all," and insurances for sums under £300 were not encouraged by the companies. (Premiums of a few shillings were as tiresome to them as cheques for a few shillings were to the bankers of the period.) An estimate made in 1872[3] suggests that the growth of fire insurance immediately after 1869 may have been somewhat faster than the growth of insurable property, but certainly not much faster. When insurance against new types of risk began to develop in the 'eighties, insurance against fire was probably as complete as the standing reluctance of the insurer to take on doubtful propositions and of the owner of insurable property to appreciate his risks will ever permit, except perhaps in agriculture.

There had been a constant rise and fall of companies; but there was no serious change in the total after 1831–2[4]. Some

[1] They are used in Coode's *Report*; by Brown in *S.J.* 1857; and repeatedly by Walford. Returns were made of agricultural insurance down to 1868, though it was exempt from duty.     [2] Coode's *Report*, p. 33.

[3] Quoted in Walford, *op. cit.* III. 512. Lacking the basis of official figures, it is somewhat speculative.

[4] The date at which the position is summarised in vol. I. p. 287. Down to the 'seventies there are regular annals of the companies in Walford *s.v. Fire Insurance, History of.*

old ones dropped out or were absorbed; but, with few exceptions, they were from among those which did least business. The four companies which had been strongest early in the century, the Sun, the Phoenix, the Royal Exchange and the Norwich Union, still paid two-fifths of the percentage duty in 1851, and three-tenths in 1868. When this measure of the home business of the companies ceased[1], the Sun, which had done a third of that business in 1805 and a sixth in 1832, was still doing an eighth. The Norwich Union, however, was no longer the leading country office, having been passed both by the Liverpool London and Globe and by the Royal. The Phoenix remained the second town office; but it too had been passed by the Liverpool company, the most progressive society of the period, which grew with the cotton trade and the Lancashire towns, and took business from older institutions[2].

Of all commercial activities, insurance had probably altered least in principles and organisation. Incorporation had made no essential change in Lloyd's. There had been some spread of actuarial knowledge and exact method from the insurance of lives, where calculations of probability had been first applied, to the other fields of insurance; but this was a normal and slow process. The new developments of company law had little to say to fire and life insurance, which had always been exclusively company-businesses, or to marine insurance, which had been so in part for more than a hundred and fifty years. Some of the greater companies had done more than one of the older types of insurance—fire, marine, and life—before 1850[3]. There had been an increase in this composite class, as was natural. Towards the end of the period, established companies were experimenting with the newer types of insurance, particularly with that insurance against accidents which began—outside the Friendly Societies and Trade Unions—with the Railway Passengers' Company of 1848, and had been developed by a long line of small, experimental, and usually short-lived companies during the next twenty years[4]. But the great expansion of accident insurance, either by new or old companies, came later.

[1] The companies also did foreign business of which no measure exists.

[2] As the Liverpool it was only the tenth country society in 1841. As the Liverpool and London it was the sixth in 1851 and the second in 1861. As the Liverpool London and Globe it was the first in the country and the second in the Kingdom in 1868.

[3] Vol. I. p. 291.

[4] Walford s.v. Accident Insurance, I. 6 sqq.

One change of some importance there had been, characteristic of a time in which a certain amount of quiet combination was going on in the economic world, to the accompaniment of a distracting chorus in praise of free and open competition. In 1858, after several preliminary attempts, what came to be known as the Tariff Association of Fire Insurance Offices was formed, to introduce a uniform system of rating risks, and so allow the companies to present a united front to the public. It was the greatest success. "Several of the offices now in association" Walford, a frank partisan, wrote in 1874 [1], "were formed with the express intention of operating independently; but found it so impossible to meet the unreasonable demands of their clients, that they were driven into association." "At the present moment," he went on to say, "there are very few offices...outside the Association. From time to time 'independent' offices are established; but in a few years they usually join the Association—or die." The offices continued to fight for business, but with swords of a standard length. The public and the press sometimes grumbled about monopoly. The insurance interest replied that the system "while kept within rational limits" was "for the common good of all concerned." [2] No doubt they were right; and there is no reason to think that at this time the limits set were irrational.

[1] Walford, *op. cit.* III. 530–1. Walford was personally connected with this movement and is a first-rate authority: see the *D.N.B.*

[2] Walford, *op. cit.* III. 530.

## CHAPTER IX

## MONEY, PRICES, BANKING AND INVESTMENT

WHEN, in the year 1865, the four principal franc-using countries formed what came to be known as the Latin currency union, it occurred to a few British reformers that, by an easy alteration of the alloy in the sovereign and a slight reduction of the gold in the American dollar, a uniform international gold currency might be created on the basis of £1 = 25 francs = 5 dollars. The "Teutonic nations," it was thought, would be too intelligent to stand out; and "a bag of the new sovereigns, or internationals, as they should be called, would go everywhere."[1] But the dollar was buried under greenbacks in 1865–6: within a few years the franc was shaken by war and indemnities: no British statesman, it may be assumed, ever gave the proposal ten minutes serious thought; and when intelligent Teutonic statesmen placed the currency of new Germany on a gold basis, economic nationalism decided that 20 marks gold should just not be the equivalent of the pound sterling. So Lord Liverpool's sovereign, with its subordinate silver and bronze, remained unaltered and unchallenged—the chief coin of the world.

When Peel had finished his bank-note legislation of 1844–5[2], it is probable that the circulation of gold coin in the United Kingdom, or in Britain, had not much exceeded that of the notes. The notes in the United Kingdom were nearly £40,000,000. The coin may have been £46,000,000. Twelve years later, with the arrival of the new gold and the rigid limitation of note issue, the notes had fallen somewhat; the gold had increased by over 50 per cent.[3] It was demonstrable that recent price fluctuations had had little or nothing to do with the trifling changes in the circulation of notes. William Newmarch, who had helped to demonstrate this, was in a position to speak of

[1] *Economist*, October 27, 1866, commenting on an article in the *Edinburgh Review* of October, 1866, on "International Coinage," which reviewed among other books Soetbeer, G. A., *Produktion der edlen Metalle*.

[2] Vol. I. p. 521 *sqq.*

[3] Newmarch estimated the gold in 1844 at £46,000,000 and in 1856 at £75,000,000. Palgrave, R. H. J., *Notes on Banking* (1873), p. 49, quotes Newmarch as saying £36,000,000 for 1844. But Newmarch corrected this, *History of Prices*, VI. 702.

bank-notes as "the mere small change of the ledger."[1] They became in time still smaller change. During the next twenty-five years they seldom exceeded by more than a few millions the figure of Peel's day; and in 1887 they were below it. Meanwhile the gold coin of the United Kingdom had increased to between two and three times the figure of the notes in circulation, that is to say to over £100,000,000[2]. With this position, after forty years working of his Acts, Peel, there can be no doubt, would have been content.

The note held its ground better in Scotland than in England because wages could be paid in £1 notes. A revival of the £1 note in England was sometimes discussed. By 1875 there were bankers in favour of it. But Walter Bagehot, the ablest of them, hesitated. "At first I own I should have a doubt about it," he said, though he admitted that it "might be rather advantageous than otherwise."[3] He still feared money panics and runs of small note-holders on the gold. In 1886, when possibilities of economy in the use of gold had come to the front with falling prices, a Scottish banker was advocating the £1 note as a gold economiser before the Bankers' Institute of London[4]. But his argument was not conclusive and politicians were nervous of touching the currency. The £1 note, and note policy generally, remained subjects of only academic discussion until 1914. This was natural. There was never any lack of cash for wages or retail trade, and all large transactions had been settled by bill of exchange or cheque for a long time.

Down to 1853, the London Clearing Bankers[5] had still

[1] *Presidential Address, Economic Section, British Association*, at Manchester, 1861. Compare the full discussion and figures in Tooke and Newmarch, *History of Prices*, VI. 583 *sqq.*, 701 *sqq.* and the triumphant conclusion in v. 344, against those who had held that bank-note-issue was a determining cause in price fluctuations. Cp. also vol. I. p. 534.

[2] Ireland had a disproportionate note circulation, £5,726,000 out of £39,166,000 for the United Kingdom in June, 1886. She also probably had a disproportionate gold circulation. In 1875 R. H. I. Palgrave estimated that of £100,000,000 of gold coinage existing in the United Kingdom only £67,000,000 was in England. (*S.C. on Banks of Issue*, 1875, IX. Q. 5915 *sqq.*) Cp. Palgrave's *Notes on Banking*, p. 49. Palgrave's 1875 estimate was high. The estimates for the 'eighties (Palgrave, 1883: the Mint, 1888) put the gold at 257 or 260 per cent. of the notes. *U.S.A. Monetary Commission*, 1910. *Statistics for Great Britain*, etc., p. 75.

[3] *S.C. on Banks of Issue*, Q. 8015.

[4] Kerr, A. W., *Scottish Banking*...1865-96 (1898), p. 96.

[5] Cp. vol. I. p. 283. Lists of the London clearing bankers at various dates are given in Martin, J. B., *The Grasshopper in Lombard Street* (1892), p. 169 *sqq.*

adjusted their accounts with Bank of England notes, and the Custom House required payment in notes[1]. In Scotland it had not been "the general practice for a customer to draw cheques ...for his individual payments. If he has to make twenty payments in the course of a day he will go to the bank in the morning and draw out in one sum a sufficient amount of notes to make all these payments."[2] By 1855 all London Clearing and Custom House business was done by cheque. "By far the larger amount of transactions"[3] were so conducted, the Governor of the Bank of England explained in 1857. A private banker from Ipswich said that the banking habit had increased four-fold of late among farmers and shopkeepers: "almost every farmer, even those paying only £50 per annum rent, now keep deposits with bankers." London cheques for quite small sums, "very frequently under £2," came down from poulterers, green-grocers and pork-butchers; though farmers did not yet send cheques to London[4]. As time went on the deposit produced the cheque, and there was a tendency for the cheque to super-sede the inland bill as a means of payment. In 1841 an expert had placed good trade bills "with the security of the drawer, acceptor, and perhaps twenty endorsements on the back, in the first class of our currency." There was "no purpose of money except wages" to which bills were "not applicable in the pro-vinces...though not seen in London in making payments."[5] The endorsements show how freely they circulated. In 1851 farmers commonly bought on the basis of a "good bill at three months," which bankers procured for them[6]. By 1873 the freely circulating bill of 1841 was unfamiliar to an experienced country banker, though the bill discounted once and sometimes rediscounted was familiar enough. The proportion of bills dis-counted to deposits had fallen considerably, so far as could be ascertained, since 1851[7]. Instead of discounting a bill, the

[1] S.C. on the Bank Acts, 1857 (x), Q. 97 (T. M. Wegeulin, Governor of the Bank of England).

[2] Gilbart, J. W., The Principles and Practice of Banking (ed. of 1873, describing the practice of the 'forties and 'fifties), p. 495.

[3] S.C. on the Bank Acts, Q. 671.

[4] S.C. on the Bank Acts and the recent Commercial Distress, 1857–8 (v). Evidence of W. Rodwell, Q. 1331 sqq.

[5] Leatham, W., Second Series of Letters, p. 37–8, quoted in Palgrave, Notes, p. 36–7.

[6] Newmarch, "An Attempt to ascertain the Magnitude and Fluctuations of the Amount of Bills of Exchange...in Circulation," S.J. 1851, p. 164.

[7] Palgrave's Notes, as above.

banker would make an advance on security taken, or on personal credit, against which cheques could be drawn. In Scotland the practice of carrying away notes for the day's payments was "very much modified—the English system of cheques being more common."[1] The forecast made in 1873, that in the circulation of the whole country cheques would "tend to supersede"[2] bills still further, proved correct. A decided decline in inland bills was registered again in 1885[3]. It was connected with the growth of cash payment, which meant cheques and the newer telegraphic transfers. As for coin, that formed not 1 per cent. of the payments into the banks in London and only about 6 per cent. in Manchester, in the early 'eighties[4]. The late Victorian British currency system and habits were established.

Rare as the use of coin was, the whole currency rested on its thin plate of gold. A most important part of British trade was with countries where the plate was thicker, but of silver. Now there had been vicissitudes in the supply and relations of the precious metals such as had not been known since the sixteenth century. After a long spell of low gold output in the known world, that of the Ural mines had greatly increased during the 'forties, reaching the then remarkable figure of £3,400,000 in 1846[5]. The effects of the Californian gold began to be felt in Europe in 1850. On September 3, 1851, the finding of gold in New South Wales was reported in London. The mere announcement influenced trade, freights, and prices; for California had shown what would follow. Together with older sources of supply, California and Australia raised the world output of gold during the decade 1851–60 to not far short of four times what it had been in 1841–50, and to nearly ten times the output of 1831–40. There was a slight fall from the high level of the 'fifties during the decade 1861–70, and a further fall in 1871–80; but the world output for 1871–80 was still more

---

[1] Note to the passage in the 1873 edition of Gilbart quoted above.

[2] Palgrave, *Notes*, p. 37.

[3] *R.C. on Depression of Trade*, Q. 582. Evidence of the Chief Receiver in Bankruptcy. For the general decline in inland bills see Jackson, F. Huth, "The Draft on London and Tariff Reform," *E.J.* 1904: "a great deal of business ...that used to be financed by inland bills is now financed by banker's overdraft."

[4] Pownall, G. H., in 1881 quoted in Nicholson, J. S., *Money and Monetary Problems* (ed. 1897), p. 143.

[5] Tooke and Newmarch (quoting a Consular Return of 1847), v. 531.

than eight times that of 1831–40[1]. Yet even this great output added only a very small percentage annually to the existing stock. So durable is gold.

At first the new gold went mainly into coinage. During the eight years from 1848 to 1856, England, France, and the United States together coined no less than £207,000,000[2]. It has been estimated that not more than 14 per cent. of the output of the 'fifties was absorbed in industry and the arts[3]. Twice, in 1854 and in 1856, France alone coined over £20,000,000 worth in a year. The new Empire was made glorious with gold. Afterwards industrial uses absorbed much of the annual increment, mounting to about 60 per cent. in the 'eighties. By that time, also, there was a steady drain to India. Experts thought that it might amount to £8,000,000 a year[4]. It was a new thing, dating from about 1870. Formerly the East had been content to take and sterilise silver in jewellery and hoards. Now she was sterilising gold also.

Throughout the era of the Second Empire, the currency of France, and to a lesser degree that of the other members of the Latin Union, had been effectively bimetallic. Gold had been coined in such quantities, not because it alone was standard money as in Britain, but because it was for the time being the more abundant metal. The French mint took the surplus gold and the French people, great coin users, were glad of it. But at an international monetary conference held at Paris in 1867, all the nations represented, except Holland, were in favour of the gold standard[5]. After 1871, the new German Empire, composed of states all of which had hitherto employed a silver standard, turned to gold. The United States were working out of the greenback period which had followed the Civil War into a period of gold and silver. In 1873 they declared the gold dollar the sole 'unit of value.' France, driven on to paper in 1870–1, like all nations unhappy in war, resumed specie pay-

---

[1] The accepted figures, based on the calculations of Soetbeer and others, and given in the *Dict. of Pol. Econ.* II. 220.

[2] Tooke and Newmarch, VI. 154.

[3] *Dict. of Pol. Econ.* as above, article by S. M. Leathes.

[4] Evidence of S. Pixley before the *R.C. on Gold and Silver, First Report*, 1887 (XXII), Q. 175, 180.

[5] Cp. Pierson, N. G., *Principles of Economics* (1902), I. 403–49; from the Dutch standpoint, but containing the best short account of the monetary history of the later nineteenth century, written by a man who had taken part in it both as economist and statesman. Pierson was prime minister of Holland. Cp. the historical section of the *Final Report* of the *R.C. on Gold and Silver*, 1888 (XLV).

ments in November, 1874. By an agreement of January 1 of that year, she and the other states of the Latin Union had restricted the coinage of large silver, the five-franc pieces. This first step towards the abandonment of genuine bimetallism, which implies a mint open for whichever metal is more abundant, foreshadowed a growing currency demand for gold. Britain, although she had cut her use of coin to a minimum, required an increased stock year by year for her increasing population and trade. Most other nations, whether they were or were not in a position to adopt gold as their standard, were anxious to add to their stores of it. Thus, in the later 'seventies, the currency, industrial, and hoarding demands for gold were all insistent.

By that time (1876–80) the United States alone were producing in a year considerably more silver than the whole known world had produced yearly in 1851–60; and Mexico alone not very much less[1]. In the 'eighties their output went far higher. It was the fast growing silver production of the early 'seventies which had made the Latin Union decide to restrict its free coinage, for fear lest the currency should become all silver, at a time when Germany's change over to a gold basis was throwing yet more silver on to the market. In 1878 the Union stopped coining large silver altogether.

The gold price of silver in London had remained extraordinarily steady from 1800 to 1870. It was rarely more than 1d. and a small fraction above, or a fraction of a penny below, 5s. the standard ounce. The fall, slow at first and then rapid, to 4s. $4\frac{1}{4}d.$ in 1880, and to 3s. $5\frac{11}{16}d.$ in 1889, was a movement without a precedent in history, either in speed or in amount. Legislation in the United States compelling the Federal Government to coin unnecessary silver dollars, or issue superfluous notes against silver bullion, had failed to check the fall[2], which acted to some degree as an export bounty for the silver-using countries of the East, whose silver costs of production rose more slowly than the gold price of rupees, dollars, or taels fell[3].

There can be very little doubt that the marked upward heave of general prices between the triennium 1849–51 (a time of free trade and of quiet after storm) and the triennium 1868–

[1] Cp. *Dict. of Pol. Econ. s.v.* Silver, III. 395 and authorities there quoted; *R.C. on Gold and Silver, Report,* as above.

[2] The literature of the subject is vast: see the summary and references in Taussig, F. W., *The Silver Situation in the U.S.* (1893) and Conrad and Elster, *H.WB. s.v. Silber und Silberwährung.*

[3] "A fall in the Indian exchange will give a bounty to exporters from India if it is caused by a fall in the value of silver...which is felt in other countries

70 (also a time of free but quiet trade, with no war until August, 1870[1]) was closely connected with the great addition to the world's stock of coined and circulating gold, which was accompanied by a growing use of paper money in its various forms. Whether the general fall after 1873 was mainly, or to an important degree, due to causes connected with the precious metals was much debated at the time and remains perhaps more doubtful. Special causes for any particular fall could easily be assigned—virgin soil for wheat; metallurgical inventions for steel; the revolution in the transport system of the world for most things[2]. It could be argued that there was a fast growing use of bank money everywhere, which relieved pressure on gold; that the output of gold was still great, and that any slight contraction of it hardly affected the world's golden stock. Why then should gold prices fall? But those who pointed to the insistence of the new currency demands for gold; to the depletion of the stock available for circulating currency by the demand from industry and the hoarder, whether Hindu ryot or rajah, or Western State hoarding for financial security or for war[3]; to the way in which silver had been discarded and gold required to do its work; to the effect of the silver situation on the low gold prices which, for a time, might be accepted for Eastern produce—those who pointed to these things as the most important, though not the sole, causes of the unquestionably increased purchasing power of currencies based on gold, had the better of the argument, even if they could offer no precise measure of that importance for which they argued. So a strong Commission, set to inquire into the matter in 1886, was subsequently to report[4].

before it is felt in India: this will happen if more silver is raised in the West or less silver is wanted there; or if" etc. Alfred Marshall, 1888, *Memorandum for the Gold and Silver Commission: Official Papers* by A. M. p. 195. These hypotheses fit the facts of the period. Cp. the price diagram, p. 378 below.

[1] War was responsible for the rather higher level touched in 1861–6.

[2] As argued at the time by Wells, D. A., *Recent Economic Changes* (1889).

[3] "War Ministers, Indian peasants, and American negroes began to hoard gold." Alfred Marshall, *Memorandum*, as above, p. 21.

[4] *R.C. on Gold and Silver, Report*, as above. The report lays stress on the relative unimportance of increased supplies of silver and decreased supplies of gold (§ 22, 44 of Part 1) and tends—though there were great differences of opinion among the Commissioners—to assign most importance to the abandonment of bimetallism. Economists, it is hoped, will pardon this summary of a controversy which in its day strained the acutest minds. Keynes, J. M., *A Treatise on Money* (1930) II, 164, argues that "for the decade ending about 1886 this explanation [i.e. the explanation suggested above, but stated by Keynes more briefly and more absolutely] is probably accurate."

In some important external aspects the banking organisation, through which Britain economised cash and accumulated capital, altered curiously little in the forty years after Peel's Acts. No doubt the Acts themselves stiffened it somewhat against change. When Peel came into power in 1841 there had been 321 private banks and 115 joint-stock banks in England and Wales. In 1875 there were still 252 private banks, and about 120 joint-stock banks whose business was strictly English. The corresponding figures for 1886 were 251 private and 117 joint-stock. The private banks to which Peel had left issuing rights in 1844 numbered 207; in 1875 there survived 114; in 1880, 104. There were still 74 in 1890. The general types of Peel's day had not changed, though their relative importance had. They had been, and they remained, very varied in function and size. There was the group of the old London 'general purposes' private banks. There was the large and important group of London firms, classed as private banks, which did specialised business mainly connected with foreign trade and investment—merchant bankers, and houses like Rothschilds, Barings, Morgans or Lazards[1]. There were country private banks, some of which now had many branches; and there were the joint-stock banks, both London and country, with branches or without. Above all stood The Bank, both its written and its unwritten constitution unchanged—although Tooke in 1856 had thought it "hardly possible to suppose" that the written part, Peel's Act, could be "maintained much longer"; although Mill had explained in 1857 that this Act's whole theory was wrong; and although Walter Bagehot, in 1873, had put forward a considered plan for a change in the unwritten constitution, with its short-term Governorship and its exclusion of true bankers from the Board[2].

Even the development of branch-banking between 1844 and 1886 seems less remarkable in retrospect than it did to some contemporaries. The policy was nearly as old as the joint-stock

[1] For 1841, vol. I. p. 512. A few of the joint-stock banks of that date were the young chartered colonial banks (for which see Baster, A. S. J., *The Imperial Banks*, 1929). The figures for 1875 are in App. XVIII of the *S.C. on Banks of Issue*: they do not distinguish this class, of which there were at that time 17. The figure for 1875 includes 60, and that for 1886, 77, London 'private banks.' A large number of these at both dates were of the Rothschild and Baring type. These can be picked out from the detailed lists of the *Bankers' Almanac*. Lists of Banks of Issue were published officially. For 1890 see the *Dict. of Pol. Econ.* I. 94. For Peel's Acts, English, Scottish and Irish, vol. I. pp. 522–6.

[2] Tooke and Newmarch, v. 612; Mill before *S.C. on the Bank Acts*, 1857, Q. 2284; Bagehot, *Lombard Street*, ch. 8.

bank itself. Its pioneer in England, the Manchester and Liverpool District Bank, had sixteen branches in the year after the Reform Bill[1]. Among the older joint-stock banks to which Peel had left rights of issue, the National Provincial of London, and among those without issuing rights, the London and County, were the most active in spreading their offices during the 'forties and 'fifties. By 1864 the former had no less than 119 branches and the latter 127. The Manchester and Liverpool District came third, with 34 branches. Deducting these, the remaining 114 averaged only just over four branches each. All told, there were 744 joint-stock bank branches and 272 private bank branches in 1864; for many private banks had one or two sub-offices, though only three of them had so many as ten. Twenty-two years later, again deducting the three joint-stock banks with most branches, the remaining 112 averaged ten branches each. The leading three were the London and County with 165, the National Provincial with 158, and the Capital and Counties with 99 branches. Six others now had more than 50, and some few private banks, like the firm then known as Lloyds Barnetts and Bosanquets, were spreading branches fast. These were important changes, but there was no radical transformation[2].

In Scotland the change was less because the banking system in the middle of the century had been more mature. Peel had regulated the issues of nineteen Scottish banks; all joint-stock; all furnished with branches. There were five more of the same type which did not issue. Failure and absorption had reduced the total to thirteen by 1864, all banks of issue; and to ten by 1886. Branches had been planted out freely—it was the old Scottish policy[3]—so freely that in 1858 a Select Committee of the Commons supposed there were as many bank offices, head and branch, in Scotland as in all England[4]. Probably there were not nearly so many[5]; though in proportion to population there were very many more. This Scottish excess of banking facilities

---

[1] Vol. i. p. 279.

[2] For 1864, *Return of all Banks...in England and Wales*, 1865 (xxx), the last full return. For 1886, the *Economist, Banking Supplement*, and the *Bankers' Almanac* for 1887.

[3] See vol. i. p. 267.

[4] *Report*, § 76.

[5] There are no returns for 1858; but the 1864 returns show 550 private and 861 joint-stock banking offices, head and branch, in England and Wales: 607 of all sorts in Scotland. Compared with population, the Scottish figure is astonishing.

continued. The ten banks of 1886 had 949 branches. England and Wales, with seven times the population of Scotland, had only about 2500 bank offices including the smallest agencies[1].

The small number of the Scottish banks and the concentration of the principal head offices in Edinburgh made joint action easy. There had been a clearing system in operation, at first for notes alone, since the eighteenth century. It was older than the Clearing House in London[2]. When the Western Bank with 101 branches failed in 1857, the others stilled the panic by agreeing, after a slight hesitation it is true, to accept its notes in the ordinary course of business[3]. In 1863 they all at once instructed their branches to follow promptly changes in the Bank of England discount rate[4]. By 1865, the last of them had abandoned old-fashioned banking secrecy, and all published annual reports with abstract balance sheets and statements of profit. In contrast with English diversity, "a uniformity of practice in the conduct...of business had been obtained throughout the whole of Scotland," before the 'seventies[5]; so that it was easy to make concerted changes, as when in 1885, feeling the pinch of hard times, all the banks together withdrew the old clients' privilege of interest on their daily balances[6]. Many years later, the smooth uniformity of Scottish banking practice still seemed "almost incredible from the English point of view."[7]

The Scottish banks had always had correspondence with London. Early in the century, they had settled their clearing balances with drafts at ten days on the Bank of England[8]. Peel's Act, by which they were permitted to increase note issues beyond a fixed minimum only against coin held in their head offices, made their relations with the Bank more intimate. They

[1] I make the number in the *Bankers' Almanac* for 1887, 2533.

[2] Kerr, A. W., *History of Banking in Scotland*, p. 81, 221. For the advantages of the concentration in Edinburgh, cp. Palgrave, *Notes on Banking*, p. 11 and the quotation from the *Bankers' Magazine* of 1876 in Powell, E. T., *The Evolution of the London Money Market* (1915), p. 510.

[3] Kerr, *History*, p. 262. Two recent books, Munro, N., *The History of the Royal Bank of Scotland* (1928) and Rait, R. S., *The History of the Union Bank of Scotland* (1930), do not add much of general interest to Kerr's narrative.

[4] Kerr, *History*, p. 270.

[5] Palgrave, *Notes*, p. 11 and Kerr, *Scottish Banking during the Period of Published Accounts*, 1865–96.

[6] Kerr, *Scottish Banking*, p. 10.

[7] Withers, H., *The English Banking System*, U.S. Monetary Commission, 1910, p. 49.

[8] Kerr, *History*, p. 221.

acquired the habit of drawing the extra coin necessary at harvest and other times of expanding note issue from its Newcastle branch[1]. Meanwhile the increased prosperity of Scotland was linking them closer to the London Money Market. They sent much "superfluous money" for use there by the bill-brokers in the early 'fifties[2]. At that time Scottish merchants seldom kept accounts in London or accepted bills payable in London, so far as is known[3]. By 1873 the situation was reversed. It was "quite an exception with large mercantile houses" in Scotland "to accept a bill payable there." They accepted those bills on London which the whole world wanted; for bills not payable in London were "simply unmarketable."[4] And the Scottish banks had "all their spare money...in London... invested as all other London money"[5] was.

Down to the 'sixties, the Scots worked their London business through agencies. In 1855 however the Clydesdale Bank had taken Roundell Palmer's opinion as to whether it could legally open in London without sacrificing its issuing rights in Scotland. Palmer said it could, but it did not[6]. In 1864 the National Bank of Scotland did; and in 1868 the Bank of Scotland[7]. The Royal Bank followed in 1874[8]. By 1883 all the important Scottish banks had their London offices. They had survived a Parliamentary attack in 1875, consequent on the 'invasion' of Cumberland by the Clydesdale Bank, which led to the inquiry of that year[9]. The law, it appeared, was on their side; but equity would seem to endorse a Bill drafted by Goschen, that never became an Act, under which a Scottish joint-stock bank, like every English joint-stock bank, must choose between a London office and its right of note issue[10]. The Scots retained both,

---

[1] *S.C. on the Bank Acts*, 1857–8, Q. 3186 (Sir George Clark).

[2] *Ibid.* 1857, Q. 5151 (D. B. Chapman of Overend and Gurney).

[3] *S.C. on Banks of Issue*, 1875, Q. 28 (a Scottish witness referring to "thirty years ago" with an "I daresay").

[4] Rae, G., *The Country Banker* (1885), p. 87.

[5] Bagehot, *Lombard Street*, p. 32.

[6] Macleod, H. D., *Theory and Practice of Banking*, II. 400.

[7] Kerr, *Scottish Banking*, p. 13.          [8] Munro, *op. cit.* p. 267–8.

[9] *S.C. on Banks of Issue*: evidence was published but no report.

[10] In fact between an English domicile of any sort and its right of note issue, but London was in Goschen's mind. His Bill—*A Bill to amend the Bankers Acts*—suggested that "the power of any banker to...issue notes, whether in England or in Scotland, shall...be subject to the condition that such banker shall not...have any house of business...in the other of the said parts of Great Britain." Macleod (II. 397) was very truculent about this. The Scots' argument was that Irish and Colonial issuing banks had London offices, so why not theirs?

probably because the commercial and political worlds were no longer much interested in problems of issue. So the whole British army of bankers was concentrating on Lombard and Threadneedle Streets.

The Scottish contingent was much the most uniformly drilled and organised, its movements and resources the best known to those whom it served. England had her metropolitan and country, her North country and South country, customs and practices. Her private banks still preserved the old secrecy[1]. Not quite all the joint-stock banks issued reports and balance sheets even in the 'eighties. Only one provincial bank had yet imitated the Scottish raid on London. This was that active and "octopus-like establishment" the National Provincial, which had sacrificed its issuing rights to establish its position at the heart of the banking world[2]. When it announced its intention, in 1864, the *Economist* rightly thought that it was "long since so great an event had happened in English country banking."[3] The normal English bank, however, like Scottish banks before the 'sixties, went on doing its London business through an agent from among the old metropolitan firms.

London itself was not a fully organised banking unit even at the end of the period. In the early 'fifties, jealousy between the private and the joint-stock banks hindered co-operation. The joint-stock banks had started new policies. They "entered more and more into competition with the private banks, and by their practice of allowing interest on deposits [which the private banks did not do] began to accumulate vast amounts."[4] In June, 1854, however, a sort of treaty was concluded, when the private banks admitted the new-comers—some of them nearly thirty years old—to the conveniences of the Clearing House. After ten more years, in April, 1864, the Bank of England itself condescended, and was allowed, to take a hand in the clearings, besides acting as banker to all other clearers. In the interval, in 1858, Sir John Lubbock had started the 'country clearing,' by which country banks could write off claims against one

[1] The first agreement of some of them to publish accounts came only in 1891.

[2] See the account in *S.C. on Banks of Issue*, 1875, Q. 1815 *sqq.* The octopus metaphor is in Phillips, M., *A History of Banks...in Northumberland, Durham and North Yorkshire* (1894), p. 117. The National Provincial had opened at Newcastle in 1865.

[3] June 4, 1864.

[4] *Report of* 1858, § 7, and evidence of D. Salomons, of the London and Westminster, Q. 1130.

another, through their London agents. By 1871 all of them were doing so[1].

But cohesion among the English banks was still very imperfect, and arrangements for joint action in emergency did not exist. In a sort of song of triumph over the rapid and unexpected success of the joint-stock banks, Walter Bagehot, in 1873, noted as a dubious point their lack of care for ultimate reserves[2]. They left that to the Bank of England. The Governor of the Bank had noted the risk in 1857, when it was much smaller. But at no time in the 'seventies or early 'eighties, so far as is known, did the Bank negotiate with the banks about it, nor the banks with one another. Indeed the Bank itself had been slow to recognise fully its own position as a central bank, in the sense in which that term is used to-day, a position which no charter or Act had assigned to it. It was still halting somewhat between the interests of its shareholders and those of the nation, when Walter Bagehot "finally established with unanswerable brilliance and cogency"[3] the functions and duties of a central bank, in 1873. In 1876, an English expert was complaining that the "homogeneity" which made it easy for the Scots to "decide on a common course of action" was "difficult, if not impossible, with English bankers."[4] In 1879 a financial writer noted that although "the lenders of money in Lombard Street are all within a stone's throw of one another...the Channel might run between them, instead of a dark, narrow little street, for all the interchange of information or assistance that goes on...in times of panic neither would fortify his neighbour with ready money or help him with information."[5] Perhaps he exaggerated a little. Perhaps the Lombard Street men would have replied that Scotland had just had a great banking catastrophe and England had not[6]. Yet certainly there was not much conscious organisation, beyond that for clearing accounts; so little that George Rae in 1885 was explaining to banking readers that a certain desirable reform would require "a greater degree of concert and a livelier sense of a common danger, on the part of English banks, than exists at present."[7]

---

[1] *Report of* 1858, § 7, for 1854; Gilbart, *The Principles and Practice of Banking* (ed. of 1873), p. 452–3; Macleod, *op. cit.* II. 192, and Martin, *The Grasshopper in Lombard Street,* for the later events.  [2] *Lombard Street,* p. 254–5.
[3] *Report of the Committee on Finance and Industry,* 1931 (Cmd. 3897), p. 15.
[4] Croft, C. W., in the *Bankers' Magazine,* quoted in Powell, *op. cit.* p. 510.
[5] Ellis, A., *The Rationale of Market Fluctuations,* p. 36.
[6] See below, p. 383.  [7] *The Country Banker,* p. 40.

The chances of a strain at the centre had been increased by the arrival in the city of other people besides the Scots. Before 1850 there were a few well-established Americo-English merchant banking houses, such as Peabody's of London, or the firm which was to become Brown, Shipley & Co. of Liverpool, later also of London[1]. They were already so strong in the early 'fifties that it was usual for "the shipper of goods here for America" to draw bills "upon a great American house in this country for them."[2] But in 1857 Peabody's came on the Bank for help[3]. Firms, most of which were bankers, at least by continental definition, and whose names were seldom British, were rising in London or arriving there from Europe and America on the track of the Barings and the Rothschilds. Some had come to London, or risen in London, as exchange dealers and acceptors of foreign bills long before 1850. Such were Huths', Doxats', and Raphaels'[4]. But like the Rothschilds and Barings before them, they were turning more and more to the issuing of loans for foreign governments and foreign railways. They were joined by others to whom, whatever their original character, issuing, perhaps linked with concession seeking, was the main chance.

The Hambros came from Copenhagen about 1848. They were taking up Danish loans in 1849–50, Sardinian and Peruvian in 1851–2[5]. Bischoffsheim and Goldschmidt, of Paris, Frankfurt and elsewhere, had an office in London from about 1850, and were prominent in the issuing world between 1866 and 1875. Frühling and Göschen, originally dealers in exchange, acquired special interests in Egypt. J. S. Morgan & Co. succeeded to the Peabody business during the American Civil War; in 1871 they were competing with the Rothschilds over the finance of the French indemnity loan. Speyers of New York came to London in 1862, and were issuing American railway bonds ten years later. There were Oppenheims, Schroeders, and Erlangers; there was Baron Hirsch, son-in-law to a Bischoffsheim; and there were others, European or American and generally

---

[1] Jenks, L. H., *The Migration of English Capital to* 1875, p. 94; Cole, A. H., "Evolution of the Foreign Exchange Market of the U.S.," *J.E.B.H.* May, 1929, p. 391.

[2] *S.C. on the Bank Acts*, 1857, Q. 5134 (D. B. Chapman of Overend and Gurney).

[3] Evans, D. M., *The History of the Commercial Crisis*, 1857–8, p. 49 n.

[4] Powell, *op. cit.* p. 386.

[5] *Fenn on the Funds*, 5th ed. 1855, p. 151, 200, 241.

Jewish, some of whom went down in the troubles of the 'seventies[1].

"Since the Franco-German war," Bagehot wrote in 1873, "we have become to a much larger extent than before the Bankers of Europe."[2] "The German Government, as is well known, keeps its account, and a very valuable one it must be, at the London Joint Stock Bank."[3] What other governments, crowned heads, and personages kept valuable accounts in the secret places of the private banks could be a matter only of conjecture, not of common knowledge. No doubt the accounts were there. During the next twelve years most of the continental public banks, as distinguished from the private international issuing houses, opened offices in London. The Crédit Lyonnais and the Deutsche Bank are cases in point. Not one of these institutions or individuals but was in a position to draw, directly or indirectly, on the reserves of the Bank of England. There was foreign money on deposit and foreign money at call or short notice. The whole scale and range of operations had widened since the 'forties; and cables had shortened notices since the 'sixties. The mobile deposits in the British joint-stock banks had enormously increased. These were the considerations which made Bagehot insist, not that there was grave danger—"I am by no means an alarmist," he said—but that there was a delicate problem presented which had been imperfectly studied. "Money will not manage itself, and Lombard Street has a great deal of money to manage."[4] Happily there was never a risk of Britain's becoming involved in anything but little wars, between 1873 and 1886, and her economic complaints during those years were of the wasting kind, not of the feverish kind which makes panic. Also she had learnt by trial and error, if not by profound speculative study, some useful rules of thumb for the maintenance of her financial health. Her leaders might fairly have argued, after watching Europe and America in 1873, that at least they knew more about these things than their neighbours[5].

Following very often a Scottish lead, the joint-stock banks of England had been extending their functions. The "vast amounts"[6] which they had accumulated by allowing interest on deposits had been employed very largely in the purchase of bills.

---

[1] See the account of these firms in Jenks, *op. cit.* p. 267–8, also p. 171.
[2] *Lombard Street*, p. 17.  [3] *Ibid.* p. 312.  [4] *Ibid.* p. 20.
[5] Below, p. 381 *sqq.*  [6] Above, p. 344.

They have "decidedly run into our business," the managing partner of Overend and Gurney said in 1857[1]. Overend's, the bill merchants, 'the bankers' bankers' of the early nineteenth century, liked to have as much bank money as possible lying at short notice with themselves. The joint-stock people were doing more of their own bill-dealing than the private firms had done.

Subsequently, but with more hesitation, the joint-stock banks encroached on another field, that of the 'accepting houses,' mercantile firms who employed knowledge and capital in accepting—and so making more marketable—foreign bills on London. Again Scots led the hunt for new business. One of the charges of the more staid English bankers against the raiders from the North in 1875 was their 'undesirable' practice of accepting. The London and Westminster made a virtue of having refused "many accounts of great value, simply on the ground that they would involve foreign acceptances."[2] In fact it did very little accepting, either foreign or domestic. In 1870 it had among its liabilities only £759,000 of acceptances, against £19,600,000 of deposits. The acceptances were presumably not foreign. But the Union of London, which at the same time had £4,100,000 of acceptances and £10,000,000 of deposits, must surely have dabbled deep in the undesirable practice to do so large a business[3]. Even in 1883, all the Scottish banks together had only £4,800,000 of acceptances and drafts—not all foreign —against £83,000,000 of deposits. The acceptance figure, however, had increased by 85 per cent. since the totals were first made available in 1865[4]. The business was growing, but the evidence does not allow of its exact study.

Experts believed in the 'eighties that this growth was "due mainly to that exceptionally good department of acceptance business supplied by the Colonial banks drawing on London, and not so much to mercantile acceptances."[5] The Scottish bank office in London was helping the colonial bank to remit,

---

[1] S.C. on the Bank Acts, Q. 5210 (D. B. Chapman).

[2] S.C. on Banks of Issue, Q. 7318. W. H. Crake, the director giving evidence, was himself in a mercantile house and had a clear, old-fashioned, view of the line between his two activities.

[3] Half-yearly reports quoted in the Economist, August 6, 1870.

[4] Kerr, Scottish Banking, p. 119, and History, App. B.

[5] Kerr, History, p. 315; originally written in 1883. The statement is introduced with "it would seem that...." Kerr was a working banker. It was suggested in 1875 that the Union Bank's big accepting business was due to connections with a large Indian bank. S.C. on Banks of Issue, Q. 6944.

a most unobjectionable practice. Like all accepting of 'finance bills'—which was not a new thing[1]—it might involve some divorce of the balance of indebtedness from those movements of goods which lie behind the mercantile acceptance proper. There were obvious risks in this divorce, but also the great conveniences which had first brought it about. Finance bills could be created abroad to assist remittance at times of the year when trade bills, representing actual goods shipped to England, were scarce—between clips in Australia, or between cotton and wheat crops in America. And the British banks were as good judges of foreign and colonial bankers' credit as the accepting houses could be of merchants' credit. No doubt their activities and those of their overseas banking correspondents—many of whom had themselves come to London—were curtailing the field of the private acceptor. A wool grower need not comprehend bills, nor a merchant in Sydney establish his credit with a London accepting house, when everything to do with wool finance has been taken over by the Sydney and London offices of the Bank of New South Wales[2].

Among the new minor activities of the banks was the business, "begun of late" Bagehot said in 1873, of collecting "people's...incomes for them." Not only were coupons on bonds and debentures "handed in for the bank to collect"; but "often enough" the banker was expected to keep the bond and cut off the coupon himself. "And the detail of all this is incredible, and it needs a special machinery to cope with it."[3] The joint-stock banks had first set up that machinery, as Bagehot pointed out, and the private banks often lacked it[4].

[1] See below, p. 371. The acceptor of such a bill undertakes to put money at the disposal of the drawer just as if he had bought goods from him. He of course trusts the drawer to repay at a convenient time.

[2] By 1886 there were 28 Colonial Joint-Stock Banks with London offices: the Bank of N.S.W., which had 171 branches, was the biggest: *Economist, Banking Supplement*, 1887. Cp. Baster, A. S. J., *The Imperial Banks*.

[3] *Lombard Street*, p. 279.

[4] Existing English bank histories usually say nothing at all about such internal functions and their modern development. The histories are antiquarian, personal, and external. See *e.g.* Grindon, L. H., *Manchester Banks and Bankers* (1877); Martin, J. B., *The Grasshopper in Lombard Street* (1892); Phillips, M., *A History of Banks, Bankers and Banking in Northumberland, Durham and North Yorkshire* (1894); Cave, C. H., *A History of Banking in Bristol* (1899); Bidwell, W. H., *Annals of an East Anglian Banking House* (1900); Easton, H. T., *The History of a Banking House* (Smith, Payne and Smiths) (1903); Lloyd, S., *The Lloyds of Birmingham* (1907); Matthews, P. W. and Tuke, A. W., *A History of Barclay's Bank* (1926); Saunders, P. T., *Stuckey's Bank* (1928).

While new banking activities developed, some old ones decayed. Of these, perhaps the most important was the Scottish system of cash credits or cash accounts, by which promising young men even "from low situations" could get credit from the banks, provided they could find a couple of bondsmen, that is, sureties[1]. It had been the habit of English writers on banking ever since the 'twenties to praise the system freely. They were still doing so in the early 'seventies[2]. But it was already in decay. Certainly it was moribund within a few years; for by 1896 "the day of the cash account was practically done,"[3] and such customs die hard and slow.

Not that an able Scot from a 'low situation' had fewer opportunities of getting help from banks than before. The cash credit system had grown up when such a man had no banking account. It had helped him to get one. Already in the 'fifties Scottish operatives kept accounts, and the Glasgow banks had savings departments open at night to assist them[4]. By 1875 there was about one banking account to every two Scotsmen of twenty years old and upwards, in all 418,000 accounts[5]. Any serious and promising young man would have one. There were branches everywhere: the agents knew their men. Bank funds accumulated and in the 'eighties were seeking employment at low rates. The cash account, which had involved a formal bond[6], gave way to less formal and cheaper methods of attaining the same end.

The state left the more important banking functions completely free. Legal relaxation of the usury laws, begun in 1833, had been carried so far by 1839, and their evasion was so well understood, that their complete abolition in 1854 (by 17 and 18 Vict. c. 90) did little more than recognise an established freedom[7]. The function which the state did regulate, that of

---

[1] See vol. I. p. 269.      [2] *E.g.* Palgrave's *Notes on Banking*, p. 13.
[3] Kerr, *Scottish Banking*, p. 121. The system, Kerr adds, was "at its best during the period of free issues," *i.e.* before 1845.
[4] *Report* of 1858, § 33.
[5] *S.C. on Banks of Issue*, App. 7. There was no doubt some duplication of accounts.      [6] Cp. Kerr, *Scottish Banking*, p. 121.
[7] Vol. I. p. 347-9, 509. For the abolition see Levi, L., *History of British Commerce*, p. 355. The Act of 1833 referred to in vol. I. p. 509 did not affect the Bank of England only: all three months' bills were put outside the usury laws. Longer dated bills soon followed. By 1839 (2 and 3 Vict. c. 37) usury had vanished from the law of personal contracts; but a man could commit usury over land!

issue, was becoming less important every decade. But the state had tried for many years to give stability to joint-stock banking by making rules about the constitution of the banks, or by denying them constitutional privileges reputed dangerous. Their growing stability owed little to these rules or these denials. For ten years after the first modern joint-stock bank was opened in London, in 1834, such banks had not even enjoyed the elementary right of suing and being sued in the names of their officers. They had got on quite well without it. They used trustees[1]. When Peel initiated the registration of joint-stock companies in 1844 he framed a special Act for banks (7 and 8 Vict. c. 113)[2]. They could only register if their capital was at least £100,000 and their shares of no lower denomination than £100. When in 1855 parliament began to feel its way towards a general law of limited liability, banks were at first excluded (from 18 and 19 Vict. c. 133). In 1857 Peel's bank registration Act was repealed and replaced (by 20 and 21 Vict. c. 49), yet the exclusion was not raised[3]. But after the catastrophes of 1857[4], and some shocking cases of bank failures with unlimited liability, parliament changed its mind, and by 21 and 22 Vict. c. 91 allowed new banks to be formed with limited liability, and old banks to register as limited[5]. Liability for notes however was in no case to be limited. Finally, the generalised limited liability Act of 1862 (25 and 26 Vict. c. 89) covered banks together with all other associations of seven men. But by that time effective bank creation was nearly over. The old and strong banks looked down on the 'limiteds' and thought that registration might impair their own credit. Sixteen years later, none of the Scottish banks was limited under recent legislation, and there were 69 unlimited banks in England and Wales, including nearly all the most important joint-stock concerns—the London and Westminster, the Capital and Counties,

---

[1] Vol. I. p. 510.

[2] *An Act to regulate Joint-Stock Banking in England*; this is the Act referred to in vol. I. p. 511 n. 2. See Shannon, H. S., "The Coming of General Limited Liability," *E.J. (Hist.)*, 1931, and the very good short account of Joint-Stock and Limited Liability in Levi, *op. cit.* p. 333 *sqq.*

[3] This was a special *Act to amend the Law relating to Banking Companies*: the general Act of the year dealing with Limited Liability is 20 and 21 Vict. c. 78, concerned mainly with the winding up of companies.

[4] Below, p. 368 *sqq.*

[5] By 1864 there were 33 new banks registered under the Acts of 1857 and 1858, and 12 which existed before 1857 and had also registered. *Return of all J.S.C. formed or registered since 18 and 19 Vict. c. 133*: 1864, LVIII. 291.

the Manchester and Liverpool, the York City and County, and Stuckeys, to name only a few well-known firms in various districts[1]. But the failure of the criminally mismanaged City of Glasgow bank in October, 1878, killed unlimited joint-stock banking, as it were in a night[2]. Frightened shareholders, shuddering at the object-lesson of losses six times the amount of the losers' holdings[3], put pressure on directorates. "Many responsible holders of shares" in banks with unlimited liability "showed a desire to sell out."[4] Parliament (by 42 and 43 Vict. c. 76 of 1879) facilitated a change over to limitation, bringing into existence the principle of reserve liability, by which companies might increase the nominal amount of their shares, but might call up the difference between the amount actually paid on each share and its nominal amount only in the event of the company's being wound up. Within five years all banks of importance had taken action under the new law. They did so, however, in such sweeping fashion that, what with capital authorised but not called up before the Act and the new reserve liability created under it, to every pound share in a British joint-stock bank the average shareholder of 1885–6 was liable to add four more pounds, in the event of its failure. This was not an unlimited liability, but it would have seemed singularly like one had there been much banking in Britain so unsound as that of the City of Glasgow[5]. Security lay not in the law but in the management.

By the time that Bagehot published his *Lombard Street*, Palgrave his *Notes on Banking*, and the Committee on Banks of Issue the results of its inquiry (1873–5), the organisation by which all free British capital was sucked into the London money market was functioning almost perfectly. Compared with other

[1] See the *Return of Unlimited and Limited Companies*, 1878–9, LXV. 479, and cp. Macleod, *op. cit.* II. 400; Rae, G., *The Country Banker*, p. 260. Some of the older Scottish banks were limited by charter, Kerr, *History*, p. 306.

[2] Below, p. 383.

[3] This is not an exact statement of the final position: it refers to the call of 500 per cent. on the capital stock made at the end of November, 1878, to meet losses. The announcement of the bank's suspension of payment had appeared on October 2. Kerr, *History*, p. 294–8.

[4] Sir Felix Schuster: *Banking Interviews, U.S. Monetary Commission*, 1910, p. 34.

[5] The banks "so broadened the basis on which their credit stood, as to leave their liability practically unlimited"—Rae, *The Country Banker*, p. 261 (written in 1885).

national organisations, or lacks of organisation, it had been highly efficient even twenty years earlier. In the interval, Scottish and provincial branch banking had drawn in almost the last of those rustic hoards which country folk had kept "in their desks and cupboards"[1]; and a smooth open channel had been cut down which the aggregated northern surpluses flowed South. The channels from East Anglia, the South-West, and rural England generally, had been cut long before. Wealth slipped along them easily and without sound, very often from some placid Quaker pond in the country to a more or less Quaker reservoir in Town. Agriculture prospered. Country ponds overflowed. From Town, what was not used there ran out into the industrial districts, by way of the discount or rediscount of manufacturers' and merchants' bills. These were the greatest days of the London bill-brokers, the Lombard Street Houses[2].

In the 'fifties and subsequently, their business, except in moments of aberration, was to advance money on fine trade bills which fell due for payment in regular sequence day by day; although advances on dock warrants were one of their subordinate 'lines.'[3] The leading group were no longer bill-brokers in fact. In the 'fifties Overends repudiated the title, though everyone applied it to them. "We are not bill-brokers," they said: we are "money dealers."[4] Brokers in the strict sense, men who merely found bills for money and money for bills, always existed: they got a commission like any other broker, and were a distinct and inferior, though relatively numerous, group[5]. Distinct also was the tiny and interesting group of the money-brokers, "the great go-betweens in the banking and discount community and the Stock Exchange,"[6] men who moved

---

[1] A Scottish banker, W. B. Gordon, to the *S.C. on Banks of Issue*, Q. 4028.

[2] Chapman, of Overend and Gurney, had explained to the *S.C. on the Bank Acts* of 1857 how they discounted for Lancashire and Yorkshire with the aid of the rural surpluses put at their disposal by the bankers: Q. 5100. Cp. Jenks, *The Migrations of English Capital to 1875*, p. 246, who perhaps overrates somewhat the subsequent decline of the bill-brokers. For their importance in 1910 see Sir Felix Schuster, as above, p. 43.

[3] Chapman, as above, Q. 5104–6, 5198–9, 5203.

[4] *Ibid.* Q. 4931, 5098. "We then acted as brokers" he said (Q. 4881), referring to the usury-law days.

[5] Powell, *The Evolution of the London Money Market*, p. 378; *The English Banking System*, U.S. *Monetary Commission*, p. 62. By 1931 these 'running brokers' were reduced to 8. *R. of the Committee on Finance and Industry*, p. 43.

[6] Evans, D. M., *Speculative Notes and Notes on Speculation* (1864), p. 88–9.

about daily to ascertain what floating surpluses were available, and what were likely to be the demands upon them from bill-brokers and stock-brokers, insurance companies, financial houses and sometimes banks. In the heads of these men the supply and demand curves for 'short money' crossed. They earned their living by arranging transactions for a commission at the day's equilibrium price. Even in the 'sixties their numbers were contracting[1]: not until the telephone reached the city did their function become superfluous.

The money-dealing bill-brokers stood at the centre of the short-money market. They bought bills to hold until maturity, and bills to sell to bankers and others who wanted them. The bills which they sold they guaranteed. Overends, in their great days, held no Consols or other securities whose price might fluctuate, only the bills and allied documents recording obligations of definite amount due for payment at precise dates[2]. This was the foundation of their practice of trading on borrowed money payable at call or short notice. Trust in the leading houses was so implicit that bankers were by no means the only depositors with them. Their position was always delicate, though in quiet times safe. But with the smallest breath of distrust among their depositors, the least fear that the parcels of bills falling due on any given date might not be met, strain almost intolerable set in. On one bad day in 1857 "a single discounting house paid...£700,000 to depositors and £100,000 to discounters."[3] It had to discount for its name's sake, although its working capital was so horribly fluid. Which house it was is easily guessed.

Until the limited liability legislation of the mid 'fifties, the business was all in private hands. Two discount companies had been established before 1858, one of which, the National, was successful from the first and by 1866 was in a strong position[4]. Others—they were never very numerous—rose and fell, among them Overend and Gurney Limited, which under its new designation found a public eager to subscribe in 1865, and crashed to ruin in 1866. Three only, including the National, were of importance in the early 'seventies; and of these two amalgamated

---

[1] Evans, as above: "not so numerous as they were"; mostly elderly men.
[2] Chapman, Q. 5104, 5216.
[3] Sir G. C. Lewis discussing the crisis of 1857, December 4, 1857. *Hansard, Third Series*, CXLVIII. 155.
[4] For its position in 1866 see *Fenn on the Funds*, 9th ed. 1867.

to form the Union with a capital of £1,000,000, 50 per cent. paid, in 1885[1]. The Union, the National, and about a score of private firms made up the 'discount houses' of the mid 'eighties[2]. The business had changed little in character and lost nothing in absolute, though perhaps something in relative, importance since the 'fifties. The lesser firms, other than the pure brokers, bought bills mainly to sell again. The greater both sold and held. The delicacy of the business had not decreased. It was a banker with late nineteenth century experience who said, early in the twentieth, that "the liability of the bill-broker is one which can only be met in ordinary times...in troubled times he is at the mercy of the banks and of circumstances."[3]

In its relation to the ordinary workings of British industry and commerce, the London short-money market was important mainly as a furnisher and economiser of circulating capital. Except when it was very feverish, it did not interest the investor who was neither manufacturer nor merchant. It was of more immediate importance to the merchant than to the manufacturer, because the circulating element dominates commerce. The mechanism of the discountable bill helped the creation of fixed capital—the textile engineer, it might be, drawing on the mill-owner—but fixed capital as such was never the concern of Lombard Street. The provincial banker gave every assistance to men whom he trusted, allowing them ample overdrafts at all times; but even he regarded plant, machinery "or works of any description"[4] as ideally bad security for loans. Almost all the fixed capital of manufacturing industry, as it existed in 1850, and the overwhelmingly greater part of the additions and renewals made during the next thirty-six years, came from what the economists of the age called—with more reason than

---

[1] The *Economist* (July 14, 1866) spoke of "a great many" new companies, but there were not really many. By February 12, 1870, it is taking interest only in the "three principal" companies—the National, the General and the United —and the six or seven "eminent" private firms. For the amalgamation, *Banking Interviews*, as above, p. 104 (the manager of the Union).

[2] In 1931 there were 3 public companies, 4 private companies, and 17 private firms. *R. of the Committee on Finance and Industry*, p. 43.

[3] *Banking Interviews*, p. 42 (Sir Felix Schuster).

[4] Rae, *op. cit.* The overdraft in the economic life of the industrial districts deserves a special study—if the facts are available. The sort of provincial banker who was dying out at the end of the nineteenth century used to speak of the men he had 'made' and wonder whether the modern type of banking would do the work so well.

their critics have sometimes allowed—the abstinence of those
steady manufacturers whom the provincial bankers trusted[1].
Creation of fixed capital through the husbanded reserves of
industrial companies was known but not yet important[2]. When
he was doing well, when, in later economic jargon, he was
drawing 'quasi-rents,' sort-of-rents; either rent of special ability,
or rent of mere good-luck, or rent from the ownership of capital-
goods of which the world's stock was for the time being inadequate[3]; then the manufacturer improved or extended his
mill or his works. Britain, until the 'eighties, was so often an
owner of capital-goods of which the world was short that—
acting through her more fortunate and able manufacturers—
she could for a time make some of those goods yield these rents,
not mere fine-cut competitive profits; and with the rents she
could build more works and more mills. From the standpoint
of economic theory she was the world's great quasi-rentier.
If, however, from some doubt of the near future, she hesitated
to 'fix' her rents and her profits in plant to the normal extent,
and her manufacturers left money on deposit with their bankers,
Lombard Street got an abnormal supply and it was 'cheap.'
This was perhaps the main link between the Street and the
course of domestic fixed-capital investment[4].

But if, even in the 'eighties, most of the additions to industrial
capital were still made directly by those who owned and managed
industrial establishments, the early railway age had familiarised
a great part of the nation with the attractions, methods, and
risks of centralised investment and speculation. Railways had
been promoted locally and London capital had at first been shy
of them. That phase was nearly over before 1848 when, as
Tooke wrote, "in every street of every town persons were to be
found who were holders of railway shares."[5] Dealings were
concentrating in the Stock Exchange. Whole grades of society
to whom Lombard Street remained mysterious, even after
Bagehot revealed it, had acquired some crude knowledge of
Capel Court. Railway Gambling, pilloried by Tooke in capital

[1] Cp. R. of Committee on Industry and Finance, p. 162.
[2] For the importance to-day see e.g. Pigou, A. C., A Study in Public Finance
(1928), p. 78 n.
[3] See Marshall, Alfred, Principles of Economics, Index, s.v. Quasi-rent.
[4] Cp. below, p. 379, and p. 385.
[5] History of Prices, v. 234. Cp. throughout Jenks, op. cit. p. 131–2 and passim.
All discussions of investment, here and elsewhere in the text, are much indebted
to Jenks.

letters, had turned into the soberest investment. By the 'eighties railway stock was, after Consols, the banker's ideal security[1]. Down to about 1850, well-managed banks had doubted the propriety of advances on it: they had left much of that work to an ephemeral type of concern called an exchange company. When the exchange companies had bought experience and died, the joint-stock banks took the business over[2].

With railway stock as a universal family investment, for all families which had anything to invest, went the other public utility stocks—of gas, water, dock and telegraph companies— and those of the joint-stock banks themselves. (Cemetery, pier, and market companies might become family investments locally; but they were in a lower grade[3].) City articles in the daily papers and the growth of a financial press spread information of varying quality. Continental railways, North and South American railways, colonial railways and loans, and the funds of all the more reputable governments became in turn investment, as opposed to speculative, securities—the kind of thing which a country lawyer might not question if found among the inherited capital of a maiden lady. All this paved the way for the entry of new classes of companies, and eased the work of those promoters who had to induce, first, narrow financial circles, and then the ordinary public of investors, to take an interest in them.

The list of companies provisionally registered in 1853[4], though a large proportion of them never got to work, shows where the main interests of promoters and investors lay just before the legislation of 1855–62 finally cleared the ground for the joint-stock age. Out of a total of 339, there were 80 railway schemes; 54 gas schemes; 35 insurance schemes; various mining, shipping and trading schemes; but only 30 for "conducting manufactures, working patents, etc." The total amount of capital even nominally involved was, by later standards, insignificant. Numbers and nominal capital remained low until 1862. For the five years ending in 1861, the annual average was 381 companies with a total nominal capital of £21,000,000. In 1864 there were registered 975 companies with a nominal capital of

[1] Rae, *op. cit.* p. 101–2.

[2] The definite evidence for these statements is Scottish (Kerr, *History*, p. 248), but they are no doubt generally true of England.

[3] There are a number of these in the 1853 returns of *All Applications for Charters with Limited Liability under* 1 *Vict. c.* 73 (1854, LXV. 611), including the London Necropolis Company. For piers, see below, p. 518.

[4] *A. and P.* 1854, LXV. 597.

£235,000,000[1]; and the figures for 1865 were 1014 and £203,000,000. After 1866 came a precipitate fall to a level not much above that of 1857–61. The nominal capital figure of 1864–5—a figure more important in the psychological than in the economic history of joint-stock enterprise, though in the psychological history very important—was not again reached until 1881–2; but even in the least active years of the 'seventies the annual crop of registrations was almost what it had been in 1864–5, and by 1887 it was twice as great[2].

The registrations of 1863–5 contain all the types of ten years earlier, though in different proportions[3]. Naturally there are fewer home railway companies, though it was a period of vigorous railway building. A few durable industrial registrations—the Shotley Bridge Iron Company; Chatwood's Safes; John Brown; Charles Cammell—stand out of a crowd of seven-man projects, industrial and commercial, which never came to anything. The railway waggon building business was developing in the hands of companies, as might perhaps have been expected[4]. There was a fresh spawning of joint-stock banks, British and overseas. A novelty which caught the public eye was the hotel company: the Randolph at Oxford was registered in April, 1863, and 46 others were registered that year[5]. There was also a crop of Indian tea-planting and similar enterprises. Of considerable importance in the general history of investment was a group of finance companies, or investment trusts, modelled on the Franco-Jewish *Crédit mobilier* of ten years earlier[6]. Their directorates were "a combination of the mercantile and banking elements"[7]: the International Financial Society of 1863 included Morgans, Heaths, Göschens, Huths, Sterns and Dobrees. Their objects were miscellaneous—com-

---

[1] The amount paid up was barely a tenth of this however—£24,229,633.

[2] The figures are in the annual returns, summarised in the *Statistical Abstracts* and in the *Economist*. The earlier ones are discussed by Leone Levi in an article on Joint-Stock Companies in *S.J.* 1870, p. 1–41 and by Max Wirth, *Geschichte der Handelskrisen* (2nd ed. 1874). And cp. Jenks, *op. cit.* p. 238 *sqq.*, the latest discussion.

[3] See the detailed *Return of all J.S.C.* of 1864.

[4] Cp. above, p. 98.

[5] For the public eye see Evans, *Speculative Notes*, p. 166–7.

[6] Perhaps the best contemporary account of the *Crédit mobilier* is that of Max Wirth, *op. cit.* (the first edition was 1858), p. 268 *sqq.* Cp. Art. *Finanzierungsgesellschaften* (by R. Liefmann) in Conrad and Elster, *H.WB.* IV. 261. See below, p. 364.

[7] *Economist*, August 22, 1863. See too the *Economist's Review* of 1863, February 20, 1864.

pany and loan flotation, concession negotiation, the assistance of other enterprises of all kinds, "in a word...all such operations as an intelligent and experienced capitalist might effect on his own account with a capital of millions."[1] In particular they gave British-promoted railways overseas, in their early stages, the help which British banking had hesitated to give to home railways when still a little speculative. The nature of the work which they set out to do can best be illustrated by a list of the chief enterprises in which one of them, the rather absurdly named Crédit Foncier of England, was interested after four years of life. They were the City of Milan Improvement Company, the Varna and Rustchuk Railway, the Belgian Public Works Company, the Irrigation Company of France, the Imperial Land Company of Marseilles, and the Millwall Docks[2].

By that time, August, 1867, "small dividends, if any,"[3] were being paid by the finance companies, and their shares were all below par. Several had died and the type had lost vitality. A variant and less adventurous type appeared with the Foreign and Colonial Government Trust of 1868. Its intention was "to give the investor of moderate means the same advantage as the large capitalist"[4], by spreading for him the risks of investment in government bonds over a wide range of countries, from Austria and Australia to Turkey and the United States. It was followed by the Submarine Cables Trust of 1871 and by others; but the type was not very important down to 1886[5]. Its object was security; that of the finance company had been enterprise. Mistakes were made by the directors of both types, but naturally fewer by those who looked to security.

The company uprush of the 'sixties was so swift and dramatic that its immediate importance in the economic life of the nation may easily be overrated. Exact measurement is impossible, but

---

[1] Prospectus of the General Credit and Finance Society quoted in Jenks, *op. cit.* p. 249. There is a very severe contemporary judgment of the companies in Levi's *History of British Commerce*, p. 429–30.

[2] *Economist*, August 24, 1867, "The Crédit Foncier of England."

[3] *Ibid.*

[4] Quoted in Powell, E. T., *The Evolution of the London Money Market*, p. 469. Jenks overrates these companies. They handled a very small part of the business of investment at this time. The accounts in Grayson, T. J., *Investment Trusts, their Origin, Development and Operation* (New York, 1928) and Glasgow, G., *The English Investment Trust Companies* (1930), are slight.

[5] Only 12 were quoted on the Stock Exchange list in 1886. The oldest then surviving (2) dated from 1871; 3 from 1873; 4 from 1879; 1 from each of the years 1881, 1883, 1884—*Economist*, October 7, 1886.

a contemporary estimate suggested that not 10 per cent. of the authorised capital of new companies registered was paid in prompt cash. The figure for 1863–6 is £35,600,000 out of a nominal capital of £373,000,000. This was only a small fraction of the national savings[1].

Far more important than many of the conspicuous flotations of new companies and new kinds of company was the process, gathering momentum gradually during the 'sixties, and 'seventies, by which old businesses were 'limited' and the flow of outside capital was directed into them. For this work there specialised out, in the best known instances from among accountants, a small group of men who came to be known as financial agents or investing agents. To them, as they acquired reputation, propositions were submitted by prospective vendors, representatives perhaps of an engineer who had died "leaving his business to his sons, who had been educated at college, and had paid no attention to business."[2] Thirty-nine such propositions out of forty, a leading financial agent told a Select Committee in 1877, had been refused by his firm because they came from firms on the down-grade trying to save themselves by 'limitation.'[3] Yet that single firm had averaged some £2,000,000 of flotations a year in 1867–77[4], and in sixteen years had found employment for the capital surpluses of 5000 rich men. Most of the companies floated by them had been large, but there were also "many private companies of small capital."[5] Latterly, trained valuers had always been employed at an early stage to assist the agents in their decisions, because in some of the first 'limitations' the company had been formed with a nominal capital which proved to be excessive, and as the Act of 1862 had not provided for reduction of capital, there had

---

[1] The estimate was that of the *Economist*, discussed by Leone Levi in "Joint-Stock Companies," *S.J.* 1870. Jenks' statement (*op. cit.* p. 238–9) that "during the early 'sixties" there was a "transformation of a considerable part of British trade and industry into companies with limited liability" is too strong. In industry the transformation was insignificant, in trade not considerable. Cp. above, p. 138 and p. 311.

[2] David Chadwick before the *S.C. on...the Companies Acts*, 1877 (VIII. 419), Q. 2008. His evidence in 1877 and before the *S.C. on Limited Liability Acts*, 1867 (X. 393) is the source of information. He had practised as an accountant since 1842; from 1860, with the new legislation, he became mainly an investing agent. *S.C.* of 1867, Q. 835 *sqq.* There were other firms of the same type—Q. 2157.

[3] Chadwick, Q. 2092.

[4] Q. 1993–5, 2081.

[5] Q. 1999.

been a burden of uncalled liability[1]. When the agents had received the valuers' report they offered the proposition "by private circular or prospectus to their friends." The statutory seven men to sign the memorandum of association were taken from these friends and those of the vendors. In a typical arrangement for a capital of £100,000, the vendors would take some £30,000; the agents' friends the same; "and we should feel certain before we registered...that the whole of the remainder would be subscribed." The agents in question always pressed for the appointment of a well-paid manager. "The nearer you can approach to the management of a private concern the better." This was how the work was done, or was said to have been done, by a firm who boasted that they had no connection with the Stock Exchange; that there was no jobbing "and very seldom any advertising"; and that nine-tenths of their flotations since 1860 were still not only afloat in 1877 but "eminently successful."[2] There were no doubt less thorough, less scrupulous, and less successful firms who may not have charged so much as the 1 per cent. on the capital floated which was Messrs Chadwick's substantial fee[3]; but it was in some such fashion, business-like and well considered, that the more important 'limitations' of the 'sixties and 'seventies and the increasing number of the 'eighties were carried out. Usually the capital remained in few hands and the company private or semi-private; but at the close there was a group, though a small group, of industrial securities regularly quoted on the London Stock Exchange[4].

[1] The legal provision for reductions of capital was one of the main points discussed before the committee of 1877.

[2] The quotations are from Q. 2041, 2075, 2007, 2045, 1991. Chadwick gave much the same evidence in 1867—Q. 835 *sqq.* The success of his flotations, if stated accurately, was in marked contrast with the fate of new joint-stock companies generally. Cp. Macgregor, D. H., "Joint-Stock Companies and the Risk Factor," *E.J.* December, 1929. Prof. Macgregor's statement that "conversion of family businesses into companies was a later development [later than 1880] facilitated especially by the Act of 1900, though referred to as a growing practice by the Committee of 1895," needs qualification.

[3] Q. 2114.

[4] The group classed as 'Commercial, Industrial, etc.,' given in *The Times* in June, 1886, is extraordinarily small. From 14 to 18 is the number usually quoted and of these by no means all are industrial. Bryant and May, Price's candles, and Spratt's dog biscuits are quoted fairly regularly. In most of the not very many 'industrials' dealings were decidedly intermittent. *The Times* list is of course far from exhaustive but it contains those 'industrials' which interested the general investor.

It would be unwise to reduce the economic history of Britain to a running commentary on the health or fever charts of the London money market. But, given the appropriate text, they provide decidedly the best approach to a greater and more complex story, the story of the contacts between the British economy—with its fully-used capital, its short-money market, and the growing 'anonymity' of its commerce and industry—and that world economy with which it was involved, and without which it could not even endure, still less prosper.

'Money' in London had never been so cheap for so long as it was between the middle of 1848 and the end of 1852. Nor had bread, since back in the eighteenth century. The island was tolerably active throughout those years, and very active in 1852; but at least until 1851 much of the world was neither. Europe was slowly getting back to work after famine, revolution, and war. France was being turned again by plebiscite into an Empire. Meanwhile her railway building was held up. America, however, was in high activity. Men poured into her much faster than ever before—three hundred and seventy-nine thousand of them in 1851[1]—and the forty-niners had set out to get the gold, singing "Oh California! that's the land for me." American prosperity always told in Britain; but at that time there might well be more than a year's lag. It took four months in 1848 for the first gold news to reach Washington, by way of Panama. In fact it was about the turn of 1850–51 that British exports "began to exhibit the influence of the large consumption in California."[2] Nine months later came the Australian news, which worked much more quickly. Meanwhile, shipment to California from all quarters had been for the time overdone, so that in the middle of 1851 "all new supplies of goods were wholly unsaleable"[3] there. Cotton and colonial produce were abundant, and the year closed with prices low and the Bank of England rate of discount about to fall from 3 per cent. to $2\frac{1}{2}$ per cent.

In the course of 1852, while prices were rising steadily and freights to Australia precipitately, for nearly nine months the Bank rate stood at 2 per cent. Yet employment was very good

[1] The U.S.A. received 114,000 foreign immigrants in 1845. There was a steady rise to 1851: a halt for two years: a rise to 428,000 in 1854: then a fall to a minimum of 89,000 in 1863. *Final Report of the Industrial Commission*, 1902, p. 958.

[2] Tooke and Newmarch, v. 258.

[3] *Ibid.* v. 261.

and wages began to follow prices—first, most naturally, among the shipwrights. The rate of discount was low in spite of trade activity because America, once more an avid purchaser of all kinds of goods, was paying in gold, and the Australian gold was beginning to arrive, so that the Bank in July, 1852, held £22,000,000 of bullion; more than it had ever held before. It held only a few hundred thousand pounds less in December.

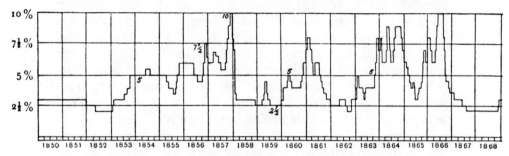

Bank of England minimum Rate of Discount, 1850-68.

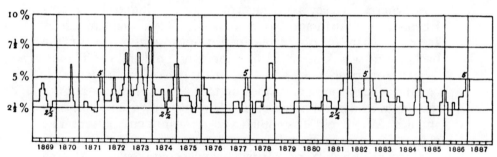

Bank of England minimum Rate of Discount, 1869-86.

"Many political economists even talked of a future time when ...the ordinary ornaments and utensils would be of the most massive auriferous manufacture"[1]; and less foolish people supposed that the rate of interest was permanently down. Old loan contracts were revised and new ones made on very easy terms. The banking world reflected with satisfaction that at least there would never be another gold panic[2].

It is easy to develop the earth with capital at 2 per cent. The men of the early 'fifties set about it. In 1852 Thomas

---

[1] Evans, D. M., *The History of the Commercial Crisis*, 1857-8, p. 9: the political economists are not specified.

[2] Evans, *op. cit.* p. 9 n.

Brassey, who had only averaged one small foreign railway contract a year since 1847, had taken five, including 113 miles of
the Nantes and Caen and 539 miles of the Grand Trunk of
Canada. In 1853–4 he took seven more, though not so large[1].
In France the Saint Simonians had made a religion of earth
development, a religion of which the new Emperor approved.
They were dreaming of the Suez Canal; making the P.L.M.;
founding the Lyons gas and water works[2]. In 1852 appeared
the two great companies for the development and encouragement of everything, the *Crédit foncier* and the *Crédit mobilier*.
Money was to be lent on the security of land; state loans were
to be underwritten; railways financed; ports developed; gas
companies created; Paris rebuilt—the whole nation helped and
stimulated and inflated. In 1853 the Darmstadt Bank for Trade
and Industry was founded to do in Germany all that the *Crédit
mobilier* was to do in France, and more[3]. Soon there was hardly
a state, however small, in the old German patchwork which had
not its credit bank. Nations borrowed. Railways were a-making
everywhere. Brassey's contracts of 1852–3 included the Dutch-
Rhenish, the Turin and Novara, and the Royal Danish. These
are only a handful of samples of European enterprise. In the
background was America, full of men and gold and confidence.

The American gold and the Australian which followed it
could not keep the Bank's stock up to the level of 1852—nor did
the Bank, a business house after all, in any way desire that they
should. Much gold was coined and went into circulation. The
circulation increased at least 50 per cent. between 1844 and
1856, mainly after 1850[4]. British exports contained a large proportion of capital goods, and another large proportion of goods
—for the Australian markets and the like—which, although not
capital goods, were necessarily sold at such long usance that
the returns for them were hardly in sight. For the time being
they were lent without return, like the railway metal and the
locomotives for lines whose capital was held in Britain. There
were also cash calls in London on foreign railway and government securities, much as in 1846[5]. Moreover, throughout 1852,
while the Bank of England rate was at 2 per cent., that of the

[1] See the table of his contracts in Jenks, *op. cit.* App. A, quoted above, p. 237.
[2] Cp. Levasseur, E., *Histoire des classes ouvrières et d'industrie en France de
1789 à 1870*, II. 48c and Clapham, J. H., *The Economic Development of France
and Germany*, p. 383 *sqq.*
[3] Wirth, *op. cit.* p. 285 *sqq.*
[4] Tooke and Newmarch, VI. 699, 701.       [5] Vol. I. p. 529.

Bank of France, which had gone back to cash payments only in August, 1850, was 3 per cent. Possibly some fluid international capital left London for Paris, and some which might have gone to London may have gone to Paris direct[1]. French historians have claimed that London gave way to Paris as a capital market at this time[2]. English historians would recognise at least a period of dual control.

Working together, these forces tugged at the gold in the Bank from December, 1852. The Bank put its rate up twice in January, 1853—prematurely, as its critics and the public thought[3] —again in June and once again on September 1, when it was known that the harvest had failed. Wheat prices were running up, to touch 80s. at Christmas. A winter of abnormal food imports threatened. So at the end of September the rate was raised once more. Even then it was only 5 per cent. As £2,600,000 of gold came from Australia in October and November, it stayed there[4]; although Turkey and Russia went to war and corn trade with the Black Sea stopped. If corn buying in America were to reverse the Atlantic flow of gold, as it might, there was now always the flow coming up from the far South. True the Bank had only £15,000,000 worth at the end of 1853; but down to 1851 it had never had more.

In March, 1854, war with Russia began. In the money market there was scarcely any disturbance. It was local war, not high seas war, like the old wars with the French. The gold flowed up easily from the South[5]. War reduced supplies of some important raw materials; helped to keep corn dear for two years; required remittances of treasure to the Near East and stimulated war industries at the expense of others. These things apart, what economic discomfort coincided with it was due mainly to other causes, such as the overbuilding of ships, a bad harvest in 1855, and temporary checks to the course of American prosperity; although heavy war remittances, coinciding with the failed harvest of 1855, kept the Bank rate particularly high

[1] This is uncertain. A difference of as little as 1 per cent. was not at that time sufficient to move capital in the form of bills. The argument which demonstrates this is probably best known from Goschen's *Theory of the Foreign Exchanges* (1865); but it is clearly set out, like so much else, in Tooke and Newmarch, v. 313. It is there argued that though even a difference of 2 per cent. would not move bills, it would "pretty certainly" divert investment.

[2] *E.g.* Levasseur, *op. cit.* II. 483.

[3] Tooke blamed it for keeping so long at 2 per cent. and then moving so fast (v. 280); but then he generally blamed it.

[4] Tooke and Newmarch, v. 299.          [5] Much of it *via* Egypt.

during the last months of the war (October, 1855–May, 1856). Even then, however, it was argued, and probably with truth[1], that the main cause of the stringency was not pressure of military necessity but the blunder of the Bank in reducing its rate to $3\frac{1}{2}$ per cent. in the previous June, when its vaults happened to be full, instead of keeping them full to meet the emergencies of an unfinished war.

Economically speaking, the country slipped out of war in 1856 as easily and smoothly as it had slipped into it in 1854. "In the import markets," Newmarch wrote about the end of the year, "there has been a quiet and steady business; in the Manufacturing Districts, a fair share of prosperity, but entirely free from excitement or speculation."[2] He and his aged partner Tooke, "already turned of fourscore,"[3] were satisfied that the high rate of discount which had ruled since 1853—the Bank rate, after a drop in the summer, jerked up to 6 and $7\frac{1}{2}$ per cent. in October–November, 1856—was "to be traced, in its origin and continuance, to extended demands for capital for the purpose of new, distant, and costly enterprises."[4] Resolute critics of the Bank Act, they registered with satisfaction that for nine years prices had either changed abruptly while the note circulation had been constant, or had gone down when notes went up and up when notes went down. They were convinced that, but for the new gold, the Act of 1844 could not have remained unbroken through the war; and that even the Act of 1819 might have been in danger[5].

From the heart of the money market the directing partner of Overend and Gurney supported them. "We have had an extraordinary amount of bullion arriving from Australia," he said in 1857, "and even from America, entirely beyond all

[1] Tooke and Newmarch, v. 318: compare the bullion figures in VI. 557, £18,360,000 in June, 1855, and £10,430,000 in January, 1856.

[2] v. 337.

[3] v. p. ix in the Preface dated February, 1857. From this time forward the historian loses Tooke's sound sense, economic insight, and exact knowledge of monetary and commercial affairs. Very little has been written in any language about those aspects of economic history on which he and Newmarch were specialists which does not come, directly or indirectly, from them. The preceding pages are no exception.

[4] v. 345.

[5] See Newmarch's evidence before the S.C. on the Bank Acts, 1857, Q. 1423 sqq. and the relevant passages in the History. Cp. an able letter from 'A Banker' in the Economist of February 21, 1857, who argued that loans and discounts might go down when circulation went up because the main users of bank notes had no bank accounts.

calculation, coming from the bowels of the earth, which has kept us alive during this extraordinary demand upon us for bullion for war and other purposes. We have looked to the arrival of these steamers from Australia as much almost as to anything else, to know whether we were safe in going on with our business."[1]

This was said in evidence before a Committee on the Bank Acts in June, 1857. Mill and Newmarch condemned them. Lord Overstone and G. W. Norman defended them. An aged representative of the Birmingham School, who recalled 1797 perfectly, attended to advocate plenty of money and a currency divorced from gold and silver[2]. The Governor of the Bank explained the working of the Bank rate and within what limits it could influence market rates and the exchanges. He also reported that since January 1, 1851, £109,500,000 of gold and £25,800,000 of silver had been brought into the country from the places of origin, and that £139,900,000 worth of treasure had been exported, taken into circulation, or consumed in industry[3]. He noted the result, that whereas the Bank's metallic reserve had averaged £15,000,000 in 1851 it had latterly been about £10,500,000, but he did not stress the associated risks in relation to a much expanded trade. Yet he and his colleagues were aware of them. All the year they were guarding their reserves with high rates—$5\frac{1}{2}$, 6 and $6\frac{1}{2}$ per cent.—and were refusing to discount long-dated bills[4]. India had been on fire since March. Delhi was not taken until September 20; but the British harvest was good and there was no reason whatever, at the beginning of September, to anticipate acute financial distress. At that time the Bank was negotiating with the East India Company for the shipment of £1,000,000 in silver to the East[5]. It did not carry silver to that amount, and for years had been in the habit of buying it for Eastern remittance with gold. Paris was the best market; for the bimetallic currencies had been filling up with gold and ejecting silver so freely that in the eight years from 1850 to 1857 Europe sent East some £57,000,000 of silver,

---

[1] Chapman, before the same Committee, Q. 5310.

[2] John Twells, of Spooner, Attwoods and Co., Q. 4366 *sqq.* Let merchants find gold and silver when foreigners want them, he said. We did very well without metal for twenty years and he supposed we could again. Cp. vol. I. p. 311, 535, and Keynes, J. M., *A Tract on Monetary Reform* (1923).

[3] Evidence of T. M. Wegeulin, Q. 15 and *passim.*

[4] And were warmly commended for so doing by the *Economist*, April 4, 1857.

[5] Evans, *The History of the Commercial Crisis*, p. 63.

nearly twice as much as she received from the producing countries[1]. This particular contract was only a small item in the great account.

It had barely been made when bad news began to come from America, on September 15. In the year 1856 more than a fifth of the British exports had gone to the United States. Of foreign government securities ordinarily listed one-third were American. "Some persons estimated" the British holdings of American stocks and bonds at £80,000,000[2]. Liverpool and Glasgow were especially sensitive to any slight tremor from the other side. Now there came a jarring shock. American railway securities began to fall. A big Trust Company in Ohio collapsed. Banks first suspended payment in Philadelphia and Baltimore. Soon 62 out of 63 in New York followed. Railways pushing out into the West, which was Illinois in those days, went bankrupt; "and discounts ranged from 18 to 24 per cent."[3] For a time business all but stopped in the three Eastern gateways of the United States.

By October 27 the Borough Bank of Liverpool and two or three large Scottish mercantile houses were down. On November 7 Dennistoun & Co. of Liverpool, Glasgow, New York, and New Orleans, "American bankers and exchange brokers," failed for over £2,000,000. A few days later a London bill-broking house failed for more than £5,000,000. The Western Bank of Scotland broke on the 9th. The City of Glasgow Bank suspended payment on the 11th[4]. Next day, when, as the Governor said, discounts "had almost entirely ceased in London except at the Bank of England,"[5] the Chancellor of the Exchequer, following the precedent of ten years earlier, authorised the Bank to break Peel's Act if necessary. This was to enable it to discount freely, to support anxious banks or bill-brokers, and to carry out its bullion contract with the East India Company, which had begun to ship the silver about October 31. So long as it issued more notes than the Act allowed, the Bank was not to discount below 10 per cent.

In the week before the letter was sent the Bank had poured

---

[1] The figures, as known at the time, are in the *Report* of 1858, § 2.

[2] *Report*, § 15.

[3] Dewey, E. R., *Financial History of the United States* (1903), p. 263.

[4] The story of failures here given comes from Evans, *op. cit.*, a contemporary account written from Birchin Lane, Lombard Street, in 1859. Dennistoun's eventually paid in full: the City of Glasgow Bank resumed payment.

[5] Quoted in the *Report* of 1858, § 17.

more than £1,000,000 of gold coin into Scotland, where conditions were panicky; and £250,000 into Ireland[1]. The small savings-account depositors of the Glasgow banks wanted gold, not the famous Scottish notes. "These people who came for money would not take the notes of any bank," a Scottish director said[2]. Although the Bank had been moving up its discount rate steadily, and with great judgment as capable critics allowed[3], and had already pushed it to 10 per cent. by November 9, the paralysis of private discounting and this gold drain from the uneasy North forced it to use its extra-legal powers. (The stolid English shires, whose harvests had been good, were actually sending gold to London[4].) But for the drain to Scotland on November 9–11, the Directors thought, they might have got through legally. As it was, at night on the 12th, though there was still over £5,000,000 of gold in the issue department, their banking reserve was only £581,000. Their next return showed that they had fed it in the interval with £2,000,000 of extra-legal notes[5]. But "these steamers from Australia," and the high rate of discount which kept capital in London, soon helped the bill-brokers to resume their interrupted business. "It is expected," the *Economist* reported on November 21, "that by far the larger proportion of the £525,000 brought by the steamer *Australasian* from Alexandria will be sent into the Bank in a day or two." Gold also came back from Scotland. On Christmas Eve the Bank reported a stock of over £10,000,000 in the Issue Department; dropped its discount rate from 10 to 8 per cent.; thereby automatically cancelled its extra-legal powers of issue, and registered the end of the gold crisis. That crisis had been essentially internal. "With a foreign drain we have learnt by experience efficiently to cope," as Disraeli said in the House[6]. The Bank had been coping with it, or with the risk of it, in the approved way when the clamour of Glasgow spoiled its operation.

---

[1] *Report*, § 27.    [2] Quoted in *Report*, § 33.
[3] *Economist*, November 14, 1857.
[4] Evidence of W. Rodwell of Ipswich before the *S.C. of* 1857–8, Q. 1604. 'All' country banks were sending, or were ready to send, gold to London. He knew of no case of the reverse process.
[5] Of which less than £1,000,000 went into circulation. As the banking reserve of notes and coin stood at £1,553,000 on November 18 it could be argued that the "actual infringement was less than half-a-million" (*Economist*, November 21), *i.e.* much less than the gold sent to Scotland.
[6] December 4, 1857. *Hansard, Third Series*, CXLVIII. 159.

The business crisis was less easily passed, though its acute phase was short. There had been two important bank failures outside Liverpool and Glasgow—iron-country failures, at Newcastle and Wolverhampton. Apart from the merchants, the iron industry with its American connections showed most wreckage. Industry as a whole escaped lightly. Among the broken merchants, very many were described as in the German or North European trades[1]. The catastrophe had been worldwide, and Britain was among the least sufferers. Hamburg, which linked Northern Europe to America and England, and made heavy use of the bill on London, was among the greatest. "All transactions," in that community of merchants, "abruptly stopped and a complete dissolution of society threatened."[2] Every Northern and Central European business centre was affected, even so far East as Austria and Poland. The troubles had come, as Disraeli put it with his customary incision, "not from the mismanagement of the currency of this country, but from the mismanagement of the capital of Europe."[3] All the bubbles, blunders and dishonesties of five years' European exuberance and experiments in credit were tested or revealed.

In Britain, inquiry uncovered rather more than the usual proportion of common fraud, and the usual high proportion of stupidity—fictitious bills, "false reports and manufactured dividends,"[4] mixed up with credulous advances by banks to firms of doubtful stability, and the naïve belief of the self-making man that rising prices and expanding trade will put everything right on the day. It was noticed that, as compared with 1847, there were fewer failures of houses of good repute[5]. Almost everywhere the immediate cause of trouble was some stoppage in anticipated remittances from America. These remittances might be due for goods actually shipped, or they might be due under the system of open credits, by which British 'foreign banking' firms allowed themselves to be drawn upon to specified amounts by American, and other, correspondents, trusting that they would be put in funds by the correspondent before the liability incurred on his behalf matured. With banks shut all down the Atlantic coast, the most honourable American cor-

[1] There are complete lists in Evans, p. 180 sqq.
[2] Wirth, op. cit. p. 390.
[3] In his speech of December 4 quoted above.
[4] Evans, p. 47 n.: applies to the Western Bank of Scotland, the Liverpool Borough Bank, and the Northumberland and Durham District Bank.
[5] Report, § 35.

respondent might fail to remit. The use of these open credits, this international accommodation paper, not based like the old trade bill on actual mercantile transactions, was harshly criticised. Some people called it a novelty; but the Governor of the Bank of England rightly said that it was "not a new thing at all."[1] Presumably there has been some 'accommodation paper' ever since there has been 'paper.' Its use by solid and honourable firms who know one another's position is unexceptionable, and it oils the wheels of trade. It is also the familiar instrument of fraudulent 'kite-flyers.' There is evidence for a considerable extension of its use, especially in the North European trade, just before 1857. That was natural in those years of quickened communication and experiments with credit. It was also natural that the experimenters should not always be the solid folk, and would contain a full share of the rogues. Into which class should be placed a Newcastle firm that, starting with £2-3000 in 1854, failed for £100,000 of foreign credits in 1857 is uncertain[2]. At least its career illustrates the defects of the system. The old experienced merchant bankers of London who thoroughly understood the business, as the Governor knew, came through without disaster, if not untouched.

The trouble in Britain was due mainly, apart from fraud and crude incompetence, to the general reluctance to keep even small tanks of capital stagnant. Everybody wanted it to circulate and fructify the ground. They trusted to their regular or emergency feed-pipes—bankers to depositors and the Bank; bill-brokers to bankers, depositors and the Bank; acceptors on open credit to those sanguine and prosperous Americans, or to someone in Northern Europe. Blocks in the feed-pipes had produced a brief unpleasant drought. The Bank at once tried to force the brokers to keep fuller tanks by stopping discount for them altogether[3]. It would make quarterly advances to them, at the regularly recurring times when tax and government dividend money was off the market and in the Bank; but for the rest they must take care of themselves.

The sanguine Americans were justified in 1857-8[4]. All their

[1] *S.C. of* 1857-8, Q. 1690 (T. M. Wegeulin). In spite of his evidence, the *Report*, § 40, states boldly that "this practice appears to have grown up of late and to be principally connected with...the North of Europe." The evidence as a whole bears out the statements in the text—*e.g.* John Ball's, Q. 1663 *sqq.*; and Wegeulin's.

[2] Described in the *Report*, § 40.

[3] *S.C. of* 1857-8, Q. 616-18, 688.   [4] See *Economist*, January 2 and 30, 1858.

banks except those of Pennsylvania had resumed payment by the new year. The most important British firms in the American trade which had stopped were able ultimately to pay in full. Early in January, Paris and Hamburg were discounting at 5 per cent.; London at 4 per cent. before the end of the month. On January 27 the Bank had £15,000,000 of bullion; "half a million was overdue from Australia"; and America was again shipping gold. "There was never a more severe crisis nor a more rapid recovery."[1] The deep permanent springs of the world's wealth were intact. The gold which fascinated men into widening their outlets and clearing their channels remained abundant; and Britain's sustained exports of capital were increasing her claims on them yearly.

Yet the complete recovery of trade and industry, as opposed to the recovery from the acute phase of the crisis, was slow. For two years, except for a month in 1859 when there was a scare on the Stock Exchange[2], Bank rate was at 3 per cent. or less. Only at the very end of 1860, when South Carolina had already seceded from the Union, did it rise above 5 per cent. for the first time since 1857. In leading articles with titles such as *When will trade revive?* expert journalists had explained in 1858 that the business world could not be expected to recover its tone all at once[3]. Europe had been very badly shaken. British exports to America in 1858 were lower than they had been in any of the previous four years. As partial compensation, exports to India in 1858 were more than twice what they had been in 1853. The construction of the Indian railways, pressed forward for reasons of high policy after 1857, was absorbing capital goods and would open new territory to trade. On the other hand, Europe, though shaken, was now following hard after Britain on the tracks of industry and economic enterprise. She could do more of her own railway promotion and contracting, and was less dependent on the island for capital goods.

There was war in Europe in 1859. The rise in the Bank rate at the close of 1860 was due not to trade activity, nor to a failed harvest—harvests since 1857 had been good or fair—but to fear of war in America. When Mississippi, Florida, Alabama, Georgia, Louisiana and Texas—all cotton states—seceded in

---

[1] *Economist*, January 30.

[2] Described in Evans, *op. cit.* p. 148 *sqq.*; and see the *Economist*, April–May, 1859.

[3] *Economist*, January 5, 1858.

January, 1861, it rose for a time to 8 per cent. Gold was being taken out to buy silver for India; and India's claim on silver was said to be due to "wild orders"[1] for cotton, from men who in imagination saw the American supply cut off. It was not in fact cut off until much later. Anglo-American trade in 1861 showed a large increase in the American export of goods, sold eagerly by Americans while there was still time, and such a fall of British exports to America that gold moved West instead of East[2]. But as home trade was slack, Europe restless, and the Indian and other trades not active enough to counteract these deadening forces, the gold movement was easily arranged and the Bank rate was dropping during all the latter part of the year. It remained very low all through 1862. Mainly because of the check to Anglo-American intercourse, the years 1861–2 yielded the only horizontal section of the mounting curve of the aggregate import and export trades of the United Kingdom between 1850 and 1884[3]. The low Bank rate registers the same fact on a different scale. Between 1862 and the surrender of Lee at Appomattox on April 9, 1865, although Anglo-American trade as a whole did not improve, England was finding elsewhere outlets and sources of supply sufficient to enable her trade curve to resume its steep upward course—the French treaty of 1860 and its successors helping[4].

Apart from the cotton industry, with its principal source of supply closed, and silk, at last obliged to face French competition naked, 1863 was a very good year for British manufacturers and an excellent one for merchants, financiers, and company promoters[5]. In industry, much of what Lancashire and Glasgow lost, Yorkshire and Dundee gained. The heavy trades were particularly active. There had been good harvests and bread was cheap. A money market flurry at the close of the year only illustrated the growing efficiency and speed of control in London and Paris. There had been heavy cotton buying in India, Egypt and Brazil. Bullion was wanted for all three. The Bank of England pushed up its rate far and fast, once before and once after Christmas. The Bank of France did the

---

[1] *Economist*, February 9, 1861.

[2] Cp. Chapman, S. J., *The History of Trade between the United Kingdom and the United States* (1899), ch. 4.

[3] The curve referred to is not the crude curve, but the curve reduced by index-numbers to the values of 1889, given in Bowley, A. L., *England's Foreign Trade in the Nineteenth Century*.

[4] See above, p. 244, 247.     [5] See the *Economist's* Review of the Year.

same. "The scarcity rates of 7 and 8 per cent. had the effect of drawing to these cities in a very short time large amounts of capital from Germany, Holland and other places where the cotton pressure was not felt,"[1] so that the rates could be reduced as promptly as they had been raised.

Of really low rates in 1864 there was no question. Although America was now sending much treasure—from the Golden Gate to England direct, as more convenient in war time[2]—and Australia always sent it, the various demands easily carried off the supply. Wholesale prices for the year were a little higher even than they had been in 1857; and early in the year they were much higher, in spite of ample harvests in 1863. Bankers had to support a very vigorous home and foreign trade. Bills were many and discounting active. The new finance companies were making a sometimes experimental use of British capital abroad[3]. Other new companies readily absorbed any surplus funds available. There was less money than usual left on deposit for bankers to handle. Every now and then some drain, or anticipated drain, of bullion to one of the war-time sources of cotton supply, or some market excitement with which cotton was sure to be connected, drove up the Bank rate from the year's base, of about 6, to 8 or 9 per cent.[4] During the last of these spells of dear money, in September and October, a downward trend in prices and business was noticeable. The cotton market was beginning to discount the impending defeat of the South[5] and activity was slackening in other fields.

After so exhausting a war, and before the Atlantic cable was laid, peace in the United States could not at once restore Anglo-American trade. British exports to America were indeed nearly five millions less in the first eight months of 1865 than in the corresponding period of 1864. Europe was politically restless. Bismarck was sparring for position with Austria. There was an election due in England about midsummer. The slackening of business which began in the autumn of 1864

---

[1] *Economist's* Review of the Year, p. 2.

[2] £5,700,000 came that way in 1863 and £6,900,000 in 1864. *Economist*, April 26, 1865.

[3] Above, p. 358.

[4] According to the *Economist* (May 19, 1866) "but for admirable management" the international bullion drains would have caused a panic in 1864. The steady inflow of treasure must have greatly aided free and confident management by the Bank.

[5] Cp. *Economist*, April 22, 1865, on the fall of Richmond (Va).

continued. The Bank rate dropped steadily in nine months from 9 to 3 per cent. Then suddenly, in September, British exports leapt up by what was at that date the very remarkable figure of over £3,000,000 in a month. The delayed United States demand was beginning to tell; and there were others. The rise continued through the winter, and Bank rate went with it. During the first four months of 1866, the United Kingdom actually exported 30 per cent. more in value than during the corresponding months of 1865, though the price level was much the same. At the end of April, the period of rather dear money naturally resulting from this expansion of business, gave way to actual stringency. "The best informed people" felt no doubt that treasure was being withdrawn from London by "the foreign governments now preparing for war."[1] Stringency was followed by panic; by 10 per cent., the classical panic rate; and by a Chancellor's letter authorising a breach of the Bank Act. Overend and Gurney Limited had failed on Friday, May 11th, for over five millions. Exactly a month later the "foreign governments" began their war.

There was little that was international about the crisis, except some of its consequences. In spite of the preoccupation of the continental capitals with war risks, the rate of discount on May 10th was only 4 per cent. in Paris, 5 per cent. in Vienna, 6 per cent. in Turin, and 7 per cent. in Berlin[2]. There was no fresh gold drain of importance; nothing revolutionary in the course of trade; no abnormal locking up of capital in distant enterprises. It was a panic in every sense, and it was purely British. Those in the City who knew had long ceased to believe in Overends. Walter Bagehot had thought their failure possible "any time these three months."[3] When they became a limited company, in 1865, he had welcomed the change sardonically because now it would be "essential to publish an account of the nature of their business."[4] Everyone knew that its nature had changed since 1857. In 1860 the firm had been strong enough to try a fall with the Bank of England; but it had been beaten. It had withdrawn a huge deposit at an inconvenient

[1] *Economist*, May 5, 1866.

[2] Wirth, *op. cit.* p. 424. Those who recall August, 1914, and know the diplomatic history of 1866, may find these rates significant—highest in the capital where war was being most consciously planned.

[3] *Economist*, May 12, 1866 (assuming, as one safely may, that Bagehot wrote the article). Cp. Charles Oppenheim's letter to the *Economist* of December 22, 1866.                    [4] *Economist*, July 15, 1865.

time as a fighting protest against the Bank's policy of not discounting for the bill-brokers—and it had put the deposit back again. "The Bank of England could not afford to be frightened"[1]; and it was not. The Overends of the 'sixties handled many things besides fine trade bills—finance paper of the more doubtful kinds, and what were known as the 'finance securities' of railway promoters and great contractors. These were bonds, debentures, and what not, issued by the directors-to-be to the contractor before the public had subscribed, and turned by him into cash, often on very onerous terms[2]. The inner city knew or suspected all this. To the outer city, and the country, the name of Overends was still a symbol of credit, and when it was blown upon you could trust nobody. Besides Overends the Bank of London went down and, fitly enough, Sir Samuel Peto's great contracting firm, known all over Europe and much of America for its daring promotions[3]. There was a winnowing out of light stock-joint enterprises of all sorts. Up to August 4th the wind had carried away a hundred and eighty of them[4].

At no stage had the Bank been seriously short of bullion. The trouble had been with the banking reserve of notes and coin: though the Governors managed to see the crisis through without feeding the reserve with extra-legal notes. Yet, in the general collapse of credit, Bank notes were in great demand. Even in July the number in circulation was nearly £6,000,000 above normal. Foreigners, supposing the catastrophe worse than it was, withdrew some capital from London. There was war on the continent. Early in July the banking reserve ran low a second time. As a result of all this, Bank rate remained at 10 per cent. for no less than three months—in fact, until peace between Prussia and Austria was certain[5].

---

[1] *Economist*, May 21, 1860. The *Economist* of the 'sixties and 'seventies, under Bagehot (1860–77) was so well informed and well written that it will always remain a chief authority for these years. A better cannot be found; and there was no Select Committee and Report in 1866 as in 1857–8.

[2] See the full account of this class of 'security,' which had become common "in the last few years" in the *Economist* of April 28, 1866 (before the crisis) in connection with failures of well-known contractors and the revelation of their methods.

[3] Cp. vol. I. p. 408–12 and the *D.N.B.*

[4] Wirth, *op. cit.* p. 431–2, a good account on the whole, based mainly on the *Economist*.

[5] The gold in the Issue Department never got really low, *i.e.* there was no serious foreign drain. It had been £12,000,000 on January 10. It was £11,300,000 on May 23, its lowest point. It touched £14,200,000 on June 27; was at £12,700,000 on August 8; and then rose again.

Given the circumstances, there would have been a panic under any banking law. Peel's Act and the doubts about its suspension increased the panic at home. Suspension, when it came, gave an exaggerated importance to the panic abroad. "The French fancy we have suspended cash payments," Bagehot wrote on the 19th of May[1]. Their fancies had probably not been calmed by the diplomatic circular of May 12, in which Lord Clarendon explained to all our representatives at foreign courts that the ordinary business of Britain was really quite sound[2]. Much trouble would unquestionably have been saved had Peel's Act contained what Bagehot called an "expansive clause," that is a clause providing for, and safeguarding, excess emergency issues without the terrifying incursion of a Chancellor's letter. If such a clause is not inserted, Bagehot wrote, "the Act will be repealed soon."[3] He was wrong. There was not even an official inquiry into the crisis[4]. As for the Act it survived, without any expansive clause, to be suspended in August, 1914.

It survived so long partly because there was never 'ten per cent.' again until 1914. Once the rate began falling, in August, 1866, it did not stop until it reached 2 per cent. in the following July. There it remained for fifteen months. Commerce recovered slowly from the shock of 1866. Owing to a run of bad harvests, bread in London in 1867 was almost 50 per cent. dearer than it had been in 1864, and it did not begin to fall until the middle of 1868[5]. Dear bread meant a sluggish home trade in 1867–8. In spite of high corn prices, the general course of wholesale prices, including the corn, was downward from 1866 to 1870, which suggests an inactive overseas trade[6]. In fact, although overseas trade grew absolutely, per head of the population it was stationary. By 1869, corn and bread were again cheap, and the start of a spell of furious railway building in America suggested that trade activity in Britain might come in again, as so often before, on an Atlantic wind. The raised basic level of the rate of discount in 1869–70, as compared with

[1] In the *Economist*.
[2] It was printed in all the papers and is translated in Wirth, *op. cit.* p. 434–5. The diplomatic mind naturally assumed that our business was unsound and that we were trying to conceal the fact.
[3] *Economist*, May 19.
[4] Though there was a motion for a Royal Commission on July 31 (*Hansard, Third Series*, CLXXXIV. 1706) moved by Mr Watkin. The Ministry had changed since May. Both Northcote and Gladstone, the in and the out, argued that inquiry would do no good.
[5] See the diagram, p. 460.          [6] See the diagram, p. 378.

1867–8, registers a growing activity. The omens had suggested quick growth in 1870. Lancashire was busy in January. By May trade revival was "general and marked."[1] But Bismarck and Napoleon, France and what would soon be Germany, willed that the later months of 1870 should be anxious and unprofitable; the early months of 1871 more anxious still.

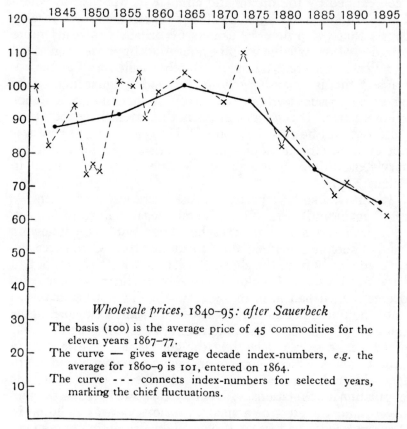

*Wholesale prices, 1840–95: after Sauerbeck*

The basis (100) is the average price of 45 commodities for the eleven years 1867–77.

The curve — gives average decade index-numbers, *e.g.* the average for 1860–9 is 101, entered on 1864.

The curve - - - connects index-numbers for selected years, marking the chief fluctuations.

How strong the economic and financial position of Britain was, and—as some might say—how sluggish her imagination, is suggested by the stability of the Bank rate while war was in the making and British neutrality, as it appeared for a time, in the balance[2]. 'Six per cent.' came only after the armies had clashed on the frontiers. It did not stay long. With Sedan the

[1] *Economist*, February 5, and May 14, 1870.

[2] Over the question of Belgium, it will be recalled. Cp. Morley's *Gladstone*, book VI, ch. 5. Gladstone was facing the possibility of having to send "12,000 or 20,000" men to Antwerp.

end seemed already in sight. The British people were doing what one of their ablest diplomatists had hoped they might do to the last in 1791—looking "at the French story like spectators in a theatre."[1] The play grew pitiful, tragic, ominous, with the terrors of the siege and the Commune. When every value seemed uncertain in the smoke hanging over Paris, the spectators held their breath. Their money did not stir. 'Two and a half per cent.'[2] Then effective peace; for the Communards, New Caledonia; for their countrymen at home, the toil and achievement of an unbelievable recovery; for Germany, the spending of France's milliards and confidence without limits, a confidence which spread among, and beyond, her German-speaking neighbours. Unlimited confidence and immense achievement in America also. Between Europe and America, Britain; cooler than any and more experienced in the treatment of economic fevers—in controlled excitement; making; lending; banking and carrying for the world; profiting by the free trade which she had taught, and which so many nations now seemed to have at least half learnt. Her wholesale prices rose some 20 per cent. between the middle of 1871 and the middle of 1873; the prices of many of her capital goods vastly more. Her overseas trade curve climbed precipitately. Her wages were very high and her bread reasonably cheap.

Excitement, control, and the pressure of trade on liquid capital resources are all to be read in the Bank rate chart for 1871–3, with its mounting basic level and its succession of steep-sided summits overtopping each other[3]. That the last summit is 9 and not 10 per cent. means that, by the experience which she had bought, by good management and perhaps some good fortune, Britain escaped the extreme phases of crisis and panic through which most trading and industrial nations had to pass in 1873. (But she was left with a deferred liability to be met in 1878[4].) No wonder that men who understood the forces

---

[1] *Cambridge History of British Foreign Policy*, I. 206. (Lord Auckland to his brother.)

[2] The rate was 2½ per cent. when Paris surrendered. It rose to 3 per cent. in March when the financing of an indemnity was anticipated, but fell again to 2½ per cent. during the Commune. "From the long suspense which has prevailed, and which has checked new undertakings of every kind, there has perhaps never been a greater accumulation of money in Lombard Street." *Economist*, April 15, 1871. As peace was not signed until May 18, and arrangements for the indemnity loan were finished in July, the accumulation remained: Bank rate was 2 per cent. in July. By October 11 it was 5 per cent.

[3] Above, p. 363.　　　　　　　　[4] Below, p. 383–4.

playing on Lombard Street from all the world, in these turbulent years, were oppressed with the responsibilities of those in charge of its ultimate reserves.

In the German lands and their neighbours 1872 was the great year of company promotion[1]—for railways, banks, building societies, credit institutions, public utilities, and all sorts of industry, especially blast-furnaces, iron works, and engineering works. There was furious land speculation in Berlin, growing like a Chicago and for a time the dearest town in Europe. Vienna too was developing, and completing her education in modern business methods and practices: there were thirteen Princes, one Landgraf, and sixty-four Counts on the boards of the Austro-Hungarian railways by 1873[2]. Paris had rebuilding to do, but the French were in sober mood. They had little capital to spare for that imaginative enterprise in which they had led Europe twenty years earlier. In 1872, although they raised more money for public loans and joint-stock business than any people in the world, they appear to have put less into joint-stock business alone even than the Italians[3]. France had claimed their money and French enterprises must wait. This saved them from the worst of the trouble when it came.

America was in a position from which it was not easy to escape without damage and discredit. She had a post-war depreciated currency; she was opening up half a continent, with furious energy; in spite of her disordered currency, she was becoming the world's greatest producer both of gold and silver; and she was also the world's greatest debtor nation, having borrowed both to develop and to fight. In 1868, when 100 dollars currency were worth only 71·5 dollars gold[4], the Treasury was in the habit of selling by auction the gold it got from import duties, which were payable in coin only, under a war-time law. New York's Black Friday, September 23, 1869, was the destructive local crisis resulting from the attempt of Jay Gould

---

[1] The best contemporary account of all the antecedents of the crisis of 1873 is in Wirth, *op. cit.* p. 450–614. Modern accounts for Germany are in Sartorius von Waltershausen, *Deutsche Wirtschaftsgeschichte, 1815–1914* (1920), p. 261–81, and the books there referred to. A general sketch in Juglar, C., *Des crises commerciales* (1889), p. 390 *sqq.*

[2] Wirth, *op. cit.* p. 491.

[3] Tables published in the *Moniteur des Intérêts matériels* quoted in Wirth, *op. cit.* p. 469.

[4] Dewey, *Financial History of the U.S.A.* p. 376; Dewey also gives a good general sketch of the American situation.

and James Fisk to take advantage of this interesting arrangement by cornering the free gold and inducing the Treasury to
limit sales. After 1869 the currency position improved; by
1872, 100 dollars currency were worth 89·4 dollars gold, and
resumption seemed near. But if America got into financial
trouble, there were sure to be voices raised—of greenbackers,
cousins to the Birmingham school—who would look to plenty
of paper money for a cure.

The construction of 6167 miles of railway in the United
States during 1872 brought the figure for four years up to
25,000 miles[1]. Naturally the iron industry was inflated, with
many others. Yet America had never bought foreign manufactures so heavily; and she bought mainly in Britain. She had
now to find large sums to pay for carrying services which before
the war she had performed for herself; and there was already
a great deal of American money being spent by travellers and
residents in Europe. She had paid her adverse balance of indebtedness partly with gold, but very largely with promises—
bonds, national, state, and railway. The position was delicate
and for her European creditors and clients dangerous. She
might easily be forced to curtail her imports. Bankruptcy, if
only of a few railways, would help to adjust her balance of
indebtedness. It might come without being designed by anyone[2].

It was hard that Austria, turned out of Germany by Prussia
in 1866, should have been the first to suffer when what might
justly, if vulgarly, be called the Prussian boom of 1871–3
collapsed. But it was so. Austria's 'Krach' came early in May.
"For the first time," an Austrian who went through it recorded
with a certain sombre pride, she suffered from this "aristocratic
complaint of civilised states...and therewith in some sort paid
her entry fee" into their circle[3]. Her sufferings, which did not
very nearly concern Britain, but had repercussions through all
Germany, have left their mark on the Bank rate chart in the
first summit of 7 per cent., in June, 1873.

Through the summer months, collapse, liquidation and the
resulting slack trade spread from one business centre in Europe

---

[1] See Adams, C. F., *Railroads: Their Origin and Problems*, 1878; Johnson,
E. R., *American Railway Transportation*, ch. 3.

[2] The delicate position of a young country which has overborrowed was
illustrated painfully in 1930–1.

[3] Wirth, *op. cit.* p. 461.

to another, without much more actual panic[1]. Stock Exchange values fell, and then commodity prices, except unfortunately that of corn, which was rising. France began to suffer, not for mistakes of her own, but through the shrinkage of demand for such things as her silks and wines. In London, discount had slipped down to 3 per cent. in August, and nothing worse than a period of slack trade seemed impending for "John Bull... throned untouched on his money bags," as a touched continental pictured him[2]. Then, on September 20, came cabled news of a crash in New York—some banks down; others closing their doors to avoid a run; a moratorium demanded for savings banks; a temporary closing of exchanges. Railway speculation, with all that accompanied it, and the locking up of capital in lines for the time unprofitable, had combined with the uncertainties and the opportunities for doubtful business provided by a depreciated paper currency in a gold producing country to bring things to a head. European capital had for some time fought shy of new American railway bonds. All kinds of expensive financial devices had been adopted to keep construction, and the companies, going. With the crisis, these devices became difficult or impossible to maintain. As a palliative, government undertook to provide more circulating medium by buying United States bonds with greenbacks recently withdrawn from circulation; but President Grant resisted the pressure put upon him to adopt a thoroughgoing policy of inflation[3]. When the liabilities of bankrupts came to be reckoned for 1873, they amounted to 93,000,000 dollars in New York alone, as against 21,000,000 dollars in 1872[4].

The American crisis completed the discomfiture of Europe. Speculation on margins had been common during the boom. The collapse of American securities started or hastened the general collapse. German financial centres, headed by Berlin, which had got through the summer, could not stand these autumn gales. Railways, banks and building societies went down. There was heavy mortality in industry, with capital reductions and combinations of over-capitalised firms. Whether

[1] There was something described as a panic at Bologna in July. Wirth, *op. cit.* p. 588.

[2] Wirth, *op. cit.* p. 594.

[3] Dewey, *op. cit.* p. 372.

[4] For all the United States the rise was from $121,000,000 in 1872 to $228,000,000 in 1873. The figures illustrate the concentration of the hurricane on New York.

there was more than the normal amount of dishonesty accompanying so widespread a madness of greed is hard to say; but it was natural to think so, when such people as the cashier of the Prussian Mortgage Bank, the Director of the People's Bank at Essen, a French ex-minister, and even business men from careful respectable Switzerland, became convicts[1].

In England the situation was worst, as might have been expected, on the Stock Exchange. There November 6 and 7 were days of panic—but Consols moved only a point or two. America, France and Germany had all been drawing on the London gold. British bankers had been drawing on their deposits at the Bank. Both reserves were low at the end of October, and the rate had been moved up steadily since mid-September from 3 to 7 per cent. It was moved again twice in November, just stopping short of the true panic rate of 10 per cent., but getting high enough to tell the continent that John Bull was touched at last. There was nothing in London to compare with the catastrophes of New York, Vienna and Berlin; although for a moment suspension of the Bank Act was feared. But as the reserve in the Banking Department was never reported below £8,000,000, nor the gold in the Issue Department below £18,600,000, the fear was unreasonable. Nine per cent. worked perfectly and very fast. By the middle of December there was a banking reserve of more than £12,000,000, and a rate of 4½ per cent. There had been losses and failures but, as yet, nothing extraordinary or discreditable.

By contemporaries the after effects of the crisis of 1873 were naturally confused with the early stages of the great price fall of the late nineteenth century, which began among them but was not in any true sense their consequence. A fall from the level of 1872–3 was inevitable and was anticipated; but a ten year fall, which was to draw out into a twenty year fall, was outside the experience of the generation which had to bear it. Five years of slow trade after so general an upheaval might perhaps have been anticipated: there had been four between the Overend crisis and the revival of 1870. But it is unlikely that any one could have guessed that, after a short and delusive recovery in 1879–80, the fall would be resumed at the old rate[2].

This resumed fall was the more discouraging because it might well have been thought that with the failure of the City of Glasgow bank on October 1, 1878, the full penalty of 1873 had been

[1] Wirth, *op. cit.* p. 569–70.  [2] See the diagram above, p. 378.

paid. Though active and pushful, with many branches and a deposit business of over £8,000,000, the City of Glasgow had for years been of ill-fame in the inner banking world[1]. It had suspended payment in 1857 but had reopened after a month[2]. Whether it had ever been genuinely solvent since was doubtful; certainly it had been insolvent for years before 1878. Some of its bad debts ran back to the cotton famine[3]. Latterly, as appeared after the crash, it had systematically treated these debts as assets. Four debtors only, from the class which in America and Germany had been sifted out in 1873, owed and would never pay £5,793,000[4]. Gaol for its directors and its manager brought Britain into line with Europe, but did not help the firms which were dragged down with it, the shareholders with unlimited liability, or the army of small depositors. There is no more miserable episode in the economic history of the age. To it, and the resultant depression, has been attributed the ruin of the great majority of the Scottish trade unions[5].

Desperate as it was in Scotland, the City of Glasgow crisis was easily handled by the Bank of England with a short spell of 6 per cent. The Bank had only to go so high once again in the next decade, at the beginning of February, 1882, when the *Union générale* stopped payment in Paris. The Union, whose foundation in 1878 marked the return of France to large-scale imaginative enterprise, was among the most fantastic and ambitious creations of the time[6]. With a clerical and aristocratic clientele, it was a promoting, finance and holding company of the widest kind, whose special interests—as became the clientele—were in the Hapsburg lands. Its failure was the outstanding event in a Parisian crisis, against the repercussion of which on gold and the exchanges, the Bank of England defended itself again by the precautionary 6 per cent.

This was only an episode, and from the British standpoint an unimportant one, in a long stretch of fourteen years (1873–87) for the whole of which the average Bank rate was barely

---

[1] Kerr, *History*, ch. 25.

[2] Above, p. 368.

[3] Giffen, *Essays in Finance, Second Series*, p. 152. From the Essay "On the use of Import and Export Statistics" (1882): "the rottenness disclosed... having been largely due to the excessive investment of capital in the Eastern trade in the times of the cotton famine."

[4] The *Scotsman*, October 19, quoted in Kerr, p. 297.

[5] Webb, S. and B., *History of Trade Unionism*, p. 334.

[6] See Juglar, C., *Des crises commerciales* (1889), p. 447; Wirth, *op. cit.* p. 621–643.

3 per cent. There was no war in Western Europe. European harvest fluctuations were losing their power to hurt, since corn was coming to England more uniformly all round the year. For Britain the era of bank failures was over. America was more cut off by tariffs and more self-sufficient in capital goods than she had formerly been; Britain rather less confiding in her American and general overseas investment. Even the making of 35,000 miles of American railway in 1880–83, and the reaction which followed, did not leave such deep marks on British industry and the London money market as corresponding events had left ten years earlier. That quiet era in Lombard Street which helped a bad Bank Act to work without further inquiry was due partly to the removal of old dangers and fears; partly to accumulated experience in the Bank parlour, and to the way in which other parties in the Street had learned how to tackle old or new dangers. But things would not have been so quiet but for that numbness in the industrial and commercial life of the country which marked the years of falling prices and quickened international competition. When producers and dealers had surplus funds, there was hesitation about turning them into new machinery and plant or developing the business: money lay longer on deposit, and there was more of it to handle than Lombard Street could manage profitably[1]. Removal of dangers and increased wisdom may well explain the saving of Lombard Street from 10 and 8 per cent. The rare appearances of 4 and 5 per cent. require a less gratifying explanation. Reviewing the evidence given before that inquiry into Trade Depression with which the period closed, Alfred Marshall could find no proof that the general economic welfare of the country was abnormally depressed; but he admitted a severe "depression of prices, a depression of interest, and a depression of profits."[2] His admissions sufficiently explain the chill and heavy air of Lombard Street.

[1] Cp. above, p. 356. The statement that "money lay longer on deposit" is an inference from the other facts of the situation. I know of no precise authority for it.
[2] Before the *R.C. on Gold and Silver*, Q. 9824.

# CHAPTER X

# THE ECONOMIC ACTIVITIES OF THE STATE

JEREMY BENTHAM, it may be recalled, had once advocated the handing over of all Poor Law work to a National Charity Company[1]. As a rationalist son of the eighteenth century, he assumed that particular governments are likely to be both incompetent and corrupt. As a liberty loving philosophcr, it was his axiom that "all government is in itself one vast evil."[2] But he held that whatever limited amount of this evil thing might remain should be rationally organised, very well served, very well informed, careful to put its information at the disposal of the public, consistently hostile to all kinds of monopoly, and watchful over the nation's health. His scheme of ministries was so exactly thought out that a twentieth century committee faced with the same problem arrived independently at a closely similar result[3]. (The scheme of course contained a Minister of Health, not to provide for disease but to anticipate it.) Inspectors reporting to Secretaries of State, recording registrars whose statistical results are widely published, and expert central civil servants are all typical Benthamite officials. When Edwin Chadwick and Walter Bagehot inclined towards different forms of railway nationalisation in the 'sixties[4], because railways were of the nature of monopolies, neither was outside the Benthamite tradition.

From the victory of 1832, which he just did not live to see, until the usury laws were abolished in 1854 and examinations initiated for those entering the civil service in 1855[5], there had been a bit of Bentham in every great reform, destructive or

---

[1] See vol. I. p. 312. The notion was not original. It had been discussed, in various forms, a century earlier. See Charles Davenant's *Essay upon the Probable Methods of making a People Gainers in the Balance of Trade*, Section 3.

[2] Quoted in Leslie Stephen, *The English Utilitarians* (1900), I. 287.

[3] *Report of the Machinery of Government Committee* (1918), Cd. 9230; and see Webb, S. and B., *English Poor Law History: The Last Hundred Years* (1929), p. 816–17.

[4] Above, p. 189.

[5] The first Civil Service examinations were qualifying, not competitive. Effective competition only began in 1870. See Morley, *Life of Gladstone*, I. 509–12; II. 314.

creative. No doubt he would have criticised each new thing. The examining of civil servants, for example, was not linked with the economical device which he had suggested of inviting them to tender against one another, so that the state might know which of them would do the work cheapest[1]. But he would have recognised, and probably overrated, his own touch; just as he had been glad to treat "Master Peel" as a "model good boy" when that associate of his prime enemy Eldon reformed the criminal law, made the new constabulary, or behaved in some other way like a pupil[2]. Indeed nothing could have been more to his taste than the 'Peelers,' since to him security was the primary condition of happiness, equality only a secondary.

Some old regulations and functions the state had abandoned, or was in course of abandoning. But it had been reformed in head and members—parliament, civil service, municipalities, guardians of the poor. It was stronger for the reforms. Without overstepping Bentham's circle, it had become stronger still by extending its activities, sometimes against the wishes of those who were readiest to invoke Bentham's principles, and by creating new instruments *ad hoc*. Success with the Penny Post had certainly increased its prestige[3]. It was at length publishing accurate statistics of trade and shipping, and of the output of minerals. Though it had no trustworthy agricultural statistics, and had made no attempt to gauge the production of manufactured goods, it had completed in the census of 1851 a remarkably ambitious statistical account of the whole kingdom— so ambitious that in later census years a number of the most valuable economic chapters were not continued. It had registrars of births, deaths and marriages, of friendly societies, and of joint-stock companies. It had poor law inspectors, textile factory inspectors, inspectors of railways, of weights and measures and of mines. In Scotland it had fishery inspectors, who branded herrings for market and linked the inspectorates of the nineteenth century with those of the eighteenth. For the sake of decency, safety or health it forbade women to work in mines; it even interfered a little with the labour contracts of male miners[4]; it laid down rules for the construction and working of steamships; and it had begun to build up a sanitary code to be

[1] Leslie Stephen, *op. cit.* I. 286.
[2] *Ibid.* I. 226–7; and cp. J. S. Mill, *Autobiography*, p. 99.
[3] And success with the Post Office Savings Banks after 1861 increased it further.
[4] See vol. I. p. 576: wages not to be paid in taverns, etc.

enforced with the aid of medical officers of health and various inspectors. It had just brutally interfered with liberty in the interest of security by ordering that every child born in England should be not only registered but vaccinated (16 and 17 Vict. c. 100)[1]. It had revived and strengthened the ancient laws which forbade the payment of wages—but not of all wages—in truck. It was working out a code which treated the seaman "as if he were a mere child,"[2] a code under which anyone might be punished who boarded a ship within twenty-four hours of her arrival in port and asked a sailor to lodge with him[3]. It had regulated the price of 'parliamentary' railway travel, though it had abandoned the Assize of Bread. Within a few years it would regulate in great detail the sale, if not the price, of gas.

The world of industry was become very intricate and in some ways increasingly dangerous. Men's minds and consciences were more sensitive than their grandfathers' had been. They asked for themselves and, when they had influence with government, for the people, a wide and specialised security that the grandfathers had not thought about. The state, purged and trained fine, better informed and better equipped, could supervise the carrying out of its decisions with a certainty which would have been nearly unthinkable two generations earlier. Whatever the conscious or sub-conscious doctrines about the proper sphere of its action by which legislators were influenced, it was probable, perhaps inevitable, that the organism of state, more sinewy and efficient, would also become more active. Among the legislators, whose often inconsequent and party-blinded votes determined its activities, were some not yet convinced that it ought to leave foreign trade and navigation alone; others certain that it had not gone nearly far enough in promoting health, safety, and the good life; some few who held with Bentham that there was one strongly fortified monopoly yet to be stormed—that of the land with its land laws[4]. Such groups were ready to use the machine of government at

---

[1] *An Act to extend and make compulsory the practice of vaccination*: 1853. The Acts for Scotland and Ireland only came ten years later, following a second English Act, rendered necessary by the comparative failure of the first.

[2] Jevons, W. S., *The State in Relation to Labour* (1882), p. 69. Jevons quotes most of the 'interferences' mentioned in the text. References are to the fourth edition, ed. F. W. Hirst, of 1910, in which the paging differs from the first.

[3] See below, p. 410.

[4] Cp. Walpole, Sir Spencer, *The History of Twenty-Five Years* (1904), I. 39 *sqq.*

opportune moments to gain their ends. There were those waiting outside parliament and outside the electorate who, when their time came, would be readier.

The average legislator, a man of property, reasonably content with the growth of wealth under a system of modified freedom, and proud of the economic leadership of his country, was averse from radical measures either of reaction or reform. Not until the difficult times of the late 'seventies would he be likely to listen to advocates of either, and not with any eagerness then. His leaders were not radicals of the left or of the right. Of the two dominating parliamentary gladiators whom he cheered[1], one had grown into economic liberalism empirically and by inheritance from his master Peel: there was no scrap of Bentham in Gladstone's intellectual and moral makeup. The other, who with the detachment of an alien genius could step outside his age and watch it, had done no more than acquiesce in certain economic liberalisms as appropriate to that age and useful to his party. They were expedients not principles, and it is of the nature of an expedient to be short-lived. But for the present they served.

In the year after Disraeli died, the most observant and acute economist of that generation put into words what in fact had been the normal attitude of government towards economic affairs, if one is to judge by the statute book. "We must rid our minds," Stanley Jevons wrote[2], "of the idea that there are any such things in social matters as abstract rights, absolute principles, indefeasible laws, or anything whatever of an eternal and inflexible nature." And again—"We must neither maximise the functions of government at the beck of quasi-military officials, nor minimise them according to the theories of the very best philosophers. We must learn to judge each case upon its merits."[3] Herbert Spencer, who may well have been the very best philosopher whom Jevons had in mind, broke out in 1884 into a last grumbling cry for *The Man versus the State*. Conscious of the state's growing power, and familiar by profession with the views of those thinkers who welcomed it, he made his protest against, among other things, the Public

[1]      "Yonder and close to Mr Speaker's chair,
         Enfolding all things in a net of words,
         Stands our first gymnast."          Wilfrid Blunt,
                                                   *The Idler's Calendar.*

[2] *The State in Relation to Labour* (1882), p. 6.
[3] *Ibid.* p. 171.

Libraries Act, "by which a majority can tax a minority for their books."[1] He was late, even belated. It was doubtful, too, whether the challenge came fitly from an evolutionary philosopher. Should one grumble at the amalgamation of the three hind toes of *eohippus* into the single hoof of *equus*, even if *equus* kicks one with it? In any case, statesmen and legislators were not regular readers of Spencer.

Mill they were at least supposed to have read: he stood for political economy. When a man set out between 1848 and 1886 to invoke, to attack or to defend, political economy, he generally meant Mill, if he meant anything[2]. Professed students as a rule still built on Mill or adjusted their thought to his[3]. Now in his theory of the state Mill had given cautious empirical innovators like Jevons all the justification they required, and plenty of encouragement to more radical reformers. In particular, his book had, from the first, been Bible and Fathers to those few who wished to reform the land law or the practices of land-holding.

Land being "the original inheritance of the whole species," its appropriation was in his opinion "wholly a question of general expediency."[4] Whatever "sacredness" property might have did not "belong in the same degree to landed property." The legislature might "if it pleased convert the whole body of landlords into fundholders or pensioners." And more dogmatically—"whenever, in any country, the proprietor, generally speaking, ceases to be the improver, political economy has nothing to say in defence of landed property as there established. In no sound theory of private property was it ever contemplated that the proprietor of land should be merely a sinecurist quartered on it." The conditions justificatory of the existing

---

[1] *The Man versus the State*, p. 10.

[2] See, for example, Ruskin's criticism of Mill in *Unto this Last* (1860); noble and perverse, sometimes even stupid.

[3] As in the Introduction to Henry Sidgwick's *Principles of Political Economy* (1883). And compare a passage in the *Economist* of May 17, 1873, obviously written by Walter Bagehot: "the writer of these lines has long been in the habit of calling himself the last man of the ante-Mill period....All students since begin with Mill....They see the whole subject with Mill's eyes." Alfred Marshall was working out his principles; the *Economics of Industry*, written in conjunction with Mrs Marshall in 1879, was beginning to tell; his thought was influencing pupils and scholars; but it was hardly yet a force in public affairs during the early 'eighties. See J. M. Keynes' *In Memoriam. Memorials of Alfred Marshall* (1925).

[4] Book II, ch. II, § 6.

form of landed property were "insufficiently realized even in England." In Ireland, with some "very honourable" individual exceptions, they were "not complied with at all." This plain speech about Ireland, and the report of Peel's Commission[1] on Irish land which lay behind it, were the intellectual legacies of the 'forties to the next decades. When in 1870, after many proposals and experiments by others, Gladstone brought in the regulative, but far from revolutionary, Bill which opened the late nineteenth century era in Irish land legislation[2], Mill was with John Bright among the small group of public men who wrote and spoke in favour of buying out the landlords—'converting them into fundholders'—and setting up peasant proprietorship out of hand[3]. As the Abbé Sieyès, also a logical individualist, had said long before, he did not want to abolish property but only to change the proprietors.

In another matter of state which cuts deep into the problems of property and its distribution, the law and taxation of inheritance and bequest, Mill remained to his death in 1873 only the philosopher who raises a standard—a standard to which few men had rallied even a dozen years after he died. For drastic reforms he certainly thought the times were not ripe; nor would be soon. (There had been no killing to ripen them as in Ireland, a cynic might have said.) The right of bequest he held to be a necessary corollary to any right of private property: the state must protect it. But inheritance was another matter. Through all his editions, his standard flew with the legend—"were I framing a code of laws according to what seems to me best in itself, without regard to existing opinion and sentiment, I should prefer to restrict, not what any one might bequeath, but what any one should be permitted to acquire, by bequest or inheritance."[4] He was generous. He was no envious egalitarian. He would permit a man to inherit "the means of a comfortable independence." In all this, whether he realised it or not, he was working tacitly for the

[1] The so-called Devon Commission: *Report of H.M. Commissioners of inquiry into the State and Practice in respect to the occupation of Land in Ireland*: 1845 (XIX–XXII).

[2] It merely confirmed Irish tenant-right customs; asserted that tenants' improvements were tenants' property; and arranged for damages in cases of unfair eviction. See Locker-Lampson, G., *A consideration of the state of Ireland in the Nineteenth Century* (1907), p. 339.

[3] See his *Speeches and Chapters on the Irish Land Question*, 1870.

[4] Book II, ch. II, § 4.

state. What power and knowledge would be required for the efficient administration of such a system? Impossibly great powers, he held, "unless the popular sentiment went energetically along with" the law. Still very great, it might be added, even if popular sentiment did.

Not contemplating a law of this kind as a near possibility, Mill applied the thought underlying his advocacy of it in his theory of taxation. Here he laid down very plainly the route along which the state would in fact travel within twenty-five years of his death. "I conceive that inheritances and legacies, exceeding a certain amount, are highly proper subjects for taxation: and that the revenue from them should be as great as it can be made without giving rise to evasions...such as it would be impossible adequately to check. The principle of graduation (as it is called)...seems to me both just and expedient as applied to legacy and inheritance duties."[1]

Mill never favoured the principle of graduation as applied to property or income taxes, even with a view to "mitigating the inequalities of wealth."[2] Not because he had the least dislike for mitigation of inequality by the state, but because he was always anxious in no way to discourage earning and saving. Therefore, in the state of his dreams, he would concentrate the differential taxation, with its mitigating effects, on inherited wealth. He discussed, very hypothetically and with many reserves, an income-tax not graduated but differentiated—"with one uniform rate for all incomes of inheritance, and another [lower] uniform rate for all those which necessarily terminate with the life of the individual."[3]

In his first edition, he had regarded the impossibility of finding out what people's incomes really were, "in the present low state of public morality," as an "insuperable" objection to any income tax at all. The word "insuperable" vanished from the later editions; yet after his death his authority could still be quoted for the view that "the fairness which belongs to the principle of an income-tax cannot be made to attach to it in practice," and that therefore the tax "should be reserved as an extraordinary resource for great national emergencies, in which the necessity of a large additional revenue overrides all objections"[4]—for war-time in short. Strong and well-informed as the state was growing, he did not anticipate the

---

[1] Book v, ch. II, § 3.  
[2] The same section.  
[3] Book v, ch. II, § 4.  
[4] Book v, ch. III, § 5.

further growth, nor that parallel growth of wealth held in joint-stock and so taxable at the source, which would make these objections sound oddly antiquated to men of the next generation.

Another fiscal policy which Mill stamped with an economist's approval would also have called for much government activity— the taxation or absorption of future additions to incomes derived from the ownership of land. "This would not properly be taking anything from anybody; it would merely be applying an accession of wealth, created by circumstances, to the benefit of society, instead of allowing it to become an unearned appendage to the riches of a particular class."[1] He broadcast this explosive seed in 1848, and left it to the chances of political weather and soil, thorns and stony ground.

Mill's doctrine of the land, a rigidly Benthamite and Ricardian development, formed the intellectual bridge between the radicalism of the early nineteenth century and the socialisms of the late. He was deeply interested in socialisms[2]. His discussion of some of those of his own day, which after his first edition became more sympathetic while remaining faithfully critical, did not apply to developed doctrines of what came later to be called state socialism; but in his condensed handling of communism he touched on many of the valid general arguments bearing on systems in which "the land and the instruments of production" are to be the property "of communities or associations or of the government." Of these systems he had little economic fear. For the reasons which made men welcome them he had a great sympathy. "If...the choice were to be made between communism with all its chances and the present state of society with all its sufferings and injustices...all the difficulties, great or small, of communism would be but as dust in the balance." But he had humane fear lest "the absolute

---

[1] Book v, ch. ii, § 5.
[2] He has sometimes been criticised for neglect of those early English socialists whose writings have been so much discussed since the publication (in 1899) of Prof. Foxwell's classical Introduction to Menger's *Right to the Whole Produce of Labour*. No doubt there was some neglect; but he only professed to discuss "the most prevailing forms of the doctrine" of socialism. He knew William Thompson, author of *The Distribution of Wealth*, well (*Autobiography*, p. 125), but evidently thought that his doctrine was not "prevailing." Foxwell overlooked this passage in the *Autobiography* when he wrote (*op. cit.* p. lxxviii) that "he [Mill] must have heard of Hodgskin from his father, and of Thompson, with whom he had much in common, from Bentham."

dependence of each on all, and surveillance of each by all," should "grind all down into a tame uniformity of thoughts, feelings, and action," and so intensify a prime and "glaring evil" of existing society, "in which eccentricity is a matter of reproach."[1]

Seeing that the laws of private property had "never yet conformed to the principles on which the justification of private property rests,"[2] there remained much destructive and creative work for the state to do before the ultimate place of property could be determined. From the first, Mill had approached the matter with scientific reserve and complete personal disinterestedness. He felt that an age of experiment lay ahead. "We are too ignorant either of what individual agency in its best form, or socialism in its best form, can accomplish, to be qualified to decide which of the two will be the ultimate form of human society."[3] Had he inserted the words "or what combination of the two," he would have anticipated the essence of all that advocates of the one or the other, when converted by experience to scientific reserve, are saying to this day.

Among the most urgent creative work which, in Mill's opinion, the state still had to do was law-making to encourage the diffusion of property. Hence his support of peasant proprietorship, limited liability, co-operation in all its shapes, more flexible laws of partnership, any and every movement of legal reform which might help to multiply small capitalists. It was when discussing partnership that he stretched out a hand to the industrial socialists and reaffirmed his "conviction, that the industrial economy which divides society absolutely into two portions, the payers of wages and the receivers of them, the first counted by thousands and the last by millions, is neither fit for, nor capable of, indefinite duration."[4] He had not in mind communal or state ownership of the means of production, but a diffusion of property with co-operative ownership. Yet although he had no great faith in the state, and had a horror of the spiritual tyrannies of communism, his influence tended to increase the strength and activity of government in his own generation, and still more in that which followed him. It was vain for Herbert Spencer to decry as inimical to *The Man* that

[1] Book II, ch. I, § 3: the paragraph on communism. The passage "If the choice were to be made" etc. is not in the first edition.

[2] The same section. This passage is in the first edition.

[3] The same section. [4] Book V, ch. IX, § 5.

institution through whose decisions and legislative experiments alone "the ultimate form of human society" could be determined.

In spite of Mill's many editions, his recognised authority, and his influence on thinkers, there remained down to the 'seventies—and indeed later, as Jevons' forcible repudiation of any absolute political economy shows—a widespread opinion that the science prescribed, as from some pulpit of Mammon, eternal laws of state inaction. While Mill was arguing that the Irish land bill of 1870 was not nearly thorough enough, persons of importance were attacking it as contrary to the laws of political economy; and a disciple of Mill felt himself called to explain at length in an inaugural professorial lecture how "there is no security that the economic phenomena of society, as at present constituted, will always arrange themselves spontaneously in the way which is most for the common good."[1] Emphasis lay on the "as at present constituted." Cairnes was no socialist or paternalist. When in doubt leave things alone, was his maxim. But, like Mill, he was very sure that on a great number of questions there was no doubt. He had made a masterly study of the economics of American slavery[2], and he had taught political economy both in Dublin and in Galway. So anxious was he to dissociate his science from the stupid and interested *laissez-faire* of those in possession, that he claimed for it a complete detachment from particular systems, whether individualist or communist, which many of its early masters would have repudiated: "it stands apart from all...and is absolutely neutral as between them."[3]

Meanwhile another Irishman had started an attack on the whole method of Mill's master Ricardo, and had advertised the discredit into which it was falling among many German scholars[4], while Jevons, in a brilliantly written but conspicuously one-sided book, had suggested a revision of the fundamental economic analysis of value[5]. By the 'eighties, "disputes as to

[1] Cairnes, J. E., "Political Economy and Laissez-faire" (1870), in *Essays in Political Economy* (1873), p. 250-1. Cairnes added "What did we hear during the discussions on the Irish Land Bill? Political Economy again and again appealed to as having pronounced against that measure."

[2] *The Slave Power* (1862).            [3] *Essays*, as above, p. 251.

[4] T. E. Cliffe Leslie, *Essays in Political and Moral Philosophy* (1879). The Essays cover the years 1870-9.

[5] *The Theory of Political Economy* (1871 and 1879): cp. the criticism of Jevons in Keynes, J. M., *Memorials of Alfred Marshall*, p. 23.

particular doctrines" seemed to be broadening into "more fundamental controversy as to the general method of dealing with economic questions."[1] These were controversies of experts. The outer half-informed world, which was slowly learning that economists did not always teach strict *laissez-faire* from a pulpit, was in some danger of beginning to think that they did not know what they taught. When one of them reverted to the strict doctrine, in criticism of Gladstone's Irish Land Bill of 1881, Gladstone, in a phrase that stuck, said that he argued "exactly as if he had been proposing to legislate for the inhabitants of Saturn or Jupiter."[2] The banishment of political economy to Saturn became a catchword. In 1883, another economist set down his impression that the hostility of "influential artisans to the traditional Political Economy" had not diminished; it had "only changed somewhat from sullen distrust to confident contempt."[3] It was in this unfriendly atmosphere that Jevons underlined the scientific and 'each-case-on-its-merits' method of approach to problems of state action—a good method, but one which risks falling behind the act.

As yet the sphere of the state had not been greatly widened. Railway nationalisation had been talked about by a few people and dropped[4]. Land tenure reform in Britain had not got beyond the very modest inroad on the Common Law made by the Act of 1883[5]. Extension of factory and safety laws went on; but no fresh principles were applied. The Poor Law, untouched in all essentials, was being administered during the early 'eighties in as strict and individualistic a spirit as was compatible with its essence of Tudor paternalism. But, whether through indifference or contempt for "the traditional Political Economy," or through perfectly consequent use of the explosive material put into it by Mill, the inhibitions which had surrounded proposals for further state action were breaking down in many active governing minds. "The pet idea" of "the liberalism of to-day," Peel's aged and mighty disciple wrote to his political confessor in 1885, "is what they call

[1] Sidgwick, *Principles*, p. 6. And see Keynes, J. N., *The Scope and Method' of Political Economy* (1891).

[2] Hansard, Third Series, CCLX. 895. Debate of April 7: the economist was Professor Bonamy Price.

[3] Sidgwick, *Principles*, p. 6.

[4] Above, p. 189–90.

[5] Above, p. 256.

construction,—that is to say, taking into the hands of the state the business of the individual man."[1] This was when Joseph Chamberlain was advocating peasant proprietorship, the large-scale acquisition of land by local authorities, a graduated income tax, and the break up of great estates; and when Randolph Churchill, from the other side, had already spoken favourably of radical housing reform, "the public wash-houses of Mr Jesse Collings," and the "idea of compulsory national insurance."[2] Mill would have given patient consideration to all these ideas, and resolute support to most of them.

A liberal-minded historian of finance was writing in 1887–8 that "the most striking and most disheartening feature of the last few years" had been "the disastrous expansion of the national expenditure."[3] He was thinking of budgets which dealt with figures in excess of £90,000,000, and of a revenue from taxes in the United Kingdom which had risen sharply from £69,800,000 in 1880–1 to £76,600,000 in 1885–6. There had been little wars in those years; and the warship costing more than £750,000, and now no longer an ironclad, had arrived. Modest as the figures of 1885–6 seem to a later age, the period of a rather rapidly accelerating growth in taxation and expenditure had in fact begun; but only just. The annual average tax revenue of the United Kingdom had grown since the 'forties as follows[4]:

| | | | |
|---|---|---|---|
| 1841–6 | £52,100,000 | 1871–6 | £65,300,000 |
| 1851–6 | £54,400,000 | 1881–6 | £72,900,000 |
| 1861–6 | £62,900,000 | | |

Compared with the growth between the 'forties and the 'sixties, or with that between the 'sixties and the 'seventies, that in the last decade of the period might well seem disheartening to an economist-politician bred in the school of Gladstone. Gladstone was in power, yet circumstances had been too strong for the man who had never seen the least glint of romance in public expediture.

[1] Gladstone to Lord Acton. Morley: *Gladstone*, III. 173.

[2] Churchill, W. S., *Lord Randolph Churchill*, I. 251. For insurance see below, p. 434.

[3] Buxton, Sydney (Lord Buxton), *Finance and Politics*, II. 319.

[4] These are not the ordinary figures of revenue, but the tax-revenue proper, *i.e.* they omit Post Office receipts, Crown Lands, and certain Miscellaneous receipts. As usually quoted, the figure for 1851–6, for example, would be £56,900,000.

Financially speaking, Gladstone had generally been in power. Of the thirty-six effective budgets following that of 1850 he had himself introduced thirteen; lieutenants in his ministries had introduced eight; and Stafford Northcote, an ex-lieutenant enlisted on the other side but full of respect for the strategy of the old warrior, another seven. Behind the power of Gladstone stood the shadow of the great name of his master Peel. In 1884, Gladstone, aged seventy-five, was combating a financial heresy with memories of the days when he himself, "a Parliamentary youngster," had been "extremely captivated" by it; but Peel "put an extinguisher upon me in half a minute and declared that he would not entertain for an instant a proposition such as this."[1] Argument followed, but first the great name was invoked; and it is hard not to believe that to Gladstone's loyal and reverent mind the invocation was the essential thing. To him the age of Peel was as the age of Homer when heroes fought and ruled. He looked back to it during his last years "with immeasurable yearning."[2]

The heresy concerned the doctrine of the Income Tax. About the history of that tax the financial narrative of the Gladstonian era may most fitly be grouped. For a whole generation after the victory of free trade in 1842–52 customs policy almost ceased to be a matter for discussion. Chancellors showed their skill in the choice of occasions for remission of duties; or by that mastery of their detail, still bewildering down to 1860, of which Gladstone had the secret; or by the economy which made abandonment of lucrative duties possible. When Gladstone's work was complete, the customs schedule was almost as short as the authors of the *Report* of 1840 could have wished[3]. About many forms of internal taxation there was even less difference of opinion than about the customs. Surviving excise and licence duties disappeared with universal approval whenever the chancellors could afford to do without them. Tories and Whigs had cut at the excise between 1823 and 1840. Peel, with the income tax in hand, dropped the glass duty in 1845. The duty on bricks went in 1850; those on soap, dice, and advertisements in 1853; the newspaper tax in 1855; the paper duties, after

---

[1] See Hubbard, Rt. Hon. J. G., *Gladstone on the Income Tax. Discussion...in the House of Commons on 25 April*, 1884, *with preface and historical sketch* (1885).

[2] *The Personal Papers of Lord Rendel* (1931), p. 132.

[3] For the detail of customs reduction see above, p. 219–20, 242 *sqq*. For the *Report* of 1840, vol. I. p. 496.

a famous fight between Gladstone and the Lords, in 1861. By the 'eighties, apart from the liquor excise, only the excise duties on patent medicines, playing cards, and plate remained[1].

So with the licences. The complex licences for 'the trade' necessarily survived. With them survived the licences for makers and sellers of tobacco, because it was taxed, and for dealers in plate and patent medicines, also taxed; for makers of the taxed playing-cards; for various responsible professions, such as solicitors and auctioneers; for game dealers, hawkers, pedlars and pawnbrokers. In a different class were the gun, game, and dog licences. But the licensing of those who sold tea, coffee, cocoa or pepper had been dropped in 1869; of soap-makers, paper-makers, still makers, makers of watch-cases and sellers of playing-cards in 1870; of horse-dealers, with the horse duty, in 1874[2].

On all this there was substantial agreement. Agreement about remission of taxes is easy. But as time went on, continuous remission told in favour of the retention of the debatable income tax. Gladstone was tied throughout to a personal and, as it must seem, somewhat perverse view by his loyalty to Peel, his own early opinions, and the triumphant success of the arguments with which in his first great budget speech of 1853 he had "marked it effectually as a temporary tax."[3] The view, so far as a Gladstonian view can be summarised in few words, was that the tax was unpopular, necessarily unequal in its incidence, very apt to encourage immorality among taxpayers, very useful for raising money in great emergencies, and to be borne by the nation as a sort of penance so long as it went to war or tolerated extravagance. He once told Bright that the income tax even promoted extravagance, because money was so easily raised by it[4]. That was just before he fought the election of 1874 on its abolition[5]. He lost. Ten years later he was

[1] Buxton, *op. cit.* I. 95, 123, 266–8. For the commutation of the malt-tax into a beer-duty in 1880 and the intricate history of the tax, see Buxton, *op. cit.* II. 276 *sqq.*

[2] Buxton, *op. cit.* I. 92, 104, 188; II. 375.

[3] He had criticised Peel's original proposal to revive it: W. E. G. to R. P. November 4, 1841; Parker, *Sir Robert Peel*, II. 502. For the sweeping success of his arguments in 1853 see Northcote, Sir Stafford, *Twenty Years of Financial Policy* (1862), p. 185. The speech was issued as a pamphlet, in which the phrase quoted comes on p. 34.

[4] *The Diaries of John Bright* (1930), p. 269.

[5] He was thinking of abolition so early as August, 1873: Morley's *Gladstone*, II. 478.

'promising a right honourable friend' that 'a sufficient number of years would pass over the heads of Englishmen before they had another opportunity of abolishing it.'[1] They have passed. Had anyone interrupted, 'why did you not get rid of it when they restored you to power in 1880?' who can doubt that he would have countered in stately confidence with some reference to extravagant Disraelian imperialism, and the cost of peace with honour—"peace with honour on tick," as his unstately lieutenant Harcourt put it?

When a revived income tax was discussed in the reign of George IV, no advocate had spoken of it as temporary, though that may have been in some minds[2]. But when Peel begged the gentlemen of England to give him 7d. in the £ of all incomes over £150, to help him to wipe out Whig deficits and reform the tariff, he asked for only three years certain, with two more if his work were not done in the three. He got what he asked, in spite of the opposition of John Russell and Richard Cobden[3]. When 1845 came, he had no difficulty in turning the two years into three, in order to make certain of finishing his work. By 1848 his party was broken up; there had been famine in Ireland, panic in London, and revolution abroad. Revenue was coming in so badly that the Whigs asked not for repeal but for 1s. in the £ for five years. They got 7d. for three. In 1851 and 1852 the tax was renewed for a year only, still on the old basis, and its prospects seemed uncertain[4].

J. R. McCulloch had declared against it in his *Treatise on Taxation* of 1845. Mill's new book had said that the objections to it were "insuperable," because of the low state of public morality. A strong committee, appointed at the instigation of Joseph Hume in 1851 to inquire into *The Present Mode of Assessing and Collecting the Income Tax*, had made no report. It had served only to give limited publicity to a very complex scheme, suggested to Hume by William Farr the statistician, for taxing not income but property, at varying rates according to its value, the nature of its tenure, and the age of its owner[5]. It was the contemplation of such intricacies which made Glad-

---

[1] In the debate of April, 1884, quoted above.
[2] Vol. I. p. 329 *sqq.*
[3] Parker's *Peel*, II. 524; Morley's *Cobden*, I. 240–3.
[4] Buxton, *op. cit.* I. 91, and see Moneypenny and Buckle's *Disraeli*, III. 361.
[5] The evidence is in *Reports, Committees*, 1852 (IX). Farr's scheme is in App. X and Q. 4853 *sqq.*

stone cling later to a hint from Samuel Gurney—"whatever your plan is, let it be simple."[1] An official who came before the committee had said that evasion would "go on increasing with the existence of the tax";[2] but he had not given very much evidence of fraud. Mill in his evidence had been less gloomy about public morality than in his book, but, in company with other witnesses, had stressed the great defect of the tax—its failure to discriminate between what came eventually to be called earned and unearned incomes[3].

The opinion of the commercial and professional classes was naturally with Mill. They were the more anxious for reform because income tax payers in general were becoming accustomed to think of the tax as a permanent thing—and no wonder, after ten years. There was a section of the middle class, organised in the Liverpool Financial Reform Association, which wished to see the treasury filled entirely through this and other direct channels of taxation. Pamphleteers were saying that Mill's "insuperable" was based on a needlessly gloomy reading of public morality; or that they could not "for a moment conceive that any large proportion of the community" would "consent to annul" a tax which was now bringing in more than a ninth of the public revenue[4]. A representative of the propertied middle class so solid as J. G. Hubbard, the Deputy Governor of the Bank of England, in his *How should Income Tax be levied?* of 1852, had shown no objection to the tax on principle—provided always that there was differentiation between what he called industrial and spontaneous incomes[5]. Hubbard was pertinacious. He was the 'honourable friend' whose case—the same case—Gladstone was overwhelming with precedent and oratory in a thin House thirty-two years later.

Hubbard's pamphlet was supposed by some contemporaries

[1] Morley's *Gladstone*, I. 460–1.
[2] Q. 292: Pressly of the Inland Revenue.
[3] Q. 5222 *sqq.* (Mill); Q. 5448 *sqq.* (Ch. Babbage).
[4] Symons, J., *A scheme for direct taxation for* 1853; Coleman, J., *Some observations on Direct Taxation in reference to Commercial Reform.* For an attack on the Liverpool Association, see Maitland, J. G., F.R.S., *Property and Income Taxes: the Present State of the Question.* Among the other pamphlets of the time are Hemming, G. W., *A just Income Tax how possible*; Major, M. H. C., *A review of the Income Tax...with suggestions for Removal of its Present Inequalities*; *Derecourt on Taxes and Duties*; and cp. Seligman, E. R. A., *The Income Tax* (1911), p. 136 *sqq.*
[5] He also wrote in 1853 *Objections to a Reform of the Income Tax considered, in two letters to...The Times.*

to have inspired the proposal in Disraeli's strangled Budget of December 1852 that business, professional, and farming incomes should pay only three-quarters of the rate to be levied on incomes from realised property[1]. As Disraeli sat on the Committee of 1851-2, there is no need to assume this; though no doubt the support of a conservative Deputy-Governor of the Bank was welcome. Nor need one endorse Gladstone's view that Disraeli's proposal was "flagrantly vicious."[2] Possibly, as Gladstone used to say, it was made "without any communication with the Revenue departments";[3] but Disraeli had before him their official evidence, so that is immaterial. Differentiation would no doubt have been hard to arrange, with the administrative experience then available; but if incomes could be differentiated according to their size—and Gladstone himself in the next year taxed those above £150 at one rate and those between £100 and £150 at another—it should not have been impossible to differentiate according to source, had it been thought desirable.

Gladstone's Budget speech of 1853, which "changed the convictions of a large part of the nation on the income tax,"[4] diverted liberal opinion from the policy of differentiation, and determined the form of the tax for the next half century, seems less convincing to-day than it did to contemporaries. He set himself to prove that landed incomes did in fact, as things worked out, pay the equivalent of a higher rate than many other incomes, because they were taxed gross and were encumbered with mortgages, annuities, and jointures. He made play with the fact that traders 'assessed themselves.' He objected strongly to any differential taxation of incomes from the funds, on the curious ground that, because much of the national debt had been raised with promises that its income yield should not be taxed, it would be a breach of public faith to tax that yield differentially; though it was no breach merely to tax it, provided you taxed all other incomes just the same[5]. He used the old 'inquisitorial' argument, which had carried so much weight with Adam Smith, against the inquiries which differentiation

---

[1] The *Economist*, December 18, 1852. See Buckle's *Disraeli*, III. 425, 431.
[2] Morley's *Gladstone*, I. 436. From one of W. E. G.'s fragmentary notes.
[3] From the speech of 1884.
[4] Northcote, *Twenty Years of Financial Policy*, p. 185. "When I became Chancellor...an immense majority would have voted for the plan of differentiating the income tax," Gladstone in 1884.
[5] The same point is made more fully in the speech of 1884.

would involve. He had no difficulty in showing how insensibly one type of income merges in another, and what varying combinations of interest on fixed capital, akin to land, with earnings of management were to be found in Hubbard's 'industrial' incomes[1]. He used Gurney's excellent practical plea for simplicity. He begged the House not to 'break up' a tax which was a working engine for emergencies. To avoid all uncertainty, he asked it to vote this bad useful tax for seven years at dwindling rates, while commercial reform went forward. At a known and anticipated time, the nation might, if it chose, see the last of it.

War came next year to spoil his plan. He doubled the income tax. When he returned to the Exchequer to foot other men's bills, in 1859, he raised the tax automatically from the uniform 5d. to which it had fallen to 6½d. or 9d., according to the size of the taxed income, getting about a seventh of his tax receipts from this source[2]. The income tax was degenerating into a chancellor's umbrella, to be put up or down according to the signs of the financial skies.

In 1861, over Gladstone's resolute opposition and by a majority of only four, Hubbard secured a Committee to inquire into its *Mode of Assessment and Collection*[3]. The Committee, if not packed, was heavily weighted with Hubbard's critics— Gladstone, Northcote, Lowe—and was given no assistance by the government[4]. The evidence of the Inland Revenue officials examined was hostile to reform, but hardly conclusive: they were "in terror of their master's wrath," Hubbard wrote long after[5]. There was naturally much business and professional evidence in favour of differentiation; and there was no decisive evidence against Hubbard's other main proposal, to tax net rather than gross income. Mill, warmer than in 1851, sparred cleverly with Lowe in support of Hubbard. Lowe sneered at "this income tax," and made lawyers' points about life tenants of settled property. Mill retorted that such people had no obligation to save like ordinary recipients of life incomes[6].

---

[1] He asked how profits from Barclay and Perkins' brewery, or the income of Miss Coutts from the bank, could claim to be not what Hubbard called 'spontaneous' incomes.

[2] Buxton, *op. cit.* I. 188.

[3] *Reports, Committees* 1861 (III. 1).

[4] Hubbard's pamphlet of 1885 (quoted p. 398 above), Preface, p. 6.

[5] *Ibid.* p. 7.

[6] Mill's evidence, Q. 3538 *sqq.*

Newmarch the statistician was on Mill's side, and Farr, while not abandoning his intricate programme for the taxation of property, "certainly" preferred Hubbard's plan to the existing system[1]. The plan, put into a draft report, was then voted down; and the Committee reported that it was "brought to the conclusion that the objections which are urged against it [the tax], are objections to its nature and essence rather than to the particular shape which has been given to it."[2] But the Chancellors and the future Chancellors who formed the majority went on using it. There was never another inquiry, official or unofficial[3].

Gladstone's proposed abolition in 1874 seems uncommonly inopportune in retrospect. The boom was just over. The great price-fall had begun. That empire had come into being which taught men the value of new and costly weapons. But these things were hidden in August, 1873, when he made his plan. It was not the shameless electoral bribe that his enemies said. In view of his record, failure to make it, in some season of fair weather, would have been greatly to his discredit. The weather seemed fair, and the other side had dallied with repeal. Northcote, when he reached the exchequer, gave the country two years of a twopenny income tax—keeping the machine mounted for emergencies but running it at an uneconomically low pressure. The emergencies soon came, and with Gladstone back in power the machine was driven harder than ever. By 1885-6 an eightpenny income tax was bringing in nearly a fifth of the tax revenue.

Gladstone never discussed the tax at length as part of a system planned with an eye to exact distributive justice. His view of taxation was simple—a necessary evil, to be reduced to the practicable minimum. In his old age he rejoiced that his strength had been spent in pulling things down, in "opening doors and windows," not in doubtful construction[4]. But, had he ever been able to get rid of the income tax, he would not have relieved property of that small contribution to the needs of the state which was all that he ever wished any 'interest,' or section of the community, to make. In 1853 he had explained

---

[1] Newmarch, Q. 326 *sqq.*; Farr, Q. 2713.

[2] *Report*, p. iv.

[3] "It is probable that, during his [Gladstone's] time, his influence on financial opinion will be sufficient to prevent any further examination into the merits of the case, or any attempt to establish the tax on a broader foundation and a juster basis." Buxton, *op. cit.* I. 113 (1887-8).

[4] *The Personal Papers of Lord Rendel*, p. 95.

that the alternative to an income tax was a combination of some tax on "visible property" with increased legacy duties and a licence duty for all traders, instead of only for some. If he had been successful in 1874, the death duties would have been "reconstructed and enlarged."[1] For this he himself had prepared the way when, in 1853, he added to the small old probate duty, and to Pitt's legacy duty on successions to personal property, that parallel duty on successions to real property which Pitt would also have imposed, had not Fox and the landed interest thwarted him[2]. It was the first new tax levied since Waterloo and it proved not very lucrative. The three 'death duties' together yielded about £3,000,000 a year in the 'fifties.

Thirty years later they were substantially unaltered, though improved in various details, especially by Gladstone himself in 1880 and 1881. By 1886, with the growth of national wealth, they produced all together upwards of £7,000,000. Of this sum £4,000,000 came from the probate duty, the most universal of the three. It was derived from £140,500,000 worth of property passing at death. So lightly did the state press on inheritance. It had not yet listened to Mill, though disciples of his would soon gain its ear.

Customs and excise had provided about two-thirds of the tax revenue in the 'fifties: concentrated on a handful of semi-luxuries, they still provided more than a half. 'Stamps'—which included the death-duties, paid by stamp—had then brought in not quite one-eighth: now they brought in rather more than an eighth. Those taxes on comfortable people's surpluses which the income tax had in part replaced—the house duty, the remnants of the old land tax, and the 'assessed' taxes on certain luxuries—had produced about a twentieth (some £3,000,000) in the 'fifties. House and land tax now produced just over a thirtieth[3]. An income tax at 8d., as levied in 1885 and 1886, ranked almost with the customs as a revenue yielder,

---

[1] Gladstone, in the *Nineteenth Century*, June, 1887; an article quoted in Buxton, *op. cit.* II. 167.

[2] Pitt's original proposal applied only to collateral successions. In 1805 he extended the legacy duty to bequests payable out of, or charged on, real estate; Buxton, *op. cit.* I. 118. And see Morley's *Gladstone*, I. 463.

[3] The Land Tax, fixed and made redeemable by Pitt in 1798, had been redeemed unequally in different districts. Where it survived it affected the selling value of land. It was of no importance in nineteenth century fiscal history, though in the 'eighties it still yielded over £1,000,000.

producing £15,600,000 to their £20,000,000, out of a tax revenue of rather more than £80,000,000.

That national debt should be reduced systematically was an axiom both of Gladstone's and of Mill's political economy. But they also agreed that it was better to remove bad taxes, so setting free productive powers, than to hurry forward the reduction of debt[1]. The debt as Gladstone found it was nearly all in 3 per cents., the loans of higher denomination having been converted by Robinson, Althorp and Goulburn between 1824 and 1844. There had been both capital reductions and capital additions since the 'twenties[2]; additions for freeing the slaves, feeding Ireland, and helping West Indian planters; reductions from tax surpluses and the falling-in of annuities. As a result, the total capital amount of the debt was not very much less than it had been when Sir Henry Parnell drew up his programme for liberal financial reform in 1828–30. Funded and unfunded debt together were put at £808,000,000 for the year 1828. For 1850, the corresponding figure was £787,000,000, and for 1852, £779,000,000. The 3 per cents. had risen to par in 1852; they had only touched it once before since 1755. They held about par until the middle of 1853, but never saw it again until the 'eighties.

Gladstone had tried to snatch the moment for another conversion. He was too late. His complex scheme for creating a fair sized block of $2\frac{1}{2}$ per cents. was explained on April 8, 1853. The French Toulon fleet was then at Salamis, and Stratford Canning had reached Constantinople three days earlier to play his strong lone hand[3]. Only a tiny block of $2\frac{1}{2}$ per cents. resulted. Those 3 per cent. stockholders who had declined the treasury offer, and were to be paid off at par, got their cash in January, 1854, when the 3 per cents. were dropping towards 90 and the money was wanted for a probable Russian war. War added to the debt some £36,000,000—the cash price of a squadron of twentieth century battleships—and no more conversions were attempted until 1888[4].

[1] Mill, *Principles*, Book v, ch. vii, § 3.

[2] See vol. I. p. 318–19. The debt figure given there (£780,000,000) is the funded debt only. It is a round figure because the exact calculation of the burden of the annuities is difficult. See Buxton, *op. cit.* II. 203.

[3] *Camb. Hist. of British Foreign Policy*, II. 364–5.

[4] The story of the conversion is in Buxton, *op. cit.* I. 127–9.

The 'sixties saw a brief debt panic. In 1865 Jevons had argued that British coal was giving out. Mill had concluded that therefore the existing generation and its immediate successors were "the only ones which will have the smallest chance of ever being able to pay off" the National Debt[1]. So Gladstone put aside an extra half-million a year, whereby the debt might be paid off in 250 years, if there were no more wars; and Disraeli also did a little. In 1875 Northcote did something more systematic, in the creation of the new sinking fund. The annual debt-charge was to be raised, and reduction of debt out of realised income to go on more regularly and faster. Wars and other emergencies came to derange the programme, but the principle was maintained. Payments to the debt-charge in 1885–6 were almost as great as they had been thirty years earlier, just after the Crimean War[2]. At the close of the financial year 1885–6 the total liability, comparable with the £779,000,000 of 1852 and the £808,000,000 of 1856, was £742,000,000, against which might now be set such tangible assets as the telegraph system, probably overvalued however[3], and Disraeli's appreciating Suez Canal shares. The achievement was not heroic in a richening country; but growing riches made the fallen liability very easy to bear; and there was a good deal of coal in hand, though Mill was not yet proved a false prophet.

Outside the sphere of taxation, the state of the 'fifties was still using some of its strength in that breaking down of barriers which gave Gladstone so much healthy pleasure. The last scrap of the navigation laws, the monopoly of the coasting trade, was cleared away in 1854 (by 17 and 18 Vict. c. 21). With it (by 17 and 18 Vict. c. 90) went the shrivelled body of the ancient usury law. Systematic evasion had long since robbed it of vigour. Even in Queen Anne's day it had not been allowed to interfere with "parliamentary securities."[4] In 1833 the Bank of England had been empowered to disregard the legal rate of 5 per cent. in the short money market, and had done so for the first time during the commercial difficulties of 1839[5]. The crisis

---

[1] Hansard, Third Series, CLXXXII, 1525. Mill's speech of 17th April, 1866, referring to Jevons.

[2] In 1885–6, £28,000,000: in 1858–9, £28,400,000.

[3] Above, p. 209 n. 4.

[4] See 12 Anne, St. 2, c. 16, *An Act to reduce the Rate of Interest* [i.e. the rate more than which it was usury to charge] *without any Prejudice to Parliamentary Securities.*          [5] Vol. I. p. 518; and see p. 347–9, 509.

of 1847 had finally proved the usefulness of a flexible bank-rate. So, by permission and evasion, the money market was freed. In practice, the usury laws served only to interfere with mortgage operations, when the mortgage could not be arranged on a 5 per cent. basis, and occasionally to make a railway company in difficulties issue 5 per cent. debentures below par, because it might not create 5½ per cents.[1] The law had been "practically swept away in all cases except where real security was given,"[2] as Campbell said in the Lords; and even the sphere of real property had been invaded; for usury, *i.e.* interest beyond 5 per cent., was already sanctioned for the convenience of building societies.

The repealing bill was introduced, very appropriately, by Gladstone as Chancellor of the Exchequer and James Wilson, founder of the *Economist*, as Financial Secretary to the Treasury. There was really no debate in the Commons; though one member thought fit to make a bad point against Peel's Bank Act by arguing that if the law restricted the creation of bank money it ought also to restrict interest. In the Lords, the bill was managed by Lansdowne, who quoted John Calvin's critique of usury doctrine. It was blessed by three Lord Chancellors present, past, and future[3]. It repealed Acts, and parts of Acts, stretching back for England to Henry VIII; for Scotland to James VI; and for Ireland to Charles I.

By an odd accident, the state, again working through Gladstone, had revived in 1843 a quaint, exceptional bit of labour legislation which only expired in 1856—the law regulating working conditions among the coal-whippers of London Pool. 'Whipping' was the job of filling and hoisting baskets of coal from the hold and emptying them into barges. In 1831 the Thames coal-code of 1807 had been repealed[4]; and the statutory control of whippers' wages, which had led to notorious abuses, lapsed. But in 1843 joint action by the City Corporation and the coal-whippers had produced a private bill which Gladstone took over, for the registration and employment of the whippers under commissioners. Its excellent intention was, in modern terms, to decasualise the work and secure jobs for gangs of registered whippers in regular rotation. The men, some em-

---

[1] See Gladstone's speech in the Commons, Hansard, Third Series, CXXIV. 929.
[2] Hansard, Third Series, cxxv. 581.
[3] *Ibid.*
[4] The code described in vol. I. p. 234-5.

ployers, and the clerk of the Thames Police Court believed that it succeeded. Renewed several times, in 1851 after full inquiry, it was allowed to expire in 1856, on the ground that it had done its work in delivering the men from "a state of squalid poverty."[1] Shipowners had bargained for its expiry by promising to start an office of their own and never to hire men or pay wages in public-houses. With this the Board of Trade was content. The question was never reopened, because the old-style whippers were passing away.

The connection of the coal-whippers with London and tide-water helps to explain this long-lived regulation. Parliament never controlled the loading of colliers at Whitehaven or the unloading of railway trucks. But the Thames flows by Westminster, and seamen, in one way or another, had always been a concern of the state. Navigation laws were but recently repealed. With them had gone laws, and clauses, requiring shipowners to adjust the numbers of seamen and apprentices to tonnage: as a result, the 31,636 enrolled apprentices of 1850 had fallen to 13,826 by 1854[2]. But, while abandoning this type of regulation, the state had been acquiring a new solicitude for the welfare of the seaman and of the traveller by sea, shown in a series of Passenger Acts, Merchant Seamen's Acts and Steam Navigation Acts, and embodied in the great consolidating Merchant Shipping Act of 1854 (17 and 18 Vict. c. 18), a code of two hundred pages[3].

All seagoing ships must have an appropriate equipment of boats and life-buoys. Seagoing steamers must have safety-valves to their engines; they must carry fire-hoses; when built of iron they must have watertight compartments; they must provide shelter against the weather for deck-passengers. The right of inspecting steamers lay with the growing marine department of the Board of Trade. For the general supervision of maritime affairs, an Act of 1850 (13 and 14 Vict. c. 93)[4] had

[1] See George, M. D., "The London Coal Heavers," *E.J.* (*Ec. Hist.*), 1927, p. 244. This paragraph is based on Mrs George's article.
[2] From a return quoted in the House by Cardwell, May 18, 1854. Hansard, Third Series, cxxxiii. 571.
[3] The early Passenger Acts are 43 Geo. III, c. 56; 9 Geo. IV, c. 21; 5 and 6 Vict. c. 107 (see Walpole, K. A., in *T.R.H.S.*, 1932: cp. p. 232 n. 2, above). The early Merchant Seamen's Acts are 7 and 8 Vict. c. 112 and 8 and 9 Vict. c. 116. The Steam Navigation Acts are 9 and 10 Vict. c. 100; 11 and 12 Vict. c. 81 and 14 and 15 Vict. c. 79.
[4] The Mercantile Marine Act.

called into being elective Local Marine Boards in all active ports, to co-operate with the Board of Trade.

Beyond the safety clauses, the consolidating law, which repealed forty previous Acts, contained sections dealing with these marine boards; with shipowners' liability, wrecks, salvage, lighthouses, pilotage, registration and tonnage; with the keeping of logs; with boats, lights, crimes and deaths at sea; with marine store dealers, and with the rights, obligations and welfare of seamen. The marine store dealers'. sections (§ 480 *sqq.*) are curiously out of keeping with the reputed spirit of the age. Among various burdens laid on those who dealt in "anchors, cables, sails, or old junk, old iron, or marine stores of any description," was an obligation not to "purchase marine stores from any person apparently under the age of sixteen years." No doubt the clause was aimed at pilfering by ships' boys; but that does not make it less paternal or, with its "apparently," more easy to administer.

From the seamen's acts of the 'forties the law of 1854 took over the 'lime-juice clauses' and, in general, the attempt to provide a minimum of medical comfort and enough breathing space in the fo'castle. It carefully regulated apprenticeship, now become voluntary. It contained a whole wage-paying code, but no wage regulation. And it made premature solicitation of seamen by lodging-house keepers illegal. While leaving carefully untouched the central economic problems of value and the balancing of the factors of production, capital in ships and seamen's labour, the law had finally added a whole new province to the territory of the state.

It was a province difficult to administer, because the necessary disciplinary powers of shipowners and shipmasters, and the loneliness of the high seas, could often cover offenders' tracks[1]. In 1867 the 'lime-juice' and seamen's accommodation clauses of the Act of 1854 were improved, and the seaman was given a claim—obviously not easy to enforce—for wages during any period in which he was sick owing to the master's or owners' neglect to supply him with proper food and medicine[2]. In the early 'seventies there was a Merchant Shipping Act every other

---

[1] See, *e.g.*, the evidence given before the *S.C. on the Merchant Seamen Bill*, 1878 (XVI. 77).

[2] The Act is 30 and 31 Vict. c. 124. Up to this time the 'lime-juice clauses' had not been successful: there was still much scurvy. Simon, Sir J., *English Sanitary Institutions*, 2nd ed. 1897, p. 301–2.

year[1]. The seaman's friends in parliament were fighting those who made profitable capital of coffin ships, or risked men's lives by overloading. The last of the series was the Act of 1876 (39 and 40 Vict. c. 80) which at last declared the sending of an unseaworthy ship to sea a misdemeanour; regulated the stowage of grain and deck cargoes; and introduced the load line named after Samuel Plimsoll, once secretary of the Great Exhibition and from 1868 to 1880 radical member for Derby, who more than any one was responsible for the shipping legislation of these years[2]. When Plimsoll left parliament there came a halt in protective lawmaking for seamen, though the principles of the existing law of wages, apprenticeship, and certification of masters were extended to the English fisheries in 1883[3]. The Scottish fisheries had their own law and their old-established Board. It was in their interest that an Act of parliament of 1884–5, not applicable to England, dealt in its ninth clause with the construction and hooping of herring barrels[4].

John Bright had called the Ten Hours Bill of 1847 "a delusion practised on the working classes," which at "no distant day" would have to be repealed, because wages would fall[5]. In 1855 Harriet Martineau was foretelling that, if employers had to fence machinery thoroughly and carry the burden of mill accidents, they would "retire from occupations so intolerably burdensome."[6] But Queen Victoria's acceptance of a gold medal from the operatives at the hands of Lord Ashley, when the Ten Hours Act came into force in 1848, symbolised the state's definite approval of the policy[7]. Flouting Bright and Miss Martineau, not only real wages but even cash wages rose[8],

---

[1] In 1871, 1873 and 1875; 34 and 35 Vict. c. 110; 36 and 37 Vict. c. 85; 38 and 39 Vict. c. 88.
[2] Plimsoll lived till 1898. See the *D.N.B.* and his retrospective evidence before the *Labour Commission, Sec. B* (1892, XXXVI. part 2), Q. 11,244 *sqq.*
[3] By 46 and 47 Vict. *An Act to amend the Merchant Shipping Acts*, 1854–80, *with respect to fishing vessels and apprenticeship to...fishing...and otherwise.*
[4] 48 and 49 Vict. c. 70.
[5] Speech of February 17, 1847. Hansard, Third Series, LXXXIX. 1136.
[6] *The Factory Controversy. A Warning*, p. 41. This was when the Factory Law Amendment Association was compaigning against the Law and against Horner the Inspector. Hutchins and Harrison, *A History of Factory Legislation*, p. 113–16.
[7] 'Alfred's' *History of the Factory Movement*, II. 285.
[8] As Bright argued, owing to Corn Law Repeal. Trevelyan, G. M., *The Life of John Bright*, p. 158.

and the cotton mills of the later 'fifties were thought to be in danger of outrunning the supplies of cotton. The Ten Hours Act had soon required amendment, but. was never repealed[1]. It had been evaded by a system of relay working, until the supplementary and perhaps more important Act of 1850 (13 and 14 Vict. c. 54) ordered that women and young persons should work only between 6.0 a.m. and 6.0 p.m. or between 7.0 a.m. and 7.0 p.m., with an hour and a half for meals, and should cease work at 2.0 p.m. on Saturdays. By an odd anomaly, the Act did not apply to children, and so had to be supplemented in 1853. Yet it established *la semaine anglaise* by law[2], and gave the short time committees of the North the basis for that general limitation of hours which they had always desired; although J. M. Cobbett's attempt to clinch the matter for them with a Bill which required the factory engines to stop between 5.30 p.m. and 6.0 a.m. failed[3].

The textile manufacturers' old and not altogether unfair grievance, that they were pilloried beyond their deserts, and singled out among manufacturers to be dragooned by masterful Inspectors like Leonard Horner, remained unabated until 1860. In 1847 Mark Phillips of Manchester had asked, as many had asked before and since, why there should be this indirect limitation of adult labour in one field only; and John Bright, referring to what to-day would be called welfare work in his own mills, had suggested that the law, by treating the master as the natural enemy of the operatives, would embitter industrial relations and spoil such work[4]. The manufacturers in the 'fifties had their Factory Amendment Law Association, which achieved something against Leonard Horner, their chosen enemy among Factory Inspectors. But the delayed and partial answer of the state to Mark Phillips' question came in 1860 and 1861, not in the form which they desired, but in the form of Acts "to place the employment of Women, Young Persons, and Children in Bleaching and Dyeing Works," and "Women, Young Persons, Youths and Children in Lace Factories under the Regulations of the Factories Acts."[5]

It was not suggested by reformers that these industries were

---

[1] Or rather was only repealed to be strengthened, in 1874, by 37 and 38 Vict. c. 44.
[2] See below, p. 448.
[3] In 1853. Hutchins and Harrison, *op. cit.* p. 110.
[4] Hansard, Third Series, LXXXIX. 1083, 1136.
[5] The Acts are 23 and 24 Vict. c. 78 and 24 and 25 Vict. c. 117.

particularly harmful, though all had their abuses: they were simply those nearest to the textile industries proper, the territory easiest to occupy. By infection from their neighbours, they had often already acquired factory habits. Dewhurst's of Salford, dyers and finishers, a firm "among the largest in the trade," was working factory hours, and rarely overtime, in 1854–5[1]. The rush of the finishing business, when merchants were hurrying to ship, did however mean spells of overtime throughout the trade. But the works did not employ an abnormal proportion of women and children. They were manned by "a very respectable class of work-people,"[2] who made good money. Employers, especially the larger bleachers and dyers, were not as a body hostile to the prospect of regulation. They justified their occasional long hours by explaining the cause, and by pointing out that the pace of work was not set by machinery; that there was a good deal of "stand off" in the course of the day; and that the workpeople were unusually healthy, especially the bleachers. The facts were not disputed; but logic and geography were against one set of living rules for spinners and weavers and a different set for bleachers and dyers. Hence 23 and 24 Vict. c. 78 of the year 1860. It was in the debates on this Bill that Sir James Graham, an upright embodiment of the Peel tradition and the mid-Victorian state, announced his conversion to 'factory principles.'[3]

In 1860 lace had just ripened for the control which this standard statesman was now ready to apply. When the Children's Commission had inquired in the 'forties, more than half the lace machines were worked by hand and in private houses. Besides, there was the true hand-made lace. Factories were not dominant and so the industry was reckoned unfit for regulation. This obstacle, Tremenheere reported in 1861, "may now be said to have ceased." Machine-made lace had become a factory product. Of 3000–4000 machines, "not more than ninety," and they old-fashioned, were "worked by hand in private houses."[4] So, with some unimportant adjustments, the textile code for 'protected persons' might be applied to the trade; and it was.

---

[1] *Report of the Commissioner appointed to inquire how far it may be advisable to extend* [the Factory Acts] *to bleaching works* 1854–5 (XVIII. 1), p. xvii.

[2] *Ibid.* p. vii.

[3] On May 9, 1860. Hansard, Third Series, CLVIII. 984.

[4] *Report on the expediency of subjecting the Lace Manufacture to the...Factory Acts*, 1861 (XXII. 461), p. 6.

By this time many reformers were dominated less by the particular evils of child labour than by its general interference with education. The educational aspect is prominent in the series of reports on children in "trades and manufactures not already regulated by law" which the Commissioners of the 'sixties issued between 1863 and 1867[1]. Just as prominent is the continued use of even the youngest children, for labour "in private houses" in the most insanitary conditions, and in the fields, wherever they were good for it. The unregulated sections of the lace manufacture yielded ugly evidence. So did hosiery and straw plaiting and other light trades. The common age at which to begin the work of seaming knitted gloves was five: a witness had seen "many as young as" three and a half[2]. Four years old was a usual, three and a half or three a not uncommon, age for entering the straw plaiting 'schools.' Things were much the same in pillow lace 'schools,'[3] and not very different in the horribly overcrowded 'mistresses' rooms' in which machine-made lace was finished[4]. As jobs got heavier, the demand for very young children to do them slackened. In the Birmingham trades, although work sometimes began at seven years old, nine or ten was much more general[5].

The fact that a child started to earn relatively late was no safeguard against ignorance, overwork, degrading conditions or excessive hours. There were the wretched little mould runners of the Potteries, hurrying with their loads for twelve hours a day in and out of temperatures of 100 to 120 degrees—a fire and ice purgatory in winter time; the child nailers in their "private houses"; the savage children of the brick-fields; the chain-smiths' boys distorted by wielding hammers too heavy for their strength. It was among the Midland metal-workers and at Sheffield that the Commissioners, their minds running on education, put questions to which were given such answers as these—"a King is him that has all the money and gold";[6] "the devil is a good person; I don't know where he lives"; "all go in the pithole, when them be buried; they never get out or live again."[7]

State control in the Potteries, in the Birmingham area, in

---

[1] Usually quoted as the Children's Employment Commission. The Reports are in 1863, XVIII; 1864, XXII; 1865, XX; 1866, XXIV; 1867 (agriculture), XVI.

[2] *Second Report*, 1864, p. xxxvi.   [3] *Ibid.* p. xxxix.

[4] *First Report*, 1863, p. 184.   [5] *Third Report*, 1864, p. x.

[6] *Fourth Report*, 1865, p. xv.   [7] *Third Report*, p. xvii.

the metallurgical trades wherever found, except the more modern branches of engineering, and at many other points on the industrial field, was made difficult by the prevalence of child-hiring, not by the firm but by the workman[1]. Dish, saucer, and plate makers hired the mould runners. The masters said they could not "correct it—without incurring the risk of exciting tumult."[2] In the Birmingham trades, most of the children and many 'young persons' were hired "by the adult piece-worker."[3] In iron-works, puddlers, shinglers, and forgers took on the lads. In the chain and nail and lock and saddlers' ironmongery trades, boys were rarely hired by the firm; "never in small works."[4] "We employ the anchor-smiths and they employ a mob or gang"[5] is a typical bit of evidence. Boiler-rivetters did the same in Lancashire. And at Sheffield "the workers even in factories keep much of the old independence of their masters, in fact, are more in the position of small masters themselves."[6] So the Sheffield men always had been, and would remain.

Yet there was legislation while the Commissioners' reports were coming in. The first report made plain that the old laws protecting climbing boys were inoperative in most places, "the metropolis and some other towns excepted."[7] Many pitiful cases came to light of children killed while climbing. There was a slave-trade in boys. "In Liverpool," said a master sweep, "where there are lots of bad women you can get any quantity you want."[8] On that report Charles Kingsley wrote his *Water Babies*, and left Mr Grimes the sweep eternally stuck in a chimney. Parliament at once accepted a restraining Bill of Lord Shaftesbury's (27 and 28 Vict. c. 37); but two years later the fifth report showed that the restraint was ineffective. It estimated the sooty and sore army of the climbing boys at two thousand[9]. Even in 1875, after yet another law, a working sweep believed that "there is plenty of boys climbing in large towns."[10] By a second Act of 1864 (27 and 28 Vict. c. 48) the six trades first reported on, which included the deadly lucifer match making, had been put under factory law. As one of them, fustian cutting, was not a mill industry, the term factory was defined

---

[1] Cp. above, p. 128.  [2] *First Report*, p. xxviii.  [3] *Third Report*, p. xi.
[4] *Ibid*. p. 12.  [5] *Ibid*. p. 19.  [6] *Fourth Report*, p. 2.
[7] *First Report*, p. lxxxiii. See vol. I. p. 577-8.
[8] *Ibid*. p. lxxxviii.  [9] *Fifth Report*, p. xxi.
[10] R.C. *on the Working of the Factory and Workshop Acts*, 1876, XXIX. App. D, p. 149.

in relation to the six trades as "any place in which persons work for hire."[1] No objection was made to this novel definition. The *Economist*, which in 1847 had compared the Factory Acts to the Corn Laws, was writing that no one who knew how they had "worked in Lancashire and Yorkshire had any doubt *now* of the wisdom of those measures." Its sole concession to former principles was that it called them "the Children's Factories Acts";[2] which they were not.

The way was clear for that general widening of the law which the Commissioners desired. It was made by the intricate Act of 1867 (30 and 31 Vict. c. 103) which put a very long list of named industries, together with any place in which fifty or more persons were employed in any manufacturing process, under the factory code and the Home Office Inspectors—with a large number of exceptions and reservations, and some special prohibitions of women's or children's labour in dangerous processes, such as glass-melting and metal-grinding[3].

With the Factory Act was associated a Workshop Act (30 and 31 Vict. c. 146) covering all children, young persons, and women engaged in handicraft, "with or without wages," in "any room or place whatever" in which the employer had "the right of access or control." Thus it covered an employer's family but not his outworkers. Hours were made more elastic than in the factories; control and inspection were entrusted to the local sanitary authorities. The Act was vague and only permissive. The local authorities were supine, in country districts generally, but also in many towns. The task laid on them was heavy, but often it was not even faced. Three years later, in the area of one chief factory inspector, out of 352 authorities reported on, 172 had taken no steps whatever to enforce the law and only 110 had arranged for frequent visitation of workshops[4]. To correct these omissions, the inspection, but not the sanitary control, of workshops was transferred in 1871 to the Home Office staff, who thus became the too busy overseers of some 110,000, instead of only 30,000, work-places of all sorts and sizes[5].

When they were grappling with this heavy duty, Forster's

[1] A discussion of this is in Hutchins and Harrison, *op. cit.* p. 155.

[2] *Economist*, May 21, 1864.

[3] It has been held that the exceptions and reservations "nullified half the good the regulation might have done." Hutchins and Harrison, *op. cit.* p. 169.

[4] *Workshops Act, return on the enforcement*, 1870, LIV. 555.

[5] Hutchins and Harrison, *op. cit.* p. 230-1.

Education Act of 1870, with the corresponding Scottish Act of 1872, was applying the only general cure for child labour, direct compulsion to attend school. Meanwhile the textile unions of the North were working behind the women's petticoats for a 54-hour week: they got 56½ hours in 1874. The last of the doctrinaires were arguing that the law should not touch the liberty of adults, even of adults in petticoats. Advocates of woman's right to compete with the uncontrolled adult male supported them. Like the *Economist* of the 'sixties, they thought in terms of Children's Factory Acts. But their parliamentary leader, Henry Fawcett, Professor of Political Economy in the University of Cambridge, was well beaten when he moved "to omit the word woman" from the textile factory bill of 1874. The law was barely deflected by their efforts from a course long since set[1].

This was important, because in 1878 factory law was consolidated into a single great Factories and Workshops Act (41 and 42 Vict. c. 17)[2]. The work had been prepared by a commission appointed in 1875. Its evidence and reports are full of administrative problems, and only touch here and there on such gross abuses as fill the pages of earlier inquiries. The worst of these had at least been scotched; and "direct compulsion" to schooling, "accepted...with surprisingly little opposition," had "already produced satisfactory results."[3] The slight deflection of the law concerned grown women, as Fawcett and his supporters wished. The amendment "to omit the word woman" was, it is true, beaten on clause after clause. But the commissioners had suggested that at one point existing law might be reversed: under it, all dwelling-houses where women and children followed handicrafts were liable to inspection. They thought that by including women at this point the law went too far. The reversal was effected by a clause in the Act exempting from inspection workshops "conducted on the system of not employing children and young persons"—to the benefit of woman-driving laundry-men and milliners.

The essentials of the law, which now covered nearly all the 'in-working' manufactures of the country, had not been greatly changed since they had been worked out for the textile mills

---

[1] This episode is fully described in Hutchins and Harrison, *op. cit.* ch. IX.

[2] It repealed nineteen Acts, or parts of Acts, back to Peel's *Health and Morals of Apprentices Act* of 1802.

[3] *Report*, p. lvi.

in the 'thirties. Brief general statements about sanitation and safety leave room for the improved level of both towards which the inspectorate had been working. The standard day contains 10 hours work; Saturday 6½ hours. In most industries this standard day must fall between 6.0 a.m. and 6.0 p.m., or between 7.0 a.m. and 7.0 p.m. A child is anyone under 14, a young person any one under 18. A child between 10 and 14 when at work must be a 'half-timer,' a type which a generation of lawmaking had defined[1]. But the employer's obligation to see that factory children receive half-time education is retained "as a privilege, not imposed as a burden."[2] (The country had set its heart on education for all: the privilege would be continuously challenged.) From a few occupations women and children remain excluded[3]; but the list is not increased. They are excluded also from nightwork, except some 'male young persons' in metallurgy. Besides the group of women put outside the law, women and children employed in their own homes are also excluded, if no power is used and no hired persons found there. Such people had not been excluded under the Act of 1867. Outworkers proper all remain outlaws.

After 1878 the state, thinking that its work was good, rested from this sort of law-making for five years. There had not been so long a pause since 1844. A law of 1883 which ended it belongs to the old series. A fresh series, the late Victorian, was only opened in 1886 with an Act 'to regulate the Labour of Children and Young Persons in Shops.'[4] The commissioners of 1875 had glanced at that class of labour, but had decided to pass by on the other side[5].

But, during the pause in factory legislation, parliament, urged on by those most concerned, had written a fresh page in the law of employment. At common law, an employer's liability to the public was very different from his liability to his servants. If his servant caused injury to a third party, the employer was liable, even if the servant was doing what he had been told not to do. But if the employer had taken reasonable safety precautions, he had no liability should one servant hurt another.

[1]  Since the Act of 1844: see vol. 1. p. 576.
[2]  From the *Report* of 1876, p. lvi.
[3]  They are, for all females, coal-mining and glass-making; for girls under sixteen, brick-making; for boys under twelve, glass-making; for children under eleven, fustian-cutting and metal-grinding. An odd arbitrary list.
[4]  49 and 50 Vict. c. 55.
[5]  *Report*, p. xxiii.

The Employers' Liability Act of 1880 (43 and 44 Vict. c. 42) started the process of assimilating the position of servants to that of the public. In the extreme case of the railways, the assimilation was complete. A shunter and a passenger killed by a negligent driver were all one to the new law. For other employments it did not go so far. Seamen, domestic servants, and those not employed in manual labour it did not touch[1].

Actual wage rates, except those of government servants, the Gladstonian state had not thought of touching. Nor had it strengthened the existing law against wage filching by payment in truck. There was no general Truck Act between that of 1831 and that of 1887 which, like the Shops Act of the previous year, belongs to the late Victorian group of labour laws[2]. The only legislative sequel to a wide, if not exhaustive, inquiry made in 1871[3] into survivals of truck was an Act of 1874 intended to check, not truck proper, but old abuses connected with frame rents in the outwork knitting industry[4]. There was a remnant of truck in that industry among about 1200 workers on the borders of Nottingham and Derby; but this was left to time and the old law, together with a good deal of open or veiled truck at the company shops of Welsh iron works, the stores of Lanarkshire collieries, and other places[5]. The few surviving middlemen truckers, in scattered outwork trades like knitting and nailing, were often publicans at whose houses the goods were handed in[6]. They were hit hard when in 1883 the rule against wage paying at public houses, which had been a part of the law of coal mines ever since 1842, was extended to every occupation, even to agriculture: "no wages shall be paid to any workman at or within any public house, beershop, or place for the sale of any spirits, wine, cyder, or other spirituous or fermented liquor, or any office, garden, or place belonging thereto."[7]

Lord Ashley's Coalmines Act of 1842 was a labour law not concerned with the shafts and workings. Those of the 'fifties were safety laws concerned with little else, and of incalculable value. By 1855 there were general rules for all mines, and

[1] See *Dict. Pol. Econ.* s.v. "Employers' Liability."
[2] See vol. I. p. 410, 562 *sqq.*
[3] *Report of the R.C. on Truck*, 1871, xxxvi.
[4] See vol. I. p. 563–4.
[5] *Report* of 1871, p. xxx (hosiery) and *passim*, and see below, p. 456 *sqq.*
[6] *Report*, p. xxvii, xxx.
[7] Barmen naturally excluded. The Act is 46 and 47 Vict. c. 98.

provision for the making of special rules for each[1]. It was in preparing these last that the inspectors learnt what further securities all the mines required. By 1860 (by 23 and 24 Vict. c. 151) a timid step was being taken beyond Ashley's Act. It had not allowed boys under ten to go down the shafts. Now they might not go under twelve, unless furnished with a certificate that they could read and write. Winding engine men must be eighteen years old: under the Act of 1842, a lad of fifteen at the engine might hold men's lives in his hand. But the words most important for the future were in §29, which empowered the colliers in every mine "to station a Person (being one of the Persons...employed in such...Mine...) at the Place appointed for...weighing...in order to take an account thereof," and see to it that when they were paid by weight they were paid fair. A fierce struggle in Yorkshire lay behind that clause[2]. For years after 1860 it was fought or evaded by the coalowners. An Act of 1872 strengthened the position of the checkweighman a little; but not until 1887 did the law become all that the miners desired[3]. Yet the first recognition in 1860 of the bare right of a representative of the men to put his finger somewhere near the pay-sheets is the decisive historical moment.

The state had waged unsystematic war on disease with whole regiments of ill-assorted Acts ever since the pioneering Public Health Act of 1848, passed in cholera and typhus time[4]. Strategy had been halting because the state at once distrusted and over-trusted its tactical agents, the local authorities. There was in parliament a Whiggish suspicion of corporations not so long ago reputed corrupt. At the administrative headquarters there was a Benthamite faith in the expert, propagated by the first chief of staff, Edwin Chadwick. The whole tradition of local government, however, as the eighteenth century had bequeathed it, favoured permissive rather than compulsory legislation and a great reliance on that municipal initiative which

[1] Cp. above, p. 100. The series begins with 13 and 14 Vict. c. 100: "Whereas it is expedient that Provision should be made for the Inspection of Coal Mines," etc.

[2] See Webb, S. and B., *History of Trade Unionism*, p. 289–92.

[3] Under the consolidating Act, 50 and 51 Vict. c. 58.

[4] The tangled history of sanitary legislation is given in full in the *Second Report of the Royal Sanitary Commission*, 1871 (xxxv), p. 7 *sqq*. For the Act of 1848 see vol. I. p. 545.

produced local Acts of Parliament. Whig distrust of borough finance had made the Municipal Corporations Act of 1835 severe; and it was rigidly interpreted in the light of the expanding legal principle of *ultra vires*. It may be assumed that the Common Law would not have hindered an old unreformed borough from spending borough money on a fountain, had it been moved to do so; but special Bath and Wash-house Acts had been thought necessary in the 'forties to enable "inhabitants of towns through the Town Council to supply themselves with the means of cleanliness."[1] Without an Act, general or local, such obvious expenditures might be held to be *ultra vires*[2].

The General Board of Health of 1848, Chadwick's and Ashley's Board, was a patent replica of the Poor Law Commission of three—"two Lords and a Barrister, to preserve the health of the living," as it was said, "and then, after a year or so of doubtful success...a Physician to bury the dead";[3] for Dr Southwood Smith was only added at the time of the Metropolitan Interments Act of 1850. The Barrister and the Physician were salaried. The Board in the first instance worked through the Guardians of the Poor[4]. It could only force a corporate borough to accept for its Council the functions of a Local Board of Health, or force such a Board to be elected elsewhere, when the area in question had an abnormally high mortality. The ordinary procedure was for a town to petition to have the Act applied. At the end of five years only about two millions of urban population had come under it[5]. For twenty years more it was hardly felt except in urban and urbanised areas. In

[1] *Second Report of the Royal Sanitary Commission*, p. 15.

[2] According to Brice, S., *A Treatise on ultra vires* (1893), Preface, the doctrine is "of modern growth" and is "first prominently mentioned...in equity...in 1846." It was mainly applied, in the first instance, to Railway Companies. Robson, W. A., *The Development of Local Government* (1931), p. 194–6, seems to hold that the Municipal Corporations Act of 1835 (5 and 6 Wm. IV, c. 76) left corporations free to spend money on, and levy rates for, any object which was "for the public Benefit of the inhabitants" (§ 92); and that the doctrine of *ultra vires* was applied to them by false analogy. To me § 92 of the Act appears more restrictive, though it seems to give great liberty of expenditure to any borough so rich in rents and profits that it has no need to levy rates. The decision is for lawyers.

[3] Dr H. W. Rumsey, *Essays on State Medicine*, quoted in Simon, *English Sanitary Institutions*, p. 214.

[4] See its *First Report*, 1849 (XXIV. 1). "The Legislature contemplates the Poor Law Union...as the chief local administrative body," p. 24.

[5] *Report* for 1854 (XXXV. 1), p. 14.

1868 Suffolk had only three Local Boards, all in towns; the Welsh counties, excluding Glamorgan, an average of less than three; Hereford only two; Northampton and Huntingdon each only one[1].

Down to 1854, when the first General Board lapsed and Chadwick's official career ended with it, he and Ashley and Southwood Smith worked incessantly, advising and circularising where they might not command, promoting Common Lodging House Bills, Burials Bills and a whole series of minor drainage and waterworks Bills to confirm the provisional orders of the Board. If Chadwick had won all his battles, the Board would have secured complete control of burial throughout the country, and London would have had a unified system not only of drainage but of water supply. But as the Board said in its last report, "extensive interests" were "unavoidably interfered with" by its plans—undertakers, cemetery companies, water companies and engineers[2]. Chadwick was an awkward subordinate and no handler of men. His later official chiefs attacked his policies. Parliament became restive about centralisation and swept the Board away. For four years a precarious one-man board without salaried members replaced it, to be succeeded in 1858 by a department of the Home Office[3], and in 1871 by the Local Government Board.

The pace slackened after Chadwick left. Instead of the autocratic, single-minded, and clumsy-penned sanitarian, who respected no one, the sociable Tom Taylor was promoted secretary. He found time amid his sanitary duties to write plays[4], and died editor of *Punch*. Chadwick's allies, although they knew all his weaknesses, felt that they had been watching "the failure and foundering of a life-boat"[5] when he fell; but a group of health Acts of 1855, including that which created for London the Metropolitan Board of Works (18 and 19 Vict. c. 120), was some consolation. Within the next few years, the

---

[1] *Return...of the Local Boards*, 1867–8 (LVIII. 789).

[2] *Report for* 1854, p. 48. The report is self-defensive, self-righteous, very Chadwickian.

[3] Medical work came under a Committee of the Privy Council in 1858. See the evidence of Tom Taylor, the Secretary, in *First Report of Royal Sanitary Commission*, 1868–9 (XXXII. 303).

[4] *Our American Cousin* appeared in 1858. In 1857 he read to the Social Science Congress a paper on *Central and Local Action in relation to Town Improvement*, criticising centralisation.

[5] Simon, *op. cit.* p. 236.

Metropolitan Board took in hand the arterial drainage of London and cut the great outfall sewers, North and South, to Barking and Plumstead Marshes.

Eleven years later, the state moved forward again, its memory for sanitary needs having been jogged by a return of the cholera. The Sanitary Act of 1866 (29 and 30 Vict. c. 90), which included London, made sanitary inspection obligatory on local authorities and overcrowding a nuisance; and for the first time empowered a Secretary of State, upon complaint received, to compel those authorities to remove nuisances and to provide sewers and water supplies. "The grammar of common sanitary legislation acquired the novel virtue of an imperative mood."[1] It was time.

Sanitary law in the late 'sixties was scattered about in local acts, factory acts, burial acts, lodging-house, vaccination, alkali, smoke and food adulteration acts, with its core in the Public Health Act of 1848 and the Local Government Act of 1858[2], which had altered the constitution and powers of the Local Boards. The administering authorities overlapped, yet did not cover the whole field. The sewer authority was normally the Vestry; the nuisances authority the Guardians of the Poor. Even the greatest local authorities might be apathetic. Liverpool, anticipating parliament, had appointed the first British Medical Officer of Health in 1847[3]: Manchester did not follow for twenty-one years. In industrial matters especially, as the history of workshop inspection shows, there was a clear reluctance to adopt sanitary law as such; although the early 'sixties had seen the discreditable spectacle of tiny insanitary urban and rural districts adopting the Local Government Act with its sanitary obligations, which they neglected, to escape a recent Highways Act and keep their roads in their own hands, also to be neglected[4]. The very capable Royal Sanitary Commission of 1869–71 recommended that "all powers requisite

---

[1] Simon, *op. cit.* p. 300. The bill, it should be added, was planned by Simon, as medical officer to the Committee of the Privy Council, and H. A. Bruce, later Lord Aberdare, then under-secretary at the Home Office, in 1864, before the cholera.

[2] This Act, 21 and 22 Vict. c. 98, was "to be construed with the Public Health Act of 1848 as one Act."

[3] Hope, E. W., *Health at the Gateway*, a sanitary history of Liverpool (1931), p. 43.

[4] Robson, *op. cit.* p. 43–4. See the *Return of Local Boards* of 1867–8, which contains twenty-nine districts with populations under 2000.

for the health of towns and country should in every place be possessed by one responsible local authority";[1] but that is an ideal not even yet fully attained.

The report of this Commission served as basis for the Act of 1871 (34 and 35 Vict. c. 70) which created the Local Government Board; for succeeding Acts which concentrated sanitary power in the Board's hands; and for the consolidating Public Health Act of 1875. Unhappily for the cause of health, the Local Government Board absorbed, and on its sanitary side was dominated by, the old Poor Law Board. Now the Poor Law Board had a bad sanitary record. Only four years back, it had just been wakened from its "long sleep" of sanitary neglect[2]. Its system was formal and bureaucratic. It subordinated the medical consultant at headquarters to the administrative official. The district inspectors on whom it relied lacked medical knowledge and had been well trained in economy[3]. Although the Local Government Board was now obliged to establish medical officers of health everywhere, it acquiesced in a system inherited from the Poor Law. Its officers were usually 'part-timers,' whose often exiguous salaries might be expected to measure the amount of attention which they would give to their duties. Preventive policies, whether of destitution or sickness, had not flowered in the old Poor Law atmosphere. Wide gaps in the nation's health defences, still to be found in the twentieth century, might have been stopped thirty years earlier, if the Local Government Board of the 'seventies had made full use of the powers which the legislation of 1871–5 gave it, and of the medical knowledge and facilities for inquiry then available. When cholera strode north-westward from Egypt in 1884, the Board ordered a hurried medical survey of its coastal defences, of whose condition it appears to have been quite needlessly ignorant, only to find that the inferior sort of local authorities had "since their constitution done no efficient work," and that some of them showed "no desire even to be properly instructed as to the sanitary requirements of their districts."[4] There had been twelve years in which to instruct and if necessary coerce them.

[1] *Report*, 1871 (xxxv), p. 3.

[2] Chance, Sir W., *The Better Administration of the Poor Law* (1895), p. vii. See Webb, S. and B., *The English Poor Law*, part II, p. 319, 622 and *passim*.

[3] Based on Simon, *op. cit.* p. 387 *sqq.* Simon witnessed what he regarded as a retreat from policies which he had himself initiated, and may have been over-hard on the L.G.B.; but his authority is high.

[4] Report of Dr Ballard, quoted in Simon, *op. cit.* p. 404.

The survey of 1884–6 was called off before it was finished, and the age closed—cholera at its end as at its beginning—with a country much healthier than it used to be, but not nearly so healthy as it might have become, had administration done all that the law now permitted.

The Poor Law Board, whose traditions dominated the early days of the Local Government Board, had lived a threatened life of twenty years (1847–67) and had only been made permanent four years before it was absorbed[1]. That desperately unpopular extra-parliamentary body, the executive Poor Law Commission of 1834—"the three bashaws of Somerset House," had handed over to the parliamentary President of a phantom board in December 1847, when, as a result of the Irish famine and the bad trade of a year of crisis, the figures of pauperism were abnormally high. The executive Commissioners, in the thirteen years since 1834, had mapped out most of the country into the new type of Poor Law Unions, and had seen a workhouse of some sort established in nearly all of them[2]. Contrary to the expressed opinion of the *Report* of 1834, they had acquiesced, as a matter of administrative convenience, in the establishment of general mixed workhouses of the type which, when found under the unreformed system, had supplied the reporting Commissioners with their most beastly illustrations of abuse. "We recommended [in 1834] that in every Union there should be a building for the children, and one for the able-bodied males, and another for the able-bodied females; and another for the old; we supposed the use of four buildings in every Union," Nassau Senior said indignantly, many years later, protesting against what had become the universal policy[3]. But a single building was easier for the Assistant Commissioners to get built—few existing country poor-houses proved fit for

---

[1] A general reference can here be made to Webb, S. and B., *English Poor Law History: the last Hundred Years*, 2 parts, 1929. For the next generation it will be the classic narrative. Its best predecessor is H. Preston-Thomas' translation of Aschrott, P. F., *Das Englische Armen-Wesen*, first published in 1888. References below are to the second English edition of 1902. At some points Aschrott is, in my opinion, more useful than Webb.

[2] See vol. I. p. 465–6, 581–2. On p. 582, l. 5 the figure of out-paupers in 1848 should be 1,571,000 not 1,877,000.

[3] Before the *Poor Relief Committee* of 1861 (1862, x, Q. 6905). In Webb, *op. cit.* p. 129, he is quoted as saying "and another for the sick" instead of "for the old": it comes to much the same, no doubt. The explicit advocacy of "separate buildings" by the Commissioners of 1834 is on p. 306–7 of the *Report*.

any of the uses suggested—and much easier for Guardians to manage. Besides, it was hoped that able-bodied people would seldom go into workhouses at all; so it seemed wasteful to provide two separate ones for them. Indeed, the scanty evidence suggests that the Assistant Commissioners who did the local work never seriously considered the policy of classification by houses, and that the central body made no attempt to press it. They relied on regulations to secure classification inside 'the house,' with disastrous results, especially for the children and the sick[1].

The policy of not relieving the able-bodied except in the workhouse had broken down against the facts of London life and the sullen resistance of the industrial North. The new Board of 1847 confirmed the breakdown, after five years trial. It was "not expedient," ran the circular of August 25, 1852, "absolutely to prohibit out-relief even to the able-bodied."[2] (The most extreme advocates of the principles of 1834 had never suggested its abolition for widows and other impotent poor, who could most conveniently be relieved at home.) In each succeeding decade, the number of Unions to which prohibitory orders applied contracted, and the population of those to which they did not apply grew[3]. What had been thought of as a national policy in the 'thirties had become, by the 'seventies, a policy applied only to men in overcrowded rural Unions—and even there with exceptions. No doubt it had helped the good work of turning agricultural labourers into navvies, urban carters, railway men, policemen and emigrants[4]. A later generation has learnt the risks of relief systems which give insufficient encouragement to mobility and occupational adjustment. But it was hard that these risks should have been averted for forty years at the sole cost of the bread-and-cheese fed labourers, with their 9s. to 11s. a week.

Throughout the 'fifties the statistical position of poor-relief improved steadily. Starting in 1850 with a mean figure of a million people, or 5·7 per cent. of the population of England and Wales, in receipt of relief at any one time, it closed in

[1] Historians had overlooked this decisive divergence from 'the principles of 1834' until its history was written by Lord Passfield and Mrs Sidney Webb.

[2] *Fifth Annual Report of the Poor Law Board*, p. 22, quoted in Webb, p. 151 n.

[3] The prohibitory order is that of December 21, 1844: the laxer order, used for the towns, is that of December 14, 1852. Cp. Aschrott, *op. cit.* p. 165.

[4] The direct encouragement of emigration by the Poor Law authorities was insignificant. Above, p. 233.

1860 with 845,000, or 4·3 per cent. Of these, the number relieved indoors remained extraordinarily constant, at from 110,000 to 125,000[1]. As there was no important change in law or policy, it may be concluded that the statistical improvement registered, in a rough negative way, the share of the least fortunate in that improved national well-being which marked the decade. The Guardians had settled down into their local policies of administration and relief—by no means uniform, in spite of orders from the Commission or the Board—and these policies were becoming routines. Wage-earners and their families, especially in the towns, had lost none of their horror of 'the house'; nor had there been any change in their willingness to accept outdoor relief in emergency. The elective Guardians acquiesced in the outdoor system, and the central authority was in no position to coerce them, even had it resolutely wished to do so. It never raised any objection to the very general practice of giving a shilling or two a week to aged destitute folk in their own homes. Consequently, the mean number of those relieved 'out' remained nearly seven times that of those relieved 'in,' after a quarter of a century of the new Poor Law.

Those relieved 'in' included growing numbers of a class whose very existence the *Report* and legislation of the 'thirties had barely recognised—the vagrants, professional or occasional[2]. The able-bodied vagrant, and the vagrant is normally active if not always fit, had been offered 'the house' like any other able-bodied man of no resources. If he was a work-seeker become destitute, he would accept reluctantly; if a professional, with his whole heart. From Union workhouse to Union workhouse was an easy day's walk; and at the end was accommodation which the professional found perfectly satisfactory. In the metropolitan area not even a short day's walk was necessary. Various attempts had been made, during the later years of the original Commission and the early years of the Board, to deal

---

[1] The figures are summarised for the whole period in Aschrott, App. II. Figures from before 1849 (*e.g.* those quoted in vol. I. p. 582) are not comparable, being on a different basis. (See Mackay, T., supplementary volume to Nicholls' *History of the English Poor Law*, App. p. 603.) The figures here used are based on the winter and summer returns, January 1 and July 1, for each year.

[2] Cp. Webb, p. 402 *sqq.*, and Nicholls-Mackay, III. 371 *sqq.* The *Report* of 1834 gives two pages (338–40) to vagrancy and simply recommends "that the Central Board be...directed to frame and enforce Regulations as to the Relief to be afforded to vagrants...."

with the situation by law or by administrative order; but very little had come of them. A few Unions had started what in later years were known as casual wards; but most simply put the vagrants for their night's rest on the men's side of 'the house.' Especially in London, the crowding of workhouses with undesirable vagrants was causing anxiety at the Board in the late 'fifties. Plans were drawn up in 1857-8 for the creation of special metropolitan "asylums for the homeless poor"; but they came to nothing at that time[1].

At the close of the year 1860, in which the figures of poor-relief had touched a minimum, the Thames froze and a great weight of snow fell. For a month (December 17, 1860 to January 19, 1861) outdoor work was held up as it seldom is in the British climate. It was reckoned later that there was an abnormal increase of some 40,000 in what contemporaries, in the undiscriminating language of Poor Law circles, called "metropolitan pauperism."[2] Charitable people got to work; a relief fund was opened at the Mansion House; the meanness, incompetence, corruption and bumbledom of many London Poor Law authorities were pilloried[3]; and there was talk of the Poor Law having broken down. An echo of the old, and still strong, dislike of centralised administration was heard in the suggestion, very seriously made in Parliament, that the Poor Law Board with its orders was the main source of evil. Remove it, so the argument ran, and enlarge the unit of Poor Law administration; then a sufficiency of able, public-spirited men will come forward to take over and reform the system[4]. The Board, it is to be remembered, was not yet on a permanent footing: it had been created for only five years, but had been periodically renewed as a reasonably successful experiment.

For three years a strong parliamentary committee, whose leading members were Charles Villiers, Robert Lowe and Lord Robert Cecil, examined the law and its working, with special reference to the problems of London. While it was sitting the

[1] Cp. Ed. Twisleton's criticism of the reformed Scottish Poor Law of the 'forties for its neglect of such provision: vol. I. p. 587.

[2] *S.C. on Poor Relief, Report* (1864, IX. 157), p. 3. There are preliminary *Reports* and evidence in 1861, IX.

[3] For the intricacies of London poor relief, and the local Acts, see Aschrott, p. 71; Nicholls-Mackay, III. 486; Webb, *passim*.

[4] See the Debates of February 1861 in Hansard, Third Series, CLXI. 237, speech of Mr Ayrton. Ayrton was arguing for the abolition of any parochial independence and for the concentration of power in the Union.

American Civil War created fresh problems in Lancashire; but with these, as matters of special emergency, the committee did not deal.

Early unemployment difficulties in the cotton area were met by that lax administration of out-relief, to retain which the North had fought the Commissioners[1]. Poor-rates had been low in Lancashire, so for a time there was a margin to draw upon. Yet single parishes soon began to complain of their burden—too soon, critics suggested; for, as Charles Kingsley wrote to the *Times*, the poor-rate was far heavier in Hampshire than in Lancashire[2]. But Lancashire could make its voice heard in parliament. So early as August 1862, under 25 and 26 Vict. c. 160, it had been decided that when the rate in any parish rose above 3s. in the pound of rateable value the other parishes of the Union must share in it. If the Union rate got above 5s. the Poor Law Board might order other Unions to share, but only cotton-area Unions, that is to say Unions in Lancashire, Cheshire or Derbyshire. Such rates in aid had been contemplated even in the Elizabethan law[3]. A new principle was, however, inserted in this Act of 1862, at the instance of Cobden and the Lancashire members. The burdened Unions were given emergency borrowing powers. Hitherto there had been no legal borrowing for poor-relief anywhere.

Then came the Public Works Act of 1863 (26 and 27 Vict. c. 70) under which the Treasury and the Public Works Loan Commissioners were empowered to lend to Unions and local authorities on the security of the rates, for drainage and other works of permanent utility, with a view to providing for the unemployed. Not many cotton operatives helped to make the new drains. There were not 2300 of them on all the subsidised public works in January 1864, and not 4000 in December[4].

---

[1] The fullest account from the side of administration is in Nicholls-Mackay, III, ch. 18. See also Arnold, R. A., *History of the Cotton Famine* (1864 and 1865) and especially Watts, J., *The Facts of the Cotton Famine* (1866).

[2] The columns of the *Times* for November 1862 contain much correspondence. Kingsley was rather violent and laid himself open to rejoinder. The *Times* itself in an article on "The Distress and the Resources of Lancashire" (Nov. 13) pointed out temperately that the seven South-Western counties had a poor-rate burden 120 per cent. above that of Lancashire.

[3] See 39 Eliz. c. 3 (1597). In § 2 it is provided that other parishes in the Hundred may be rated for the needs of a necessitous parish; or the County to relieve the Hundred. So far as is known, these powers had been very rarely used.

[4] Watts, *op. cit.* p. 320. Probably these were not the spinners, etc. to any great extent, but general labourers from the mills, stokers, porters, etc.

For many operatives, the Unions with the consent of the Poor
Law Board adopted the famous device, of which Lancashire
was very proud, of giving relief on condition not of hand-work
but of head-work; so many hours of education per week. With
the aid of much private charity, and a straining of all the
principles of non-intervention at the request of its prophets, the
crisis was passed—though with a national pauperism figure for
1863–4 higher by 200,000 than it had been in 1860. By 1866,
however, it was back, not at the exact figure of 1860, but at the
1860 ratio to population of 4·3 per cent.

Meanwhile the Committee had reported cautiously, and
cautious action was being taken on its recommendations. "The
continuance of a central authority" it had declared to be
"essential," and it wished to see the authority placed "upon
a permanent footing."[1] Hence permanence for the Board in
1867, and for its successor the Local Government Board of
1871. The Committee was further of opinion that the law had
not broken down in 1860–61; that there had been much abuse
of the charitable attempts to supplement it; and that the London
Unions could have handled the emergency, though not easily.
It saw no reason to interfere with the existing system of medical
relief, although Poor Law medical officers had complained
loudly before it of the arrangement which gave them "a fixed
amount of money for a very variable amount of work."[2]  It
thought that workhouse education was "on the whole satisfactory,"[3] but it advocated the provision of separate Poor Law
schools wherever practicable. There were already some.  It had
much to say about the religious difficulties in the workhouses
and the grievances of Roman Catholics. There was a recommendation that "the general question of extending the area of
rating," *i.e.* the policy of rating by Unions, not by Parishes,
should be "further considered by the House";[4] there was decided advocacy of more thorough classification of the mixed
multitudes who came within the view of the law; and there was
a proposal that the burden of metropolitan vagrancy should be
shouldered by the whole metropolis[5].

The suggestion of the Committee about Union rating; the

---

[1] *Report* of 1864, p. 11.

[2] Evidence of J. Rodgers, M.D., Q. 13,334.

[3] *Report*, p. 36.

[4] *Report*, p. 44. In its particular context this recommendation only applies to
London Unions.

[5] These are only the more important recommendations.

satisfactory experience of Union as opposed to Parish rates under the Lancashire emergency system; and the well-known fact that parochial parsimony was a main cause of the social evils of the close parish, in which liability for the poor was kept down by keeping down the cottages, led to the decisive Union Chargeability Act of 1865 (28 and 29 Vict. c. 79)[1]. There had been a common Union fund for certain general purposes from the first. Since 1834 the charges thrown upon it had increased. Now the Union became the financial unit for all purposes. No parish could evade its share of the burdens of poverty in its district by arranging that potential paupers should tramp to work in it from neighbouring higher-rated open parishes. The Act was a logical development of the Union policy of 1834.

A still prompter outcome of the *Report* of 1864 had been the Metropolitan Houseless Poor Act of that year (27 and 28 Vict. c. 116) which established a common metropolitan fund upon which Guardians might draw to make special and appropriate provision for casuals and vagrants. It was a success. Classification of 'paupers,' so long urged by the wise, was at last becoming a reality. The Metropolitan Poor Act of 1867 (30 Vict. c. 6) and later supplementary Acts helped it forward. The common fund was made available for expenditure on asylums, small-pox and fever hospitals, poor-law schools, training-ships, and other specialised relief institutions and policies. The Metropolitan Asylums Board was created and was soon doing work of the highest social value[2]. Disgusting conditions in workhouse sick-wards and infirmaries, where paupers suffering from disease of every kind were tended only by other paupers, had been exposed in the *Lancet*; and Gathorne Hardy, President of the Board, had declared in the House in 1867 that the sick were "not proper objects" for the traditional deterrent workhouse policies. "We must peremptorily insist," he said, "on the treatment of the sick...being conducted on an entirely separate system."[3] The last President of the Board, Goschen, in his last report, was even toying with the possibility of extending "gratuitous medical relief beyond the actual pauper

[1] Questions arising out of 'settlement' were those which most interested poor-law reformers of the years 1850–70. See, *e.g.*, Pashley, R., *Pauperism and the Poor Laws*, 1852.

[2] See Webb, *op. cit.* p. 321.

[3] Hansard, Third Series, CLXXXV. 163. Quoted in Webb, p. 319, but with "different system" for "separate system."

class."[1] There was thus official driving force behind the new movement. But, outside the metropolis, the Unions were hard to drive. Improvement in workhouse infirmaries was already noticeable in 1869; but even the largest towns and Unions had made very little progress with specialised institutions by 1886.

Slack trade in the late 'sixties brought with it a slight statistical increase of pauperism. For four years (1868–71) the mean number of persons relieved, 'in' and 'out,' stood at just over a million, or 4·6 per cent. of the population. The mean number of able-bodied adults relieved 'out,' excluding the vagrants, was still almost equal to the whole workhouse population[2]. (In the 'fifties it had usually been greater, and in the difficult early 'sixties much greater.) Its persistence was a standing challenge to the many individualist thinkers and public men who hoped that progress, economic, social and moral, might one day render a Poor Law superfluous, and who believed that it was their clear duty at least to get rid of outdoor relief to able-bodied adults, by some process of depauperisation, possibly drastic. In 1870 Henry Fawcett was teaching Cambridge, and in 1871 telling the country in his *Pauperism: its Causes and Remedies*, that "it would be far better altogether to abolish the Poor Law than that the present state of things should continue."[3] His own aim was not to see the law repealed but "by gradual steps to discourage and ultimately to abolish outdoor relief."[4] Herein he was in the strict tradition of 1834, an appeal to which carried weight; for the tradition of 1834 had been hallowed by thinkers and Poor Law administrators much more than it had been followed or understood. In this case at least, it was rightly interpreted.

The spirit which inspired Fawcett also inspired the Local Government Board of the 'seventies and its inspectorate. There began what has been called the crusade against outdoor relief[5]. A few Boards of Guardians joined early from conviction. Others gradually felt the pressure of official reforming opinion. Down

---

[1] Quoted in Webb, p. 322.

[2] The mean workhouse population was 137,000 in 1867 and 158,000 in 1869. The 'outdoor able-bodied adults, excluding vagrants,' rose to 150,000 in 1870. The figures and the totals are not terrifying to the modern mind.

[3] *Pauperism*, p. 41.

[4] *Ibid.* p. 24.

[5] Prof. William Smart's phrase in the historical survey of the Law prepared for the Royal Commission of 1908–9, Vol. XII (1910, LI). A full discussion with bibliographical references is in Webb, *op. cit.* p. 435 *sqq.*

to 1877, from trade-boom into trade-slump and with a growing population, the mean number of persons relieved declined year by year. The whole number of those relieved 'out' fell to less than four times the number of those relieved 'in'; the able-bodied adults relieved 'out' to less than half the workhouse population[1]. There was a trifling rise in 1879–83; but in 1884–6, when the country was worried about depression in trade and industry, the ratio to population of those relieved by the Poor Law was lower than it had ever been before (2·8 per cent.) and the mean number of able-bodied adults relieved 'out' was much smaller than it had been in the trade boom of 1871–3[2]. How far this result merely registered an administrative achievement, accompanied by increased reliance on private charity and on what Thomas Chalmers had called "the many indefinable shifts and capabilities of the pauper himself,"[3] and how far it marked a national advance in forethought and average well-being, cannot be determined with certainty. There was crushed misery in the social depths and grinding strain in strata above them. But though profits were depressed and there was much unemployment, there had been a rise in average well-being. The able-bodied rustic pauper was a type almost extinct; and as the Minority Report of the Commission of 1885–6 pointed out, in spite of "the stricter enforcement of tests in the administration of the Poor Law...the aid...so widely given by friendly and trade societies limited or deferred the pauperisation" of the industrial unemployed[4]. There were reserves to draw upon, if scanty reserves.

As for true vagrancy, it remained pretty intractable, although, with the aid of the central authority and a law of 1871[5], guardians outside London had been giving it special attention and organising casual wards ever since 1867–8. Unhappily no proper attempt was made to sift destitute work-seekers on tramp from professional vagrants. The casual ward, like the workhouse, was made deterrent for all. So, very often, were

---

[1] The figures for 1877 are: 'indoor paupers,' 150,000; able-bodied adults relieved 'out,' 73,000; ratio of all paupers to population, 2·9 per cent.

[2] Figures for 1886: total, 781,000; indoor, 186,000; able-bodied outdoor, 78,000.

[3] See vol. I. p. 367.

[4] *Minority Report*, p. xlix. Cp. above, p. 385 and below, p. 477. In Fawcett's discussion of pauperism unemployment was ignored.

[5] 34 and 35 Vict. c. 108. See Nicholls-Mackay, *op. cit.* III. 384 and Webb, *op. cit.* p. 411 *sqq.*

those labour yards which throughout the whole period Guardians opened up and down the country in times of bad trade, requiring a usually repellent and not too useful task to be done in exchange for a modicum of relief. With easy-going Guardians, on the other hand, the yard might, and did, become a mere pretext for relief—the kind of thing against which the inspectorate of the 'seventies crusaded.

It was to avoid if possible these equally anti-social extremes that Joseph Chamberlain, during the unemployment of 1886, issued a notable circular from the Local Government Board suggesting to Town Councils the initiation of really useful relief-works, like the sanitary undertakings of the Cotton Famine[1]. The circular had no prompt effect. Chamberlain was soon busy with other things. But it was a signal flown by that new Liberalism which was so little to Gladstone's taste.

At that very time a Committee was inquiring into what was called National Provident Insurance. Commissioners on Friendly Societies, reporting in 1874, had described as a National Friendly Society a scheme laid before them by a very distinguished group of people, which proposed to extend existing, but little used, facilities for buying annuities from government through the Post Office, so as to allow of similar voluntary purchases of insurance against sickness, old age, and burial. The plan was to provide complete state security for thrift, in place of the insecurity of most existing Friendly Societies. The Commissioners could not see their way to recommend it intact, and nothing important was done[2]. Then, in November 1878, an article appeared in the *Nineteenth Century* with the prophetic title "National Insurance." Its author, the Rev. W. L. Blackley, a Hampshire rector, later a canon, followed it up next year with "Compulsory Providence as a Cure for Pauperism" in the *Contemporary Review*. In 1882 he founded the National Insurance League for propaganda work. He was untirable. Within a few years, there was "hardly a platform in any important town on which he had not stood."[3]

---

[1] *Sixteenth Annual Report of the L.G.B.* p. 3. Circular of March 15, 1886. See Webb, *op. cit.* p. 367, 644–8.

[2] *Report of the R.C. on Friendly Societies*, 1874 (XXIII. part i), p. cxcvi. The memorandum is in App. IX. It was signed by both Archbishops, six Bishops, seventeen lay peers, thirty-five M.P.'s, etc. For the Friendly Societies at this time see below, p. 471 *sqq.*

[3] Blackley, M. J. J., *Thrift and National Insurance* (1906), a memoir and reprint of the articles referred to. The National Friendly Society was a part

In the 'eighties therefore National Provident Insurance meant what was known as the Blackley scheme, a rather crude proposal by which £10 was to be compulsorily deducted, through employers, from the wages of all young people between seventeen and twenty-one, and handled by the state through the Post Office[1]. Both sexes and every class were to make a similar payment, as their contribution to a national need; but only the wage-earner was to be given 8s. a week in sickness, and 4s. a week on reaching the age of seventy. Actuaries said the scheme was unsound: they were probably right. Officials said it could not be worked: they were no doubt wrong[2]. Compulsion, and the suggested contribution by those who would not benefit, were offensive to the average opinion of the day. The whole scheme was unwelcome to the vested interest of the Friendly Societies in voluntary thrift. The Committee of 1885–7 thanked Canon Blackley but decided to wait for the "further development of public opinion."[3] That would come; but when it came, bringing national insurance and old age pensions, the pioneer canon and his League were already in danger of oblivion[4].

The Scottish Poor Law had only been revised, by very conservative hands, in 1845[5]. It had immediately been subjected to the strains of famine in the Highlands and the Western

of John Acland's *Plan for rendering the Poor independent on Public Contributions* of 1786. In 1787 Joseph Townsend, in his *Dissertation on the Poor Laws*, proposed to make Friendly Societies universal and compulsory. There were several similar schemes. Those of Tom Paine, for old age pensions, kept alive the idea of public provision for age. Then interest in the subject lapsed. In 1837 Lord Lansdowne spoke favourably of public superannuation schemes. In 1867 Major Corrance advocated state assistance to the Friendly Societies (see Lamond, R. P., *The Scottish Poor Law*, 1892—originally 1870—p. 282). Before 1878 John Walter, M.P , of *The Times*, was advocating compulsory insurance: *Economist*, November 6, 1877.

[1] The scheme varied from time to time. This was its shape in 1885–7. There is a short summary of it in H. Preston-Thomas' part III, "Old Age Pensions," of the 1902 edition of Aschrott, *op. cit.*

[2] Their view was restated by Sir Robert Giffen before the *R.C. on Labour* (*General Session*), 1893–4 (XXXIX), Q. 7015 *sqq.*

[3] *S.C. on National Provident Insurance Report*, 1887 (XI. 1), p. ix. The Committee began work in 1885 but was interfered with by Home Rule crises and General Elections.

[4] Oblivion may be hastened by his omission even from the footnotes of the short section on National Insurance in Webb, *op. cit.* p. 615-21. It is hardly fair to the English pioneers to credit so much "to the example of Prince Bismarck's legislation" (p. 615). Hence this note.

[5] See vol. I. p. 365-9, 585-8.

Isles and of bad trade in the industrial districts. The ancient distinction between the 'legal' or 'enrolled' poor and the 'occasional' poor had been retained. 'Occasional' poverty was conceived of as due to sickness, accident, or other temporary incapacity; but in the bad year 1848 the Scottish Board of Supervision had been legally advised that "able-bodied persons ...unavoidably thrown out of employment" might be treated as occasional poor, and given temporary relief[1]. Before any serious use had been made of this opinion, it was overruled by the courts. Test cases decided in 1852 that the able-bodied had no right to parochial relief "in any circumstances"; and that their children, inseparable from the parents, had no right either. So the Scottish law stood throughout the period, envied by those drastic English depauperisers who were aware of it[2].

While these test decisions were being made, the business of providing Scotland with poorhouses was going forward. Most of the work was done between 1848 and 1865; but remnants of the pre-poorhouse system survived 1870. Before the revision of the law, there had been only a handful of hospitals and work-houses in the greatest cities. The usual practice had been for the parish authorities to hire ordinary houses for the accom-modation of the sick and impotent 'enrolled poor,' or to board out both them and the destitute children. There were still a number of these bad, overcrowded, ill-furnished, promiscuous parochial lodging-houses in 1861; though by 1870 they were "fast disappearing."[3] Boarding-out of the children, whether orphan or deserted or separated from vicious or impotent parents, had worked well, especially in rural districts. It was continued, though not universally, after the poorhouses were built. Crofters made excellent foster-parents; the literacy of the poorest Scottish homes led on to education; and so the lot of many Scottish poor law children was in every way preferable to that of the ordinary English workhouse child[4]. By 1870 England was inquiring into the matter, with a view to possible imitation. There had been some sporadic boarding-out by

[1] Vol. I. p. 588.

[2] The cases are M'William v. Adams, and Lindsay v. McTear. The original decisions were of 1848: the business of appeal was not completed till 1852. Macqueen, J. F., *Reports of Scotch Appeals*, I. 120, 155.

[3] *Report on the Boarding Out of Poor Children in Scotland*, by J. J. Henley, Poor Law Inspector, 1870 (LVIII. 73), p. 8.

[4] *Report of* 1870, p. 35. Cp. S.C. *on the Operation of the Poor Law in Scotland*, 1868–71, *Report*, 1871 (XI. 389), p. xi.

English Guardians before that time. The inquiries of 1869, and the philanthropic agitation which had preceded them, led to a rather grudging official encouragement of the practice in England; but not until 1889 was the old and excellent Scottish system "whole-heartedly and permanently adopted"[1] by the Local Government Board.

Poor Law Unions had not been imposed on Scotland. Her large parishes never united for any purpose except the erection of what came to be known as combination poorhouses. Owing to the late dates of erection, these houses, the visiting inspector from England reported in 1870, had not "the repulsive features of those English workhouses that were built immediately after the passing of the Poor Law."[2] In 1870 only twenty-six parishes in the whole country had their own poorhouses. They were nearly all in and about Edinburgh and Glasgow[3]. The total of Scottish poorhouses was sixty-three, most of them 'combinations' serving whole counties, or great parts of counties, and incredibly small, judged by English standards, for the populations which they served. Sutherland had a population of 24,000 in 1871. The county combination house at Portinleek had room for 50 people. At the other end of the country, Kirkcudbright combination house could take 250 out of a population of 36,000. And because of the innate distaste of the Scot, especially the countryman, Highland or Lowland, for the poorhouse and all that it implied, even the scanty accommodation was not fully used. This distaste had been utilised by the Poor Law authorities to cut down outdoor relief. Claimants were offered 'the house' as in England; shied at it; and lost their claim. "Oh, Sir, they winna bide," said the governor of the Dalkeith house, when asked why it was so empty. "Oh, plenty of them sent here, but they just come in at the tae door and they gang out at the tither."[4]

The result of this and of kindred policies was that, in a growing population, the number of enrolled or registered poor relieved at any one time remained remarkably constant at between 70,000 and 80,000 from 1850 to 1870; and declined there-

[1] Webb, *op. cit.* p. 275. For the literature of boarding-out, see notes to Webb, p. 271–2.

[2] *Report*, p. 7.

[3] Details are in the *Reports on...the Poor Law in Scotland*, 1868–9 (XI. 1), App. 16, and 1870 (XI. 1), App. 15.

[4] Evidence of Sir John M'Neill (1868–9, XI, Q. 1382), quoted in Lamond, *op. cit.* p. 114.

after to 59,000 in 1886[1]. Besides these, there was a group of their dependents, wives and children, which averaged rather more than half the number of the enrolled. And there was a handful of casual poor with their dependents, kept small by the rigid Scottish law, which before 1870 averaged at any one time about 7000, and after 1870 was worked down to less than 5000. Yet, in spite of the very different principles and application of the English and Scottish laws, the net results, when both had been stiffened after 1870, were curiously similar. In England, by 1886, the mean number of persons relieved at any one time had been reduced, according to official figures, to 2·8 per cent. of the population: in Scotland to 2·5 per cent.[2]

The Scottish reaction to that slight increase of poor-relief during the late 'sixties, which in England had produced Fawcett's *Pauperism* and the crusade of th inspectors, had been a movement which invoked the name of Chalmers and urged a return to the ancient voluntary parochial system of relief[3]. Benevolent men in Edinburgh founded an Association for Improving the Condition of the Poor, and endowed the Chalmers Lectures on Pauperism. They also procured a parliamentary inquiry into the operation of the Poor Law in Scotland, hoping that the law might be condemned. The Committee, reporting in 1871, blessed the law and most of its operations, though it found the Scottish system of medical relief casual, unsatisfactory, and inferior to the English[4]. But it advised a stricter application of the poorhouse test, and it was "not prepared to accede to the suggestions made from many quarters, that a discretion should be given to parochial boards to grant relief out of the poor-rates to able-bodied poor in cases of commercial distress."[5] So it provided an official basis for that stiffening of administration which in Scotland, as in England, marked the close of the age.

It was remarkable that the state, whose inroads on individual liberty Herbert Spencer resented and Stanley Jevons watched

---

[1] Figures in the first *Report on...the Poor Law in Scotland*, 1868–9, App. 3, and in the *Statistical Abstract for the United Kingdom*; criticism of them in Lamond, *op. cit.* p. 129 n. They are not very good statistically.

[2] Neither figure is very satisfactory. The English is an average of one summer and one winter day; the Scottish is the figure for May 14.

[3] Lamond's book was originally written to combat this movement.

[4] *Report*, 1871, p. x.

[5] *Ibid.* p. xi.

with critical impartiality during the early 'eighties[1], should have managed thus to restrict its most ancient 'socialistic' activity within the very narrowest bounds—less than 3 per cent. of the people 'paupers' at any one time. Severe administration had been needed to attain this position, as has been seen. Dogmatically harsh though reforming administrators might appear, they had a noble conception of their duties. But for a few score thousand unhappy incapable folk, for whom the workhouses could be reserved, they believed that growing wealth, growing personal thrift—both were in fact growing[2]—and tonic refusals of poor relief might finally make a Poor Law superfluous. They stood towards that law much as Gladstone had stood towards the income-tax in the 'seventies. A little more prosperity, a little more thrift, joined with the better organisation of private charity to which they were pledged[3], might, they thought, get rid of all that was worst in it; just as to Gladstone only a few more years of peace, and another touch of retrenchment, were needed to finish off the bad tax.

Thinking, as they did, in terms of 'pauperism' and 'the principles of 1834,' they were not very open-minded to new policies, which might perhaps get rid of the 'stigma of pauperism' in other ways than by pressure. The best of them were making conditions of relief more tolerable for the few—young, aged, or infirm—whom they recognised as legitimate wards of society; but only deterrent methods for the able-bodied were recognised in strict Poor Law and official circles, in spite of Chamberlain's recent unemployment circular. Prospects opened out by Canon Blackley did not attract them. They probably agreed with Herbert Spencer when he wrote—"habits of improvidence having for generations been cultivated by the Poor Law, and the improvident enabled to multiply, the evils produced by compulsory charity are now proposed to be met by compulsory insurance."[4] That was indeed a proposal, as Spencer noted with disgust, both of Bismarck the militarist and of some Englishmen who reckoned themselves peaceful reformers of the left. A new territory for the state to occupy was being opened up.

---

[1] Above, p. 389.          [2] See below, p. 450, 477.

[3] The history of the Charity Organisation Society is told, without much sympathy, in Webb, *op. cit.* p. 455–68. For the other side see Loch, C. S., *Charity Organisation* (1892). The Society was founded in 1869.

[4] *The Man versus the State*, p. 28.

# CHAPTER XI

## LIFE AND LABOUR IN INDUSTRIAL BRITAIN

THE Britain of 1851 had seemed crowded. Yet the crowd thickened fast during the next thirty-five years. While Ireland was emptying, though still over-full for a rural country, the sweeping upward curve of British population steepened in the 'seventies, and flattened out the merest trifle in the 'eighties[1]. Medical knowledge and sanitary law had pushed death back. The crude death-rate in England and Wales, which had been 22·2 per thousand in the 'fifties, was 19·1 for the 'eighties. William Farr's modest ambition of 1854, an urban death-rate of 20 per thousand[2], had been almost reached. London got below 21 in 1883, though Clare Market and other black patches had still a rate nearly double that, ten years later[3]. These were figures better than France or Belgium or Prussia could show; but not so good as they might have been if administration had kept pace with knowledge and the law. And young children still died about as fast as they had died twenty years earlier[4].

This was partly because the flow of life had hardly slackened. The birth-rate reached its recorded maximum—35·5 for England and Wales and 34·9 for Scotland—in 1871–5; and although after that the fall began which perhaps is not yet over, its effects were hardly perceptible until the late 'eighties. In the years about 1880, no important town in the island had a birth-rate below 30, not even Brighton; and some of the industrial towns had rates approaching 40. The gap between birth-rate and death-rate was wide almost everywhere. In this country, of whose people something like two-thirds were real townsmen, the average natural increase, the simple excess of

---

[1] There is a convenient collection of facts here used in the *Statistical Memoranda and Charts...relating to Public Health and Social Conditions* of 1909 (Cd. 4671).

[2] *S.C. on Public Health Bill and Nuisances Removal Amendment Bill*, 1854–5 (XIII. 413): Farr's evidence, Q. 1554: he thinks 20 per thousand 'practicable.'

[3] A part of Clare Market in 1891–2 had a rate of 41·32 and 800 people to the acre. Jephson, H., *The Sanitary Evolution of London* (1907), p. 363–4.

[4] For continental and infantile death-rates see Charts 2 and 5 in the *Statistical Memoranda and Charts*.

births over deaths, was more than 14 per thousand yearly. Towns had at least become habitable. They were not devouring an immigrant population, killing more men than they bred, as in the eighteenth century.

Ireland had been emptied, first by famine and pestilence and afterwards by the emigrant ship; but emigration from Britain, even when it approached 200,000 a year, as it did in the slack trade of the early 'eighties, made room for less than half of the new lives. At that time, the births always exceeded the deaths by more than 400,000 a year. As the new population grew to working age, the automatic operation of the industry state, guided only by the unseen hand of self-interest, found jobs for them, on the whole with astonishing success. (The number of jobs on the land was stationary or declining.) Some were blind-alley jobs and some were sweated; but the expansion and perpetual diversification of manufacturing and distributing processes provided very many fresh ones which were neither. For the census of 1881 it was necessary to make a new and much enlarged dictionary of occupations, which contained between "eleven and twelve thousand...having each its name."[1] It began with the all-rounder, the bambler, the barker and the bat-printer. Towards the end came the western-man, the wheel-glutter, the whim-driver and the whitster[2].

As some slight offset to British emigration, the 'seventies and 'eighties saw an appreciable increase of foreign immigrants which produced, in a few narrow areas, fresh competition for some of the humblest jobs. Down to the 'sixties, immigrants, apart from the Irish, had been almost all selected men of business or skilled craftsmen, successors to the Ricardos, Angersteins, van Mierops and Rothschilds, the Vulliamys and Bartolozzis of the eighteenth century[3]. These Germans, Greeks, Swiss, Jews of all nationalities, occasional Frenchmen, and Americans like George Peabody, were an invaluable and quickly assimilated addition to the human capital of the

[1] *Census of* 1881: *General Report* (1883, LXXX), p. 26.

[2] *All-rounder*, a man who can perform any process in boot-making; *bambler* is neither in the *N.E.D.* nor in the 1927 *Dictionary of Occupational Terms*; *barker*, of trees or of leather; *bat-printer* is not in the 1927 *Dictionary*, probably connected with the making of 'bats' for pottery kilns; *western-man*, a boatman who takes out pilots; *wheel-glutter*, one who mortices hub and fixes spokes of wheels, also a smith who fills up small V-shaped spaces in metal wheels; *whim-driver*, or *whimseyer*, a rag-cleaner in a shoddy mill; *whitster*, a foreman bleacher.

[3] Cp. vol. I. p. 289. Justin Vulliamy was clock-maker to George III.

country. There had been a few humbler folk, especially in the foreign quarters of London; but from the national economic standpoint they were negligible. At the census of 1871 there were only 105,000 people of foreign birth returned in Great Britain. Of these, 34,000 were Germans, including German Jews, and 18,000 were French. By 1881 the total had not risen beyond 124,000, of whom 60,000 were in London. The Russian, that is the Polish, Jews were now bracketed second, at 15,000, with the French, who had declined. There was a sharp increase after 1881, following on anti-Semitic movements in central and eastern Europe[1]. The resources of the Jewish Board of Guardians in London were strained in dealing with the destitute[2]. Complaints of underselling, based on underliving, came from the Gentiles of the East End, at a time when such irresistible competition was specially painful. The pressure was chiefly felt by the bakers, cigar-makers, and tailors; above all by the tailors. London had to face a disquieting social problem. So, on a small scale, had the tailoring quarters of Manchester and Leeds; but there was no national problem. There were only a few thousand foreigners in all Scotland, of whom an important section were seafaring Scandinavians; it is not likely that the whole foreign-born population of the country in 1886 was equal to the British emigration of that single year; and although among the East End Jews the second generation, now springing, would tend to remain a race apart, it would be more nearly assimilated to its economic environment than the first had been.

The decline in the London death-rate by about three per thousand between 1851-3 and 1881-3 was one statistical measure of what Shaftesbury, giving evidence for the last time before a Royal Commission in 1884, the year of his eighty-third birthday, called the 'enormous'[3] improvement in housing and sanitation during those thirty years. His mind was still haunted by memories of his earlier discoveries—the room with a family in each of its four corners: the room with an open cesspool immediately below its boarded floor: the room in which man and wife took turns at night watching a hole in the floor which led direct to the drains, to save their baby from

---

[1] See the *Memorandum on the Immigration of Foreigners* (by H. G. Calcraft), c. 112 of 1887.

[2] *Ibid.* p. 11.

[3] *R.C. on the Housing of the Working Classes*, 1884-5 (xxx), p. 4.

rats[1]. He had seen such things during his days at the first Board of Health, in the early 'fifties, days when even "in the mansions of the West End the cesspools were regarded as equally sacred with the wine cellars,"[2] although cesspools had already been completely cleared out of the City; days when some of the London Water Companies had their intakes below Teddington Lock[3], although in a hot summer a few years later—that of 1858—"the pestilential smell from the Thames" became so intolerable that there was "a question of changing the seat of Parliament."[4] The Metropolitan Board of Works was at that time cutting the arterial drains which carried off the London sewage and solved the parliamentary difficulty[5]; but Hammersmith in 1860–1 was still laced with foul sewers and ditches. It contained also "a morass of several acres...having no outlet, which received the sewage from a large area, the noxious emanations from which must be regarded as highly detrimental to health," as the Medical Officer put it[6]. There was still a great deal of 'town spring water' drunk in London; the Shoreditch officer in 1860 said he had "hardly ever exposed a sample of it to the heat of a summer day for some hours without observing it to become putrid".[7] In 1856 there was plenty of pig-keeping in Westminster; and in Fulham were mountainous dustheaps of the kind which made the fortune of Mr Boffin. Sanitarians considered them "a most injurious and offensive nuisance."[8] All these nuisances were but gradually abated. There were two courts in Islington of which the Medical Officer reported in 1863 that "young children cannot live in them. All that are born there, or are brought to reside there, are doomed to die within two years."[9] The return of cholera in 1866 revealed the "criminal indifference to the public safety"[10] of the Southwark and Vauxhall Water Company.

---

[1] R.C. on the Housing of the Working Classes, 1884–5, Shaftesbury's evidence, Q. 36–38.

[2] Simon, Sir J., English Sanitary Institutions (2nd ed. 1897), p. 252.

[3] Jephson, op. cit. p. 71: they were instructed to arrange intakes above the lock by 15 and 16 Vict. c. 84.

[4] Malmesbury, Earl of, Memoirs of an ex-Minister, diary for June 23, 1858. Under June 27 comes the footnote, "Although Mme. Ristori...sniffed the air with delight, saying it reminded her of her dear Venice."

[5] Jephson, op. cit. p. 90; and above, p. 423.

[6] Ibid. p. 101. Jephson's book is based on the reports of the M.O. of Health, now in the library of the London County Council.

[7] Ibid. p. 105.          [8] Ibid. p. 115–16.          [9] Ibid. p. 177.

[10] Dr Simon's report of 1869; quoted in Jephson, p. 192.

Slaughterhouses, cowhouses, piggeries and private manure-mixing yards in closely settled areas were worrying the Health Officer of St Mary, Newington, in 1871.[1] New drains in the 'seventies were sometimes as bad as the old. Shoddy houses were being built on old dustheaps, as University College and Hyde Park Gardens had been built before them; even a 'small town' grew up in Wandsworth on six or seven feet of made ground, made of filth[2].

The chaos of London government left the capital a medley of well and ill-administered sanitary areas, with inadequate central control of internal or external dangers. The Metropolitan Board of Works supervised the main sewers, main streets, and other principal works of the London area, but had no inspecting or coercive powers over the vestries. Only in 1866 did the Thames Navigation Act (29 and 30 Vict. c. 89 § 63–9) authorise regulation of the drainage of up-stream towns in the interests of London. Not until 1878 (under 41 and 42 Vict. c. 32) was the Board empowered to issue general regulations about foundations and building materials, so as to get rid of shoddy houses. Yet there was motion. The first stone of the Embankment was laid near Whitehall Stairs on July 20, 1864. The Embankment did not only give the river a better scour and London a highway of dignity. It covered a great low-level sewer which intercepted the drainage of all the slopes above it. Under the legislation of the 'seventies, the Board began the clearance of insanitary areas; and an improved public opinion told on the administration of all but the very worst of the local authorities. The death-rate was falling towards William Farr's ideal. But the infants were dying as before, and the growth of London was always setting new sanitary problems. By the mid-'eighties, the Thames sewage trouble had recurred, about the outfalls made a generation earlier. When some Royal Commissioners embarked at Woolwich in 1884, the river "for its whole width was black, putrid sewage, looking as if unmixed and unalloyed. The stench was intolerable." They thought this "a disgrace to the metropolis and to civilisation."[3] So settling tanks and the transport of the sludge to sea in barges had to be provided.

---

[1] Jephson, p. 246–7.
[2] Jephson, p. 228, quoting the M.O. of Shoreditch: cp. vol. I. p. 539.
[3] *R.C. on the effects of the discharge of Metropolitan Sewage into the Thames*, 1884–5 (XXXI. 341), *Second Report*, p. ix.

Not until the passing of the London Public Health Act of 1891 were some sanitary rules, which had been applied long before in the country at large, made universally applicable in the territory of the new County Council. Towns which had always had a single central authority were in a position to make prompt use of the general health legislation, so much of which was permissive, or to promote local acts of their own. Birmingham under Joseph Chamberlain is a case in point[1]. Most of the great towns had handled their water supply with vigour. Liverpool had struggled resolutely with the exceedingly difficult problems of sanitation and health in a seaport, originally ill-built, and full of not too sanitary Irish immigrants[2]. But in most manufacturing towns industrial were apt to outweigh sanitary considerations. There was little interest in smoke abatement and, with slow means of transport, a strong desire to keep people near their places of work. None of these towns had such large, comfortable, and relatively healthy residential areas as London. Many had more difficult sites. Birmingham stands on high and open ground where wholesome drainage is not too difficult; the Tyne is tidal up to Newcastle and the Clyde to Glasgow; but the towns of the West Riding and the Lancashire Pennines, in their narrow, hard-sided valleys, had no light task when, and if, they wished to alter their lay-out, or decided no longer to drain into the small and obvious river— Calder, Aire, Don or Irwell. Above Manchester, the Irwell has already passed some half-dozen manufacturing townlets and towns. In hot weather in the 'eighties it stank there much, one supposes, as the Thames had stunk at Westminster in June 1858[3]. The Calder and the Aire stank also, though perhaps not so badly as in earlier hot summers[4]. But Parliament never sat by any of them, and their stench is recorded in no *Memoirs of an ex-Minister*.

So, in spite of municipal governments which had at least opportunities for sanitary efficiency, round about 1880 none of the greater towns, except Birmingham and Bristol, had death-rates below that composite rate of Eaton Square, Clare Market

[1] Cp. below, p. 492.

[2] See Hope, E. W., *Health at the Gateway* (1931), *passim*; and below, p. 493-4.

[3] Memories of a boy who sometimes played by it, at an exciting place where a little clear stream, which had cut a canyon eight feet deep in red sandstone, ran under trees into the foul current.

[4] An old Leeds resident, in 1903, spoke of the great improvement in the stench of the Aire during the previous half-century.

and the Old Kent Road which stood for London. Newcastle, Sheffield, Leeds and Leicester were within a few points of it; Manchester, Glasgow and Liverpool were decidedly worse. Yet the cities of Britain were among the healthiest in the world, and were certainly the healthiest of the Old World. The death-rate of New York was worse than that of Manchester; those of Paris and Berlin worse than that of Liverpool; and that of the whole city which the Victorians knew as St Petersburg nearly 25 per cent. worse than that of a small, selected, black London area such as Clare Market. The census of 1891 would show that more than 11 per cent. of the population of England and Wales, and nearly 20 per cent. of the Londoners, lived more than two to a room, 'under conditions of over-crowding' as then officially defined[1]. No comparable figures exist for the foreign capitals; but there is no great doubt that, had they been collected, they would have been worse, except possibly in New York. The English sanitarians were never content, rightly; but there was something to show for fifty years' work when Edwin Chadwick, who was born in 1800, died in 1890.

"Hitherto it is questionable if all the mechanical inventions yet made have lightened the day's toil of any human being." So Mill wrote in 1847, and so the text of the people's edition of his *Principles* stood in the 'eighties[2]. Only "just institutions and the deliberate guidance" of the increase of mankind, he thought, could resolve the question. There was not much trace of this guidance in 1883–6. Certainly institutions had been made somewhat more just. What lightening, if any, had there been of the day's toil? Whether appropriate or not when written, was the question as it stood in the people's edition of Mill misleading?

Some heavy, even murderous, jobs had been killed, or nearly killed, by machinery since he first wrote. There were few 'bottom-sawyers' left; few, if any, carpenters worked out in fifteen years by handling the great jack-plane[3]. The sewing machine

---

[1] Cp. below, p. 490 *sqq.*

[2] Book IV, ch. VI, § 2. This is one of the many famous phrases of his which have too often been quoted without being dated. The fact that he allowed it to stand until his death does not prove that he reconsidered it. He described the United States as a country "in which the doctrine of Protection is declining, but not yet wholly given up" (Book V, ch. X, § 1) in all his editions.

[3] For bottom-sawyers see vol. I. p. 445. The jack-plane was a favourite illustration of Alfred Marshall's.

must have lightened an incalculable number of days' toil. It was easier to mind a completely self-acting mule than to push about the carriage of the old hand-mule. The power-loom shed was noisy, and its looms had been speeded up; but work in it was certainly lighter, day for day, than the bowed, endless, insanitary monotony of that lower-grade hand-loom weaving of the 'thirties and 'forties which alone had been completely superseded. Scything is a noble art; but it cannot be argued that a full day's scything is lighter than a full day's management of a reaper; nor that a day in an un-mechanised copper or lead mine is lighter than one in a fully equipped colliery.

Yet if mechanical invention was killing off some heavy jobs, it had made and was making others—stoking and coal trimming in a gale, or in the Red Sea; puddling, and all the exacting work of blast furnace and steel furnace; the long day, heavy with responsibility, of the signalman or the engine-driver; and scores of laborious and often dangerous tasks in gas works, chemical works and engineering shops. An hour's work in the caissons, or on the cantilevers, of the Forth Bridge may well be called heavier than one put in under Rennie on Waterloo Bridge. So the enumeration might go on; but no balance could ever be struck. For it is not even quite certain that twelve and a half hours' work, paced by the "wheels of iron," in the early cotton mills was heavier for the child than twelve and a half hours of the many different drudgeries to which he might have been assigned before the inventions[1].

It is hard to say how common twelve hours' drudgery for children had been before the inventions. After them, it was certainly common in the mills; and that was the justification for those factory laws to which, although the Ten Hours' Act had passed when he wrote, Mill gave a single page, containing no information, and occupied almost entirely by a protest against the extension of the laws to women. One object of the early acts had been to bring the child mill-worker's day more nearly into line with the customary working day of average adult wage-earners[2]. Cam Hobhouse had told the House of Commons in 1825 that, from inquiries which he had made, it appeared that ten and a half hours, and in winter in some cases eight and a half, was an ordinary day's work for "machine-makers, the moulders of the machinery, house-carpenters,

---

[1] Cp. vol. I. p. 371, 565. Twelve and a half hours was the day in the "best regulated" mills of the 'twenties. Hansard, XIII. p. 643.    [2] Vol. I. p. 377.

cabinet-makers, stonemasons, bricklayers, blacksmiths, mill-wrights," and many other craftsmen[1]. There were trades with longer regular hours; outwork of all kinds in which inclination or necessity determined the working day; continuous processes with twelve-hour shifts; and all sorts of emergency arrangements. But something like ten and a half hours was normal for the man or woman working to an employer's direction, or on his premises. So it remained down to 1848, and later. Its persistence, combined with the increased strain of some tasks connected with machinery, was probably the cause of Mill's dreary questioning[2].

A rather long day's work was normal in all serious occupations during the early 'fifties, not merely for wage-earners. It was the otherwise unimportant Factory Act of 1850 (13 and 14 Vict. c. 54) which, besides introducing the legal 60-hour week for women, really started the *semaine anglaise*, by ordering the stoppage of work at 2 p.m. on Saturdays[3]. As the textile factory code was extended to other trades, a Saturday half-holiday became the rule. The building trades, never under factory law, were securing it by negotiation or strike during the 'sixties[4]. But until 1854 even so capitalistic an institution as Lloyd's was open on Saturday afternoon[5]. At that time carpenters and joiners were working from 52 to 64 hours a week, according to the season, much as in 1825. So were bricklayers, and presumably the rest of the building trades. The week of a compositor in London was 63 hours all the year round. That of the engineer and the iron-founder was the same. Textiles, building, metal-working were all more or less in line, with a tendency for the state-protected textiles, once so far in the rear, to get a trifle ahead of the rest, because of the law and their women and children[6].

[1] Hansard, XIII. p. 1008.

[2] There is no reason to think that Mill had really studied the problem: he just threw out his suggestion.

[3] Under the Act of 1844 (7 and 8 Vict. c. 15) work, for protected people, stopped at 4.30 on Saturdays.

[4] See the evidence given before the *R.C. on Trades Unions* of 1867–9; R. Applegarth, for the carpenters, Q. 192; E. Coulson, for the bricklayers, Q. 2295; J. Wilson, a builder, Q. 4396.

[5] Wright, C., and Fayle, C. E., *A History of Lloyd's*, p. 356.

[6] The history of the day's work in the various trades is summarised in the *Statistical Tables and Report on Trade Unions* of 1887; Burnett's Report (LXXXIX. p.715). See also Wood, G. H., "Some Statistics relating to Working Class Progress since 1860," *S.J.* 1899, p. 640–2.

For twenty-four years the 60-hour textile week stood. Then, in 1874, it was cut to 56½ under 37 and 38 Vict. c. 44. In the interval, some of the trades, by negotiation, strikes and threats of strikes had, in their turn, got ahead of the textiles. The English building trades did not manage to force their summer hours below 61½ or 61, either before or after 1874; but they got their winter week down to 48 hours or under; their average to something near 55, or less when inevitable weather stoppages are taken into account. By judicious use of the brisk demand for labour of all kinds in 1872, they made it 54; where it stayed. Both the engineers and the iron-founders, and with them necessarily the mass of the shop-working metal-workers, had brought their normal hours down to 57 before 1861. There was a pause; and then, with the boiler-makers and like the compositors, they utilised the splendid opportunity of 1872, when the A.S.E. averaged only 0·9 per cent. of its members unemployed, and the little close society of steam-engine makers only 0·6 per cent., to extort from employers with books full of orders the 54-hour week which became standard throughout their group of trades[1]. In Scotland the engineers beat the week down to 51; but they could not hold it there. When the bad times came, in 1879, employers took back the half-hour a day by which Scotland had got ahead of England. With unemployment figures in the metal-working unions ranging from 11 to 22 per cent., the men were in no position to fight. The week's work of 54 or 54½ hours, to which these unions of representative trades settled down in the 'seventies, was not to be changed for many years. It was never universal, and it was of course extended by overtime when trade was brisk, or reduced by short-time working, especially in the textile industries, when it was slack. But it was as typical of the fourth quarter of the nineteenth century as the 63-hour week had been of the first and second quarters. To that extent, at least, the day's toil for human beings had been lightened. Guidance of the increase of mankind had nothing to do with it: that palliative Britain, in her strong international position, did not yet require. In the background, mechanical invention, by increasing the divisible national dividend, had a great deal to do with it. In the foreground, institutions and laws, become more just, were directly responsible for the example set in the textile factories, and

---

[1] Unemployment figures are also in the *Report* of 1887, and have often been reproduced.

were partially responsible for the greater ease with which a trade union or group of half-organised men could negotiate or fight for a shorter day. In this matter of the day's work, the law or the union is more important than in the matter of wages. Wages may rise 'of themselves', when the balance of supply and demand is definitely favourable to the wage-earner. Between 1850 and 1886, the wages of the almost completely unorganised women in the cotton industry rose, it has been reckoned, in the ratio of 59 to 98; those of the women in the woollen industry, still less organised, in that of 62 to 96; those of women agricultural labourers in Northumberland, not organised at all, in that of 67 to 100[1]. In wage bargains made between individuals, the worker may ask for more pay, or the employer may propose it to attract him. Individual demands or employer's proposals for a shorter working week, though not impossible or unknown, are much less practicable and less common.

The rise in women's wages which accompanied the shortening of hours, a rise which in the cotton industry has been estimated at 66 per cent., is only a special case of that general wage rise which marks the years 1850–86 from the years 1830–50, when wages in general were almost stationary[2]. There were interruptions and set-backs in the rise after 1850. In most trades there was a slight fall, in some a sharp and painful fall, between 1874 and 1886; but when the chief occupations of the country are taken together, and when allowance is made for the steady transfer of labour from worse to better-paid occupations, wage-rates in the mass, so to speak, are estimated to have fallen during the twelve years not more than in the ratio of 156 to 148[3]. This cut away only a fragment of the gain made between 1850

[1] Wood, G. H., "Factory Legislation considered with reference to the Wages of the Operatives," *S.J.* 1902, p. 284–320. The Northumberland figure is for the period 1850 to 1883: figures for 1886 were not available. There is of course a margin of error in all such calculations. Textile wages are especially difficult. But the margins of error are relatively narrow and there is a very close agreement among statisticians about the general course of wages in this period. This explains, and justifies, the concise treatment in the text.

[2] Vol. I. p. 548, 561.

[3] The calculation is that of Wood, G. H., "Real Wages and the Standard of Comfort since 1850," *S.J.* 1909, p. 91–103. The article summarises and carries on the work done by Mr Wood and Prof. Bowley in the *S.J.* during the previous ten years and in Prof. Bowley's *Wages in the United Kingdom* (1900). It is the basis of the diagram on p. 452 below. Prof. Bowley calculated the fall from 1874 to 1886 to be rather greater—in the ratio of 142 to 130.

and 1874; for the figure for 1850 which corresponds to the 156 of 1874 is 100, the base line of the calculation. Even the fall after 1874 was more than compensated—on the average; not for everyone—by a contemporary fall in the cost of living.

These figures are statisticians' weighted index numbers, based on all known representative and trustworthy series of wage-rates, including those in agriculture. From the standpoint of national welfare they are the true figures, or at least the truest available, because they take account of the differing numbers of people earning the different rates of wage at successive dates[1]. As there was a continuous movement from lower to higher-paid occupations, not so much by individual wage-earners as by their children, this is a vital consideration. The relatively ill-paid agricultural labourers, to take the outstanding case, were a much smaller fraction of the whole body of wage-earners in 1886 than in 1850; and so, in any exact discussion of national welfare, it would not be proper to give their low wage so much weight for the former year as for the latter. But the 'average wage-earner' whose receipts, given equal regularity of work, rose between 1850 and 1886 in the ratio of about 100 to 148, is not a man of flesh and blood. He is the result of dividing the estimated aggregate amount of wages paid by the estimated number of wage-earners in all the occupations dealt with; a most important figure, but not human.

A man who had worked at the same trade from the Great Exhibition to the eve of Victoria's Jubilee, without losing any of his efficiency, could not show a rise of 48 per cent. in his weekly wage like this 'average wage-earner'; though one who had left the land as a young man for some urban job might well show more. The man who had remained in the station of life in which he was born had, on the average, lived to see a rise in his weekly or hourly rate of pay of something like 30 per cent. About this figure different trades and jobs fluctuated.

The English agricultural labourer came rather above the general average for the wage-earners of unchanged grade. His rise was some 40 per cent. But for the sharp drop after 1877, it would have been over 48 per cent. Trades already fairly well paid in 1850, like printing and engineering, had made less

[1] Chart 4 in the *Statistical Memoranda and Charts* of 1909 gives the unweighted average of wages, not taking account of changes in the sizes of the wage-earning groups. Bowley's weighted average, calculated in 1900, in a rather different way and with rather different material from Wood's, was almost identical, but gave a slightly smaller rise, 1850–86 (*Wages in the U.K.* p. 132).

progress: the former is credited with a rise of only 16 and the latter of only 25 per cent.[1] All the heavy trades come out badly, because iron and coal were specially hard hit in 1886. One

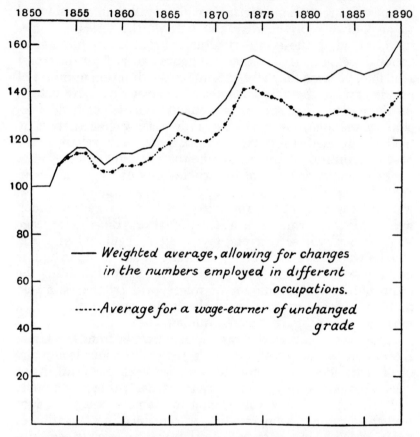

Course of Average Wages in Industry and Agriculture, as percentages of the average of 1850. Based on Wood, G. H., "Real Wages and the Standard of Comfort since 1850," *S.J.* 1909.

calculation gives the miners a rise of only 8 per cent.[2]; but it is agreed that in 1874 their wages had been from 60 to 70 per cent. above the level of 1850[3]. The building trades, untouched by

[1] These are Wood's figures. Those of Bowley show a rise of 21 per cent. for printers. But the results are very close.

[2] Wood. Here there is a more serious discrepancy in the statistical conclusions, as Bowley's figure is 20 per cent.

[3] There was a very rapid rise almost, if not quite, to the level of 1874 in 1886–91. This is one of the cases in which the 1886 figures are not representative.

machinery, working a shorter day and—by general consent—
working slower, had at the same time managed to increase their
standard pay by some 50 per cent.[1]

Cotton, with its difficult statistics and shifting mechanical
practice, shows a rise, for men as well as women, well above the
national average of 30 per cent., largely because jobs with the
same name did not remain really the same. Only the mill
mechanic, whose function did not change and whose wage rose
from 27s. to 32s. (21 per cent.), comes below that level. The
average wage of the various kinds of male jenny or mule
spinners—a group of unequal units—rose in the Manchester
district from about £1 to £1. 15s., or 75 per cent. That of the
carding over-lookers, whose job was fairly constant and not ill
paid at the start, nevertheless rose from 27s. to 39s. 10d., or
47·5 per cent. For the whole cotton industry, men women
and children, the rise in average wages, taking into account the
constant increase in size of the better-paid groups, has been
estimated at 59 per cent.; and other methods of calculation have
yielded an even higher figure[2]. It is certain, at least, that the
great cotton industry as a whole—a complex of industrial grades,
not a single job like bricklaying—had made not less than 48 per
cent. improvement, which is the weighted figure for Britain.

It is possible that, in the particular year 1886, as compared
with the particular year 1850, the position of wage-earners in
the mass, and as individuals, was a little worse than the wage-
rate arithmetic suggests. There was heavy unemployment in
1886. Except 1879, it was the worst year of that late period for
which the growing supply of trade union unemployment pay
figures begins to facilitate close discussion. In 1886, the Iron-
founders had on the average 13·9 per cent.; the Associated
Blacksmiths 14·4 per cent.; the Boilermakers and Iron Shipbuilders 22·2 per cent. of their membership drawing out-of-
work pay. Those are the extreme figures; but both the Amalgamated Engineers and the United Carpenters and Joiners had

[1] According to Wood. Bowley gives 42 per cent. which illustrates the close
general agreement in these calculations. For the pace of building see above,
p. 159.

[2] The 59 per cent. is Wood's figure (S.J. 1909) "based on an entirely new
method, which discards...earnings in separate occupations, but takes into
account the average earnings of all the operatives engaged in the industry as
estimated by Ellison and others". Bowley, in *Wages in the United Kingdom*, made
the rise 72 per cent.

over 7 per cent., a rather high proportion for these late nine-teenth-century records[1].

By the standards of the time, 1850 was certainly a prosperous year. It has been suggested, on the evidence of the trade-union records[2], that a general unemployment figure of 4 per cent. might be assumed for it, as against one of 9·5 per cent. in 1886. But trade-union unemployment figures at their best, that is from 1875 onwards, are very incomplete. The farther back they go, the scantier and less typical do they become. For only a handful of unions do figures from the 'fifties exist at all. Even for the 'seventies and 'eighties, there are no series of importance from the textile trades; necessarily none from the outwork trades, whose members were seldom in unions; none from the miners; and none from the whole fields of agricultural, casual, unskilled, and women's labour. It is probable also that the ranks of the trade unions, especially in their early days, contained the picked and the fortunate men of their trades; and that the slack worker, who perhaps drank the money which might have gone in a union subscription, or the feeble worker of sub-normal capacity who took no interest in unionism, was likely to be the first to be discarded by an employer. From 1869 to 1886, and after, the Amalgamated Tailors never once showed an average unemployment figure so high as 0·6 per cent. Most creditable to the union and to its select membership of 12,000 to 15,000, in the 'seventies and 'eighties; but is it to be supposed that the grotesquely cheerful figure of 0·46 per cent. unemployed in 1879 can give any indication of the probable amount of unemployment and under-employment among the 170–180,000 tailors and tailoresses, mostly outworkers, in Britain in that bad year?[3]

During the fourth quarter of the century, textile mills and mines were apt to counter slack trade by short-time working or fewer shifts. Of this the available figures tell nothing. It was not a new practice; but in earlier years complete stoppages of

[1] For the thirty years 1860–90 the average unemployment figure of the A.S.E. (the modern A.E.U.) was 4·35 per cent.

[2] By Wood in the *S.J.* for 1909, as above, p. 102. The 4·0 for 1850 is given with a query; 3·9 is suggested without one for 1851. It is also the figure given in the *Statistical Memoranda and Charts* of 1909, p. 44. For prosperity in 1850 see the evidence in Tooke and Newmarch, *History of Prices*, VI. 249 *sqq.*

[3] The figures for 1881 were—tailors, in England and Wales, 108,000; in Scotland, 21,000: tailoresses, in England and Wales, 53,000; in Scotland, 3,000. *Census of* 1881 (1883, LXXX and LXXXI).

work were commoner. During the very bad trade of 1847–8 both methods are found in use. In June, 1847, of 40,000 mill hands in Manchester, the mills of 12,000 were stopped. How many more were working short time we do not know. Horner, the great factory inspector of the North, reported in June, 1848, that "as many mills have already closed and a large proportion have shortened their time of working,"[1] the ten-hour law was being applied quite easily.

In the 'fifties, the textiles were relatively more important than in the 'eighties. There was still a great deal of outwork in them; in the clothing trades far more. In important sections of the metal trades the outworker and the small master were typical[2]. For outworkers and small masters, under-employment, a bit of work here and a bit there, all at inadequate pay, is often widespread even in those good times when complete unemployment is rare. Agricultural labourers in 1850 formed a much larger part of the community than in 1886, and there can be no doubt that their chances of unemployment were also larger; though there are no statistics of unemployment among them for either date. It is probable, therefore, that good years in the 'fifties, such as 1850 and 1851, were far nearer in the aggregate of unemployment and under-employment to later bad years, such as 1886, than any calculation based on the handful of existing early trade-union figures would suggest.

A bad year in the 'fifties could be very bad indeed. Even on the basis of the trade-union figures, 1858, the year after the great commercial crisis, was worse than 1879 or 1886; and the average of the eight years 1851–8 was only a fraction better than the average of 1881–8, years in which the air was full of talk about unemployment and depression. So, even if the particular year 1886 was worse than the particular year 1850, as it may well have been, there is no reason to discount the wage rise which occurred between the 'fifties and the 'eighties by assuming any parallel increase in the average amount of unemployment in groups of years. Alfred Marshall astonished a Royal Commission in 1888 by telling them that in his belief there had not been "a larger number of people unemployed during the last ten years than during any other consecutive ten years";[3] and

[1] Quoted by Wood in *S.J.* 1902, p. 314; where the Manchester mill figures are also quoted.

[2] See above, p. 126, 131.

[3] *R.C. on Gold and Silver*: Marshall's evidence, Q. 9828. Presumably when he said a larger number he meant a larger proportionate number.

even though his decade included 1879 as well as 1886, it is more than likely that he was right. Statistical certainty was, and remains, impossible.

In some trades and places, during the 'forties, payment of wages in truck, in spite of the Truck Act of William IV and its many predecessors, had meant an effective reduction of the nominal wage[1]. The system, even when not seriously abused, was generally disliked by wage-earners as an infringement of liberty, and more bitterly by their wives. It died slowly. In 1863 miners are protesting against it with a vehemence which suggests widespread survival[2]. But though, in the 'seventies and 'eighties, there was still both corrupt and economically, if not legally, defensible trucking, there was hardly enough of either to affect any general conclusions which may be drawn from the course of money wages. Only in one district, and that very remote, was truck "in an oppressive form...general"[3] by 1871—the Shetland Islands, where the peasant knitters and fishermen, ignorant both of money and of prices, were at the mercy of dealers who paid them in bad 'goods,' precisely as English foggers and bagmen had paid nailers and knitters[4], and sometimes still paid them. It was reckoned in 1871 that 14,000 Midland nailers were 'trucked' by the foggers. The Truck Act "was simply disregarded";[5] and the truck was in every way corrupt. The trucking fogger, often a publican, paid in bad dear goods, and undersold the honest master. His subject nailers dared not invoke the law. In hosiery, however, at the same date, the system was almost extinct. The few middlemen's shops, in northern Nottinghamshire and the edge of Derbyshire, were said to serve not more than 1100 or 1200 knitters. The new hosiery factories had a clean record[6]. Truck of a corrupt sort was still practised by some of the mining 'butties' and 'doggies' of the Midlands and the South-West[7]. It was found occasionally, as might have been expected, in such outwork

---

[1] See vol. I. p. 409–10, 562–5.

[2] *Transactions of the National Association of Miners of Great Britain*, 1863, p. xi, quoted in Webb, S. and B., *Industrial Democracy*, p. 317, n. 2.

[3] *R.C. on Truck*, 1871 (xxxvi), p. xliv: a whole volume of the R.C.'s *Report* (1871, xxxvii) was given to evidence from Shetland.

[4] Vol. I. p. 564.

[5] *R.C. on Truck*, p. xxv.            [6] *Ibid.* p. xxx.

[7] *Ibid.* p. xxv. A complaint of 'butties' paying miners in liquor is in the *Transactions of the National Association* of 1863, quoted above.

industries as gloving and lace-making, where conditions nearly resembled those of nail-making or knitting. In remote places, works of almost any kind might occasionally start a shop, a 'tommy' shop, as a matter of convenience; and the working of the shop might become corrupt[1]. But the only large-scale survivals in 1871 were those in coal and iron areas where the system had been common twenty years before.

Once upon a time, in the steep remote valleys of South Wales and Monmouthshire, the company shop had been a blessing, a mine inspector said in that year[2]. Many employers held that it was so still. It did not now pay out wages in goods, for that was illegal. But as cash wages were only paid at long intervals—monthly at Ebbw Vale; sometimes only every twelve weeks at Rhymney—men might be given advances on account, to cover their shop purchases. Careful men avoided both the advances and the shop, which is its chief condemnation. The companies ran some shops direct; some were farmed. The stuff supplied in the bigger ones was generally good but dear. Dearness was defended on the ground that the shops gave credit, while outside tradesmen asked for cash. Had pay-days not been so far apart, and had all the men been provident, credit would not have been necessary. The men, provident or not, naturally wanted short pays.

The shop was common also at the Lanarkshire and Ayrshire coal and iron works; and so were fortnightly or monthly pays. Perhaps 25,000 workers in that area were affected in 1871[3]. Sometimes there was actual compulsion to frequent the shop; but as a rule the long pays provided it with customers, as in Wales. Prices were habitually high, and goods, at least sometimes, inferior. All the best men and their wives hated the business. They did not go to law about it because the Truck Act was not properly adjusted to Scottish legal procedure. The aggrieved party would have had to prosecute. So the Act was "in abeyance altogether."[4]

How far this iron and coal truck, or semi-truck, was corrupt, wage-encroaching as well as unpopular, it is hard to say. There

[1] R.C. on Truck, p. lxxix. At Stephen's shipbuilding yard on the Clyde a store started by the men with the help of their employers had degenerated into a sort of truck-shop, the firm having allowed the store-keepers to make deductions from wages to cover accounts due. It was closed early in 1871.

[2] Ibid. p. v.

[3] Ibid. Q. 8575. Evidence of Alexander Macdonald. The Scottish evidence is discussed in the Report, p. xv sqq.     [4] Ibid. p. xx.

were certainly corrupt patches; there were also large healthy areas. Evidence of deliberate use of the shop to secure labour cheap, as among the nailers, is scanty. The Commissioners of 1871 were no doubt right when they argued that weekly pays would dispose of nearly all the attendant evils, if the shops were maintained. No law in that sense was passed, or even suggested, and there was no revision of the Truck Acts until 1887 (50 and 51 Vict. c. 46). But short pays became commoner. Company shops declined. By 1886–7 truck proper had sunk into insignificance, though there were still a few 'tommy' shops in lonely places, such as the chair-making villages of the Chiltern Hills. Some grievances akin to that of truck proper survived to be dealt with in the late Victorian Truck Acts—excessive charges by the employers for materials, or power, or powder, or candles used by workpeople; and those fines for irregularities and blunders which, in bad hands, might amount to systematic deductions from wages. But these were occasional and limited evils[1].

Part of the under-employment and unemployment in out-work industries, throughout the period, was connected with the technical innovations which were changing them in turn into factory industries; but how serious this 'technological' unemployment was in any given trade, or at any given date, is most difficult to determine. It had been very serious among hand-loom weavers of cotton, flax and worsted, from the 'twenties to the 'forties. There was no doubt a good deal of it among them in the 'fifties, and some later. But after the year 1860 it was unimportant, because the hand-loom was now only used for specialities or oddities; and for these it was discarded gradually. In woollen and silk-weaving, the transition from hand to power was so long drawn out that large-scale unemployment was avoided: death and the transfer of the younger generation did most of the work[2]. There may have been some technological unemployment among nail and chain-makers, handmade-lace workers and frame-work knitters, as machinery slowly conquered their trades[3]; and there must have been a little at every other particular industrial revolution. But at the most con-

---

[1] For the survivals at the end of the period see the article "Truck" in *Dic. Pol. Econ.* Very little was heard of it before the *R.C. on Labour* of the 'nineties.

[2] See above, p. 28 and p. 83.

[3] For the growth of factories in chain-making see *R.C. on Labour*, 1892 (xxxvi. Pt. 2), Q. 16,890 *sqq.* There is no suggestion of unemployment.

spicuous revolutions of these years there is no evidence that
the amount was important; and when revolution was slow the
final turn to machinery might well prove a godsend to those
affected. Clothing became a factory industry so gradually and
so partially, and the clothing factory was such a blessing to
sewing women and sewing girls, that the certain and grave evils
in the trade were never connected by any responsible person
with the coming of the factories; rather with its delay. Though
hand shoe-makers, in some places, struck against machinery
at first, and probably suffered in consequence, on the whole
it did very little harm to these 'seat men' as they were called.
"The most competent machine workers" were "continuously
recruited" from among them[1]. There were all kinds of half
machine jobs to which the less adaptable of them could turn.
And as easy processes passed into girls' hands, the male shoe-
makers, following sound advice given them by well-wishers,
deliberately kept their own numbers down[2]. The industry of
the country as a whole was expansive enough to absorb those
who, if they had not been so excluded, might have become
stickit shoe-makers. And the bespoke trade was always there
for the best craftsmen, just as in tailoring. The wages of hand
shoe-makers certainly went up during the years when the
machine was coming in, which they would not have done had
machinery made any considerable number of them redundant.
As factories spread in the Midland metal trades, small masters
passed into them without, it would seem, any general gap of
unemployment. There, as in the clothing trades, it was among
late surviving outworkers that under-employment, sweating,
foul working conditions, and all evil things were commonest at
the close of the period. They were a handful of outworking
locksmiths who in 1892, "in bedrooms...and in wash-houses
and all about", worked, when work was to be had, from "six in
the morning to ten at night and all night on Friday,"[3] so that
their employers might undersell properly equipped factories.
For these locksmiths a final industrial revolution was much to
be desired, even if it should bring any added risk of formal unemployment, which was unlikely.

[1] Leno, J. B., *The Art of Boot and Shoe Making* (1885), pp. vii, 210.
[2] *Ibid.* p. 210: "The rank and file, acting under the advice...tendered thro'
the pages of *St Crispin*, set sternly to work to reduce their numbers." Leno had
been editor of *St Crispin* and also of *The Boot and Shoe Maker*.
[3] *R.C. on Labour* (1892, xxxvi. Pt. 2): evidence of E. Day, Q. 18,128, 18,229.

Although no complete or scientifically accurate cost-of-living index for industrial wage-earners from the 'fifties to the 'eighties has yet been constructed, the broad facts are not in doubt. That the money cost of living, on any given scale, including rent, had not gone up perceptibly is certain. The available evidence suggests that it may have fallen a trifle. Bread prices had fallen sharply[1]. Londoners, during the ten years 1850–9, had paid an average price of 8½d. for their four-pound loaf. For the seven years 1880–6 the figure was just above 6¾d.

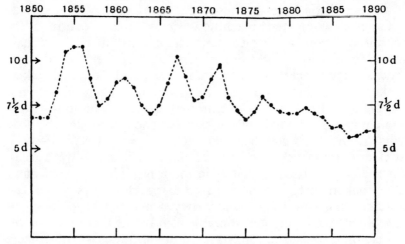

Average annual price of the 4-lb. loaf in London.

Even in the seven years of high prices and high wages, 1870–6, it had only been 8d. In 1887 it fell nearly to 5½d. (When Victoria came to the throne, a cheap year for the period, it had been 8½d.) Of other food prices important for the wage-earning consumer some, such as meat, had risen; but bacon had fallen and so had sugar and tea. Altogether they showed a definite fall. If the prices are taken of all those commodities of ordinary consumption, including bread, for which records are continuous, it appears that a miscellaneous collection of them which would have cost on the average 17s. 8½d. in the decade 1850–9 could have been bought for 16s. 2½d. in 1880–6. The difference would not have been so great but for the Crimean War and the price

---

[1] The general statistical discussion is in Wood, "Real Wages and the Standard of Comfort since 1850," *S.J.* 1909, quoted above, on which this account is based. The London bread prices used here are those given in the *Eighteenth Abstract of Labour Statistics* (1926), p. 143.

rise of the 'fifties. In 1851-2 the collection could have been bought for 15s. 6d. But even this low figure was above that of 1886 (14s. 7d.); and the figure of 1886 was never exceeded during the remainder of the nineteenth century. When Victoria's second jubilee came to be celebrated in 1897 the four-pound loaf in London stood at 5½d. and the cost of the same collection of commodities of ordinary consumption was down to 13s. 8½d. Trade-union unemployment was at 3·5 per cent. The people had votes: they cheered the Queen and a majority of them voted Conservative. It is not surprising. The mills of God, with a little supervision from man, had ground out, if not all that vision-seers had hoped, still some very sound nourishing stuff worth conserving.

How far the fall in retail commodity prices was offset by a rise in urban rents is much harder to estimate, for lack of figures[1]. Estimation is complicated by changes in housing. The normal wage-earning townsman of the 'eighties was rather better housed than his father had been. So far as is known, there had been a rise in average rent from about 4s. to about 5s. 6d. a week[2]. It has been suggested that perhaps half of this rise represented the price of better housing—more space, more conveniences; the other half, the increased rentable value of urban land and the increased costs of building, due mainly to higher pay and easier working conditions of men in the building trades. If this is approximately correct, the unavoidable rise in rent—that is, the extra cost of accommodation not better than the average accommodation of the 'fifties, estimated at about 9d. a week—would not quite absorb the net gain on bread and other articles of consumption[3]; and so the rise in money wages would be all available for improvement in the standard of living, including the rather better houses, unless unemployment had got worse, which is at least not demonstrable. It is unlikely

[1] This discussion of rent also follows Wood, *op. cit.* p. 95, and has no more authority than he claimed for it in view of its scanty foundations. I know no other treatment of the subject; though material for a fuller one should somewhere be procurable.

[2] The latter figure is of course much more certain than the former. The full inquiry made twenty years later (*Report on the Cost of Living of the Working Classes*, Cd. 3844 of 1908) showed *e.g.* that in Oldham, where 64 per cent. of the population lived in four-room houses, average rentals for such standard accommodation varied between 5s. and 6s. Outside London, the *maximum* rental for such a house only exceeded 6s. in eight out of the sixty-three towns reported on. There had been only a slight upward price movement since 1886.

[3] These estimates and hypotheses are again Wood's.

that more exact calculations, which could probably be made, would modify this conclusion much. In substance it was that of all observant contemporaries[1].

Among those conveniences for which the smaller householder paid increased rent, besides 'company's water' and gas-fittings and the like, were a whole range of public enterprises directly or indirectly beneficial to him, and all either new or improved since the Public Health, Public Baths, Common Lodging Houses and Public Library Acts of 1848–52. The trouble of collecting from small occupiers the Poor Rate, upon which other rates had been piled, had been recognised by law early in the century, and rating of the owner rather than the occupier had been permitted[2]. This compounding system was extended by the Small Tenements Act (13 and 14 Vict. c. 99) precisely in 1850, when the new municipal activities were just beginning[3]. If the annual rateable value of any tenement was below £6, the rating authority might deal with the owner. Local acts pushed up the figure. Finally, under an act of 1869 (32 and 33 Vict. c. 40), rendered necessary by the Second Reform Bill and the linking of rate-paying liability with the franchise, a uniform system of compounding was introduced for the whole of England and Wales. The rateable value below which compounding was permitted was raised to £20 a year for London, £13 for Liverpool, £10 for Manchester and Birmingham, and £8 for the rest of the country[4]. Rateable value being lower than renting value, this meant that the ordinary wage-earning householder everywhere paid nothing beyond his rent for all that the rates helped to provide—police and fire brigades; sanitation and vaccination; street maintenance and lighting; the growing provision of parks, open spaces, libraries and public baths; the whole business of poor relief, and the specialised hospitals which in a few of the greatest towns were growing out of it; and that new educational system which, although its cost to the rates had been casually estimated by Forster, when introducing the Bill of 1870, at much less than 3d. in the £ in the great majority of cases[5], was already, after fifteen years, drawing from the local exchequers what seemed the immense

[1] Cp. similar evidence about agricultural earnings, above, p. 284–7.

[2] By 59 Geo. III. c. 12, § 19.

[3] As the result of a recommendation from the *R.C. on the State of Large Towns and Populous Districts* of 1845: see vol. I. p. 544.

[4] Cp. Aschrott and Preston-Thomas, *The English Poor-Law System*, p. 80, 183

[5] Cannan, E., *History of Local Rates in England*, p. 137.

sums of £5,500,000 in England and Wales, and £1,360,000 in Scotland[1].

Reasonably efficient local government, a measure of clean-liness and order, some opportunities for rest and education, were the least that the towns owed their people. The debt was paid, if not in full, at least much more honestly than it had been a generation earlier. Peel Park by Manchester[2], the memorial to the lost leader of Free Trade, and Victoria Park in the London East End, both opened in the 'fifties, are perhaps not very radiant; but they, and their counterparts in other cities, must be judged before the background of the report of the Com-mission of 1845: "the great towns of Liverpool, Manchester, Birmingham and Leeds, and very many others, have at present no public walks."[3]

The central government, by the system of grants in aid of certain local services, contributed something towards their cost[4], besides providing the armour of political security and order for the body economic. The triumph of Peelite and Gladstonian finance was that this had been done with less and less pressure on the taxpayer, especially the wage-earning tax-payer, throughout forty years. It was estimated for 1882 that whereas the average amount of taxation per head in "the middle and upper classes" had increased by a bare 10 per cent. since 1842, in spite of the much greater increase of average wealth, in the "working classes" there had been a decline of 5 per cent.[5] In view of the rise in wages this meant, according to the esti-mate, that the average wage-earner with a family, who had paid out 16 per cent. of his income in taxes in 1842, paid only 7⅓ per cent. in 1882. Probably the position of the non-wage-earning family had been equally favourable when the income-tax stood at 2d. in the £ under Stafford Northcote; but in 1882 Gladstone's cabinet had ruthlessly pressed it up to 6½d., to pay for Disraelian imperialism and its own unanticipated military

---

[1] Compared with a total local expenditure of £62,000,000 for Britain and a national expenditure for the United Kingdom of under £90,000,000.

[2] Actually, in Salford.

[3] Quoted in vol. I. p. 545.

[4] Less than £5,000,000 in the mid-'eighties.

[5] By Prof. Leone Levi in S.J. March, 1884. The estimates are at best rough and must not be pressed; but they have been used, as reasonably trustworthy, by Prof. H. Clay in E.J. March, 1927.

obligations[1]. This was the year England went to Egypt and the year after Majuba Hill. Even so, the small actual increase of "middle and upper class" payment per head must have coincided with a decrease in the percentage of the family income paid out, though not so great as in "the working class."

Women's wages, poor as they still were if regarded as the livelihood of independent citizens, had risen in almost exactly the same fashion and ratio as those of men, where the woman was a regular whole-time wage-earner of industry or agriculture. Indeed, in the early 'eighties, the wage position for such women appears to have been relatively rather better than that of men. All wages had fallen since the slump of the 'seventies; but as women did not work in coal or iron or ship-building, they had escaped some of the most plunging falls[2]. The wages of domestic servants had also risen, perhaps in the same ratio; but in that great career which, in 1881 as in 1851, employed more than twice as many women and girls as all the textile industries put together, so much of the wage is paid in the most variable and unmeasurable kind that it has hitherto defied statisticians. Who knows whether the maidservant's food and housing and treatment by her mistress had improved at just the same rate as her money wage?[3]

What the improvement had been in the endless varieties of whole-time and part-time outwork—stitching trades of every kind, and a score of others such as box-making, brush-making,

---

[1] Imperialism and imperialistic obligations which, according to Lord Passfield, helped greatly to make socialists out of radicals: Webb, S., *Socialism in England*, p. 16.

[2] See the full study of *The Course of Women's Wages during the Nineteenth Century* by G. H. Wood, with a bibliography, published as Appendix A to Hutchins and Harrison, *A History of Factory Legislation* (1903). Wood's diagrammatic treatment shows that women's wages "on the whole...have not been so fluctuating" as those of men. He adds: "This is probably due to the rapidity with which wages change in the coal and iron and steel industries, where women are not employed" (p. 283). He also shows that women's wages, so far as known, were a little higher (about 5 per cent.) in 1883 than in 1886. Part of this small loss was recovered by 1888.

[3] An attempt was made to collect some statistics in 1886. Only 567 returns from large households were secured. Thirteen years later a fuller inquiry yielded an average wage for indoor domestic servants of £17. 16s. 0d. a year in London; £17. 6s. 0d. in the three chief Scottish towns, and £15. 10s. 0d. in England and Wales outside London. No attempt was made to value the board and lodging, because so "extremely difficult." *Report on the Money Wages of Domestic Servants* (by Miss Collet), 1899 (XCII. 1), p. iii.

or artificial flower-making—it is also quite impossible to calculate. These trades were the resort, among others, of the perfectly helpless, who perhaps lived partly on poor relief, and of wives who wanted to add to the family income. The finisher of shirts "is generally elderly, infirm, penniless, and a widow... she is nervous and timid and takes work at whatever price it may be offered to her....The young wife of the clerk with regular employment takes sealskin capes home from the warehouse where she worked as a girl."[1] It is very likely that the competition of such people had prevented the pay, for any given number of hours' work, in these trades from rising so much as the pay for corresponding work at the spinning-frame had risen. But young, quick and strong whole-time workers in them could make what was about the normal woman's pay in the poorer London artisan class of the 'eighties—10s. or 12s. a week. The Government paid 12s. to the charwomen of Whitehall, though 14s. was a common wage in the City and even 15s. is heard of[2].

About 20s. a week was the maximum for any ordinary woman worker, in a factory or at home. It was sometimes exceeded by a weaver minding four looms in Lancashire. At Oldham such a weaver could make up to 22s. 8d.; but the average earnings in that district were from 13s. to 19s.; in the Manchester district from 13s. to 15s. a week[3]. From nowhere in the Yorkshire woollen and worsted towns is a wage higher than 18s. reported: representative wages are the 10s. 9d. of 'preparers' and the 14s. or 15s. of weavers at Bradford. A pound a week was the top figure for 'clippers' and 'scollopers' in the Nottingham lace trade, and for circular-frame knitters in that neighbourhood. In the Staffordshire potteries, 3s. a day on piecework is given as the maximum: the normal pay for day-work was only 1s. 4d.[4] In the factories of East London, which were thoroughly representative of the miscellaneous

---

[1] Collet, Miss C. E., in Booth, *Life and Labour of the People in London*, IV. 259, 295. The inquiry was made in 1888 and all figures here quoted from Booth apply to that year. There had, however, been little change since 1886; and the object here is not precise statistical accuracy for a particular year, but illustration of the general position of the 'eighties.

[2] *Ibid.* IV. 260; VIII. 270.

[3] These are rates for 1882 and 1886 quoted in Bowley, *Wages in the Nineteenth Century*, p. 119.

[4] From the *Returns of Wages published between 1830 and 1886* (1887, LXXXIX. 273). The wool, lace, knitting and pottery wages quoted all refer to 1883.

factory industries of the country, ranging as they did from book-binding, through confectionery, to corsets, matches, rope and umbrellas, the maximum of 20s. was never exceeded[1]. It was not touched in book-binding, confectionery or matches; not nearly touched in rope, where 11s. was the limit. Nowhere was it at all common. Except in fur-sewing, the most degraded of East End trades, ordinary full-work pay varied between 8s. and 16s., or between 10s. and 18s. for such people as the umbrella-makers or the better-class tailor's machinists, working in. Among outworkers, although a full heavy week would yield an elderly seamstress only a few shillings, there were those who could make their 20s. during the season (Easter to August) on good 'order work.'[2]

Between London and the typical manufacturing towns there was thus no marked gap. Everywhere the mass of full-time women workers made from 10s. to 14s. a week[3]. Only from the smaller towns of outlying manufacturing districts are definitely lower ranges reported—from 6s. to 15s. in the woollen mills of Stroud, or from 6s. 6d. to 11s. 6d. in those of Kendal. At Stroud probably, and at Kendal certainly, the earnings of the largest group would be below 10s. There would no doubt be corresponding ranges for outworkers in small towns, and for the surviving industrial outworkers in country districts; but the wages of these classes have been little recorded or inquired into.

The mass of wage-earning women in 1881 were still in the same great groups as in 1851—domestic service; the textile industries; the stitching industries; the washing industries[4]. The country having grown richer, there was a higher proportion of domestic servants. Including those on the farms, 11 per cent. of the whole female population as against 10 per cent. were in service. Neither the textile workers nor the stitching women had increased nearly so fast as the population; the women tailors had increased much faster. Machines accounted for these things. New industrial occupations for women were

---

[1] Booth, *op. cit.* IV. 318, a tabular summary.

[2] *Ibid.* IV. 258.

[3] The *Wage Census* taken by the Board of Trade in 1886, published in 1889 and later, which is the basis for all wage statistics of that year, gives an average wage for women of 12s. 8d. and for women and girls combined of 11s. 3d. The figures collected nearly all came from the textile trades, but evidently serve as a good sample for women's wages generally. Cp. the discussion in Wood, *The Course of Women's Wages*, as above, p. 260-1, 280.

[4] Above, p. 23-5.

developing slowly, though domestic and outwork jobs were passing into factories, both in the staple and the miscellaneous industries. But girls, it may be recalled, had proved competent to act as telegraph operators; and by the end of the decade there would be nearly 23,000 female clerks as compared with the 19 of 1851[1].

Factory Acts and Education Acts had kept the very youngest children from work, and so had subtracted something from family incomes. The subtraction, however, can seldom have been great. Under the Elementary Education Act of 1880 (43 and 44 Vict. c. 23) a certificated child of ten, and any child of thirteen, could begin earning. The early Factory Acts had put the normal age at nine, reduced in 1844 to eight for half-timers. In other industries, during the 'forties, regular work had usually begun between seven and eight. If there were babes making lace, straw-plait and hosiery, then and later, there were also boys of twelve to fourteen not yet at regular work in some trades and places. In the Birmingham trades of the 'sixties, nine or ten was the most usual working age; and the great engineering works of Lancashire employed only a handful of boys under thirteen, though no doubt some of the boys who came to them as improvers had run errands first[2]. London had never found much regular work for children under ten or twelve[3]. The obligation to keep them at school would hardly affect the economy of the average Londoner's household. It was among agricultural labourers that the curtailment of the child's earning years was most felt. And, of all classes, farmers had been the most critical of the new compulsory schooling. The clause of the Act of 1876 (39 and 40 Vict. c. 79), which allowed its relaxation during six weeks a year for children employed in agriculture, had probably been acceptable to all parties concerned.

For family earnings in the 'eighties there are not even 'misery' statistics, like those which gave the maxima for whole families of hand-loom weavers earlier in the century. But from the end

---

[1] *Census of* 1891: Occupations, 1893–4 (CVI, England and Wales; CVIII, Scotland). It appears from the figures that the woman clerk was commoner in Scotland than in England. For telegraph operators, above, p. 209.

[2] *Children's Employment Commission: Second Report*, p. xxxvi (lace and hosiery), p. xxxix (straw-plait); *Third Report*, **p. x** (Birmingham trades), p. 186 (Lancashire engineering).

[3] Cp. vol. I. p. 567.

of the decade onwards calculations and house-to-house inquiries began to be made which throw light back upon it:
since these things do not change rapidly in a few years. Only
the house-to-house inquiry can supply perfect data. In the
'eighties, many married women were in whole-time work everywhere, especially in textile districts; but common statistics do
not tell how many of these were childless, or the wives of sick
men, or of ne'er-do-wells. Nor can they tell of part-time work
done at home, nor of receipts from washing and charing done out.
Opportunities of work for children over school age varied: they
were the best in the textile towns; worst, for girls, in the
mining villages. In no rank of life do full-earning children
normally stay for many years in the home, a fact which the
inquiries from the end of the decade confirm. By far the
largest wage-earning group of all, the girls who go into service,
take their wages with them. "The match-girl and the jam-girl
and the rope-girl...generally live at home";[1] but for all the
trades of London, the regular wage-earners additional to the
head of the house ranged from a minimum of 0·55 per household to a maximum of only 2·15, in the early 'nineties. Calculations made for a selected group of these trades, substantial
trades like engineering, printing, railway service and the police
force, suggested that on the average additional family earnings
might amount to between 25 and 30 per cent. of those of the
male head of the household[2]. When, in 1899, house-to-house inquiry for a population of 46,754 was first made at York, in a
very different industrial atmosphere, it appeared that the additional earnings of every kind, excluding payments made by
lodgers, came within a small fraction of 30 per cent. of the
father's income[3]. The proportion is not likely to have been less
in textile and light-metal-working districts. In colliery districts, one working lad living at home would supply as much.
London and York between them represented most of the miscellaneous occupations of the country, and the York inquiry went
to the very bottom of society. The close agreement between it
and that of London, conducted in a totally different and much
less personal fashion, suggests that for urban England an addition of from 25 to 35 per cent. of the earnings of the male head

[1] Booth, *Life and Labour*, IX. 380–1. The volume only appeared in 1897, but
its basis was inquiry made in 1888–91.

[2] *Ibid*. The actual average arrived at was 26·9.

[3] Rowntree, B. S., *Poverty, a Study of Town Life* (1901), p. 83. The facts were
collected in the autumn of 1899 (Preface, p. ix).

of a working-class household by the other members may have
been about normal. Perhaps it was the same in the country;
but that is much less certain.

The entry of a boy or girl into the serious business of earning
was often casual, usually informal. Since the Children's Employment Commissioners of 1842–3 had been so much impressed by the vitality and the abuses of apprenticeship[1],
abuses had certainly declined, and so had apprenticeship. But
in modified forms, almost entirely without legal or official
sanction, it had persisted, or grown up, in a number of those
callings for which some formal spell of preparation was specially
desirable. And the social problem of 'overstocking with apprentices,' which had vexed municipal authorities of the
Middle Ages and Elizabethan legislators, still troubled Victoria's later years.

Throughout the textile trades, and in many others, especially
the rougher factory trades, formal apprenticeship was all but
extinct[2]. The child doffer picked up his simple job, became a
piecer, and with luck a spinner. Luck was needed, because the
spinner usually employed, and paid, two piecers. The sister of
the girl who was about to leave the mill learnt standing by her
loom, and then took it over. Lads were hired by the men who
ran sub-contract gangs in the heavy-metal industries, or went
into them under their fathers. On the other hand, the outworking journeymen of the older Sheffield trades, masters of
a sort, had some rigid rules of admission, which generally
favoured their own sons; and so had a number of other small
unchanged crafts, coach-builders, basket-makers, coopers and
the like[3]. The conservative shipwrights had not even abandoned
the formal indenture, though it was dying[4]. Among pattern-
makers in engineering shops apprenticeship was universal, and
five years was the minimum: often it extended to the age of

---

[1] Vol. i. p. 571.

[2] There were, however, survivals among specialists connected with the textile
trades, such as beamers, stuff-pressers, overlookers. See Webb, S. and B.,
*Industrial Democracy* (1897), p. 460 n., 463, 478. The section on apprenticeship,
p. 454–81, deals with the trade union aspect of the subject thoroughly.

[3] For Sheffield, *R.C. on Labour* (1892, xxxvi. Pt. 2), Q. 19,772; Webb, *op. cit.*
p. 458; vol. i. p. 571. For the other crafts, Webb, *op. cit.* p. 462 n., referring,
however, primarily to limitation of numbers by regulation of admissions, not to
regulation of apprenticeship conditions.

[4] "Till recently...the bulk of our apprentices used to be indentured": A.
Wilkie before the *R.C. on Labour* (1893, xxxii), Q. 21,462.

twenty-one[1]. The Admiralty still insisted on a full seven years' apprenticeship for all naval engineers[2]; but among engineers and boiler-makers generally, a rather informal spell, usually of two years, as a factory apprentice, plus a similar spell as an improver, was the rule[3]. There were standing controversies with employers over the ratio between the number of learners and of finished tradesmen. In Scotland, lads were so keen to get into the shops that some employers tended to overstock, by adopting what the men properly regarded as the outrageous ratio of one to two[4].

Machinery, always changing and always more easily minded, had broken down the engineers' attempt to retain an apprenticeship like that of their forerunners the millwrights; though the A.S.E. still kept up an ineffective struggle for the rights of apprenticed, as against 'illegal,' men[5]. It was the same wherever the machine had touched an old handicraft. The best cabinet-makers were still apprenticed; but in London, with the coming of machine-made furniture, apprenticeship was dying. Finished craftsmen, if wanted, were brought up from the country. But only a few were wanted, in London or anywhere else[6].

The building and printing trades, as might have been expected, retained apprenticeship in form and, to some extent, in fact. Young stonemasons were apprenticed to employers, but were nearly all masons' sons whom their fathers pushed on quickly. The apprenticeship described in masons' trade union rules was something far more formal; but then it applied only to the rest. In the other building crafts, the position was somewhat similar, but even less rigid. There was a theory in the unions, and some practice, of five to seven years' training; but unapprenticed men, who had picked up their trade somehow, had no great difficulty in practising it, especially if they practised where they had not picked[7].

---

[1] R.C. on Labour (1893, XXXII), W. Mosses, Q. 22,449.
[2] Ibid. Q. 24,548. This was abandoned in 1890.
[3] Ibid. Evidence of R. Knight of the boiler-makers, Q. 20,683.
[4] Ibid. J. Lindsay of Glasgow: Q. 23,288-9. These disputes were regulated by the treaty of 1893: Webb, op. cit. p. 457.
[5] The struggle was kept up "on the whole down to 1885." Webb, op. cit. p. 472.
[6] Evidence for the Alliance Cabinet Makers before R.C. on Labour (1892, XXXVI. Pt. 2), Q. 19,178 sqq. By that time apprenticeship in London was said to be extinct: Q. 1973-5.
[7] Compare the evidence of rather ideal policy given before the R.C. on Labour (as above), Q. 18,512-13 (an employer), with the account of the working of the system in Webb, op. cit. p. 460-1, on which this paragraph is based.

In printing the thing was much more formal and regular. Compositors claimed that it was universal. Certainly the unions required it[1]. The best employers endorsed the requirement. But there were plenty of compositors outside the unions, and innumerable small master-printers who would take on men who could work up to their rather low standard. The unions had failed completely to control entry to the trade: men who had merely picked it up could get, not only into the little shops, but even into the unions themselves.

Except for a remnant of reputedly 'overstocked' and under-trained apprentices to the Thames lightermen[2], and the gentlemen apprentices of the greater shipping companies, the system was extinct in all the industries of transport. The lad came on as he could, say from engine-cleaner to fireman, and so to the driver's foot-plate, if he had it in him to drive and was chosen from above. In the coal-mines there was no kind of apprenticeship, and the miners' unions took no more interest in it than did those of the cotton spinners. Probably a majority of trade unionists shared this indifference, making not even a nominal effort to control access to their trades[3]. There were skilled and apprenticed men outside the unions; but a system for which only a minority even of unionists were ready to fight had lost all national significance. Of course boys and girls still had to learn; but just how the vast majority of them learnt, or what the relations of learners to practisers should be, was neither the affair of the state nor of any lesser social organisation.

Even in the harsh 'forties, great numbers of wage-earners, in agriculture as well as in industry, managed to find contributions to some village club or town burial society or, if more fortunate, to one of the friendly and provident Orders which were springing up and splitting off, and spreading with extraordinary speed from town to country[4]. The Lancashire cotton area was the forcing ground of burial clubs, the birthplace of the collecting friendly society[5], and the headquarters of that representative Order, the Manchester Unity of Odd Fellows,

---

[1] *R.C. on Labour* (1893–4, xxxiv), Q. 22,624–5, G. D. Kelly of the A.S. of Lithographic Printers; Q. 22,799 *sqq.*, H. Slatter of the Typographical Association, who mentions the existence of much informal 'apprenticeship' in London. For union weakness in London, see above, p. 169.

[2] For whom see *R.C. on Labour* (1892, xxxv and xxxvi. Pt. 2), Q. 7469 *sqq.* and Q. 14,081 *sqq.*

[3] Cp. Webb, *op. cit.* p. 473–4.          [4] See vol. I. p. 588–9.

[5] *R.C. on Friendly Societies*, 1874 (xxiii. Pts. 1 and 2), p. xci.

in the 'forties still an unregistered organisation, because its structure did not comply with existing friendly society law. After examining the Odd Fellows' Grand Master, whose name was Smith, a Committee of the House of Lords in 1848 had been almost terrified at its strength. "The Order," they reported, "has reached such gigantic Proportions, and attained such extraordinary Popularity, that it seems to possess the greatest Attractions for the younger Portion of the Labouring Class, and threatens to supplant all minor Institutions of the Kind."[1] They had been told of a membership of 260,000[2] and an income of £340,000. They had no present reason to doubt the loyalty of the Odd Fellows; but it was the year of Revolutions, and they felt bound to remark that such "an affiliated Body with such resources...must become highly dangerous, if it should ever be turned from its legitimate objects." It is not easy to picture those whom Lancashire has always known as the Oddféllers in the rôle of Jacobins or Carbonari, even in 1848; but the Lords were taking a distant view. They went on to pillory certain 'objectionable' customs of the Order—"the Employment of secret Signs, the Circulation of Lectures, and the Introduction of Funeral Orations after the Burial Service." The Grand Master had been quite unable to comprehend their anxieties about these things.

This inquiry bore on proposals for legislation, which in the end, by 13 and 14 Vict. c. 115, enabled the Orders to come within the scope of the law[3]. The Manchester Unity entirely approved: it had of late lost £4000 to an embezzling secretary, because it had no legal status[4]. If its lodges now 'turned from their legitimate objects,' John Tidd Pratt, the Registrar of Friendly Societies from 1846 to 1870, might hope to know[5]. But in fact the Orders were, and remained, singularly innocent

---

[1] S.C. of the H. of L. on the Provident Associations Fraud Prevention Bill, 1847–8 (XVI. 249), p. 4.

[2] According to later statistical work, this should have been 249,000: Neison, F. G. P., "Some Statistics of the Affiliated Orders of Friendly Societies," S.J. March, 1877, p. 45–6.

[3] The earlier friendly society law had only made provision for, and offered registration to, unitary societies, not for what were classed after 1850 as 'societies with branches.' The Odd Fellows were registered in 1851: see vol. I. p. 590 n.

[4] Evidence of W. B. Smith before the S.C. of the H. of L. as above, Q. 87.

[5] The Registrar's unforgettable name was a power for good in the societies: 'if you do so-and-so you will have Tidd Pratt upon you,' it was said (Brabrook, E. W., Provident Societies and Industrial Welfare, 1898, p. 12). He was a voluminous writer, an F.S.A., and a founder of the Reform Club.

of revolution. Even in 1848, from 15 to 20 per cent. of the Odd Fellows were "in a station of life to forego their claims" on the funds[1], subscribers who were not a liability, tradesmen, some medical men, and in the country many of the clergy. As patrons and friends, these mingled with the artisans and operatives, the upper-grade wage-earners, who formed the rank and file. It is fairly certain that the lodges, with their ceremonial, "their jewellery and haberdashery," encouraged what modern Moscow calls a bourgeois ideology[2].

Burial clubs were widespread in the 'fifties, but outside the cotton country they were not very important[3]. Inside it their hold was extraordinary. Of 80,000 inhabitants in the Poor Law Union of Stockport, more than 49,000 were insured for burial in 1853-4. There were at least 46 district societies in Wigan. A witness before a parliamentary committee spoke for societies with a membership of 90,000 in Liverpool[4]. The Blackburn Philanthropic Burial Society, founded in 1839, in 1850 had over 45,000, and by the early 'seventies 130,000 members—the child could be entered at 16 weeks old—out of a total burial society membership of perhaps 750,000 in all England at the latter date[5]. From time to time public opinion was alarmed by horrible cases of the murder of insured children, and the law was called in to impose preventives; but it was never shown that murder was common, or that it was a special product of child insurance[6]. People have been murdered at all ages for the sake of the money which their deaths will bring to the murderer.

Closely associated with the burial clubs, because they too insured against death, were the general collecting societies, so called because they lacked the personal intimacy of a village social club or Odd Fellows' lodge. Liverpool was their place of origin, the Royal Liver of 1850 their representative institution. Above them again, linking the wage-earners' provident to the ordinary insurance society, were profit-making companies like the Prudential, which began industrial insurance

---

[1] *S.C. of the H. of L.* p. 5.

[2] The rather superior reference to jewellery is in the *R.C. of 1874*, p. xxxiv. Most of those who signed it had decorations or court dress.

[3] Lists for 1850, compiled from the returns of the Registrar, are in Walford, C., *The Insurance Cyclopaedia*, IV. 565.

[4] *S.C. on the Friendly Societies Bill*, 1854 (VII. 127), Q. 1395 (Stockport), Q. 1080 (Wigan), Q. 1321 (Liverpool).

[5] *R.C. of 1874*, p. xciii, c; and for 1850, Walford, as above.

[6] *S.C. of 1854*, p. iv, v; *R.C. of 1874*, p. cxxxiii.

in 1854 and was the first company to take infant lives. Its membership, drawn from many classes, had passed 1,000,000 by 1872[1].

Down to that time, village clubs, dividing societies—vulgarly, share-outs—and public house 'free-and-easies' had made small pretence to actuarial knowledge. Good-fellowship was the foundation, calculated providence only a light upper storey. The village labourer of the 'seventies, it was said, could not tolerate a club with "no beer, no feast, no fire."[2] Nor were the finance and management of the collecting societies generally satisfactory. Their finance depended too much on 'lapses'; it was to their interest to evade obligations by declaring that subscribers had lapsed[3]. Even the great Orders, between 1850 and 1875, still lay wide open to the actuarial criticism which had been directed against them in the 'forties, when they had not quite emerged from the good-fellowship phase[4]. The Manchester Unity began regular valuations before 1870, to find that few either of its lodges or its districts were technically solvent[5]. The Foresters, next to the Unity in size, had never even ascertained their deficiencies down to 1875. The cure, often heroically applied, was to meet threatened insolvency by levies or curtailment of benefits. The defence of such action was that benevolence, self-denial, and mutual help were of the essence of a friendly society.

But the relative insecurity of the best societies, the competition, chicane, and actual fraud of the worst, kept government uneasy. The state had long dabbled in insurance, by offering annuities suited to the needs of the people through savings banks and associations. Few had been taken. Gladstone, inspired by William Farr the statistician, had planned in 1864 a whole system of annuities and life insurances, to be worked through the Post Office. For once, a financial plan of Gladstone's miscarried. It was curtailed in parliament and little used in the country[6]. But the somewhat exaggerated criticism of

---

[1] R.C. of 1874, p. cxxviii sqq.

[2] Ibid. p. xxi, from the report of Sir George Young, one of the Assistant Commissioners.

[3] Ibid. p. cix.                    [4] See vol. I. p. 591.

[5] R.C. of 1874, p. xxxvii. Cp. Baernreither, J. M., English Associations of Working Men (Eng. trans. 1889), p. 273, 383. There was great improvement by 1886. See S.C. on National Provident Insurance, 1887 (XI. 1), p. vii.

[6] Walford, op. cit. v. 478–9, 483. Walford prints Farr's Memorandum. Baernreither, op. cit. p. 340; Hansard, Third Series, CLXIII, debates of March 4 and 7.

friendly societies which Gladstone had allowed himself stimulated reform in the Orders. Penetrating inquiry by a Royal
Commission, which sat from 1871 to 1874, "rather frightened"[1]
the worst of the collecting societies and led to some setting in
order of houses. From the Commission's work emerged the
consolidating Friendly Societies Act of 1875 (38 and 39 Vict.
c. 60). It recognised more completely than any earlier law had
the federal nature of the Orders. It brought down many rotten
societies of every type, which could not comply with its rules,
and led to improvements in the finance and management of
the survivors[2].

The federal Orders gained ground everywhere at the expense
of the purely local type of society in public house, schoolroom,
dissenting chapel, or place of business, which early legislation
had favoured. Even before the Act, the local clubs were ful-
filling the prophecy of the Lords' Committee of 1848: "we
cannot stand up against" the Orders, they were saying[3]. In
the decade after the Act, 9283 registered societies were turned
into registered branches of Orders[4]. The Foresters had been
the chief gainers. They had absorbed thousands of country
clubs. By 1886 they had over 5000 'courts' and over 667,000
members[5]. The Manchester Unity of Odd Fellows at that time
was not quite so large, but its membership was above 600,000.
Even in Scotland, for every local club of the old type registered
in 1886, there were eight branches of the general Orders of
English origin—Foresters, Odd Fellows, Rechabites, Shepherds. Scottish invasion of England was only indicated in a list
of public houses, filling several folio pages of an official publication, in which met branches of the Grand Independent
Order of Loyal Caledonian Corks. It is to be supposed that this
Order resembled the Royal Antediluvian Order of Buffaloes, of
which the Commission of 1871 had reported—"it is said to be
wholly convivial." Working men's clubs, convivial and political, were also registered as friendly societies in the early

---

[1] *R.C. of* 1874, p. cxxv.

[2] *Report of the Registrar of Friendly Societies* (J. M. Ludlow) *for* 1885 (1886,
LXI); *S.C. on Friendly Societies* 1888 (XII. 119), Ludlow's evidence, esp. Q. 9;
Brabrook, *op. cit.* p. 60.

[3] *R.C. of* 1874, p. xxiv.

[4] *Report for* 1885, p. 3.

[5] The Foresters had 84,000 members in 1848, 135,000 in 1858, 349,000 in
1868, and 491,000 in 1876; Neison in *S.J.* 1877, p. 60. The figures for 1886 are
in Baernreither, *op. cit.* p. 372–3.

'eighties. How far potation in all these was checked by the Order of Total Abstinent Daughters of the Phœnix the reports do not say[1].

The serious Orders, and friendly societies generally, spent far more money on sick benefit and accident than on funeral allowances; the Manchester Unity, for example, about three times as much[2]. Only in the 'eighties did they begin to study superannuation allowance at all carefully[3]. In constitution they were self-governing; in spirit, as in name, friendly. Collecting societies, on the other hand, specialised in death. To the Registrar of the 'seventies and 'eighties, J. M. Ludlow, they were "necessary evils"; evil, because they lacked self-government, had a "vast official network," and were too much mixed up with child insurance; necessary, because they met a want in those lower social grades where there are seldom reserves enough to provide for the emergency of the grave[4]. Many of the crude old burial clubs had vanished; but the term survived at Blackburn, whose Philanthropic Burial Club shared with the Royal Liver, the Liverpool Victoria, and the Royal London the distinction of having more, far more, than 100,000 members. It will be noticed that three of the four were domiciled in Lancashire[5].

Altogether, the collecting societies of 1885–7 had upwards of 3,000,000 'members'; the single club societies of the old-fashioned type certainly more than 2,000,000; and the federal Orders about 1,750,000. The figures are for Britain. In addition, there was an overflow of the Orders into the dominions, colonies, and even foreign countries[6]. There is some overlap in

---

[1] These details are from the *Report for* 1885 and the *R.C. of* 1874, p. xxxi.

[2] Expenditure is analysed by Neison; *S.J.* 1877. It is interesting to notice that in 1848–52 the Odd Fellows (Manchester Unity) issued 4721 'travelling cards'; in 1868–72 only 2204. This overlap of functions with the trade unions has not, I think, been studied.

[3] "Still in its infancy," Baernreither, *op. cit.* p. 423.

[4] Ludlow's evidence in 1888, as above, Q. 8, 75.

[5] The special success of the burial societies in Liverpool and Lancashire generally, and the frequency of Irish names among witnesses at all inquiries into them, suggest that they owed a good deal to the poor Irishman's desire for a corpse-wake.

[6] *Report of the Chief Registrar for* 1886 (1887, LXXVI), *Report for...*1887 (1889, LXXI. Pts. 1 and 2): *Dic. of Pol. Econ.* s.v. "Friendly Societies," for the statistical position, which is not perfectly clear owing to the neglect or intermittence of returns to the Registrar by the societies. No attempt has been made to give a picture of such associated movements as those of the building societies and the savings banks; partly for reasons of mere space and partly for

the figures, and the friendly society movement overlapped other movements. A Forester might insure members of his family in the Royal Liver. An Odd Fellow might well be also a co-operator and a trade unionist. The minimum certainty is that nearly 4,000,000 adults, mostly wage-earners, were active participants in the life of the societies; and that many, possibly millions, more were in a position to make some formal provision for themselves or their children by way of insurance. In addition were the large sums which these people, or people like them, had put into savings banks, building societies, and trade union benefit funds. Foreign visitors, who studied the Britain of the 'eighties against Friedrich Engels' background of the Britain of the 'forties, were writing of "the complete revolution...in the lives of a large number of English workmen" and of "an improvement...beyond the boldest hopes of even those who, a generation ago, devoted all their energies to the work."[1] Of this revolution and this improvement the friendly societies were at once a witness and a cause.

It is not easy even to guess what a representative wage-earner during this generation of progress, self-help, and Gladstonian finance was thinking—or should one say feeling?—about the economic order of society and his place in it. "A thousand times in a thousand shapes," when moving among "the distressed operatives" of the previous generation—the average men of the Chartist age—a friendly inquirer heard one and another of them say "that he had a right to a better condition, inasmuch as he had taken a part in raising society to the conditions which established a higher average of comfort than that to which he could attain."[2] This was the plain, sound, raw material of average working-class opinion or instinct out of which, with the tools of Ricardian economics and the measuring rod of Patrick Colquhoun's estimate that the wage-earners received a bare quarter of the national income, scattered thinkers of that generation had constructed those theories of value, doctrines of the right to the whole produce of labour, which

reasons suggested in the remarks on savings banks in vol. i. p. 592. Co-operation and trade unionism, which have points of contact with the friendly society movement, have been discussed elsewhere.

[1] Baernreither, *op. cit.* p. 5.

[2] Taylor, W. C., *Notes on a Tour in the Manufacturing Districts of Lancashire* (1842), p. 155.

Karl Marx was subsequently to put into crabbed dialectical shape[1]. Very often, no doubt, among the enemies of the new Poor Law who had supplied so many recruits for Chartism[2], the claim to a better condition had meant little more than a claim to poor relief as a right. Tom Paine and Cobbett had taught this. The people, they said, were owed compensation for land filched from them. The compensation was already payable in part through the rates. These ought to be supplemented, so Paine had argued, by unconditional payments to enable the poor man to set up in life and to provide for his old age, which should come from death duties on landed property[3]. How far, or how well, the sound had carried of the more refined arguments used by that group of writers whom modern scholars have called the Ricardian socialists is uncertain[4]. The scarcity of their books and pamphlets suggests a rather short radius and an indistinct hearing. But, either directly or relaid, Paine and Cobbett had certainly 'come through' well, and were easy to 'get' at long range.

So in all probability was 'Bronterre' O'Brien, the thinker of Chartism, for he had written in half-a-dozen popular journals and could hold a public meeting "for four and even five hours"; though a mere "three hours was about the usual time he occupied."[5] O'Brien had said that property was theft, long before Proudhon coined that glittering phrase which later he alloyed with qualification. O'Brien had called capital accumulated labour. He had maintained that the French Revolution had been a failure because rent was still payable to individuals and not to the state. He had argued that the nation alone should decide how much land any person or family ought to hold; and had asked why individuals, and not the public, should secure

---

[1] See generally Foxwell, H. S., Preface to Menger, *Right to the Whole Produce of Labour*; Beer, M., *History of British Socialism*; Dolléans, E., *Le Chartisme* (1913); Hovell, M., *The Chartist Movement* (1918), esp. ch. 3, "The rise of anti-capitalist economics."

[2] See vol. I. p. 583.

[3] Paine's *Agrarian Justice*.

[4] Those of Hodgskin, author of *Labour Defended...or the Unproductiveness of Capital Proved* (published anonymously in 1825), were spread fairly well by his lectures at the London Mechanics Institution. See Halévy, E., *Thomas Hodgskin* (Paris: 1903).

[5] Gammage, R. G., *History of the Chartist Movement* (first published in 1854), p. 77. O'Brien wrote in *The Poor Man's Guardian*, *The Northern Star*, *The National Reformer*, *The British Statesman*, *Reynolds' Newspaper*, and probably in other journals.

the increment of value that results from the opening of a new mine or the building of a town[1]. Like all Irishmen, he cared most for agrarian socialism, about which he was still writing in *Reynolds' Newspaper*, long after the political collapse of Chartism, down to his death in poverty in 1864[2]. But he had defended with almost equal zeal Owen's notion of a currency to be based on units of labour, the precious metals to be retained only as a matter of international convenience, until such time as labour should be equally productive and equally rewarded everywhere[3].

The little Owenite church, to which alone into the 'forties it was customary to apply the epithet socialist, had kept its faith in community distinct from other reformers' faiths, though it was often sympathetic towards them. In its Halls of Science, in grimy streets, the faithful had sung hymn Number 129[4]:

> Community, the joyful sound
> That cheers the social band,
> And spreads a holy zeal around
> To dwell upon the land.

In *The Book of the New Moral World*, Part v (1844) the old prophet, never disheartened, had preached the old faith, adding to it the pregnant suggestion that the state should buy up the new railways and broad strips of land on either side of them, to be so laid out that there, on the land, joyful communities might bring in the New World without any harsh breach with the Old. But the church was then weakening. Men had passed through it into other communions. Their interest in its distinctive teaching decayed; though their love and respect for the prophet never. By 1846, the Social Institution in John Street, one of its early homes, had become the Literary and Scientific Institution[5]. The *Reasoner*, edited from that year to 1861 by G. J. Holyoake, reasoned more about utilitarian morals, re-

---

[1] His opinions on these questions are fully illustrated in Dolléans, *op. cit.* I. 84, 98, 99. He had not preached confiscation of the land, merely state purchase as it came into the market. His moderation resembles that of Thomas Ogilvie's *Essay on the Right of Property in Land* (1781).

[2] Beer, *op. cit.* II. 240; Dolléans, *op. cit.* II. 486, and for his agrarian socialism, Niehuus, H., *Gesch. der englischen Bodenreformtheorien* (1910), p. 99 *sqq.*

[3] See the article in the *Northern Star* for 29 March, 1845, quoted in Dolléans, *op. cit.* I. 104.

[4] Podmore, F., *Life of Robert Owen*, II. 472; the hymn is from the hymn-book of 1840. Cp. *A Bibliography of Robert Owen*, Welsh Bibliographical Society; 1914.

[5] Podmore, *op. cit.* II. 581.

publicanism, and secularism than about community. Even the co-operative workshops of 1848–54, into which had been poured the enthusiasm—and the money—of men who had learnt under Owen, and of that other band of prophets who had taken the name of Christian Socialists, and had preached "production...by the Trade Unions"[1] to the Amalgamated Engineers in 1852—even these workshops, imperfect embodiments of the complex community as Owen had conceived it, yet seemingly for that reason more likely to endure, had shown a discouraging instability[2]. But the simple two-storey structures of the co-operative stores were rising and standing. Here the tools of social faith were put to definite limited uses, instead of being strained and broken in attempts to construct an ideal city out of refractory material at once. As soon as the small job was done, bigger ones were to be put in hand. About, and from, the stores should spread the whole Co-operative Commonwealth. But the immediate business was to get them built[3].

When Owen died in 1858 there can have been few people left to call themselves socialists, though the growing body of co-operators all looked to him as the preparer of the way. The leaders of Chartism were scattered or dead. Many had emigrated. Some were lecturers, journalists, doctors, lawyers—democrats all, but of no uniform type. Those who had ever had it, had lost the hope of quick success for any doctrine or social reformation. William Lovett, the noblest of them, in early life "half an Owenite, half a Hodgskinite, a thorough believer that accumulation of property in the hands of individuals was the cause of all the evils that existed,"[4] lived on till 1877. As he had always known that a new moral world was unlikely to arise among an uneducated people, it was probably with no regret that he gave the best of his later years to the cause of popular education. Meanwhile old Chartists of the rank and file acted with left-wing liberals and radicals, and thought more of the democratic conquests yet to be won than of any changed social order which might perhaps follow them. After all, the Charter was a political programme, and there had never been any agree-

---

[1] Ludlow, J. M., in the *Economic Review*, April, 1892, quoted in Raven, C. E. *Christian Socialism*, 1848–54 (1920), p. 299.

[2] See Raven, *op. cit.* and above, p. 144–5.

[3] Above, p. 308 *sqq.*

[4] Francis Place's description of him, from the Place MSS. quoted in Hovell, *op. cit.* p. 56. And see his own *Life and Struggles of William Lovett* (1876; new edition, ed. R. H. Tawney, 1920).

ment on social doctrine. In the Gladstonian age, the political objectives were being reached one by one; through the rhythm of good and bad times economic progress was obvious. There were still bad laws to be broken down; abuses to be cleared away; all that work of demolition and 'opening of windows' in which Gladstone delighted and was glad to co-operate[1]. Nearly all the best minds among wage-earners and their friends were as fully occupied with the task as he. Like him they were working with confidence and in hope; for though the ageing Chartist might look back to brave days of drillings, imprisonments, and 'sacred months' of general strike, with the regrets of an old fighting man, it was fairly evident that, however bad to-day might be, the former days were not better than these. There was motion, and with that, as all the signs suggest, the average industrial wage-earner, down to the trade collapse of the 'seventies, and perhaps after, was reasonably content. A natural revolutionary he had never been. Chartists had always found London politically apathetic—because too well paid, they thought[2]. Radical reformers of all sorts, during the thirty years after 1848, must often have noticed the same apathy in the whole country. There is little doubt that Karl Marx did, whatever his opinion of the pay.

London was his headquarters for nearly twenty-five years[3]. In the British Museum, among the blue-books and the economic literature of the centuries, *Das Kapital* took shape. But the first part only appeared in 1867 in German, and in 1873 in French[4]. Engels' preface to the first English edition is dated November 5, 1886. He can hardly have meant the dating as a grim joke. Neither he nor Marx had humour; and he prefaced it by repeating Marx's opinions that "England is the only country where the inevitable social revolution might be effected entirely by peaceful and legal means." However, as he noted that "Marx never forgot to add that he had hardly expected the English ruling classes to submit without a 'pro-slavery rebellion' to this peaceful and legal revolution,"[5] it is just possible

---

[1] See above, p. 404.    [2] See vol. I. p. 584.    [3] He died in 1883.

[4] The French edition was "entièrement revisée par l'auteur," and in it some Englishmen read their Marx during the next twelve years. The rest of the book only began to appear in German in 1885. I doubt if one professed English economist, or socialist scholar, in five has studied the latter parts closely to this day. They have had no influence whatever on English socialism, and were first translated, at Chicago, in 1909.

[5] Preface, p. xiv.

that he thought of the English edition as an explosive. He had anticipated revolution in England within three years in the 'forties: in 1886 he was sure that "the sighed for period of prosperity would not come."[1] If he did suppose that he was touching off the powder, he was wrong. Marx, even at second hand, has had little influence on English thought; on English action, almost none. The untranslated Marx of the 'seventies and early 'eighties was read by a mere handful of students and people curious in continental economics. No one added an appendix on Marx to Mill's discussion of socialism. When younger economists wrote volumes of Principles they ignored him, like Sidgwick, or later noted his blunders in stray magisterial asides, like Marshall[2].

During the whole of Marx's residence in England, no contribution of any importance to technical socialist thought was made by an Englishman[3]. The instinctive socialism common among men well below the half-way line of society was dulled by better times. Trade union leaders were busy breaking down fences and promoting their group interests in society as it was. They had not much time for society as it might become. But meanwhile Mill's influence, far more effective in keeping men's minds open to possibilities of social change than any socialist dogmatics, was spreading among all those who thought. With it spread generous and confused criticism of industrial society from the prophets of the age—Carlyle, Kingsley, Ruskin. None was more critical than Mill himself, in the restrained passion of those ordered paragraphs available latterly in cheap editions for the people. His care for individuality—"the importance, to man and society...of giving full freedom to human nature to expand itself in innumerable and conflicting directions"[4]—kept him hostile to all precise and authoritarian forms of socialism, with their 'over-government'; but, as the later editions of his *Principles* had shown, and as his *Autobiography* of 1873 and his posthumous *Chapters on Socialism*

[1] Preface, as above; cp. vol. I. p. 580.

[2] Sidgwick's *Principles* (1883) has no index; I do not think there is a reference to Marx in the text. There are three concise references, showing characteristically thorough consideration of Marx's arguments before their rejection, in Marshall's *Principles* (1890).

[3] Beer, *op. cit.* II. 189, has claimed Richard Jones' recognition, in his *Text-Book of Lectures* (1852), of capitalism as "but a stage in the economic development of mankind" as a contribution of considerable interest; but it is hardly technical socialist thought.

[4] *Autobiography*, p. 253.

of 1879[1] showed more evidently, he had been making through-out his life a "greater approximation, so far as regards the ulti-mate prospects of humanity, to a qualified Socialism."[2]

His doctrines of the land and of inheritance were themselves revolutionary, judged by the common standards of the day; while his tenacious belief in the social value of a diffusion of property, his co-operative enthusiasm, and his dislike of the prospect of eternal wage-paying and wage-earning, had kept him in sympathy with the three strongest currents of action among wage-earners—those represented by the friendly and building societies, the co-operators, and the trade unions. But in thinking of the future he was haunted by the ghost of Malthus; and, almost to the time of his death, he had taught a wage doctrine not only unspeakably distasteful to wage-earners but also, as with his usual candour he had himself admitted, wrong[3]. Both the teaching and the recantation helped to produce among them that "confident contempt" for "the traditional political economy" of which economists wrote ten years later[4]. This contempt had been embittered by the fashion in which economic thinkers, not excluding Mill himself, had often written about the relation of Malthus' teaching to wage problems[5]. So, great as was Mill's indirect influence on thinkers in all social ranks, there were obstacles to his direct in-fluence on the world of labour. It was natural there to assume that political economy, and he, taught just what the stupider members of the propertied classes had implied that they taught[6].

In 1879–80 there appeared to that world, indeed to all British worlds, a new prophet with a gospel. First published at New York in 1879, and republished there twice in 1880, Henry George's *Progress and Poverty* went through ten London editions between 1881 and 1884. The prophet followed his book, and proved not less moving with the spoken than with the written word. There was every sign of a religious revival. *Progress*, an unsympathetic contemporary wrote, was circu-lated "like the testament of a new dispensation. Societies were

[1] Published in the *Fortnightly Review*.

[2] *Autobiography*, p. 191. There is a more decided profession of qualified socialist faith on p. 231-2. But the *Chapters* harmonise with the phrase quoted.

[3] The old wages-fund doctrine, which appeared to set rigid limits to the efficacy of movements for the increase of wages: see *Dic. Pol. Econ.* s.v. *Wages Fund.*

[4] Sidgwick, *Principles*, p. 6.

[5] It was easy, if incorrect, to infer from Mill that in a growing population wages could not rise.          [6] As sketched above, p. 395-6.

formed, journals were devised to propagate its saving doctrines, and little companies of the faithful held stated meetings for its reading and exposition."[1] Not Mill before him, nor Marx after, ever had such honour in Britain. Though five minutes' simple arithmetic with the income-tax returns would have displaced the keystone from the arch of Henry George's doctrine, his wage-earner's record, magnificent ardour, honest care for the poor and the disinherited, apocalyptic American eloquence and short way with Malthus, combined with the smooth soaring curve of the doctrinal arch, made disciples everywhere, even if the discipleship of many was short. "The limit to the population of the globe can only be the limit of space":[2] so much for Malthus. "What I, therefore, propose as the simple yet sovereign remedy, which will raise wages, increase the earnings of capital, extirpate pauperism, abolish poverty, give remunerative employment to whoever wishes it, afford free scope to human powers, lessen crime, elevate morals, and taste, and intelligence, purify government and carry civilisation to yet nobler heights, is—*to appropriate rent by taxation.*"[3] That is the arch. And the keystone is—"*to abolish all taxation save that upon land values.*"[4] Whether or not land values should be specially taxed is a reasonably simple problem in applied economics. Mill always had a clear view of it. The suggestion that a European state could live by such taxation alone is of course absurd. But George had watched the magical growth and gamblers' distribution of the land values of California. He had seen poverty beside the home of the speculator in real estate. These things obsessed him. And indeed the land values socially created in nineteenth-century America would have gone some way towards maintaining even a Federation of States, could it have got control of them wisely and in time.

George's function in Britain was that of a ferment. The single-taxers were never more than a sect, like the pure Owenites before them. But the crusade set men thinking about inequality, and stirred old memories among many who were never professed disciples. Thomas Spence[5] and Tom Paine, Cobbett and the early socialists, the Chartists, the radicals of every shade, Mill himself, Joseph Arch and Joseph Chamber-

[1] Rae, J., *Contemporary Socialism* (2nd ed. 1891), p. 441.
[2] *Progress and Poverty* (an ed. of 1884), p. 94.
[3] *Ibid.* p. 288: italics in the original.
[4] *Ibid. loc. cit.*: italics in the original.
[5] See vol. I. p. 313.

lain, all had been land reformers of one kind or another. Feargus O'Connor had collected the pence of hard-pressed industrial wage-earners—who themselves perhaps, or whose fathers, had come into industry from the countryside—for that National Land Company which was the last, and rather unhappy, product of Chartism. A few small holdings "on a high plateau exposed to all the winds,"[1] at Minster Lovell in Oxfordshire, still survived as its memorial. Mill had founded the Land Tenure Reform Association in 1870–1, and had put on record in its programme that "an active and influential portion of the working classes had adopted the opinion that private property in land was a mistake."[2] (He thought not; but was sure that it had been abused.) He had always been as willing as George himself to annex unearned increment for society by taxation; but he had no delusions as to its amount. In the year when George first toured the country (1882) Alfred Russell Wallace had published his little book on land nationalisation, dedicated to the working men of England[3], and with a few friends, most of whom had much less experience than George of the wage-earner's life, he had founded the Land Nationalisation Society. Also in the year of the first tour, and again quite independently of it, H. M. Hyndman, who had studied Marx and sought his friendship, republished Spence's lecture on *The Real Rights of Man*. A year later, in September, 1883, the Democratic Federation which Hyndman had helped to found in 1881, and which had put land nationalisation into its programme[4], turned itself into the Social Democratic Federation and became, within a short time, a powerful organisation of socialist propaganda.

Its leaders thought meanly, not of George, but of his system, as semi-Marxists and builders on the socialist element in Mill's teaching well might. During the second tour (1884) Hyndman disputed publicly with George in St James's Hall on socialism *versus* the single tax. Without the prophet from California, the socialist could hardly have secured so large and respectable a sounding-board. And the ferment which George set up was equally useful to William Morris's Socialist League, to the newly founded Fabian Society, and to other more obscure

[1] Jebb, L., *The Small Holdings of England* (1907), p. 121. The holdings were still there in 1907.

[2] Quoted in Beer, *op. cit.* II. 241.

[3] It had three editions in 1882; the third, with about 250 pp., sold for 8*d*.

[4] But not a prominent part of it.

organisations. Adherents of Henry George's views in their "little propagandist societies...gradually developed in many cases, into complete Socialists."[1]

The foreigner could note; the statistician could prove; and old wage-earners might remember, that there had been "a complete revolution...in the lives of a large number of English workmen"[2] since Peel's day. But there was squalid poverty and misery enough still in the depths. The sharp crisis of unemployment in 1878–9 had opened the possibility of a fall into the depths to skilled men who as a rule moved above them. When George first visited England, unemployment among the trade unionists, as it happened, was abnormally low; but from the year of his second visit to that of Victoria's jubilee it was persistently and abnormally high. Engels, convinced that it was merely a disease of capitalism, was prophesying with a gloomy satisfaction that "the sighed-for period of prosperity would not come"[3]; and even those people who looked with most complacency on the improvement in the wage-earner's position could say no more than that "the aid...so widely given by friendly and trade societies limited or deferred the pauperisation"[4] of their members, when unemployed. (There are no statistics of the unemployment in those depths from which membership of a trade or friendly society was all but unattainable.) Though there was no good reason to suppose that, in the familiar jingle of pessimism, the rich were getting richer and the poor poorer; and although statisticians were engaged in estimating that more than five-twelfths of the whole national income of Britain went to the manual labour classes in 1883, as compared with considerably less than a third fifty years earlier[5],

---

[1] Webb, Sidney, *Socialism in England* (1890), p. 21. According to Beer, *op. cit.* II. 245, "Some four-fifths of the socialist leaders of Great Britain in the 'eighties had passed through the school of Henry George." I am not in a position to check this fraction, but the impression which it is meant to give is certainly correct.

[2] Above, p. 477.

[3] In fact, trade union unemployment was at a minimum, just over 2 per cent., in 1889–90.

[4] Above, p. 433.

[5] Giffen, Sir R., "Further Notes on the Progress of the Working Classes," *S.J.* 1886, reprinted in *Essays in Finance: Second Series*. Giffen estimated a national income for Great Britain in 1883 of £1,198,000,000 and a 'manual-labour class' income of £515,000,000. (In *Socialism Made Plain* (1883), which had a circulation of about 100,000, the Democratic Federation was saying that the workers'

this estimated share—had they agreed about it—might very well seem entirely inadequate to the sons, now educated and voting, of those men of the Chartist age, who had held that their contribution to the progress of the country gave them "a right to a better condition."[1] The sons did not need either to read or to believe Marx's dialectics of value, nor to be in any sense revolutionary, in order to come to this opinion. It might, and usually did, serve merely to stiffen their backs in some wage fight or in some wage negotiation diplomatically conducted by their leaders.

The world was still full of inequality. Democrats of all shades chuckled over Joseph Chamberlain's gibe at those of the old governing class who "toiled not neither did they spin," and welcomed his advocacy of a graduated income-tax. Whatever Henry George may have failed to do, he had proved to demonstration, though not for the first time, how in one great field at any rate inequality was a result, not of over-riding economic forces, but of an alterable human law of property. And meanwhile Gladstone was making solemn fun in the House of Commons of an elderly, conservative, director of the Bank of England, who for a generation had urged the differentiation of the income-tax on the ground that all incomes were not equally 'earned';[2] while Gladstone's political opponents, and some of his recent allies, were denouncing him for his very restrained, if perhaps not very wise, handling of property rights in the Irish Land Act of 1881[3].

The representative wage-earner had not begun to call himself a socialist by 1886; far from it. But many politically active wage-earners, especially in London, had. From the stock-in-trade of radicalism, some of the more socialist pieces were being brought down from the upper shelves of the mind. Disraelian conservatism and Tory democracy could repudiate *laissez-faire* without denying their past. It was probable that the new electors in town and country, while conservative in many things, would not use their votes to maintain permanently

share was £300,000,000 out of £1,300,000,000.) His corresponding estimates for the period just before 1843 were £432,000,000 and £122,000,000. Colquhoun for 1812–15 had estimated a bare quarter.

[1] Above, p. 477.                                           [2] Above, p. 401.

[3] See *e.g.* Locker-Lampson, G., *A Consideration of the State of Ireland in the Nineteenth Century* (1907), ch. xv. It was over this Act that the Dukes of Argyle and Bedford parted from Gladstone.

both the rights of private property, as understood by the average middle class mind of the 'seventies, and that slender taxation of the greater, and the 'unearned,' private incomes with which Gladstone was content. The minds of electors, to whatever social class they belonged, were not all clear or far-sighted or likely to remain consistent. Though there were close independent thinkers, and would be disinterested voters, in all classes, the view which majorities would take of the economic order and of the voter's place in it, and of the changes immediately necessary, would depend on the political programmes put before them, and on the pressures which economic forces in the whole world—for these all played on Britain—might exert on individual voters. It was now certain that, as time went on, more and more drastic proposals for change would find their way into the political programmes, even though at the time of the Irish Home Rule controversy British economic issues had fallen for a time into the background. The pressures of the outer world on Britain were exceptionally severe; and the relaxation which was to come shortly could not, in 1886–7, be foreseen. Engels might prove to be right this time. Prosperity might not return. If so, it was not unlikely that the average wage-earner's thought about society would move, as fast as thought ever moves in Britain, from right to left.

## CHAPTER XII

## THE FACE OF THE COUNTRY, 1886–7

WHEN Victoria's jubilee was approaching, most people in Britain were within earshot of the crash or mutter of a town by day. Many of those who were not, unless they lived North of the Highland Line, could yet catch the clank of trains in a still night. Few railway lines had been built of late, so the clank had not often come as a new sound of the night. Here and there it had, preceded by some fresh gash in a hillside or some raw embankment abutting on a viaduct of unweathered brick—common sights forty, and thirty, years back. But in most places the railway had sunk into the landscape, like the road and the canal before it. All that it brought in sight and sound had become established, and familiar as the uninterrupted spreading of the mutter of the towns. Towns had become the birthplaces not merely of "a large part of the British race," as William Farr had anticipated in 1851, but of the major part[1]. Its critics called the race street-bred. If the streets were not really England, they seemed so to most Englishmen; and London streets were England to nearly one Englishman in seven. So the streets should be looked at before the fields, or the hills, or even the sea-coasts.

Whilst giving evidence before the Royal Commission on the Housing of the Working Classes in 1884, Lord Shaftesbury said there had always been "the greatest desire in London and other large towns that every man should have his own house... It would be a great blessing. But in such a vast city as this it is next to impossible."[2] He had in mind principally the congested core of London across which his name would soon be written, such districts as that of which another witness reported that five families to six rooms was about the average[3]. Yet, even in London, Shaftesbury's ideal was much more nearly realised than his words suggest, more nearly perhaps than he knew;

[1] Vol. I. p. 537.
[2] *R.C. on the Housing of the Working Classes*, 1884–5 (xxx), Q. 40.
[3] *Ibid.* Q. 1948. There was a good deal of evidence to suggest that, in such areas, there had been an actual increase of overcrowding in the early 'eighties.

for he had lived to face the worst, and all that was terrible was reported to him[1]. It is true that when he spoke more than a fifth of the people of London were living under what would later be defined as conditions of overcrowding, that is more than two to a room;[2] but as soon as you got away from the central and other specially congested quarters, with their big old houses gone to decay, there began those long unlovely streets which still were urban England—'two parallel walls of brick pierced with holes.'[3] In them a man with a family might have a house, such as it was. Since in all London there were less than eight people to each inhabited house, and since both the tenement houses and those of the rich and the fairly well-to-do with their servants would often contain more, the house with five or six people in it was obviously the commonest of all[4].

It might be a wretched thing, jammed against its neighbours and overcrowded like any tenement house in Clerkenwell or Whitechapel: it was likely to be that in inner London. In inner East London, mixed up with the older bigger houses, were the "houses of three rooms, houses of two rooms, houses of one room—houses set back against a wall or back to back, fronting it may be on to a narrow footway, with posts at each end and a gutter down the middle."[5] In Bermondsey there were plenty of two-room houses, the rooms one above the other. The people preferred them to tenements; and though all were old, "very few were built back to back."[6] In newly built districts on the Middlesex side, there was "only a small demand for houses which are subdivided into separate tenements."[7] The artisan demand, as opposed to that of the unskilled, the floating and the semi-criminal population of the true slums, was for three, four and five-room houses, especially four-room. A company

---

[1] Cp. p. 442 above.

[2] All references below to overcrowding refer to 1891, when statistics were first collected (*Census of* 1891, 1893–4, CVI). The conditions in 1886–7 would be nearly identical. The census definition of 'more than two' to a room is used, because no other is available for most towns, not Charles Booth's definition of 'two or more' to a room, which is retained for purposes of comparison with Booth's *Life and Labour* in the *New Survey of London Life and Labour*, I (1930), p. 150, 169, etc.

[3] Pasquet, D., *Londres et les ouvriers de Londres* (1914), p. 45.

[4] The census 'house' was "all the space between the external and party walls of a building"; its 'tenement', each separate occupation (cp. vol. I. p. 547). For all London the population per house was 7·82 in 1881 and 7·72 in 1891.

[5] Booth, *Life and Labour*, I. 30.

[6] *R.C. of* 1884–5, Q. 4622.        [7] *Ibid.* Q. 12,203.

which was trying to provide for the artisan what he wanted, and what he could afford, found nothing so popular as "our little four-room cottages." They found too that their larger houses, including some of the four-room, were "almost invariably let partly to lodgers."[1]

What kind of a London was growing up of itself, and how Londoners lived when they had room, is best shown in some such place as West Ham, although West Ham was not technically London. As an urban area it had only come into being since 1850. Its statistics have never been much complicated by the homes of the well-to-do. It was too new to have many houses either of the old Middlesex sort, once prosperous now broken into tenements, or of the old room-above-room Bermondsey sort. It had not attracted the philanthropist or the building company with a conscience. It was a 'builder's' town, for wage-earners and lesser city workers—'clerks on thirty bob.' Here not more than about 10 per cent. of the population lived 'under conditions of overcrowding,' and the representative inhabited house contained almost exactly six people and a half. This house was at least four-room, or there would have been a great deal of overcrowding, and is perhaps best pictured as holding a family and a lodger or lodgers. 'Our lodger' was almost as normal in Cockney life as he is familiar in Cockney rhyme. If the house had six or seven rooms, it was likely to contain two families[2].

The impossibility of every man having his own house, in London's central area, had produced the model dwelling movement connected with the names of George Peabody and Sydney Waterlow. About the same time (1861-2) they had begun the erection of what to the eye of to-day are their "large and dreary block tenements."[3] Peabody's trustees carried on the work after his death in 1869. Since 1863, Waterlow had been working through the Improved Industrial Dwellings Company to show that sanitary housing could be made to pay. He succeeded, on an average weekly rental of 2s. 1¼d. a room. By 1884 his company had built, or had in hand, tenements for 25,000

---

[1] *R.C. of* 1884-5, Q. 12,062, 12,124.

[2] A common arrangement in the Canning Town dock area was two families to a house, with three rooms per family, plus a common kitchen, etc. *S.C. on Artisans and Labourers Dwellings*, 1882 (VII. 249), Q. 1430. Statistics of housing, when not otherwise stated, are from the Census of 1891.

[3] Wood, E. E., *Housing Progress in Western Europe* (New York, 1923), p. 13.

people[1]. The Peabody Trust, at a rental of $1s.$ $11\frac{1}{2}d.$ was in course of providing for about 20,000[2]. Waterlow's success was drawing out imitators, as he had hoped it would. Up and down inner working-class London, above the huddled 'gardens' and 'rents,' the blocks of 'models' were rising. But they housed only a tiny proportion of the Londoners. Their erection, Charles Booth wrote, "an effort to make crowding harmless, is a vast improvement, but it only substitutes one sort of crowding for another. Nor have all blocks...a good character, either from a sanitary or a moral point of view."[3]

Outside London, the more completely an English town had taken shape under the pressure of nineteenth century conditions, the more likely was it to be a place of numberless little houses, and to conform to Shaftesbury's ideal of a house for a man. But if the pressure had been mainly applied rather early in the century, there was considerable risk of there not being enough room in the houses, judged by the standards of the 'eighties, for the men, their families, and the occasional lodgers; unless an active municipality had been recently at work. Very early in the century "every workman had a home of his own," in Birmingham[4]. There was "never any serious overcrowding," Joseph Chamberlain said with justified pride in 1884: "we have no flats and no cellars." "Nor do working class families often take in lodgers," he added. It was under his guidance, in 1875–6, that the city had utilised current legislation to carry out one of the earliest schemes of slum clearance: it had also acquired, and greatly improved, its water supply, completed a sewerage system, and brought in a new and strict set of building by-laws[5]. It averaged only five people to each house, and so had very little technical overcrowding.

At Liverpool the municipality had a far worse inheritance. It had taken action early. Even in 1860 it had begun "some large blocks of dwellings out of our own corporate estate."[6] Latterly, under local acts and national legislation, it had been closing bad tenements as nuisances, scheduling insanitary areas, and acquiring house property to demolish it. But in the 'forties,

[1] Waterlow's evidence before the *R.C. of* 1884–5, Q. 11,905 *sqq.*
[2] *Ibid.* Q. 5063, 11,570–1. Cp. *S.C. of* 1882, Q. 1897, 2589.
[3] *Life and Labour*, I. 30. There is a full study of the 'models' in vol. III.
[4] Vol. I. p. 37.
[5] Chamberlain's evidence to the *R.C. of* 1884–5, Q. 12,359 *sqq.*
[6] *R.C. of* 1884–5, Q. 13,421 (evidence of an ex-mayor of Liverpool).

just before effective sanitary legislation began and before the city had adopted proper building by-laws, builders had endowed it with 14,500 houses in 2500 blind courts—the houses facing one another at 10 or 12 feet range, and backing on to similar houses[1]. They usually had an attic, two rooms, and a cellar which down to 1871 had too often been a tenement, and was sometimes "secretly occupied" still[2]. Fourteen hundred of the worst of these court houses had been swept away by the authorities, mostly since 1882. In spite of the many surviving, the city, young and vigorous, could show a house population of under six and an overcrowding percentage of probably not more than twelve[3].

The textile towns of the North—Manchester, Salford, Blackburn, Bolton, Oldham, Preston, Bradford, Halifax, Huddersfield—with other representative industrial towns such as Leeds, Sheffield, Nottingham and Leicester, all had an average house population within a few points above or below five. Yet, so inadequate was the accommodation of the cottages in the originally stone-built and not easily remodelled towns of the Yorkshire valleys, that they were among the most overcrowded places in England—Bradford, Halifax and Huddersfield having a slightly larger proportion of their population living more than two to a room even than London[4]. The number of two and three-room 'inhabited houses' in these places was evidently still very great. The overcrowding was less in Leeds, much less in Sheffield, and very much less in the cotton towns. Preston had remarkably little, and even Manchester-Salford, where there were many architectural survivals from the bad days described by Friedrich Engels, had less than West Ham[5]. The grimed and slated little red-brick houses of the Lancashire side, under their low grey sky, held a population in the main comfortable and well satisfied with them, itself, and its county.

[1] R.C. of 1884–5, Q. 13,336 sqq. See Hope, E. W., Health at the Gateway, Ch. IX, where on p. 158 a photograph of one of the old courts is reproduced. And cp. vol. I. p. 16, 546.

[2] R.C. of 1884–5, Q. 13,467 (another witness).

[3] The proportion of the population 'overcrowded' in 1891 was 10·9. The number of people per house was 5·99 in 1881 and 5·68 in 1891. This comparatively rapid motion suggests that overcrowding may have been perceptibly worse in 1886 than in 1891.

[4] London, in 1891, 19·7; Huddersfield, 19·9; Bradford, 20·1; Halifax, 21·3.

[5] Manchester, 8·2; West Ham, 9·3. For Engels' Manchester, see vol. I. p. 538; for some survivals Marr, T. R., Housing Conditions in Manchester and Salford (1904).

Most comfortable of all, judged by the tests of average house population and overcrowding, were towns which had been comparatively little affected by the first uncontrolled movements of population and the attempts to house it, such as Derby, Nottingham and Leicester. These three had average house populations below five and overcrowding percentages of only from two to four. In view of the decisive and degrading influence of the early nineteenth century Irish immigration on housing habits and housing conditions[1], it may be noted that whereas 9 per cent. of the Lancashire population in 1851 had been actually Irish born, the corresponding figure for Derbyshire was 1·5, for Nottinghamshire 0·9, and only 0·7 for Leicestershire[2]. Leicester had been spared a social disease, and had made good use of its immunity: in Liverpool "most of the inhabitants" of those insanitary courts were Irish in 1884. If a reforming municipality began to flush the courts in the morning, they were foul again at noon[3].

Bristol and Newcastle had inherited awkward sites and some of the ancient houses of historic seaports, split, like those of London, into tenements. Away from its centre, parts of which were "worse than Whitechapel,"[4] Bristol had also inherited quantities of small two-roomed cottages; for the housing standard of the West had been low both in town and country. Like London, it had made a beginning with model dwellings—two blocks of them with 131 'lettings' in 1884. This did not greatly help; and the two-room cottages drove up both of its test figures[5].

North of the Tees, not only in Newcastle but in Gateshead and Sunderland and throughout Northumberland and Durham, those figures were exceedingly bad; but the reality was rather better than the figures. The inherited town house of the North-East coast was either the large house fallen to tenements, or a smaller house of two storeys built for tenements—"each storey being a complete small house of itself"[6]—or some variant of

---

[1] Cp. vol. I. p. 62.    [2] *Census of 1851. Occupations*, etc. I. ccxcv.

[3] *R.C. of* 1884-5. Evidence of H. Farris, Q. 13,463 *sqq.* The quotation is from Q. 13,626.

[4] *Ibid.* Q. 7018. Whitechapel was the synonym for bad housing conditions in the 'eighties.

[5] *Ibid.* Q. 6947, 7018; and cp. vol. I. p. 547. For country housing in the South-West, below, p. 510.

[6] *Ibid.* Q. 7452. And cp. vol. I. p. 27-32, on Scottish and North Country housing. For the larger North Country, or Scottish, rooms see Q. 19,396 and vol. I. p. 29, n. 6.

the one-roomed or two-roomed Northumbrian miners' and agricultural labourers' cottage. There had been in fact, and there remained, an approach to housing conditions typically Scottish. Population per house in the towns was nearly as high as in London, and the habit of living more than two to a room was far more widespread. The rooms may have been larger on the average, as they probably were in the Scottish towns, and certainly were in the Northumbrian, as compared with the South Country, agricultural districts. It was just as well; for in Sunderland over 32 per cent., in Newcastle over 35 per cent., and in Gateshead over 40 per cent. of the whole population lived 'under conditions of overcrowding.' The census officials who first reported on the matter, not fully apprehending the local peculiarities, were puzzled to find that their figures showed more overcrowding—more cases of three people in one room or five in two—in Northumberland and Durham when all the towns were excluded than when they were included[1]. But it was natural that the old Northumbrian one or two-room way of living should survive least altered among the pits or in the dales.

The old Scottish urban way was little touched, whether in the towering many storied houses of Edinburgh and Stirling; in the three and four-storied ones among which burrowed the Glasgow wynds; in their fellows of grey granite at Aberdeen; in the two-storied, often of two flats as at Newcastle, common in the smaller burghs; or in the one-storied, 'single end' or 'but and ben,' which linked town to country and collected about the coal mines and iron works[2]. The Scottish way of living had been got by ancient country habit out of ancient town necessity, and it was a one or two-room way, very tough and indestructible, as were the eighteen inch or two foot stone walls of the houses which encased it. "The single-room system," the Commissioners of 1885 reported in a not quite lucid phrase, "appears to be an institution co-existent with urban life among the working classes of Scotland."[3] In Edinburgh the house of a skilled man—Scottish witnesses called it a house, though English Commissioners said tene-

---

[1] *Census of* 1891: *Final Report*, p. 22. This would of course have been a surprising result south of the Tees. The officials noticed that the 'percentage of over-crowding' dropped plumb from 34 in Durham to 16·5 in the West Riding.

[2] See the *Report on Housing in Scotland* of 1917, p. 41–2, 47, 49.

[3] *R.C. of* 1884–5: *Scotland* (XXXI of 1884–5), p. 4.

ment—was "generally a room and a kitchen";[1] sometimes two rooms and a kitchen. The unskilled man had just a room. There were 14,000 'single-room houses' in the city, and 19,000 'houses' which had only one room with a window to it, though 5000 of them had two rooms of a sort[2]. About a quarter of the whole population of Glasgow lived in one-room 'houses.' The Bridgeton division was the masterpiece. In 1881 it contained 8946 families of all sizes, from the widow living alone upwards. Of these only 882 had more than two rooms fitted with windows[3]. The municipality of Glasgow, under its own Acts of Parliament, had done some admirable slum clearances and street making since 1866; but it could not change the system[4]. For the whole of urban Lanarkshire, out of 176,000 families, 42,000, or not 24 per cent., had 'houses' with more than two rooms fitted with windows. The granite streets of Aberdeen were less congested: nearly 40 per cent. of its families were in that favoured position. Dundee was more congested: the percentage of favoured families there was under 24. All this is for 1881; but, in the nature of the case, the position was changing very slowly[5]. It is not surprising that the Scottish census of 1891 did not imitate the English by applying a persons-per-room standard of overcrowding. The arithmetical results would have been disastrous. More than half the urban population would have appeared overcrowded; although a Glasgow official in 1884, taking a cubic-foot-of-air-space standard, had maintained that not more than 5 per cent. of the Glasgow houses could be so described[6].

Experts of the Peabody Trust knew that their models "would not fill if erected in the outskirts";[7] and it was noticeable, towards the end of the decade, that working class tenement blocks filled much better in Westminster than in Deptford[8]. Pressure was so great West of the City that blocks of flats were being built for the use of the more comfortable classes. "Dined with Willie and his wife," John Bright noted in his diary, on April 10, 1883: "their rooms or *flat* in Victoria Street not so

---

[1] *R.C. of* 1884–5, Q. 18,594.
[2] From the *Census of* 1881: in App. to the *R.C. Report of* 1884–5.
[3] *Ibid.*                                    [4] *S.C. of* 1882, as above, Q. 736.
[5] It had changed comparatively little by 1917.
[6] *R.C. of* 1884–5, Q. 19,508.         [7] *R.C. of* 1884–5 (xxx), Q. 11,701.
[8] Booth, *op. cit.* III. 5.

inviting as a *house* would be."[1] Before 1880 such buildings had been rare; though inner London had always provided lodgings for every social grade, and had specialised in chambers and apartments for single gentlemen. Her comfortable, normal, family men had standardised continuous houses like the wage-earners of the outskirts, not in low, but in high unlovely streets and squares and gardens—basement; portico; stucco or brick front; four stories, and attics for the maidservants; with mews, and sometimes a scrap of slum round the corner. The type was reproduced with variations in the inner residential belt of many English towns, becoming rarer as you went North, partly because the inner parts of industrial towns were less fit and less prized for comfortable residence, partly because more spacious ways of living could be got relatively near.

In London they could only be got with any ease in the true suburbs, with some of which communications were defective, judged by a rising standard of mobility, although it was com-munication—the radial railways—that had made them. The suburb was much the same all over the country. It had real gardens, if ever so little, and shrubs and hedges of holly or privet. When, as a suburb, it was old, there would be imbedded in it houses restrained, balanced, usually rectangular in mass and fenestration, of red brick or stuccoed, inconspicuously roofed, dating from before the railways and the publication of *The Stones of Venice* (1851-3). But whether old or new, the suburb was dominated by what average builder-architect opinion had made out of the Gothic Revival and John Ruskin. Slated roof and gable were assertive. There might be patterns on the slates. There was likely to be a wooden or iron finial on the gable end, and perhaps machine-made open work on its crest. Latterly, the half-timbered gable had become prominent. Turrets were possible; curved bays or some deliberate avoid-ance of the rectangular almost certain. True Gothic windows were awkward and scarce, but some of the windows could be given round heads; others small panes. Worked stone, for beauty and diversity, would be mixed with the normal brick in various ways, if only in the single bow window of the smallest semi-detached villa residence, or in the diminishing perspective of bow windows along the stretches of continuous house between the true suburb and the town. Attention had

[1] *The Diaries of John Bright* (1930), p. 498.

been called to the Venetian decoration of wall veils with inset marble slabs;[1] so there could be patterns of red brick on white, and of blue on red. Porches gave great scope for Gothic detail, because they need not be comfortable[2]. It was on a porch, but of a public-house in Ealing, that Ruskin had seen in 1873 brickwork "which would have been in no discord with the tomb of Can Grande, had it been set beside it at Verona."[3] Discord with the best Italian Gothic had not, however, been universally avoided.

The suburbs had no bounds. They shaded away into the country; and even villages remote from London had often been suburbanised, judged by the standards of the country squire. "The enormous rise in the value of all sites within easy reach of great towns or railway stations," wrote the Hon. George C. Brodrick in 1881, "sometimes offers to great landowners an inducement to sell which they cannot resist. In this way... detached portions of great estates...are bought up by land-jobbers and sold in petty blocks to retired tradesmen. The villa-residences of such immigrants from towns, fronting the road in unsightly rows, with an acre or two of freehold land at the back of each, are a characteristic feature of many country villages, and have been too much overlooked in popular descriptions of rural England."[4] The village as popularly described was not extinct. It had hall and parsonage and perhaps another house or two whose inhabitants, unlike the "immigrants from towns," took "an active part in county interests."[5] But one had to go into the depths of the country to find it. When found, its houses might be quite untouched by the Gothic Revival, unless the parsonage had been rebuilt lately, or a hall of no pretensions had been replaced by something gabled and arched, possibly with stained glass in it and a pitch-pine staircase[6].

Apart from the definite encroachment of towns, suburbs,

[1] See Ruskin's Preface to *The Stones of Venice*.

[2] An architect who has been consulted writes of the average designs of this period—"all houses had as many gables as could be crowded on to them, and as great a variety of building materials as the designer could assemble."

[3] Ruskin, Preface to the 1873 edition of *The Stones of Venice*, p. vi.

[4] Brodrick, *English Land and English Landlords*, p. 154. "But this class," he adds, "though of great importance to election agents, fills a very small place in the agricultural economy, or even in the social life of an English county."

[5] *Loc. cit.*

[6] Cp. Cobbett on the earliest Gothic revival houses quoted in vol. I. p. 36.

pits and factories, and of the railways with their brood, the country itself, if thought of as a series of landscapes, had not changed so very much since Cobbett rode about baying at tax-eaters and Scotchmen and pitying the fortunes of the poor. It had become increasingly difficult, even during Cobbett's lifetime, to find landscapes with "those very ugly things, common fields" in them[1]. In a few places, bits of the patchwork of the "ugly things" had survived until a main railway line was driven across its shots, headlands and gore acres[2]. You could see it from no main line now. Only well-informed people knew where to look for accidentally preserved specimens. Naturally there were rather more remnants of the Scottish equivalent, the runrig field, in the untouched Hebrides; there was some runrig too in Ireland; perhaps a few fields cut up into 'quillets' in Wales. In England there were men "still living who had held and worked farms under" the "inconvenient rules" of the open-field system, and who knew the "meaning of its terms and eccentric details";[3] but even the memory was perishing. The thing itself had gone out of the English scene for ever.

At a time when it seemed not unlikely that they would follow it, the surviving commons and wastes had been maintained by acts of deliberate policy, in that dwindled and regimented state into which they had fallen by the 'seventies. In the really fertile parts of the country, few of any consequence had escaped enclosure by the end of the first quarter of the century. The survivors were most numerous and extensive on the sandy soils. Few had yet been turned into golf links. Fewer had kept much of their former economic character. There was not a great deal of firing gathered or turf cut, not many goats and swine fed, on your average English common. Often the suburbs had got all about it, as they had got about some of the almost unrecognisable 'moors' of the industrial North[4]. Among them it served its purpose, yet not the old purpose. Well beyond the suburbs, gypsies might still find camping ground on it; but vagrant life had been much confined and policed. Peter Bell

---

[1] Vol. 1. p. 20.

[2] As can be seen in some of the early plans for the Eastern Counties Railway, the present L.N.E.R. line from Liverpool Street to Cambridge.

[3] From F. Seebohm's Introduction to his *English Village Community* (1883). p. xiv.

[4] There was still a little heather on Kersal Moor (Manchester); not any, I think, on Woodhouse Moor (Leeds).

no longer lay out beside his asses. By the time that George Borrow died in 1881, there was little left of that society of the open sky among which the Flaming Tinman had travelled and fought[1]. There were the county constabulary and the Commons Preservation Society.

The hill commons of the West and the North had been regulated or portioned out, but not otherwise greatly changed. A wire fence now divided the Wasdale fells from the fells of Ennerdale; but the intakes had gained no ground on the lower slopes—if anything they had lost since the dales became more accessible. Not even as a romantic possibility was the carrying of cultivation, "rich as that of a flower garden...to the very tops of Ben Nevis and Helvellyn,"[2] any longer anticipated. Whether wanderers from the towns below or the grouse deserved more consideration on Kinder Scout; whether the sheep with their shepherds or the deer and their gillies had the best title to the use of the Cairngorms—about these things there was discussion; and there would be more. But in the true Highlands, except at the prescribed times, there were fewer men than ever amid the loneliness of "the seven bens and the seven glens and the seven mountain moors."[3] In the Pennines, solitude could be found without much seeking, all the way from Kinder Scout to Cross Fell; although the railways pierced the hills, and the smoke of Cheshire and Lancashire broke against their southern ranges, blown on the South-West wind.

For over two centuries there had been little forest in Britain. The English landscape was full of trees but astonishingly empty even of woodland. Not five per cent. of the surface of the country was wooded, in spite of the hedgerow and roadside timber, the parks and gardens and spinneys. In Scotland the percentage was less than four. The work of clothing Scotland with trees, undertaken in the eighteenth century[4], had been checked after the decade 1820-30. When the railway age came, a line was driven through the best wooded districts, Athole, Badenoch and Strathspey, and much of the standing timber went in sleepers. It was said that by 1872 Scotland had 200,000 acres less forest than she had just before Waterloo. There had been

[1] There was most of it in Scotland, where the vagrant 'tinkler' survived.
[2] Macaulay's *Essay on Southey's Colloquies on Society, ad finem*.
[3] A favourite refrain of Catriona MacGregor, later the wife of David Balfour of Shaws.
[4] See vol. I. p. 13-14.

some replanting since. Interest in forestry was reviving. The woods of Scone, Blair-Atholl and Strathspey were considerable, and much of the timber was magnificent. But the ground lost to forest had not been regained; there was little management, as a trained forester understands it; and to a visiting continental expert, Scotland, with its great spaces and forest climate, seemed a land of infinite lost opportunity[1].

In England opportunity was far less, but what there was had not been seized. The state took little interest in oak, for oak had no longer its immediate fighting value. The state was not yet wise enough to interest itself vigorously in any timber with a view to the long future. Schemes for replanting in the New Forest, after what was called the Deer Removal Act of 1851, were stultified by the opposition of the commoners and the public. The commoners were no doubt shortsighted but wise in their generation. Very possibly the public was wise for future generations. England was so full that she had to balance forest against 'open space.' But a little more modern forest might have been made there in Hampshire. As it was, some 40,000 acres of William's hunting ground lay "bare and unproductive," if beautiful[2]. "Before long it will *not be here*," M. Boppé, the Forest Inspector from Nancy wrote in 1885, "that a professor of Sylviculture...will choose to pitch his tent." Only in the Forest of Dean did he find a little workmanlike management on Crown land[3].

Where the town and suburban railway crawled round the trees, as at Epping, the transition to open space was inevitable. The other fragment of the old forest of Essex, Hainault, was disafforested in 1851 and its deer removed or destroyed, like those of the New Forest. It had melted into common agricultural land, all but a remnant, which still retained some of the ancient woodland peace and survived to become an open space in the twentieth century. Much of Epping had been nibbled away by unlawful enclosure. In the 'seventies, when the Corporation of London began to take interest in its future, barely 3000 acres of open waste remained. In 1878 came the *Act for the disafforestation of Epping Forest and the preservation and management of the unenclosed parts thereof as an Open Space* (41 and 42 Vict. c. 213), as a result of which, after long

[1] *S.C. on Forestry*, 1884–5 (VIII. 779), Q. 319 *sqq.* (Scottish evidence): p. 45 *sqq.*, Report of M. Boppé of Nancy on the British forests.
[2] *V.C.H. Hants*, II. 454.          [3] His *Report*, as above.

arbitration, Queen Victoria proclaimed it free to her people, from High Beech, on May 6, 1882. The securing of it had cost the City more than a quarter of a million pounds[1].

For the rest, plantation had gained ground here and lost it there, but was nearly all of one uneconomic kind. In Nottinghamshire, since the dissipation of Sherwood, woodland had increased and was increasing. But as was said later, in words which would have been approximately true of the whole country, the increase was "almost entirely due to...the luxurious value of forest trees and coverts,"[2] as beautifiers of a landscape and shelters for game. There were a few remnants of ancient woodland, in Sussex parks, or the New Forest, or Savernake; there was some planting of native forest trees; but most nineteenth-century planting had been of conifers, those upstarts of the English woods[3]. These had won their way into good society and become part of England. Soon poets would think of the Sussex pines much as they thought of the Long Man of Wilmington, forgetting that the upstarts were little older in the county than the Brighton Pavilion.

Among the plantations and the hedgerow elms which made England seem so green and heavily wooded, when viewed from ground level, on that level itself green had been spreading in slowly from the West—from the "land not of farmers but of graziers"[4]—since the repeal of the Corn Laws. But as yet the amount of land newly laid down, or tumbled down, to grass was not great enough to affect the colour scheme of the island much. If a man could have flown high over it at the time of the first Reform Bill, again at the time of the Crimean War, and again at the time of the third Reform Bill, his broad visual impressions would have been much the same. Over the fens, unless he were there when the corn was young, he might even have noted less verdure on his third flight than on his first: many of Cobbett's "bowling greens,"[5] now safely drained by steam and the suction pump, had gone under the plough. On his second flight, he would have missed the glint from the thousand acres of water in Whittlesea Mere. It had just been turned into arable, after a great struggle and one failure: the

[1] V.C.H. Essex, II. 623–4. Hainault Forest was an attractive place as described in the 'seventies and 'eighties.
[2] V.C.H. Notts, I. 380; and vol. I. p. 9–10.
[3] See vol. I. p. 9 sqq.
[4] Cobbett's description of the Yorkshire dales and other parts of the north-west, quoted in vol. I. p. 50.  [5] See vol. I. p. 8.

young wheat was on it already in 1853, and still recurred in its proper rotation, a generation later[1].

And the pattern of the island surface had not changed very much, either in design or in size, since the last open fields had been cut out of it. The big, rational, more or less rectangular 'several' fields of the final era of enclosure required no fundamental alteration, and had received none. The campaign of the agricultural reformers against unnecessary hedgerows, in districts enclosed earlier or anciently, had been vigorous and effective in places since the 'forties[2]. It had enlarged bits of the pattern, and made it a trifle more uniform. But there were whole counties and regions in which very few hedges had been grubbed up. There was not one in which a field system previously irrational, judged by the standards of the strict agricultural economist and agricultural mechanician, had been thoroughly rationalised. Just a little squarer; just a little larger; just a little less 'nook-shotten'[3]—there had been no more change in the pattern than that.

One change there was appropriate to the age in which England, as Ruskin said, had become "the man in the Iron Mask," the outbreak of wire in the fences which made the pattern. When John Leech and Robert Smith Surtees died in 1864, it was still almost unknown. Leech's Mr Briggs did not come to grief over it: the cry of 'ware wire' is not heard in Surtees' hunting stories; although there is a reference to a farmer who mended a broken fence with a bit of wire rope in the last of them. In the 'seventies, so the memories of old riders to hounds tell them, the wire began to be a nuisance. With the 'eighties, it became common; occasionally it was barbed[4]. A country already fenced had less use for it than countries of prairie and sheep-run; but you could not possibly go far without meeting it, either as primary or secondary fencing. Where the business of fencing was new, as on the Cumberland fells, its meagre economical lines might run for miles.

---

[1] Wells, W., "The Drainage of Whittlesea Mere," *J.R.A.S.* 1860–1. For the amount of change in the country at large from arable to pasture by 1886, see above, p. 284, below, p. 504.

[2] Above, p. 267.

[3] Full of nooks and corners—" will sell my dukedom
          To buy a slobbery and a dirty farm
          In that nook-shotten isle of Albion." *Henry V*, Act III, Sc. 5.

[4] Both the hunting information and the Surtees information come from Mr W. H. Macaulay of King's College, Cambridge.

The crops that filled in the pattern of Britain had changed even less than the pattern itself, except that wheat had shrunk by about 900,000 acres, between 1874–7 and 1884–7, and the whole acreage under corn by rather more. A little rye was still grown, because saddlers and packers of pots wanted rye straw; but rye had long ceased to be a British crop. There were the three standard grain crops; the three principal root crops; the clover, rotation grasses, vetches and lucerne; very little else. Flax had dwindled to a mere 2000 or 3000 acres; and there were no other industrial crops of any significance. The potato acreage had grown steadily, though not so fast as population. It was still well under 2 per cent. of the cultivated area, much less relatively than in neighbouring European countries. There was a small, almost fixed, acreage under hops; some scores of thousands of acres in cabbages and other miscellaneous crops; and the same in orchards. In many districts there had been no orchard extension, and a backward and negligent orchard practice, as in most of the apple orchards of the South-West. But in the whole country the area under fruit was growing slowly[1]. Gladstone's advice to depressed agriculturalists that they should get a living by making jam may have had something to do with it, though growth began before depression.

In its broad features cropping was uncommonly simple. Everything but the staples had been subordinated to the point of neglect. The system had grown up when the staples were in no danger. The danger to some of them, which had threatened since 1875–9, had not yet led to any important adjustment, beyond the obvious one of an addition of some 2,000,000 acres to the permanent pasture. This was merely an acceleration of an existing process which, working slowly at first, had turned into additional grazing land perhaps 5 per cent. of the area of Britain, and 9 per cent. of the cultivated area, between 1850 and 1886. By that amount the face of the country had become permanently greener.

Although in some counties the suburb had spread far into the villages, the great houses of England—Tudor, Jacobean, but predominantly Hanoverian and Whiggish[2]—stood secure in their parks, little changed and seldom deserted since Whigs

---

[1] A verbal summary of the agricultural statistics of the period.
[2] See vol. I. p. 35–6.

began the work of Reform. The fanciful mind may picture them listening, with no fear but some high-bred bewilderment, to the noises of a populous, steely, and democratic time. "Our land laws were framed by the landed interest, for the advantage of the landed interest," a man bred in one of them was heard saying a few years later: "we are now come, or are coming fast, to a time when Labour laws will be made by the Labour interest for the advantage of Labour."[1] That need not mean the near fall of Blenheim, or even the change of Stowe into a school. Randolph Churchill was impulsive. He might be mistiming events, or he might be quite wrong. Still change really seemed to be coming. Was even decay possible?

In sixty years few great houses had been built, and not many of the second rank. New Balmoral had grown out of the "little castle," itself new, "with numerous small turrets, and white-washed," which Prince Albert had found there in 1848[2]. A few more noblemen's castles had been built or rebuilt in one or other of the Gothic styles. Rather lower in the scale came such places as Peel's Drayton Manor, where a house "neither Italian nor Elizabethan, but relieved in its outline by towers and turrets," had succeeded the plain rows of window and short square chimney stacks of old Drayton Hall[3]. Other manors and halls had felt the hand of the time spirit; but they were a minority. Only on the villa level had he found a field reasonably clear.

Of farmhouse and farmstead building there had been a great deal, so long as agriculture had prospered. There were not many of the "rickety and shapeless"[4] houses now left in the home counties, nor in any county of vigorous agriculture, whether it was mainly pastoral like Cheshire or mainly arable like Norfolk and Lincoln. When an important farmhouse was old, it was generally a manor house, become the headquarters of a modern farm with modern buildings attached. Except for these, there were not anywhere on the larger farms many houses older than the last era of enclosure; and old farm buildings were rarer than old houses. Even on the smaller and smallest farms, houses had nearly all been rebuilt, or in

---

[1] Lord Randolph Churchill in 1892; *Life*, by Winston Spencer Churchill, II. 459.

[2] *Life of the Prince Consort*, II. 109. It was built by Sir Robert Gordon, brother of the then Lord Aberdeen.

[3] There are pictures of both in Parker's *Peel*, vols. II and III. The quotation is from Murray's *Guide to Staffordshire* (1874).

[4] Vol. I. p. 34.

some way modernised, although this was not so true of the
Western side of the country as of the East. It was least true
of Wales, where there was no sharp line between farmhouse
and cottage. Everywhere, it was on the border line between
farm and cottage, or among the cottages below it, that the
oldest dwellings and types of dwelling were to be found. And
these were most numerous all along what it would soon become
the fashion to call the Celtic fringe[1].

On its furthest edge were the 'black houses' of the Lewis:
"the cattle occupy one end...the walls range in thickness from
3 to 6 feet, and are built of two tiers of stones with a wall of
turf between. The roof is of somewhat loose thatch...the
floor is of clay in most instances. The human portion of the
dwelling is usually divided into a 'but' and a 'ben.' In the
living room the fire is in the centre of the floor, and the smoke
finds its way out as best it can, there being usually no chimney.
...In the cattle end the manure is allowed to lie all the year
until it is required....The houses are often end to end and
back to back."[2]

That is a good black house. In the worst, cattle and people
lived "in the same undivided space."[3] Variants of the type
were to be found scattered in many parts of the Highlands and
Islands; but on the mainland they were said "to be disappearing" in 1884[4]. Even in South-Eastern Scotland there had
been still a few "of the old turf houses" in 1870;[5] Dumfries
had been full of the one-room Scottish stone houses with their
box beds; and Ayrshire full of what were described as hovels[6].
Twenty years later, although the turf houses seem to have disappeared from the Lowlands, "in some of the older and inferior
dwellings, both in the north and south...there was actually
only one large room."[7] (So there was in very many of the
Scottish miners' houses at the same date[8].) But taking rural

---

[1] The phrase is credited to A. J. Balfour in 1892: see the *Times*, March 24,
1930.

[2] This is 'the black house' as it remained in the twentieth century: *R.C. on
the Housing...of Scotland*, 1917 (Cd. 8731), p. 211. There is a similar account
in the *R. on the Crofters and Cottars in the Highlands and Islands* of 1884 (XXXII),
p. 48.

[3] *R.C. on the Housing of the Working Classes: Scotland* (1884-5, XXXI), p. 9.

[4] *Loc. cit.*

[5] *Fourth Report on Children and Women in Agriculture* (1870, XIII. 177), p. 19.
Cp. vol. I. p. 29.

[6] *Ibid.* p. 20 and vol. I. p. 29-30.      [7] *R.C. on Labour*, 1893-4, XXXVI. 9.

[8] See Keir Hardie's indignant evidence before the *R.C. on Labour* (1892,

Scotland as a whole, it was supposed that there might be more three-room than one-room dwellings. The standard labourer's house everywhere was still the one-storey, two-room, 'but' and 'ben,' like those of the Lewis, except that it was, in Hebridean language, 'white'—that is to say mason built—not 'black.' Scottish rooms as compared with English were big, and these houses were probably better than the worst in England, better for example than a one-storied mud-walled Somerset hovel, with "two compartments each being about three yards square," described by an angry reformer in 1872[1], and possibly still standing in the 'eighties. The Scot used his space in the ancient way. "The practice of putting one or more beds in the living room is inveterate, and to insist on a departure from it is much resented."[2] Of some other things he had not always learnt the use: the constant abuse of privies when provided had greatly hindered their provision. Yet of the better Scottish cottages it was said that "comfort was written both inside and outside them."[3]

The Welsh equivalents of the worst Scottish hovels were the so-called ink-bottle houses of squatters in the Mid-Welsh hills, rough one-room affairs with a central chimney from which they got their name. These had become rare; but there were still one-roomed mud-walled cottages, with chimneys of wattle and daub, in the South-West, and one-room "square box" stone cottages in Anglesey, all furnished with cupboard beds of the old sort. In general the Welsh cottages were inferior to the English and, it would seem, less roomy than the Scottish. Their users still had something to learn. Even when the cottage was fairly good, its chimney might be blocked up by the occupant, and its slops might be thrown out of the door[4].

In England the one-room cottage hardly existed South of the Tees, though the two-room was still common. Northumberland and Durham had a few with a single big room, 24 feet by 16, and a small loft above. Cottages of this type were being built down to about 1848; and there were said to be still far too

xxxvi. Pt. 2), Q. 12,482 sqq., and the evidence of a colliery official that when his firm built two-room houses the tenants sublet one of the rooms, Q. 13,458.
[1] Heath, F. G., The English Peasantry (1874), with a picture of the hovel.
[2] R.C. on Labour, 1893–4, as above, p. 24.
[3] Ibid. p. 24, 33.
[4] Ibid. p. 22–3. Cp. Doyle's Report on Wales in R.C. on Agricultural Depression, 1882: cottages generally worse in Wales than elsewhere: sometimes mere hovels.

many of them twenty years later. At that time (1867–9) the situation was changing fast owing to active cottage building by landlords, the most popular type of house among the North Country labourers being the so-called 'two-ends,' with a couple of big divisible rooms on the level, like the Scottish 'but' and 'ben.'[1] It was a house with no 'upstairs,' such as had worried Cobbett greatly in the 'twenties[2]. This type, and South Country 'upstairs' types with more rooms, had become general North of the Tees by the 'eighties[3].

Similar rapid improvement had been made in the Lothians. So early as 1870, a Scottish expert maintained that in no county of England was the "average so good as in Berwickshire."[4] There is no reason to reject his evidence; for the really ancient type of Scottish hovel was so primitive that it could hardly survive in a vigorous neighbourhood, whereas in England types slightly better in their day survived nearly everywhere to be denounced in the 'eighties. The typical lowest grade English cottage could be found in nearly every rural district, though by no means in every village, from Lincolnshire and East Anglia to Cornwall. It was "of mud, clay lump, or lath and plaster."[5] The living room was some 9 feet square. There was a single bedroom, or perhaps a room and a bed-closet. In the worst of all—there were happily few of these—the ceiling was only 6 feet high, or even less, and access to the bed-loft was by ladder. Now and again there was no privy; there was never a good one[6].

Such places were mostly found on land which had once been waste, as in Cornwall or Hereford, or in that class of village which was still described as 'open.' Down to 1865, the working of the Poor Law had perpetuated the distinction between the close and the open parish—the former controlled entirely, or almost entirely, by a single landlord; the latter in many hands[7]. It had been to the interest of the landlord of

---

[1] R. on Employment of Children...and Women in Agriculture (1867-8, XVII), p. 65. Report of J. J. Henley on Northumberland and Durham.

[2] See vol. I. p. 31.

[3] In the Northumberland Union of Glendale, in 1890-2, 67 per cent. of the population living in small tenements (i.e. tenements of less than five rooms) lived in tenements of one or two rooms. R.C. on [Agricultural] Labour, 1893-4 (XXVII. Pt. 2), p. 100.

[4] Fourth R. on Children and Women in Agriculture (1870, XIII. 177), p. 19.

[5] R.C. on [Agricultural] Labour, 1893-4 (XXXV), p. 33. C. M. Chapman's description of the C grade English cottage.

[6] Loc. cit.        [7] Cp. p. 431 above, and vol. I. p. 467-8.

the close parish to have relatively few cottages, occupied by families in good regular work, and so to limit the liability of his parish for poor rate. Casual workers and undesirable families were left to the open parish—from which their surplus might tramp to work, when wanted in the close. The Union Chargeability Act of 1865 (28 and 29 Vict. c. 79), by spreading the rate burden evenly over the whole union, had removed the main incentive to keep down the parish stock of cottages, and had combined with good prices and rents to make the quarter of a century from 1854 to 1879 one of very active building of 'estate cottages.' The example had been set well before 1850, by such landlords as the Duke of Bedford[1], and it had been extensively followed, as in Northumberland and Durham. But, even with good will and some economic incentive, the business of transformation had been slow and remained incomplete. For at no time had the building of good cottages paid.

A Commissioner who, during 1868, had visited 300 parishes in Norfolk, Suffolk, Essex, Sussex and Gloucester had been entirely satisfied with only two[2]. He had found places in which the lowest grade one-bedroom house actually prevailed. The worst, he reported, belonged to squatters, speculators, or the parish—these last old poor law cottages, which poor law reform had superseded but not destroyed. Elsewhere, ancient freehold or copyhold cottages in the hands of what literary people called the peasantry, or cottages owned by small squires with nothing but their land to live by[3]—the cottages of Old England in short—were among the worst. A more fortunate Commissioner of 1867–9 reported much good building in Lincoln, Nottingham and Leicester; but also that the lowest cottage type survived there in most open villages[4]. In Northamptonshire's many close villages—it is an attractive county for the resident landowner—cottages were usually new and excellent, the three-bedroom type predominating. In open villages they were of all sorts, some vile. Much the same was true of Cambridge, Bedford,

---

[1] Vol. I. p. 472.

[2] Fraser, the Rev. J. (later Bishop of Manchester) reporting to the *C. on Children and Women in Agriculture*, 1867–8 (XVII), p. 11 *sqq.*

[3] For the first class, see Boyle, R. F., in *C. on Children and Women in Agriculture*, 1868–9 (XIII), p. 128; for the second, Joseph Arch's *Life*, p. 127.

[4] Stanhope, E., in 1867–8, XVII. 91 *sqq.* His eight worst villages contained 24 three-bedroom cottages; 193 two-bedroom; and 178 one-bedroom. The average number of dwellers in the one-bedroom cottages was 3½.

Buckingham and indeed of most counties South of the Trent; except that the Fens, unsuitable for gentlemen's places or easy sanitation, had a high proportion of vile cottages, and that the South-West, especially Somerset, had also a high proportion[1]. From Somerset in 1868 there came the gloomy news, which might perhaps have been anticipated, that "the worst...are generally the small freeholds, inhabited by the person who owns them."[2]

The general situation for Southern England in 1867–9 was summed up thus by a Commissioner who had conducted inquiries in Surrey, Wiltshire, Warwick, Worcester and Hereford: the cottages that landlords built, "and they are building a great many, are almost universally good."[3] There was even reasonable complaint that the greatest landlords, with their urban-rural rent rolls and their policies *de grand seigneur*, had set impossible standards of excellence, so that the small squire was being indicted for his poverty, like the indwelling freeholder of Somerset.

North of the Trent, Derbyshire had many new cottages and a standard above the English average. Yorkshire was said to be "vastly superior to the South." In most parts of the county there was "much comfort in the cottages,"[4] not to mention the gardens and cowgates. In North Lancashire it was the same; in Cumberland and Westmorland worse; but as these were small-holding regions, where living-in was usual, the housing of the handful of manual labourers was a subordinate matter[5].

One tendency these inquiries, made just before 1870, had registered in counties so different and far apart as Lancashire and Somerset—that a three-bedroom cottage was apt to have a lodger in its third room, unless this was prohibited by the owner. However, the building of three-bedroom and other types of cottage went steadily on so long as agriculture prospered, and did not quite stop when distress began. There was a touch of the Gothic revival in some of these mid-nineteenth century estate cottages, perhaps an arched window head or a slightly ornate chimney; but most new cottages, whether estate or not, were plain brick boxes or pairs; tiled in some districts; more often slated; very seldom thatched. Thatch recalled old

---

[1] From the various assistant-commissioners' reports in 1867–8, XVII and 1868–9, XIII.

[2] Boyle, in 1868–9, XIII. 128.

[3] Norman, F. H., in 1868–9, XIII. 69.

[4] Portman, E. B., in 1867–8, XVII. 105.

[5] Tremenheere, J. H., in 1868–9, XIII. 142–55.

bad memories. Slate, distributed easily from Wales or West-morland by rail, had become the symbol of progress. When Joseph Arch's father died in 1862, leaving a freehold cottage to his son, Joseph not only put in windows—practicable windows presumably—but he "took off the old thatched roof ...and made it as smart and comfortable as it is to-day."[1] In every way Joseph was a man of his age.

Scotland still kept its bothies for unmarried farm labourers, but they were declining. They had never been much used in the West, where farms were small. The Lothians, Perth, Fife, Forfar and Kincardine had been their headquarters; and in the far North the arable country on the shores of the Moray Firth. Originally comfortless enough, some at least were reputed very comfortable by 1870, especially those which had a married woman in charge as cook and caretaker[2]. By the end of the 'eighties, the system was said to be "unknown in the Lothians" and decadent in Fife[3]. The bothy for unmarried women, which had been familiar in Haddington and Edinburgh so late as 1870, and was found occasionally elsewhere, seems to have dis-appeared. While it existed, its occupants had often been re-cruited from among the Edinburgh Irish. In spite of the general decline of the bothy system, many of the worst sort of bothies for men survived into the 'nineties, to be labelled "dens of dirt and confusion" and "a disgrace to Scotland."[4]

For England and Wales, some statistical material collected in 1891-3 pictures in arithmetic outline the state of the rural cottages, when the work of the 'seventies and 'eighties was done. At the census of 1891 tenements were enumerated, and the small tenements were defined and distinguished from the large. The definition of a small tenement was one of four rooms or less. On the land, tenement and cottage were almost synonymous: there was no regular tenement dwelling in the urban sense. The sample figures collected rather later[5] showed that a re-spectable percentage of the population did not live in 'small tenements' at all, but in five-room, or even six-room, cottages. These figures came from six widely scattered and representa-tive districts so far apart as Lincolnshire and Somerset; but as

[1] Arch's *Life*, p. 57.
[2] *Fourth R. on Children and Women in Agriculture*, p. 21 *sqq.* Cp. vol. I. p. 31.
[3] *R.C. on* [Agricultural] *Labour*, 1893-4, XXXVI. 28.
[4] *Loc. cit.*
[5] For the *R.C. on Labour; General Report on Ag. Lab. in England and Wales*, by W. C. Little (1893-4, XXVII. Pt. 2), p. 99 *sqq.*

they excluded Wales and the 'two ends' cottages beyond the Tees, no doubt they exaggerate somewhat the proportion of 'large tenements,' as defined by the census, among the cottages. They make it over 19 per cent. Possibly 15 or 16 per cent. would be near the mark for the whole country South of the Tweed. The census statistics of small tenements in rural districts showed that just over 14 per cent. of the 'small tenement population' lived in one or two-room tenements. Owing to the five or six-room cottages, the small tenement rural population was less than the agricultural labouring population, perhaps 20 per cent. less, because the bigger cottages would generally house the biggest families. Further, the two-room tenements of England and Wales included the roomy and popular 'two ends' dwellings of the North. It is probable, therefore, that not more than some 11 or 12 per cent. of the rural labouring population was left in the bad, cramped, two-room, and very scarce one-room, cottages of central and southern England, or of Wales. That was far too much, even though such a house, if in fair condition, might be tolerable for a young married couple, an old man and wife, or some similar little family group. But unquestionably the percentage would have been higher had it been reckoned at any earlier census, and very much higher at that of 1851. The Somerset hovel which stirred the reformer of 1872 to indignation contained one old man: the occupants in the 'forties had been a man and wife and six children[1].

Since Augustus Petermann mapped the results of the census of 1851[2], there had been few important changes in the geographical distribution of industries in Britain, and hardly any of first-rate magnitude, judged merely by their effect upon employment. Most industries had expanded; but as a rule they had expanded in and from their old headquarters. The cotton areas; the coal areas; the wool and worsted areas; the endlessly varied industrial areas of the Birmingham country and of London, were bigger and denser. There had been important changes in their internal organisation and structure. Some few urban industries had declined, locally or even generally; but none of them were great, and their decline had not affected the life of the areas, or the look of the country.

[1] Heath, F. G., *The English Peasantry*, p. 48.
[2] See the census map at www.cambridge.org/9780521101004

Some rural industries had been dissipated, or had condensed into towns and manufacturing villages, with the spread of machine production; or had been part dissipated and part condensed; but the dissipations and condensations were relatively small. Yet the more important of them had national significance.

Hosiery showed a still incomplete condensation into industrial villages and towns, but no other change of importance. Its headquarters were fixed before 1851; and the number of people engaged in it in 1891 was very nearly what it had been forty years earlier. (The output was of course enormously increased.) The rural, domestic, and by-industries of straw plait and lace showed both condensation and dissipation. Down to 1870-80, rural straw plaiting had held its own fairly well in the belt of country from Buckingham to Suffolk, where Petermann registered it. So late as 1874, a hall was built at Hitchin to which country workers might bring in their plait[1]. It recalls the central cloth and linen halls of earlier rural industries. Numerically, the combined plait and straw-hat industry seems to have shrunk between 1851 and 1881; but the available figures are not perfectly comparable[2]. Strictly comparable figures for 1881 and 1891 register the marked shrinkage of the 'eighties, when the rural industry was going down before imports of Italian and Japanese plait, and the urban industry was assuming more of a factory character, as at Luton. In the 'nineties, the plait hall at Hitchin became a Mission Church.

Country lace-making had vanished almost completely from Buckingham, Devon, Northampton and the other counties in which it had been something of an industry in 1851. The number of people engaged in making lace, either by hand or machine, fell by nearly a half between 1851 and 1891. In the latter year, more than two-thirds of the 35,000 engaged in the manufacture were in the town of Nottingham, and most of the small remainder in other North-Midland towns; though fair quantities of home-made lace still came from Devon. Of other

[1] Hine, R. L., *The History of Hitchin* (1929), II. 431. The hall was sold in 1898. In 1867 in S. Beds and N. Bucks 'all females,' and many males, plaited straw. *Children and Women in Agriculture*, 1867-8 (XVII), p. 134. Plaiting was very important in Herts in the 'sixties: Evershed, H., "The Agriculture of Hertford," *J.R.A.S.* 1864. There were still over 2000 women and girls employed on it in South-West Suffolk in 1871: in 1881, only 781: in 1891, none. *V.C.H. Suffolk*, II. 248.

[2] The census classifications of the two years are not on the same basis.

industries which showed numerical decline, linen and silk were the chief. Linen had long been drawing out of England into Ulster. By 1891 it had become completely insignificant; and it had ceased to be a great industry even in Scotland[1]. The transfer had been so continuous as to be almost imperceptible: it had left no important gap, few decaying mills, no districts once industrial quickening back into agriculture. Hand-loom weaving was nearly dead, and most of the mills had been put to other uses or rebuilt for them. The decay of hand-loom weaving in silk, though less thorough-going, partly explains the numerical contraction of the industry; but there had been also what might be called absolute decline of manufacturing power in certain branches and localities. Yet there was still a little silk-working in every county, if not in every place, where Petermann had found it[2]. The two most considerable changes in the geographical distribution of the industry, its slow and now nearly complete disappearance out of London, and its recent growth in the West Riding[3], were after all but tiny and indistinct features in the industrial map, obscured by the smoke and growth of the towns.

Indistinct and tiny also were the traces left by the extinction of hand-loom weaving, and the concentration on a few Gloucestershire Cotswold valleys, in the old woollen industry of the West. Forty years were needed to reduce the whole working staff from about 24,000 to about 10,000, in all the counties westward from Wiltshire and Gloucester. The slow ebb had left behind it some weavers' cottages available for other people, and a number of mills in green West-country valleys, most of which had been diverted to fresh, often odd, uses—they made umbrellas, or hairpins, or sporting goods; few having slipped into a decay which in such surroundings might have been pleasing enough. Wales still had her diminutive rural spinning mills, and something which could be called a cloth or flannel industry in every county, though her whole wool-working population—mill people and the surviving cottage weavers—could have been fitted easily into a dozen fair-sized Yorkshire mills[4]. Scotland also retained a scattered domestic and semi-domestic industry, with important factory

---

[1] Above, p. 85.

[2] The reference is to the Census of 1891, as indicating the situation at the close of the period.           [3] Above, p. 87-8.

[4] The distribution in 1901, when there were still a few wool-workers in every Welsh county, is shown on the map in Clapham, J. H., *The Woollen and Worsted Industries*.

concentrations much where they had been in 1851: there was no radical change in the industrial map[1].

The greatest change in the whole island was of a type which can only occur rarely in an old industrial country—the shifting of the primary metallurgical industries to fresh sources of ironstone and to the sea. Neither Middlesbrough nor Barrow, still less Frodingham, is marked on Petermann's map; though Middlesbrough might have been called a town in 1851. Nor does the map show an important iron industry at Cardiff or at Newport. By the late 'eighties, more than a quarter of the British ironstone miners were working in the Cleveland hills, and a third of the British pig iron was made in and about Middlesbrough. A community, perhaps more highly specialised than any which earlier industrial change created, had risen around its blast furnaces[2]. Quite recently another mineral industry had appeared. So early as 1859 salt had been struck by boring at 1200 feet, South of the Tees, and in 1874 at 1127 feet, North of it. By 1882 the engineering difficulties had been mastered: brine was being pumped: salt was being made. Ten years later the annual output would be well over 200,000 tons[3].

The growth of Barrow-in-Furness had been more remarkable than that of Middlesbrough because more varied. Only in 1844–6 had the railway line which made the place been laid out. Cumberland hematite was being mined at that time for shipment to Staffordshire and South Wales;[4] and a few charcoal iron furnaces lingered on in the Furness fells. When the Barrow docks were opened in 1867, the Barrow and Workington districts were smelting an important part of the local ore; by 1875 the whole of it. In 1880 the largest iron steamer yet laid down, except the *Great Eastern*, was building at Barrow. By 1885 Cumberland and Furness were producing more than a sixth of the total 'make' of pig iron; and Barrow was busy with her iron and steel-making, with ship-building, and with marine engineering[5].

[1] But all Scotland only had 44,000 wool-workers in 1891, against 203,000 in Yorkshire.
[2] See Ch. III above, *passim*; and Lady Bell, *At the Works*, for the community.
[3] Grigg, R., "On the Middlesbrough Salt Industry," *Trans. Inst. Mech. Eng.* 1893; *V.C.H. Durham*, II. 293.
[4] Above, p. 49 and vol. I. p. 50, 189.
[5] Cp. the table on p. 49 above: Stileman, F. C., "On the Docks and Railway Approaches at Barrow-in-Furness," *Trans. Inst. Mech. Eng.* 1880: the historical account of Barrow given before the *R.C. on Depression of Trade and Industry*, 1886, Q. 2183 *sqq.*

The tracking southwards of those ironstone beds in the lias formation which had made the fortune of Cleveland had led, first to mining—or rather open working—of ore in an agricultural district of North Lincolnshire, and later to the erection of modern blast furnaces there, in the fields of Scunthorpe and Frodingham. The process had been repeated further south in Leicester, Rutland, Northampton and even Oxford; but only in Northampton had the furnaces followed the ore workings, and marked a rural area about Kettering and Wellingborough with the signs of the iron age. By the mid-'eighties its output was not far behind that of Lincolnshire. The other counties sent their ore North and West into districts marked for the iron age long before, districts most of which were now declining as iron makers and dismantling antiquated blast furnaces, without thereby losing an industrial and metallurgical character, or causing any deep change in the face of Britain[1]. A few fresh derelict patches, with their "scum of dross, old plash of rains and refuse patched with moss," stood out in landscapes which, at best, had shown only a grim plutonic beauty. Such patches were familiar in counties where the smoke hung low. No one as yet had taken in hand their salvage; though often some new smoke-making use was found for parts of them in course of time.

Away in South Wales and Monmouth, where iron-making and the steel-making which now went with it were well maintained, any derelict patches were back in the hills: iron-making did not die, it moved to tide water. The raising of native ore had nearly stopped, and it was easier for the coal to slide down the Glamorgan and Monmouthshire valleys than for the sea-borne ore, first Cumbrian then mainly Spanish, to be dragged up them. Some of the up-valley iron works were still smelting in 1885; but most of the smelting was done along the coast, from Swansea by Cardiff to Newport. The valley works of Ebbw Vale, Rhymney and Blaenafon all now smelted at Newport. While in Glamorgan more than four furnaces in every five were cold, together with all those in the upper valleys of Monmouth, at Newport twenty-one out of the thirty-eight large modern ones were in blast[2].

The ironstone mines of Britain reached their maximum output in 1882. The decline which followed was to prove not a fluctuation but a permanent shift to a somewhat lower level.

[1] See the *Mineral Returns* for the underlying facts.
[2] *Mineral Returns* for 1886.

It had not, however, affected the new geography of the industry. None of the areas now at work was in danger of going derelict. The position in 'half precious' metal-mining was greatly different: the stagnation of tin-mining since 1870, a sharp contraction in lead-mining since 1877, and the almost complete collapse of copper-mining, had scarred the face of the country. Scars left by declining or derelict lead workings were mostly hidden in the folds of Welsh or Pennine hills. Nor were the derelicts as yet very many; for the decline of output from its maximum was not yet 40 per cent., and to this decline most mines had contributed. But in the year of Victoria's Jubilee the whole output of fine copper from British ores was 889 tons: it had been 13,540 tons in 1860[1]. Old and famous Cornish districts were gaunt with abandoned mines and impoverished villages. The mines still working had a weak hold on life. Tin-mining held its own fairly well, but did not grow. There was gloom in Cornwall and her miners were taking their skill beyond the seas[2].

For lost copper-mining the Duchy had some compensations on her long double coast-line. Fishing was still reasonably vigorous, fresh mackerel and mullet sent to London having replaced losses in the export of barrelled pilchard to the Mediterranean[3]. China clay, quarried within easy reach of the sea and whitening the country-side, was taken in increasing quantities both coastwise and abroad, in vessels which could make even the smallest Cornish ports[4]. Potato-growing and market-gardening were now old-established at selected points on the southern coast. Flower-growing for the market had just reached the mainland from its original headquarters in the Scilly Islands, where it first became remunerative about 1880[5]. Perhaps more important still was Cornwall's share—not yet very great but to her valuable—in those large-scale migrations to the sea for recreation and residence which had flooded Brighton and Margate before the railway age[6] and, helped by increased earnings and savings in all ranks of society, had been carried by the railways to make or remake, after the pattern of the day, small hamlets and ports all round the island.

[1] The 1887 output was an absolute minimum: it was 1472 tons in 1886 and 1456 in 1888. In 1856 Cornwall alone had produced 13,274 tons: that was its maximum.

[2] Above, p. 104: Jenkins, *The Cornish Mines* (1927): *V.C.H. Cornwall*, I. 570.

[3] *V.C.H. Cornwall*, II. 582–6.

[4] *Ibid.* II. 577–8.     [5] *Ibid.* II. 578.     [6] Cp. vol. I. pp. 8, 9.

The second, the railway, stage in the resultant shiftings and fresh permanent accumulations of people had been indicated distinctly even in the census of 1851. Among the towns which had grown fastest during the previous decade were two pure seaside residence and recreation towns, Southport and Torquay[1]. Since 1851 each successive census had registered the arrival of fresh places in this class. Their rise had usually been marked, among other things, by the establishment of a pier company. Brighton had been equipped with her chain pier since the time of George IV and no ambitious 'resort' was perfect without some such accessory. Southport got its company, with 117 foundation shareholders, in 1859. Three years later a company was founded to provide, by means of a pier, "an extensive and agreeable promenade at Blackpool, Lancashire, over the sea, at high water." A year later again—the thing was infectious—a pier company was promoted for Lytham[2]. Lancashire had capitalised some of her prosperity into promenades just when the War of Secession was interrupting it. Recovering, she had built a second pier at Blackpool, with other facilities. And now, East, West, and South about Britain, where the seas were not too abruptly deep or too stormy, the new-style piers straddled into them on their iron legs. At its extremity the standard "iron promenade pier not made for trade"[3] swelled out to carry a pavilion. Brighton had a pavilion, though on land. Margate's second pier, of 1856, lacked the swelling[4]. This was added after 1871, "to meet the requirements of visitors,"[5] and on it the appropriate pavilion was built. The piers were as symbolic of what archaeologists call a culture as are axe-heads and beakers and other durable products of man's handiwork. This is not the place to speculate on their duration and uses, or to interpret their symbolism. There they stood. No visitor to the island could miss them. From them the least seafaring of the islanders could watch his ships go by with the joy of vicarious ownership.

[1] Weber, A. F., *The Growth of Cities in the Nineteenth Century* (New York, 1899), p. 55, groups Southport and Torquay with Birkenhead, Cardiff and Grimsby—all growing fast—as seaports; but that is not the explanation.

[2] *Return of all Joint Stock Companies Formed or Registered since 18 and 19 Vict. c. 133. 1864* (LVIII. 291): under 1859, 1862, 1863.

[3] *Harbour Authorities: Return of Works executed within the last Twenty Years*, 1883 (LXII. 433). The harbours are in alphabetical order. The quotation refers to Skegness.    [4] For the first, see vol. I. p. 8.

[5] *Return of Works*, as above, under Margate.

The maritime resources and maritime dominion of Britain had never been more apparent, even to ignorant watchers. Her shallow seas were thronged. The sailing tonnage of the United Kingdom, though sinking, was as great in 1885 as it had been in 1850; the steam tonnage was nearly 4,000,000 greater. The steam tonnage alone had all but twice the capacity, and many times the carrying power, of the whole merchant navy of sixty years earlier. Perhaps a third of the world's sea-going ships were on the British register; of the world's steamships nearly five-eighths[1]. The last and finest of the clippers were on it also.

For their help, the Trinity House of Deptford Strond, as it was still called in official language, and the Commissioners of the Northern Lighthouses were perfecting their lights and buoys. There was now left undone very little building or placing that could possibly be of use. In Northern waters, the Skerryvore lighthouse had been finished by 1843. At the gates of the Channel, the Bishop's Rock was lighted in 1858 and the Wolf Rocks in 1869. The new Eddystone, stronger and safer than the old, came into use in 1882. The Thames estuary triangle, between the North Foreland lighthouse and the floating lights of the Gunfleet and the Nore, had long been studded thick with buoys, lights, and beacons[2]. The lights there fell on clouds of sail and small shipping; for against every steamer which made the port of London there were still between two and three sailing ships, mostly small coasters; so that the average size of all the ships entering the Thames with cargo was still only about 230 tons. At Liverpool the situation was very different and was becoming more different yearly. In 1873, the steam ships and sailing ships using the port had been equal in mere numbers. In 1884 the ratio was two to one: by 1889 it would be three to one. The average ship entering with cargo was of well over 500 tons. At Cardiff it was of about 400 tons. In fact the trade of the Thames retained traits of an earlier time, which that of Cardiff or of Liverpool had lost[3].

[1] *Tables showing the Progress of Merchant Shipping*, 1902 (Cd. 329), p. 48-51.

[2] Cp. vol. I. p. 7-8, and see the series of *Reports...by Trinity House of Deptford Strond and the Commissioners of Northern Lighthouses, e.g.* for the new Eddystone, 1883, LXII. 211.

[3] For harbours, docks and port facts and statistics in the 'eighties, see Harcourt, L. F. V., *Harbours and Docks* (1885), and Dorn, A., *Die Seehäfen des Weltverkehrs* (1891), 2 vols.: very thorough. Detailed figures of trade at the various ports are in the annual *Trade Returns*, and summary figures for all the more important ports in the *Statistical Abstracts for the U.K.*

Though it was no longer usual to speak of London and the 'out ports,' as if these last were of little account, London remained the greatest port of Britain and of the world—judged by all tests but one. The tonnage entered and cleared was between 50 and 60 per cent. greater than that of the Mersey; the aggregate trade was more valuable, but as an exporter of British produce London was now far behind Liverpool; for cotton manufactures still made up more than a quarter of the British exports, and they were not the only goods shipped principally from the Mersey. Yet London's great and various import and re-export trade, together with the growing size of ships, had called for a long series of additions to the dock system of the Thames. After more than twenty years during which no works of importance had been undertaken[1], early in the free-trade era the Victoria Dock below the mouth of the Lea was begun, to be opened in 1855. In 1864 the Commercial Docks in Rotherhithe were extended and their control amalgamated with that of the adjacent Surrey Docks. The Millwall Docks in the Isle of Dogs had been made, and an existing cut just North of them had been turned into the South West-India Dock, by 1870. After a halt, the Albert Dock between the Victoria and Gallions Reach was opened in 1880. Its opening led to the transfer of the Peninsular and Oriental sailings from Southampton to the Thames. Lastly, miles along the Essex shore, the Tilbury Docks were dug out of the Chadwell Marshes, and opened in 1886. In spite of amalgamation, there were still four distinct dock companies: these movements down stream were steps in a race for the sea, and for the patronage of the big ships, between the London and St Katharine's Company, which owned the Victoria and the Albert, and the East and West India Company, which replied to the Albert with the Tilbury[2].

Under the competent monopoly of the Mersey Docks and the Harbour Board, a trust which did not work for profit, the long chain of Liverpool Docks had reached the mouth of the estuary with the opening of the Langton and Alexandra basins

[1] Since the opening of St Katharine's Docks in 1828 (vol. i. p. 5). Dates of later docks are in Harcourt, *op. cit.*; Dorn, *op. cit.*

[2] The other companies were the Surrey and Commercial and the Millwall. There is remarkably little official information about the port of London in the Free Trade era. Parliamentary Papers are abundant for 1795–1801: there is a Report on Docks of 1823; and one on the State of the Port of London of 1836. The next Report is of 1902.

at the northern end in 1881. The construction of independent docks on the Cheshire side had begun in the 'forties; but this incipient Birkenhead system had been incorporated with the main system in 1855, since which date management had been unified and construction continuous. Between 1846 and 1881 nearly 250 acres of docks had been added on the Lancashire shore alone; and eventually for more than seven miles "the monumental granite, quarried from the Board's own quarries in Scotland" fronted the river, "in a vast sea wall as solid and enduring as the Pyramids, the most stupendous work of its kind that the will and power of man has ever created." So a Liverpool historian has described it, not without justification[1]. By this "vast sea wall," not yet at its full length, a quarter of the imports—by value—and more than a third of the exports of the whole United Kingdom moved with the tides.

In 1886 Liverpool was, as it were, pausing at her "stupendous work" to see what would come of a rival undertaking, long discussed, sharply fought over, and that year begun—the construction of the Manchester Ship Canal[2]. It was aimed explicitly at her dock traffic. Its completion, so many people supposed, might mark the end of her great era of economic and geographical expansion.

Glasgow, who like Liverpool had drawn life from the Atlantic trade, had no such anxieties. Unlike Liverpool, with her suburbs and daughter towns she was her own industrial *hinterland*. She had made for herself Port Glasgow at a time when it was not certain that engineering skill would be able to bring modern ships to the Broomielaw. But Port Glasgow was no longer needed. By judicious utilisation of the scour of the current and heavy labour in dredging, widening and embanking, the engineers in a whole century of work had turned the river Clyde up to Glasgow Bridge into something which gave foreign visitors "the impression of a magnificent canal,"[3] 150 yards wide and 24 feet deep at high water. A couple of docks led out of it; but the river itself, with its quays, was Glasgow harbour. What competition she had to fear came from below,

---

[1] Ramsay Muir, *A History of Liverpool* (1907), p. 301.

[2] Its history belongs to the next generation.

[3] Dorn, *op. cit.* II. 1015. A concise history of the Port, by Sir W. H. Raeburn, Chairman of the Clyde Navigation Trust, appeared in *Brassey's Naval and Shipping Annual*, 1928. See also Macgregor, G., *A History of Glasgow* (1881). Some information has also been supplied by the General Manager of the Clyde Trust.

where the Clyde needs no deepening and the recent completion of the James Watt Dock at Greenock invited ships to turn in. But Greenock, though well placed and active, was hardly to be counted a rival of the city which with her suburbs had ten times Greenock's population.

From Greenock to the Glasgow quays on the South bank, and about Dumbarton on the North, lay the Clyde shipyards, many, efficient, and as the pioneering work done in them merited, dominant—Napier's, Elder's, Denny's, and the rest. They had been offered every opportunity and had neglected none, opportunities in coal, in iron, in skilful and tenacious labour, in an engineering tradition which reached back to James Watt, and a tradition of shipwright's work soundly based in wood. Two-thirds of the steam tonnage of the United Kingdom was either built or engined on the Clyde. So were a great number of the steamers, particularly of the mail steamers, used by foreign countries. One-sixth of the tonnage built in the United Kingdom in 1881–6 was for foreign account; and the Clyde did the greater part of this trade.

At Hull, the gate of Yorkshire and the third port of Britain—Glasgow judged by the value of her trade being only fourth—dock-building was as essential to trade as at Liverpool. Without it, loading and unloading in the Humber could only be by lighter. The half circle of small inland docks about the old town was complete before 1830. The additions of the 'forties and 'fifties along the waterside—a railway dock and others—had raised the dock acreage to 48 by 1863. Between that year and the completion of the Alexandra Dock, east of the town, in 1885 the acreage was almost tripled[1].

These four great ports—the Metropolitan; the Northern industrial, West; the Northern industrial, East; and the Scottish industrial—had sucked in an inordinate share of the expanding trade of the country. The coming of the railway and the great ship had meant stagnation or decadence to many harbours all round the coast, some of which fifty years earlier had served areas really important, others areas important to them. There had still been some 1300 tons of shipping a week, exclusive of the fishing boats, making use of the port of Whitby in 1863: there were barely 500 in 1882[2]. The fenland ports, Boston and Lynn, if not actually decadent, had lost greatly in national

---

[1] Dorn, *op. cit.* II. 988; Harcourt, *op. cit.*; *Return of Works*, Hull.
[2] *Return of Works*, 1883, as above; Whitby.

importance since the invasion of the fens by the railway[1]. It
was reported in 1883 that no sum worth mentioning had been
spent on harbour works at Boston for over twenty years. There
came into it weekly from 500 to 600 tons of "sloops, schooners,
brigs, barques and screw steamers."[2] A coast railway had cut
the lines of supply and distribution to and from the sandy little
ports of North Norfolk. On the Suffolk coast, nearly two ships
every week had still made Southwold in 1863: there was not
one a fortnight in 1882. The rail from Hailsworth and improvements at Lowestoft were indicted as the causes, though nature
had collaborated in destruction[3]. To some of the Cinque
Ports she had long been unfriendly: Winchelsea and Hythe
had been stranded for generations,—

> "and near and far across the bar
>     the ploughman whistles at the plough."[4]

Now the big ship and the railway were finishing what nature
began. Sizable vessels were no longer built at Rye. Its tonnage of trade was not half that to which Whitby had fallen[5].
Like Whitby and other harbours in reduced circumstances,
Rye was learning to eke out a living by the entertainment of
paying guests.

On the Bristol Channel, the trade of Minehead and the other
small ports of West Somersetshire had "very much decreased"[6]
since the railway from Taunton was finished in 1874. Trade up
the Gloucester and Berkeley Canal had sunk very low by 1875;
but the opening of the Sharpness Docks at the canal mouth
in that year was restoring it. Bristol's trade had never declined,
had in fact grown steadily since the railways came, but the city
had to struggle with her awkward situation upstream in a part
of England relatively unpopulous and non-industrial. Considerable improvements had been made since 1860 in the river
harbour works. A company had finished the Avonmouth
Docks in 1877—at almost twice the estimated cost. Later, the
Corporation had interested itself in the docks at Portishead.
But the aggregate tonnage frequenting the port in the 'eighties
was only about half that of Hull; the tonnage engaged in

[1] Cp. above, p. 199. In the sixty years 1831–91 the tonnage using the port
of Lynn increased by less than 40 per cent., that of Boston by barely 30 per cent.
[2] *Return of Works*, Boston.
[3] *Return of Works*, Southwold.
[4] John Davidson, *A Cinque Port*.
[5] Above, p. 67, and *Return of Works*, Rye.
[6] *Return of Works*, Minehead.

international trade was not a quarter; and, to those familiar
with the ports now dominant, it was "difficult to realise" that
Bristol "was once the second port of Great Britain."[1] Though
neither decadent nor stagnant, as she had been when Dupin
visited her in the 'twenties[2], she had been outpaced, not, however, since the railway age but before it.

The tale of little ports choked by coastal railways and the
ease of distribution from bigger neighbours could be told all
up the West coast of Wales, England and Scotland—Car-
marthen, Aberystwyth, Carnarvon, Lancaster, Ayr, Troon.
The trade of Aberystwyth in the 'eighties was only a quarter
of what it had been twenty years earlier: the digging of Glasson
Docks at the mouth of the Lune had not saved Lancaster from
a similar, if less abrupt, decline[3]. Like the stranded ports of
the East coast, those of the West had often started new careers
as watering places; but Lancaster had powerful neighbours
carrying on this business, for the profitable pursuit of which
she stood in any event too far up the river. So the capital to
which Liverpool owed allegiance, though not without an industrial life of its own, had a population little greater than that
of King's Lynn, the half-discarded seaport of the Fens.

The railway had made far more trade than it had choked,
but not so many ports. Some of its comparatively few creations
had been out of nothing, like Fleetwood and Barrow. Others
had been made out of nearly nothing like Grimsby, whose
population increased fourteenfold between the census of 1831
and that of 1891[4], or Cardiff where the increase was thirteenfold.
Of those not made but remade, Southampton was the chief.
Left far behind the ports of the West and North in the seventeenth and eighteenth centuries, it grew very slowly until the
coming of steam. Through railway communication with London
had been completed in May, 1840. Two years later the Royal
Mail Steam Packet and the Peninsular and Oriental Companies
made Southampton their headquarters[5]. At that time serious
work on docks and quays and channels had hardly begun. It
had continued ever since, the railway and dock companies

[1] Harcourt, *op. cit.* I. 530. Cp. Dorn, *op. cit.* II. 1062 and *Return of Works*,
Avonmouth.
[2] See vol. I. p. 6.
[3] *Return of Works*, Aberystwyth, Lancaster.
[4] Population in 1831, 4200, in 1891, 59,000.
[5] Sherrington, C. E. R., *Economics of Rail Transport in Great Britain* (1928),
I. 24, 42.

working hand in hand[1]. The tonnage which cleared from the port in 1851–2 had been 213,000; in 1882 it was 909,000, although expansion had been checked temporarily by the transference of the Peninsular and Oriental sailings to Tilbury. But all through this later period, Southampton was far ahead of Bristol in aggregate tonnage, and very far ahead of her in ocean-going tonnage.

Cardiff had sprung above Newcastle into the position of the world's greatest coal exporter and, for mere tonnage cleared with cargo in the foreign trade, into that of the third port of Britain; for coal is bulky. "At Cardiff one sees nothing but coal, coal dust or coal-blackened faces, and talks of nothing but coal," the foreign visitor said[2]. The Bute family, who owned it, had begun the docks which bear their name in 1839; but the main dock and harbour development had been in the 'fifties and 'sixties; and the great growth of the coal export trade had come with the victory of steam at sea during the 'seventies and ˙ ˙ghties. It had now outrun the port facilities of Cardiff, those of Penarth across the bay, and the much inferior facilities of the other South Welsh harbours. In November, 1884, work had been begun nine miles to the South-West on one of the greatest harbour-making enterprises of the century, the construction of Barry Docks by the Barry Dock and Railway Company, to handle the overflowing coal[3]. Barry would be more easily accessible for ships than Cardiff, but was not yet ready to compete with her.

Railways had not made Tyneside; it was Tyneside that made them. Nor had they undermined the coal trade from the North-East into London; though they had set limits to its expansion. The Tyne still shipped some 4,000,000 tons of coal a year coastwise, principally to the Thames; and the Thames took in from the Tyne and elsewhere 4,750,000 tons. In coastwise and overseas coal trades combined, the Tyne was very near to Cardiff. Its general trade was much more important; its aggregate trade very much more valuable. Under its Improvement Commission, constituted by Acts of 1850 and 1861, it had been dredged and quayed, provided with docks on its lower

[1] *Return of Works*, Southampton Docks.
[2] Dorn, *op. cit.* I. 1048.
[3] Contemporary admiration is in Harcourt, *op. cit.* I. 525; Dorn, *op. cit.* II. 1050. The general character of the trade of Swansea and Newport resembled that of Cardiff, bulk cargoes of coal and iron out, of ore timber and provisions in, dominating all three.

course, and with a swing bridge in place of the old low bridge
of Newcastle—fitted to carry whatever Armstrong, Palmer, or
Wigham and Richardson might put into it. At its mouth, the
two great breakwaters begun in 1856 were still unfinished.
There had been damage by storm, changes of plan, shortage
of funds; but the work was going forward[1].

Such deliberation in coastal works had been more the habit
of the state than of a local commission; though the Tees
southern breakwater, built of Middlesbrough slag and concrete,
and started by local enterprise in 1863, took more than twenty
years to finish[2]. Towards the close of the early railway age,
when the navy was still under sail and the *entente cordiale* with
France had just broken down, the state had begun to build
the 'national harbours of refuge and defence' at Dover, Portland and Holyhead. Convicts worked at Portland from 1849
to 1871 on the long breakwaters of rubble stone which had
never been much used either for defence or refuge. At Holyhead, the rubble mound, also begun in 1849, was left to con-
solidate before it was given a worked stone superstructure.
That was finished in 1873. It enclosed the New Harbour which
had a limited value in the age of steam. Dover Pier was the
first large breakwater designed as an upright wall of masonry.
It too was begun in the 'forties, and finished, with an extension
of the original plan, in 1871. But the complete design for the
harbour, "the most important of all the harbours started by
the Government," had not been carried out when that description of it was written in 1885. It remained in the "most
unfinished state" of them all[3]. There had been a long peace
in the Channel, with the retrenchment which accompanied it
in the Gladstonian age; there had been revolutions in both the

---

[1] *Return of Works*; Tyne Improvement Commission: Harcourt, *op. cit.* I. 318.
With the Tyne harbours must be classed Sunderland and Hartlepool, whose
joint trade was about a third of that of Newcastle and North and South Shields
in the 'eighties, in tonnage; and in general character similar.

[2] Harcourt, *op. cit.* I. 200. The South breakwater, "approaching completion"
in 1883, was finished before 1886. The North was only begun in 1882.

[3] Harcourt, *op. cit.* I. 333. The official literature extends from the *R. on
the alleged deficiency of Protection for Ships on the North-East Coast of England
and the North-West Coast of Wales*, 1836 (XVII) and the *R. on the most Eligible
Situations for Harbours of Refuge in the Channel*, 1845 (XVI); through the
*Quarterly Reports of the Engineers on the Harbours at Dover*, etc. 1850–75; to
the *R. on Harbour Accommodation*, 1883 (XIV), with some discussion of convict
labour and the *Return of Works*, quoted above. The works themselves are
described and discussed by Harcourt, *op. cit., passim.*

merchant service and the royal navy; and the Admiralty Pier served cross-channel traffic adequately.

These old-planned state enterprises had been carried out with little use of the new structural material—concrete. They need not have neglected it, for its value in harbour work was known even when they were originally designed. Italians, it is said, had been the first to repair masonry under water with concrete applied in bags. Poirel had used it for the port of Algiers in the 'thirties, both in mass to set under water and in artificial blocks to replace stone in rubble-mound breakwaters. He had given his methods to the world in a stately quarto in 1841[1]. England was rather slow to follow him, in spite of the reduction of risks due to improvements in cement[2]. By the 'sixties, concrete was being extensively used for dock walls; but in the mid-'eighties, all that could be said of breakwaters was that few were "constructed entirely without it."[3] One, however, was nearing completion in 1883 which was made of nothing else—that of Newhaven, designed to protect a system of modern harbour works, the start of which went back to an Act of 1862, from the south-westerly swell driving into Seaford Bay[4].

Concrete had first been used in Britain, on a large scale and under difficult conditions, in the construction of the new South breakwater at Aberdeen in 1870–3:[5] the concrete wall protecting the seaward slope of the slag-mound breakwater slowly pushed out on the South side of the Tees came rather later. Aberdeen and the other East Scottish ports had not enjoyed the commercial opportunities of Glasgow or Hull. As shipbuilders and shipowners they had declined with the decline of wood. But trade had increased and equipment with it. There had been most increase in the Forth. Leith had extended its two piers, each now more than half a mile long. It had a dock system which, like nearly every British dock system, contained both a Victoria and an Albert. Its trade was comparable in value with that of Southampton, but in character more metropolitan, with a dominance of imports and re-exports, as in the port of

---

[1] Poirel, M., *Mémoire sur les travaux à la mer*.

[2] Cp. above, p. 44.

[3] Harcourt, *op. cit.* I. 141; for its use at Millwall Docks in the 'sixties, I. 416.

[4] *Return of Works*, Newhaven: Harcourt, *op. cit.* I. 134, 345. The works were only started effectively after a second Act, of 1878. The old wooden jetties mentioned in vol. I. p. 3, had served until the 'sixties.

[5] *Trans. Inst. Civ. Eng.* xxxix. 127, and Harcourt, *op. cit.* I. 131.

London[1]. Grangemouth, controlling the eastern end of the Forth and Clyde canal, had become the leading timber port of Scotland: she could pass Baltic supplies across to Glasgow by water and save the Scandinavians the navigation of the Pentland Firth. There was coal-handling also for her and for the other harbours on both sides of the Forth.

Dundee had kept her quays and docks along the Tay well in line with the needs of her very active industries—"right well and practically arranged" the foreigner called them, adding, however, that "other things of note beside harbours and factories Dundee cannot display."[2] Aberdeen had her old and new breakwaters, and a spacious Victoria Dock, as the chief elements in a first-rate equipment; but her foreign trade was hardly commensurate. Judged by the standards of the day, she had too poor and empty a *hinterland* for an international port of the first, or indeed of a much lower, rank[3]. But she was busy with a coasting trade—mainly in granite and cattle—which occupied seven-eighths of the still considerable tonnage that frequented her harbour.

The coasting trade, so important at Aberdeen, Bristol, Newcastle, London, and in all ports from the lower ranks not here set out, must not be thought of as a mean or secondary thing because it was so little discussed at the time and has been so very seldom described. It has always been a principal source of Britain's wealth, since few important places are far from tide-water. For the entire United Kingdom—which, in this connection, cannot be divided into Britain and Ireland, for statistical reasons—the coasting trade was somewhat greater in cargo tonnage than the whole of the overseas trade proper. That was largely because of the coastwise trade in coal, and of that Anglo-Irish trade which from a British standpoint might almost be regarded as foreign. But besides these, there was a huge miscellaneous coasting business, carried on in small and not well known 'liners,' in second-rate steam 'tramps,' which would fit a little home-seas carrying into their world-wide wanderings in search of profitable cargo, or in the Thames barges, or in those "sloops, schooners, brigs and barques"[4] which poked into all the third-rate harbours where big ships

---

[1] Cp. Dorn, *op. cit.* II. 1006, 1067.    [2] *Ibid.* II. 1009.
[3] She appears only among 'other ports' in the *Statistical Abstracts*.
[4] Above, p. 523.

could not go. By a last gesture of confidence and faith in freedom, the coasting-trade had been thrown open to the ships of all nations: the foreigner had not secured one-half of one per cent. of it. The trade still bred seamen, as it had once bred Captain Cook.

In the true overseas trade, of vessels entering United Kingdom ports with cargo, just a third—by tonnage—had been foreign in 1875-7. By 1885-7 the proportion was barely a quarter. The rest, with the coastwise shipping, was British. Clippers that brought wool round the Horn; square-topsail schooners doing the odd jobs of the narrow seas; steam tramps with wheat or cotton or pitch-pine from American ports; liners from all the great harbours of the world—the pageant of sea-power had at no time been so varied or so stately. And now at length had become fully true of the men of Britain and their ships what was said in the seventeenth century of the Dutchmen and theirs—"the which except they stir, the people starve."[1]

[1] Above, p. 22.

# INDEX